THE

LIFE AND LETTERS

OF

BARTHOLD GEORGE NIEBUHR.

ESSAYS ON HIS CHARACTER AND INFLUENCE,

BY

THE CHEVALIER BUNSEN,

AND PROFESSORS BRANDIS AND LORBELL.

NEW YORK:

HARPER & BROTHERS, PUBLISHERS,

329 & 331 PEARL STREET,

FRANKLIN SQUARE.

1852.

PREFACE.

No justification could be needed for offering to the English public a life of Niebuhr, but it seems necessary to explain how far the present work can claim to be considered as such.

It is founded upon one entitled "Lebensnachrichten über Barthold Georg Niebuhr," which is chiefly composed of extracts from Niebuhr's letters; though a short narrative, intended to explain these, and fill up the chasms they leave in his history, is prefixed to each of the periods into which it is divided. The principal editor of "Lebensnachrichten" was Madame Hensler, Niebuhr's sister-in-law, to whom most of the letters are addressed, and who thus states the views with which she performed her task:

.... "The reader will not need to be reminded that the extracts from the letters form the most important part of the work.

"As I have already observed, these are not to be judged from the point of view which would be taken by an editor of Niebuhr's learned or general correspondence: such a one would have made a very different and a much more copious selection, and would probably, too, have followed critical rules which were beside the aim of the present work. This aim is simply biographical; to communicate whatever can throw light upon his natural capacities and dispositions, his mental development, his studies, his mode of thought, his views of life, the State, art, and literature; his relations as a citizen, a friend, and a member of the domestic circle; his large and profound sympathies; his keen sense of the noble and beautiful; his zeal for justice and truth; and, not less, his faults and weaknesses, for these too, neither ought nor needed to be glossed over. Niebuhr was not so poor in great and amiable qualities, as to require an artificial light, in order to retain the esteem of those whose esteem he would have valued; and while his letters contain many beautiful traits which a regard to others forbids us to publish, they contain nothing which could have brought our friendship for him and our love of truth into collision.

"Whether some of the letters retained might not have been omitted, and others inserted with advantage, is a point on which judgments will naturally differ. . . . .

"The greatest possible care has been taken to avoid any thing like indiscretion toward the living, or a profanation of feeling, which Niebuhr would have regarded as belonging to the inner sanctuary of the heart. Perhaps, in some cases, this scruple has been carried too far (for instance in omitting expressions of affection in the letters to his betrothed), and possibly too, some things may unawares have been retained, in which one better acquainted with the circumstances may perceive allusions that escaped the selecter."

I believe none who have paid attention to the subject, will deny, that the editor has, in the main, accomplished her purpose, and presented a picture of Niebuhr as a man, and in his private relations, which, in point of completeness and fairness, is excelled by few biographies; but it is equally certain that the account of his public career is very incomplete, and by no means one that enables the reader to perceive the relation in which Niebuhr stood to his times. The biographical notices in the present work are shorter than Madame Hensler's narrative on which they are based, but they also comprise a considerable amount of additional information, derived partly from other publications, partly from conversation with intimate friends of Niebuhr.* Several letters too have been added, throwing additional light on his public life. Thus, it is believed, that something has been done toward supplying the deficiency alluded to, though far less than still remains to be done. It was hoped that much more might have been effected, but Niebuhr's memorials and dispatches, as well as some valuable collections of his letters (especially those to Valckenaer and many of those to De Serre), still remain inaccessible to his friends.

Of the letters given in the "Lebensnachrichten," about half have been translated. In the selection of these the aim has been, while omitting those which could be interesting only in Germany, and avoiding repetition, where it was possible, to maintain the relative proportions which their various topics assume in the original, and thus to reproduce with faithfulness, on a smaller scale, the portrait there exhibited. Those who know the "Lebensnachrichten" will probably regret that none of Niebuhr's letters on learned subjects have been inserted; but it seemed desirable to confine this selection to those of general interest, and should the present work meet with a favorable reception, it is intended to publish, in another

* Such information as helped to explain or illustrate the letters has been added in notes, in cases where it would have broken the thread of the narrative if inserted in the Introductory Notices.

volume, the letters referred to, together with the most valuable portions of his smaller writings.

In reading Niebuhr's letters, it must be remembered first, that they were hasty compositions addressed to his most intimate friends, and hence in giving them to the world, Madame Hensler has deemed it necessary frequently to omit single sentences or expressions, which explains the somewhat abrupt and obscure style of many passages; and secondly, with regard to his political sentiments, that it was necessary, in Germany, to observe great caution in the publication of facts or opinions on such subjects; and therefore these letters give no *complete* view of what he thought and felt, even on the passing events of the day: nevertheless it may be hoped that he will not be misunderstood in England, and that those who occupy themselves with political questions will lay his words to heart.

In conclusion, the translator begs to express the warmest acknowledgments to those friends of Niebuhr who have aided in the progress of this work, especially to His Excellency Chevalier Bunsen, without whose encouragement and assistance it would never have been undertaken, and to Professor Loebell, for his "Letter on Niebuhr's Character as an Historian," and to Professors Brandis and Welcker, to the former of whom it has been indebted for most of the original information which it contains.

CONTENTS.

CHAPTER I.

CHILDHOOD AND YOUTH.

CHAPTER II.

COLLEGE LIFE.

LETTERS.

LETTERS.

CHAPTER III.

RESIDENCE IN COPENHAGEN.

LETTERS.

CHAPTER IV.

JOURNEY TO ENGLAND AND SCOTLAND.

LETTERS.

CHAPTER V.

OFFICIAL LIFE IN COPENHAGEN.

LETTERS.

CHAPTER VI.

THE PRUSSIAN CIVIL SERVICE.

LETTERS.

LETTERS.

LETTERS.

CHAPTER VII.

PROFESSORSHIP IN BERLIN.

LETTERS.

CHAPTER VIII.

RETURN TO PUBLIC LIFE.

LETTERS.

CHAPTER IX.

RESIDENCE IN BERLIN UP TO JULY, 1816.

LETTERS.

CHAPTER X.

MISSION IN ROME.

LETTERS.

1817.

LETTERS.

1818.

LETTERS.

1819.

LETTERS.

1820.

LETTERS.

1821.

LETTERS.

1822.

LETTERS.

1823.

LETTERS.

CHAPTER XI.

RESIDENCE IN BONN.

LETTERS.

1825–1831.

LETTERS.

MEMOIR OF NIEBUHR.

CHAPTER I.

NIEBUHR'S CHILDHOOD AND YOUTH, FROM 1776 TO 1794.

BARTHOLD GEORGE NIEBUHR, the historian of Rome, was born at Copenhagen, on the 27th of August, 1776. He was the son of Carsten Niebuhr, the celebrated traveler. His family, for as many generations as any thing is known respecting it, had been settled in Hadel, the northwestern province of Hanover, where they occupied a small freehold that had descended from father to son.

Carsten Niebuhr, being a younger son, had not inherited the family farmstead, and as his ardent love of knowledge prompted him to seek some occupation which would afford more scope for its gratification than the agricultural operations that filled up the life of the peasants around him, he determined to become a land-surveyor. For this purpose he applied the small capital which his father had left him, to his support while studying under private tutors at Hamburgh, where he acquired the rudiments of a learned education, and afterward at the University of Göttingen. When in 1757, the Danish government resolved to send an expedition of discovery to the East, Niebuhr was recommended by his tutor, Professor Kästner, one of the most distinguished German mathematicians of that day, to Count Bernstorff, who had applied to him for a person competent to conduct the geographical portion of the researches. After two years spent in preparatory studies, he received the rank of a lieutenant in the engineers, and in the autumn of 1760, set out on his travels with four companions, who each undertook a separate department of scientific research.

The difficulties and privations of the journey through Arabia, in 1763, proved so excessive that all Niebuhr's fellow-travelers sank under them within a year, and he was left to pursue the journey alone. He not only resolved to do so, but endeavored to supply, as far as he was qualified, the place of his fellow-discoverers.

From this journey he returned to Copenhagen in 1767, after an absence of six years. Here he employed himself in revising his journals, and those of his fellow-traveler Forskaal, for publication.

He was on the point of undertaking a journey into the interior of Africa, when he fell in love with a young orphan lady, the daughter of the late physician to the King of Denmark. Though he had reached his fortieth year, this was the first love he had ever experienced, and its sincerity and depth may be judged of by the fact of his abandoning all the plans he had formed for his future life, and, instead of continuing the adventurous career which till then had alone possessed any charms for him, resolving to settle down quietly in Copenhagen. He married in 1773, and had two children by his wife—a daughter, Christiana, born in 1774, and his son Barthold.

His position in Copenhagen became far less agreeable after the fall of his patron, Count Bernstorff, to whom he was personally much attached, and at length he requested his discharge from the military service, and an appointment of a civil nature in Holstein. He was accordingly made secretary* to the province of South Dithmarsh, and removed with his family to Meldorf, its chief town, in 1778.

The province of Dithmarsh, formerly a republic, and celebrated for its defense of its freedom, still retained certain privileges, and a free and independent communal constitution peculiar to itself. The inhabitants were of the same Frisian race as those of Carsten, Niebuhr's native province; were a free peasantry like them, each man occupying and cultivating his own little freehold, and possessed the industry, frugality, and sturdy independence which usually characterize their order. The circumstance that his childhood and youth were passed among such a population, probably contributed to the strong interest and sympathy with which Niebuhr always regarded this class. Frequent references occur in his letters to the peculiar institutions of these districts, and his practical acquaintance with them was often brought to bear upon

* Land-schreiber.

his researches into the political and civil organization of other countries, ancient as well as modern.

The external features of the country were not at all picturesque. Marshes extended over the greater portion of its surface, which was neither diversified by trees nor rising ground. Meldorf itself was a little antiquated country town, that had formerly been of much greater importance as the capital of the republic, but had sunk into decay through the ravages occasioned by repeated sieges; and its remoteness from any high road prevented an influx of trade, which might have revived its prosperity. Many of the old-fashioned houses were now unoccupied, and the quiet of the place was rarely broken by the carriage-wheels of a passing traveler, for it had no visitors but such as were drawn thither by some personal interest.

The want of any natural beauty in the scene of his early life rendered Niebuhr long insensible to impressions from this source. Thus, writing from Edinburgh in 1798, he says, that Nature has denied him the taste for picturesque scenery, but given him instead a perception of the sublime. In later years, however, he was keenly sensible to the charms of a beautiful landscape.

It will be readily conceived that Meldorf was, in many respects, an unfavorable position for Carsten Niebuhr, whose previous life had been passed, almost ever since he had been grown up, in the excitement of traveling through previously unexplored eastern regions, or amidst the society of the scholars and statesmen of Copenhagen. The fame of the celebrated traveler occasionally attracted a stranger, and many friends came to visit him; but sometimes for months together he saw no one beside the inhabitants of the little town. Of these the clergy and officials of the place formed the circle with which the family associated. Among them there were few—and for a long while perhaps none—who had any taste for intellectual pursuits except so far as they were connected with their peculiar vocation. Carsten Niebuhr, however, employed himself in a most conscientious discharge of the duties of his office, and occupied his spare hours in building himself a house and laying out a garden, from which he then scarcely expected he should live to gather the fruit, but most of whose trees he long survived. Moreover, though accustomed to mix with the highest classes, he had never lost his fellow feeling with the peasantry to whom he belonged by birth, and when among his relations, whom he loved to visit, he could completely accommodate himself to their habits and enter into their modes of thinking. His son says of him, "He was and remained throughout his life a genuine peasant; with all the virtues and also the little failings of his order. He was certainly self-willed and obstinate; it was almost impossible to talk him out of any idea he had once taken up. This held good, too, of his favorable or unfavorable prepossessions with regard to persons. His character was perfectly irreproachable, and his morals extremely strict and pure. He was in all relations of life unexacting and self-sacrificing."

Of Niebuhr's mother there exist very few notices. From the circle in which she was brought up, she was, in all probability, a woman of education and refinement. She is described as having been of a nervous, sensitive temperament, probably in great measure the effect of her very delicate health; as excitable and warm-tempered, but at the same time easily pacified, affectionate, and tender. Her son is said to have resembled her much in person as well as in character.

An unmarried sister lived with her, with whom she usually spoke Danish, so that the children learnt both that and German as their native languages.

The parents, especially the father, seem to have devoted themselves to the training and education of their children with an attention rarely seen; but the frequent indisposition of Madame Niebuhr, with whom the air of the marshes did not agree, and his own ill-health, occasioned many interruptions to the otherwise happy tenor of her son's childhood. The boy had been very strong up to his fifth year, but he then had a dangerous attack of ague, which seemed quite to alter his constitution, for it became and remained through life very irritable, and highly susceptible both to mental and atmospheric influences. He had also several severe illnesses and accidents in his childhood. One of the latter was a bite from a dog, which obliged him to submit to very painful treatment; and all these circumstances contributed to increase his constitutional nervousness and timidity. Indisposition often rendered it needful for him to be kept within doors, and his mother's anxiety, which was heightened by her own delicate health, often unnecessarily prolonged these periods of privation from air and exercise.

On the whole, however, he and his sister led a very merry life, romping about with their playfellows in a spacious house, or in large court-yards and gardens. When Niebuhr was about five years old, he took great delight in watching the erection of his father's house at Meldorf. The elder Niebuhr was his own architect, and the child soon learnt to draw plans by watching his father at work, and asking him questions; he was constantly at his side during the progress of the building, and long afterward retained an intelligent recollection of the proceedings of the workmen. His father was never weary of providing occupations and entertainments for his children. He had a skittle-ground made in the large court-yard, and in the winter a Russian mountain was put up in the garden. A very considerable collection of seals and coins was made for them, from which on Sundays they were allowed, as a treat, to take casts, and they eagerly studied heraldry in connection with these. The father even applied to several of his learned friends in Copenhagen for specimens to enrich this collection. He was not less willing to devote his own time to their pleasure. In summer he would help his son to build fortifications in the garden according to the rules of military art, which he afterward taught the boy and his companions to attack and defend, likewise according to rule. In winter he often used to collect other children at his house in the evenings, and then set them to dance while he played for them on the violin. The Christmas festivities were seasons of unbounded enjoyment to Niebuhr in his childish years. He thus describes his blissful feelings, as a child at this festival, in a letter dated Copenhagen, December 30th, 1797:—"I had the evening at liberty. I locked myself up in my own room, and luxuriated in the recollections of my departed childhood, whose best and sweetest pleasure was my intense happiness at these Christmas festivals. I was of a grateful disposition; a little thing would make me as happy as a prince, and I was not ill-behaved in my glee, which is as natural to many children as elation in prosperity is to grown-up people. A many-colored tissue of bright memories floats over to me from those times, of which the most distinct images are connected with my eighth year. But with all of them there is associated a peculiar charm of eager outstretched expectation and dazzling surprise, succeeded by a vehement feeling of delight, occupation, and gratitude. Happy is he who begins anew to recall with joy those scenes which he once fancied barren of interest, and afterward was obliged to rouse himself by reflection to prize, and contemplated with mournful feeling, as not only lost to him, but dead even in memory."

With such an education, it was natural that the children should grow up good and intelligent, but the boy early gave indications of his extraordinary talents. His instruction in reading, writing, and arithmetic, seems to have begun in his fourth or fifth year, with his sister, under a tutor. He early distinguished himself by his quickness, ready apprehension, and sure retention of what he learned, and, according to his sister's account, he soon got before her. He had always finished the tasks that were set them sooner than she had, and then would roguishly dance round her, singing

"Rest is sweet when work is done."

Niebuhr says, in his Life of his father, "He instructed both of us in geography, and used to relate stories to us from history; he taught me English and French—at all events much better than I could have learnt them from any instructor the place afforded, and also a little mathematics, in which he would have gone further had he not been discouraged by the want of liking and talent in myself. It must be confessed that he grew weary of teaching, whenever he found any want of seriousness and interest in his pupils, for he never could understand how it was possible that they should find a difficulty in receiving, with delight and attention, any kind of instruction whatever, as he himself had always done."

These instructions must have commenced early, for in December, 1782, when Niebuhr was six years old, his father writes to his brother-in-law, Eckhardt, "Barthold has begun to-day to learn the Greek alphabet, and shall now proceed to write German in Greek characters." Somewhat later, writing to the same individual, he says, "He studied the Greek alphabet only for a single day, and had no further trouble with it; he did it with very little help from me. The boy gets on wonderfully. Boje says he does not know his equal; but he requires to be managed in a peculiar way. May God preserve our lives, and give us grace to guide him aright! Oh, if he could but learn to control the warmth of his temper; I believe I might say his pride. He is no longer so passionate with his sister; but if he stumbles in the least in repeating his lessons, or if his scribblings are alluded to, he fires up instantly. He can not bear to be praised for them, because he believes that he does not deserve it. In short, I repeat it, he is proud; he wants to know every thing, and is angry if he does not know it. May the Almighty guide and direct him!" Then he continues, "My wife complains that I find fault with Barthold unnecessarily. I did not mean to do so. He is an extraordinarily good little fellow, but he must be managed in an extraordinary way, and I pray God to give me wisdom and patience to educate him properly."

The Boje mentioned in this letter, was the editor of the "Deutsches Museum," one of the earliest literary periodicals, not exclusively learned in its character, that appeared in Germany. He thus stood in connection with most of the literary men of the day, and was himself a man of high intellect and taste. He had been appointed prefect of the province in 1781, and his settlement in Meldorf had an important influence on the life of the Niebuhrs. His society, and that of his wife, afforded the elder Niebuhrs, with whom they became very intimate, that unreserved intercourse with intelligent and highly cultivated people which they had previously missed at Meldorf, and Boje's large circle of friends imparted variety to their social life. The boy gained still more from these friends. He was allowed free access to Boje's extensive library, which was particularly rich in English and French as well as German books, and gained thus much information which he could not have acquired elsewhere. But most of all, Boje's æsthetic and poetical turn of mind awakened in the child similar impulses, which would probably have otherwise remained dormant, as his father's cast of thought was essentially prosaic, and his method of education intentionally calculated to repress the imagination and to exercise the other faculties. How keenly alive he was to poetical impressions appears from a letter of Boje's, written in 1783: "This reminds me of little Niebuhr. His docility, his industry and his devoted love for me, procure me many a pleasant hour. A short time back, I was reading 'Macbeth' aloud to his parents without taking any notice of him, till I saw what an impression it made upon him. Then I tried to render it all intelligible to him, and even explained to him how the witches were only poetical beings. When I was gone, he sat down (he is not yet seven years old), and wrote it all out on seven sheets of paper, without omitting one important point, and certainly without any expectation of receiving praise for it; for, when his father asked to see what he had written, and showed it to me, he cried for fear he had not done it well. Since then he writes down every thing of importance that he hears from his father or me. We seldom praise him, but just quietly tell him where he has made any mistake, and he avoids the fault for the future."

The child's character early exhibited a rare union of the faculty of poetical insight with that of accurate practical observation. The amusements he contrived for himself afford an illustration of this. During the periods of his confinement to the house, before he was old enough to have any paper given him, he covered with his writings and drawings, the margins of the leaves of several copies of Forskaal's works, which were used in the house as waste paper. Then he made copy-books for himself, in which he wrote essays, mostly on political subjects. He had an imaginary empire called Low-England, of which he drew maps, and he promulgated laws, waged wars, and made treaties of peace there. His father was pleased that he should occupy himself with amusements of this kind, and his sister took an active part in them. There still exist among his papers, many of his childish productions; among others, translations and interpretations of passages of the New Testament, poetical paraphrases from the classics, sketches of little poems, a translation of Poncet's Travels in Ethiopia, an historical and geographical description of Africa, written in 1787 (the two last were undertaken as presents to his father on his birthday), and many other things mostly written during these years. His father probably in one way indirectly assisted these imaginative tendencies by his habit of relating his travels to him.

"I well remember," says Niebuhr, in the Life of his father, "how he used to tell me stories in my childhood about the East, and the structure of the universe; particularly in the evening, just before bed-time he would take me on his knee, and feed my imagination with these instead of fairy tales. The history of Mohammed, of the early Caliphs—especially of Omar and Ali, for whom he had the deepest reverence—of the conquests and spread of Islamism, and the virtues of the heroes of the new faith, with the history of the Turks, were early imprinted on my memory in the most lively colors; nay, works on these subjects were among the first books put into my hands.

"I remember too, how, one Christmas Eve, when I must have been in my tenth year, he heightened the delights of the festival, by taking out of the almost magnificent chest which held his manuscripts, and was revered by the children and all the household, like the ark of the covenant, the volumes which contained the information he had collected in Africa, and reading them with me. He had taught me to draw maps, and now, encouraged and assisted by him, I soon produced maps of Habbesch and Sudan. . . . . .

"He entered with the utmost indulgence and sympathy into my half old-fashioned, half childish ideas; helped me in the details of my castles in the air; conversed with me on all the topics of the day, and strove to give me clear conceptions of whatever subjects we talked upon—among other things, of fortifications, by encouraging me to measure out and excavate polygons under his eye, and with books and plans at hand."

From a letter of his father's, it appears that Niebuhr was able to read any English books without help when only in his eighth year. Somewhat later, Madame Boje, who was an admirable French scholar, kindly undertook to teach him that language, which he had begun with his father. The death of this lady, in 1786, was the child's first experience of heart-sorrow. After the funeral his mother found him in the garden, rolling on the grass almost wild with grief, and it was a long time before he recovered his spirits. This had the effect of turning his attention still more exclusively to the serious occupations to which he had been previously inclined, and in consequence his progress was more rapid than ever.

In his eighth or ninth year he had begun to receive private lessons, principally in the classics, from one of the masters of the Gymnasium. As the linstruction in the ower classes of the school was defective, his father wished to keep him at home till he could at once enter the highest class. The master, however, was so deficient both in abilities and attainments, that his incapacity could not escape the boy, and with a child's love of mischief he used to tease him by learning his task within the appointed time, in order to oblige the tutor to read further than his preparation reached, when their respective positions were almost reversed, the boy assuming the character of a teacher, while the master had to sit by his side as a learner.

This state of affairs must have had a very injurious influence on the boy's character, as well as on the progress of his education, had not its effects on the one hand been neutralized by his unbounded desire of knowledge and remarkable abilities, and on the other by his good and affectionate disposition. But it is certainly surprising that he should have made such extraordinary progress in spite of it, and still more so that it should never have caused his industry to flag. He tells us, however, that his father assisted him in his Latin, and read Cæsar's Commentaries with him, in which he, very characteristically, paid much more attention to the geography than to the grammar.

It is mentioned that from about this time the young Niebuhr shared the warm interest in literature which prevailed in Germany toward the close of the eighteenth century, and eagerly welcomed the appearance of any new work from the pens of Klopstock, Lessing, and Goethe. But that interest in politics, which became the master-spring of his life, was first awakened at about the age of eleven. It is said that when the war with Turkey broke out in the year 1787, it so strongly excited the child's mind, that he not only talked of it in his sleep at night, but fancied himself in his dreams reading the newspapers and repeating the intelligence they contained about the war; and his ideas on these subjects were so well arranged, and founded on so accurate a knowledge of the country and the situation of the towns, that the realization of his nightly anticipations generally appeared in the journals a short time afterward. Of course this is not to be regarded as indicating a miraculous gift of prophecy in the boy, but only as showing with what distinctness all that he heard transferred itself to his imagination, and how capable his understanding was of combining the ideas he had received in their true relation to each other. Partly through his father's narratives, partly through his own geographical studies, those regions were as familiar to him as his native province. He had studied the nations inhabiting them, and their mode of warfare, in history and the accounts of travelers, and had taken great pains to gain accurate conceptions of the character and conduct of the various commanders in the war, from the journals and other sources of information. There are still extant some letters which he wrote at this time to his uncle Eckhardt, containing the grounds and proofs of his predictions.

This faculty of divination exhibited itself again during the early part of the French Revolution; when in several instances he not only anticipated the course of events with reference to the progress of the war, but also the direction which popular movements would take, the plans and objects of the revolutionary leaders, and the results of the measures adopted by the various parties, with so much correctness and precision as to excite the astonishment even of the eminent statesman Count P. A. Bernstorff, that such a mere youth should have so just and acute an appreciation of men and events. With equal correctness and certainty did he guess the plans of the commanders during the war, from the marches and position of the armies, in which his exact and detailed geographical knowledge served as a guide to his judgment. He retained this faculty to a considerable extent during the whole of his life, but he possessed it in a higher degree in his earlier years, when he could concentrate the whole power of his mind on impressions of this kind.

From the time when the Turkish war broke out, therefore, his attention was fixed upon historical events. But the disturbances in the Netherlands in the Emperor Joseph's time, excited in him a still stronger interest than the Turkish war, and it was heightened by his acquaintance with a fugitive named De la Vida, who took up his residence in Meldorf.

It happened about this time that many friends of Boje's and Niebuhr's came to visit them from Copenhagen and Germany; several foreigners also came to Meldorf to make the acquaintance of the two authors. But the friend who had the most important influence on Niebuhr's studies was the well known poet Voss,* who had married Boje's sister.

During the frequent visits made to their brother by Voss and his wife, an intimacy sprang up between him and Niebuhr, which was only terminated by death. Voss soon discovered the wonderful talents of the boy, won his attachment by many acts of kindness, and assisted him with advice and guidance in his classical studies. He found his reward in the boy's affectionate reverence for him, and adherence to his counsels.

In the conversations which took place among these friends and

* The translator of Homer, author of "Luise," &c.

foreigners during their visits to Holstein, the boy, then eleven or twelve years of age, was frequently called to take part, and not seldom information was asked of him regarding geographical, statistical, historical and other subjects, and given in a manner which excited their astonishment. His father used often to talk of this with great pleasure in later years, when his darling son had become his joy and pride. His statistical knowledge was even then extraordinary; he was frequently assiduously engaged in subjects of this nature, such for instance as working out lists of mortality.

All this would no doubt have rendered him vain or proud, but that his simple education in strict principles of obedience, the example of his father, and frequent expressions of his mother showing how little she valued such things, proved a sufficient counterpoise. Against vanity he was moreover protected by an instinctive love of completeness in knowledge, and a repugnance to all merely superficial brilliancy. Pride might have proved a more dangerous enemy, as he could not remain ignorant of his own superiority, had not his generous and loving spirit enabled him to appreciate every genuine manifestation of humanity, and taught him to look up with deep humility and admiration to those great men of ancient and modern times, whom he regarded as heroes in thought and action.

In later years he was indeed conscious of his own value, and felt deeply hurt, when he thought himself not appreciated, or treated with intentional neglect, but he never over-estimated himself; in his letters we find frequent and touching proofs to the contrary. He displayed much magnanimity in his readiness to recognize eminent qualities and merits, even when they might come into collision with his own claims. No trace of envy, nor the slightest disposition to detraction, could ever be perceived in him. He inherited the distinguishing characteristics of his father, integrity and truthfulness—qualities that were so inherent in Carsten Niebuhr, that it was utterly impossible for him even to feel tempted to transgress their laws. Hence dishonesty and untruthfulness, with the vain love of display so often combined with them, were of all faults those which Niebuhr most detested.

Little variation occurred in his life during three years, beyond the incidents already mentioned. Materials for the acquisition of knowledge were not wanting to him. Travels, especially in the other quarters of the world, were at all times his father's favorite reading, and of lighter literature he was able to obtain a constant supply from Boje, whose library was liberally stocked with works of this class.

He was now entering on his thirteenth year, and his father, feeling that the desultory instruction he had hitherto received was insufficient for him, determined on sending him to the Gymnasium at Meldorf, a step which appears to have been in accordance with the boy's own inclinations. In a letter dated November, 1788, Carsten Niebuhr says: "Barthold has not troubled his head so much about the Turks and the Emperor for some time past, but has made up his mind to enter the highest class at Easter, and is therefore busily engaged with the history of literature. He revels so in the Latin authors that I am almost obliged to restrain his ardor." He was not however exclusively absorbed in books, as, from a passage in one of his mother's letters written about this time, it appears that he was of great service to his father, during the autumn, in the financial calculations connected with the collection of extensive state revenues in South Dithmarsh. At Easter, 1789, Niebuhr entered the school, where he found himself at once by far the youngest, and considerably the most advanced in his class. In spite of this he was a favorite with his schoolfellows, a sure proof that he did not presume on his superior knowledge in his behavior toward them. He remained, however, at school only till the Michaelmas of the following year, when the Principal, Dr. Jäger, found it necessary to dispense with his attendance, on the departure of most of the seniors, and the entrance of a much younger and less advanced set of boys into the highest class. Dr. Jäger offered, however, contrary to his usual practice, to give him an hour's private lesson every day, which, he said, considering Niebuhr's attainments and industry, would be sufficient to prepare him properly for the university.

This offer was gladly accepted, and the daily lesson was continued till Easter, 1794. Dr. Jäger read with him the more difficult passages of the Greek and Latin authors, and gave him hints which enabled him to read them by himself, to study grammar and Greek composition, and to exercise himself in Latin composition.

Other branches of knowledge he pursued by himself, except that his father occasionally assisted him in mathematics. There still exist plans of his daily studies, written at this time, which evince his extraordinary industry. More than half of each day he devoted to hard work, some hours to general reading, and a very short time to recreation and social pleasures. Yet in later life he often accused himself of indolence. The only ground he could have for this complaint was, that he prosecuted his studies rather under the guidance of inclination, than with reference to any definite object, and hence those subjects, which from being less attractive to him cost him the most effort, were placed in the background. He certainly suffered at this time from the want of any competent guide. He read largely, and collected an immense amount of information, more indeed than he was able to digest properly, and there was no one who could teach him how to systematize his hoards of knowledge. He afterward became aware of this, and was often much depressed by perceiving the confusion of ideas that resulted from it, particularly during the period from 1796 to 1798. When, as was not unfrequently the case, he found himself wandering involuntarily from the direct course in the studies he had undertaken, and perceived how much this habit of mind precluded his reaping due results from his labors, he complained with great bitterness of his self-incurred deficiency in energy and strength of will.

In 1791 he was confirmed by a clergyman of Meldorf, who was a friend of the family.

The French revolution, which broke out about this time, excited a strong interest in him from its commencement. Its effect on his mind differed, however, from the impression it produced on most of the young, and many of the elder persons of that day, who saw in it the promise of an era of glorious liberty, and many of whom carried their enthusiasm to such a height, as to view the most horrible excesses, simply as deplorable but inevitable steps in the transition to a higher development of the human race. Hence arose a universal agitation, which brought forth many melancholy results in the schisms that took place between men of different views, the arrogant tone of triumph which the enthusiasts assumed in their speeches and writings toward those whom they deemed the unenlightened and timorous men of the opposite party, and the divisions that ensued among friends and families. Niebuhr had studied history with an earnestness and thoughtfulness unusual at his age, and early recognized the workings and tendencies of the democratic movements. The horrors of anarchy and popular tyranny, which that revolution exhibited with such fearful distinctness, filled him with deep sorrow, and anxious misgivings for the fate of the rest of the world. He reverenced liberty, when obtained through self-sacrifice and persevering effort in conformity with the law; and thus, in later life, he cherished a great respect for the Roman plebeians, who had conquered their rights and their constitution by such means alone. But all that tended to lawlessness, to the overthrow of social order, to establish the sway of mobs and demagogues, he detested from his earliest youth, because he saw therein the germs of future barbarism. Doubtless, however, he would not have acquired these views so early, nor entertained them through life with such unalterable firmness, if, on the one hand, they had not received confirmation on so gigantic a scale from those great events; and if, on the other, he had not brought to bear on all that was passing around him a most rare faculty of observation and combination, even at this early age. It is impossible to estimate how much the formation of his opinions may have been influenced by his father's way of thinking, whose preference for the English, and antipathy to the French, were perhaps even exaggerated,* yet it can not be doubted that his political sentiments were founded upon a real personal conviction.

In the course of the year 1792, the elder Niebuhr resolved to send his son to spend some time in Hamburgh, at a school which was then the most celebrated of its kind in Europe for instruction in modern languages and commercial science. Its founder and head master, Büsch, was an old friend of his, and the author of numerous highly esteemed works on commercial subjects.† Büsch's school was nearly unique of its kind, and attended by pupils from all parts of Europe. His circle of acquaintance was one of the largest in Hamburgh. All the learned and intellectual society of the city assembled at his house; all foreigners of dis-

* "He saw in that nation [the French] our natural hereditary enemies; and I remember he was delighted when the War of the Revolution broke out, not because he sided with the counter-revolutionary party, but because he hoped that the conquered German and Burgundian provinces might be regained—provinces which he always included in Germany when teaching his children geography." *Life of C. Niebuhr, by his Son.*

† Of which the most remarkable are—"Outlines of a History of the most eminent Commercial Enterprises of the World," "Handbook of the Collective Commercial Sciences," and "the Library of Commerce."

tinction brought letters of introduction to him; and his wife enlivened by her wit and intelligence the society which then counted among its members the poet Klopstock, the geographer Ebeling, and the more celebrated physician Reimarus (the first who practiced inoculation, and who distinguished himself in that day by his advocacy of free trade and political reforms), and among its occasional guests, Lessing and other noted literary men. The young Niebuhr was not to be placed merely on the footing of a scholar, but was to be admitted to the social intercourse of the house. This resolution seems to have been prompted by Carsten Niebuhr's wish that his son should choose a diplomatic career, for which he regarded a residence in Büsch's house as an excellent preparation. He also wished that his son, who had lived up to this time entirely at home, should acquire a wider knowledge of the world and the tone of good society, and learn to take an interest in subjects relating to practical life. He felt too that his boy's attachment to home was excessive, and that his too eager pursuit of his studies threatened lasting injury to his health. The visit was offered the young Niebuhr as a reward for his industry, his father sincerely believing that it would conduce as much to his pleasure as to his improvement. He was, however, disappointed in his expectations. The youth was received and treated most kindly by Büsch, but the continual whirl of amusement and occupation in the house, the contrast presented by the ordinary topics of conversation and the pleasantries in so mixed a society, to those he had been accustomed to, produced a most painful impression on his mind. He felt restless and dissatisfied in this new world, where his most cherished sentiments were unregarded or misunderstood. It was indeed natural that the elder men around him should take little notice of the thoughts of a youth of sixteen, yet in many respects he could not but feel conscious of his own superiority to them. Klopstock and Ebeling, however, liked and appreciated him, and in their society he felt at ease. The former frequently invited him to his house, and this acquainatnce was the most valuable result of Niebuhr's stay in Hamburgh, for he was too home-sick to make much progress in his studies. He implored his father to allow him to leave, declaring that his residence in Hamburgh was an utter waste of time; and when his father did not immediately accede to his request, repeated his entreaties with such vehemence, that the elder Niebuhr yielded, and fetched him back after a three months' absence. It may be doubted whether he would not have acted more wisely for his son's true interests, if he had stood firm; for though it is very probable that young Niebuhr would have advanced less rapidly in his studies amidst the distractions of Hamburgh than in the quiet of home, the life in Büsch's house, among young people of his own age, would perhaps have furnished precisely the discipline needed to neutralize the effects of his solitary education at home, which had stimulated the precocity of his intellect, and the over-sensitiveness of his temperament. Perhaps in after life Niebuhr's defect as a practical statesman, was that he set too high a standard for mankind at large, instead of taking them as he found them, which made it difficult for him to work with others, and rendered him liable to despair of men and classes, as soon as he detected their moral deficiencies. This tendency—the natural result of his own disinterestedness of character, and the unusually high moral tone of the society in which his early years were passed—might have been corrected, had he been forced to come into daily contact with a number of young men of about the average stamp, at an age when he could not have made them treat him otherwise than as one of themselves.

His return to Meldorf was, however, a great immediate comfort to his family, as his father was soon after seized with a dangerous and tedious illness, which for a long time incapacitated him for performing the duties of his office. During his convalescence Niebuhr undertook the financial part of his duties, and the fact that he was capable of performing them at so early an age, may be regarded as the first indication of his future eminence as a financier.

After this interruption Niebuhr resumed his studies, and his private lessons with Dr. Jäger. From this time he employed himself in collating MSS., which Münter sent him from Copenhagen, and Heyne fron Göttingen. The latter wished that the superintendence of Niebuhr's studies should be confided to him, and it was his father's intention to send him to Göttingen after he had passed through the two years' course of study in his native university of Kiel, necessary to render him eligible for receiving any official appointment in his own country.

His favorite intercourse during this period was with a young man named Prehn, a few years older than himself, who had been a playfellow of his childhood, and was now appointed secretary to the prefecture. The two friends, who were very different in other respects, had a common interest in pursuing their researches into the constitution and condition of their native province.

The time from Michaelmas, 1792, to Easter, 1794, was spent in his father's house, amidst the employments and circumstances already mentioned. He was now more occupied than formerly with the study of modern languages. With French, English, and Italian he had long been familiar; the sale at this time of some books cast on shore from a wreck incited him to learn Spanish, and, soon afterward, Portuguese. A letter from his father, dated December, 1807, gives a summary of the languages with which he was acquainted. "My son has gone to Memel with the commissariat of the army. When he found he should probably have to go to Riga, he began forthwith to learn Russian. Let us just reckon how many languages he knows already. He was only two years old when we came to Meldorf, so that we must consider—1. German, as his mother tongue. He learnt at school—2. Latin; 3. Greek; 4. Hebrew; and besides, in Meldorf he learnt—5. Danish; 6. English; 7. French; 8. Italian; but only so far as to be able to read a book in these languages; some books from a vessel wrecked on the coast induced him to learn—9. Portuguese; 10. Spanish;—of Arabic, he did not learn much at home, because I had lost my lexicon, and could not quickly replace it;—in Kiel and Copenhagen, he had opportunities of practice in speaking and writing French, English, and Danish; in Copenhagen, he learnt—11. Persian (of Count Ludolph, the Austrian minister, who was born at Constantinople, and whose father was an acquaintance of mine), and 12. Arabic, he taught himself; in Holland he learnt—13. Dutch; and again in Copenhagen—14. Swedish, and a little Icelandic; at Memel —15. Russian; 16. Slavonic; 17. Polish; 18. Bohemian; and, 19. Illyrian. With the addition of Low German, this makes in all twenty languages. Forgive this effusion of my heart concerning my son. I did not mean to boast of him."

During these years, Niebuhr often grieved over the progress of events in France. The scenes of horror in 1791–3, almost disgusted him with Europe, and he and his sister often turned their thoughts toward America, hoping to find there, with a few friends, the repose which seemed to have forsaken the old world.

Even then his mind was often visited by that anxiety about the retrogression of the present generation toward barbarism, which troubled the last months of his life. In later years, he would certainly never have thought of America as a place to settle in. Both the want of any proper nationality among that amalgam of races, and the absence of any historical antecedents in their circumstances, as well as the predominance of the mercantile interest, and the want of literary society, would have prevented that country from ever becoming a congenial residence to him.

CHAPTER II.

NIEBUHR'S COLLEGE LIFE, FROM 1794 TO 1796.

AT Easter, 1794, Niebuhr commenced his studies at the University of Kiel. He found his position and society here infinitely more agreeable than in Hamburgh. Indeed, he could hardly have been more favorably situated, for the students were at that time in general characterized by industry and morality, while most of the professors were men of distinguished talent, and appear to have shown great kindness in admitting the students to friendly intercourse with themselves. He found in the aged Professor Hensler, who was head physician to the University, and a friend of his father's, a man full of intellect, feeling, and information, to whose house he had constant access. Of all the professors, there was none who attracted Niebuhr's lasting affection so much as Dr. Hensler; but in his house he found another friend, who exercised a still greater influence over him—one in fact, who, by what she was, and what she did, affected his development and his destiny more, perhaps, than any other human being. She was the widow of a son of Dr. Hensler, who had died very young, and from that time she had resided with her father-in-law, to whom she supplied the place of a daughter. She was a woman of strong and healthy mind, with much decision of character, combined with deep feeling and no ordinary cultivation—one of those women whose clear and correct judgment and ever-ready sympathy render them through life the person to whom all their friends instinctively turn for advice and assistance. She was six years older than Niebuhr—a circumstance which prevented any shyness and restraint on her side, while the unusual maturity of his character rendered him not too young to be a companion to her.

The professors with whom Niebuhr chiefly associated were, besides Hensler, Hegewisch, author of "The History of German Civilization," &c.—a man of considerable talents and attainments, but of no great depth as a critic; Cramer, a well known professor of Roman law; and Reinhold, author of "Letters on the Philosophy of Kant," and several other philosophical works, one of the first who drew attention to Kant's philosophy, which he expounded in his lectures.*

Among the young men he soon made the acquaintance of several with whom he afterward formed sincere and lasting friendships. Of these, were Conrad Hensler, a relative of Dr. Hensler's; Thibaut, afterward a celebrated professor of jurisprudence in Kiel, and subsequently in Heidelberg; a M. von Späth, who had previously served in the army; and a French emigrant, named Dachon de Billière, a man of eccentric character but high principle.†

Reinhold, who had just removed to Kiel from Jena, excited so great an enthusiasm for the study of philosophy that the better class of students were ashamed to neglect it. This had an elevating influence, too, on their moral character. Reinhold also founded a club, to which both the professors and the students were eligible, where the meetings were designed principally for scientific conversation, and concluded with a frugal supper. Niebuhr became a member of this club, but he did not join in any of the societies confined to the students.

He studied at Kiel till Easter, 1796. During his first year, he attended lectures on German and Danish history, by Hegewisch; on jurisprudence and the institutes, by Cramer; on logic, metaphysics, and moral philosophy, by Reinhold; on natural philosophy, organic and inorganic chemistry, by Eimbke; on æsthetics, by Nasser. What lectures he attended during the latter year of his stay his friends can not recollect with certainty: most probably some on anthropology by Hensler, and the Pandects by Cramer. Philology and history continued to be his favorite pursuits, but he carried them on by himself, and attended none of the college lectures on these subjects, excepting the two courses by Hegewisch, before mentioned. Though in later life he was far from possessing a metaphysical cast of mind, it appears that at this time he devoted himself with great zeal to the study of philosophy, particularly the system of Kant. The Greek and Roman classics were at all times the most attractive to him; but while at college he only permitted himself to read them as a sort of reward for industry. When reading the ancients, he completely lived in their

* He was son-in-law to Wieland, and the predecessor of Fichte at Jena.

† Though he did not stir from his house for weeks together, he spent nearly all his leisure hours in reading travels, many of which he obtained from the elder Niebuhr; and he used to beg him to send him none in any country nearer than Turkey, because all that described European countries reminded him so strongly of the Revolution that he could not bear to read them.

world and with them. He once told a friend, who had called on him and found him in great emotion, that he often could not bear to read more than a few pages at a time in the old tragic poets; he realized so vividly all that was said and done and suffered, by the persons represented. He could see Antigone leading her blind father—the aged Œdipus entering the grove—he could catch the music of their speech, and felt certain that he could distinguish the true accent of the Greeks, though he could not reproduce it with his barbarian tongue.

His liveliness of imagination, and quickness and depth of feeling, rendered his mental condition extremely variable; his sense of enjoyment was so keen, that any thing which gave him pleasure would at times affect him even to tears, while, on the other hand, trivial circumstances would occasion him an unwarrantable degree of annoyance, or even excite him to. momentary asperity. His sensitive physical temperament aggravated this tendency, and when he was suffering in body or had over-studied himself, he became dull and incapable of mental exertion, and in such cases he would often fancy that his faculties were giving way; but an interesting conversation with a friend, or a literary work of importance, was sufficient to recover him from this state, and restore him to his mental powers.

The series of letters to his parents only extends to the middle of December, 1794, when it is interrupted, and we have no more addressed to them from that time to January, 1798. Of all that he wrote in the succeeding years, but few have been preserved. After the death of his father, he requested to have them returned to him, and all except those inserted in the "Lebensnachrichten" were destroyed when his house at Bonn was burnt down in 1830. Were the complete series still in existence, there would be little to add to their records of his life up to the time of his father's death.

The following extracts will give a picture of his life and mind during the first year of his university career, beginning when he was seventeen years and a half old.

I.

TO HIS PARENTS.

KIEL, 11*th May*, 1794.

MY DEAR PARENTS—When I remember the anxiety and sorrow we felt at parting, my gloomy ideas of this place, my melancholy at being transplanted, from my quiet peaceful occupations in the midst of you all, to this noisy town, and the deep silence of my solitary room, &c., how glad and thankful I am to have found every thing better than my expectations. I would give a great deal—yes, what I prize most of all, some days of my future stay with you—if you could know a little sooner how happy I am, if you could know it at this moment while I am writing.

On Friday morning I paid my calls. I found neither Dr. Hensler nor Hegewisch nor Cramer at home: thence I went to call on Ehler, who was supplying the place of Fabricius, as Dean of Philosophy, during his travels. Then I took a walk, and enjoyed, even to sadness, the beauty of the scenery, the blue sea, the flowery meadows, the green forest, and the singing of the nightingales. Hensler sent for me to come to him at six. You may believe I did not keep him waiting. I had expected a friendly reception, but not such a one as I found. I was shown into his library, where he came to me, and accosted me with such hearty kindness that he won me instantly. Other people came in afterward; but they did not put a stop to our conversation, indeed Eimbke rather helped it on. As I went away, Hensler told me I might come again as often as I liked; and he would do with me as he had done with some of his young friends before, send me into the library if he was busy. I shall certainly not neglect this opportunity of gaining both information and enjoyment. I told him of my great wish to see Reinhold, and he promised, when he saw him, to try and get me an invitation. Yesterday I found Hegewisch at home at last, but only for a few minutes; he had to go to an examination. He was very friendly, and said he hoped we should have many walks together. By his invitation I remained with Mrs. H., the first cultivated woman I have seen as yet in Kiel, except those whom I may have seen at the windows perhaps without knowing them. Carl Cramer's* misfortune was the subject of our conversation. She was so polite as to invite me to call frequently. Thence I went to the Library, where I made the acquaintance of Kordes, who was extremely civil to me.

I have just returned from Dr. Hensler's again. I am to call on Reinhold to-morrow. Hensler has obtained permission for me to do so. I am in a fever of impatience. Hensler assures me, he never saw any man whose first address so instantly prepossesses you in his favor and so irresistibly wins your heart. If I could but feel as free with him as with Hensler! I am convinced that Hensler takes a great interest in me. My ideas about the origin of the Greek tribes, the history of the colonization of the Greek cities, and my notions in general about the earliest migration from west to east, are new to him, and he thinks it probable that they may be correct. He exhorts me to work them out, and bring them into as clear a form as I can. But he will only allow me to study philosophy for the present; I am to let other matters rest, or at least do very little in them. I think, however, he will let me do more as soon as my progress in philosophy will allow of it without injury to my health, about which I have consulted him. I am much pleased to find that Hensler agrees with my political principles; and he is equally pleased that Reinhold agrees with him. My dinner society is very good. Among others I single out the advocate Jahn as a man of talent; but I have not yet had much conversation with him. Hensler has arranged my course of study thus:—Ger-

* The brother of the professor of this name before mentioned, and likewise a professor in Kiel. He lost his professorship at this time, owing to his openly expressed admiration of the French Revolution.

man History, with Hegewisch; Jurisprudence, with Cramer; Logic and Metaphysics, with Reinhold; and Æsthetics.

II.

KIEL, *27th May*, 1794.

I just fancy myself back again among you all with great vividness, and can assure you honestly, that it gives me much more pleasure than pain. I prize the advantages of Meldorf, and can tell you, that though I am very happy here, I learn nothing, putting Reinhold's instructions, and some other things, out of the question, compared to what I could at home, in my own room; for as to German History, I already know nearly all that comes in the lectures, and could learn more by myself. But this I say only to my most intimate friends, and to them in such a way that they can see I am very well contented here on the whole. I have now, I think, completed the circle of my more intimate friends, and do not mean to extend it. It consists of Reinhold, Hensler, Hegewisch, and, among the young men, Purgstall, Maisl, Meier of Altona, Thibaut, and Conrad Hensler.

Of philosophical books which I do not understand, I have so far a superfluity. Since I heard that Fichte has begun to defend the right of insurrection (which, however, Kant and Reinhold abhor), and to deny the obligation of treaties, I begin to fear that men are abusing the mysteries of philosophy, from which I expected, and still expect, the elucidation and solution of the most important questions, to the establishment of the most dreadful sophisms, or at least that a skillful hand may so abuse them. And then, if philosophy itself be turned against the cause of right and civil order, and the power of the mob be backed by the authority of brilliant fallacies, what refuge from their united tyranny is left us but death?

I long to get back to my ancients, my best friends, to whom I owe all my thoughts, at least on such subjects, to Aristotle and Cicero. Oh that it were permitted me, if only like the last of these, to attain an imperfect wisdom, and to expound it with his majesty of style!

III.

KIEL, *7th June*, 1794.

This day twelvemonth was a memorable one to me. It was the day I left Meldorf for Hamburgh. I do not know whether the recollection of it is cheering or depressing, but I am very fond just at present of looking back upon many things that occurred this time last year. This day month too, I left you for the second time in my life. The first month in Hamburgh did not pass away with such happy speed as this has done. There I suffered from illness and melancholy; here I enjoy health and spirits. And even if I had learnt little or nothing of lasting value to me, except from Reinhold and Hensler (though I have learnt a great deal besides), should I have cause to regret that I can not pursue my favorite study here, at least never with sufficient assiduity? Ought not the prospect of finding no insuperable difficulties in philosophy, to rejoice me as it does, even though I may never be able to master it entirely, but only to comprehend its general outline? I do not flatter myself with the idea that I shall ever become, properly speaking, a critical philosopher. No, that I dare not hope for, because I can not devote my whole life to this study, and indeed think I can employ it more profitably in active exertion. The philosopher's satisfaction ends with speculation. But, as Bolingbroke justly remarks, he who speculates in order to act, goes further. I could wish I had it in my power to do this, and to that end, should like to devote two years to philosophy, and then to study jurisprudence as long as might be necessary. But if I must be content with one year of philosophy, and even divide the latter half of that with jurisprudence, I will at least as far as I can, strive to gain a thorough insight into the system of the Critical philosophy, and when I have once got on the right track, follow it perseveringly till I have found either truth, or the impossibility of truth. It would certainly have been a good thing for me, to have inured myself previously to meditation, by the study of other systems of philosophy; and yet on the other hand, as it is, I can plant every thing in a fresh soil; no preconceived notions stand in the way of those which Reinhold communicates to me. If it were possible for him to develop all his ideas (or even some of them) in my mind with half his clearness of thought, how would even my skepticism vanish! But unfortunately I have only been able so far to clear up my ideas to a very small extent, and have to struggle with obscurity on all sides. True, it is gradually dispersing, and has already given way on some points; still, I constantly feel my weakness, and wish for more power of thought than I possess. We have now come to the faculty of Cognition, consequently have finished the Representational faculty. In the holidays I intend to study all we have gone through as thoroughly as I can, that when Reinhold returns, I may lay before him the principal points which I do not understand.

I have received the globe through H., and with the assistance of that and Dalrymple's Collection of Voyages of Discovery, I mean to begin a description of the South Sea; this will form the subject of my first essay; the second will be on the regions about Greenland, Iceland, and the doubtful Friesland, with reference to the voyages of the Zeni. It may also include some islands, probably fabulous, and certainly not now in existence, which on this, and other old globes, are placed between Europe and America. You see how busy I am. Whether I shall be able to accomplish all this, time will show; but it is a work in which no one can help me.

I have caught a little cold, so I did not get up till nearly six this morning, and have not done much to-day beyond beginning my researches concerning Solomon's Islands, about which our globe gives quite new results. Yesterday and to-day I have read a great deal in Pope, and it has quite refreshed me.

How much I shall have to read merely about Solomon's Islands! Are they really the New Hebrides of Bougainville, Cook, and Forster? or are they the Britannias of Carteret and Dampier?

I often take walks with Maisl. Our conversation is mostly about history; for as he attends Hegewisch's lectures on Universal History, as well as those on German History, he repeats to me the most important of Hegewisch's propositions in a condensed form, which I am often forced to dispute, but have notwithstanding almost as great a respect for Hegewisch's learning as for Hensler's, which is saying every thing.

I have not as yet fully explained to any body but Hensler, my ideas about the colonization of Greece, and the whole of Asia Minor, including Armenia, from the West. For the peopling of the rest of Asia, I assume,

1. the Aramaic or Assyrian race, to which belong the Arabs, Jews, Syrians, Assyrians, Chaldees, and Medes, of more or less pure descent; 2. the Indo-Persic; 3. the Tartar; 4. the Mongul; and 5. probably the Chinese race. Taking this as a basis, we can proceed further, and shall obtain every where at last the same result, viz., that these great national races have never sprung from the growth of a single family into a nation, but always from the association of several families of human beings, raised above their fellow animals by the nature of their wants, and the gradual invention of a language, each of which families probably had originally formed a language peculiar to itself. This last idea belongs to Reinhold. By this I explain the immense variety of languages among the North American savages, which it is absolutely impossible to refer to any common source, but which, in some cases, have resolved themselves into one language, as in Mexico and Peru for instance; and also the number of synonyms in the earliest periods of languages. On this account, I maintain that we must make a very cautious use of differences of language as applied to the theory of races, and have more regard to physical conformation, which latter is exactly the same, for instance, in most of the Indian tribes of North America. I believe further that the origin of the human race is not connected with any given place, but is to be sought every where over the face of the earth: and that it is an idea more worthy of the power and wisdom of the Creator, to assume that he gave to each zone and each climate its proper inhabitants, to whom that zone and climate would be the most suitable, than to assume that the human species has degenerated in such innumerable instances. Here is one of the most important elements of history still remaining to be examined, that which is, in truth, the very basis upon which all history must be reared, and the first principle from which it must proceed. This of all subjects should be thoroughly investigated in the first place; and then (to which philosophy is necessary) a universal history ought to be written, which should exhibit all nations from the same point of view. This point of view Reinhold beautifully defines as the relation between reason and sensation. When this universal history is completed, the separate history of each country should follow. This is the way in which I would teach history, if I had Hegewisch's learning and position. But the latter I wish for less and less the more I know of it. H. began to talk to me one day as if he wished to attract me to the academical profession; but withdrew his proposals, when I assured him that I should desire a life of greater activity, and more opportunity to make myself useful, especially in such times as ours. This he quite approved of, and advised me, therefore, zealously to study Roman law, and pitied me for having to devote so much time to other things; but as to this too every thing depends upon the point of view from which we regard our studies, and the manner in which we pursue them. I have not yet told Hensler of our projects, because they are growing rather problematical to me; but he bids me take courage whatever happen, for, he says, I should be certain to rise by my own exertion without any occasion for servility. That I voluntarily go to no parties, has his full approbation. They rob me of the evening and the morning hours; and, what is still worse, of the calmness of mind which must be undisturbed by dissipation, if one is to work.

IV.

KIEL, *6th July*, 1794.

My health is but indifferent. Hegewisch leaves this week, and then the lectures on German History will be over. I mean to employ the hours I shall then have at liberty, in walking to Düsternbrook, with a book, and reading there till toward noon. Of course, I shall not at first take the "Critique of Pure Reason," or the "Theory of the Representational Powers," to amuse myself with; but a simple historical work or a poet, Hume, Demosthenes, Pope, or something of that kind. The "Critique of Pure Reason," however, is not comparatively so very difficult, and some chapters seem to me quite easy to understand, very forcible, and when you are able to enter properly into their spirit, very clear. Hensler thinks me already quite competent to take the "Critique" in hand, but forbids me to do so on account of my health.

My acquaintance with M. has been put a stop to by the difference of our principles; and what is strange, not in politics, but philosophy. He denies the freedom of the will, and the moral law; is a fatalist and indifferentist: I subscribe to Kant's principles with all my heart. I have broken with M., not from any dispute we have had, but on account of the detestable conclusions which necessarily follow from his opinions, conclusions that absolutely annihilate all morality. I really loved him notwithstanding, but with such principles I could not be his friend.

V.

KIEL, *20th July*, 1794

You will see from the above that I am in good spirits. My occupations acquire new charms for me, and grow easier too, the further I advance and the more I get used to them.......

My head swims when I survey what I have yet to learn—philosophy, mathematics, physics, chemistry, natural history. Then, too, I must perfect myself in history, German and French, and study Roman law, and the political constitutions of Europe as far as I can, and increase my knowledge of antiquities; and all this must be done within five years at most, so far as a foundation can be laid in that time, for truly it will not allow me to accomplish more than that with regard to most of these things; and it would be hard indeed if I could not find time and opportunity afterward to complete the superstructure. I *must* know all these things, but how I shall learn them, Heaven knows! That I shall require them, as a learned man, or in any position I may occupy, I am fully convinced.

VI.

KIEL, *27th July*, 1794.

My health and spirits are quite restored, my dearest parents. I feel that I have made some progress in philosophy, and cleared the way for much more, so that I have not labored in vain. I see at last what I have yet to learn, and why I must learn it. I have received much assistance lately in this respect from a treatise of Spinoza's, which has wonderfully strengthened my mind and cleared up my thoughts....... I mean to make an abstract of all the best works that I read in every department of my studies, and arrange every subject under certain heads....... I think I shall make the most rapid progress in knowledge, by perfecting my acquaintance with the sciences that I have begun. In the seven years between this and my twenty-fifth year, I should like to lay a foundation in all the sciences that will be useful to me, so that afterward I might be able to keep pace with the progress of the age on all subjects, and to advance before it on some points, which I shall be all the more capable of doing from understanding them in their connection with the rest. I think that then (though I might reach my thirtieth year before completing the work that would only serve as an introduction to any creative labors of my own in science), I should know all that Bolingbroke requires for a competent statesman. And though I have quite lost the foolish ambition which made me think of aiming at high offices of state, the inward gain would still be left me, the consciousness of having developed my powers, and rendered myself fit for usefulness.

VII.

KIEL, 2*d August*, 1794.

......I now know who are the men worth knowing at the university, and can reckon all the best of them among my friends, or at least my acquaintance. We form a sort of circle, which Thibaut and I had thought of bringing together in a literary club, but we shall hardly be able to manage it this winter.

Purgstall's love for Greek is on the wane, since he took to spending the Saturdays and Sundays in the neighboring country places; and it makes me dislike the hour from six to seven, that I sacrifice to him out of friendship. I am vexed at it, and yet I do not like to let him see this, lest he should lose all liking for the lesson; in other respects I like him as well as ever; perhaps, too, he is suffering from home-sickness.

I hope much from the winter, when I shall take advantage of the long candle-light evenings in a warm room. The winter after, I shall spend at home, and go on with philosophy, ancient literature, my researches in Greek history, and mathematics. How much I shall be able to get through then in six or seven months! I should like at that time, by way of practice, to deliver some lectures on the principles of the Critical Philosophy to my friends. I should not bring forward any new doctrines; I have not capacity for that. Probably I might throw light on some points, but history is my vocation, and to that I shall perhaps some day make my philosophical acquisitions subservient. I shall very likely attend lectures on the Institutes this winter. Reinhold's "Letters,"* to say the truth (and a great part of the "Elucidations"), are, to my taste, as insipid as his "Theory" is delightful.

If I could introduce to you the friends with whom I am on terms of intimacy, or describe them to you, you would say I had chosen well, and esteem me happy to have found such in Kiel. Of some, I say myself, and you know I am not over-modest, that they are better than I; of most, those would say so, who know us and are impartial...... In Thibaut I have nothing to censure but a little obstinacy, and a leaning to democracy, which does not, however, prevent my loving him, since it seems to me excusable in him, considering his descent from the refugees of the last century; his apparent coldness gives way with frequent intercourse, and changes into the sincerest friendship; more industry, more vigor of intel-

* The Letters on Kant's Philosophy, mentioned above.

lect, more irreproachable virtue and integrity, can not be desired in a human being than he possesses.......

VIII.

KIEL, 21*st August*, 1794.

......Yesterday afternoon I felt very gloomy; I set off to Hensler's to cheer myself up. I went into the library, and had not been long there, when the servant was sent to ask me down stairs. I found, besides Hensler's wife and daughter-in-law, the mother and sister of the latter—consequently countrywomen of mine from Dithmarsh—and several others. I felt then really, to a painful degree, the timidity and bashfulness before ladies of which I wrote to you lately. However much I may improve in other society, I am sure I must get worse and worse every day in their eyes; and so, out of downright shyness, I scarcely dare speak to a lady; and as I know, once for all, that I must be insupportable to them, their presence becomes disagreeable to me. Yesterday, however, I screwed up my courage, and began to talk to Miss Behrens,* and young Mrs. Hensler. Now, in gratitude and candor, I must confess that they were sociable enough toward me to have set me at my ease if my shyness were not so deeply rooted. But it is of no use. I avoid them, and would rather be guilty of impoliteness, by avoiding them, than by speaking to them, which I should now feel to be the greatest impoliteness of all. At last, however, especially through taking a walk with Hensler and Dr. Behrens, I got so roused up that my awkwardness vanished, and I went home cured. Thus I was healed by Hensler's words and looks.

IX.

KIEL, 7*th September*, 1794.

......On Monday afternoon I received, through Purgstall, an invitation from Madame de R. to spend the evening with her. She had been two days floating about on the sea between here and Alsen, or whatever other more flowery mode of expression she may have selected. I tell you—and I do not know how I shall keep it to myself in Meldorf—she was insufferable, beyond comparison worse than on any former occasion. With a tone of great unction, she began to hold forth in such an absurd style, upon philosophical subjects, that I could not conquer myself so far as to let my silence be construed into assent. My objection was indeed as modestly urged as if it had been directed against Reinhold himself; that I held due to the lady; but it only caused the fair philosopher to produce her fancied arguments with all the greater earnestness. Positively I can not conceive how we could all take her for a philosopher. She is nothing but a miserable twaddler, shallow and insipid, words without ideas. Then, too, I have learnt to see through her conversational artifices. Three times, if not more, have I heard her tell the same anecdote; twice within the last few days has she repeated the same thing. We were talking about Providence. The lady said (God knows from what author she took it) that Providence could be proved more convincingly from the arrangements of nature, than from the course of history; and I maintained the contrary. Providence, I said, like the existence of God, was a matter of faith, not of demonstration; it lay beyond the province of reason, as the "Critique" beautifully shows

* Who was afterward his first wife

But if our aim was to find a support for our transcendental faith, we could not, strictly speaking, rest safely on arguments about the arrangements of nature, which could not do more than strengthen the belief in a supremely wise Cause of the universe, and could not even place this quite above the reach of attack from materialists. We must look to the succession of historical events for a confirmation of this faith. Perhaps it was the desire of confounding the lady-philosopher by a paradox, that incited me to lay down this, in itself, very tenable proposition. However, it was a barricade which, with all her loquacity, she could not get through. But before either she had owned herself vanquished, which she never would have done, or I had abandoned the strife from politeness, behold! there came the master, Reinhold himself, and she was silent. I might have talked on unrestrained, for I knew very well that, to be consistent, Reinhold must have agreed with me. I have been summoned to her house several times since, and on Thursday was even invited to dinner. She has left now. Has Hamburgh changed this woman, or did we see her in Meldorf through colored glass? It was our frivolity, good nature, vanity, and all our respective peculiarities of thought and feeling, which we discussed till we brought ourselves into a community of sentiment, and one and all got our heads heated about a woman for whom the heart must remain cold, unless it have run full speed from our control, and is seeking the first gate to stop at (for her heart is nothing but a voice, and has long ago evaporated into breath, like camphor in the air). I repeat, it was our own weakness and sentimentality that allowed us to find every thing ideal in this woman, as raw expositors do in the Bible; which is all the more natural in seclusion, in proportion as we have endeavored to do full justice to what we do not possess ourselves, and the more ambitiously we strive not to be exposed to the imputation of stupidity, from a want of appreciation. We were blind to overweening pretensions (which certainly indeed did not come up to those of yesterday); lectures, which were meant for the nourishment and satisfaction of her unbounded vanity, we believed to be devoted to our improvement; literally the very same questions have been put to us again upon these lectures, till we were weary of them, and now as mechanically as if the word-machines, then perhaps new, were by this time quite worn smooth with use. We submitted to receive honor from her. However, the delusion is over with me—a delusion that has been dissipated simply by reflection. For she has done me honor now too, and no sort of neglect or jealousy has warped my judgment. The honor that is my due can only be conferred on me by men like Reinhold and Hensler, for they have it in rich abundance to bestow; but not by any presumptuous dispenser of a usurped possession. I will receive roses and myrtles from female hands, but no laurels; I only wish that I may plant them, and then be crowned by three or five men......

X.*

KIEL, 29*th October*, 1794.

......It is certain that I feel the loss of all much more deeply, now that I have enjoyed these lost blessings again for a short time in such full measure, than I did before, when I lived in complete ignorance of the future, and then too forgot so many things almost entirely in the complete novelty of my position. What I miss, and always shall miss, you know;

* Written after having returned from Meldorf.

and I am not sure that it is good for me to dwell upon it. My isolation —not isolation from strangers, that is salutary—but isolation from my own family, from those who are nearest and dearest to me in the world—this is what would still frequently depress my spirits, if I did not strive with all my might not to feel it. The beginning of next month shall find me diligent; as intent upon banishing troublesome thoughts as upon advancing in knowledge. Knowledge, what is commonly called learning, mere dull memory-work, will never be the aim of my exertions. The one thing needful is, to cultivate one's understanding for one's self, so as to render it capable of production. He who merely crams himself with the conceptions of other men's minds, clothed in forms foreign to his own nature, will never accomplish much. Quiet and independent energetic industry can alone attain to what is true, and bring forth what is really useful. . . . . . .

XI.

KIEL, 16*th November*, 1794.

. . . . . . I am now accustomed to my solitude, and do not get gloomy when I am alone the whole evening, and work till eleven o'clock.* . . . . . . Yesterday evening I was much pleased to hear of the new plan of education in France. "Go thy way, and sin no more." That is all that lies in our power. . . . . . . It would heartily rejoice me if I could some day conclude a history of all those horrors, with the account of measures through which a great nation might become happy and truly enlightened, and should live to witness the result of these judicious plans. . . . . . .

Hensler cherishes views with regard to my future career, in which I can not fully concur. He wants me to be a natural philosopher, and to make the natural history of antiquity the special object of my investigations This is a good and worthy and beautiful pursuit for those who like it; but from the peculiar direction of my mind and talents, I believe that nature has intended me for a literary man, an historian of ancient and modern times, a statesman, and perhaps a man of the world; although the last, thank God, neither in the proper sense of the word, nor in the horrible one that is usually associated with it. Meanwhile, my individual taste will certainly carry the day; and, if my name is ever to be spoken of, I shall be known as an historian and political writer, as an antiquarian and philologist. I study the sciences, which Hensler would make my ultimate object, merely as the means of procuring greater richness of ideas, rendering my heart and head clear and bright, or rather subjecting my poor heart, which will go on sentimentalizing and blundering, to my head. Meanwhile, I constantly become more and more estranged from the world, in the ordinary sense of the term; but the less I mix myself up with it, the more affectionately do my thoughts turn to you; and I trust that some day, through my love, obedience, and the fruits of my honest endeavors, I may, if not reward you for your love, at least prove that it has not been thrown away. Therefore forgive me when I am prolix, and forget myself over my writing. I acknowledge how much I owe to your care and affection, and I only regret that you were not stricter and more severe with me; for what would have hurt and pained me at the time, would now be

* While it appears from Letter III., that he considered it late when he was not up before six in the morning.

very beneficial to me, and I should ere this have attained much that still costs me an effort. Therefore I would warn every one, whose child shows a bad disposition, to hold him in while he is young, for there is not much fear of breaking his spirit. His innate impudence will protect him from this; and I feel, by myself, that our faults can not be torn up with too much violence in childhood, before they have taken too deep a root. It is not every one who is so deeply in earnest in the effort to overcome his faults as, God knows, I am. For many others, therefore, it is yet more necessary; and it is better for him who has a proneness to frivolity and other vices, to "suffer in the body that the soul may be saved."......

XII.

KIEL, 23*d November*, 1794.

I will not deny, my dearest parents, that I was distressed and hurt by the undeserved tone of displeasure which seemed to prevail in both your letters. You are dissatisfied with me because I seek no society, or rather because I avoid parties.......But you will allow that I am at the University, not to lead as pleasant a life as I can, but to turn all my time and powers to account. And believe me, dearest parents, it would be impossible to be as happy in much society as I am in the feeling that my solitude is well employed. When I have completed my studies I will enter the world. Woe be to the fool who enters it before he has knowledge enough to compensate for its emptiness......My dear parents, do not misunderstand me. I do not mean to be an oddity, and I am not a misanthrope. ......If my letter has really the morose tone which you, dearest mother, think you perceived in it, it was certainly quite accidental. It may be that the strict mode of life which I impose upon myself gives a sort of rigidity to my manners and every thing about me, even to the tone of my letters. But, believe me, I am none the worse for it. I must do one of two things; either I must accommodate myself to the manners of our vicious, effeminate, and feeble age, or I must keep my own manners, consequently my own tone and mode of thinking and speaking. In the first case, I may, perhaps, please a great part of my contemporaries, but certainly not the better part, nor myself, nor posterity. In the second, I must indeed offend the partisans of the first, but it will be possible for me to live so as to deserve my own approbation, and so as not to pass away with the great multitude of my nameless contemporaries.......

XIII.

KIEL, 30*th November*, 1794.

......I spent an evening with Behrens lately, and we laid a wager. He asserts that within a year, more than one revolution will break out, and I assert the contrary. On the other hand, I have offered to lay a wager with him, that in four years a monarchical government will be re-established in France.* I find myself constantly confirmed in this opinion as I read the English history, which I do a good deal in my leisure moments. If I had time, I should like to get more facts together, and as it is, I have found in the very rare notices which are inserted in the notes to Algernon Sidney's "Discourses," and seem to be quite unknown in

* If Niebuhr had said *five* years he would have gained his wager. Napoleon was created First Consul on the 10th of November, 1799.

Germany, very striking and extraordinary parallels. Unfortunately I have no time for employments of this kind at present! And yet history grows dearer and dearer to me, so much so that my ardor in reading history interferes with my zeal for philosophy, while no philosophy can blunt my inclination to history......Salchow came in just as I was writing about him. We took up our usual occupation. I am dictating to him a short outline of the history of the French war. I am astonished at my own memory, for I still remember with great distinctness the merest trifles that have occurred from 1792 onwards.

XIV.

KIEL, *6th December*, 1794.

......This day is the anniversary of Algernon Sidney's death, one hundred and eleven years ago, and hence it is in my eyes a consecrated day, especially as I have just been studying his noble life again. May God preserve me from a death like his, yet even with such a death, the virtue and holiness of his life would not be dearly purchased. And now he is forgotten almost throughout the world, and perhaps there are not fifty persons in all Germany, who have taken the pains to inform themselves accurately about his life and fortunes. Many may know his name, many know him from his brilliant talents, but they formed the least part of his true greatness.......

What I am dictating to Salchow is not a history of the Revolution, but merely a brief outline of the war, and is really a recreation which serves to exercise my memory. This trusty servant has preserved dates for the last two years of which I have rarely thought a second time. Among the many whimsical crotchets which have plagued me from time to time, I once took it into my head that it injured the judgment to strengthen the memory, and therefore resolved to give up the latter. But nature was kinder to me than I deserved. I retained every thing without effort, and now I am as anxious to strengthen the one as the other.......

My dictating to Salchow is no secret, and as my attempt seems likely to turn out very well, I do not care into whose hands the paper may fall. I do not copy it; what I have once given forth I do not like to see again. It is too insignificant to be worth printing; in manuscript it might be useful to an officer.

Niebuhr's intercourse, however, during his college life at Kiel, was by no means confined to the professors and students of the University, but he was admitted into a circle of the intellectual society of Holstein, which then comprised some of the most highly gifted persons of that day in Germany.

The little city of Eutin, delightfully situated on the wooded shores of an extensive lake, about twenty miles from Kiel, formed a sort of centre to this circle. It had formerly been an imperial bishopric, and was afterward secularized and transferred to Oldenburg, with which duchy it came into the possession of Denmark but still retained a separate administration, the president of which at this time was Count Frederick Leopold Stolberg. His elder brother Christian—married to a sister of the two Counts Reventlow—lived at no great distance on his estates. The two brothers, belonging to one of the most ancient families in Germany, were both well known as poets and public men, though the younger was much the more distinguished of the two. The elder was a man of noble and pure mind, and sincere religious feeling, and possessed talents of no mean order, but he had not the originality nor the fiery depth of feeling which characterized Count F. L. Stolberg. The latter was full of genius, life, and affection, but already disturbed by the consciousness of those deficiencies in his hereditary creed and church, which led, three years later, to his making a profession of Catholicism. The secretary to the government was Nicolovius, afterward minister of public worship in Prussia, whose acquaintance Niebuhr seems to have made at this time, and to whom several of his letters are addressed. Voss was rector of a gymnasium at Eutin, and the amiable and intellectual philosopher and poet Jacobi, likewise resided there at that time. Near Kiel lived Count Frederick Reventlow, Curator of the University of Kiel, a man of intellect, integrity, and high cultivation; a conservative in politics, and a strict Lutheran in religion. He had lately returned from his mission as embassador in London. His wife, a sister of Count Schimmelman, the Danish minister of finance, exercised, by her brilliant powers and unaffected religious fervor, scarcely less influence over the circle of their associates than himself. The professors Hensler and Cramer belonged to this coterie. All its members were conservative in their principles excepting Voss, whose views, indeed, were so little in unison with those of the rest, that they were already beginning to divide him from his friends.

Niebuhr spent his long vacations with his parents, but his shorter ones were generally passed at Eutin, on visits to Voss, Jacobi, or Count F. L. Stolberg. Of these Jacobi had the greatest influence over him. The union in Jacobi, of candor, amiability, high refinement, and calm philosophic thought, with taste and susceptibility of feeling, particularly attracted him. The predominance of the moral sentiment in both, and their intense reverence for all that was exalted and holy, was a link between them, and Niebuhr's letters show that there were few to whom he could so unreservedly unbosom himself. His friendship with him was only broken by the death of the latter in 1819. Niebuhr also made the acquaintance, about this time of Schlosser,* the brother-in-law of Goethe, mentioned in his "Dichtung und Wahrheit," and the poet Baggesen,† whose talents he greatly admired, though he regretted his unsettled life and character. During the second year of his college life Niebuhr became acquainted with Count Adam Moltke, then residing at Kiel, who was several years older than himself, but admitted him to as close an intimacy as if they had been on a footing of equality. They soon became bosom friends, and retained their affection for each other through life. Moltke is thus described, as he was a few years later, by the son of an intimate friend of both himself and Niebuhr.

"Count Adam Moltke had lived from about the beginning of the present century at Nütschau, an estate in Holstein, which he had received as a compensation for the loss of the fief formerly held by his family in Zealand. Outwardly gifted with a magnificent manly figure, a noble forehead and flashing eyes, inwardly overflowing with energy, and rich in imagination, the principles of the French Revolution had taken a powerful hold of his mind, and for years he was among its warmest and certainly one of its purest adherents. After having visited a great part of Europe, and undergone many a bitter grief, he retired to Nütschau, where he strove—apart from political employments, but full of interest in public events—to endure the iron age in patience with a strong resignation. He needed but a few hours' sleep, and sought to still his inward restlessness by the earnest and continuous study of history; in particular he made himself acquainted with the development of the Italian Republics of the middle ages in its minutest details. He often endeavored to give a poetical form to his mental life, or to present an historical picture of the well known political relations of past times, but he was unable to clothe the ideas floating in his mind, in shapes sufficiently clear and distinct, to render them fit to go forth into the external world. Thus it was denied him to take an active part in history either by word or deed; but as in his ardent and stirring youth he had

* Author of several papers on various subjects connected with jurisprudence, and the translator of Aristotle's Politics and Longinus on the Sublime.

† Professor of the Danish language and literature in Kiel. He had considerable celebrity as a poet, both in Danish and German. His best poem in the latter language is, "Parthenäis oder die Alpenreisen."

exercised an irresistible influence over every one who came in contact with him, so when a man he brought life and energy into every circle he entered. 'He had reached the perfection of his nature,' wrote Niebuhr, in 1806, of this the dearest friend of his youth; 'he had tamed the lion, the restless spirit within him, and was employing his Oriental fire in the animation of Greek forms.' "

Niebuhr's letters to Moltke, of which the following are some extracts, are all that have been preserved of his correspondence during this epoch.

XV.

TO COUNT ADAM MOLTKE.

KIEL, *4th August,* 1795.

I went to your library yesterday to fetch Frisch, for which I thank you in your absence. Remember Hickes, for truly in the sweat of our brow must we learn our mother tongue, for the jargon which we speak is no longer a language. Our forefathers were better off before the Thirty Years' War. Then there was but one speech for gentle and simple, and that was German. Ours is like our jurisprudence, the Divine-Mosaic-Roman-Lombard-canonical-German-statutary code, as some one calls it. Our language is Greek-Roman-Gallic-German-provincial. That most disastrous of wars, which made our princes absolute sovereigns, the Protestants of Upper Germany Catholics, and those of Lower Germany orthodox—which permitted the Jesuits to flourish, desolated the whole land, robbed the Empire of its independence, and our towns of their power—that lamentable war has ruined our language forever. And this want of a language adapted at once to literature and popular use, is a curse that rests perpetually and exclusively on our nation.

Let us deliver ourselves from this yoke as far as we can! One man has done so, and the result will be, that this element of his intellectual greatness will cause his songs and orations to live longer than those of all our other German sages. I refer to Voss, whose "Luise" has lately afforded me such unequaled enjoyment, that it were a sin against friendship on my part, if I, knowing the existence of such a masterpiece, did not invite you also to contemplate and admire it. He may be (and will be perhaps, for after ages) to Germany, what Homer and the most perfect of the Greek poets were to their nation. Did he meet with such a reception as they found among their unrivaled fellow-countrymen—were his idylls publicly recited to the people, and his songs sung in popular assemblies, how much might such a teacher accomplish! He would effect more that was really good and great than *the only true philosophy*, should that ever be discovered. I should like to prescribe Voss and Lessing, for you and myself, as our exclusive aliment. Voss forbids every author but Lessing, whom he deems perfect, except that he wants rhythm; he did not, indeed, name himself as the second, but no doubt he knows what he is, and would despise the false modesty of refusing to confess it on a fitting occasion. Forsake even Klopstock, and measure yourself by the severe standard of these men; such at least is my resolution. Not without reason do I speak thus warmly of "Luise." It has done what a book scarcely ever did before—drawn tears of delight from my eyes. It is a striking example that to move the reader most deeply, the author must be in perfect repose, and the style of his whole work calm and mellowed. We can never sufficiently study and examine this late-born Greek. I, at least with Homer, Sophocles, Æschylus, Pindar, Horace, and him, would willingly resign all the other poets in the world: yet this is too hastily written—I could not relinquish Theocritus and that German-Greek, Gessner. It will seem strange to you, perhaps even ridiculous, that I should pass over Klopstock. It has cost me much to do so, but if strict justice be done, I fear he will not stand before the Greek tribunal. I must except the most finished of his odes, which Alcæus himself need not blush to acknowledge, were they ascribed to him, and also the "Republic of the Learned," a thoroughly German work. Voss's criticism has robbed me of the "Grammar," and I am ashamed of the praise I once bestowed on it. But then, alas, the "Messiah!" This rigid justice is a sacrifice, and as you know how I revere this great creator, or rather resuscitator, of our literature, you will appreciate it as it deserves. I have sat at his feet, and am at least not ungrateful.

If you are frequently kept waiting for an answer when you expect one soon, there shall, at least, be no delay whenever business is concerned. So much for excuses and promises. I wish you health and happiness!

NIEBUHR.

XVI.

MELDORF, *in October*, 1795.

The service you have done me is, as you know, most essential. This book shall occupy not a little of my time this winter, and it gives quite a different insight into our language, usually treated so ignorantly by all our modern grammarians; for who can pronounce what a certain thing ought to be, and what it ought not to be, without having traced it to its origin, and thence derived the laws of its after course? Wolf, in Halle, makes himself indeed somewhat ridiculous by his exaggerated praises of grammatical studies even of the most trivial nature, for he ascribes far too much of the literary disgrace of our modern times to the neglect of such pursuits, but there is too plainly some truth in what he says. But to adduce the ill-effects on their respective languages, of the rules laid down by the Alexandrine, and recently by the Florentine Academies, as an argument against all attempts to give a language fixed grammatical forms, is quite wrong. For these Academies set to work in the wrong way, they took their forms from the writers of their golden age, and in every age when much has been written, and by men of talent, the language has swerved from its original use. But it is only from its primitive style that rules can be drawn why a man must express himself thus, and no otherwise, if he will speak Greek or German. No instance from the most intellectual and fertile author of the most brilliant period can justify, or even excuse, his successor for the use of an expression which offends against those fundamental laws. For the former had no more liberty than I have. The case is different with secondary meanings and shades of meanings, which depend more on the spirit of the age. I am not bound to remain absolutely faithful to the sense which the most ancient writers may have affixed to a word; if the sense ascribed to it by the moderns is more suitable, I may make use of it, and perhaps it is even the duty of an author to obey custom in such a case, in order to make himself intelligible. But it would certainly be advisable for our philosophers to examine into the primitive meaning of the words which they employ; they would not then impose on them so much more than they can bear, and it might lead them to some conclusions which would render many an acute dissertation unnecessary. Hence I most earnestly wish to see such an examination undertaken, and to see it employed as the foundation, at least in part, of the history of philosophy. It has long been my conviction that such an investigation must begin from the beginning, and gradually descend to our own times, if it is to get behind the scenes of the history of systems and opinions, and I was not a little pleased to find from Jacobi, when he was in Kiel, that he quite agrees with me. . . . . Before all things I must say a little more about Jacobi. He seems to me to gain indescribably by personal acquaintance, and to display in all his manners, and his whole being, a noble nature, which his later writings do not show in its simplicity.

To me this shows how a man of great endowments may fall into thoroughly bad mannerism, and if this once happens, there is a danger of his sinking into it ever deeper. But as to the man himself, his kindness and gentleness, his singular urbanity, his eloquence, the grace of his manners, and the rich unbroken flow of his discourse, I find that none of his many admirers have praised him too highly; on the contrary, all these qualities singly and in combination surpassed far and far every expectation I had previously formed. You know, or may guess from a conversation we had not long before your journey, that my opinion of him had been somewhat lowered by the judgment of men whom I respected. I silently asked his forgiveness for it as soon as I saw him, and still more when I knew him better, for I had this good fortune, and was able to ask his opinion on many subjects. Rejoice! He says Fichte is among the first of men and philosophers, and is on the right road, &c. . . . .

While Niebuhr was on a visit to Eutin in January, 1796, Dr. Hensler received a commission from the Danish minister of finance, Count Schimmelman, to ask the young Niebuhr if he were willing to accept the post of private secretary to him for a few years. Some of Niebuhr's productions had excited Schimmelman's interest, and he had also frequently heard of him as a young man of very eminent talent from his brother-in-law Count Reventlow, and the Stolbergs. Dr. Hensler, who was on the point of setting out for Eutin, took Count Schimmelman's letter with him, and communicated it to Niebuhr. Both he and Hensler felt some hesitation at the interruption it would cause to his studies; still they both perceived the great advantages of such a connection, not only as regarded his future position, but also his improvement in practical knowledge.

Hensler knew also, that although only nineteen years of age, he was sufficiently well grounded in knowledge, and ripe enough in understanding and character, to perform the duties that would devolve upon him to Schimmelman's satisfaction, and to enter on the great world without peril to his industry and morality. Stolberg and Jacobi strongly urged his acceptance of the offer. Niebuhr referred the decision unconditionally to his father. The elder Niebuhr, who could conceive of no pleasure so great as that of visiting foreign countries, had originally wished that his son should follow in his steps, and carry out the enterprise which he had himself contemplated. He became afterward convinced that his son's delicacy of health would prove an insuperable obstacle to such plans, but still wished him to travel within the limits of the civilized world; and when he hoped to see him filling some diplomatic office, it is hard to say, whether he most desired it for its own sake as an honorable post in the service of the state, or because it would involve a residence abroad. For the present, he advised him to accept Count Schimmelman's offer, but only in the first instance for a year, or a year and a half, so that he might afterward be at liberty to pursue his studies abroad.

The offer was therefore accepted, and Niebuhr, who had to enter on his post at Easter, left Kiel early in the spring, in order that he might spend some weeks first with his parents. Moltke accompanied him to Meldorf. While there, he paid a visit to Dr. Behrens, the prefect of North Dithmarsh, and the father of his friend Madame Hensler. At the house of the latter he had already been introduced, as we have seen, to her younger sister. He had also known Dr. Behrens for some time, and had a high esteem for him and his wife, but his usual shyness in the society of women had prevented his ever entering into conversation with the daughters. Now, however, he had a common topic of interest in speaking of Madame Hensler, and he soon became deeply impressed with the nobleness and worth of Amelia Behrens, though he did not express his feeling, and indeed scarcely ventured to encourage the idea that she would ever return his attachment

CHAPTER III.

NIEBUHR'S FIRST RESIDENCE IN COPENHAGEN. 1796—1798.

COUNT SCHIMMELMAN was the son of a man who had made an immense fortune by contracting for the army, and was afterward ennobled and made a count. This second count was for thirty years minister of finance and commerce in Denmark, which under his administration enjoyed a high degree of prosperity up to the time of the ruinous war with England at the beginning of this century. The termination of the slave trade and the emancipation of the negroes in the colonies, were owing to him (though he was one of the largest landed proprietors in the West Indies), and he was also the author of many other measures for the amelioration of their moral and physical condition. Affairs of state did not, however, engross his whole attention; he took a warm interest in science and art, and willingly extended help and encouragement to those engaged in their pursuit. Yet this extraordinary man was small almost to insignificance in person, of a nervous and sensitive temperament, and so retiring and humble in his manners that a stranger would have fancied him quite oppressed with diffidence. His house was the resort of all who were distinguished for talents or cultivation, whether foreigners or residents in the city. Copenhagen itself was perhaps at that time in its highest prosperity; its trade was extensive and flourishing; the government was greatly respected both at home and abroad. Commerce was carried on with great activity; travelers from all regions, and natives of every part of the globe, were to be seen there.

On his arrival in Copenhagen, Niebuhr was received by Count Schimmelman with a friendliness which at once inspired him with a very agreeable idea of his new position. His first impressions were not contradicted by his further experience. In a short time he had so won the esteem and confidence of Count Schimmelman, and discharged the duties intrusted to him so completely to his satisfaction, that the count had hardly any secrets from him, and used to converse with him openly and familiarly on the weightiest matters of state. Others also sought his society, not only because he was a favorite with Schimmelman, but for the sake of the more than ordinary life and interest which his intellect and vivacity imparted to general conversation. His position in Schimmelman's house, and the consideration which his father enjoyed, gave him access to the houses of the highest families and the most distinguished officers of state and scholars in Copenhagen, as well as those of the principal merchants.

At first, Niebuhr was highly delighted with this new world, but he soon found that society took up too much of his time, and interfered with the calmness as well as the leisure requisite for study during the hours that Schimmelman did not require his services. The consciousness that he was thus wasting his time, and the self-dissatisfaction that ensued, affected his health and spirits, but he now found it difficult to draw back. This was particularly the case with regard to the parties at Schimmelman's house. The countess, who had delicate health, and on this account usually excused herself from attendance at court, and visits out of her own house, was nevertheless extremely fond of society, and apt to require rather too much attention from her acquaintance. She invited Niebuhr to join in her parties, which he at first did very willingly, but when, feeling the necessity of economizing his time for better objects, he gradually withdrew, it produced an unpleasant state of feeling between him and the countess. This lasted so long as he remained in the house, and rendered his position there often extremely uncomfortable, but after he had left it, the offense was forgotten, and he continued to see her on the footing of an intimate friend.

In the month of August, however, the Prime Minister, Count P. A. Bernstorff, offered him the post of supernumerary secretary at the Royal Library, with no salary in the first instance, but with permission to travel abroad after a time. He at once accepted this offer, but in compliance with Count Schimmelman's request, remained in his service till the count could find a suitable person to take his place. As Schimmelman was not able to do this for some time, Niebuhr continued to act as his private secretary till May or June, 1797.

Niebuhr had accepted the post at the library, in order to extricate himself from the whirlpool of society into which he had been drawn, and to have the power of laboring with less hindrance in those fields of science to which his taste still chiefly inclined. He partially succeeded in this attempt, but not to the extent he had hoped. His talents for public business were already so conspicuous, that Schimmelman often intrusted commissions to him, which he always willingly undertook; and he was also disturbed in his pursuits by attractive offers from other quarters. For instance, he writes to Mrs. Hensler as early as August, 1796, "I have received from France, the offer of a post of literary activity, which would have involved an immediate journey to Rome. How much there was against the thing you will see yourself. I informed Schimmelman of it, who saw what attractions it held out to me, but at the same time was not blind to its disadvantages." On Mrs. Hensler's expressing her fears about plans of this nature in such perilous times, he replies in September, "It appears to me that you see more cause for alarm than really exists. At any rate, I decided long ago not to venture on this seductive step. How indeed could I bear to live so far from all who are dear to me—among a nation to whom in general I have an aversion? A wish was afterward expressed to see me in the suite of the next Danish embassy to Paris, without any suggestion of the kind on my part.* You know that this accords with similar wishes of my father's. For the present, however, I have declined the proposal. You know that I am appointed secretary at the library. This is exactly what I could have wished; it releases me from obligations which had been imposed upon me over and above my personal duties to Schimmelman—from waste of time—from all bustle and distraction—gives me the hope of living with Conrad Hensler this winter, and of going abroad next year to prosecute my studies with all earnestness. How much I mean to profit by this journey, and feel that I need to profit by it, I have already told your father Dr. Hensler."

Niebuhr remained therefore during the winter of 1796–97, at Count Schimmelman's, in his former position. In the course of this winter he frequently saw Baggesen, with whose intellect and geniality he had been already charmed when in Holstein, but whose instability of character both in thought and action he always deplored.

In the spring he left Count Schimmelman's, and hired apartments in the city, but remained on his former terms of friendship

* Probably by Grouvelle, who was at this time the French minister in Copenhagen, and who tried much to attach Niebuhr to himself.

and intimacy with the count. As a proof of the esteem in which he was held by him, it may be mentioned that in August, 1797, Schimmelman offered him the situation of Consul-general in Paris during the war. His official duties in this post would probably have led him to visit the southern provinces of France, and a portion of Spain. Before Niebuhr had fully decided whether to accept it or not, the place was applied for by a man whose years and length of service entitled him to consideration. The greater quiet and freedom from interruption in his new situation was very beneficial to Niebuhr. In August, 1797, he paid a visit to his friends in Holstein. He first went to Kiel, where he spent a fortnight, and met Amelia Behrens almost daily at the house of Dr. Hensler. The impression which she had made on him a year before was renewed and deepened. His secret wishes could not escape the eye of Madame Hensler. She spoke openly to him on the subject before he left for Meldorf, begged that while there he would seriously examine his feelings and his position, consult his parents, and regulate his conduct toward her sister accordingly. The following letter he wrote to her in reply:

XVII.

MELDORF, 20*th August*, 1797.

Yesterday was the fourth evening since our conversation—a conversation which will remain eternally imprinted on my memory. Since then, I have not only visited a new place, which till now has always been enough to run away with my imagination, but have also revisited those spots, which, from the number and vividness of my associations with them, were wont to banish for a time all other thoughts. I have seen my parents and sister, my acquaintances, and our friends, the Voss's—but the remembrance of those last hours is still fresh in my heart, as at the first moment of our parting.

I never grieved more at having reached the end of a happy time, and yet never felt so full of joy and hope as in these last few days. You and your friends made me very happy while I was with you. I told you my sorrows, and you comforted me; I rejoiced with the purest joy in the affection and virtue of my beloved friends; they were all crowded together in Kiel, and knew and loved each other well. You brought me nearer to those, who, though the dearest on earth to you, were as yet almost strangers to me. I felt that my friends loved me, and I had no thought beyond the present; at last, dear friend, you did more than this; you had guessed my wishes, and seen that I dared not express them; you gave words to my timorous thoughts, and in so doing suffered me to cherish them. What a change for one who had before stood alone, and looked on solitude as his doom!

At every moment that I have had to myself for reflection, I have pondered on the idea, and asked myself whether the reality would be as happy as the prospect was entrancing. I found the question very simple, and the answer was, "Were I to obtain the blessing of which I am not yet worthy, I should have more than I ever ventured to desire, and my happiness could only be disturbed by my own fault!" It is not necessary to know your Amelia long. Can one help believing in her at first sight? Why should I repeat what you know already, that her presence gave me such unspeakable, heartfelt delight! The first speaking glance of her clear, beautiful eyes, her richly-cultivated mind, that reveals itself so simply and unassumingly, almost timidly; her purity, her tenderness, shine out in all her words and motions, and would be evident to one less susceptible than I am. I see no shadow, not even a cloud, to dim this sunshine, when I think only of myself.

Your objection that Amelia is nearly three years older than I, and that even equality of age is in general undesirable, is I think inapplicable in my case;—and then I have two remarks to make as regards myself:—First, that two years of strenuous endeavor, during which the possibility of the new position you have pointed out to me, would fill my mind with pictures of a happy future, would resemble hot, sunny, fertilizing days, in which the fruit which has long hung green and hard upon the tree, rapidly receives color, perfume, and ripeness; without metaphor, that these two years would make me worthier of Amelia. Secondly, that the advice of a wiser friend has ever been invaluable to me, because I am apt to neglect the small duties of daily life; this you see in our friendship, and how much more with such a being if she were wholly mine! But I dare not think too constantly about it, for the more vividly I picture to myself such unclouded happiness, the more painful becomes the doubt whether Amelia will ever consent to unite herself to me. Just what makes me see that in a connection with her I should gain a sure guide, and many wounds of my heart would be gently healed—namely, her decidedly superior maturity of character—must prevent her from thinking of me. We all strive after something above us, to support and elevate us, and will she alone be unable to estimate her own worth in comparison with others'?

I wait with impatient desire for your next letter. I wonder whether you have as much hope as when we parted, or whether you will advise me to suppress the beautiful thought before it grows into an unconquerable longing.

After staying three weeks with his parents, he returned to Kiel. The following letter to Moltke shows with what result.

XVIII.

KIEL, *October*, 1797.

Dora and I send you and your wife this messenger, because we can not bear to wait several days before writing to you, especially as our letter would be a long time on the road; so you will receive this before another, that Dora wrote to you two days ago, which announced as close at hand what has now really taken place. I am in far too great an agitation to say much. Each of you take one of our letters; Dora's will tell you the most. Yesterday evening, at Dora's house, Amelia decided in my favor. Her heart had already decided. Love can distinguish between truth and pretense. She assumed no girlish affectation when Dora gave words to feelings that had before scarcely expressed themselves, and joined our hands. This pure simplicity, this Roman decision, in a gentle heart, made my happiness perfect, and made it possible. A long time of trial, full of doubt and uncertainty—servitude to win a love, that can not be sustained by gallantry and pretty flatteries, but must take root in the heart—would either have frightened me away, or harassed me to death; and yet one scarcely sees any thing else, except where the suitability of the connection is calculated, and every thing negotiated by the papa and mamma on each side. I long considered this servitude as the only means of becoming intimately acquainted with a girl, for the gulf, which custom and our folly have placed between young men and women, seemed to me impassable. And so it would have been to me, had not Dora's heart and Dora's wisdom allowed me to follow my nature completely. I know that I have earnestly endeavored not to deceive Milly. In our conversations when we met, I spoke to her from my inmost heart, and took pains to discover to her, what, if concealed, might have deceived her, and made her very unhappy hereafter; for I thought myself bound not to deny what still clings to me from former evil times as a stain to be washed out; but I hope to God, that happiness, and the power of love, this new unknown force, and above all, the contemplation of the proud joy in her angelic heart, and an openness that will rather gain than lose through absence, will purify me before we can be united—for absence is before us. The letter Dora wrote to you the day before yesterday will have told you all about it. It is inevitable, and you will not misunderstand me when I tell you, that I do not now view it with dread. O who could feel themselves separated, when in spirit and in love they are so inseparable! I embrace every effort, every toil, every sacrifice, for all will render me worthier of my Milly. It is true we have a long future before us, but who knows how it may be shortened? And if I, who have not your equability, can not promise Milly your evenness of temper, your constant warmth, I can promise her inviolable truth, and ever-growing, exclusive love. And woe to him who does not repose with full confidence upon the truth of a pure-hearted maiden! I shall assuredly know neither suspicion nor jealousy. And she who equally possesses both our hearts, our Dora, who can now live wholly for us, and is through us brought back to the world, will unite us by the rarest bond. Thank you, dearest of friends, as much as it is possible to thank, for the kind solicitude that you shared with Dora. My heart was sealed up, and my courage gone. Many a pretty face, and here and there a bright creature, had given me a passing pleasure, but only once had the thought of a connection risen vividly before my mind; and when the event made me angry with the maiden and despise myself, yet consider myself happy that the delusion was over, my heart seemed quite dead. I believed no longer in that energetic feeling which irresistibly fixes our destiny.

. . . . Milly has a Roman character, and this was always my ideal of a citizen's wife; pride, intellect, the most retiring modesty, unbounded love, constancy, and gentleness. In history we only meet with such women among the Roman matrons—the Calpurnias, Portias, Arrias. Soft, weak, tender girlishness, would neither have elevated nor strengthened my character. I must stop. This is too confused, and I must go and take these pages to Dora, and then go to Milly and her mother, who willingly consents. Farewell.

The following is an extract from a letter of Conrad Hensler's to Niebuhr, on this occasion:

"Dearest Niebuhr, doubly and trebly do I wish you joy. I could form no slight expectation of *your choice*, but it is far exceeded. So much intelligence and affection, such purity of mind and clearness of judgment, such depth of feeling, such overflowing affections—such as your Amelia is, so ought she to be who is to be your companion for life. How beautiful is her seriousness—even her reserve! She does well to maintain her reserve, for if she breaks through it, her feelings overflow. So self-relying, so unexacting, and yet such delicate and tender feelings, such fullness of affection! With what sweet open cordiality she greeted me—she who formerly was so reserved and distant; it was so visible what a claim it gave me upon her to be your friend. And when I saw her again, when she was cheerful, even merry (your letter had arrived), how beautiful was the smile on her countenance!"

After Niebuhr's return to Copenhagen, he continued to fulfill his duties as librarian during the winters of 1797-98, and also diligently carried on his own studies in private. As his wishes still inclined toward a professorship in Kiel, where he hoped to lead the quiet and studious life most suited to his disposition, he directed his reading at this time principally to philological and historical subjects.

His letters to his betrothed show that, though no longer suffering from unsatisfied aspirations of the heart, his over-active intellect occasioned him many hours of depression and lassitude. Unconscious of the disproportion between his mental and physical powers, he exerted the former without regard to the latter; and when experiencing the natural consequences of such a course in the loss of mental tone, he reproached himself bitterly for indolence and want of proper discipline of the mind. He found a still stronger source of dissatisfaction with himself, in the belief, that from the inadequacy of his education in childhood, and his too early introduction into the distractions of the great world, his mind had received a wrong direction; that the creative faculty which requires self-concentration had been lost, and but poorly replaced by the power of acquiring and elaborating the ideas of others. He seems to have thought that his mind, which might have been a lamp, had become a mirror.

The following extracts from his letters will serve to illustrate this period of his life:

XIX.

TO COUNT ADAM MOLTKE.

Written in April, 1796, *at* COPENHAGEN.

It is rather through accident than fault of mine, dear friend of my heart, that you have had no letter yet worthy of the name. Yours of the 25th of March did not reach me till the 8th of April...... I can not imagine who has given himself the trouble to interrupt our correspondence, for an inexplicable delay has taken place somewhere. As long as no letter had arrived from you, I hesitated whether to write or not, and the following reasons decided me to wait...... I wanted you to know all about my situation here. At first it promised wonders. I was very happy, though not so much as with you at Kiel. I was made much of, my work was easy, and I got on well with it. I was treated like a friend, and found myself in a family, whose head, at least, commands my deepest reverence. Then the variety of people whom we see here, afforded me a fund of entertainment, though I could not help despising most of them. One sees queer puppets here. To write to you then would have been like writing in a fit of intoxication or a dream. The intoxication has evaporated, and the dream is fled. What I say to you now, is what you will always hear from me: I am quite convinced that, as matters stand, I could not have had a happier lot than that which has fallen to me. Not a *happier*, for whether a different turn of events—the obligation and the leisure to devote myself to hard study—might not have been more *wholesome* for me, is another question. Such a vocation would at least have conduced much more to my peace of mind. That this is now often much disturbed by the nature of my position, that I have a thousand temptations to yield to a frivolous vanity, a detestable desire to please; that there are numberless amusements to entice me; that the tone universally prevalent among the people with whom I have to do, allures and tempts me to ease and indolence, you will readily conceive, and will forgive your friend if he should now and then go astray. Yet you will understand, and indeed you told me long ago, that good-fortune had done every thing possible for me in this situation. A pleasant life, Schimmelman as a friend and instructor, freedom from all pecuniary cares during my youth, the best opportunities of being initiated into statesmanship with Schimmelman, of advancing in scholarship, by means of the library here; it is my own fault if such advantages remain unimproved. But they are like precious gold-mines, that rarely lie on the surface of the earth, and require much toil to bring their treasures to light. I did not believe at first that it would be so difficult to profit as I ought by these gifts of fortune. This was my dream, the illusion of my intoxication. I over-looked the hindrances. It is not Schimmelman, nor the work he gives me to do, that takes up my time and worries and harasses me. I really do not regret being obliged to stay at home every evening from eight till eleven, because of the society I meet there. But what does vex me now (at first it was neither so bad in itself nor so noticeable) is that our reading is so often interrupted, so unconnected, that such precious time is thus wasted. Even the heartfelt delight I have in Schimmelman, and all that he says, can scarcely make me forget it. I often laugh at the countess's plans and speeches, especially her philosophical discourses; seldom let them provoke me; never talk with her on philosophy. What annoy me most are our parties, especially the stiff, lifeless, horribly aristocratic, state assemblies, though these do not come very often. Perhaps I shall manage to get excused from them altogether. All the time they consume is utterly wasted. I think you can hardly imagine how I love that noble Schimmelman. For you do not know him but by daily intercourse, by living with him from morning to night as I have done for this month past; from morning, when we work together, to night, when we read together. His integrity, his cheerfulness, his really great intellect, his freedom from prejudice, his consistency—ought I not to esteem myself most happy in having all this daily before my eyes as a model of excellence? One thing that I particularly like in him is his habit of acting without much talk. The only thing that I should wish to see altered in him is that he should be more careful of his time. He has a great quantity of work, it is true, but he does not know how to economize the time that is so invaluable. Hence also, business gets into disorder, and he feels more over-burdened than he really is. I have become acquainted with Grouvelle, and have the freest access to him. He speaks of you with the interest of a friend, and the admiration of an upright and enlightened man. How we made acquaintance with each other, and got so intimate the first day, that he did not even wait for a request on my part to open his house to me, I must reserve till my next letter which you shall have a week after this, if God permit. If possible write to me.

XX.

COPENHAGEN, 23*d April*, 1796.

I have just found from a letter of Hensler's—and it has given me a painful surprise—that your wedding took place on Wednesday, therefore without your having let me know one word about it. This breach of promise on your part has wounded me deeply and painfully, so that I hardly know whether to be more grieved or angry. I not only, when on my journey, stole time from sleep to write to you; I wrote to you also on the first morning that I spent here, and when, after a three weeks' delay, I received a short answer, I sent you in return a letter which was at least much longer, and, however much it might be wanting in arrangement, elegance of style, or profound thoughts, certainly expressed the warmest friendship. And you have not even time for two lines to enable me to celebrate your festival! You chose an earlier day than you told me—you made it impossible for me even to guess that it was to take place so soon. You always said that you would let me know when your marriage day was fixed. You told me so many times. How am I to explain this, Moltke? For amid the joy that your happiness really gives me, I still feel the sting of deeply-wounded friendship. Have I displeased you? Have I offended you by act or omission? Truly I am conscious of nothing, and if any thing of the kind had happened would willingly wash it out with tears, or my blood. Do you blame me? Then why now, more than at any other time? Once you loved me; did you not allow me to lay open my faults before you, when I would not suffer you to think better of me than I deserved? What has opened your eyes so suddenly, and why would you not open them before? I know in my conscience that I never wished to deceive you. I love you deeply, with all the strength of my heart, with a love that will stand all trials, and will never conceal our friendship, even in the midst of your bitterest enemies. This I have already shown here, but not all who call themselves friends do the same. In spite of my impatient desire for letters from you, in spite of our wish and resolution to hear often of each other's welfare, in spite of your reproaches when you thought *me* careless in writing, I am left in ignorance of the most important day of your life, and even now know nothing of it, but from others! I thought I perceived a visible coolness in the only letter you sent me here. O Moltke, I love you; I am jealous and eager for your love. Can any one have stolen it from me? Explain yourself, and let us not become cool or mistrustful. You would despise me if I were to permit such an injury to pass unresented; but I should despair of all friendship if you could mistake the spirit of this letter. No, you are no hypocrite; you never dissembled. At our last parting, your heart was certainly mine, for you said so. I entreat you, make all clear between us. I love few as I do you, but if it must be, if I must lose you, an open, bleeding wound were better than a hidden one, than a disease of the soul which would at last fill the whole heart with bitterness, and the mind with night. Am I unjust to you? No, for I accuse you of nothing. Fears, anxiety, mortification, are not accusations, but you must answer me as quickly as possible, within three days at the most after receiving this letter, or I shall hold all my fears for truth. Through your silence you have not received the "Nedham," the token of my joy at your union. Did you wish not to have it? I am so vexed and unhappy that it is impossible for me to speak a single word of joy. Do not be offended at my warmth. Only set my mind at peace, and I will write to you immediately; but first of all, I pray for God's blessing on you and your wife, and give my love to her, who has certainly no part in your fault. NIEBUHR.

XXI.

9th December, 1796.

......What do you say to the *moral* tone of our poets? Our philosophers and scholars have long since distinguished themselves in that respect. But Schiller's Almanac for this year!!! It is a comfort to me to be able to share my exasperation at it with Baggesen; for all the rest of the "literati" here are unanimous in its praise. The Germans admire its wit and raciness, the Danes find so much "smag" in it, and such "deylige" verses.* The lady at our house is of the same opinion, and is never weary of extolling it, though, perhaps, she does so chiefly to provoke Baggesen and me. Do you know Falk's Satires? the prayers in the last Göttingen Musen-Almanac,† and another in the Deutschen Merkur?‡ If you have read them, did you not rejoice in the hope of a German Juvenal? And has not your pleasure been converted into indignation by the scurrility and the hackneyed witticisms of his "Pocket Book?" It is time to attack this evil very seriously. I write to you about it, because I could fain do it myself. Do you in Holstein read as little as we do here? It seems as if the literature of Germany were visibly on the decline. Schiller and

* Smag, taste; deylige, charming.
† Published by the celebrated Poets' Club [Dichter Verein] at Göttingen, numbering among its members Voss, the Stolbergs, Bürger, Holty, Müller, &c. Boje was its editor for some time, afterward Bürger.
‡ Edited by Wieland.

Goethe are worse than dead. Wieland's Agathodæmon is insufferable. The new generation is dwarfish. Is Voss to stand alone? Even Klopstock has by no means distinguished himself in his last production. O confess it, Moltke; the bloom of our literature is over, and, besides the usual course of nature which has proved itself the same in all nations, it is the French revolution, our infamous policy, and shameful undervaluing of our own people, the want of cultivation among them resulting from this general indifference, and the desecration and shocking abuse of philosophy, that have brought us to this wretched pass. Innocence and light-heartedness have vanished. I must break off, dissatisfied with what I have written. I have been on the point of tearing up my letter, but I will venture to send you the stuff, for I have a presentiment that our correspondence may suffer a long interruption, and I really feel as if I must write to you. I wanted to add:—and we can only make satires to mock our own degradation, or a history that would have the effect of a satire. This afternoon Kirstein, who much admired the Almanac, has had the candor to send me the masterly review of it in the Nürnberger Zeitung. Give yourself the pleasure of reading the avenging article. I shall copy that, and not write another word against the gentlemen. Baggesen entreats your wife for an answer. I have understood, dear Moltke, how happy you are going to be! I rejoice with you in your happiness, and in the thought of what an excellent father you will make. Dear friend, we shall have but a short time together next summer, but I should like to have a few days alone with you. I enjoy the very thought of it. I shall at least enjoy them by anticipation. We shall hardly go to Italy together now. Probably you will not even visit Switzerland? . . . . . .

XXII.

EXTRACT FROM AN UNFINISHED LETTER TO HIS PARENTS, PROBABLY NEVER SENT.

COPENHAGEN, *5th March*, 1797.

. . . . . . You will not be sorry to hear, my dear parents, were it only as a good testimonial of your son, that notwithstanding the short time which I am able to devote to Persian, my progress is very considerable; that in ordinary authors I can already understand the sense of whole periods, and have only to contend with single words, for which the Dictionary gives several meanings, among which the sense must decide. It will please you too that Ludolf is extremely well satisfied with me, and even finds his expectations exceeded, so that, with the help of Arabic, he now thinks it possible for his pupil to acquire such a close acquaintance with the Persian, as at first he always represented as quite unattainable. But you will be still more glad to hear that Ludolf shows himself more and more a warm and sincere friend, as he perceives the success of his undertaking, and that he removes, by a thousand little marks of his good will, all the scruples which I might otherwise feel at such an apparently unnatural connection as that between a man of his standing, and a young scholar as yet undistinguished. He not only takes a sincere pleasure in forming a connoisseur and student of his favorite language, it gives him delight even to have some one with whom he can converse about his general reading (for though not ignorant of European literature, he is not well versed in it), and still more, to be able to describe with enthusiasm, yet without fearing to make himself ridiculous, his youthful years in Constantinople, which place he much prefers to Europe.

But I shall only allow myself to fancy that all this may give you half as much pleasure, my dearest parents, as you have given me in consenting to my plan of going to England next year. The necessity of being burdensome to you is certainly more unpleasant to me than to you; but your ready consent, and the conviction that so it is best, set my conscience at ease about the matter. I shall, therefore, next summer (if a devastating revolution has not broken out in England first) read and make extracts from the seven or eight folio volumes of Mirchond, in the Radcliffe library at Oxford, read as much as possible of the more or less important Persian classics which are preserved there in great number, and write notices of them which may lay the foundation of a *Bibliotheca Persica*. As it is impossible, between now and then, to gain more than a mere school-boy knowledge of Arabic, and as it is besides by no means advisable to try to embrace everything, I shall devote all my attention there to the Persians....

It is a great pity that you, my dearest parents, will always persist in fancying that the praises I bestow on Persian literature proceed from partiality only, and are not deserved. If I could but translate something for you, or lay before you English translations! Hafiz has been compared to Anacreon, and it has been considered a great compliment to him; but the pseudo-Anacreon, who is commonly read for the genuine one, and even the few remains we have of the real poet, are not to be compared with some of the best odes of the poet of Schiras, selected in the Asiatic Miscellany. In general, the Persians stand far behind the Greeks. Firdusi has natural disadvantages from the immense length of his poem (of 60,000 distichs at least, four times as long as both the poems of Homer) and from the circumstance that he wrote in rhymed, decasyllabic iambics, which we must take into the account if we compare him with Homer. But is it not extraordinary enough that it is possible to compare him with such a poet even if he loses by it? The excessive grammatical freedom of the Persian language, and its corruption with Arabic, are very injurious to it; still no language is so sweet and fascinating.

I will now tell you of a proposal which will not be indifferent to you, and I hope not disagreeable.

Since the war, which has ruined the commerce of England and Holland in the Levant, there is an opening for Denmark to carry on a trade there, particularly from the port of Altona; and it is hoped that the peace, or rather the treaty of subjection to France, will not injure these prospects. For this object, consulates are in course of establishment in all quarters of the Levant; and as a consul is to be appointed at Constantinople as well, with a liberal salary moreover, Schimmelman has proposed to me to fill this office, after a time, for a few years, in which he has perhaps been chiefly actuated by Ludolf's earnest assurances that the school of the East is in that city. On my return the desired professorship would certainly be given me.

You see, my dear parents, that I lay this project openly and honestly before you, and leave it to my dear father to discern for himself, and communicate to you in particular, dearest mother, the great advantages it presents. Without taking Ludolf's assurances that people there are much happier and better than in Europe for much more than the expression of a warm and tender heart, and well knowing that just what must make that place so peculiarly dear to him, parents and home, is an objection to every one else; yet I must put it to you, whether, for a young man who is fond of antiquity and has made it his study, a life of some years in Greece (through which my way would lead me, after I had spent a few months in Portici, which I could examine more in detail on my return), would not be the most desirable thing imaginable? Whether Constantinople, in whose great library are preserved all the extant works of value in the Persian language, and which would afford me living practice in writing, speaking, and intercourse with the natives, would not be much more interesting than, for example, a European capital? And whether it would not be very advantageous for a young man (and this is no slight consideration) who has had the misfortune to be known too early, and has thereby become more inconsistent, more showy, and less solid than he ought to be, to find such a retreat, where he might acquire greater serenity and a more complete cultivation of mind? What outward things society, intercourse, civilization, and the like can give, I have, to a considerable extent, enjoyed, and am not wholly unthankful for it; but my inward cultivation, during many periods of my life, has been unhappily only too much neglected.

I am, however, particularly glad that it is not to be for long, but only for a few years. Schimmelman can not be at a loss for a consul there, and so we may reckon upon it with certainty, that no forced prolongation of my stay can arise from this source, which would otherwise, I think, be the greatest objection to the plan. It is true letters take a month in going from here, or from Holstein by way of Vienna, before they reach their destination; and it would be still more impossible to wait for answers there than it is between Copenhagen and Meldorf. But if it is true that we have no advantages without corresponding disadvantages, and that we always must submit to this condition, we ought not, I think, to condemn such a plan on account of this circumstance, as, on account of the quieter life I should lead there, I should certainly be able to write, in comparison, more to you, and more interestingly than I do here. So tell me, dearest parents, what you think about it.

XXIII.

TO MADAME HENSLER.

COPENHAGEN, *8th July*, 1797.

......Schimmelman had a favorite idea lately, which he was extremely anxious to carry into execution. He read me an excellent paper that he had written upon the subject. He wished, namely, to make known the actions of the Government in the most complete and authentic manner. For this purpose he wanted to set up an official journal, uniting correctness with a high moral tone, and announcing the measures proposed by the Government, their adoption as laws, all important acts of the executive, particularly all the appointments to offices, perhaps the names of all the candidates, giving at all events a trustworthy account of the one chosen, and of all the leading questions of the day, &c. Such a paper, circulated gratis through the whole country, could hardly fail of producing the effect that Schimmelman hoped and intended, of bringing more life into the relation of the subject to the Government....... You may see by this how little Schimmelman keeps to the beaten track.

I spent a delightful evening with him yesterday, and staid very late. We could not get away from each other. It was a most lovely summer day; the soft air—the beauty of the sea-shore (and it was the first time this year that I had gone that way)—the sense of having performed a task really worth doing, and of use to Schimmelman, to whom I was bringing it—a serene and happy mood that has hardly been interrupted since our last parting—a strong attraction toward Schimmelman himself—all this happy combination of circumstances completely took possession of me, and put me into the brightest state of mind. I could feel sure too that I gave pleasure to my noble-minded friend.

XXIV.

MELDORF, *24th August*, 1797.

At last I am able to announce to you the decision of my political fate.* . . . . . .

In order fully to understand, and to give lectures upon ancient literature, and ancient history, which forms a part of it, it is, in my opinion, absolutely necessary that I should have read through all the ancient writings still extant, at least once, with the closest attention—the more important works many times—and acquired a living and familiar acquaintance with each period. There may possibly be some exceptions to this rule in the case of special sciences, which must forever remain a mystery to the uninitiated. This undertaking was carried out by Milton long ago. There would scarcely be found many to do it now, but it seems to me that it is what I undoubtedly ought to attempt.

A profound and practical acquaintance with the grammar of the two classical languages must be obtained, partly by means of the various treatises on that subject, and partly from the literature of the languages themselves. A systematic philosophy, as the groundwork of all settled convictions, and all accurate thought; what is perhaps still more important, method in thinking, writing, and studying; added to these, various exercises in the art of composition, and a thorough command of our mother tongue, are indispensable requisites for any one who steps forth before the public, and seeks to obtain a high standing. It is no more than a man demands of himself.

These then are the preliminary tasks that I should have to execute, before I could accept a professorship in Kiel without a blush, and discharge its duties without disgracing or overworking myself. As one can not do every thing, and, least of all, prolong one's preparations *ad infinitum*, it appears to me that other studies which H. and my father wish me to undertake, must only be carried on in subordination to this object.

I have, perhaps, already reminded you of Hume's example, who, in order to bring his mind, which had got into confusion in consequence of an ill-regulated education, into the right track again, and to strengthen his powers by peaceable seclusion, lived unknown for several years in La Flêche, and then came back another man from what he was when he left home. Now, it is true it would be presumptuous to institute a comparison, which would allow me to hope for such results as proceeded from Hume's talents; and besides, he and I should have different requirements and ideals of happiness; but an analogy may nevertheless subsist.

* See page 66.

I do not think of traveling so long as three years.

What do you say to my spending this winter in Kiel, as I am no longer bound to my post in Copenhagen either by duty or interest? It would be no mere pretext, and no doubt a decisive argument with Schimmelman, that if I go back and resume my former mode of life, my health will return to its former indifferent state...... In Kiel, as my father knows, I should be able to carry on all my studies with the aid of Hensler's library.......

XXV.

MELDORF, 27*th August*, 1797.

I can not help writing to you again to-day. You know that my emotions are apt to carry me away with their violence. Thus your letter has made me so wild with delight that I have felt full of affection to every creature that has come in my way.......

My father, my dear father, clings with such conviction and firmness to the idea of some journey or other, that he would consent with reluctance to an earlier settlement in Kiel. He would consent, for he would be ready to sacrifice any thing to me now. I, too, can not help believing that if it were possible for me to win such an affection as might deepen into a heartfelt willingness to unite herself eternally with me, absence and distance, cheered by such a prospect and trust, and unremittingly devoted to my cultivation, could be only beneficial to me. I should see a foreign country, and must be a gainer by it. A somewhat lengthened preparation for the holiest society, when one has been already long accustomed to think of oneself as engaged, must, it seems to me, have great advantages. And so many of my present deficiencies I might strive to supply. Dear friend, I should not like to owe any thing to fortune, to her prepossessions in my favor, nay, not even to your sisterly interest in me. You will surely not misunderstand me here. What we do not possess in and through ourselves, is not truly ours. I will strive and toil not to be unworthy of your sister, and to deserve, if I can not win her affection. So much is in my own hands.

The idea shall not have uncontrolled sway; the annihilation of a ruling passion that must be conquered, is too terrible, and the higher and intenser its life, the more convulsive is its resistance to extinction. And must I not fear the possible necessity of its extinction? Its seat in my heart is light and warm, my life is joyful and deep, my mind open to all, all that human love can embrace.

The first few days, my mother showed some annoyance at the length of my stay with you, and she was displeased too with my carelessness in dress, and my refusal to pay all sorts of visits. But the mother's love soon prevailed. Her affection for me was always vehement, and therefore always exacting. I have told you that I have inherited the vehemence and sensitiveness of my disposition, together with my features, from my mother. To-day is my birthday, and all my family have greeted me with the warmest affection. One word more about my sister. She seems to me so worthy of love, that she must win yours too some day.

Farewell.......

XXVI.

MELDORF, 31*st August*.

......You accuse me of a propensity to idealize.

I am sorry that you do not give me credit for sufficient true-heartedness to love the Beautiful devotedly without the necessity of coloring it more highly by any imagination. If it were as you say, I should be fated to turn perpetually to new objects, till cold experience gradually taught me better, and warned me against such folly with bitter mockery—till I sank into hopeless misery. Such a warmth is not that of life but the unhealthy and transitory glow of fever.

If I have any thing to thank nature for, her best gift to me was a correct and very rapid judgment, a facility in detecting every thing false, incorrect, untrue, that can hardly be imposed upon. While I am ready to adopt any well-grounded opinion, my inmost heart revolts against receiving the judgments of others respecting persons, and whenever I have done so, I have bitterly repented of it.

Manly worth, elevation of intellect, and enthusiasm, are to me the noblest things on earth, superhuman, and the best pledge of our higher destination, heavenly origin, and divine illumination. I can not worship the abstractions of virtue—she only charms me when she addresses herself to my heart, speaks through the love from which she springs. I am not blind to the faults of those I love, because I do not speak of them. Either faults cease to exist where there is true excellence, or they are only imperfections. I have never fancied any one perfect, indeed I have rather been liable to err through mistrust and suspicion. I really love nothing but what actually exists: virtue, love, sincerity, purity; where these are, what more need I seek for? I believe that where these qualities are irradiated by the joyousness of innocence, and fortified by a clear, active, cultivated intellect, we have, without any idealizing, the only thing that remains to us from the golden age.......

If you reveal my wishes to Amelia, you must let her know that she is not the object of a blind passion—that it is my first endeavor to acquire her esteem.

XXVII.

MELDORF, 6*th September*, 1797.

Even while I was writing my last letter to you, I began to feel the sort of stupor and gloom creeping over me that I have on my dark days. Whether this is physical, or whether the dazzling brightness of a succession of happy days is necessarily followed by a fit of exhaustion, when external circumstances do not feed the flame, is a mystery to myself. I have at last succeeded by strenuous efforts, in driving away the blackest clouds and to-day your welcome letter has kindled a fresh life-giving spark within me.

But all my life this inequality of spirits has been my torment. When ever I have worked hard, of course I mean in special investigations which only serve as means to an end, or amidst the confused heap of materials required by some other object, I seem as if paralyzed. When a few days have elapsed, and my new acquisition has fallen into its place, then comes my brightest time. But meanwhile I am good for very little.

The lot of the scholar working amidst his books is a wearisome one.

He is ever treading on the brink of pedantry, a yawning chasm, in which, if we were laughing on the subject, we might say he would be buried in dust and dead leaves, if he made a false step. He has to extract honey from wormwood. He must constantly keep his mind on the stretch; can only succeed by slow degrees in his task of self-culture, and measures every thing by an ideal standard, which he is often unable to attain from the poverty of his materials—still oftener from his own want of talent. Sciences which are entirely based on speculation, such as philosophy and mathematics, are free from this disadvantage; and all occupation with them refreshes and quickens the mental powers, when one has fairly got into their spirit. Neither are those liable to get depressed by their studies, who collect and compare, often without the least philosophy, single interesting things, such as natural objects. But he who studies grammar, and rhetoric, and style, seeks and deduces rules and laws, or learns those that others have found, which are indeed important to him as regards the refinement of his taste, and perhaps something higher, but which are so dry—taken singly, for the most part so unimportant—must constantly stimulate his ardor, and keep his affections in play, or he will be in danger of either relaxing his exertions, or acquiring a mechanical pleasure in mere words. In the study of history there is a much higher species of interest. But its immense extent, the difficulty of imprinting all that is needful on the memory, the almost greater difficulty of steadily maintaining a correct point of view, the toil of collecting the most interesting fragments from innumerable books and relics, while conscious of their incompleteness, the repulsive task of wading through an immense amount of what is bad (though in this respect people generally of their own free will do more than is necessary), until at last you have so far reduced all to order, that you can begin to mould the mass into a beautiful form (which it takes years to do)—these preparatory difficulties almost overpower any one who perceives them.

I have long attributed to this cause, and to the still worse state of the professional sciences, which have long been an empty husk, the inertia of the best intellects among us. The life of the ancients in small States, was like that in a large family; even Rome itself was, in reality, as a State, confined within its walls, and to the spots consecrated to the popular assemblies, notwithstanding the enormous extension of its boundaries.

War and the discharge of public functions were extremely liberal occupations, and it was considered that good sense and practice were sufficient qualifications for either. Then there were very few, whose minds had not been developed by the active discharge of these functions, which were not confined, any more than learning, to a particular class. We see nothing among ourselves that can be compared to the indefatigable power and activity of the ancients. They were at all times *men* and free citizens. We are obliged to make a special class of learned men; and, in consequence, we lose sight of the world, of active life, of the best part of ourselves, of reality; and cling to book-knowledge alone. A few escape this fate, to whom their kind genius has given the good fortune and the energy to separate the kernel from the shell, in spite of all difficulties, and to keep their hearts warm and active.

The ancients invented the sciences; the elements of which were not diffused among the vulgar, producing a shallow knowledge; men sought for insight in converse with sages, and there were only two kinds of knowledge, the common and the philosophical. We lose the simple aspect of nature long before we are able to comprehend the expositions of philosophers. We hear, as children, that the earth turns round the sun, before the words can convey any idea to us; for the senses will not suffer the imagination to grasp an image of such magnitude. It is the same with every thing. On all hands there abound crude doctrines, patchwork theories, assertions on authority.

It is impossible for us to see as clearly as the ancients did. And then their philosophy of human affairs does not satisfy us: we rack our brains and split hairs, and, after all, do not think. Why were they so free from the monstrous absurdities by which we are surrounded?

I have wandered far from my subject, but all that I have said has a bearing upon it; for what I mean is, that there are two things which have a very mischievous effect upon my mind—the disadvantages of my occupations, which are, nevertheless, the only ones open to me in these days, and my own inequality of temperament.

......I must tell you a little about my life here. My friends evince the deepest affection for me; but I am almost frightened to see the exaggerated opinion my father has of me, and his propensity to look upon all his aspirations for me as so certain of accomplishment, that he regards every difficulty I see in the way as mere nonsense. One trait that is common to all of us, has often deprived us of many a happy hour, we are too apt to be irritated by opinions opposed to our own, and, instead of testing them, either to reject or be persuaded into them. You may find in this an explanation of many points in my character, particularly my habit of hasty, passionate condemnation.

XXVIII.

MELDORF, 18*th September*, 1797.

......I have written a tremendously long letter to Desaugiers* about the unhappy revolution in Paris,† and endeavored to set in the clearest light the merits and the innocence of the now proscribed party, and the black guilt and inexpiable crime of the triumphant faction, with all the force of language and logic at my command. It is the only homage which a remote foreigner can bring to oppressed virtue. This has cost me much time and paper......

I am quite decided not to go to Paris at present. It is a lucky thing for me that the post there, which was offered to me, has fallen to another candidate. I could neither endure the sorrow of seeing such a complete triumph of villainy over virtue, of barbarism over intellect and accomplishments, nor yet of listening to the shameless insults and groundless impu-

* The French Chargé d'Affaires at Copenhagen.

† The Revolution of the 18th Fructidor, when the democratic majority of the Directory, alarmed by the growing influence of the moderate and monarchical sentiments in the nation, which threatened the ascendency of the violent Jacobin party, resolved to overturn the Constitution, surrounded the Councils of Five Hundred and of the Ancients with troops, dispersed the majority of the members, annulled the motions unfavorable to their interests, and condemned the leaders of the opposite party, including most of the men of genius and principle in France, to transportation to Guiana. The immediate results of this revolution were the abolition of the freedom of the press, and of the institution of juries, and the re-enactment of the laws enjoining the banishment of the nobles and priests.

tations heaped upon the proscribed by their victors; and as little could I submit to the degrading humiliation of associating with men whom I abhor.

XXIX.

TO AMELIA.

COPENHAGEN, *4th November*, 1797.

Your remembrance and your image, thank God, are always present to me. Hence my solitude depresses me less than it ever did before; hence, in society, I feel more strange, embarrassed, and unsympathizing than ever. The first is good, but the second frightens me, and I feel that it is not right. Schimmelman and Prehn are the only persons with whom I speak of you. No one else has any idea of our engagement. A greater change has taken place in my character than at any former time. I shall certainly be further than ever from foolish and unworthy conduct. Till now, I have been very idle. Strictly speaking, nothing has yet been done. Of course, I am never quite without reading. Homer, Plato, and Cicero lie before me; but I have only read a little of Homer. The constant fogs and clouds prevent me from going on with astronomy. Here, too, I perceive with humiliation the bad effects of my long continued careless inobservance of nature, and feel the necessity of a tolerably intimate acquaintance with phenomena before proceeding to science, at least, if I am to learn it independently and with insight. Beyond the first evening I have not had any pleasant time yet with Schimmelman. We have been interrupted by strangers. I am fairly besieged with invitations; but I have now an object, and work toward it without suffering myself to be drawn aside. I owe it to you that I am infinitely more tranquil than I ever was before. You will certainly change your wavering, restless friend into a firm, calm man, worthy of your love.

XXX.

11th November.

......I have had numerous invitations. You know that I did not wish to see Grouvelle again, and certainly meant not to visit him. This I kept to, and should have continued to do so, but he, not to be repulsed, sent my friend Desaugiers to me, with an invitation; and, moreover, with strict orders to bring me back with him. He has once since then forced me to come to his house in the same way. I confess that I have no pleasure even in my intercourse with Desaugiers, though he has an excellent heart, because he is always occupied with ideas which have become abhorrent to me, since it has grown so evident that the fearful tragedy is issuing in a disgusting farce, as if in both halves it were played by devils. I plainly declare that I do not wish to have any thing to do with Grouvelle, whose society was once sought by all the refined and intellectual world of Paris. I feel that such intercourse does me no good. It is dazzling outwardly, but hollow, mere empty talk; it goes against my conscience. Nothing but the impossibility of escaping from it without an open breach, has made me put up with it so long. My staying away, making difficulties, or giving downright refusals, would have made any one else give me up as an obstinate fellow. Desaugiers has here no more intimate friend than myself; perhaps not even among his early acquaintance. But here the difference between the friendship of our circle and that of foreigners is most striking. The life and food of our intimacy is the communication of our inmost thoughts, absolute confidence, constituting an individual relation. But between foreigners there is nothing but a higher degree of kind feeling, if help is wanted, openness and confidence; otherwise, the attention of both is only directed to outward objects. The relation is easily broken, and may be dissolved by a neglect in the *degree* of attention.

XXXI.

TO HIS PARENTS.

COPENHAGEN, 2*d January*, 1798.

I will not begin my first letter in the new year to you, my dearest parents, with general wishes for your happiness, for you will take these for granted, knowing them to be ever in my mind; but with wishes for the health of us all, for an uninterrupted harmony of feeling, and for external prosperity. With regard to the last, I have for some time past felt much inquietude, which I no longer hide from you, since the moment of decision, one way or the other, is daily approaching. Probably rumors of a French expedition against Hanover and Hamburgh may have reached Holstein, even the newspapers have alluded to it, and it has long attracted our attention. We can scarcely picture to ourselves, in all their details, the frightful consequences of such an enterprise; but it would be childish not to see that the French, after coming so far to destroy English commerce, would inevitably require us to close the Sound to all English vessels, and place a garrison in Friedensburg to insure our compliance. However, no salvation could have been looked for from a continuance of the war, if the late King of Prussia had lived. His death, combined with the great impression which the conduct of Austria made on Germany, awakened at first great hopes; and we ventured to look forward to seeing a powerful, well-supported Prussian army on the Rhine. Nor were we deceived in the disposition of the young king; we must not call him cowardly and weak because he surrendered the last yet unconquered fortresses on the frontier of Germany, for his kingdom is as yet unprepared, and, at the first outbreak, the enemy's forces could occupy all Lower Saxony and Westphalia before any opposition could be offered by a Prussian army. Thus all persons here, who are informed as to the movements of the great powers, live in a state of the most anxious expectation. An army is forming, all officers and soldiers on furlough are recalled, and Magdeburg placed in a state of defense. If France makes a sudden incursion, Prussia will scarcely venture upon a war for the recovery of Hanover. If Prussia has time to prepare, will she not require all the assistance from Holstein which the latter can afford, after having already contributed to the defense of the line of demarkation?

And is not the cause of Hanover and Hamburgh our own? Must we not submit to every demand of France, when she has possession of these? Will she not occupy Holstein, even though we may endeavor to satisfy her by submission? Thus fearful is our position as long as France holds her present views. And it is not probable that she will give them up as long as the war with England lasts. And a termination to this, by means of a fair peace, seems at present hopeless. The congress of Rastadt may decide the fate of Hanover; but even if the dangers now threatening us are diverted for a time, it is but too probable that, at a future period, we may find submission to France the only means of saving the existence of our State.

So the most earnest wish for us all must be peace, and the independence and inviolability of our soil. Holstein, which contains all that is dearest to me in the world—you, and those whom I have made mine by choice—and which will, perhaps, be the scene of my future life, is unquestionably in danger. If we can gain time, it is certain that a courageous resistance—let it be understood, a resistance to which we bring our utmost resources—might preserve our soil from devastation, and all we love from the horrors of war, and so fearful an enemy as the French armies of the Rhine; and no less certain that we can not in any case lose more than by sacrificing Prussia, if Prussia is willing to rise.

But if we choose this plan, we must count the cost of all our sacrifices, and make an unalterable determination not to survive disgrace. . . . .

XXXII.

COPENHAGEN, 30*th January* 1798.

The kind manner in which you, my dearest parents, have received my account of Moldenhawer's proposition has given me great pleasure.* My last letter renders any further details unnecessary, and you will there find all your questions already answered.

It has rejoiced me to see that you, dearest father, express a just indifference as to the kind of appointment I may receive, provided that it affords us a sufficient income, and a sphere of action at once useful to others and congenial to my talents. My engagement has placed me in a narrower circle and led me to renounce all plans involving uncertainty as to results, a great length of time for their execution, or a residence in any distant country; thus freeing my mind from many chimeras, and unsettling yet impracticable projects, and fixing my thoughts with infinitely greater earnestness on what lies near at hand, and the use I can make of it, in my time as well as in my occupations.

We can not now build castles in the air, to be realized in some distant future—of a residence of some years abroad during my youth, which should procure me cultivation and polish almost without effort on my part. My travels can now—and in this light I have always viewed them myself—be only diligent study on an ever changing scene. . . . .

XXXIII.

COPENHAGEN, 2*d February*, 1798.

I shall therefore decline Moldenhawer's offer unreservedly. I am now most anxious to hear your opinion of Schimmelman's proposals, which have at least this recommendation, that they come from a man who, I may almost say, loves and trusts me as a son, who has my welfare at heart, and who is capable of sympathy, affection, and enjoyment to a degree very rarely to be met with. In accepting them I should, it must be confessed, involve myself in government business, but only partially so, and I could easily withdraw as soon as a chance of a professorship in Kiel offered. Business of this kind is not new to me, and presents no difficulties.

* Niebuhr here refers to an offer that he had received of the chair of ancient languages and literature in a philological academy about to be founded in Denmark.

For the chief talent I possess, or have preserved, besides that of memory (and, indeed, it is the cause of the latter), is a very quick comprehension of the matter in hand, a correct and clear perception, which almost invariably seizes at once on the true state of the case. This saves me an infinite amount of time, and as we should restrict our society to a very narrow circle, I should still have leisure enough not wholly to lose sight of my favorite pursuits.

Amelia would wish my journey to be shortened, and I agree with her. England, and at the most two or three months in France, now full of vain glory over her triumphs, will furnish me with sufficient instruction, and a vast field for observation. But time must decide for us on this point.

You ask after my health, dearest father. For some time it was not as I could wish—my head was unusually heavy and stupid. My labors in the cold halls of the Library brought on another attack of my complaint.

I have re-arranged and supplied the deficiencies in one portion of the historical department. But my health is not so bad as last spring, when I was imprudent enough to go straight to work in the halls of the Library heated and lightly dressed as I had come from Count Ludolf's.* Sometimes, too, I read there extracts of works which I can not well take home with me; thus I have lately read parts of Theophanes, and Luitprand on the Byzantine Empire, and yesterday meditated on some passages of Xenophon concerning the Greek tactics, which I have been studying among other things this winter, and of which I have obtained a tolerable conception, especially those of the Macedonians and Lacedæmonians.

XXXIV.

TO AMELIA.

COPENHAGEN, 3*d February*, 1798.

......How will you bear my asperities and all my faults? There are defects of temperament which can scarcely be conquered. My irritability, my egotism, is of this kind. To efface these without filling their place with any other feeling produces apathy and injures the character. Love may conquer them. To be strong in love is the only way to become noble, and all softening through education, which is not based on love, is merely pernicious. I remember that I was terribly passionate in my childhood, but being often reproved for it, strove with such success to attain indifference, that for a time I was as if dead, and only by degrees recovered at all a vivid feeling of real injuries. It would have been better to have let me alone, till nobler feelings had replaced this vehemence.

XXXV.

TO HIS FATHER.

COPENHAGEN, 13*th February*, 1798.

.....In the great world here every one lives in a constant round of gayety, and the same is true of the other classes, according to their different ranks. Business is hurried through, to leave time for amusements. These form the staple of conversation, and one party furnishes the poverty-

* The Austrian embassador, who had kindly assisted Niebuhr in his Persian studies.

stricken materials for another. Next to these, politics possess the strongest interest, yet even they not a very vivid one. In some houses they are the all-important topic, and swallow up every thing else. One would think there could now be but one voice on these questions, that the Gallomaniacs must be silent, and the arch-aristocrats descend from their claims and their credulity, but unfortunately it is quite the contrary. The former ignore all the excesses of the French government, and openly rejoice in its overweening power, while the latter are filled with indiscriminating anger.

Thus it is impossible to agree with either side, and to avoid the dislike of both. For my part I really do not seek disputes, though my position has exercised my lungs, my tongue, and my logic considerably.

The apprehensions, of which I lately wrote to you, dearest father, may apparently be laid aside for the present. The firmness of the King of Prussia seems to have diverted the French from their project of occupying Hanover, and without ceremony taking it away from the King of England, according to the same rule of force by which they seize on every thing that excites their desires. Probably, too, the consciousness of their irresistible strength, as it has induced them to make some temporary concessions, will enable them to exercise coercion at any future moment as successfully as at the present. Who knows that they are not hoping to find some ground of quarrel with Hamburgh, by means of their commissioner in that city, and that they may not yet bring forward at Rastadt a demand for the sequestration of Hanover? for as they treat justice with contempt, they invariably contrive to throw the blame of the failure of their attempts at peace on their adversaries, whereas their own requisitions are always unprecedented, and such as the opposite party can not concede. To hear such conduct defended, and the principle advocated that the utmost possible increase of their power is to be desired—a principle whose partisans, though for the most part hypocrites themselves, talk as if the right were exclusively on their side, and calumniate and misrepresent the opinions of their antagonists—is, indeed, perfectly intolerable. I am very curious to see whether any of our convoyed vessels will be captured; whether the defense of our ships of war will be regarded as a crime; whether requisitions will be made to Hamburgh to close the Elbe, and expel all emigrants, and similar demands made to this country; whether Grouvelle will be sent as minister to Sweden, and Leans-Bourdon, the thoroughly Jacobinical commissioner at Hamburgh, be made embassador here in his place—all possible contingencies, and all dreadful to us.

I foresaw the absorption of Switzerland. As to England, I am in a state of doubtful expectation. I do not believe in a naval expedition against her. Would it were true! for a dozen barges filled with bombs would infallibly destroy the monster, if it were not dispersed or shattered by the waves. The good fortune and boldness of the French causes me much more alarm. Several squadrons, starting from several different points, and consisting of a multitude of armed vessels of all kinds, might attack the English coasts at the same time; could they succeed in landing troops every thing might be feared from the bravery and discipline of their soldiers, the unserviceableness of the English forces, and from the rebels in Ireland, and the traitors in England......

XXXVI.

TO AMELIA.

COPENHAGEN, 2*d March*, 1798.

......As I was standing here about noon, the sun shone so warmly into my dull room, and the sky was so brilliantly blue above the high roofs of my neighbors, that I could not refrain from going out into the fresh air, which I have not tasted for a long time, and not desired for still longer. The air was even more refreshing than I expected, and allured me on and on, though there was as yet no sign of life in grass or tree, no sign of richness or beauty. There is a great charm in the mildness of early spring, it affects the feelings so gently and soothingly. You reminded me once, that the first time we saw each other at your father's, I told you of my dislike to bright winter days. This feeling is still invincible, and the cloudy autumn, and the depth of winter, whose shadows invite to social pleasures and to meditation, are as dear and welcome to me, as the shivering spring is disagreeable. The latter, indeed, generally brings sickness to me, for the unhealthy air after the rough cold winds of winter, and the exhaustion of my solitary toils, is more than I can stand; and then, too, nothing is so hateful to my eyes as the dead earth in the glare of light. Certainly we ought not to allow ourselves to be too much under the control of such impressions, but one can not entirely get rid of their influence where they are very strong.

XXXVII.

TO HIS PARENTS.

6*th March*, 1798.

I have only spoken warmly of Souza two or three times to you, and yet he has gained a very high place in my affections.

Perhaps it falls to the lot of very few young people to have advances made to them by so many of the most remarkable men of the day as my good or evil genius has brought me in contact with; and no one has displayed more cordiality toward me, a more decided wish to contract a lasting friendship with me, than this most amiable man. Jacobi had prepossessed him in my favor, and Schimmelman had strengthened the impression; thus he saw me through my friends' eyes. I have by no means availed myself of his advances to the full extent, but I have nevertheless seen enough of him to love him heartily, and to possess full intimacy with him.

He has a great amount of information, is a very good speaker, has seen a great deal, is a very thinking man, and has withal, the very agreeable characteristic, that by the kindness of his manners, nay, even by the nobleness of his physiognomy, he draws out those with whom he converses, so that with him you find, you can not tell why, that you have a much greater flow of words, and more available thoughts, than in ordinary conversation. Unfortunately he has been recalled hence very quickly, and goes on Friday to Hamburgh; I am uncertain whether to engage in business of his own, or to enter on a dangerous mission from his court, for on this subject he observes a silence that I have no right to break. My journey to England pleases him much; he has visited that country, and has a real attachment to it, though not so strong as he once had. He has given me a letter to one of his friends, Sir Thomas Rivers, and offered me one to Lord Lansdowne, and one to Mr. Wyndham, in order that I may be personally acquainted with the English minister; but I hesitate about making use of the last. Sir Thomas Rivers is a great scholar. Count Rantzau gives me a letter to William Roscoe, and I reckon on having letters from you to Schönborn, Rennell, and Russell. Moldenhawer gives me introductions to Watson, Former, Ford, and Bryant; and Torkelin has offered me one to Lord Moira.......

XXXVIII.

KIEL, *13th May*, 1798.

......The weather was beautiful when I got to Hamburgh, and when I inquired at the coach-office for Jacobi's, a note was handed to me whose contents were equally delightful and unexpected, for it contained an invitation to stay at his house; thus the main object of my journey was much facilitated. But this offer stood in the way of other plans, for how could I stay away any length of time from Jacobi, after he had treated me with so much kindness.......

I hope I have learnt much from Jacobi this time, his society is more improving than that of any other man I know; he treated me like a brother, and my conversations with him are among the best hours of my life. Souza was equally affectionate. Klopstock was unchanged, and delighted to see me. We arrived here yesterday. The Henslers remain in town till Friday. The Vosses arrive this evening, and we shall most likely go with them to Eutin. We shall visit Moltke afterward.

To these letters may be added a few extracts from Niebuhr's Diaries, which are calculated to throw light on his character during this period of his life:

Probably written in the autumn of 1794.

"I made it my first occupation to-day to pursue my meditations on what experience and reflection have shown me to be the daily duties of pure morality and wisdom, and to note down what should serve me as a guide and rule. This new essay is to be instead of that which I wrote in the spring, and of which I am now almost ashamed, though I do not like to destroy it. On the other hand, it is a cheering witness to me that I have not worked in vain, but have really advanced in goodness and knowledge. How weak I was this spring; how governed and led by passion and vague opinions! I could not say positively, *I will;* I was obliged to make it conditional, and so accomplished nothing. Now, I do not ask myself whether I can do a thing, I command myself to do it. I hope I have by this time brought my passions tolerably under control. Vanity is now the chief enemy that I have to contend against, and absence of mind; uninterrupted work is the best defense against both. In this, therefore, I must not relax, and hence must be on my guard against society and dissipation."

A page, written probably in the spring of 1797, contains the following passages:

"I have been too remiss; I must be more strict with myself if I am to reach my goal with honor."

"So long as we receive what is delivered to us, with the ears and eyes rather than with the understanding, we can not survey it with rapidity and insight; hence, also, depth and comprehensiveness of view are impossible. Words are the dangerous shallows that so often obstruct my progress. O, what will help me to inward, voluntary, deep thought? What will break the talisman that still keeps me spell-bound under the yoke of imagination?"

"One hour, at least, every morning to be devoted to clearing up my thoughts on a given subject.

"Two hours to mathematics, algebra, chemistry, natural philosophy.

"An extensive knowledge of *facts;* astronomy, mathematical and physical geography; these are the rational and scientific basis of political geography, ancient as well as modern, and of history.

"General laws of material nature, and meteorology.

"Description of natural objects, animal, vegetable, and inorganic.

"Distinct consciousness of the rules of my moral being. Philosophy.

"As my historical study, to work out the chapter on chronology and chronometry; also (before my return) that on grammar.

"The problem is to get through the greatest quantity possible each day, taking care, at the same time, not to overstrain the power of application.

"1. To avoid all that taxes the powers fruitlessly; all dreamy activity.

"2. Self-examination; clearness of thought; accurate definitions; exercises of the imagination.

"3. Diligent reflection; weighing the work performed; zeal; to harden myself against effeminacy."

In another paper, probably written rather later, which, as it is said to be intended only for his own eye, can not be inserted, he expresses "the holy resolve, now more and more, to purify his soul, so that it may be ready at all times to return without fear to the Eternal Source from which it sprang."

There are several papers of a similar kind in his diaries, which express the purest resolves and purposes of a noble youthful soul; and through all there breathes the spirit of the purest morality, and severe self-judgment.

After passing the winter in Copenhagen, he returned to Holstein, in April, 1798, in order to spend a few months there before setting out on his travels to England. His chief aim in going thither, beside the general advantages of a residence in a foreign country, and the further prosecution and extension of his studies, was to brace up and strengthen both his mental and physical energies, in preparation for active life. He felt that the one needed bracing, since from never having been obliged to regulate his habits according to those of others, except during the short time that he was at Count Schimmelman's, he had become too dependent on the little details of life ; and the other, in order to counteract a certain one-sidedness in his cast of mind that had caused him to neglect entirely the study of natural objects. He felt that he stood, so to speak, outside the world of realities;—that nature and human life—the various functions of civil life which are closely connected with the internal economy of the State, were unknown regions to him, which it was necessary for him to survey before he could take a comprehensive view of the relations of the external world, and of the various conditions of humanity, either as a scholar or a statesman.

His three months' stay in Holstein passed away very happily in the society of those who were dearest to him on earth.

CHAPTER IV.

NIEBUHR'S JOURNEY TO ENGLAND, AND RESIDENCE IN LONDON AND EDINBURGH, FROM JUNE, 1798, TO NOVEMBER, 1799. —VISIT TO HOLSTEIN, AND APPOINTMENT IN COPENHAGEN, MAY, 1800.

TOWARD the end of June Niebuhr sailed from Cuxhaven, to which place his father had accompanied him, and landed, after a tedious voyage of more than a week, at Yarmouth.

Of Niebuhr's residence in England, we have no account but from his letters to his betrothed; no others of that date have been preserved. Those to his parents, which were so unfortunately burnt, contained many details of general interest respecting English political and civil institutions, the character of the nation, and remarkable individuals. The letters to his betrothed are of a more personal character. They afford a general view of what he learnt during his absence, and the advantages he derived from it; and, above all, a delineation by his own hand of the inward workings of his own mind, and the characteristics of his nature, from which we can see how thoroughly he knew, and how severely he criticised himself, and watch the struggles of a noble spirit to realize its highest aspirations.

In his journal there occurs the following list of the aims which he wished more especially to keep in view, during his stay in London:

"I will strive to obtain by reading and inquiry.

1. A more complete notion of the constitution of England.
2. A fuller acquaintance with its topography.
3. A knowledge of the ordinary measures, weights, prices, &c.
4. Information respecting the character, talents, and lives of distinguished persons.
5. " " " literary institutions, education, schools.
6. " " " mode of life of the different classes.
7. " " " imposts.
8. " " " army and navy.
9. " " " banks and trade.
10. " " " literature of all kinds, authors; publishing trade.
11. " " " East and West Indies.

In Dalrymple's library, to make catalogues of the Hindoo books under the following heads :

(*a*) Those concerning the Hindoo nation,
1. Matters relating to antiquities, history, and national character.
2. History of the provinces and of the Mogul Empire.
3. Modern history since the fall of ditto.
4. Descriptions of single provinces.

(*b*) Those concerning the Company,
1. Its charter and privileges.
2. Its direction, trade, and European affairs.
3. Its establishments in the East Indies, their constitution and administration."

Niebuhr became acquainted with many distinguished men in England and Scotland. The first friendship which he formed in London was with the aged Schönborn, who resided there at that time, and acted sometimes as Secretary of Legation, sometimes as the Danish Chargé d'Affairs, of whom a spirited and well written memoir appeared in 1836, entitled, "Schönborn and his Contemporaries." He was a very original man, of remarkable talents and information; profoundly versed in ancient and modern systems of philosophy, and familiar with the ancient writers on mathematics and natural philosophy. He had been for four years Danish consul at Algiers; was a contemporary and friend of Klopstock and the Counts Stolberg, and known in his earlier years by several poems in the Pindaric style, which appeared in the Deutsches Musæum and other periodicals. At a later period he returned to Holstein, where he retired into private life. His friendship with Niebuhr subsisted till his death. At the time of which we are now speaking, it was the depth of his intellect and the uprightness of his character which won Niebuhr's respect and attachment; it was not until a later period that his young friend learnt to estimate the warm affection which flowed in the depths of his soul with almost youthful enthusiasm, while outwardly he appeared cold even to indifference.

Niebuhr had letters of introduction to many of the political characters of that day, as well as to most of the noted men of letters. He only availed himself of a few of the former class, but the latter procured him almost every where a friendly reception through the reputation which his father enjoyed in England. Those with whom he became most intimate were, in England, Rennel, Russell, Marsden, Banks, Dalrymple, Mallet du Pan, and some others, but especially Wilkins, who had been, from 1760 to

1786, in the civil service in the East Indies, was one of the founders of the Asiatic Society in Calcutta, and has since acquired celebrity by his grammars and lexicons of Sanscrit and other Oriental languages, and his translations of various Oriental works. In Edinburgh, where he entered himself as a student at the University, Niebuhr's chief friends were, Playfair (with whom he renewed his acquaintance at Rome many years after)—Coventry, Robinson, Hope, Gregory, Home, Rutherford, Walker, Grant, who had long resided in the East Indies, and above all Mr. Scott, an old friend of his father's in India. He became acquainted with a great number of his fellow-students, but formed no intimacy with them; there were only two among them, named Moorhouse and Lambe, to whom he became really attached. His acquaintance with the English men of letters was only slight, owing to his visiting London during the summer months, when nearly all of them were absent.

He always retained a great predilection for the English nation. Their great consistency of character, their general strict integrity, and their great truthfulness, raised them in his estimation above every other nation, excepting his own; and therefore he was more disposed to form lasting connections with individuals belonging to it than with any other foreigners; in fact most of his foreign friendships were with Englishmen.

The subjects which Niebuhr principally studied in Edinburgh, were mathematics and the physical sciences; among the latter chiefly natural philosophy, chemistry, agriculture, and mineralogy. Philological and historical studies he only prosecuted by himself, and by way of recreation. In these departments he regarded the learned men there as incomparably inferior to the Germans. But besides the scientific knowledge which he acquired in the course of his attendance on the college lectures, he gained during his visit, through observation, intercourse, and research, an insight into the mutual relations of the various parts of the state machine, which it would have been impossible for him to obtain elsewhere. The information which he thus acquired, may certainly be considered as the real foundation of his political and financial eminence, although he attended no lectures on these subjects in Scotland. He indeed frequently expressed the opinion, that finance, considered in its practical application, was rather an art than a science, and could not be handed down from the professorial chair, but was only to be learnt by personal investigation, and study.

Niebuhr often acknowledged with thankfulness how much England had taught him. He had previously been only capable of making such additions to his knowledge as he could derive from conversation, or books; now he had learnt to read nature also, and the objects that spoke to the eye alone. He felt too that he had gained much in courage, experience, and aptitude, through this tour.

He left London, toward the end of October, for Edinburgh, where he remained about a year, made some little excursions into the southern part of the Highlands, and then returned, by way of Manchester, Sheffield, &c., to London, where he only staid a few days on this occasion. He had, in the first instance, formed plans of more extended travel in the interior of England, chiefly in order to visit the great manufacturing towns; he also wished to have penetrated further into the Scottish Highlands; why these schemes were only partially carried into execution, will appear from his letters to his betrothed, which, besides some recollections of his own verbal accounts, are the only source from which any records of this period of his life have been obtained.

In the beginning of November, 1799, Niebuhr returned to Holstein, and spent the following winter there among his friends. In the middle of April, 1800, he proceeded to Copenhagen, where he met with a hearty welcome from Count Schimmelman, and was received with great kindness by the Crown Prince.

A few weeks after his arrival, he was appointed Assessor at the Board of Trade for the East India Department, and secretary and head clerk of the standing Commission of the affairs of Barbary (or the Direction of the African Consulates), with a salary which was not indeed large, but sufficient for his wishes, and for a quiet retired life, such as he and his Amelia had firmly determined to lead; a life that was in accordance with their tastes, and from which they were both resolved not to depart, in spite of all allurements to the contrary.

EXTRACTS FROM NIEBUHR'S LETTERS DURING HIS STAY IN ENGLAND AND SCOTLAND, 1798-1799.

XXXIX.

TO AMELIA.

CUXHAVEN, 28*th June*, 1798.

Good morning, dearest! You are most likely writing at this moment, and so we may fancy ourselves sitting opposite to each other: this sense of your nearness consoles me for our separation, and its good effect will be strengthened when the compulsory, prison-like inactivity to which I am doomed at present is succeeded by uncontrolled activity: then I shall look up to you in thought, to see if your glance of satisfaction sets the seal upon my performances, or your sad eye says that I have failed in my duty.

I have been sitting in a little room here for several hours this morning. which I have spent in reading an English magazine, and have been very agreeably surprised by one of its articles—a notice and specimens of a poem that has just come out, "Naucratia, or Naval Dominion," by H. G. Pye. There is a great bustle in the house, and the mingled sounds of children crying, nurses singing, people shouting, the loud voices of the Englishmen calling to the waiters, and the still more resounding and unintelligible conversation among themselves, has as stunning an effect upon me, sitting all alone in my little room, as the noise of a set of drunkards upon their sober comrade. Meanwhile, I have already found that necessity is an excellent teacher—that nothing makes us so active as having no one to help us, so discreet as having to rely upon ourselves alone, so self-collected as feeling our own individuality sharply outlined off from all others, which must be the case with the utter stranger; and thus I am full of hope that the bitter cup of separation will strengthen my enervated soul as much as we expect, and immensely invigorate my energies. That must be our best consolation.......

XL.

LONDON, 21*st July*, 1798.

I find very little that interests me in the mere external appearance even of the most remarkable city; and London, however little it resembles our towns, has extremely little variety in itself. Perhaps, on this account, I am not adapted for a traveler, and still less because what is foreign has, in general, little attraction or value for me.......

The day before yesterday, I presented my father's letters to Russell, Rennell, and Mallet du Pan, and enjoyed a very pleasant day in consequence. The two first are very unaffected, warm-hearted men, who were evidently glad to see me, and do all in their power to help me.

What Mr. Russell has done, out of regard to my father, would not often be done with us; and it is perhaps the main distinction between our method of treating a stranger and that here, that we more quickly conceive a personal attachment and try to give pleasure; while the English, in the same case, spare no pains to be of use, but leave their friend to seek out his amusements for himself. Russell has had a fever, and is still taking quinine; he looks older than my father and seems much more infirm nevertheless, he took me yesterday to Sir Joseph Banks and the British Museum, where he introduced me to all the curators; asked Dalrymple to introduce me to the meeting of the Royal Society, and finished by introducing me to a Dr. Gartshorn, who has asked me to dine with him to-day Rennell's kind, simple, animated face impresses you still more agreeably, and it is principally through him and his directions that I can obtain what may prove the way to my appointment in Kiel. He has a family, and speaks with so much feeling of the happiness he enjoys in it, that I wish above all things to win his confidence and get intimate with him. Marsden, whose book is so excellent, seems jovial and open-hearted; he interests me much, and I should fancy him a most highly cultivated man; but he is probably too wealthy and too fashionable to admit me to familiar intercourse.

The dinner at the Royal Society fully justified the sentence that has often been passed upon such meetings. It was a feast, and the conversation extremely indifferent; in fact, below the every-day conversation of learned men in Germany. We must not be unjust to ourselves: it is our own fault that we are not nobler than we are in general; but whether the Good and the Beautiful find a temple in more hearts here in England, is a great question, and worth the solving, if it can be solved. Every body here is in action; idleness and half-done work are certainly less common than with us; practical ability is certainly more general—a false show of knowledge rarer; a smooth exterior gains little respect; the word of a man may be depended on, and I believe the better sort trouble themselves little about the opinion of others. But it can not be denied that mediocrity is very common, and is by no means looked down upon: that, as Schönborn says, it is a question whether genius is an attribute of this nation, and certain that true warm-heartedness* is extremely rare; a little of the fog that "Allwill"† talks about seems very prevalent—hence, also, the great indifference, the one-sidedness, the self-will. You see that novelty has not so raised my opinion as to place me in danger of having, hereafter, to moderate a flaming enthusiasm. It would indeed need much to make me feel here as in my fatherland—to make other advantages compensate for the absence of that harmony of sentiment, which made me happy in the society of our friends, even before you were mine.

I think that most learned men here, as elsewhere, look more to the authority that a man brings with him, than to his talents and intellect. My father's name, which is very celebrated here, introduces me every where. But I look forward with pleasure to the time that will transfer me from a rather too conspicuous position to the quiet of Scotland.

XLI.

LONDON, *27th July*, 1798.

......London does not exercise a cheering influence on me, though I have had occasional hours of intense enjoyment here......

I owe my pleasantest moments in London to the arts. My good fortune has ordained it so, that a splendid collection consisting of paintings of the Italian school, with some antique busts and vases, which is about to be disposed of, has been on show for the last few weeks. It contains pieces by all the greatest masters; but after the *chef-d'œuvres* of Raphael, &c.,

* *Innigkeit.*—The term warm-heartedness is scarcely an adequate translation of the German word, though perhaps the nearest to it our language affords. *Innigkeit* implies depth and sincerity in addition to warmth of feeling.

† Allwill's Letters, a novel, by Jacobi.

the Lucretia of Guercino has filled me with more admiration than any thing else. It was almost the first thing I had seen in England that I felt a very strong impulse to describe to you; but what words could reproduce the impression made by the countenance of this fair, youthful matron? These paintings have taught me, for the first time, how high art can rise, and how great is its power; and further, how first-rate excellence alone is worth any thing in works of art.

You have probably heard of the Shakspeare Gallery, which owes its origin to a few publishers and picture-dealers, who have brought out a magnificent edition of the poet, with copper-plates, for which they have procured drawings from the best English artists by high payment, and appealing to their patriotism (where they have it). Very few of these engravings have pleased me; but the productions of a young man, named Westall, form a decided exception. He has also drawn a series of illustrations to Milton, which indicate real genius.

I have not seen much of Schönborn for the last week past; two days he has been out of town, and on the rest I have hardly been able to find him at home. On Sunday we had another conversation, in which we came a great deal nearer to each other; at least, I have conceived a high respect for his philosophical knowledge and his extraordinary acquaintance with all the philosophical and mathematical writers. It was interesting to me to watch his bold intellect as it played with the exposition of mythology, even when he did not interpret the legends, but only imposed a meaning on them.

If we lived longer in the same neighborhood—had I systematic knowledge which I could really call my own—could I repay him with the same pure silver (all personal conversation may be compared to private banknotes, which are valueless beyond their own narrow sphere of circulation), no doubt the barriers of which I spoke to you in my last would give way.

If, even with him, I feel oppressed in finding a want of personal interest, you can easily imagine how much more this is the case with the English. The superficiality and insipidity of nearly all the conversations to which I have listened, or in which I have joined, is really depressing. As far as I hear, little is said about politics, which is a good thing—much better than our German mania for going beyond our depth on such subjects; but, that narrative and commonplaces form the whole staple of conversation, from which all philosophy is excluded—that enthusiasm and loftiness of expression are entirely wanting, depresses me more than any personal neglect of which, as a stranger, I might have to complain; for of this my share is not large, and I bear it easily. I am, besides, fully persuaded that I shall find things very different in Scotland; of this I am assured by several Scotchmen whom I already know......

I have not availed myself of my introductions to fashionable society, and hesitate considerably to expose myself to the mortification of a haughty reception, though it is also possible that they might procure for me much that would be interesting.

XLII.

LONDON, *10th August*, 1798.

......Really, in summer, London is not a very interesting city, and the libraries are at present my chief sources of information. In the morning, from eleven or twelve till toward four, I am at Sir Joseph Banks's library, which is very liberally opened to all scholars; on Thursday, during the same hours, I was at that of the Royal Society; in the afternoon I am at Dalrymple's. Sir Joseph's librarian, a Swede named Dryander, who is very civil to every one, and still more to me, as a sort of fellow-countryman, because we understand one another when he speaks Swedish and I Danish, affords me every possible facility in the use of any book which may be of importance to me.

I am extremely sorry that I have found no friend inclined to take me about, and explain to me what is most worthy of observation, nor to remove by his experience the obstacles which necessarily lie in the path of one who has not beeen accustomed to find his own way into unknown regions. I regret that Schönborn has not shown more zeal in this respect, or perhaps has not a sufficient knowledge of men and things; for I feel that this valuable time might certainly have been better spent than among books, though I am also perfectly aware that this mode of passing my time is far better than that of many travelers, who run hither and thither and look and wonder without comprehending. Vauxhall, Raneleh, Astley's, the Royal Circus, &c., &c., which one likes to see as favorite amusements of the public, are scarcely worth the money and the time. I have seen St. Paul's, and mean sometime to ascend the dome, whence there is a fine view over the city. I have also lately visited Westminister Abbey, and looked with reverence and gratitude upon the busts of so many great men. But how characteristic is the equally honorable position accorded to so many nameless and insignificant persons by the side of the noblest dead! What a quantity of nonsense is to be seen on these venerable walls! One man writes a Hebrew inscription on the tomb of his daughter; on another, I think also belonging to a woman, there is an Abyssinian inscription; Chatham has an absurdly over-burdened allegorical monument; Sidney and Russell have none at all, and on Milton's, the man who erected it gives his own name and title in several lines: Milton is mentioned in the quietest manner.

At Sir Joseph Banks's I have made the acquaintance of Dr. Afzelius, a Swede, who was with Wittström in Africa; he is by all accounts an excellent man; his exterior gives me the impression of sociability and sincerity. Africa and the new discoveries there have been the subject of many conversations with my acquaintance......

To have some society in the evening, I went to Mallet du Pan's. The party there presented the attractions and the defects of true French society;—interesting anecdotes were related in well-chosen language, but there was an utter absence of dignity, wisdom—all that speaks to the heart......

17th.—I saw last week Captain Bligh, who has introduced the Bread-fruit tree into the West Indies, and whose crew during the first attempt had mutinied, and cast him out in an open boat, in which condition he performed a voyage of many hundred miles. He has a noble physiognomy....

XLIII.

LONDON, *7th September*, 1798.

The autumn draws on, and the bright season of the year is over. With the cold foggy mornings and the dark evenings, I have grown serious too;

I feel the alterations which the change of the seasons always works in my still too susceptible organization. I always suffered so under these various changes that I used to fancy myself a new man with every season of the year, because my new sensations and emotions were so powerful just when the old ones had become so weak; and this revolution raised me heaven-high for a time. It can not deceive me now; I can not even be grateful for so delusive a favor. What is good-humor, what is gayety worth, if its source is not in ourselves? To find the inward source is what I strive after: to succeed in this endeavor demands faith in the free energy of the will for its support and animation.

Perhaps the sensations produced by the changes of the seasons have some effect upon every one whose life-thread the Fates have spun finer than that of common men.

We all share something of the nature of the world which surrounds us, and are, perhaps, in closer dependence on it than our fair dreams will allow us to confess; and the consciousness of this is doubtless the most vivid in him who strives the most earnestly to obtain deliverance from it. But if he can in some measure succeed, he will find that he has gained freedom in many other ways besides.

My thoughts often travel back a year, when I am alone and unoccupied. Then, indeed, I saw a light; but it was a light in a storm, a flickering glow, the sun had not yet risen that has now scattered the clouds from which the storm broke.

I have read a good many political writings lately, indeed, devoted a great part of the day to them. Now I have got so far that I shall soon be able to give up this employment. I have groped into every hole and corner for information, in order to obtain a correct notion of the very complicated politics of this empire, and of the present crisis, which to the superficial reader must appear a tedious confusion, barren of celebrated men—to the careful examiner, a wonderful, unprecedented, but horrible drama. My heart has been wounded more deeply with every step toward its development, and all ideal notions of the people's capability of great things in a state of liberty, which were hitherto such welcome intruders, are now fled forever. I can not bear to spoil a letter to you with the account of actions and men which do not concern us. But because it has occupied me, and because I should tell you all about it if we were together, I will say this much to you, that, in the printed documents of the conspirators, I have learnt to know men, who, while possessing almost unequaled eloquence, began a career which led them into crime, and made them the cause of deep misery to numbers of their fellow-citizens; very different men from those who are the objects of admiration to our fools; extraordinary men, but men whose existence is the curse of their country. The politics of such a party is something higher than those which we both disapproved on principle, and which I promised you to handle cautiously in spite of the current of inclination.

What I have been studying lately borders on history; it does not concern the color of the garment, but the shape of the figure; but as regards this topic also, I shall soon have reached my goal, and shall then turn my attention easily and completely from this field.

I continue to derive much instruction from the library of the distinguished man who has treated me with so much kindness, but I shall soon have attained all the advantage I want from it; that is, I shall have extended my own literary knowledge as far as time and opportunity permit, and finished a notice of the German books it contains, which I am writing for its owner, as the only way in which I can in some measure repay his kindness......

XLIV.

LONDON, 21*st September*, 1798.

......My favorite amusement here is the theatre. In spite of all its defects we have nothing like it across the water. Many foreigners, who, in general, can enter very little into the spirit of any thing truly English, find a thousand things here to carp at, and in truth there is much to criticise. But however hypochondriacal and ill-humored a man may feel, if he is not too stupid to understand a joke, the English comic stage will certainly put him into spirits again, for it is rich in interesting plays and clever actors. Tragedy has only two great artists: Mrs. Siddons, who played Lady Macbeth lately in the most elevated style, quite free from the national fault of a false declamation of the serious passages, and from every impropriety of demeanor; and a celebrated actor, who, however, stands far below Mrs. Siddons in correctness of expression......

XLV.

LONDON, 30*th September*, 1798.

Last Sunday, a heavenly autumn day, I went to see Nicolai, at Richmond. We took a boat across the Thames, and I made a pilgrimage to Twickenham to see Pope's garden. Oh! that I could thus visit with you the monuments of those men whose memory excites a wish to have lived in their times. The garden has been preserved unaltered, as Pope laid it out. The monument he erected to the mother he so dearly loved is still standing; but the cypresses that he planted round it have all died out except two, which still show here and there a green shoot. Hedges and old-fashioned flower-beds occupy the left side of the garden, and in the centre stands a bower, the trees of which have now grown to a gigantic height, and, with the recollection of the great men who once trod this sward, inspire the awe of a sacred grove. They who will may call the grotto, the cool retreat in which Pope loved to sit with his most intimate friends, a toy—to me it was more. The prospect it commands must be allowed by all to be enchantingly beautiful—the Thames and its incomparably charming banks. Before the grotto stood an old weeping-willow, now almost dead, and propped up with care, also from Pope's times. The house is not shown. It is inhabited, and therefore frequent visits would probably disturb the occupants. But it ought not to be inhabited; it ought to be a temple for the grove. The many beautiful views from Richmond also afforded me extreme delight.

XLVI.

TO COUNT MOLTKE.

LONDON, 9*th October*, 1798.

......You will have heard most of my adventures from Milly, when she had the happiness of seeing you and your wife again after your journey. In future I will send something to you also as opportunity offers. This will be rather subjective than objective. I know no nation to which I would rather belong as a citizen, than the English; not only on account of their Constitution, but from my delight in the hard-working, active intellect, and the strong, straight-forward common sense of the thinking men, and because of the superior, almost universal cultivation of the burgher class, strictly so called, and, as I believe, of the farmers, who might put to shame many a conceited scholar, and many a high-bred, polished aristocrat. Of the English scholars, on the contrary, I have a very mean opinion: I keep to my assertion, that they are without originality; also, that England can boast of no true poets at the present time. And yet literary men are the only people with whom a foreigner can come into close contact; for only a very brilliant intellect or external advantages can procure him admittance to the interior of families. These are only open to natives, and I think it right that it should be so, for, in fact, what can a foreigner bring with him, unless he be an extremely distinguished man, to make his friendship wanted, when people have been long surrounded with friends already? I positively shrink from associating with the young men on account of their unbounded dissoluteness, which makes me feel that I should be more likely to meet with uncourteousness and repulse from them than cordial friendship. You see, therefore, dearest Moltke, how lonely I still am, for you know that I do not go where I might have the entrée if I do not like the people, and you can pretty well estimate how much I trouble myself about the scholars; and that, if I should like to be a citizen of England, it would be an essential condition, not only to have Milly unalterably my own, but to plant a colony of you friends around us. Whether it will be different on the other side of the Tweed, a few weeks will show me. However, your friend is a silly child to dislike England because of the unpleasantness of his isolated position. For nature is very lovely here; it is cheering to see the cultivation of the soil, and the prosperity of the inhabitants; and the immense accumulation of industry, wealth, and resources throughout the empire is most magnificent. You very likely know from Milly, that if Schönborn were not here I should literally live in solitude. But this friend I shall never forget, and can not give you too high an idea of him; and when I am alone, my time is not wasted. I have more than ever turned my thoughts inward, and striven to attain mental freedom; I have begun to reflect more than formerly, and felt the need of extent and completeness of cultivation with a force that has shaken the empire of indolence, of "chaos and old night," and will at last assuredly destroy it. I feel that I am capable of great things, and called to perform them. I have vowed to myself to clear up the confusion that has always reigned in my mind, and to replace it by order. These efforts will gain strength in Edinburgh, whatever the professors may be, for if they can not teach me mathematics and astronomy, I will teach myself; and chemistry, natural history, and agriculture are indisputably well taught there. I ardently long to form friendships there, ascribe my difficulty in finding friends to my own defects, and regret it, but in any case mean to keep a good courage, and *look forward* to the time *when I shall be truly happy!* O, how great a thing it is to be able to express this confidence! . . . . . .

XLVII.

TO AMELIA.

NEWCASTLE, *25th October*.

A day of rest after three weary days of traveling......I will take the best hours of to-day for you, and in the occupation of telling you all that is most interesting about my journey, seek the resting-point from which to control the whirl of continual change; so I will talk to you this evening, in the gloomy, dirty inn-parlor, hundreds of miles away, as if we were sitting together before the fire.

The modes of traveling in England are very different from those which are so far in use among us, as are also the posting regulations.

Open carriages are something unheard of, even to the country people, as far as I yet know England; in Yarmouth only a sort of car is used. All burdens are carried on carts of an excellent build and extraordinary strength in general with two wheels, only the heavy wagons have four; the former, drawn by from one to four horses harnessed before each other; the latter, sometimes by eight, or perhaps even more, both for agricultural purposes or the carriage of goods. Even the common people do not willingly travel on foot, and I believe you would nowhere meet fewer people walking, than here in the country. Hence you find remarkably few footpaths, either across the fields, or by the road-side, and in consequence the country looks almost destitute of human beings, to one traveling through it. Thus, those who do not travel on horseback, must either travel by post-chaise, by mail, or by stage-coach; in any case you travel in a close carriage. The first are very pretty half-coaches, holding two; but as they cost as much in proportion as our extra-post are too dear for me. The second is a letter-post, a public undertaking; a very rapid mode of conveyance, and safe, as it has an armed guard; but inconvenient from the smallness of its build, and particularly liable to be upset. The last are something like our traveling-post, but belong to private individuals. In traveling by them you have no further trouble than to take your place in the office for as far as you wish to go; for the proprietor of the coach has at each stage, which are from ten to fifteen English miles at most from each other, relays of horses, which, unless an unusual amount of traveling causes an exception, stand ready harnessed to be put to the coach. Four horses drawing a coach with six persons inside, four on the roof, a sort of conductor beside the coachman, and overladen with luggage, have to get over seven English miles in the hour; and as the coach goes on without ever stopping, except at the principal stages, it is not surprising that you can traverse the whole extent of the country in so few days. But for any length of time this rapid motion is quite too unnatural. You can only get a very piecemeal view of the country from the windows, and with the tremendous speed at which you go, can keep no object long in sight; you are unable also to stop at any place.

In a coach of this kind I took my place on Monday morning. I found myself with two females, one of whom looked like a married woman. A good-looking man had accompanied her to the carriage, and said a "*God bless you*," by way of farewell. The woman's face was red with weeping. The appearance of these women showed that they could not belong to the wealthier classes; but this was proved by their traveling at all in this mode. I could not, however, make up my mind to what class they might belong. That in the ordinary course of things they were sure to be re spectable seemed certain to me; and that was the main thing; for on short excursions I had often found myself in the same coach with creatures of a very different kind. Meanwhile the tears of the first woman dried amazingly fast, and her countenance cleared up instantly. Thus I saw that she was either destitute of deep feeling, or had been only playing a part before. On the road an extremely vulgar shopkeeper's wife got in for a part of the way. In Hertford we picked up another companion, a middle-aged man, who at first seemed to me ill-bred but he soon gave me a much more favorable impression. I found, to my surprise, a man of rare polish and sociability, well-informed, both by reading and experience, and very witty. His name I did not learn, but we parted at York with a friendly farewell. It is said that the English are a people of few words: this is only so far true, that they would rather sit dumb than drag on a conversation by empty questions like the French Neither do they speak without consideration. Besides, formulas and formalities play a more important part in English conversation in society than in the French, which is much more unfettered. This conventional politeness I have not as yet been able to acquire, and hence I always feel embarrassed with strangers. My companion possessed it completely, and seemed anxious to make me forget my deficiencies in this respect.

On Monday, as long as daylight lasted, our road, after leaving Middlesex, with its hedges full of trees, and long, low hills, and town-built houses, lay through Hertfordshire, whose not very fertile soil, though rendered fruitful by most skillful culture, yields no profit to the husbandman, and then through barren, heathy Bedfordshire, with its miserable villages. In Northamptonshire, which did not seem much better, nightfall interrupted my observations. In Stamford, the first town in Lincolnshire, I could perceive, by the moonlight, evidences of considerable importance and beauty. The whole country, a rich, level pasture ground, evinced prosperity, and when the daylight afforded a distinct view of the rich county of Nottingham, my eyes were greeted with such a spectacle of universal rural prosperity as I had never before seen; a multitude of little peasants' cottages, all smiling, built of bricks; here and there a larger and roomier one; every thing finished to the last degree. Probably many foreigners imagine the whole of England like this; but even an unromantic expectation would be disappointed at the sight of the dirty huts and the unfruitful district mentioned before; huts to which I should prefer many a serf's dwelling. But throughout there is not a field on the way uninclosed and wild.

XLVIII.

EDINBURGH, *Saturday, 27th October.*

I arrived here about half-past eleven to-night. The last day's journey, 116 English miles, was the most disagreeable part of the whole way. From early in the morning it was damp and gloomy; in the afternoon it rained heavily. I never saw a more striking contrast than is presented by the two banks of the Tweed. Northumberland was much more beautiful than I expected, although without wood, like all this part of England. Berwick, which is on this side of the river, is in no respect superior to the common towns of poor countries, disgustingly dirty, and immediately beyond the town you enter a wild country, almost entirely destitute of cultivation. This district extends to Dunbar, a distance of eight-and-twenty miles. High hills, bare and dreary, with deep moory valleys, and over all an impenetrable mist. More in my next. I have made acquaintance on the way with a young medical student, from Sheffield, named Moorhouse, and we shall very likely lodge together. The lectures begin on Wednesday. I have seen nothing of the town yet, but now I shall run out. The country is so romantic that I shall certainly taste new pleasures here. Farewell.

XLIX.

EDINBURGH, 31*st October*, 1798.

I have just come back from a round to four of the opening lectures given to-day. An excellent practice has been established here, of reading an introductory lecture some days before the regular commencement of the course of instruction, which is open to the public, and gives an intelligent hearer a complete notion both of the talents and style of the teacher, and of the views and comprehensiveness with which he will handle his science. This day's specimens have convinced me beyond all doubt that the reputation of this University is fully deserved, and that the Professors here are all I could wish as men of profound insight, thorough mastery over their subjects, and admirable delivery. I can not say this of all of them; one Robinson, the Professor of Natural Philosophy, wasted his time with very superficial remarks on the origin and value of the sciences, and further with very unseasonable invectives against modern philosophy. However, we must not be too fastidious, if we want to learn; and the science of natural philosophy possesses sufficient safeguards against the consequences of such defects in the exhibition of its principles; attention and judgment will be able to eliminate extraneous elements; and since no one in England would obtain such a chair without an eminent acquaintance with his science, I shall willingly rank myself among his hearers. The other Professor, whom I can accept as an instructor with unqualified satisfaction, is Dr. Hope, the successor of the venerable Dr. Black, whose advanced age prevents him from continuing his labors. I have never heard or read a more concise, complete, and clear survey of a science than that with which he opened the course on chemistry. He divided it into its different branches as an art and a science, accurately defined its limits, pointed out its special interest, and that which it derived from its application to the various purposes of life and the arts, its uses and abuses, with masterly skill. The two others, Dr. James Home and the celebrated Gregory, I heard accidentally in accompanying my good friend and fellow-lodger, who is studying medicine. The former I judged to be quite a new beginner, both from his own expressions, and the style of his delivery, which was too rapid and timid; he seemed to me, however, an excellent, correct thinker. The latter, with a venerable mien, and an excellent delivery, seemed, as far as I could judge, quite equal to the reputation which he here enjoys. Casual expressions betrayed a noble mind. So much for this morning's observations, which will give you as good an acquaintance with the university as I possess myself. It has greatly raised my spirits. It strengthens my conviction of the propriety of my decision, and animates me to carry it out with earnestness.

An unexpected circumstance has obliged me somewhat to alter my plan for the employment of my time. Rutherford, Coventry, and Walker, whose lectures on natural history, botany, and agriculture, I expected to hear, give their courses, quite apart from the academical arrangements, during the summer, beginning in May. At first it was a serious vexation to me to hear this, but I soon resolved rather to give up or shorten my travels in the provinces, and, during the winter as well as summer, to give a closer application to a smaller number of subjects. You know, however, that in any case October will remain the latest period for my return.

Edinburgh is incredibly cheap in comparison with London—even cheaper than Copenhagen. I have a very nice apartment, with firing, for seven shillings a week; coals do not cost much here; in summer I shall only have to pay five shillings. The young medical student who lives with me, is an intelligent and honest fellow; we dine together at home, frugally and cheaply. I shall have a sum left now from my allowance for the purchase of books and philosophical instruments. One is not restricted by fashion here as in London. The natives of every class are distinguishable, not to their advantage, by the carelessness of their attire; and the students are as far removed from English neatness as our young men. It has taken my fancy, however, and I mean to keep faithful to it; but I have availed myself of the liberty of wearing my hair plain. In London a hairdresser costs nine guineas a year. I shall put off the remainder of the account of my journey, the description of Edinburgh, and much besides, till my next.

L.

EDINBURGH, *4th November*, 1798.

......To-morrow begin the lectures I mean to attend, and with them, the regular arrangement of my studies; and, if it is possible, the long-intended daily continuation of a letter to you: with the same intent I will employ these hours in giving you a full account of what it makes me happy to think of.

You remember the letter to Francis Scott, the old friend of my father,* and how we reckoned on his reception of me, if he should be still living. I soon learnt where a man of this name resided, and as he was distinguished from the host of men bearing the same name here, by being of higher rank, and better known, he seemed to me very likely to be the same person, and although there was still the possibility of a mistake, which would have brought me into a very disagreeable position, I felt an uncommon desire to venture on the step. So, yesterday morning, I walked to the house. While I was in the act of making inquiries to see if it were my man, and was just sending the maid in with my father's letter, on the cover of which several circumstances of his life were mentioned, to distinguish him from any other, out came Mrs. Scott, and made me certain at once that it was the very man I sought. She invited me into the parlor in a very friendly way; where, indeed, I did not find him, as he was gone out into the city, but she received me quite cordially without waiting for his return, and promised me that he would be at home to-day between the hours of service. *Nota bene* in passing: there is no nation that can be compared to the Scotch for piety; they not only go to church *every* Sunday, but to both the services; and all, high and low, conclude the day of rest with prayer and sing-

* The elder Niebuhr had known him in Bombay.

ing. At this hour, therefore, I found the venerable white-haired old man; besides himself, his wife, a young lady who seemed to be his daughter, a grown-up young man, and two boys, all evidently his family. They all seemed even to have looked forward to my coming, as if I were an expected friend. The mother greeted me as being already an acquaintance, and the old father received me with the whole fervor of English cordiality, when it is aroused from the depths in which it ordinarily conceals itself in those who have not quite starved it out. He inquired with great earnestness about all that concerned my father; the letter had given him an unhoped-for surprise, for he thought that my father had been long dead. In the course of this conversation, the whole family gradually left the room, and when we found ourselves alone, he began to speak of my objects, and to open his heart to me about the position of a young man at this university. You will readily imagine that these exhortations, which were, and could be only, addressed to my age and its usual characteristics, did not wring my conscience; for, certainly, at my age, it is impossible to be less liable to fall into youthful excesses than I know myself to be; but the noble old man spoke with such a tender anxiety, referred so solemnly to his parental cares, and his trust that he should keep his children's hearts pure, and then concluded with the words, "You are far from your parents and your friends; look upon me as your father, this family as your own; I shall regard you as my own child. However hard you work you will have leisure hours, and need recreation; seek it among us. I am at home myself every evening almost without exception, but if I should be out, my wife will be glad to see you; and if you like music, my daughter plays and sings. My eldest son, who is nearly blind, but an excellent youth, will be happy to go out with you or converse with you." He was so moved that he dried his eyes, and it cost me some trouble to repress my own tears. We shook hands, and I entered in thought a new home.

Say, dearest Amelia, is not this a happiness beyond all possible expectation? What accident could we have fancied probable, that would so instantly have removed all that is suspicious (especially to an English family) in my youth and present position, all that isolates me as a foreigner, all the insignificance of my obscurity,* and opened connections to me in which my personal sympathy will not be regarded as intrusive, my worth not measured simply as an attentive or intelligent listener; in which sympathy and intercourse may create an enduring bond, and the sight of a happy family present the image of what the future promises to us.

I am without a doubt as to my progress in all the branches of science and cultivation that lie before me; for besides mathematics, astronomy. physics, and chemistry, I wish to pay particular attention to the art of composition.

My connection with my dear fellow inmate, too, takes a more and more brotherly character; and when I have labored conscientiously, a few hours' conversation with the old man and his children will refresh me and make a new man of me. And then post-day will bring your letter, and perhaps, if we remind our friends, I may get something from them besides. So this is my present, and my immediate prospect for the future!

I have only two courses of lectures to attend as yet, one by Dr. Hope,

* *Thatenlosigkeit*, literally *deedlessness;* the not having yet accomplished any deed worthy to be named.

the other by Professor Robinson. The first is excellent. It will give me an opportunity, one way or other, of learning physics, for which I have a great inclination. Playfair has not yet begun the higher mathematics, but will do so on Wednesday; he will be my third tutor. About taking more I hesitate. My understanding counsels me not to lose the advantage of hearing Munroe's anatomy; but my feelings loathe it. Should it be the necessary price of Stewart's and Tytler's society to attend their lectures, I may resolve to pay it; but with them my lectures would mount up to six, and the consequence would be, that my daily hours of study must rise to more than twelve, which seems with me to be the limit, if not of physical strength, at all events of the power of thinking for myself. I have begun to study mathematics by myself with success, and mean to make constant use of the beautiful observatory, which is situated on a rocky hill to the northeast of the city.

I promised you, last time, some little account of the pleasant fellow-lodger with whom an unexpected chance has thrown me together. Do not picture him to yourself possessing genius, or with astonishing and comprehensive learning; no, fancy him with the more fortunate endowments of inexhaustible vivacity, unwearied activity, with a careless modesty as regards himself, and yet considerable acquirements in his own department, and a very warm heart. He is a native of Sheffield, a place where the very general, but very equable cultivation of the inhabitants, is particularly favorable to the strengthening of a sound understanding. A striking trait in his character is a too credulous good-nature, which always falls into any cunningly laid snare; and an invincible pertinacity in his good opinion of people whom he has once, although mistakenly, begun to respect. With such a nice fellow, who would not be a warm friend? And I believe we both consider each other as friends already. He is not the only acquaintance I have here among the young men; there is one of his friends whom I will tell you about in my next, only too unlike him in purity of heart.......

LI.

12th November, 1798.

......In the very first days of our acquaintance, my friend Moorhouse began to speak of an acquaintance of his who had been here some months, but whom he had not yet been able to find out. He was a young man of uncommon genius, and burning with ambition to win a name for himself in literature; with this view it was his intention to visit Germany, to learn our language, and study our literature most thoroughly, and then to introduce it to the English public. This account, of course, made me curious to see him. As soon as my good friend had found him out, he invited him, in the first joy of his heart, and in the persuasion that the acquaintance would be a mutual acquisition, to take a place at our table, and hire a room next to mine; proposals to which the other willingly assented. But in spite of his courteousness, our first conversation gave me a repugnance to the stranger. I saw in him a man, who in early youth (he is more than a year younger than I) had nipped all virtue in the bud, and trodden it under foot; and cultivated and availed himself of some superficial reading in the French materialistic philosophy, to cast a mantle of system over his weaknesses; merry and humorous, full of incessant con traditions in his thoughts and actions; not without reading, not without cultivation, but as far removed from a thinker, which is the reputation he especially affects, as from any accomplishment in the world. You can fancy that the prospect of having him for a daily companion and a next-door neighbor, was any thing but agreeable. He is, indeed, a strange fellow; for instance, horrible expressions and unaccountable behavior, are followed by asservations of his good-will, and demonstrations of liking and kindness.

The second stranger at our table is an old friend of my fellow-lodger—a young man, according to his own account, given to excesses; in whom, however, there still remains a love of the noble and beautiful; and as he is an honorable and trustworthy man, he is not personally offensive to me, however much the conversation is so, which prevails among people of such a cast. In England you would seek almost in vain, I think, for the warmth and depth of feeling which characterize our friendships in Germany; isolation is the natural position to a young man, though in individual cases high esteem and veneration may call forth warm expressions of attachment, particularly in absence. I only wait an opportunity to set myself at liberty by unloosing a bond, which, like many others, promising advantage at first, threatens to transform itself into a chain......

23d. I have seen the Scotts three times since, and their first reception showed such earnest kindness, that it is almost superfluous to say, that with them I look forward to an unchangeable, not an inconstant and capricious friendship......

The strict and rather pedantic piety of the whole family, causes me some embarrassment; still this quality seems to me truly worthy of respect, particularly in the father; and I wish and intend, as far as I can with sincerity, to conform to the Kirk. I should not like to grieve the old man, and at all events my ideas harmonize much more with his than with those of the English infidels.

LII.

EDINBURGH, 18*th December*, 1798.

The number of vigorous, thinking minds is incontestably much larger in this than in most other countries, but the bonds which hold them together are just as much weaker and slighter. Some exceptions may be made, and (although kindness and friendship can not properly be said to make an exception when we are speaking of life-giving enthusiasm) not many of our fellow-countrymen, brought up in every-day life, would be capable of feeling and expressing such hearty sympathy and cordiality as Mr. Scott's treatment of me displays. But I have never witnessed, nor heard of family life full of deep and tender affection, nor of a hearty, enthusiastic, mutual confidence between young men. I have, indeed, though very rarely, been told of ardent love between married people, which expressed itself through the deep sorrow felt by the survivor; but even this love led to no results, for in other respects they retained the same indifference to all that appears to us of the highest value. Every young man has a crowd of friends; indeed, any one can have as many as he likes. But this sort of friendship consists simply and solely in a taste for paying each other long and frequent visits, and then killing the time together either in wild excesses, or in sleepy conversation, or boisterous merriment. I have remarked and proved by experience, what, perhaps, will astonish you, that it seems very strange to a young Englishman for a young man to speak of his absent friends with warmth, and to occupy himself with thoughts of them in his solitary leisure hours; and to this void in their hearts and imaginations, perhaps their universal licentiousness may be in great measure ascribed. They are only happy in the enjoyment of sensual pleasures. They are much more ready and obliging in undertaking trouble for their acquaintance than we usually are; but it is no great merit in them; bodily activity is an enjoyment to them, and they are accustomed to it by their whole education and mode of life. I have sketched this picture from my own experience, and add that it is nevertheless true, that the English, on the average, are worth more than people of a corresponding class whom we see at home; because, in the first place, with the exception of contemptible idlers, they hardly ever are, or like to be, without employment; and secondly, they quickly obtain a practical acquaintance with a subject, because their imagination does not divide and distract their attention by presenting other interesting objects; besides, they would be without a standing or a profession if they were not active in this way, the example of which they see every where around them.

Of the female sex I can not speak from my own knowledge; out of Mr. Scott's family I have not had so much as one long conversation with any lady; I have, however, seen a considerable number, and found them extremely commonplace. On the whole, women, though treated with scrupulous politeness, are very little honored; and few men have any idea that their conversation can be an agreeable recreation. In families where freedom prevails between the young people of both sexes, and is confined within the limits of propriety (over which a strict watch is kept), the whole pleasure of their intercourse consists in pert jesting, dancing, and fun, just calculated to please and feed empty-headed frivolity. In parties, the ladies always keep together, and beyond certain prescribed formalities, are treated with perfect indifference; it would excite the greatest attention, if the least interest were perceptible in the conversation of two young people with each other.

I have wandered far from my aim, which was to complain to you how little benefit I derive from the parties, and the extended circle of acquaintance into which the point, consisting of one single family and a few friends, has expanded itself, in spite of my efforts to the contrary.

In other respects, my peace is more secure against disturbance from such sources than it ever was before, and my industry does not flag. My conscience does not make me a single reproach on this point. I hasten to conclude; I leave this letter unwillingly because it gives me the semblance of a talk with you.

LIII.

EDINBURGH, 25*th December*, 1798

......If it were possible to infuse into my friends here, in addition to their many good qualities, somewhat of the higher interest which is so natural to us, I would not complain of the interruptions they cause me; but to that they are dead, and if you can bring them so far as to allow you to speak out of the fullness of your heart, without misunderstanding and misinterpreting you, you are made to feel that you have attained the utmost you can hope for, and need never expect a return on their side. This keeps your relation to them within the same narrow limits which restrict their intimacy with their other friends, and the natural consequence is, that the interest of intercourse must inevitably diminish, unless external circumstances give it, from time to time, a fresh impulse. You must not infer from this that I am growing tired of my acquaintance, and therefore am tempted gradually to forsake them. I visit nowhere habitually, except at the Scotts', and with them I have made it a rule never even to wear the appearance of diminished attachment, because I may find less interest in their conversation. I go there generally about three times a week, and enter into whatever mode of passing the time they choose, as heartily as I can. Then, too, they really are all so good and amiable, that it is never a task to be lively in their company. The father is a man of remarkably sound, strong understanding, and the mother a refined, sensible, and good woman, although not so free from prejudices, by a great deal, as the father, who, notwithstanding his decided strictness in religion and politics, never condemns a man for his opinions without knowing him, and possesses in a high degree a large and enlightened benevolence. Their third son, a boy about fifteen, who serves in the navy, came last week to spend some time at home. He seems to be a lad of good abilities; but they complain that he is too volatile, and he is unhappily liable to convulsive attacks, so that his poor parents must have much secret anxiety; but the laws of conventionalism oblige me to lock up my sympathy with them in my own breast. I thought, at first, I might possibly take some part in the instruction of the younger sons, in order, if possible, to awaken a higher intelligence in them; but delightful as that would be, on closer consideration I found it impracticable. Besides, they have a host of instructors, though scarcely such as they ought to have. Their father seems to do absolutely nothing himself toward their education, and one would feel almost indignant at it, if the contrary were ever heard of in this country. The extent to which boys are left to themselves, and the books they have in their hands, are a subject for just astonishment. Altogether you can have no adequate idea of the carelessness upon every subject, which quickens and nourishes all the germs of corruption till their poisonous weeds take root and shoot up, and you find their consequences meeting you at every step.

I went to the Scotts' yesterday evening, to pass the happy Christmas Eve in some measure as if at home, and hoped I might, perhaps, by joining in the freedom of their festivities, get on a more confidential footing with them. I was disappointed. To-day is to the English, in their own families, something like what yesterday is to us; but it is kept in a very different way, and is more of a family feast. Yesterday is just like other days; and it is a superstitious point of distinction between the Scottish and English churches, that the former studiously disregard this festival as savoring of Catholicism. Thus I only lost the quiet solitude, the sweetest remembrancer of the many happy anniversaries of this day in years that are past, and some of the vividness with which I should otherwise have called up the prospect of enjoying it with you a year hence.

LIV.

EDINBURGH, *8th January*, 1799.

One difficulty, which even overcomes my natural inclination to take things easily, lies in the multitude of subjects which I have set myself to study and imprint on my memory in a single day, and, with one exception, on every day of the week, rendering a methodical and frugal arrangement of my time absolutely necessary. This in no wise accords with my love of freedom and dislike of restraint. I hope to bring my inclination under control: but with the imperfect mastery we generally obtain over our actions, even after effort, much necessarily remains undone; we sacrifice one thing to another. You know that it was the perception of my need of gaining manly firmness, and ripeness of intellect, together with active energy, which decided me to take this journey. Provided this healthy state of mind be secured, it is not of much consequence whether one branch of abstract knowledge, which can be acquired any where by reflection, comes a little sooner or later into my possession. But I should be unwilling to miss the opportunity of gaining knowledge of a more local character, and I should be ashamed of myself if, possessing and practicing a good method of study, I could not learn to observe, to understand, to think, and to write. My attention is much directed to chemistry at present; not that I find much interest in it for its own sake, except as an exercise of ingenuity, but rather because it may be generally useful in application, and because of nothing is it so true, that it must either be understood thoroughly or not at all.

In spite of a good deal of hard work my health is rather improving than giving way. I account for this by the healthy tone of my feelings, which always accompanies the vigorous activity of my intellect, and I try to maintain it by extreme simplicity of diet, and frequent exercise in the open air, which the dry rocky soil renders all the more agreeable. The city is surrounded by a wide plain, which is, however, high above the level of the sea; hence the air here is very pure, though often very keen from the cutting wind. The real mountains are still a long way off; who knows if I shall be able to get away from here soon enough to climb them? August is the best time for a tour in the Highlands, and it will be impossible for me to leave here before the end of that month. And then the time of my return will be drawing nigh. I wish it could be managed, for nature, when she denied me the vivid delight in soft smiling beauty, gave me a cordial enjoyment of the sublime. You would find yourself as much disappointed in your expectations of the people, as you would rejoice with your whole soul in the majesty of nature. The nation, both in the Highlands and Lowlands, is said to be given to the vice of drunkenness, and the common people not to be one whit better than with us, except that they are very hardy and warlike. The Scotch mountaineers have been savages from time immemorial, and now that civilization is gradually spreading among them, are necessarily much deteriorating, as all savages do. In order to know them on their favorable side, an acquaintance with their language is necessary, which, in my uncertainty about visiting their country, I must renounce the attempt to acquire, and to which all helps are strangely wanting.

LV.

EDINBURGH, *15th January*, 1799.

......My days flow on pretty uniformly and simply, without much waste of time in society, but not quite without periods of weariness and exhaustion. Though I am seldom caught in the snare of spirit-killing parties, the interruptions arising from my ordinary intercourse are frequent; and the difference between the English way of thinking and ours is so great, that communication by degrees comes to an end. You know, when we are choosing friends, we can not help looking for congeniality of views, trying to accommodate ourselves to theirs, and taking interest in their affairs, even when they do not enter into ours with the same warmth. To the last especially I am naturally inclined; but it is not possible for me to sympathize with my acquaintance in all their concerns. You know that there is a great want of this congeniality, even in the family where in other respects there is so much that invites me to consider myself as one of themselves. There is nothing artificial about them; that is a great point: but genuine life, interest in the noblest subjects, is wanting also, and has given way to a narrow circle of blindly received and invincible prejudices; they have so adapted themselves to the world as it goes (and you would find the same every where here), that when its evils force themselves upon them, nothing is so far from their thoughts as that the origin of these may be among the things to which they are themselves accustomed; they rather imagine that they must arise from some change or innovation in the order of things, which is essentially bad. So, likewise, authorities are every where here the most dangerous opponents, and independent thought is a stranger to all parties. Hence, in such circles, you may perhaps enjoy yourself sometimes, but you never receive a fresh impulse from them, and you must either get this from within, or go on for a time in the ordinary track. . . . .

Whatever may be my vocation in life, assuredly nothing can be more essential to the soundness of the understanding than a close and accurate insight into the great scenes of nature. Our mind is in a sickly state when we prefer to her any work of human hands or human tongues, or confine our interest to those spots which have been illustrated by human actions.

Germany, as the province of the scholar, becomes dearer to me in a foreign country, although I am reminded at every step in how deep a slumber we, as a nation, are sunk. A close accquaintance with the English literature yields me a full conviction that, at the present moment, we may claim a decided superiority in almost every branch of letters, and this superiority is candidly confessed by many, especially among the more distinguished of the younger men, and even by some older scholars. In this place especially a great number are learning German. It must be confessed, however, that most singular prejudices prevail against our country.

Formerly our learned men were regarded as very slow, narrow-minded fellows; now people are inclined to pronounce them very clever men, but to look upon them as so many conspirators against the peace of the world; an opinion that is adopted in a still more incomprehensible manner by some young profligates, and excites their delight as much as it does the abhorrence of other people. One of these asked me, with great astonishment, "Are you speaking seriously? We thought that the German men of letters were, without exception, atheists, and we admire you on that account." All we want in order to measure ourselves, as far as it is good to do so, with these Britons, is to be more active, observant, and apt in seizing hold of the right moment.

In the awakening of such a spirit I would gladly co-operate, and the plan of uniting all our friends in the same object has afforded me some pleasant day-dreams.

LVI.

EDINBURGH, 11*th February*, 1799.

I have made the accquaintance lately of two persons who read German In no place in England is there so much attention paid to German literature as here, and the number of those who know enough of German to read a little, and to procure books in our language, is not inconsiderable, but they only know such works as accident throws in their way. Kant's name is already very well known here; this is owing to various Germans, who, with unequal capabilities, have taken upon themselves the apostolic office. His works are in the hands of several scholars of this town, and an Englishman has begun a translation of them, which he carried to a considerable length, but then got tired of the work.

But the representations of his philosophy are curiously confused, and, unless I am very much deceived, it will never take root here. Among the young men there are several who mutually compliment each other with the name of metaphysicans; but this class consists exclusively of mere empty praters, who have borrowed their fine attire from books, and are incapable of any true investigation. Their ideas are in such confusion that any development or elucidation by conversation is out of the question; their results are detestable; and their empty self-complacency contemptible. Last week I could not avoid attending a breakfast where several of this sort were present, and Kant was referred to (which is the reason of my speaking of him here); it was a meeting which irritated and vexed me to such an extent that it almost made me ill. I had seen enough long before to be persuaded, and this meeting fully convinced me, that the praise which Jacobi accords to the philosophical spirit of the English nation is quite undeserved, and founded on ignorance. Those works, the neglect of which he reckoned as a great honor to the English nation, which with us are now forgotten, and have lost their authority, the disgusting sophistries of the French school of thirty years ago and more, are the chosen food of the daily increasing class of which I speak; they are extending in circulation, and are even to be found in circulating libraries in the country, and the cast of thought that results from their influence only awaits political commotions to become dominant in the nation.....

LVII.

EDINBURGH, 26*th February*, 1799.

......I have written nothing to you as yet about English literature. The reason is, that I do not see the new works. There are no reading rooms here, as there are in Paris or even in Copenhagen, in which travelers can meet with new books, and pamphlets, and literary periodicals.

My hope of finding something analogous among the booksellers, whose shops are a meeting-place for acquaintance here, is disappointed; for there is nothing but gossiping in them; and the publisher to whom Scott specially introduced me, does not seem to have made his arrangements at all with a view of enabling one to hear of new works, but rather in fact to neglect modern productions for older literature. But among all the new publications that have appeared during the last eight months, and fallen in my way, there is nothing much worthy of notice, except a voyage round the world. The English seem, in fact, to have no great author at present, not one whose words they wait for with eager anticipation, and can dwell on with love and enthusiasm. They have a good number of useful authors in the departments of mathematics and natural science. Philosophy is quite at a stand-still; and among the writers I have referred to, there is not one of brilliant and commanding genius. There are many who write history, but the best of them do not rise above mediocrity. Still, on this and kindred topics, many points of interest are brought to light, which is to be ascribed, in great measure, to the peculiar position of this country, as containing within itself much with which the rest of Europe has no connection. Taste is at a very low ebb. The public devour and admire translations of all the unnatural and marvelous tales and satires of our German dramatists and romancers; and the original works most widely read are of the same cast. Schiller is the most admired German poet. Even among the political writings, for which England has always been so famous, nothing appears that excites, much less that deserves attention. One work, however, I would recommend to you; at least the notices of it have raised my expectations very high. It is a work on education by a lady of middle age, who has been occupied in the education of members of her own family for twenty years. I have never seen a work on this subject which displays a sounder judgment, more unprejudiced views, and more penetrating observation, than this of Miss Edgeworth's, judging by the extracts from it that I have read.

LVIII.

EDINBURGH, *7th May*, 1799.

......Scotland stands, far and wide, in high repute for piety, and has done so from the commencement of the Reformation. The clergy in general are not good for much; that is allowed by every one who knows the country. The piety of the people is, for the most part, mere eye-service—an accustomed formality without any influence on their mode of thinking and acting. They say prayers, learned by rote, at their meals, even before and after tea; they observe all the ordinances of their Church, and consign Infidels, Deists, and Atheists to perdition, with the pride of a soul that knows heaven to be its own exclusive privilege. In short, I no longer blame Hume for judging the Presbyterians, in Charles the First's time, with harshness and scorn. I expected austerity among them, I find only rusticity.

I live in such a house as I have described to you as an ordinary burgher's house; in a sunny, spacious room. My host is a carpenter. He and his wife have many of the usual vices of the common people here. They are lazy, avaricious, unsociable; but withal, less dirty than most persons of their class. In the same house with me, a story higher, lives an ironmonger, to whom Moorhouse had an introduction from some tradespeople in Sheffield, the seat of the hardware manufacture. This man, who is in humble circumstances, and uneducated, has always shown himself well-meaning and honest; he is a widower, and has several children, some of them scarcely grown up yet, who are all very well disposed. Although without a mother, they seem to keep their father's house in excellent order, and to be happy and industrious. Music is their only accomplishment.

The nation has a peculiar taste and remarkable skill in this art, and the many and sweet national songs exercise and cherish the talent from which they have sprung. I have spent many a pleasant hour in listening to the singing of these good children, and always found myself a welcome visitor. This family are much more rigid in their piety than those who belong to the Established Church; they are Baptists, and have retained the most extravagant notions of the fanatics of the last century in matters of austerity. To go to the theatre, to dance, to read worldly books, are all alike inexpiable crimes. Where education and habitual culture of the nobler faculties can not exist, such a way of thinking pleases me much more than the opposite, that of the people who give themselves up entirely to amusement. They look upon me as a great scholar, and, very likely, as an unbeliever.......

LIX.

EDINBURGH, 4*th June*, 1799.

......This journey has perhaps made me a more competent man of business than I had previously thought myself capable of becoming.

From my ignorance of the internal economy of the state, and the various branches of industry that sustain its vitality, the details of public business often used to seem to me quite unintelligible, and always unconnected; but as employments of this kind acquire a meaning to me, they lose their unpleasantness, and I have to contend less with the periodical inclinations to indolence which it so often requires intense exertion of will to overcome; and as I have more knowledge of the subjects to which a statesman has to direct his attention (though heaven knows what may be my peculiar department) than many of those to whose hands they are committed either have, or have any idea of obtaining, the consciousness that I do not hold a post for which I am unfit, by mere favor, will give me redoubled spirit and energy. I intend besides to avail myself diligently of the learned institutions which Copenhagen possesses. There are some splendid mineralogical collections there, and I shall try to master this interesting and important branch of natural history. And if we believe that Providence disposes the events of our life with a reference to the same ends that appear to us important in earthly plans, we may regard the postponement of an appointment in the university as a respite allowed me in which to make up for past neglect. If nothing unexpected occur, therefore, we must, and ought to look upon our future fate as settled, at least for a good while to come. Our position in Copenhagen will certainly be, in many respects, a difficult and delicate one. But formerly other circumstances, as you know, embittered my residence there, which we shall now be able to obviate. I shall now be capable of fulfilling all duties of ceremony, and your silent admonition will arm me with energy to persevere in the cultivation of my own powers. I could wish that some happy idea may be awakened within me some day, which, when developed, might grow into a noble, beautiful, and enduring intellectual work. I would this were possible. Works on the so-called exact sciences, even if I should advance so far, could not, from the measure of my powers, and the present state of these sciences, ever become any thing of this kind. Philosophy? He who presumes to raise his voice on this subject, without having the clearest vocation, will do little good thereby. History? Its worth and importance may appear problematical; and besides I see with sorrow that, owing to the inadequacy of our knowledge, chiefly caused by the ignorance and incapacity of those who had it in their power to have furnished to us the materials of history, it is almost impossible to carry out any thing like the comprehensive and magnificent plan with which my mind has long been occupied. Thus my prospects of authorship are very limited.......

I read lately the biography of a very singular man, a Mr. Taylor of London, whom I may perhaps have mentioned to you before; for, though I never saw him, every thing that is said of him interests me as if I had known him. There is something fearful about his history and character, that makes one half afraid to seek his acquaintance. He grew up and passed his life under very unfavorable circumstances. Through a singular philosophical mysticism derived from the Platonists, he became an orthodox polytheist, and adherent of the mystical interpretation of the popular religion of the Greeks; a kind of insanity which manifests itself with a strange sublimity in his translations of the Greek philosophers, and his own writings, especially his poems. Well, this man made his choice in his earliest youth; and the maiden who won the first and only love of the boy, became the wife of the youth, when her parents wanted to force her into a rich marriage. During more than a year they had only seven English shillings a week, which he earned by copying. And although their circumstances somewhat improved, poverty was their companion during many after years. Yet their spirit was not broken. Taylor had much self-will, but, at the same time, much fortitude. But I blessed our fate that we were not born in this country. A similar lot would very likely have awaited us; for the crime of not being rich can only be atoned for here by the striving to become so; and he who tries to live for his genius without this effort, if not pensioned by some great man or by government, in which case he must renounce his independence and his pride, will sink, heaven knows where! I should like to bring the best writings of this extraordinary man for our Moltkes.

On Saturday I think of going into Fifeshire to visit a very interesting landed proprietor who has given me a most friendly invitation.......

LX.

EDINBURGH, 10*th June*, 1799.

......Among the acquaintance in Copenhagen who will probably visit us, dearest Amelia, the people we are wont to call *interesting* will form a class by themselves. They are generally the most agreeable in conversation, and yet not those whom you would take to your heart. Men of the world, although intellectual and polished, often lose *themselves* entirely, and remain a mere brilliant form without heart and soul, and cold as death. I have often suffered myself to be too much carried away by the graceful qualities of such persons, and cultivated acquaintanceships of this kind more than was wise, and more than I could persevere in. Such characters are the production of capitals and courts, and will scarcely, if ever, be found beyond their precincts. It was my fate that such men always showed a particular liking for me; and that I, in return, felt more attracted toward them than to any other acquaintance, because they could far excel every other sort of men in that animated flow of conversation, which is of all pleasures the greatest to me. For in all artificial relationships, where the barriers that divide you are not removed by personal attachment and community of interest, and the immediate concerns of each must remain unapproached, the degree of pleasure to be found in intercourse must depend upon the vivacity of mind and the individuality exhibited by each; and the colder, more general, and more commonplace our conversation, the more indifferent we must be to each other. To you, who are more used to solitude, and so implacably averse to frivolity, perhaps such intercourse may be burdensome. But you need not stand in fear of it, dearest Amelia. Neither our inclinations nor our opinions will ever bring discord between us; and, in such matters, yours will be a law to me.

LXI.

EDINBURGH, 17*th June*, 1799.

......I reckon it among the most important results of my travels, that the indifference with which I was in the habit of regarding the objects of nature around me has given way. It was a defect naturally connected with my short-sightedness; but it constantly grew upon me, through the dreamy forgetfulness of reality in which from my childhood I was allowed to indulge. As you know, I sometimes pondered over it; but without a change in my circumstances, I could hardly have succeeded in overcoming it. This indifference has now vanished. For some time past I have taken a lively interest in mineralogy, and in fact it is this branch of natural history which has brought the others also into favor with me. This interest is in great measure owing to the nature of the country, just as the opposite character of the land in which we live must produce the opposite feelings.

I have always, when I have had occasion to allude to Playfair, spoken of him with the sincere respect, with which his distinguished merit, and upright character, have inspired me from the first. But now it is long since you have seen any mention of him, and it has been with him as formerly with other men of high standing, for whom I had a real deference and veneration, but from whom I expected no indulgence, supposing them to entertain too high an opinion of my talents, yet one not excited by affection, just as it was, a year and a half ago, with the good old Hegewisch—that is, my respect was mingled with a certain degree of dread. I felt I could not come up to my own expectations, much less to his. Thus it came to pass that I seldom saw him. By accident, however, I found myself alone with him a few days ago. In the course of our conversation, we touched upon mineralogy. He offered to take a walk with me some evening soon, round the rocks on the east side of the city, which are very remarkable. He kept his word. We walked about under the steep, time-worn walls of the cliffs, and he propounded his theory of their primitive origin and nature, and of the character and composition of the different kinds of rock. It was one of the most instructive and agreeable evenings I have enjoyed this year. Unfortunately, he is going to England before long.

My little excursion is put off till next Saturday.

LXII.

EDINBURGH, 2*d July*, 1799.

I wanted to write to you on the anniversary of our last parting, but was reluctantly compelled to yield to an invitation, where the insipidity of the conversation only gave me a sense of emptiness and desolation, after which I went to the Scotts, hoping to be refreshed by their greater cordiality. I went there with the wish and hope of pouring out my feelings for once about what lay nearest to my heart. Ever since I have written to you about this kind-hearted family, however, I have complained to you of their reserve as to those communications in which the heart expands. It is quite a national trait not to dwell upon what concerns us personally, upon what fills our heart; and it is as unnatural to them to hear me speak of the topics upon which I am feeling strongly, as it would be to do the same themselves. How I shall bless the time when this constraint will be over—when in my own land, with you and our friends, even by virtue of our national usages, I shall listen to the joys and sorrows of others, not as a mere piece of news, but as a communication to which I have a right, and be as sure of a welcome when I lay open my own heart! I am far from attributing it to coldness in these good people. It is altogether national, and it is the same with every one I have known here, whatever their rank or calling, learning, or sex. Hence, also, tediousness is seldom utterly banished from social intercourse. It has quite surprised me, for example, that if you meet a person in whose family some one has been taken ill, he will hardly allude to it, beyond a short answer to your inquiries, or speak of it with any feeling. In this way, it must be allowed, people may easily be independent of each other. I believe firmly that the Scotts love their children—that Playfair is a good father; and yet the former only speak of them because they have them with them in the evenings (which is saying much here), and the boys themselves make their presence known; the latter behaves exactly as if his boy were not in the room. So far from inviting me to speak of my connections, so far from Mr. Scott making any inquiries as to my father's position (though he is nevertheless as much attached to him as possible), they have met every attempt on my part to talk to them upon these subjects, with a silence, which admits of no other explanation, than that it is not in good taste to say much about such things. They have never once asked after my mother and sister! My friends I have only been able to mention in so far as they are connected with literature; for example, Jacobi. Though probably good Mrs. Scott may see danger to religion and the church in all such philosophical personages.

LXIII.

EDINBURGH, 10*th August* 1799.

I must really now begin to tell you what I have been doing with myself since I last wrote; how I came to leave Edinburgh, what I was about in the country when I wrote to you, and how it happens that I am here again. I can not give you all the details now, but will send you all the missing particulars in my next.

I was very unwell the day before C.'s lectures concluded, and the day itself. In this condition I went to the lecture, with which my whole connection with the University is brought to a close. He hastened to conclude, as I had expected. I waited to the end in order at last to bind the Proteus to an interview. I went up to him, and we got into conversation. He said he was on the point of going to his little estate, and asked me to accompany him. A more inviting opportunity could not have offered, for it is difficult to get hold of him. There is quite a swarm of acquaintance and visitors round him, for he has the dangerous merit of making himself interesting to his friends. On the road, and in the country, I could have him to myself. He only spoke of a few days, and this accorded with my wishes. We had very stormy weather on our journey. The occasion of his trip was a fair in the town of Kinross. His country-house is a little old cottage, which has been enlarged from time to time; small and neat. Unhappily, some one was there already waiting for him, and thus our first evening was almost lost. I comforted myself with thinking of the next day, when I could ride with him to the town, and then on our return be with him for some days.

At breakfast time, C. began to beg me to wait his return here; he should be back in one or two days, and meanwhile I could make myself acquainted with the arrangements of his farm, as I had often expressed a wish to do. Besides, he would give me an introduction, of which I could avail myself during his absence, to a landed proprietor in the neighborhood, who had the direction of some interesting works. I should have enough to learn; and besides, there were plenty of books for me. One easily believes what one wishes. I staid behind. At first I enjoyed my solitude very much. I sauntered about, read a good deal, indulged in my own thoughts, looked about me, observed much; the children were my society, and it gave me pleasure to be able to win their love with the trifles which attract at their innocent age. The poor children had lost their mother, of whom her friends speak in unusually high terms. Her remembrance, too, lives undimmed in his heart. But though these poor children are left very much to themselves, it is delightful to see how kind and loving they are with each other.

The weather had now become a downright tempest, and it was impossible to quit the house. Meanwhile, day after day passed, and my friend did not come. My patience and good-temper gave way. I knew C. too well to ascribe it to an intentional slight on his part. When the weather cleared, I found that the gentleman to whom he had recommended me, was no longer at home.

At length, yesterday, I came back in an ill-humor. My first errand was to my truant friend. I have not room to tell you to-day how he came to break his word. I do not love him the less for it. Our interview was full of emotion.

LXIV.

EDINBURGH, 13*th August*, 1799.

......I will not put off telling you what prevented C. from fulfilling his promise. It is really an unhappy affair—an approaching marriage, not as yet made public, which he has resolved on against his inclination, in order to provide care and education for his children. He told me this candidly himself. I should tremble for the consequences, were not the poor women here so accustomed to neglect, that no doubt his wife will expect nothing beyond respect. Attention she certainly will not receive. Amusement, and every thing that can fan the flame of his temperament, is a necessary to him, and thereby he trifles away a great part of the respect (for every one that knows him must love him), which is really his due. Still I assure you that he is one of the most eminent and best men I know here, only he should not have been born in this country.

LXV.

BOLTON IN EAST LOTHIAN, 19*th August*, 1799.

......This last week has already brought with it more pleasure than the monotonous months I spent in the city. The rare enjoyment of finding my expectations surpassed, and, what is far more, the simple heartiness with which I was received by people, with whom I could exchange respect in the first hour, has given me quite a new view of the nation, and a liking for it, which nothing before had called out. I can now return with the conviction of having obtained a really correct view of the country, and with a just and cordial love of its inhabitants.......

LXVI.

DOUGLAS, *Tuesday*.

I was interrupted yesterday evening by the household arrangements of my good hosts.......

In Haddington, the chief town of this county, Mr. Stevenson, the acquaintance I have before mentioned to you, was waiting for me, in order to conduct me to the son of the man in whose house he had passed a year to learn farming. I expected to see a sturdy, jolly-looking rustic; I was half-abashed when a mild, refined young man entered the room, whose manners would have qualified him to appear in the most polished circles. We, of the book-world, are apt to fancy that a farmer or an artist will not pay much attention to us, if we seem inclined to meddle with the details of his calling, but probably only laugh at us in his sleeve. Mr. Adam Bogun testified by his whole behavior that he felt otherwise, and was sincerely glad to see his unusual visitor. A German tourist was to him as new an object, as a farmer from the most highly cultivated district in Scotland was to me. I soon conceived a warm interest in him, and felt convinced that he would grudge no pains to oblige me. Pleasure beamed in his countenance when he was able to show me a kindness, when he saw that he had given me a pleasure, or that I took an interest in his circumstances and his family; and when we parted, the tears stood in his eyes. As the weather on Saturday was so boisterous that traveling was out of the question, I willingly remained with him. Before the morning was over we were no longer strangers, and we sat together alone by the fire, which the horrible weather rendered necessary, chatting so familiarly, or employing ourselves with so little restraint, that my spirits were not cast down by the gloomy prospect of having to make my tour in such weather. As acquaintanceship in the country does not proceed at such a sleepy pace as in the town, where you have only too much of it, the weather did not prevent a neighbor from coming to spend the evening, though he lived a mile off. He was likewise an excellent young man, and had more education than my other young friend; had seen more of the world too; but he was such a fanatic in politics, that for several years he had forgotten his own business, and even now injures his peace and character with his foolish notions. I must pass over the Sunday that I spent in his house (for the weather still prevented me from continuing my journey), where I met a curious adventurer, whose loquacity overpowered us all; but did not prevent my accepting his invitation to call upon him. On Monday I went with my worthy young friend Bogun to see his father. The old man had risen, by his own exertions, from a very humble origin to considerable opulence. His manners are still pretty much those of the class to which he at first belonged, but with all their excellences, and natural good breeding characterized his family. A very different reception awaited me at the house of a man of noble birth, a Mr. Buchan Hepburn, to whom I had a letter of high recommendation. Whether it was that he looked down on my companion, Bogun, and therefore on me, or that he did not choose to insult with our presence a party of noble guests whom he had invited to dinner, he began immediately to tell us in very plain terms that he had scarcely any time to spare for us, on account of this party; he would show us his fields, but must hurry through them. I hastened away from him, taking leave of Bogun also, to Sir John Murray, of Kirkland's Hill, a country gentleman to whom Mr. Scott had given me an introduction. I was received by a cheerful, healthy-looking, elderly man, in a room filled with books and papers, so that it looked like the study of a scholar. He left me in no doubt that he placed full faith in his friend's recommendation. He conducted me to his family, who were assembled in a very handsome dining-room; a mother, and four daughters, very near in age, the youngest a child who had done growing, the eldest just attained to the gravity of womanhood. I told them at once of the reception I had previously met with, which did not surprise them, but they strove with all zeal to make amends for it, and we soon got into a very animated and familiar conversation.

I have told you how very much the two sexes keep at a distance from each other in this country, when they meet in parties in the towns, and how scrupulously every appearance of intimacy is avoided. Here, German manners were in fashion, and the young ladies were as artlessly friendly as if they had learnt of you and your sisters, that it is a narrow-minded prejudice to refuse ordinary confidence, and marks of sympathy in conversation, because a stranger happens to be a man. Only one of the number was good-looking. Beauty is extremely rare in Scotland. This one and the eldest displayed much intelligence and a careful education. What their father has accomplished on his farm exceeded every thing that I have yet seen. I had never met with any garden so carefully tended, so well laid out, or so cleverly managed. All this has been done without the prospect of bequeathing it to his children, and for an avaricious landlord. He had raised the produce of his fields four-fold in thirteen years, brought every thing from a neglected condition to the highest cultivation, planted hedges, diked in a strip of land, and has now only got to keep it up to its present state. His lease is for thirty years. He has brought up his two sons to agriculture; put one in charge of two outlying farms, and the other is learning under his own eye. They are all very busy in their home duties, and happy with each other. They would all please you, even the somewhat rough mother; for if she transgresses the rules of polished society, she does it with so much good-humor that you can only laugh. She smokes her pipe, laughs at it herself, but is not ashamed of it, for as she says, "it is no sin," and seems to enjoy existence more than most people. I meant to have left the next day, but I staid. We parted with the promise to meet again. Against that time Murray will write out a set of rules and experiments for me, and engaged me in return to write him an account of our methods of agriculture, at some future period. I have really learnt much more of these matters than you would suppose. I am quite familiar with the agricultural economy of Scotland, and I am convinced that I should be able to apply what I have learnt on another soil. By the end of next week I shall be in Edinburgh again.

XLVII.

EDINBURGH, 31*st August*, 1799.

......It would scarcely be possible, perhaps, for a large agricultural population to earn for themselves a more respectable character in their calling, than that which belongs to most of the inhabitants of the district through which I traveled. True insight into their business, activity, intelligence, and an unblemished reputation are the characteristics, I really believe, of the greater number of the farmers; and many of them possess a number of very good books, are fond of reading, and speak as well as the townsfolk (the Scotch, indeed, in general, do not speak well). Public-houses, or hotels, in which our country people degrade themselves, are only to be found in the widely separated villages, or in towns. For the villages are almost every where broken up, and this of itself keeps the laborers from social excesses, as they live round the farmstead in little cottages, consisting of one room, which is at once their cooking, living, and sleeping room. The object of their aspiration is to possess the reputation, the manners, and the comforts of a respectable station. They spend a great deal upon their houses, and often upon their gardens, however short a time they have them in their possession.

If I were a landlord here, I should not make much profit, for it seems to me an unjustifiable thing to drive away such people, by over-exaction, from the soil which they have done so much to improve and embellish; and it has excited my indignation to see that this is not at all taken into account. Certainly one would be far from desiring that a whole nation should resemble them, or seriously wishing to take up one's abode among them. Still the first might not be so bad after all, and as to the latter, we should only find in the long run, that we had not chosen the better part, if we adopted their tone in all things. The number of their ideas is limited, and it is inevitable but that many things should be perfectly indifferent to them, which stir our whole hearts; that they should have an inordinate amount of phlegm. I even feel myself that my stay here, and my occupation with the things of daily life, has made me liable to the contagion, and therefore should not wish to be the associate of these very worthy men for any length of time. Perhaps it has done me a little harm already; perhaps it is with the dwelling on the things of common life, as with the composition of the air that we breathe, the life-giving part of which, when pure, seems to be only fit for another world, and would consume our life here.

LXVIII.

AFTER HIS RETURN FROM ENGLAND.

TO AMELIA.

COPENHAGEN, 18*th April*, 1800.

......Schimmelman and others will see that a suitable salary is attached to the places they are endeavoring to get for me. Every thing is dear, certainly, very dear, but I am in no anxiety. We both like a simple way of life, and do not seek or require amusements. Shelter, food, fire, clothing, and joyful love will make our all. We shall enjoy a fine day in the fields as much as in a country house. Sophocles and Homer will be our substitute for the theatre; and the absence of visitors will not bring, but prevent weariness and *ennui*. The Reventlows, Bernstorff, the Rantzaus, the Kunzens, the Desaugiers are all very friendly.

LXIX.

26th April, 1800.

......My darling Amelia, I rejoice in my good fortune with feelings which are not unworthy of your love. It is now not only a duty, but my most pressing necessity, to keep all my powers on the stretch here (where there are so many examples to lure me to indolence of mind and lukewarmness of heart), and to walk circumspectly along the brink of the precipice. I bless the æra that will end this busy yet unsettled life. Idleness and aimless occupation will henceforth be no longer possible, and with my intellect calm and strong—with the consciousness of capacity for action, and of being equal to my own requirements—that sense of life, on whose intensity depends the practice of all that is right and noble, will awake once more with youthful vigor. A consciousness of love and warmth will be shed over each moment, that will make toil a pleasure. A life in the spirit; the only life in which I can be quite happy, but in which I may be more so than most.

LXX.

29th April, 1800.

......Many considerations have been suggested to me by what you tell me about the relation between parents and children, in certain families of your acquaintance. What a glorious thing is that true equality, when it is unbroken by pride, self-erected barriers, and the love of ruling on the one side! It might so well subsist between parents and children, and then their mutual relation would rest on a sure and lasting basis. But, generally, parents are more inclined to make their children minister to their own vanity, than to be moderate in their demands upon them, to keep them unexacting on their side, and, if possible, inspire a sense of their own superiority, without attempting to keep their children under undue restraint.

As regards our affairs, our income will be very limited at first; but afterward it will depend on my own exertions to make it an ample one. The Duke of Augustenburg has already expressed to Schimmelman his intention of offering me the Greek professorship if it should fall vacant. But, as far as money is concerned, the prospects are better in public life. However, we will not trouble ourselves with these considerations at present. We will content ourselves with our lot, and not suffer ourselves to be disturbed by the fears, which Baggesen and others of my acquaintance think to excite, when they say that it is impossible to live here under 1500 thalers a year.* I am quite convinced that we shall be able to manage. Do not fear that I shall suffer myself to be alarmed by the complaints and apprehensions which I have so often to listen to from others. I know what will make us happy, and what we can renounce without a painful effort, or longing wishes. Where love is the animating principle there are no dark moments of this kind. I look at our dear Moltkes in the beginning of their married life......

* Equal to about 255*l*.

CHAPTER V.

NIEBUHR'S MARRIAGE AND OFFICIAL LIFE IN COPENHAGEN FROM 1800 TO 1806.

IN May, 1800, Niebuhr returned to Holstein and married; in June he took his wife to Copenhagen, and entered on his double official duties on the 1st of July.

The young couple were in the highest degree happy in each other. Niebuhr writes thus to Madame Hensler, in the month of August: "Amelia's heavenly disposition, and more than earthly love, raise me above this world, and, as it were, separate me from this life.

"A life of full employment, combined with serenity of mind, which we shall secure by rigidly maintaining our seclusion, protects and heightens the capacity for happiness. Happiness is a poor word: find a better! Even the toils and sacrifices of business contribute to the calm self-approval, which to me is the essential condition of enduring happiness. Amelia's cheerfulness, her contentment with her lot, untroubled by any wish for something beyond it, afford me as heartfelt joy as the contrary would give me pain. Her presence and conversation keep my heart at rest and my mind healthy. Thus I am gradually recovering from the impression made upon me in past times by the delusions and contradictions of the world."

Harmonizing in all their tastes, their lives flowed on calmly and quietly; they occasionally mixed in fashionable society at the houses of Count Schimmelman, and a few others, but beyond that only joined in small parties of intimate friends. When Niebuhr was not engaged in his official duties, he returned to his favorite classic authors. His wife entered warmly into all that interested him. In the evenings he often related stories to her from the ancient writers, or read aloud to her, or looked over with her what he had himself been writing.

In the autumn of the same year, the University of Kiel offered him a professorship. He declined it for the present; partly because he thought it would be ungrateful to Schimmelman to resign his situation so soon; partly because he feared it would be regarded as an unbecoming mark of partiality if he were thus preferred to older men; partly because he really enjoyed many branches of his present occupation. He saw that he was of use, and his merits were recognized by his superiors.

In September he heard through Madame Hensler of F. Leopold Stolberg's conversion to Catholicism, which caused so much excitement in the circle of his friends. The purity of Stolberg's motives for this change is beyond a doubt. His natural cast of mind was deeply pious. The rationalism, which prevailed at that time in the Protestant Church of Germany, shocked and pained him to the last degree; and, believing that there existed no elements of regeneration within its pale, he threw himself into the arms of a church, which at least afforded more satisfaction to his devotional feelings. By this step he not only sacrificed many advantages for his family, but lost the friendship of several of those to whom he was most warmly attached, especially Voss and Jacobi, who carried their expressions of censure to actual bitterness. Voss in particular continued his attacks upon him for many years; so late as 1817 he published a pamphlet entitled, "Wie F. L. Stolberg unfrei geworden ist."* Niebuhr did not justify Stolberg's change; it grieved him deeply; he regarded it as the aberration of a tendency in itself beautiful and noble: but he was able to transport himself into Stolberg's point of view, and was convinced that no unworthy motive could have actuated him, which alone would have warranted the harsh treatment he received from many of his friends. Therefore, much as Niebuhr was attached to Voss and Jacobi, he could not at all approve of their conduct in this instance, which was indeed often a source of regret to him, the more so as the form of Catholicism which Stolberg had adopted by no means rendered him illiberal toward his Protestant friends, nor detached his sympathies from the sincerely pious among them.

Niebuhr was intending at this time to take up the study of Grecian history in his leisure hours, and write an account of the various constitutions among the Greeks. This was a design he had cherished for many years, indeed almost from his boyhood. But his studies were to some extent interrupted by the ill health of his wife, who suffered long and severely from a complaint in the eyes, during which time most of his leisure hours were spent in trying to amuse her. They passed this winter with no other draw-

* How F. L. Stolberg became a slave.

back to their quiet and peaceful enjoyment of life's purest pleasures. But the spring of 1801 brought with it threatening storms.

It is well known how deeply the English government considered itself aggrieved by the armed neutrality of the northern powers of Europe—how acts of hostility were practiced on the Danish vessels, and even on the colonies, without any formal declaration of war, and how at last, in March, 1801, Nelson and Parker appeared in the Sound, and proclaimed war at the moment of attack. Niebuhr watched the gradual approach of this calamity, and witnessed the attack and the bombardment. His feelings on this occasion, and the intensity of his sympathies, will be seen by the extracts from his letters to Madame Hensler. After this mournful episode, this year elapsed without any alteration in Niebuhr's circumstances and occupations. In the summer of 1802, he and his wife visited their friends in Holstein, who all rejoiced to see the happiness and serenity which beamed in his looks. He performed the duties of his office with ease, pleasure, and success; the sciences were a recreation to him in his leisure hours, and the cheerfulness and affection of his wife afforded a satisfaction and repose to his heart, which made it impossible for gloom or vexation to take any lasting hold on him, although with the great sensitiveness of his nature he could not always avoid passing annoyances.

During the winter of 1802–3, Niebuhr studied Arabic with great zeal, and surprised his father on his birthday with the translation of a part of Elwakidi's History of the Conquest of Asia under the first Kaliphs, from a manuscript in the library of Copenhagen. As he soon after became engaged in new and more extended official occupations, time failed him for the continuance of this work, but he did not relinquish the intention of completing it, for many years, and preserved the manuscript with that view. He also gave several lessons a week during this winter (for which he received no remuneration), on historical and philological subjects, to a nephew of Count Schimmelman's, and two other young men, sons of his acquaintance.

In the spring of 1802, he was sent by the Danish government into Germany, to transact some financial business which obliged him to visit Hamburgh, Leipsic, Frankfort, and Cassel. His wife accompanied him. On their way home they spent some weeks in Holstein.

On Niebuhr's return to Copenhagen, Count Schimmelman informed him that he was destined to a more important office. He thus alludes to the subject in a letter to Madame Hensler, written in October: "On my return, I heard from Count Schimmelman news of some importance to me. My colleague at the Board of Trade is going to resign his post, and his duties are to be transferred to me, but without any alteration of my title or salary. . . . My work will be considerably augmented by it, which I am glad of, for it is a well-ascertained fact, that the ability to work grows with the number of things one has to get through. I do not fear that it will prevent me, at least in the long run, from pursuing those studies which are my delight and my mental aliment."

The duties of his new office were very onerous; but as he had great aptitude in learning business, and could seize the details of a subject almost at a glance, he worked at once with great ease and great certainty. Thus he still found leisure for scholastic pursuits. The following passage occurs in a letter written in 1803: "I have had as much to do before at particular times, but never for a constancy. And I must look forward to its being the same for some years to come. If I can but keep my health, there will still be time left for those occupations which most deserve our preference, though we may learn to like any that tax our powers enough. There is a reward for a man engaged in active public life, which I am now reaping, viz., a fair fame, and a position that commands the confidence even of the unlearned among my fellow-citizens. Hence my employments become a positive pleasure to me. The most intricate grow easy, and I can get through them in a very short time. . . . I am at work on a treatise, as I wrote you before in few words. Its subject is the nature of the Roman public domains, their distribution, colonization, agrarian laws, &c. It is an interesting question, and I think I have taken a more accurate view of it, than has been reached before. I used to busy myself with such questions when I was still at Kiel. I wish I were as free from worldly care, and as open to new impressions now as I was then; but how much that has happened since that time has turned out better than I ventured to hope."

Niebuhr's colleague, Obelay, died in January, 1804; he was the First Director of the Bank, and practically the only acting member of the Directory. His office was immediately transferred to Niebuhr, who, at the same time, by the express desire of the

Crown Prince, undertook the direction of the East India department of the Board of Trade, the affairs of which had fallen into confusion; and he also became a member of the Standing Commission for the Affairs of Barbary, of which he had hitherto acted as secretary. His official standing and his income were considerably raised by these changes. The amount of his labor was now much increased, particularly by business connected with the commercial world, and the credit and circulation of the paper currency. The soundness of his views and the judiciousness of his measures were generally recognized, and his management of the affairs of the bank was so universally approved, that his subsequent departure from his native country was the subject of general and lasting regret. He was not merely respected by his subordinates in office, on account of his sagacity, industry, and rigid integrity, but really loved by them for the kindness with which he treated them, and the interest which he took in their welfare. Many of them shed tears when he took his leave of them.

Even at this busy period, he never quite lost sight of his favorite studies, or forsook them entirely for more than a short time together. The mornings, from ten to three, or four, were usually spent at his various offices, or, on foreign post days, on the exchange. Then came the drawing up of reports, the large business correspondence and the necessary verbal communications with other officials. When he returned home at night after all this he was often exhausted both in body and mind; but if he got engaged at once in an interesting book or conversation, he was soon refreshed, and would then study till late at night. Ancient history formed the principal part of his reading at this time, but he did not overlook the productions of modern literature. He hailed with joy every new work of importance, and put it into the hands of his wife. When they were first married, he used to read Greek with her, but afterward the weakness of her eyes forbade the necessary effort on her part, and she also found the acquisition of the grammar tedious, and therefore gave up the further study of this language; but in every other respect he always found in her the fullest participation in all that interested him. Niebuhr had little intercourse at this time with men of letters, as his engagements led him into a widely different sphere of society. He, however, kept up his acquaintance with two of his earliest friends,

Münter, the celebrated orientalist and archæologist, who was at that time Professor of Theology in Copenhagen, and Moldenhawer, the head librarian at the Royal Library in Copenhagen, and a distinguished exegetical theologian.

The summer of 1804 was a particularly busy period for Niebuhr. He writes thus to Madame Hensler: "As far as regards business, I confidently hope to be able to do something toward bringing our finances to the height of prosperity, although, perhaps, not immediately or directly. Last winter was by no means a quiet one for us. Even on Sundays, I could sometimes hardly get time to collect my thoughts a little. The winter before, I used to cheer and invigorate my mind with the study of ancient history. Now, that is out of the question. I am obliged to see and talk with so many people; some of them interest me by their quickness and intelligence, so that I enjoy the time I spend with them to a certain extent; but in the long run, we always find that where there is no bond of affection, intercourse is sure to lose its charm, and often becomes wearisome." On the week days, he had now scarcely ever time for more than a little occasional light reading. The Sundays he devoted as far as possible to his private studies, which made those days real festivals to him. In the autumn he began to get rather more leisure, which he employed in continuing the before-mentioned treatise on the Roman domains.

The intelligence of the Austrian calamities at Ulm and Austerlitz, in the autumn of 1805, which deeply affected him, led him to peruse the Philippics of Demosthenes afresh. The similarity of the position of Greece at that time to the state of Europe, and of Philip's growing power, tyranny, and oppression, to the proceedings of Napoleon, struck him so forcibly, that he translated and printed the first Philippic.

Toward the end of 1805, Niebuhr was asked by a distinguished Prussian statesman, then visiting Copenhagen on a mission from his Government, whether he felt inclined to enter the Prussian service, in the department of finance. Some weeks later he received a direct inquiry on the subject by letter. He had never before thought of exchanging the Danish service for any other, and even now he would scarcely have replied otherwise than by a direct negative, had he not just at that time felt himself aggrieved by the intended appointment of a young nobleman to a place in the finance department to which he thought that he had a prior claim, both from his official standing and past services, and also because it had been previously promised to him, subject to the approval of the Crown Prince. This incident excited in him for the moment a strong feeling of irritation. He thought that it closed the door to any further advance in his public career: he looked forward to being burdened forever with an overwhelming mass of details, and, what stung him most deeply, found himself slighted in the very quarter, where he reckoned with the greatest security on an unprejudiced appreciation, and a just approval of his services. When, therefore, these proposals were renewed by Prussia, he felt very keenly the contrast between the estimation in which he was held abroad, and the way in which he was undervalued at home. Yet he underwent a long and severe struggle with his attachment to his native land, ere he could reconcile himself even in thought to the possibility of leaving it. His answer to the proposition at the time was quite indecisive, "that he could not commit himself on the subject, particularly as he did not know what appointment was referred to." The winter of 1805–6 elapsed without his hearing any thing more on the subject. It had not occupied his mind much after the first moment; and besides, the storm of his anger had sunk to rest; his old relationships had been renewed, and nothing more had been done respecting the appointment of the young man referred to. Yet, by frequent repetition, the idea of leaving his native country had grown less strange to him, and a consideration of the satisfaction which he would derive from a wider sphere of action, and a release from all the minor details of business, forced itself upon him at times. Added to this, the condition of the Danish finances, which had been much deteriorated through the immense military establishments necessary in order to maintain a neutral position, often caused him great uneasiness. When therefore, in March, 1806, a new and unexpected proposal reached him, to enter on the joint directorship of the first bank in Berlin, and of the Seehandlung,* with the prospect and promise of further promotion, the struggle in his mind was renewed. He communicated

* A privileged commercial company at Berlin, founded in 1772, for the promotion of foreign commerce, then in a very languishing condition. The exclusive possession of the silk trade of Prussia, and of the trade in wax, was secured to it, by charter, for twenty years. The capital was raised by the sale of 2400 shares, of which the King had 2100, and only 300 were offered to the public. In 1793, the number of shares was increased to 3000, and the Seehandlung lost its monopoly of the wax trade, but was allowed to engage in general mercantile

the proposal to Count Schimmelman, who, unwilling as he was to lose him, recognized the advantages it presented, particularly as he could offer him nothing equal to it in Copenhagen. What weighed most with him on the side of acceptance, was the release from matters of detail, which he feared would permanently weaken the powers of his mind. In this post, the directorial labors, and the general guidance and control of affairs, were all that would devolve upon him.

While these negotiations were still pending, Count Hardenberg left the Prussian ministry, and was succeeded by Count Haugwitz.* At the same time rumors got afloat, which seemed not improbable, of an alliance between France and Prussia. This deterred Niebuhr from proceeding with the negotiation, both on account of his deep-rooted aversion to any connection with the then existing French government, and also the probability that such an alliance might lead to a collision between Prussia and the Northern courts, including Denmark. He therefore wrote word to the Prussian minister of finance, Von Stein, that it would be impossible for him to leave his native land at such a critical moment, and while political relations were in such an uncertain condition: but if delay were possible, he would accept the post when peace was restored in Northern Europe. Stein answered him quite satisfactorily as regarded any hostile intentions toward Denmark, and allowed him to delay his acceptance till he could free himself from his present engagements. He now decided to send in his resignation to the Danish government, which, after a fruitless attempt to retain him, was accepted.

Niebuhr took this step with a heavy heart, less on account of the fearful struggle already then visibly impending over Prussia, than because it severed him forever from his fatherland. Denmark had been the cradle of his infancy—Holstein the home of his childhood; here he had passed his youth and received his education, and it contained all who were dearest to him on earth,

and banking operations, and its creditors were guaranteed by the State. It lost immensely by large advances made to the State in 1804, 1805, and 1806, but after 1816 gradually retrieved its affairs.

* Hardenberg always opposed the treaty of Schönbrunn, signed by Haugwitz, December 15th, 1805, by which the Prussians agreed to cede Neufchâtel, Anspach, and Clève, in return for Hanover. After the treaty between Prussia and France, signed at Paris on the 15th February, 1806, by which Prussia entered into close alliance with France, Napoleon forced the King of Prussia to dismiss Hardenberg, whom he knew to be opposed to the French interest.—See Stein's Leben, vol. ii. p. 323.

except his wife. For the future he could no longer share their common interests, but must acquire new ones, which were as yet foreign to him. These considerations often filled him with sadness, and there were perhaps moments in which he would have retraced his steps if he had given way to his feelings. Madame Hensler was at that time in Copenhagen on a visit to him and his wife; they parted with the hope of soon meeting again, but with the prospect of a much bitterer parting beyond.

In September, 1806, he left Copenhagen. His friends, acquaintance, and all with whom he had been officially connected, took leave of him with every token of respect and sincere regret at his departure. He staid but a short time in Holstein. On this occasion he only visited Meldorf, where all his relations came to meet him and his wife, and bid them a sad and anxious farewell. It could not indeed be otherwise than anxious, for every one was looking forward with dread anticipations to the fearful conflict, which was to decide the fate of Europe; and their friends parted from them with the certainty that they went to meet this conflict, and were about to be involved in the thickest of the strife.

Niebuhr and his wife were not less deeply moved; they saw the whole peril toward which their path was leading them, but they went forward with the courage of resignation that was prepared to sacrifice all, where all was at stake.

Extracts from Niebuhr's Letters during his residence in Copenhagen in the Danish Civil Service. 1800–1806.

LXXI.

TO MADAME HENSLER.

COPENHAGEN, 23*d September*, 1800.

Although, in your first letter, you requested us not to speak of Stolberg's change of religion, as it was not yet made public, it would have been unbecoming to keep it a secret from Schimmelman, Stolberg's old and unalterable friend. If he had known it first, he would have spoken of it to us. We happened to be at Seelust* on the very day your letter reached us. Schimmelman was unwell, and we had a long conversation alone. Amelia has already told you what he thinks about it. Schimmelman will never become a Catholic himself; but he, too, finds the present state of Protestantism and the Protestant clergy in general, most unsatisfactory. Even if some among them really believe what they deliver from the pulpit—and if these think about it; what sort of a faith is it they preach? Can it satisfy those who long for a loving dependence on supernatural objects? I am not so much alarmed either about the intolerance of the true mystics; they never were intolerant in practice, except when they were irritated by

* Count Schimmelman's country-seat.

contempt and ill treatment, and that should hardly be reckoned as intolerance. The unenlightened bigots are those whom I fear, and they will always remain true to their nature.

LXXII.

COPENHAGEN, *24th March*, 1801.

As Milly's pain in her eye has been worse again, and is only beginning to show signs of improvement this morning, you must not be angry at my exercising a husband's authority in forbidding her to write, but be contented with a letter from me. Send this letter on to our friends, that they may know the position of our State.

You have perhaps heard, by the last post, reports of the approach of a hostile English fleet, which were brought by the captain of a merchant vessel just arrived in the Sound, and also from the island of Anholt. We did not like to send you these reports, though they seemed to us likely to be true, and when they rose to certainty it was too late. On Sunday night, however, a dispatch came from Elsinore with the intelligence that the fleet had been seen there about three miles to the northwest, off Gillelye: there is a roadstead there, where they lay at anchor the night before; but early that day they had weighed anchor, and were cruising about.

On Saturday evening, Drummond and the other negotiator, Vansittart, left, after a conference in which a very insulting requisition was made by them, and refused on our side, till the embargo should be removed. The evening before, an English frigate had arrived here, under a flag of truce, but left again on the Saturday. This flag shows that they consider themselves in a state of war with us, because they feel that they are treating us as enemies. We have not yet exercised the slightest hostility against them, but probably the moment is very near, when the first shot will be fired, and the gauntlet thrown down beyond recall. I think it more likely that blood will flow to-day or to-morrow, than that a delay will take place, which many expect. As a cannonade at Cronburg would be plainly heard in the city, if the wind is such that the English could attempt the passage (which in that case they would certainly succeed in effecting), we often listen, to try if we can catch any sounds of the kind.

Nelson's presence leads us to think, judging of him by his past conduct, that a furious attack will be made upon our harbor. Others give credence to a report that he tendered his advice against an expedition to the Baltic, and said, that he did "not choose to ensnare himself in that mouse-trap." People here are as inquisitive as they are ready to spread news. The attack upon our defenses would be a fearful thing for the town. But I hope we should be able to sustain it, for then we should reap a harvest of glory, and the nation would be awakened from its long slumber; though at a cost, indeed, that we should all long feel. If the war is once proclaimed, it is not at all likely that the enemy will content himself with blockading us, shutting us up, while we complete our equipments, and therefore, in all probability, the next week or two will decide our fate. I do not give you the details of our defenses and preparations, because no one can tell but what the mails may be already in danger. However, every body is welcome to know, that in the course of yesterday, about a thousand men volunteered to enter the service, whereas the vessels are usually manned by impressment.

It seems strange to me to be writing to you of war and armaments, or indeed of any thing beyond our own concerns. The crisis is such that it is difficult to think of any thing else, especially if one talks much about it; but it shall not so entirely fill our minds as to prevent us from talking to you, about what it is much better to be occupied with, than with a subject that merely kindles anxiety, indignation, and malignant passions. We keep ourselves composed, and continue our employments as far as we can, as if in time of peace. We are reading the Odyssey in the first translation. Milly had almost entirely forgotten it, since she read it at your father's, when you were both girls together. She thoroughly delights in Homer, and you know how beautiful she looks when she is pleased—that no expression becomes her better. Hence the reading to her is a great pleasure to me likewise. We read before, La Harpe's "Melanie." It is a fine composition; you, too, would not lay it aside without emotion. It is a rare masterpiece of great simplicity.

Milly is perfectly calm; the ladies here in general are in great terror. Schimmelman is firm and full of courage, although not blind to our danger. You, too, must all be of good courage about us, but not in too great security, as if no terrible calamity *could* befall us. How and why this is possible, the court knows perfectly, and I know it too, but can not write any thing on that subject.

As long as the defenses hold good, no balls can reach us in the Wester-street, perhaps not even bombs. This for your consolation.

LXXIII.

COPENHAGEN, 28*th March*, 1801.

We received your letter yesterday, and send an immediate answer, for it demands one with a voice of terror to which no one could be deaf. You shall have tidings from me by each post, of every thing that I hear, and can repeat. This time, I have written all that relates to our military position in the inclosed letter to Moltke; read that. I am writing to-day to my father and Behrens; exchange letters with Behrens also; one can speak and write of nothing else, and yet one grows weary of writing always the same thing. It is quite out of the question as yet for Milly to help me in my correspondence.

I wrote to you last time with apprehensions about our defenses, which I must now alleviate....... Hence I am really in better spirits—better spirits, that is, as to the result; for spirit for resistance we have, and must have, even though we fall, if we are not to disgrace ourselves. Oh that you in Holstein were but safe! Our individual lives are tolerably secure; and unconcern on that score, which would at other times be stupid insensibility, is absolutely necessary in time of war. If we survive danger, it steels our courage more than any thing else.

Your opinion of our allies is on the whole correct. I never expected any thing else from them, and hence it does not now cast me down, and I thank Heaven for this prevision of the danger in its full magnitude (your defenselessness excepted). The King of Sweden has exhibited himself in a very unfavorable light in his conference with our estimable Crown Prince. Sweden has not promised her ships till the 2d of April; she knew well enough that this would be too late. The Schonen side of the Sound is not fortified, and therefore it is impossible to close the Straits. We have been hindered in our preparations by mistakes and accidents. Fearful as is our situation, it is not without its good effects. We have been awakened from our sleep; experience has convinced us of much to which counsel could not draw our attention. No one behaves more nobly than Schimmelman. Resigned to the loss of his large property in the Plantations,* ready and willing to sacrifice the rest of his possessions, resolved not to expose us to a greater peril, in order to avert the impending one, by trusting to the chance of a favorable issue, he gives himself up to the dictates of his heart, and thinks and speaks with a dignity and nobleness, that strengthen the very peace and calmness of mind from which they spring. Only one who sees him alone, in a long conversation, can truly appreciate and honor him.

The English are still at Gillelye, and come peaceably on shore to purchase provisions.

I hear that gun-boats are to be stationed between our block-ships, and people maintain that it is impossible to storm the battery on the island. It is said that the whole of the defenses are completed. The wind is westerly.

LXXIV.

COPENHAGEN, 31*st March*, 1801.

I must announce to you, what you will expect to hear—that the English fleet is now lying as an enemy before our harbor, where it cast anchor yesterday morning, about ten o'clock, having been favored by a north wind that suddenly sprang up.......

I am too tired, and have no time, to go out and collect further intelligence. Yesterday there was mounting the highest house-tops, towers, &c., without end; then, twice I had to traverse the long way to Schimmelman's and back to the office, where we had to relieve guard; I was as tired as a poor soldier. As we expected an attack in the night, I chose to stay up. Milly, unfortunately, could not be prevented from doing the same, and it has done her eyes harm. She begs and coaxes till I give way, and then I repent of it, because the consequences are just what I anticipated.

It was on Sunday morning that the English admiral announced that he would commence hostilities.

LXXV.

COPENHAGEN, 3*d April*, 1801.

The report of our unsuccessful defense will no doubt have reached you before you receive this letter.

On Wednesdy afternoon, about five o'clock, the alarm was given on account of the movements of the English fleet.†......

When, yesterday morning, about eleven o'clock, the cannonade sudden-

* His father had bequeathed estates in the West Indies, which yielded each of his seven children £4000 to £5000 per annum. Schimmelman, who at this time was fabulously rich, lost nearly the whole of his property during the convulsions caused by the wars which so long desolated Europe, and sank into comparative poverty in his old age. His extreme disinterestedness was such, that he never sought to shield himself from the ruinous commercial crises which succeeded each other in Denmark, but was rather one of the first to suffer by them. He suffered especially by a contract which he had made with the government, to supply muskets, and which he continued punctually to fulfill, after he had found that it would be at a great loss to himself.

† Here follows the account of the manner in which the English fleet advanced, which is sufficiently well known from other histories

ly commenced with great violence, which was the only thing that could give us notice of what impended, we were excited, but still in good spirits. We had fancied that it would sound much more terrific when so close, and did not therefore believe the attack would be so furious or so general, as was really the case. I went to my office to see that the archives were all packed up. On the way, and when there, I heard various reports that two, three, or more English ships had got aground, and that they were firing with such vehemence in order to escape being boarded. Meanwhile, the firing went on with redoubled violence: toward half-past two it quite died away, and only single shots fell from time to time. I went out then to gain intelligence. The streets had become perfectly silent, and only single hollow shots were to be heard. By chance, I overheard an officer telling a citizen of a bomb that had fallen and burst by his side. At the next corner, some people were crowding forward to read a placard from the head of the police, containing directions how to act in case of a bombardment. I now return home considerably startled; I hear the single shots which I now know to be throwing bombs. I go out again, go at last to Countess Schimmelman, who had just spoken with some one of the Admiralty, and was full of terror. Soon Count S. comes with the tidings, that our block-ships on the right wing are annihilated. I had never before been so dismayed. I return home and tell Milly only a part of the calamity. I soon went back once more, learnt that the arrival of a cartel-ship from Nelson's fleet, was the cause of the sudden, incomprehensible silence of the enemy's guns; and then heard details of the fight, that were touching to the last degree. The whole city was in consternation, and the streets deserted.

4th.—Since we have not sufficient intelligence to be able to give you a connected narrative of the battle, and, besides, our situation will interest you still more than the events of the never-to-be-forgotten day, I meant to write to you yesterday about the former in the first place, and to get more information about the latter against to-day. The regular history of the action you shall have, as soon as I know enough about it myself; to-day I can only write you some unconnected particulars. We can not deny it —we are quite beaten; our line of defense is destroyed, and all is at stake, as far as we can see, without a chance of our winning any thing—without our being able to do much injury to the enemy, as long as he contents himself with bombarding the city, or especially the docks and the fleet; because we have been deceived in the plan of attack.

But while we look with sorrowful anxiety on our peril, with indignation on the authors of our mistakes, our spirit rises at beholding the unexampled heroism of our people, which gives us a melancholy joy full of affection, that does not indeed comfort us about the State, nor suffice to deceive us as to our true position, yet fills and warms our hearts, binds us closely to our nation, and makes us rejoice to suffer with it. Such a resistance was never seen. Nelson himself has confessed that never, in all the battles in which he has taken part, has he witnessed any thing that could be compared to it. His loss is greater than at Aboukir. It is a battle that can only be compared to Thermopylæ; but Thermopylæ, too, laid Greece open to devastation......

The appearance of the city [after all was over] was terrible. Every place was desolate; there was nothing to be seen in the streets, but wagons loaded with goods to be carried to some place of safety, a silence as of the grave, faces covered with tears, the full expression of the bleeding wound given us by our defeat. The bringing home of the dead and wounded, and the wretched scenes that took place then, I can scarcely allude to. Milly burst into a flood of tears, when she heard of the fate of the crew of the Proevesteen,* which was the first news we received. She was again overpowered by her grief when a false report was spread abroad, that our defenses had been deserted: she only feared a too hasty, inglorious truce.

The negotiations have been continued; but I can not tell you any thing about them, except that nothing had been decided yesterday, though Nelson himself was on shore. The truce will last at least till to-morrow morning. We must at all events be prepared for a bombardment. The worst is, the Crown batteries can be held no longer, and the enemy will scarcely expose his ships of the line, while he can bombard our docks, fleet, and city. Do not be alarmed about us in case of a bombardment. Our house is in a distant quarter, and it would be impossible really to take the city......

LXXVI.

COPENHAGEN, *6th April,* 1801.

......The truce has been prolonged since I wrote till the present time, and may last a few days longer, even though no arrangement should be concluded; which, if it could be brought to pass without exposing us to other dangers, must be earnestly desired, when we reflect calmly on our position after the battle of the 2d. You will not ascribe this wish to any motives of personal fear. Milly is indescribably calm; the reverence for our dead heroes is ever present to elevate our thoughts; the whole nation gives us an example of courage, of unmoved self-possession, than which nothing can be nobler. Danger is the best instructress; you must not therefore think of fear. But the risk to which the fleet, docks, marine arsenal, all the most important buildings of the city, that is, of the whole kingdom, would be exposed in case of a bombardment from the side of the scene of combat, is most serious. It is not inevitable I know; we have hitherto found by experience, that the English bombs are very bad, and when preparations have been made for extinguishing them, the devastation caused even by the best, may be confined within certain limits; at least so we hope. But accident may be against us; and where order and dexterity must be our safeguards, I do not expect so much from our people, as when all depends on Spartan courage. We must not shut our eyes to this; nor to the condition of the remaining half of our defenses, which, owing to the short-sightedness of their constructor, are useless, now that the right wing is broken—a defect over which I have many a time, since last summer, fruitlessly meditated. Providence has now brought us a man whose position is sufficiently high to enable him to carry out his projects; and these few days have certainly been employed in repairing the evil as far as possible. But is this enough? and if not, what slaughter must be caused by a new attack, and without our being able to revenge ourselves!

Tuesday.—The negotiatiation is still far from settled, and I can tell you nothing further without abusing confidence.

* Of which only thirty men came ashore out of a crew of between 300 and 400 men.

It is still possible that a fresh attack may be averted; if not, it will be much more dreadful for us in the city than the first. You may be certain that Milly strives to retain her self-possession. It is the sorrow for our people, and the wounds with which the State is threatened, that weigh us down: we fear a violent attack upon the remains of our fleet; not so much a bombardment. O that they would content themselves with that!

I am so depressed that I can not now give you a full account of the battle. As soon as we are quiet, you shall have it.

Adieu, you best beloved of our friends! Shall we soon be able to correspond in peace again? Will not the time come when these hours will be scarred over, and we shall return to our accustomed sphere of occupation, in which alone we can be happy and of use? This time will indeed leave a deep impression on the whole of our lives.

LXXVII.

COPENHAGEN, 11*th April.*

My last letter was written in a state of depression that I would willingly have concealed from you. But that was impossible, and the circumstances of our position only rendered such feelings too unavoidable. We were expecting (which I did not tell you) a bombardment that evening: we only reckoned on a delay from the wind, which was high, and against the enemy. It appeared as if the negotiations would come to nothing. While this, and the general flight in the city toward our quarter, and the other less exposed parts, depressed us, and filled us with grief at the fate of our country, even the gloomy turbulence of the elements contributed to our dejection.

My heart is heavy with what I have to tell you, or should have, if we could speak to each other.

The English changed their minds quite unexpectedly. The truce was renewed, and Nelson came on shore the next day to see the Crown Prince. A truce of longer extent was agreed to, and finally fixed for fourteen weeks. We shall thereby gain the opportunity of sending succor to Norway, where the people are almost dying of hunger. We shall not disarm. The militia are disbanded to attend to their farming operations.

The loss of the enemy is placed beyond a doubt by this convention. It is not very favorable to him. The utmost he could do would be to sail away, if he wished it. They will scarcely take all their ships home. Parker's son is said to have fallen. Nelson has lost three captains, two who had been at Aboukir: on the Elephant, his own ship, the captain, two lieutenants, and one hundred and seventeen men. It is said, that in another English ship, two hundred and thirty were killed. Two English ships of the line struck their flag, but could not be taken.

Thus we have, I think, won honor, and consideration throughout Europe; likewise a firmer hold on the reverence and affection of all classes of the realm.......

LXXVIII.

TO COUNT ADAM MOLTKE.*

COPENHAGEN, 22*d August*, 1801.

My Milly has forestalled me, and told you both how deeply the death of our friend has affected us, and what we beg of you. I feel, my best-loved

* On the death of his first wife.

friend, that I could only express all that crowds in upon my mind by talking to you, or by writing it all at full length.

The termination was much more speedy than we expected. We had still cherished hope. I could not conceive that fate could really be so cruel to you; as little as one can imagine a life in which every thing is the opposite of our present nature, and therefore I so long resisted the impression of all that you and our friends described. But the impossible has come to pass. As it is, I can say nothing to you, but that your misfortune has wounded us to the heart. We can not wish to comfort you, for is comfort possible to any but children, who can forget? But we can, and do entreat you to control your sorrow; we can invite you to come to us; and then, with our best powers, we can live for you and with you. The spring-time and bloom of your life are over; but, torn from the world and all its follies, you may yet enjoy another consolation, and a pure delight in the memory of the past, and in the exercise and cultivation of all the noble sentiments that fill your excellent heart. Perhaps then a prospect beyond the grave may open to your eyes, as it has before disclosed itself to wise and holy men in similar seclusion and tranquillity of mind. Faith is the child of such effort and self-collectedness alone; it has descended to many a one who has sought to attain spiritual light and purity; the fortunate rarely acquire it; they feel not the need of it; and the anguished heart, yet in suspense, can not give it entrance. I can not, like Milly, comfort you with expectations; but I believe that faith is not folly, and that we are blind here below. I should give you advice, my dear friend, but I am not able, nor worthy to do it; but, when we are together, we will turn our thoughts in the same direction, and together become good and wise. Let us see each other as soon as you can. We *can not* come to you this autumn. It would have been a greater happiness than we could have asked for, to have lived with you, when you and yours were assembled in a joyful home; our *wishes* will be fulfilled, if you will now come to our arms. I can not say more to you at present. My health has not been good for some time, and I have already fatigued myself with writing to-day. God be with you, my dearest friend, and give you strength!

Your old friend, NIEBUHR.

LXXIX.

TO HIS PARENTS.

COPENHAGEN, 20*th September*, 1801.

. . . . . I work at Arabic nearly every day now, and am satisfied with my progress. I can read most things in a simple historical account without a lexicon, and with its help, I can understand every thing; so I think I shall get on. But I do not know how I shall manage when I come to the poets, for whom I am unable to acquire a genuine taste; they are so designedly obscure, and use words in such new senses. There are some remarkable historical works in this library, particularly among the books which the Society has contributed; for instance, Elwakidi's "History of the Conquest of Irak," which Ockley did not possess, but from the "History of the Conquest of Syria," by the same author, which Ockley has incorporated into his excellent work, you can see how important it must be. He had nothing to consult about this conquest but dry chronicles.

The authors of the "Conversations," &c., must, I fancy, have lived in Egypt; for Cairo, and the Nile, and Rif, are frequently mentioned. Though their language deviates very perceptibly from the old Arabic, I still wonder, unless the author intentionally approached it, that the difference is not greater. What a wide difference we find when we come to the language of Morocco! They use, for instance, the Spanish article *de*, to express the genitive, and distort the genuine Arabic words so miserably, that it must often be quite like another language.

I have also read lately, with great interest, a good part of Josephus' "History of the Jews," for this happens to be a time in which I have not much to do. I have often wished, in reading it, to ask you, dear father, many questions relating to Palestine and Jerusalem, and to see your ground-plan, and the map of your route, for D'Anville's plan of Jerusalem must be wrong. There are a number of highly remarkable circumstances in this history, which have never yet attracted sufficient attention. For example, the horribly oppressive taxation of the Jews, under the successors of Alexander, which is also mentioned in the first book of the Maccabees: a third of the produce of grain, the half of that of the fruit-trees (therefore of the olives), a poll-tax, a salt-duty, and a so-called gift to the king. Why this seems to me so remarkable is, that I believe these imposts to have been established by the Persians; and because they entirely correspond to the Indian system of taxation, where a fourth of the net produce of the fields, sometimes even the second sheaf—as in Tanjour—is paid to the government. We can also see quite plainly in many places, the monopoly of salt by the government, as in India; and the farming of the imposts to a species of Zemindars, who came to Alexandria at a certain time of year to settle the amount of their rent among themselves, as they do in Bengal at the time of the rice-harvest. The same system of taxation was continued under the Maccabees—became still more oppressive under Herod, and if, as is very probable, though it can not be proved, it still existed under the Romans, it was no wonder that the nation felt their conquest by the Arabs a relief. With such tributes, what enormous streams of wealth must have flowed to Persia as long as the monarchy existed; and how miserable and impoverished has been, in all ages, the condition of the Oriental nations, to whom Nature seems to have given her richest territories, in order that they might not be exterminated by all these extortions, which they would have been in Europe; as Jupiter, in that old fable, lightened the sorrows of the ass, when unable to soften the harshness of his driver, by giving him stupidity and a thick hide, that he might be able to bear the blows.......

LXXX.

TO COUNT ADAM MOLTKE.

COPENHAGEN, 21*st May*, 1804.

My Milly has kept a letter to your Marie over several post days, that I might be able to write to you, dearest Moltke, at the same time. I have been obliged to wait for the holidays to do this, partly because the regular course of my employments, when I am not well, as happens to be the case now, really takes away my power to do any thing I wish; partly because I wanted to be able to dismiss these employments from my mind before I sat down to write to you. I do not know whether you have heard, that is, read, any where, how much more numerous and onerous they have become. At the new year I was made administrative director of the Bank, or, in other words, banker to the government; and three months before, the directorship of the East India office had devolved upon me. Unacquainted as you are with our public business, you can not possibly form an idea of the complicated relations with a host of people in which these employments place me, of the laborious nature of my work, and of the unremitting application it requires. This, and the kind of men with whom I have to deal, and of whom I must make friends, render my post an arduous one; the business itself is, to one used to it, not difficult to transact, though trying to the nerves, from the constant strain upon the attention which it requires; and it often has some of the interest of a game of chance, when you can depend upon yourself not to go beyond a moderate sum, and begin with the odds in your favor. Through this extension of my duties, we have now a liberal income, instead of the very narrow one with which we began; and as a complete renunciation of amusement and recreation (along with hard work and weak health), would be very trying, we must bear the increase of my work, which takes up my time and thoughts, and in so far, takes me from my Milly, with gratitude and contentment, as a necessary evil. I wish you would all—you, my friends, between the Elbe and the ocean—look at the matter in this light, and not lay it to my charge, that I have undertaken employment which it was impossible you should approve of. It would give me much pain if any one should judge my conduct in this respect with intolerance, and reproach me in secret for entering on a vocation, which, indeed, seems incompatible with all that used to be the object of our common endeavors. Physical exhaustion alone can make me unfit at times for those things, which used to be equally dear and interesting to us both; every moment of leisure carries me back to them; and if Turgot, under the severest financial labors, kept his tastes and intellect unchanged, you ought to give me credit for doing the same. While you were preparing to tread the classic soil, and when you arrived in Italy, I was living in a work that afforded me hours of the most intense enjoyment. I was straining every power of my mind in investigating the Roman history from its first beginning to the times of the tyranny, in all the remains of ancient authors that I could procure. This work gave me a deep and living insight into Roman antiquity, such as I never had before, and such as made me perceive, at the same time, clearly and vividly, that the representations of all the moderns, without exception, are but mistaken, imperfect glimpses of the truth. My studies were interrupted by a journey on official affairs to Hamburgh, Leipsic, and Frankfort; a journey which did not on the whole bring me much pleasure, because I felt it my duty to employ my whole mind on the financial matters placed in my hands; and it was necessary to associate exclusively with those who could be useful to me in this respect. On my return home, I resumed my investigations with redoubled energy, and for the first time felt strongly the consciousness, that I could produce something worthy of study, of fame, and of immortality, and the desire to undertake such a work. I began a treatise, of comprehensive scope and courageous freedom of thought, on the Roman laws of property, and the history of the Agrarian laws. An influx of business weighed me down for some time, and made it impossible for me to complete this treatise for our Scandinavian Society to which I had intended to send it; however, it shall be finished, and also a series of papers on isolated topics and periods of ancient history. My first essay will be widely condemned, and no nobleman and landed proprietor will like it, at least if he is consistent. I do not even expect it from you; but I shall write, as I think and speak, in the strength of my unalterable convictions, as the old Romans would approve and praise, were they still among us.

I could envy you the happiness of having lived so long in Rome. You will bring home ineffaceable recollections of those scenes. Shall you not see Samnium and Apuleia? That pleasure I should be absolutely unable to deny myself, if I had those means of assuring my safety which are at your command. If you get so far, think of me. Every field there is classic. I think you will hardly return without having seen the regions which equal in importance the sublimest ruins of Rome. Could you procure me at Rome one of the celebrated Samnian denarii, and an Attic tetradrachma? If you pass through Ravenna, do not overlook the tomb of Theodoric, nor the old mosaics in the churches. All travelers despise Ravenna, and yet it is the link that binds ancient and modern history together, and much has been preserved within its walls. In Venice, seek out Morelli: he is an accomplished philologist, and I believe an obliging man; and in Switzerland, I entreat you to make Reding's acquaintance, and confirm me in my opinion that he is really a great and noble-minded man, who espoused a righteous cause from pure motives.* If you can obtain there the various constitutions and projects of constitutions, which have appeared since 1798, and any important printed papers connected with the history of the Swiss revolution (if such exist), you will do me a great service. Alas, how freedom is expiring on every side! I have received American papers, from which it is undeniably evident whither Jefferson's party are tending. The regulations making in Louisiana are such that the president there will be a complete monarch. And in Europe not a man left but Carnot! Was I wrong in regarding him with such deep reverence? I have written a little Danish essay to renew the remembrance of two great men of our nation. When you come back, you shall receive it. One of them could neither read nor write, but Sertorius need not have been ashamed of him. Adieu, my dear Moltke! However we may be separated by distance, or the dissimilarity of our occupations, we shall never change inwardly, nor cease to be, in ourselves and to each other, what we were when we were simply observers of the world, contemplators of the past, seers of the possible—simply men. A senseless sophistry is raging in Germany with inquisitorial fury and monkish pride. Do not suffer yourself to be entangled in it under any shape on your return. Think of me and give our love to your Marie.

LXXXI.

From a letter without date.

I envy you the recollections of your Italian journey. It is a hard thought to me, that I shall never see the land that was the theatre of deeds, with

* Aloys Reding invariably upheld the old Swiss Constitutions existing previously to 1798, but was alternately opposed to, and on the side of the French, as they alternately favored the Unitarian or Revolutionary party, or the old Conservative party, of which Reding was the head. At this time he was peaceably exercising the functions of Landamman of Schwyz, as the constitution promulgated by Bonaparte, 19th February, 1803, had for most part restored the old condition of things existing before 1798, and pacified the country.

which I may perhaps claim a closer acquaintance than any of my contemporaries. I have studied the Roman history with all the effort of which my mind has been capable in its happiest moments, and believe that I may assume that acquaintance without vanity. This history will, also, if I write, form the subject of most of my works......

The sight of the works of art, particularly the paintings, would have delighted me as it did you. Statues have little effect upon me; my sight is too weak, and can not be strengthened by glasses, for a surface of one color, as it can for pictures. Then, too, a picture, when I have once seen it, becomes my property—I never lose it out of my imagination. Music is, in general, positively disagreeable to me, because I can not unite it in one point, and every thing fragmentary oppresses my mind. Hence, also, I am no mathematician, but an historian; for, from the single features preserved, I can form a complete picture, and know where groups are wanting, and how to supply them. I think this is the case with you also, and I wish you would, like me, apply your reflections on past events, to fix the images on the canvas, and then employ your imagination, working only with true historical tints, to give them coloring. Take ancient history as your subject: it is an inexhaustible one, and no one would believe how much, that appears to be lost, might be restored with the clearest evidence. Modern history *ne vaut pas le diable.* Above all, read Livy again and again. I prefer him infinitely to Tacitus, and am glad to find that Voss is of the same opinion. There is no other author who exercises such a gentle despotism over the eyes and ears of his readers, as Livy among the Romans and Thucydides among the Greeks. Quinctilian calls Livy's fullness "sweet as milk," and his eloquence "indescribable:" in my judgment, too, it equals, and often even surpasses, that of Cicero. The latter missed *son genre*—he possessed infinite acuteness, intellect, wit; *il faisait du génie avec de l'esprit*, like Voltaire; but he attempted a richness of style, for which he lacked that heavenly repose of the intellect, which Livy, like Homer, must have possessed, and, among the moderns, Fénélon and Garve* in no common degree. Very different was Demosthenes, who was always concise, like Thucydides. And to rise to conciseness and vigor of style is the highest that we moderns can well attain; for we can not write from our whole soul: and hence we can not expect another perfect epic poem. The quicker beats the life-pulse of the world, the more each one is compelled to move in epicycles, the less can calm, mighty repose of the spirit be ours. I am writing to you as if I were actually living in this better world, and nothing is further from the truth. Calculations are my occupation—merchants, Jews, and brokers my society. Alcibiades was not wrong when he said that among Thracians and Persians you must distinguish yourself after their fashion (if you must or will live among them, I add, for truly it is better to remain away); and thus it is my ambition to rival the Jews, and surpass our merchants, in the cunning of trade. You would not believe with what respect the Jews regard me; only they can not understand my having no private advantage in view. But I am heartily sick of this life. Have you seen the manu-

* A professor of moral philosophy in the last century, born at Breslau in 1792. He is, perhaps, best known by his translations of Cicero de Officiis, Burke on the Sublime, and Ferguson's Moral Philosophy. His own Philosophical Essays are rather popular than scientific—a philosophy of practical life.

script rolls at Pompeii, and do you know if any of them will be printed before long, and how they are to be obtained? Write me word about this—and if you are able to inquire of any one, and are a trustworthy agent, ask this: how one can obtain a copy of the Philodemus, printed in 1793? (I can now sometimes afford to buy a book, if it is not extravagantly dear). I am full of painful anxiety about politics: I have gloomy presentiments; slavery is incontestably at hand; and the pestilence spares not the innocent. Adieu, my beloved friend! give my love to your wife and your boy. I would write more were I not at the end of my paper, and the clock striking eleven.

LXXXII.

COPENHAGEN, *January*, 1806.

......*17th.*—I left the last line unfinished because I was interrupted, and now I can not recollect what I wanted to say. However, it is easy to draw a fresh thread from the same clew. By my desire, Perthes has sent you an anonymous translation of Demosthenes' first Philippic. It is by me, and if you have read it, and reflected on the mottos I have prefixed to it, or will do so, you will know what your friend thought and wished with all the powers of his soul, when you asked, "what are we to think? what are we to wish?" (By-the-by, you must keep this a *profound secret*). The publication of the pamphlet was so much delayed, that Zama had already decided the question, before I even got the proof-sheets, and so I was like one who receives a letter after its writer is dead. At the beginning of the war, which has terminated so disastrously, it seemed by no means a chimerical hope, that it might be possible to avert the fearfully imminent danger of the universal supremacy of France, and to set limits to this terrible empire. We might have expected that the Austrians would at last have learnt the art of war; it appeared as if the army were to be depended on. Russia gave her assistance with pure generosity; and Alexander seemed to recognize the whole difficulty of his undertaking; and to be ready to exhaust all his resources in the cause; his person was a bond of coalition, such as we had never had before; and, what must not be forgotten, the tyranny and barbarity of the French had kindled in the minds of all a hatred which, we believed, must burst into a universal flame. It was indeed impossible to foresee that we had made a mistake; that superior force, led with the greatest military skill, would, in the very outset of the campaign, completely dissolve an army, placed as if for destruction, and whose ruin was inevitable, even according to the old tactics, after it had neglected to change its position on the 10th and 11th of October.* It was impossible to foresee the stupidity, cowardice, meanness, venality, and, at last, treachery, that, one after the other, and finally all combined, completed the fatal overthrow; or yet the pusillanimity displayed after the final defeat. So long as the struggle lasted, I longed to be in the camp, and, though all is lost now, at least to have the privilege of know-

* He refers to the fact, that when Napoleon had succeeded, in interposing his grand army between the Austrian army under Mack, stationed at Ulm, and the Hereditary States, so as to cut of Mack's communications, and make it impossible for him to move toward Austria or Bohemia, in order to rejoin the Russian or Imperial reserves, Mack neglected to take the only road left open to him for a retreat, namely, that toward the Tyrol, which enabled Napoleon to surround him, and compel the shameful capitulation of Ulm.

ing with what alacrity, and with what a burning heart, men rush to arms in a national war; what blessedness lies in that immovable resolution, which nothing in the world can bend. The appalling misery is, that fear had paralyzed the Germans before they had measured their strength against the French; that they thought of safety beforehand. I have felt with what truth the great Ali says, "Despair is a free-man; Hope is a slave." Those who are still, or for the second time, dazzled by Bonaparte, who exult in the lustre of the modern Romans, as the moth in the brightness of the candle that is about to scorch it up, will ere long discover the monstrosity of their idol, and, with Bojokal, exclaim too late:

"Wodan and Mana, and all ye divinities! e'en though a dwelling
Earth may not yield us, still it shall yield us a grave!"

Woe to those who greeted the victories of the French revolutionary army with acclamations, who extinguished in our unhappy nation the last sparks of national love and national hatred, that the imperious French might scatter abroad the scarce warm embers with their sword! I have ever hated the French as a State, and regarded the humiliation of Germany with the same feelings that breathe through your odes. It is over, and I shall now inveigh, like the prophet Jeremiah, against those who dream of resistance, unless a case were to arise in which, like the Saguntines and Antigone, we must rather choose death. For is not death, when freely chosen and prepared for, the most solemn and beautiful thing to which life can aspire? Who could hesitate to prefer it to shameful servitude, even if he only regarded his own mental enjoyment? Meanwhile, it has not yet come to this with us in the north. Happy are we who have no children! For perhaps it might be well for whole nations to die out with this generation. With two gifts has England's genius blessed Lord Nelson and rewarded him for his deeds; that he died victorious, and therefore still full of hope, before he could know the defeat of Ulm; and secondly, that he left no children to grovel under the oppression of those whom he had so often made to pass under his yoke. We shall soon see how the French will govern the world. What we shall not see in its consummation, but can already perceive in its commencement, is the degeneration of intellect, the extinction of genius, of all free, all liberal sentiments, the domination of vice, of sensuality, not even disguised by hypocrisy; the decay of taste and literature—in this respect we are already long past the dawn. I have written so much about the general calamity, that I have little space to write of other things......

LXXXIII.

TO HIS PARENTS.

COPENHAGEN, 26*th August*, 1806.

You have no doubt, my dearest parents, looked forward to our letter with more than ordinary anxiety. Up to this time we have remained in uncertainty as to the decision of our fate;* and this is why we did not write on the last post day. To-day we have at length been relieved from our suspense by a decisive answer from the Crown Prince.

* Whether he went to Prussia or not.

My request for my dismissal went to the Crown Prince a fortnight ago, accompanied by a letter to Schimmelman that was really written from my heart. The Crown Prince received it very kindly, and returned it, begging that nothing more might be said on the subject; he wished and hoped that I would alter my intention. But what could I do? The patent was long since drawn up. I had taken an irrevocable step, and was forced to repress my struggling feelings. I now wrote direct to the Crown Prince, and upon this, the permission for my leaving has arrived to-day, in consequence of which, the matter may now be considered as settled, and can no longer remain a secret. It will therefore be generally known here in the course of a few days.

I believe that very few officials possess so high a degree of affection and popularity as I enjoy on our Exchange (I may say this without vanity, and do say it with emotion), where I have been connected with the most dissimilar classes of people by daily intercourse, community of interest, and the universal approbation which my administration of the bank affairs has received. Hitherto all who have heard that we were leaving Copenhagen, have expressed their sorrow in a very touching manner, many with tears, and I may confidently hope that my career will be held in remembrance, and my name in respect. The merchants have been some of my most intimate acquaintance, and among them more particularly some Englishmen, who, like many "*gentlemen*," of this nation, have a great liking for me, because we harmonize very much. I am fond of the English language too, and speak it more fluently than any other foreign language, indeed almost as much so as German or Danish.

Nor can I flatter myself that this universal affection and cordiality can and will be replaced at Berlin. But all will be right, if the government display firmness and dignity. God grant that they may not yield to the proposition of alienating the Westphalian provinces! Let the consequences of a spirited resolution be what they may, we are prepared for them—prepared to sink into a very narrow sphere, and to be thrown entirely on our own resources.

If possible, we shall leave within three weeks. We are hastening our preparations for departure as much as we can. Almost our only object in Holstein is to see you, dearest parents; we shall make every thing else subordinate to that. Indeed we shall only be able to stay a very short time; for it is a deviation from our route, which nothing but our fervent desire to see our parents could justify.

We shall be nearer to you in Berlin than we are here, and the permission to travel will most likely be obtained with less difficulty. But still there will be a new kind of separation between us.

CHAPTER VI.

NIEBUHR IN THE PRUSSIAN CIVIL SERVICE FROM 1806 TO 1810.

THE Niebuhrs arrived in Berlin on the 5th of October, 1806. On the 14th, came the dreadful defeats of the Prussian army at Jena and Auerstädt, followed by those of Halle, Prentlau, Anclam, &c., within a few days. The French were advancing on Berlin. In the consternation produced by the rapidity with which defeat succeeded defeat, scarcely any of the Prussian authorities, military or civil, thought of making any resistance, but fortresses and stores of all descriptions fell into the hands of the French, strengthening them at every step. Seven ministers even lowered themselves so far as to take an oath of fidelity to the French commissioner, without writing to the King for permission. Stein formed an exception. He had taken the precaution of packing up beforehand all the money belonging to the various offices under his direction, and now sent it on to Stettin, under Niebuhr's charge. A day later it would have been lost. After staying a week in Stettin, the Niebuhrs continued their journey to Dantzic, where they met with a most friendly reception from Messrs. Solly and Gibson. In a few days the surrender of Dantzic rendered it necessary to retreat to Königsberg.

All organization of the executive was now nearly at an end. Niebuhr was, however, resolved to abide by his post so long as Stein remained there. The intrigues of opposing factions rendered the condition of affairs, if possible, yet more hopeless. Meanwhile the enemy was approaching Königsberg. The royal family went forward to Memel, followed by the members of the government and the treasury chests. Niebuhr and his wife arrived in Memel early in January, 1807, after a journey across the low grounds on the shores of the Baltic, which, at that season of the year, was not only fatiguing but dangerous.

LXXXIV.

TO HIS PARENTS.

STETTIN, *20th October*, 1806.

I hope, my dear father and mother, that you received the letter safely, in which I announced to you our arrival here on Monday. That will have quite re-assured you as to our personal safety. With respect to our future fate you must not be uneasy. We have no anxiety about it. For this I have, in these serious times, to thank the education which you, dear father, gave me, and the principles to which I have ever remained true in my onward course. I shall always be able to find and to earn the necessaries of life. Should all those brilliant prospects vanish, as now seems likely, which appeared to open before us a short time ago, I can earn a living either as a scholar or a merchant; and if I did not succeed in one country, I should in another. A shelter and daily bread will never be wanting to us, and I entreat you to be convinced, that the thought that this terrible calamity will destroy our worldly prospects, which indeed were most promising, has not for a moment mingled with our bitter grief for the fate of the nation and of Europe. My position as a citizen would in happy times have been very enviable. I should have been able to suggest and to carry out many ideas under the leadership of a most eminent minister; I should have worked with pleasure and satisfaction, and at the same time have been able to reckon upon all the advantages and honors which render public life agreeable. That is now most likely over forever, but all this will not grieve me. O that we had no other grief!

We start for Dantzic to-morrow. As the French have entered Berlin, and will probably advance hither before long, we can not put off our journey any longer. The days are so short now, that we can not even wait the arrival of the Hamburgh mail, though it will most likely bring a letter from you. Till you hear again, and as long as mails run without interruption, direct to us at Dantzic, under care to Solly, Gibson, and Co.

It is a long way to Dantzic, and the season is far advanced. In East Pomerania the accommodations and even the provisions will be wretched. To me that is of no consequence, but it is to my Amelia. God grant only, that her health may hold out, and that we may reach Dantzic without an accident.

Whether we shall reach the end of our flight in Dantzic, or whether we shall still have to pursue it toward the northeast, time will show. I do not want to think about it, but we shall bear all that comes with calmness. Only do not fear that we shall want for necessary ready money; we are well provided with it.

You will, I suppose, have received through the Hamburgh journals, tolerably correct accounts of the dreadful fate of our army. For us, a light now begins to shed its ray over the frightful chaos, and to develop a picture which I must gradually summon courage to contemplate.

We have been received here in a very friendly manner, and may reckon upon a similar reception in Dantzic. We shall meet there with the excellent Colonel Von Schack, of the War Office. We became friends at once during his stay here. Such a time quickly brings right-minded people together.

It will interest you to hear that the aged General Köllarbonner is still living here. I bid you adieu, my dear parents, with a heavy heart. Probably our correspondence will be much interrupted at present, and it were hard to say whether you will look forward to letters from us, or we from you, with the greater anxiety. Be easy about us. Fare you well, and spare yourselves to us by avoiding unnecessary apprehensions. May our dear mother be supported under her sufferings.* Farewell, and yet once more farewell, my dearest parents, my darling sister, my kind aunt! Amelia begs you to give the inclosed to her sister Frederike.

LXXXV.

TO MADAME HENSLER.

KÖNIGSBERG, *28th November*, 1806.

We did not receive your letter of the 13th till yesterday, and it is the only one which has come to hand; all the earlier ones which you mention are to us as yet lost treasures. You have all heard something of us from time to time; and if no unforeseen misfortune has occurred, you must have had a continuous account of our adventures through the letters we have sent by sea, whenever an apparently safe opportunity presented itself. Our fate has been harder in this respect; for five long weeks we had no news of a single one of our friends—and this has rendered our gloomy hours still more dreary.

It is a great comfort to us to find that you are prudently looking forward to the measures which the future may render necessary. If we were still in Copenhagen, we would summon you to us, as a hen calls her chickens under her wings on the approach of a bird of prey—probably our protection would be just as ineffectual. I am thinking over every subject, considering what I may, and may not say....... Do not be uneasy; we are on the whole in good health; mine is perhaps more constantly good than usual; my Milly is not quite well to-day. The weather here resembles that of Copenhagen at this season of the year. It is a blessing to us that we are already accustomed to this climate, the rest of our companions, natives of Berlin, suffer much more from it, and are almost all ill.

I work daily with the minister,† who appears to me in all respects worthy of esteem. He is a *man* in the highest sense of the word; and, as a minister, all that I could wish.

Many government officers are now returning to Berlin, some by command, others by their own desire; I have my minister's word that we shall not be separated, that we shall meet every shock of fortune together.

In Stettin and Dantzic, I had but very little to do; here I am pretty fully occupied, and it does me a great deal of good. One is less tormented with sad reflections, and does not feel one's self useless.

Any further journey would certainly be attended with great hardships, but hardships are no longer strange to us, and you must not fear them for us; they form the smallest part of what we have to bear. We have here found very dear friends in Nicolovius and his wife, whom you know. Unfortunately they live at so great a distance from us, that we can not see them very often. The venerable old Scheffner I have not seen even once. Fichte is here too. At the house of the merchants Hay and Philipps we also find interesting society.

Would it were possible to hear oftener from you! Omit every thing in your letters which might hinder their transmission. No misfortune shall plunge me into benumbing inactivity; what we have already undergone strengthens and rouses all our powers.......

* Niebuhr's mother had been suffering for some time from dropsy.

† Stein.

If the Countess Werthern [Stein's sister] is in your neighborhood, let her know that her brother is here with all his family, and is well.

LXXXVI.

TO MADAME HENSLER.

KÖNIGSBERG, *29th December*, 1806.

The French have not advanced; on the contrary, they seem to have somewhat retired. It is inconceivable what uncertainty exists here as to the actual position of things. The delay of the French is ascribed partly to sickness—particularly dysentery—partly to the scarcity of provisions. We shall therefore, in all probability, remain quietly here till after the new year.

You must take it as a great favor that Milly is writing to you, for her eyes have been very bad; she can not write without great pain and difficulty, and is often obliged to lay down her pen. But how can we help writing to you when there is an opportunity.......

If you imagine that the general misfortunes, and the approaching danger, have produced a grave and solemn tone of thought here, in which we should find entire sympathy, you are deceived. All amusements go on just as usual. People look on the war as a subject of conversation, find fault with the English, and lay the blame of all the misery on them; abuse those who took part in bringing about the declaration of war; abuse the Russians, who, it must be confessed, behave in our country in rather an Asiatic manner; comfort themselves with saying that the French are not so bad, &c., &c.

And not one of us may cool his blood by speaking out his whole mind to them! There is an everlasting talk—mostly without the slightest comprehension of the matter—about abuses, about the aristocracy, the Russians, the misunderstood French, and the great Emperor, about ruinous measures, and so forth. Of course there are many, very many, who think otherwise; but indignation makes one's blood boil when one is forced to listen to such things.

Stein was on the point of following the royal family the same night in their flight to Memel, though ill himself, and leaving a child dangerously ill with typhus fever, when the machinations of his enemies triumphed, and he received his dismissal in an autograph letter from the King, couched in very ungracious terms. Niebuhr was resolved to send in his resignation also. The following letter to Stein, on receiving the news of his dismissal, shows Niebuhr's views respecting the state of affairs, and is characteristic of both men:

LXXXVII.

TO BARON VON STEIN.

MEMEL, *7th January, late in the evening.*

Since the arrival of Count von Lindenow, it has been rumored here that your Excellency has been forced, by the untiring malice and inexhaustible wickedness of the men who have plunged this unhappy country into ruin, to send in your resignation. To no one among the many who have heard these fresh tidings of misfortune with consternation, could the news be a severer blow than to me. The Count's verbal announcement left us, however, some hope that our anxiety might be relieved, and that your Excellency might yet receive the satisfaction due to you. I reckoned on the cowardice and half-measures of those persons, and knew that your Excellency would never be weary of making sacrifices to our unhappy country.

These hopes have now been quite destroyed by your letter, and I find myself, in the midst of this desolation, more forsaken and solitary than words can express. I thank your Excellency from the bottom of my heart, and shall ever thank you for the precious memorial of yourself which you have given me in your letter. Fate may probably never permit me to see your Excellency again, and I may soon find it almost impossible even to write to you. I should, therefore, be the more grieved if you now reproach yourself with having been the guiltless cause of drawing me into the vortex of destruction. What you aimed at was my good fortune and happiness, and these would have been attained beyond my expectations. Permit me to say, that my most faithful adherence to you resulted not alone from my deep reverence for the minister who completely fulfilled that ideal which had never before been realized for me: it sprang, also, from the consciousness that my connection with you ennobled and strengthened me; and what better blessing could I have? Even if a kind of existence be restored to this State at some future period, and your Excellency's department fall into the hands of such men as we may anticipate, my position, however bearable in other respects, would always be distasteful, because precisely the opposite would take place. I should be in danger of sinking to the level of those persons instead of rising. If, after the conclusion of a miserable peace, your Excellency had endeavored to bring the finances into order, I should have remained, however much the official salaries might have been reduced; but now my political life in this country is at an end, and no temptations shall seduce me. A few months longer I must of course endure; but then I shall seek a new destiny, and it will be found. Never, never, shall your Excellency despise me, as a man whose actions give his asseverations the appearance of frivolity or falsehood.

I am very sorry that it was impossible to write out, in a clear form, a plan for the government of the banks, with all the necessary details, of which I had finished the first sketch in Königsberg; because I hoped it would have met with your Excellency's approbation, and, in happier times, might have been carried out with great advantage. Not that such times are fled forever. What grieves me is, that the confidence with which you honored me has not been justified by any production of mine worth mention. Will your Excellency permit me still to send you this plan, should an opportunity offer? God knows that the thought of you, and the hope that your just and grave judgment might pronounce me worthy, have been my support in the most trying situations; and that the remembrance of your Excellency's kindness will be an ample compensation for whatever course events may take for me personally, in the present complication of affairs.

May your Excellency forget, under the kindly sky of your beautiful native region, the pain of seeing a country, once so dear to you, led to the verge, nay, plunged into the gulf of ruin, and the vexation of beholding all true help shamefully cast aside! May your gaze be turned away from the fogs of this degraded age, to the last rays of the departing light of all goodness and greatness; and may you leave an example to all those who find comfort and strength in remembering you!

Permit my wife, though unknown to your Excellency, to join her most sincere wishes with mine, that you and yours may meet with every happiness which is still possible in these days.

Once more, and with deep emotion, I commend myself to your Excellency's remembrance. Yours will never be extinguished in my heart....... With the deepest respect, I am ever

Your Excellency's most obedient, NIEBUHR.

Niebuhr was now undecided as to his future course. He had received proposals from Denmark immediately after the battle of Auerstädt, and subsequently from England and Russia. His heart inclined him toward Denmark; but on the whole he was disposed to refuse office entirely for the present, and thought of retiring into some obscure place, where, with the assistance of a little money that he had at command, he meant to support himself by writing, till the future should show whether, and where, there should remain a spot in Europe, not subject to the tyranny of Napoleon and the supremacy of France.

During his stay in Memel, however, he was induced by the Prussian government to take a part in the organization of the commissariat. The scarcity in the armies, as well as in the whole hunger-stricken province, which did not even contain corn enough for seed, rendered this a business of great importance, and withheld Niebuhr from pressing for an immediate dismissal. The Provincial Chamber of Königsberg * had requested the minister, Schrötter, that Niebuhr might be consulted on this subject, and he did not like to disappoint the reliance placed on his services in a moment of such extremity. His determination to remain at his post for the present, was strengthened in a short time by the prospect that Count Hardenberg, and perhaps even Baron Von Stein, might return to office.

During his stay in Königsberg, Niebuhr formed a warm friendship with Nicolovius, who was now a member of the East Prussian Consistory. Indeed, to this period of calamity he owed many connections that were valuable to him in after years; among these we must mention more particularly his friendship with Von Schoen—the enlightened and zealous coadjutor of Stein in his

* At this period the financial affairs of each province were managed by its own Chamber.

vast plans for the fundamental reform of the Prussian State—whose integrity and patriotism he esteemed as highly as he respected his intellect and penetration. Sir Hartford Jones, the traveler in Persia, interested him greatly; and for Lord Hutchinson he had personally a great regard, though, in some instances, he regretted his conduct as a diplomatist. In the course of this winter, being without the means of prosecuting his other studies, he assiduously employed his leisure moments in acquiring the Russian and other Slavonic languages.

In April, 1807, the King again intrusted Count Hardenberg with the portfolio of foreign affairs, and, a few days after, with that of the interior and of finance, (the latter in the place of Schrötter) the direction of the bank and maritime affairs, of the police, the post-office, in short, of every thing not exclusively military. The immense extent of the business thus devolving upon Count Hardenberg, rendered it necessary for him to secure the assistance of able men. He, therefore, in May, summoned Altenstein, Schoen, Niebuhr, and Stägeman to the head-quarters at Bartenstein, and transferred to each a portion of the public business, subject to his supervision. The financial department of the commissariat was intrusted to Niebuhr, and it was therefore necessary for him to repair to head-quarters. He had to leave his wife behind him in Memel, ill of a slow fever, brought on by anxiety and sorrow at the aspect of affairs, as much as by the hardships of their flight in the winter, and the wretched lodgings and food that they were obliged to put up with in the devastated province. She only partially recovered in the course of the summer.

Niebuhr had scarcely arrived at Bartenstein, when his health too sank under the continued pressure. He was attacked with typhus fever, and remained for some time in great danger. His illness was prolonged by the want of all attention, and the anxiety and depression which, in his utter solitude, he had no means of throwing off. The letters to his wife written at this time, bear the stamp of his mental dejection, and contain many passages in which he expresses his hopelessness with regard to the results of the war and the situation of the country; still his language by no means equals the intensity of his feelings at that time, because he wished to spare her as much as possible in her weak state. After remaining here and in Königsberg for some weeks, the seat of government was transferred to Tilsit.

New calamities soon drove the King and his ministers farther northward. On the 14th of May, came the battle of Friedland; on the 18th, the Russian army arrived at Tilsit; on the 19th, it crossed the Memel; on the 22d, an armistice for a month was concluded. On the 17th of June, the news reached Memel, that the French had entered Königsberg, and that the Russian army had taken up its position on the other side of the Memel. Every one now hastened to pack up his effects and papers; the cash belonging to the government was sent to Riga, and the whole machinery of the State was dissolved. The officials were left free to remain or to embark, since the greater number of them could no longer render any service after the frontier was crossed. Many went by sea to Copenhagen.

Under these circumstances, Niebuhr saw no further possibility of usefulness. He therefore decided to go to Copenhagen, and there await the decision of the fate of Prussia, before entering the service of any other State. He went to Count Hardenberg to ask for his dismissal, but the Count besought him so earnestly, even with tears, not to forsake him and the King, but to hold out to the last, that he consented to retain his post. He now left Riga with his wife, accompanied by the rest of the officers connected with the exchequer. They set out on the 10th of June; by the time that they reached Mitau they heard that a further armistice had been concluded, and on their arrival at Riga, that the articles of peace were being drawn up as quickly as possible.

On the 12th of July, the tidings reached Riga that peace was concluded. They were evil tidings, for they displayed, as a recognized fact, what all had hitherto refused to acknowledge to themselves—that for the present a successful resistance was out of the question.

The conditions of the peace, and especially Napoleon's refusal to enter into any negotiations at all till Hardenberg was removed, showed clearly in what a state of dependence he intended to keep Prussia.* To Niebuhr this attitude of subjection to France was so painful, and the state of the country appeared so hopeless, that he again sent a request for his dismissal to one of his colleagues, for him to transmit to the King. He was aware that upon the suggestion of Napoleon, and the recommendation of Hardenberg,

* Napoleon declared he would rather carry on the war for forty years than treat with Hardenberg, on which Hardenberg instantly sent in his resignation.

the King had written to Stein requesting him to resume office, but he did not anticipate that Stein would consent, in the face of the overwhelming difficulties, which would again beset him from unworthy intrigues, as well as the nearly desperate situation of the country. With his friend he would have been willing to work in spite of all difficulties and annoyances.* Meanwhile a Provisional Commission, consisting of Von Altenstein, Von Schoen, Von Klewitz, Stägeman (then Niebuhr's colleague at the bank), and Niebuhr, had been named to discharge Hardenberg's duties, until a regular administration should be formed. On hearing this, Niebuhr's friend † kept his letter back until he should obtain his decision with regard to this fresh appointment. His resolve was not affected by it. It appeared to him impossible that he could do any good in a commission where there was to be no head, but all the members were to have equal power; and that his belonging to it could only result in injury to his health—already much shattered—without answering any useful end. He had a high personal regard for the men who were named as his colleagues, but he knew also that upon many points they differed decidedly in their views of administration, so that their meetings would be liable to degenerate into mere debating clubs. The immediate object of their deliberations was the restoration of the country from the ravages occasioned by the war. For this end projects were to be at once submitted to them, including the abolition of serfdom; advances for the rebuilding of farms destroyed, and for the purchase of live stock; and the removal of restrictions upon trade and the transfer of landed property. Schoen and Schrötter were disciples of Adam Smith, and considered that their problem was the production of the greatest amount of wealth upon a given surface of land. The hitherto existing rights and privileges of the various classes, appeared to them hindrances to the free development of the resources of the country. They held it indifferent whether the present feebler proprietors remained or not, if their place was supplied by wealthier ones, and thus the greatest possible amount of profit secured. Stägeman and Niebuhr saw the dangers of this course, if carried out with a rigid adherence to theory—the likelihood of obtaining a class of proprietors who would have no moral interest in the welfare of the country, and the importance of a numerous class of small landholders—and

* See Letter xcv.

† Most probably Stägeman.

considered the promotion of the welfare of the actually existing occupants of the soil, as the true problem of the statesman. Conscious of these essential differences in the views of those with whom he was called to act, Niebuhr still begged his colleague to send in his letter of resignation to the King, who was then at Tilsit. He received a very gracious reply, in which the King expressed his regret at the state of his health, but testified his unwillingness to part with the services of a man like Niebuhr at the present crisis, and therefore requested that he would, at least for a time, devote himself to the service of the State, and to that end repair to Memel as soon as possible. It was not in Niebuhr's nature to oppose a second letter of resignation to such an expression of confidence on the part of the King; he therefore decided on accepting the appointment, and making the attempt, though he foresaw that multiplied annoyances and Herculean labors awaited him. He left Riga after a two months' residence, and came with his wife to Memel.

In Riga he had become well acquainted with the eminent mercantile houses of Klein, and Mitchell. M. Klein was so much struck with him personally, and thought so highly of his views of commerce, that he offered Niebuhr an equal share in his business, in return for which Niebuhr was to be simply employed in forming speculations. This highly advantageous offer did not, however, attract him, though it touched him deeply as a proof of friendship.

About this time he received intelligence of the bombardment of Copenhagen by the English, and the capture of the Danish fleet. He felt the calamities of Denmark most keenly, and much as he was an enemy to France, he could never forgive the English for this proceeding. When Denmark was afterward induced by it to form an alliance with France, this was always a sore point which he could not bear to touch.

Not long after his arrival in Memel, he received the assurance of Stein's entrance into the ministry, which was only delayed by illness.

LXXXVIII.

TO BARON VON STEIN.

MEMEL, 10*th January*, 1807.

I had the honor of writing to your Excellency three days ago, when I was stunned by the pain of knowing the certainty of your resignation. Allow me to-day to inclose these lines to your Excellency in a letter to a most trustworthy friend; I write for *my own sake* alone, for there is little here worth writing about; the most part of the stories now afloat are too much beneath your attention. M. Von Altenstein has now told me every thing, and Baron Von Hardenberg has communicated to me for perusal a copy of the monstrous, incomprehensible letter which decided your resolution. It belongs to history! Nothing short of such a degree of blindness ......renders comprehensible the progress of disunion which has brought this country to ruin.

Lord Hutchinson is deeply grieved by this occurrence. He requests to be most warmly remembered to your Excellency. You alone have inspired him with unbounded confidence; he reveres you, and proclaims it now more loudly than ever. The unpleasant occurrence with regard to young Walpole (who has been arrested at Goldap for traveling without Prussian passports which M. Von Zastrow had declined to give him as superfluous) has increased the unpleasant state of feeling between him and M. Von Zastrow. This does not surprise me, but it grieves me that, even with Baron Von Hardenberg, he does not feel able to speak so openly, so from heart to heart, as with your Excellency. He finds him too mild, too hesitating. Forgive me if it is an indiscretion to repeat such expressions.

The King's speech to the Parliament promises indefatigable efforts. Lord H. sees no end to the war; it must last for years. He hopes the Russians will improve rapidly under the training of circumstances; his opinion of them is much raised, chiefly, I believe, by the views of Colonel Sontag, who has now returned. But he still fears a general engagement. Your Excellency is probably aware that four English ships of the line are in the Baltic, and that a number of frigates are to come in the spring.......

As soon as the sea becomes less dangerous—two vessels are lying on the strand at this moment, and portions of the wrecks of two others—I shall request my dismissal, and embark on the first armed English ship, which touches at any point sufficiently near this place, or the place where we may be then. Should the stream of emigration carry us to Russia we may probably remain there. It seems as if that empire would not be so easily overpowered, and in the service of that State one might perchance be placed, not on the frightful ice plains of the Neva, but on classic soil beside the glorious Bosphorus and Hellespont.

It is now, I think, clearly proved that a system of compromise, and a coalition, would have led to nothing. For the cunning and intrigues, which would have insured that such a coalition should be destroyed at last with advantage to one party, were as easy to your enemies as they were beneath your Excellency and your friends.......

With deep and cordial respects, I am ever
Your Excellency's most obedient,
NIEBUHR.

LXXXIX.

MEMEL, 10*th March*, 1807.

Doubt not, your Excellency, that the K. A. [Emperor Alexander] is most desirous to have you near him; that he is worthy to have you in his service you know. Hitherto I have declined all proposals to myself from that quarter. If your Excellency does not go thither, I shudder to think of the future. Here I shall certainly soon draw my head out of the net, and then await the course of events. For the present, I am detained by the pressing wants of the country, in the relief of which I think I am of use, though the mode in which all business is carried on is enough to drive one mad. The probability of some alteration in the ministry changes daily—a sufficient proof that nothing is to be expected! Meanwhile, M. Von Hardenberg will not allow me to leave till all is decided; this, combined, as I have said, with the hope of saving the country ten to twenty per cent. in the purchase of corn, and of thus alleviating the famine, is what keeps me here in spite of my longing to get away.

XC.

TO HIS WIFE.

BARTENSTEIN, *5th May*, 1807.

A few lines, which our friend Deetz undertook to have safely forwarded, announced to you yesterday our arrival in this little city, formerly a capital. Since your letter of Monday I have no immediate news of you, though I have heard of you through Oesterreich and Woltersdorf. I find that your fever has not yet left you. I hope it may ere long. To me too it would be an inexpressible comfort to be with you again.......

Every thing is quiet, and Heaven only knows how matters actually stand, and when action will recommence. You will, however, understand, that I can not write to you about this. We have no pleasure in our residence here. Our journey from Königsberg was deeply interesting, but the most mournful I ever made in my life.

Even in the neighborhood of Königsberg we saw single ruined houses; in the villages the majority are uninhabited; no cattle are to be seen in the fields; here and there—but very rarely—you may meet with a small flock of sheep, or a few pigs; in the villages scarcely a creature appears; the few whom you do see look anxious and miserable. At Eylau the devastation has been carried up to the very gates of the town. The principal street does not look so bad as it did.

No one could give us much account of what had happened, and all seemed unwilling to speak of it; we found, however, guides to the field of battle, who explained it to us. I could not bring away any relics for you—we found nothing on the field but rags of uniforms.

You can hardly form any idea of the dearness and distress here. Memel is comparatively a cheap place, in the enjoyment of abundance. At Lord Hutchinson's I have seen Prince Czartorinsky, and at Hardenberg's have made acquaintance with General Pfuel. I did not see Rücheln in Königsberg. I must make haste or I shall lose this courier. Altenstein and I have both caught colds, but are otherwise well.

May God watch over you! I long to hear again from you. My thoughts are often with you, notwithstanding my restless life.

XCI.

BARTENSTEIN, *10th May*, 1807.

As M. Von Schoen is returning to Königsberg for a few days, I have a safe opportunity of sending you a few confidential lines.

All that we see and hear in this place is most depressing. There is discord among the generals, and the Emperor seems to withdraw his protection from Bennigsen. It has become the fashion to depreciate him, and if all treat him so, it would be no wonder if he were to lose confidence in himself. But when he is accused of intentional misconduct, an inward voice in me pronounces him innocent.

It is believed here that Dantzic is lost. God help us if it be so! But little progress is made in our affairs, and I am convinced I could direct them as well elsewhere as here. I think it is possible I may return to Königsberg for a few days on a mission from Russia.

It comforts me to know that you strive to preserve your tranquillity. Your dear letters of the 5th and 7th arrived yesterday. Even if we must renounce all consolatory anticipations of a brighter future for our country, let us not yield to despair—not even if gloomy cares and sorrow must accompany us through life. Forgive me for not writing more to you now. Every precaution has been taken to insure our safety in case of a defeat So much for your relief. Farewell.

XCII.

BARTENSTEIN, 11*th May*, 1807.

......Schoen took with him yesterday a letter to you, which will have a bad effect on you, from the gloomy prospects it contains. Others had already told me that they felt less courage at head-quarters than anywhere else. I thought it was their own fault. But hardly had we arrived here when we were overwhelmed by a flood of depressing innuendoes and diatribes—most depressing because it is clear that a system of minute attention to details in strategy has gained the upper hand, and the old Russian method of war, whose object is to bend or break, is cramped, and not allowed fair play.

I still can not be made to believe myself mistaken in regard to General Bennigsen. I know too well, from former experience, how often really clever people are misled by theories to bestow undeserved blame, and maintain unwarranted assertions, because they overlook the peculiarities of the individual case, and, instead of actual experience, which gives courage and consolation to the man whom they blame, have no recollection of the case resembling reality. But I can far less understand how it is that, a short time ago, thanks and tokens of confidence were heaped upon him, and yet he is now spoken of as a man of mediocre talents. It is said that the Emperor and King are going to-morrow to Heilsberg; probably it is a reconnoitring expedition.......I feel myself excessively fettered in writing to you; from Königsberg I shall be able to write more openly.

XCIII.

KÖNIGSBERG, 20*th May*, 1807.

Notwithstanding the distance which still separates us, and although I can not by any means consider myself as on my way back to you, yet the knowledge that I am writing to you from no greater distance than thirty-eight miles, and that my further movements can only bring me nearer to you, make my heart much lighter than it was in Bartenstein. I arrived here this morning, and am staying with Philipps. I have come here alone, charged with a mission; if possible to arrange an affair of great importance with Hutchinson, who will probably start to-morrow, by way of Pillau, for Stralsund. I have, however, little hope of success, for he has not acted in this matter as we had a right to expect from him.

I was called away here to go to him, and now I can have the delight of telling you that I have completely succeeded in my object, and have overcome all his difficulties and objections, by clearness and decision, so that now my journey, our separation, my illness, will not have been altogether in vain, for he has distinctly assured me that he would not have placed the same confidence in any other member of the Prussian government—not that any great confidence was required in this case, but his views are very singular. I have had a very disagreeable journey from Bartenstein here. I was obliged to travel all night; it has not, however, done me any harm, and a good meal has done me a great deal of good, which deserves mention after the bad food we had for so long in Bartenstein. This bad food, and the other depressing circumstances which surrounded me then, have had an injurious effect upon my health. I was obliged, by Hardenberg's desire, to bring with me a major in the army, Count Chasot, who is going to Stralsund, and who was not at all an unpleasant companion. Nicolovius has given me a letter from Lene to you, which has been five months on the road; it will give you great pleasure, particularly the lines from our little Tiny. I have received your letters of the 17th and 18th. To-morrow Hardenberg is expected here, and as the King intends going to Memel in a few days, and Hardenberg certainly will not allow him to go alone, it may be considered as decided that we shall soon return. Greet the Krüdeners warmly from me. I have but too much to say to him.

XCIV.

KÖNIGSBERG, *25th May*, 1807.

A bad swelled face detains me from the Council, and affords me a quiet evening alone in my own room—the first I have had for a long time; and I mean to spend it partly in writing to you, partly in getting rid of some of my work. I am engaged in correspondence both with General Bennigsen and Geheimrath von Popoff, which under other circumstances would be agreeable, but as things now stand is simply laborious. Then I have also to make out a plan of finance for General Budberg.* How easy, how interesting, under other circumstances—how fruitless, how discouraging in times like the present!

Here I am in much better health. In Bartenstein I was really extremely unwell, and the scarcity of necessaries was so great, that at last I could not even obtain oatmeal porridge. With the best wishes, Altenstein could do very little for me. He was constantly interrupted during the day, and had to sit up whole nights, to work. Schoen was quite absorbed in business.

The money matters which I have undertaken for M. von Popoff bring me into connection with several Russian officers. The Russians appear to have confidence in me, and if I alone had to do with them, I believe that a good deal might be brought to pass. But this can not be; for, on the one hand, it would oblige me to remain at head-quarters, and on the other, I should not be after all in my proper place. For I may freely confess to myself, that to occupy any subordinate position, in which I had not a consciousness of the real superiority of my official head, such as I had toward Stein, would be to leave the only post in which I can labor with success. The various spheres of action resemble the different regions of the atmosphere, which suit differently organized classes of men. Some are most comfort-

* The Russian General.

able in low countries; others in the ordinary middle atmosphere; others can only exist in the pure mountain air. I belong to the last class—to those who must have freedom for the soul and intellect, and for this very reason I ought not to have entered into the restraints of official life. I am often seized with regret when I think of my beautiful researches into history—my happy meditations on dark periods—my power of bringing them vividly before my mind's eye—my life in antiquity. Where is all this gone? Shall I ever renew it? Shall I ever be able to restore it to fresh life?

The 26*th*.—I was interrupted yesterday; I was about to write out for you a passage of Cicero, where he says, "My life fell in the time of a great war, distinguished on one side by enormous crime, on the other by great calamity."

To-day, there is some talk of advancing the troops, in order, at least, to save Graudenz, as it is impossible to deceive one's self any longer about Dantzic. The English ships are returning to the roads, and Kamenskoy's artillery is embarked. If the fortress had been well provided with ammunition, it might long have held out against a siege conducted in so irregular a manner. Much remains incomprehensible to me. Even if our reinforcements arrive, disease will carry many off: want and bad food exhaust the strength both of the men and horses. Our calculations as to the strength of the Russian army are quite delusive; of this I am unanswerably convinced. Bennigsen has completely lost the confidence of the Emperor, yet the latter does not interfere with him. If Bennigsen is what the Emperor and his confidential servants hold him to be, he could not be too quickly removed. In the whole chaos of opinions concerning him, this much seems to me to be clear, that he is unwilling to expose his laurels to any new risk. Whether he deserves these laurels, or owes them—after the lion courage of his soldiers—to accident and good fortune, is a question on which no light can be thrown, and shows only too clearly, by the uncertainty in which eye-witnesses are left, how little history is able to represent with strict accuracy.

You may reckon with undiminished confidence on the *courage* of the Russians, but I can not be blind to other things. However, I must not speak of this in letters. The departure for Tilsit, it is now said, will not take place before the end of the week.

Since beginning this, a considerable amount of provisions has arrived, of which I may take the chief merit to myself.

XCV.

TO STEIN.

RIGA, $\frac{16th}{28th}$ *July*, 1807.

...... At Bartenstein I was so ill with the fever which I have mentioned (which want and distress. combined with the unhealthy weather, had rendered epidemic, so that the soldiers and inhabitants were attacked by it in great numbers), that I was obliged to let all the frequently-occurring opportunities of forming interesting acquaintances pass unused; and in Königsberg we were alone, otherwise I should have taken some preparatory steps even before the arrival of your Excellency's answer, though it would have been indiscreet and presumptuous to have treated of that in your name. And thus I hope to be justified before your severe judgment. M. Von Hardenberg sent me word, and confirmed the announcement himself when we met, that he had undertaken the premiership, as far as internal affairs are concerned, only until the King should send your Excellency such an invitation to resume the ministry of the interior as would give you full satisfaction, and you should make the sacrifice to the country of returning in spite of all that has occurred. I believe that he said the same thing to the Emperor, and that the latter then firmly hoped for your speedy return as a benefit to Prussia, in which country he then took so much interest, and would have considered it his duty to do all in his power to bring it to pass. At that period, however, M. Von H., who I think wished to excite a desire in the King's mind to have your Excellency once more in his service before making any proposition to him, seems not to have made sufficient progress in this design. To me this prospect was my only consolation, but on this point I could speak better than write.

The King has now transmitted a request, and, without doubt, a very sincere one, to your Excellency, to return to him and to the country in this pressing emergency, in which none but an extraordinary man can bring help, and M. Von Hardenberg has united his earnest entreaties to those of our sovereign. We await with eager anxiety the announcement of your decision; to yourself, to the country, a most momentous one. Some believe and hope that your Excellency will accept office, and appeal to your conscience as being the only man to whom we can look. Others doubt; and I, for my own part, can fully enter into the doubts which will hold you back. You will not shrink from the task of rescuing from annihilation a country so utterly ruined, and restoring its internal energies, mournful as is the aspect it presents, gigantic the enterprise, and dark as is the future and our outward fortune. But you will shrink from it, when you think of the lasting hindrance to all comprehensive undertakings arising from the mediocrity and baseness, that can scarcely even now be dislodged from their present possession of power—and the vanity of the idea that a better day *must* follow the night of incapacity and little-mindedness, which will fill you with a sentiment of disgust beforehand. The Titans piled mountains upon mountains, and rejoiced in their might, but the stone of Sisyphus was a hellish torment. Having a presentiment that your Excellency would believe your efforts unavailing, and hence refuse to take office, I yielded to my desire to retire from public life altogether, intending to return in the first instance to my native country, collect my property together, though that is as yet but very small, and live somewhere quietly as a private man; unless your Excellency should one day summon me to engage in public business, or, contrary to my hopes, I should find it necessary as a means of support. I have not yet received an answer to my request. I fear that it will be delayed under the vague idea that I may be made useful in some way. At all events, I hope to receive a furlough, and before long it will be decided whether your Excellency accept office or not. In the latter case, I shall insist on my dismissal, being quite decided neither to take part in an ill-organized, many-headed administration, like the present Provisional Commission, nor yet to act under the worse than mediocre men of the late administration, whom I learnt to know thoroughly at Memel last winter. I have further declined a seat in the Provisional Commission, because it is impossible to transact business under such a form, and also because it is impossible to remain long a member of it without falling out with friends, when their principles are too monstrous, and the consequences they involve still more dreadful; and without exposing numberless weak points to the enemy; for great innovations are in contemplation, with regard to some of which I do not feel myself sufficiently acquainted with the particular case, while on others I am entirely unable to form a judgment.* Besides, I am a pure Mahometan—a strict Unitarian in administrative affairs, and abhor all Commissions and the like with my whole heart. Hence your Excellency will not blame me for refusing to connect myself with them, though many single oversights might be prevented by a contrary course; and will also pardon me if I should be absent on your arrival. It will be easy to decide what steps to take in that case.......

I should have liked to have added some facts which would be interesting to your Excellency, respecting the Russian and Slavonic languages; the affinity which I have discovered between them and the Persian, and how they are by no means so difficult as people believe them or make them; also about the Grusinian and Russian literature, which I have become acquainted with through a Russian work—about the noble Russian people—about the extremely interesting commerce of Riga; but it would have enlarged my letter to too great an extent. I shall take leave to do so at a future opportunity.......

XCVI.

TO MADAME HENSLER.

RIGA, 16*th August*, 1807.

For many years past (our connection will soon include the half of my life), my thoughts, as well as those of my Milly, with all our warmest feelings, have been with you on this day....... How has every thing changed since those former times when I have celebrated this day! Where is now the tranquillity with which we then contemplated the external world ten years ago, as if it could never drag us into its whirlpool? Even a year ago it was only at times that gloomy anticipations for *our own* fate rose before my eyes; my Milly scarcely felt them; and about you we had no anxieties. Now we are resigned to our own future, and I often repeat to myself the golden proverb, "He who can not what he will, let him will what he can." We shall get on thus, and with the certainty of never wanting bread, nor, wherever I may be placed, the affection and respect of the nobler among my fellow-creatures, I live with less anxiety for myself than you probably imagine. But all our apprehensions are excited for our country and for you. Manifold reports have awakened our fears that that may soon take place, which, according to the present march of events, must take place sooner or later—and what fears? We can not describe our grief and anxiety, for our expressions might be watched in several quarters; we have often expressed them to you before, and now we have nothing but helpless wishes. Oh that the storm might disperse, that we might meet once more on the undesecrated, uninjured soil of our fatherland! How it has happened that we have been obliged to give up our fixed intention of going by sea to Copenhagen this month, and revisit-

* See page 155.

ing you all before the winter, is a long story, which Milly has written to you in that letter. Had we remained in Memel, every thing would have been more quickly arranged, and we should have crossed before the season was too far advanced to permit of our return. For there, too, my dismissal would have been very unwillingly accorded, as there is a general wish to retain me in the service, though probably without any definite idea as to how I can be employed; and this incomprehensible and universal confidence in me goes to my heart. (Do not think it vanity in me to speak of this, and do not take it amiss if I ask you not to look on it as a dream of my own fancy)...... If I had received a furlough, we might have seen each other again, and refreshed our wearied spirits; now it would be too late; the matter has been put off so long, that I could not make use of leave of absence if it were granted.

Your letter of the 20th of June, is the last we have received, and this absence of letters is now doubly painful. I have been foolish not to keep a diary from the commencement of our flight, in which you all might have had a living picture of us, in the many changing scenes of our various fortunes and positions. If these pictures had been no more than peeps into the showman's box, yet still they would have had some value. Often I can not write at all, and now when I wish to do so, and am therefore better able to write than usual, I am disturbed by the doubt whether all this may not be written in vain! And that thought makes my eyes overflow. I have long had it on my mind to enter into an explanation with you on one point; not that your expressions have hurt me, but because we ought to understand each other, and because one wishes one's best friends to judge one correctly in every thing. I allude to your disapproval of my undertaking to learn the Russian and Slavonic languages, with the view of extending my studies to the other written branches of this ancient mother-tongue, which is spoken by fifty millions. It would have pleased me better if Milly had not mentioned these studies to you at all, because I foresaw that your one-sided ideas on this point would rather lead you to blame than to praise. I will not exactly say that you are entirely wrong, but I can not help thinking that you do not look at the matter from the right point of view. If I had employed a period of genial quiet—of inward life and activity, accompanied by the outward appliances necessary for bringing forth finished productions, in learning a new language, such a use of my time would most certainly have deserved blame. But at Memel, where it was impossible to free myself from the present time, and the present was full of oppressive cares—where I had absolutely no books, the case was different; and I therefore unhesitatingly include my new philological acquisitions among the things which give me the hope that I have made as good a use of last winter as was in my power. Or, if Nature had destined me for a poet, the case again would have been different; such toilsome labor is beneath the poet. But to the historian—or if that also is too high a title for me—to the historical inquirer, it is necessary to understand all nations, were it possible, in their own tongues. Languages have *one* inscrutable origin, like all national peculiarities, and he has but an imperfect knowledge of a people, who has not become acquainted with it through its own language. Any one who is conversant with the Oriental languages, must feel vexed to read what has been said and dreamed by those who have attacked the Persians and Arabs without understanding their languages. What sort of judgment of the French would be formed by a man who had read, say, nothing but "Telemachus" in a translation? It is a great pity that one can not learn all languages; however, that is so impossible that you will not suppose I have formed such a mad project. I have now probably reached the limit of my acquirements. I think I have derived this advantage at least from my studies of last winter, that I believe I have formed a far more distinct conception of the ancient and modern Russians than other foreigners, with the exception of Schlözer. My acquaintance with the Slavonic language has led me to a very important discovery in the history of races, and their original derivation, which would not be so new as it is, if more had occupied themselves with these tongues. I also read the Slavonian Bible, and that led me to a new theological hypothesis, so I have not merely added words to words, and piled my memory with dead matter. That to write is better than to learn, is indeed true for it is better to create than to be learned; but for the former I must wait for a time when the external world does not hold me fast in its iron clutches, otherwise I should only produce something mediocre, and the literary enterprises which would admit of execution now, would give as little satisfaction to my friends as my studies in philology. Will that time ever come? Till then, love, remember the saying of Nathan, "we must not require that every tree should have one bark," nor should we blame a lopped tree, if its branches no longer form the beautiful crown of its youth. Farewell! This deeply significant word I say to you with great emotion.

Stein had received the letters requesting him to resume office while seriously ill with a tertian fever. He instantly dictated a letter to the king accepting office without making conditions of any kind, recommending, however, Count Reden and Niebuhr —the latter on account of his "knowledge of finance and the French language"—as suitable persons to settle the question of the contributions with the French authorities. He arrived in Memel on the 30th of September, and immediately took the supreme direction of civil affairs, with a voice in the deliberation on military affairs.

The Provisional Commission with which Niebuhr was connected, had begun even before Stein's arrival, to sketch the outlines of those great measures of civil reform, the execution of which has rendered his short administration a memorable epoch in the internal history of Prussia, and it continued to work with him in the reorganization of the vital energies of the country. Before the end of October, an edict was issued by the king freeing landed property from various restrictions on possession, sale, &c., and another abolishing serfdom throughout the Prussian dominions; and within the following month, plans were drawn up for the entire remodeling of the administration, and the arrangement of the financial system. The latter appears to have been that in which Niebuhr was principally employed, and he also took a share in the deliberation on the other subjects.

The most urgent problem of the government was to find the means of paying the contributions to the French, which was the condition of their evacuating the country; for till the incubus of their presence was removed from the unhappy land, it was impossible to resuscitate its exhausted energies. One portion of Stein's plans for raising money was the negotiation of a loan from the Dutch capitalists, then the richest in Europe. This business was intrusted to Niebuhr, and he willingly undertook the commission, though he neither concealed from himself nor from Stein the difficulties attending its execution, in the present position of Prussia.

Accordingly on the 21st of November, 1807, he left Memel for Berlin. The journey, performed in the depth of winter, through a country devastated by war, and with a sick wife, was a toilsome and hazardous enterprise. On arriving at Berlin, in the middle of December, he was met by the intelligence of the death of his mother, who had long been suffering from dropsy. His grief for her loss was heightened by the disappointment of the hopes he had cherished of a speedy meeting after their long separation, since his business rendered it necessary for him to go in the first instance to Hamburgh. He was obliged to leave his wife behind him ill in Berlin, and proceed alone to Hamburgh, where she afterward joined him. From thence they made excursions to Meldorf and Nütschau, to visit their relations and Moltke. In the middle of February they continued their journey to Amsterdam, where they arrived in the beginning of March, 1808.

At first there seemed some chance of Niebuhr's succeeding in his mission, although it at once appeared that the Dutch capitalists would have considerable difficulty in raising the money, and the Dutch government, who also wanted to borrow, were naturally opposed to the transaction. But all hopes of the kind were crushed by Napoleon's attack on the Spanish monarchy, for, only a short time before, he had induced the principal Dutch banking house of Hope & Co., to lend a considerable sum of money to Spain, by assuring them that he had no hostile intentions toward that country. They now naturally shrank from making any advances to a state like Prussia, which seemed destined to share the fate of Spain so soon as Napoleon should have time to proceed to its annihilation. It was, however, of such urgent importance that the Prussians should at least convince Napoleon of their honest intention to pay the contributions, that Niebuhr was directed to continue every effort to induce the Dutch bankers to listen to the proposition on any terms whatever. He was therefore ordered to remain in Amsterdam, and in June, 1808, was formally accredited as Prussian minister at the Court of Holland. But as months passed away, and the course of public events seemed to remove the object of his mission continually farther from attainment, Niebuhr requested his recall. He received it in February, 1809, and was on the point of setting out on his return, when an unexpected offer to undertake the loan was made by M. Valckenaer. An agreement was drawn up between them in March, corresponding in all essential points to Niebuhr's original proposals. The readiness of Valckenaer to enter into a transaction which all the other bankers had thought too unsafe, was partly the result of his personal confidence in Niebuhr, and partly, in Niebuhr's opinion, of his own over-sanguine disposition. He was, however, indirectly encouraged to do so by the assurance of the French embassador, that the securities on which the loan was to be raised "should be respected in any case." After all, the negotiation fell through for a time, owing to the refusal of the King of Holland, on the score of his own pressing necessities, to grant his permission, without which no foreign loan could be effected.

Meanwhile, Stein's projects for the ultimate deliverance of Germany had been discovered by Napoleon, and had led to his proscription in the month of January, 1809. He had been succeeded in the ministry by Counts Altenstein and Dohna. Both of these were personal friends of Niebuhr; to the former especially he was warmly attached, but he recognized their incapacity to enter into and carry out the great projects of reform which Stein had sketched, and as he could, at all events, form no plans for his future life until the general arrangements of the different branches of the administration were completed and the appointments settled, he resolved to travel, by way of Hamburgh, to Holstein, and wait there till affairs should assume a definite shape. He left Amsterdam with his wife on the 9th of April, transacted some necessary public business at Hamburgh, and from thence went to stay with his relations in Dithmarsh.

During his residence in Holland, he had studied with great attention the condition of the country, its institutions past and present, and especially the nature and gradual formation of its soil by deposits from the sea and rivers. Few or none of his observations on these subjects will be found in the following letters; they are chiefly contained in a series of a less personal character which used to go the round of his friends in Holstein, and which have been published since his death in his "Kleine Nachgelassene Schriften."

M. Von Altenstein made proposals to him from Königsberg, where the Prussian government was still stationed, but the permanence of the cabinet seemed to him so uncertain, that he determined to await in Holstein the further progress of events. In this undecided state of affairs the greater part of the summer passed away. Much as he enjoyed the society of his friends, Niebuhr longed at last to find a settled dwelling-place and fixed employment. At length he was expressly summoned (as the return of the court and government to Berlin was still delayed) to repair to Königsberg and secure his appointment.

Here he found every thing, not only as regarded his own position, but likewise all that related to the management of public business, in as much confusion as he had expected. The disastrous war, and the insecure position in which the State was still placed, had thrown affairs into the greatest disorder, and there seemed to be no energetic hand capable of seizing the whole with its powerful grasp, and bringing order out of chaos.

Altenstein, a learned and philosophical man, but destitute of statesman-like genius or energy, had, from the very commencement of his administration, carried on the government in a spirit totally opposite to that of Stein. The project of the latter for the reform of the administration, which had already received the royal assent, was laid aside; the promise of representative institutions was recalled; no steps were taken to give an opportunity for the expression of public opinion; and he drew back from co-operation with Schoen, whom Stein had recommended as his own successor, and who was a decided advocate of popular institutions. During the unhappy campaign of Wagram, in which Austria, for the last time, attempted to stem Napoleon's encroachments, he could not resolve to take any decided part for the assistance of Austria, but let the time slip away without forming any definite plans for the future, or adhering to any fixed system of policy.

This state of things filled Niebuhr with deep solicitude. His health gave way, and he fell into a state of dejection such as he had not even experienced during the miserable years of 1806 and 1807, when, even in the depths of calamity, there had been some noble minds at the helm, struggling to save the State from absolute shipwreck. It was some relief to him when his appointment, as head of the department for the management of the national debt and the monetary institutions, obliged him once more to turn all his thoughts to active employment, by which he might hope, at least in a subordinate sphere, to effect some benefit to the State. The appointment was made in November, and in December he returned from Königsberg to Berlin.

The contract which Niebuhr had concluded with Valckenaer, had been ratified by the King of Prussia, with the most express assurances of his complete satisfaction; and, with great effort, Niebuhr succeeded in keeping the parties concerned steady to their offer till, in the beginning of 1810, the King of Holland yielded the required permission, which was in fact extorted by Napoleon from him, on his visit to Paris in the early part of that year. On the 1st of March, 1810, the loan was opened. The condition of Holland, which was utterly ruined by its annexation to France, in July, rendered it of comparatively little assistance as a financial operation, though even its partial success was greater than Niebuhr had anticipated in the then condition of Prussia, and considering that it was the only loan that had been effected on the continent since 1808. It was, however, of incalculable political value to Prussia, for it was the fear of depriving himself of the actual revenue which Napoleon expected from this source, that withheld him from attacking the existence of Prussia, when the prostration of Austria and Spain, combined with the alliance of Russia, left him free to do so; and he thus lost the opportunity, which the subsequent breach with Russia, and the invasion of Spain by Wellington, prevented his ever regaining.

Early in 1810, Napoleon had pressed for the immediate payment of the contributions, now greatly in arrears. There seemed, at that time, to be so little chance of the opening of the Dutch loan, and it was certain, even at the best, to produce such a trifling amount in comparison with what was required, that other means of raising money were imperative. The King interrogated Altenstein as to the means at his disposal for liquidating them, and found that his Minister of Finance had no plan to propose but the cession of Silesia. He next consulted Prince Wittgenstein on the state of affairs, and the latter drew up a scheme which was submitted to Altenstein, who, perceiving it to be thoroughly impracticable, refused to take it into consideration. Madame Hensler evidently refers to this plan, although she does not state that it was concocted by Wittgenstein, when she says, at this date, that "a financial project was now submitted to the King, by which its promoters fancied that they could annihilate the whole contribution and the national debt. The plan was laid before the members of the government for their consideration. Many of its most important provisions appeared to several, and particularly to Niebuhr, either impracticable or mischievous. Among these were the introduction of paper money, the redemption of the land tax, the abolition of many privileges by which the poorer classes would have been particularly affected, the seizure of all the hand-mills in East Prussia,* the imposition of a tax on consumption extending even to the products consumed in the households of the peasantry, and a tax on the license to trade." Niebuhr was, at all times, a bitter opponent of Prince Wittgenstein, whom he thoroughly distrusted. When the plan met with opposition, the King, under the advice of Wittgenstein, applied to Hardenberg for his opinion of it. The report which Hardenberg sent in, determined the King to offer him at once the post of Prime Minister, with the title of Chancellor of State, but the present ministers were to be retained in their several departments subordinate to him. Hardenberg refused the premiership on these terms, but at length effected the dismissal of the Altenstein ministry in June, 1810. In the mean time, however, he exercised great influence over the King, who had lost all confidence in the former administration.

Hardenberg's accession to power was hailed with joy by the nation at large, but Niebuhr did not share in the general impression in his favor; indeed, many years after, in Rome, he told a friend that he had indeed come to Berlin prepossessed in favor of Hardenberg, notwithstanding the laxity of his morals in private

* Each miller had a monopoly within his own district, and corn was not allowed to be carried out of the district to be ground, but many of the peasants had little hand-mills in which they ground what they wanted for their own use. The millers paid an excise tax upon all they ground, consequently the possession of these hand-mills by the peasants injured the revenue.

life, but that he had never found himself "so disappointed in any man, except in the historian, Johannes Müller." It was, therefore, unfortunate that, as the finance question was the great problem to be solved, Niebuhr was the first person to whom the Chancellor applied for his co-operation. When Hardenberg communicated the programme of his financial plans to Niebuhr, the latter expressed his unqualified dissent from them, and was so strongly impressed with a sense of their perilous nature, that he held it his duty to leave the King himself in no doubt as to his views. He sent a memorial to him, in which he openly represented the state of the country, and requested that his Majesty would release him from his post, as he could not concur in the principles of the administration, and that he would grant him instead a professorship in the university which was to be opened at Berlin in the autumn. The King forwarded the memorial to Hardenberg, who was naturally much annoyed at it, and sent for Schoen. But the latter was also opposed to his plans, and, after some further consultation, all parties transmitted their views to Stein. Hardenberg wrote to Niebuhr, upbraiding him, though in courteous terms, with his dissatisfaction at the administration, and requesting him to withdraw his resignation, as he hoped that all difficulties would soon be surmounted, and he was anxious to have Niebuhr's counsel and assistance.* But while ready to heap personal distinction upon him, he withheld that frank explanation of the line of policy he intended to pursue, which alone could have removed Niebuhr's scruples, and after negotiations, which lasted several days, he at length gave way, and offered to request the King to appoint Niebuhr historiographer in the place of Johannes Von Müller. This post he soon received, but with the condition that he should assist Count Hardenberg and the Minister of Finance with his opinions and advice when required. Stein judged much more favorably of Hardenberg at this time. It was not till after a lengthened intercourse with him, and the events of 1815, 1816, and 1817, that he gradually came to a conviction similar to that expressed by Niebuhr in his letters. He did not approve of Niebuhr's conduct in refusing to act with Hardenberg,† but his friendship still

* According to Stein's Leben, ii. 508, Hardenberg offered Niebuhr the post of Minister of Finance.

† He writes thus to Wilhelm von Humboldt: "Niebuhr declares his dissentient opinion. M. von Hardenburg invites him to discuss the matter with him, and to send in another plan: to this he vouchsafes no reply, but instead, hands in a lengthy chain of argument against Hardenberg's plan to the King,

remained unchanged toward him; and at a later period, upon a full knowledge of all the circumstances, he expressed his approbation of the course he had taken. Niebuhr would willingly have accepted office, could he have done so and remained true to his principles; but while Hardenberg offered him a high position, he knew that he was rather desired as a skillful tool than as an independent coadjutor. He remained for some time in communication with Hardenberg, who often sent him projects in which he desired his opinion, or sketches of measures, the details of which he required him to work out. Their connection, however, ceased almost entirely at a later period.

The following letters will illustrate Niebuhr's history from the autumn of 1807, to the summer of 1810.

XCVII.

TO MADAME HENSLER.

LANDSBERG ON THE WARTHA, *13th December*, 1807.

It will be three weeks to-morrow since we left Memel, and to-day we are still eighteen German miles from Berlin. A more mournful and distressing journey we could not have anticipated, even with the worst apprehensions, which the circumstances and the season of the year excited. From Memel to Berlin it is 108 miles by the nearest route, which is the one we have chosen; the other, by way of Dantzic, is still longer. However, it was our intention to have taken this latter road, because it lies through a pleasanter country, and one which has suffered less from devastation during the war; also because Dantzic is the residence of the family of our deceased friend, Mrs. Solly, and we had intended to make arrangements with them for her husband and children, as his spirits were not yet equal to it. But in Königsberg, the impossibility of crossing the Werder was represented to us in strong, and perhaps exaggerated terms; for certainly the strip of land between Elbing and Dirschau, which is all alluvial deposit from the river, is as bad as a marsh road can be in winter. It was impossible to travel along the Frische Nehrung either, because the few houses on these downs, where travelers have usually been able to find shelter for themselves and their horses (for there are no post-horses to be got on this road), have been destroyed in the war; we were, therefore, obliged to take the regular route through Braunsberg, of which we have much repented, since experience has taught us, that with post-horses and a moderately heavy carriage, it is possible to get along even on the roads most universally decried. We left Memel on the 23d of November; our departure had been fixed for the day before, but a storm rendered it impossible to cross the ferry to the Nehrung.

without bringing forward any other project—and now he wants to appear as a martyr to the truth.

"All this is nothing but a refined egotism, and an instance of the mania so increasingly in vogue on the other side of the Elbe for pouring a sauce of high-sounding, fine-lady phrases over perfectly commonplace actions."—Stein's Leben, ii. 507

This was rather opportune for me, as I had had a return in the night of some of the pains to which my last illness left me liable, which illness had been a sort of continuation of my more serious indisposition at Bartenstein. We had a comfortable journey along the Nehrung, with fine weather. We found every thing looking, on the whole, rather better than on my former journeys (this is the third time I have traveled this way) through this frightful desert, the only one of its kind in Europe. We got to Königsberg in three days. The last stage is a heath track through the fertile, and lately very prosperous district of Samland, where now the most mournful tokens of the ravages of war—ruined and deserted villages—frequently meet the eye. On Wednesday evening, we arrived at Königsberg, where we stayed with our dear friends, Nicolovius and his wife, who are two of the most pure and noble-minded human beings whom we have ever known any where. We rested there two days, as I had business to transact. Königsberg excited very melancholy feelings in us. Some of our friends have suffered more than one heavy bereavement through the prevailing epidemics; others have been cast down by other misfortunes. I never knew so much happiness destroyed in one place within less than a year, as in the circle of our acquaintance there. On Saturday we began our long journey; Milly was still pretty well—I tolerable, and freer from the disposition to hypochondriasis, from which I had suffered so long. Late at night we reached Braunsberg; we could not proceed till noon the following day for want of post-horses, and because it was necessary to get our passports viséd. We now entered one of the parts that had suffered most from devastation and pestilence. It is a magnificent country, with a very fruitful soil for a distance of ten miles from Braunsberg to the Prussian Marches, where it rises into hills of considerable height. Before this disastrous time, it was inhabited by wealthy peasants,* dwelling in beautiful villages, hardly to be surpassed by those in the best parts of Holstein. The roads, however, are of the most wretched description, and all the worse from having served so long as the high road of the armies, and for the transport of artillery, without its being possible to repair them; for now there are scarcely any inhabitants left, and horses are very rarely indeed to be seen; the land is in the stubble, and, as our hostess sorrowfully said, "bears only flowers." Owing to the badness of the roads we only got as far as Mühlhausen; and on the 30th to Riesenburg; from hence, onward, the country was flat and sandy. On the 1st Dec., a little behind Marienwerder, we entered upon the deep sea of sand which stretches from Westphalia far into Poland, and extends in Prussia to the chain of hills I have mentioned. We passed the night at Graudenz, a place of sorrowful memory. So far all had gone on well, and though we were now about to enter a Polish district, we had lost the apprehensions which had been raised that those parts were unsafe and hostile. For provisions we had been badly off; milk, eggs, butter, wheaten bread, we were obliged to take with us in the carriage, and to lay in a store of, where they were to be got; meat we could scarcely ever obtain. We were well received at

* *Bauer* means cultivator of the soil, and to Germans conveys the idea of owner of the soil also, as with them the cultivators are generally the proprietors of the land. Husbandmen, working for wages, are termed *Tagelohner*, hired day-laborers, and not *Bauern*, peasants. Thus an Englishman, speaking of "the peasantry," and a German speaking of "die Bauern," refer to two very different, and in many respects widely-contrasted, classes. This should be borne in mind in reading translations of German works on social or historical subjects.

Graudenz. I was glad to find a town which, from its proximity to the fortress, I had supposed to be destroyed, in a flourishing condition. We were shown into an over-heated room; Milly, who had already suffered somewhat from the privations of the journey, &c., became very unwell; however, we continued our journey, and on the way she grew better. On the 2d, we arrived at Culm, which is almost entirely Polish, and could get no horses; we were obliged to remain in a disgusting inn, in the midst of Polish filth. Milly lay down, but unfortunately this famous day was being celebrated at this hotel with a concert and ball. The next day we reached Bromberg. Milly's only wish was for repose, and she felt doubtful if we must not rest on the following day. This was decided by our finding that all the horses had been seized on for General Caulincourt. Milly kept her bed all day with fever and head-ache. We sent for a physician, at the recommendation of a merchant to whom I had a letter of introduction. His appearance, which gave token of extreme old age and stupidity, frightened us. The old man showed so many signs of imbecility that we were afraid to try his remedies. Another was recommended to us; but we got out of the frying-pan into the fire. It pains me to tell you of his proceedings. He would not show the prescriptions; but their effects seem to indicate that he treated the delicate woman as if she had the constitution of a horse. As he would give no counter-remedies, we helped ourselves with old prescriptions which we had preserved. We had another horrible evening and night to endure; for suddenly we heard firing on all sides. The town was full of Poles celebrating a festival after their barbarous national customs, namely, with drinking, dancing, letting off fireworks and firing muskets. Fancy Milly's sensitiveness increased to the highest point by illness, and shots and squibs and crackers let off under our window every minute! You can imagine my anxiety. She had, in fact, another attack of fever, but she entreated so earnestly that I would take her away the next day, that I yielded. We left, therefore, on the 9th; Milly still extremely weak. We had to wait a long time for post-horses, so that we did not reach Nakel till late in the evening. Here we found a good night's lodging. On the 10th she felt better. We proceeded, intending only to travel two stages. It was a very rough day, and there was some draught in the carriage. Where we wanted to stop there were no rooms to be had, so we were obliged to go further. We were confidently assured that we should find comfortable accommodation at Schneidemühl, a flourishing little town. In consequence of the roads being deep in sand and marsh, we did not arrive there till two in the morning, and here, also, we could get no room on account of the number of troops quartered there on their march. It was a dreadful moment. Milly was exhausted to the last degree. At length the post-master allowed us to go to his wife's residence. She, however, either would not or could not give us a room with a fire, and showed us into one that was cold and wet. We had, therefore, no choice but to go on at all risks. We procured horses and drove three miles further to Schönlanke. Here, likewise, we could at first get no accommodation. Milly was by this time so ill that I sat beside her in terror. At last the post-master took pity on us, and allowed us to pass a few hours in his warm room till another was heated. One is very thankful for kindness of this sort under such circumstances. At last Milly was able to lie down. She remained the greater part of the day in bed. Her former malady showed itself again. We used our remedies and subdued it. There was nothing for it but to push on. The 12th, we got to Driesen, where we happily found accommodation. But the journey had done my poor Milly no good; she was yesterday, 13th, when I began this letter, miserably weak and ill. I have persuaded her to take a day's rest here. To-morrow we shall resume our journey toward Berlin, which we most ardently desire to reach, in order to get medical advice and rest for her. We shall manage to hold out these eighteen miles, as we have traveled nine-and-twenty from Bromberg. You may fancy what a state of anxiety I am in. It is very inconvenient for us, too, that we have no maid-servant, since we have left ours in Memel; and we shall find it so likewise in Berlin, till we can get one, as I must often be away on business. We keep ourselves up with hope. Among the most consoling images it presents to us is that of seeing you and our friends in Holstein. I shall write to you from Berlin as soon as I can. Perhaps Milly will be able to write a few lines too.

XCVIII.

MELDORF, *February*, 1808.

I can not leave the place from which I wrote to you for the first time twelve years ago, without transporting myself to your presence with my pen.

Dearest Dora, we feel the separation from you most painfully. The consoling and strengthening influence of our meeting with you will long remain with us; it renewed the spring-tide of our old friendship, and new seed has been sown which will bear fruit. My aged father has become very weak, as you, no doubt, perceived during your stay here in the summer, but did not like to tell us of it. He is no more infirm in mind than he was before my journey to England; but the life and interest which his farming occupations had given him for years is quite gone, and I fear there is no other stimulant that can excite him in the same way again. His strength has failed much since the autumn, when we saw him together, and the weakness of his eyes incapacitates him from any exertion. All this makes me very sad.

I pour out my heart to you about this sorrow: I feel as if we had both for a long time past said too little in our letters about our personal concerns, on which, however, we can scarcely have any reserves with each other. Our conversations at the places where we have seen each other, have been seldom so free, that we could form a vivid picture of all your circumstances.

XCIX.

AMSTERDAM, 30*th March*, 1808.

......The golden rule of Leonardo da Vinci must now be our maxim in all things. In this way we can find peace if not personally exposed to the storm, and on this principle I am turning my time to account here, uncertain as our future is, as busily as if I were acquiring various branches of knowledge in accordance with a plan drawn up for my life. Our income has been considerably lessened by the general reduction of salaries; but that is a small matter, about which I leave it to others to complain.

For how long is our future secure in any sense! But even this does not disquiet me. Has not a year already passed since the Emperor Alexander was in Memel? Have we not got through this mournful year far more fortunately than many others? Indeed to me it has been instructive and morally improving. It is now a great comfort to have got through a whole year, especially since time advances so slowly. And during this period we have been much favored by Providence; Milly has completely recovered from an illness amidst the most dangerous circumstances; we have been spared from the immediate perils of war; an accident saved us from participation in the misfortunes of Copenhagen; we have been delivered from pestilence and from our dreary banishment; have seen you once more and are now in safety in a land full of instruction. From all this I draw consolation for the future, and thankfulness to God for my past life, which has perhaps in many ways been a better discipline for me than I have suspected.

It is on your account that we feel the principal anxiety. I would give much to know that you were not in Kiel. Of all places Kiel is the most in danger. I can not rely upon the humanity of the English to spare the defenseless asylum of the noble Queen, and I have no confidence in the fortification of the coast.

C.

TO COUNT ADAM MOLTKE.

AMSTERDAM, 18*th May*, 1808.

......Men differ widely from each other in their capacity for friendship—let me say for love. We shall not dispute the assertion of Empedocles, that friendship is always a power of attraction. But in many persons it is only a magnetic one, where the square of the distance, and the united power of several weaker magnets may, to a great extent, neutralize that of the single stronger one; so that such friendships depend too much upon proximity; and when the friends, who have been unavoidably separated for a time, are restored to each other by fate, they find themselves at first much less powerfully attracted to each other than to those with whom they have had constant intercourse during the preceding interval, even though the attachment of the latter may not be such as will stand trial. There is another power, which operates equally through all spaces, like the emanation of light—a power to which distance and separation are as nothing, because its seat is in that inward world which the mind, through her faculties of conception and imagination, creates out of and independent of the real and historical one. I thank you both that your reception of me, and our whole intercourse during the time we were together, proved that your affection for me is of this latter kind.*......

We will allow ourselves to indulge still brighter hopes from the intimations contained in Dora's last letter, and if my most earnest wishes on your behalf are but cries to an inexorable destiny, in Milly's more pious mind they are prayers. I can not express to you, how we love you both and your children, and yet I would fain do so in this time of sorrow, when

* Here follow references to the illness of Moltke's son, and the health of his wife, who was already ill of the consumption that terminated her life a few months later.

love and faithfulness are the only consolation. We have made our covenant together; you admitted your disciple to the equality of friendship, at a time when with all my other friends there could only be attachment on my side, without any claims to an equal return of confidence or affection: believing only too firmly, before it had been proved, that although I had as yet no objective power, nothing but warmth, enthusiasm for all that I undertook, there lay within me capabilities for great works, of which I then possessed only an imperfect idea, and had conceived only a vague outline. From this condition of mind, there arose within me a mortal conflict between my belief in my future high vocation, coupled with the sense of my present weakness and imperfection, and my repugnance to take a standing beside or below finished mediocrity; a conflict from which I have come out like a troop that has been surrounded, of whom a part hew their way through, while the greater number, and perhaps the bravest of them, perish upon the field. You gave me a place in your heart, not merely as believing that I might one day become all for which I had a capacity and a calling, but as if I were that already. And yet I have never been able to realize my aspirations, and have been obliged to replace the brave troops that have fallen with a sorry rabble; instead of poetry, archæology, and ancient history, I have had to cultivate finance, banking, administration—all of which, between ourselves, are (compared to my brave old comrades) a set of beggarly fellows, that sometimes almost drive me mad, especially when any thing reminds me strongly of all those whom I have lost. Sismondi's History has done this lately: I wrote forthwith to Stein, and hinted that I should like a mission to Italy, in order to compose a history of Rome (a continuation of Livy's, from the year 588 to 625) amidst her ruins. But he wrote a very friendly letter back, to say that it was out of the question; that I must remain under the yoke. God grant only—how low we are sunk to make such a prayer—that I may long have it to bear! Our prospects are very gloomy; but who can not say the same? As regards myself, my courage does not fail, though our personal interests also are seriously threatened. Milly has so fallen in love with Sismondi's Italian Republics, that she is making extracts from the book all day long. I admire him much, but all is not what it might be. The drawing is for the most part excellent, but the coloring often false. During my stay here I have busied myself with researches into the ancient races and institutions of northern Germany, and the study of the history of Holland. What a countless host of strong-minded and sound-hearted men, and how much greatness!

This, too, is not yet written. While studying it, I often forget the present; but then comes a story of the carnage at Madrid, an image of the agonies of Prussia, a recollection of my ever-beloved Denmark, and all my dreams vanish; I feel nothing but my misery. You have, I suppose, received a part at least of the journal of my travels, from Dora. It will, however, contain for you large barren steppes, and you must remember, in judging of it, that it was not written for you, nor, in fact, strictly speaking, for Dora, though many of the letters are directed to her, so that much, even in these last, can have no interest to you or her. It is my father chiefly who will enjoy them, and he wanted something to cheer him up. This object has been quite answered by them. Only one whose mind dwells entirely or principally within the limits of his daily life, could take pleasure at all times in such an unbroken description of the every-day world. I should have directed all my letters to him, but that Dora likes also to hear something of our every-day proceedings, and some other things were mixed up with them, and finally because it is a pleasure to me to write to her. You must take all this into account in reading them; we are on a classical soil, but one that is so only in a single respect. You must learn Dutch in order to read the great Vondel, and for the sake of the country, and of freedom. Vondel is a genius of the first magnitude. The language is *very easy* to learn; it cost me no tronble at all; the pronunciation is the only difficulty, and in that I want practice, because every one speaks French. One word more. When I talk about the court, I do it for my father's sake. Do not misconstrue me; above all things do not believe that I am indeed at the grindstone where the depth is polished out of hearts, which have long since been worn smooth by the friction of the world. It is nothing of the kind. Do you know what, of all things, I stand most in need of here? A Goethe, were it only his Faust: my catechism, the epitome of my convictions and feelings, for what is not contained in the existing fragment would be found in the complete work, were it written. A hundred times has the desire to complete it risen up within my mind, but my powers are not commensurate with my will. I only wish I had the Old Gentleman up here for a bit above ground! He should have work enough to do, and I would win heaven in spite of him. Farewell, my beloved ones, and give our love to your children, as if we were your brother and sister. Give best remembrances, too, to Philippina and Falk from your NIEBUHR.

CI.

TO MADAME HENSLER.

UTRECHT, *May*, 1808.

......I have heard nothing for this week past from Berlin, that is, from Stein. The fate of our poor country, therefore, is still undecided—a state of things which use alone can enable me to bear. O that Denmark's position were but more hopeful! In Memel, Denmark was often a consolation to me, and a bright spot on which my weary eye could rest. But how can I bear to deepen your sadness? You will know what it is to hear of, I believe only too many, things that formerly appeared to you to be exaggerations. What would I not give that you should have remained without this bitter experience! People here have had their troubles; they have lost much that can not be replaced, and have still heavy burdens to bear; yet the war has scathed them but little. A citizen of this town complained to me that the soldiers quartered upon him in 1795, had cost him not less than 150 guilders. I laughed in his face. Milly asks me to leave a corner for her. Read for your refreshment Sismondi's History of the Italian Republics. Thanks for your letters of introduction; but what can the natural philosophers have to say to me?

CII.

AMSTERDAM, 17*th June*, 1808.

......Here, also, they talk of changing their king, as a man might talk of changing his bailiff on his estate. This country could only lose by any change, and I should share the sorrow of the most intelligent men in such a case. The government is national and good, and the king only too humane and tender-hearted. A short time since, the signing of some criminal warrants, where he found, after second examination, that a mitigation of the sentence was impossible, literally made him ill on the day of the execution.

CIII.

1st *July*, 1808.

......I have not been well for some time, and have suffered much from sleeplessness. Often I lie awake till daylight. Yesterday I felt particularly unwell; to-day I am much better. But will it last? I have found my former experience irresistibly confirmed, that with me the body depends entirely on the mind, and that my indisposition almost always arises from some impediment to the free action of my mind, which seems to introduce disorder into all the functions of the bodily machine. When my mind is exerting itself freely and energetically upon a great subject, and I advance successfully from one point to another, displaying their mutual connection as I proceed, I either feel no physical inconveniences, or if they show themselves, they disappear again very quickly. No man can have a more vivid perception, that *creating* is the true essence of life, than I have derived from my internal experience. But if I am altogether restricted to a passive state of mind, as is the case at present, the whole machine comes to a stop, and my inward discomfort brings on an unhealthy condition of body, of which I have an unmistakeble outward sign in the contrast between the free and strong circulation of the blood in the former state, and its irregularity in the latter. Now, if it stood in our power, when outward circumstances are unfavorable to our activity in practical life, to choose at once a field of intellectual labor instead, and to transport our whole faculties into its sphere, this evil would be easily overcome; and I have often thought that in this manner one might almost make oneself immortal. But, alas, how many hindrances stand in the way! And how impossible this independence is rendered by the interruptions to our equanimity! Above all is this the case when one is engaged in public business, which has to be carried on according to prescribed forms; where one has only to execute, and can not work out an idea, but must bring every thing into conformity with established rules......

If you consider the charge of the physical well-being of the helpless an undignified employment,* I think you are mistaken; and that you attach too much importance altogether to the intellectual part of our nature in the mass of mankind. I believe that on that subject we have a totally false view in these days, and though I do not think it can mislead you, I should prefer seeing you openly espouse a contrary view, as I do myself on the firmest conviction. Do you not agree with me, that the so-called education which we claim as indispensable for the people, whether it be of a high cast, and consisting of numerous branches of knowledge and modes of applying the understanding and talents, or restricted to the first rudiments, is only valuable in so far as it is a true approximation to that free spiritual life, where the soul dwells in a world of ideas and notions, in which the world of sense is transmuted, and on which it becomes dependent? That it is, therefore, absolutely worthless—indeed, rather injurious

* He is here referring to a wish he had expressed to see Madame Hensler at the head of one of the great charitable institutions of Holland.

—when it disturbs a man destined to every-day life, in his truthful, instinctive mode of perception and action within his own sphere, and only gives him in return notions taken at second-hand, and torn out of their natural connection? And that yet this is unavoidable with all teaching and cultivation which does not go very deep? That, for instance, writing and reading, except for the purposes of business, are to the mass of the people superfluous even as a discipline for the memory, and a dangerous gift when they are used completely at random, as the common people use them, so that they acquire only a multitude of distorted notions; because, by this means, the common man is deprived of the truth his senses teach him, which nature has given him for his guidance, and becomes familiarized with another and distorted truth, which takes no firm hold on his mind, and yet robs him of the power of judging for himself? But if it be a moral rather than an intellectual culture which you ask for, this can scarcely be effected with a multitude of orphan children taken in the mass, except by selecting individuals, and by keeping those who are only fit for the usual avocations of their class as simple as possible. And I need not ask you whether this simplicity, which preserves the outlines of good and evil in human nature clear and distinct, even though it can not choke the evil, be not better than the confused ideas of morality prevailing among the higher classes, which can not really elevate and make them free, and over which at last a varnish is spread. But it appears to me that pure, uncultivated nature can not dispense with the satisfaction of all her simple requirements, and that this satisfaction is the best security for the morals of the many, as its want is usually the main source of their degeneracy, except in those who seem utterly bad by nature. A highly cultivated man may dispense with many things voluntarily, because he lives in another world. Thus the charge of physical well-being appears to me as interesting in the cause of morality, as it is in that of humanity; while, on the contrary, it is a characteristic of our age, that, amidst the ever-increasing misery of the lower classes, we are so earnestly busied in establishing schools for them; not to speak of the absurdity of the popular works which we put into their hands......

CIV.

TO COUNT ADAM MOLTKE.

AMSTERDAM, 27*th August*, 1808.

My beloved Moltke, what shall I say to you now that the blow has fallen on you, to which we all looked forward with trembling, despairing hearts, while we thought it as yet far distant? Can I, in written words, express to you our feelings, our grief on your account? Let me rather appeal to your faith in us, that you may find a vent for your own sorrow in imaging to yourself the feelings of your distant friends.

My poor, poor friend, where now, amid the wild tumults of the world, will you find a tranquil spot, in which your grief, raising you at last above the immediate pain of your loss, may restore to you the peace of mind you need for your own sake—for the sake of your children, of your friends? Not in solitude can you regain tranquillity, for the ever-turning wheel of thought within us, which, in prosperity, we fancy obedient to our will, disturbs more than the outward world; and the eye of a friend has more power than aught else to calm the heart. Come to us, as we can not yet come to you; unless this climate and place are too unhealthy for you. But we *will* come to you—I hope soon, and I hope not for a short time. And then we will strive together after courage to meet the destruction of all happiness, all hope, all joy.

Milly's tender love for your Marie, which you so well know, will tell you how great was the blow to her, when she read in the newspaper the terrible announcement, which a letter from Dora had scarcely prepared us to expect. You know that she loved no one more deeply than Marie, and that no parting, among those fate has allotted to us, was bitterer than that from her; to live with her was ever Milly's highest wish.

I understand why you have not written to us—you could not; but now, write. I promise faithfully to answer you; and am I not your nearest and dearest friend in the world, as you are mine? I entreat you to write: we will not keep silence on your grief, either now, in absence, or when we meet again. You used to write once when I did not repay you for it.

We will come to you; we will not seek to comfort you, but to infuse serenity into your mind. Pray for serenity; strive after it. It is no sin, even in the deepest sorrow; it is the necessary support to the soul on which heavy burdens are laid, without which they could not be borne to the journey's end.

Milly embraces you with warmest love. And God strengthen and preserve you!

Your Niebuhr.

CV.

TO MADAME HENSLER.

Amsterdam, *September*, 1808.

Your last letter, and indeed the one before it, are still unanswered; they would not be so, but that my zeal in corresponding has sensibly declined; and that the circular letters, which I continue in deference to my father's wishes, hinder me from writing others. No more of that; but I must not conceal from you that we are—not myself alone, but the whole public of this city—living in a state of excitement which destroys all free exercise of thought with me, and keeps me in a positive fever. I know this state of mind from repeated experience, fear it, and yet can no more keep it off, than he can who has once been a desperate gamester, when he stands as a spectator by the green table, even though he may not touch a card himself. And in this game, other things are at stake beside gold. Were it possible to shut ourselves up without becoming hypochondriacal, it would be better not to go into society oftener than once a fortnight, and then hear the purified residue of all the reports afloat within that time, than to hear them, as we do now, from their very commencement, to doubt them, examine them without data, and never know any thing with certainty, but the existence of the abyss into which we may all plunge, and to think with terror of our distant friends.

Milly will tell you how we read in the paper the announcement of Marie's death, and that we had not expected it from your letter. Moltke has not written to me, or else his letter has miscarried. God help him! His youthful vigor had been visibly affected by the vicissitudes of his early life, and by Augusta's death; and the higher rose the flame of mingled feeling and imagination within him, the more it preyed upon that inward strength with which we must bear up against sorrow, if we are not to be overwhelmed by it; and hence we can not but tremble for the effects of such a blow. O that I were but free, and could go to him! When we meet again let us all speak much of Marie. She had every perfection—brilliancy, purity, intellect, grace—and the fading away of her body had not affected the mind. She did not know what she was. No one could talk more beautifully, and no one was more unpretending. Even during her illness, when she spoke of things with a depth of insight beyond all other spectators of the same scenes, she always spoke in such a manner that the hearer could not help feeling that no one else could have said the same, and fearing to appear commonplace beside her, although the exquisite beauty of her conversation raised all around her above their ordinary tone of thought. You, too, will feel much more desolate.

Do not indulge brighter hopes for our future, because the Prussian territory is partially evacuated. For it is not evacuation, though the troops may be drawn off. It is not impossible that the convention might be ratified now; but, as matters stand, we could not fulfill it, and therefore should only pronounce our own condemnation. The impossibility is so self-evident, that I would rather touch red-hot iron than have any thing to do with the business. However, counsel comes with time: I mean for individuals themselves.......

CVI.

AMSTERDAM, 13*th September*, 1808.

We received your welcome letter on Saturday, together with one from Moltke, that was long past its time. What you tell me about his state of mind is a great comfort to me; all and every thing. I hope that he will find tears, and then activity. It used to be very difficult to me to speak to him of his departed Augusta: now that his calamity is so great and so irreparable, I desire to talk of nothing else with him but of the dear friend whom we have just lost. Then, too, I was much younger, my attention was more easily diverted, and I shrank from the aspect of sorrow. Now, all private affliction is but a contribution to that which has penetrated into the inmost corners of our land, and, under a thousand shapes, is gnawing at every heart.

Probably at the same time you receive this letter, perhaps still earlier, you will see in the newspapers an article, which is, to a certain extent, a proscription of my friend Stein.* I have seen it this morning for the first time; you may imagine with what feelings! This is my reason for writing to you to-day, for it will not only grieve you, but also make you anxious on our account. But you may be perfectly easy. My connection with Stein involves nothing that could be in the slightest degree dangerous to me. But what the consequences may be to himself I tremble to hear. With his cast of mind, where a thousand ideas, often of the most opposite description, follow each other in rapid succession, this expression of his

* Stein was already revolving plans for the future resurrection and deliverance of Germany. A letter addressed to Prince Wittgenstein on the position of affairs, containing the expression that the spirit of discontent with the French *régime* must be kept up in Westphalia, was intercepted by the French authorities, and published in the journals. Stein instantly sent in his resignation, which was not, however, accepted by the King. Napoleon did not immediately insist on his removal, because he knew that his presence was necessary to the drawing of the stipulated money from Prussia, but waited his time to ruin him.

sentiments was any thing but a deliberate plan; it was the effect of a fit of bitter feeling, which, if it had not been necessary to write the letter, and send off the dispatch just at that moment, would have given place to a completely different view before night. It is, however, very remarkable that both his sister, the Countess Werthern, and I, have entreated him, almost upon our knees, to have no dealings of any kind with certain individuals whom he believed to be honest, but calumniated men. That noble Madame Von Werthern, who reads men's hearts with a glance, told me that when she saw those persons, she often felt as if the devil himself was standing before her. Stein rebuked her for it, and was once quite angry with me, when it happened that each of us, without any concert, warned and conjured him not to have any thing to do with these people. I think I remember clearly that Madame Von Werthern once told me in so many words, that she had a presentiment that they would bring misfortune upon her brother. Is not the hand of destiny clearly discernible here? Stein always goes headlong from the fullest confidence of hope to despair, and in his judgments of people he often neglects to confirm his opinion, when once formed, by any observation of particular cases. But since his own integrity renders him much more inclined to judge favorably than to condemn, he often gives to a rogue a place in his esteem, which an honorable man obtains but slowly and with difficulty, if he has no brilliant parts to recommend him. "Have you proofs against him?" he has asked me, when I have told him that so and so would act ill in the case in question: the result furnished the proofs, and too late.

I believe, however, that the crisis is now very near, as to the approach of which we have long since ceased to deceive ourselves. A convention had been negotiated,* but was not as yet concluded. Will the thread break at once? It certainly will break, sooner or later. If so, we shall come to you, and truly we shall not be sadder than we are now, and have long been. People may say what they please of the practical utility of history; an intimate acquaintance with it is a sure preservation from being deluded into hope by many an *ignis fatuus*.

Poor Koppe, who will get into trouble, is a harmless fellow, and has a wife and children.

CVII.

TO COUNT ADAM MOLTKE.

AMSTERDAM, 30*th September*, 1808.

The news that Perthes found you well, dearest Moltke—the only news we have received concerning you for a considerable time—has quieted our fears for your health. Suffer me now to implore you most earnestly to take care of yourself, for God's sake not to lose all interest in this life, which has still such sacred claims upon you. I ask from you no more than that you should seek, rather than avoid, the alleviations nature sends you—sleep, and the gradual transition of passionate into gentler grief; that you should, if possible, moderate the vehemence of your feelings, and, however much it may cost you, keep that memory which will never leave you, apart from the present reality, which will reward you more than most others, if you turn not from it.

My dearest friend, fate gave you what you in your ardent, stormy youth,

* In Paris, between Champagny and Prince William of Prussia.

sought as your appropriate lot. Fate gave you more than falls to the share of most men—too much—since it would not leave you the possession of blessings, the enjoyment of which had made all others in life distasteful to you. You had every thing which your heart in the vague longings of youth could imagine, and you gave yourself up to this fullness of love—to the perfect earthly sphere in which all your thoughts found employment, undisturbed by the manifold perplexities which so often prevent those, whose lot it is to be driven hither and thither through a changeful and uncongenial life, from ever attaining a satisfactory consciousness of what fate has really done for them. I have seen you happier than I ever beheld any other human being, in the highest energy of your own nature, whose internal vigor had enabled it to withstand all the storms that might have devastated it; your intellect enriched, your heart ennobled and matured through love and happiness; when, as yet, you were untroubled by any fears for the life of your Augusta. I have seen you bent to the earth beneath the stroke that deprived you of your happiness; I have seen you pass from youth to the firmness of matured manhood; and attaining, under the influence of your Marie's extraordinary harmony and completeness of character, an inward strength and peace, which neither you nor your friends could have hoped to see in you in so high a degree. Your youth is over, your joys are gone; nothing is left to you but a serene activity, for yourself, for your children, for and with your friends. But the children alone afford you so many joys, and promise far more for the future; your own efforts and the affection of your friends will bring you so many hours—such as those we spent together in early days, before you had won your Augusta—that, had you not been so surpassingly happy, your life would flow by, without, indeed, satisfying you, yet still full of beauty. Altogether, when we compare the worth of his life, who, robbed of his dearest happiness, lives on to the end with a longing, glowing heart, which when fortune smiled on him, had raised him above this world, with the life of one whose heart has never thus bled, but has also never thus glowed, can we doubt whose lot has been the best, even if we look at it only on the side of enjoyment?

If our future were not so utterly undecided, and if you could leave your estate under present circumstances (which, however, you must not do, on account of your children, at a time when land is the only property not in danger of complete annihilation), we would speak of the future, and make plans for living in the same place. But this is impossible for us at present; we can not even plan definitely for a single week. I have given up all hope for Prussia, and we shall not live in Berlin; this negative expectation is the only circumstance we can look forward to as even more probable than another. Some time ago we anticipated a violent end to the long death-struggle of our unhappy State, and we then decided to spend the winter with you; now, the sickness has assumed another form, and it seems probable that I shall be forced to rend asunder the ties that unite me to the State, if I will not turn hangman, and go back to Berlin to take part in the horrible work of raising money by grinding extortions. And so we may very likely not only see each other in the course of the winter, but spend a considerable time together. . . . . .

Farewell, my beloved friend, and be strong; be at one with yourself, and think not too lightly of what is still left to you. There is an indescribable strength in resignation; on that foundation you may build up your life securely. Do not waste your energies by striving to penetrate into the eternally hidden regions—nor by endeavoring to give eternity to this world. Eternity is more real than time; let that suffice us; the earth is too small for man; and what we become conscious of in ourselves, is but the lowest part of our being; and shall we lose ourselves in questionings about this part, which seems to us the whole? Do not you act thus, but rather fix your mind on what yet remains to you, and among the rest on the affection of your friend, who loves you with his whole heart. Our love to the children.

Your faithful N.

CVIII.

AMSTERDAM, *begun 22d December*, 1808.

......Since I wrote the previous page, and, incapable of continuing, found myself obliged to lay down my paper, I have been constantly suffering in my health, and yet could not make up my mind to send for a physician. My constitution, and more especially the influence exercised on my body by my state of mind—which is always with me the true cause of health and sickness—are too unlike any thing to be found among the Dutch, for a physician, whose opinions and mode of treatment have been formed here, to be capable of taking a reasonable view of my case; so rest, and a combination of mental and physical diet, must be my chief reliance. In fact, it seems to me, that the methods of treatment in the medical art (which would so gladly set itself up for a science) must be completely different in different parts of the globe—just as civil institutions do, and must differ in different countries and nations. Thus, for example, the physicians here may be perfectly right in adapting their general treatment to colds, indigestions, and hardy, full-blooded systems, without taking intellect or feeling much into consideration. But woe to the stranger with whom these preconceived anticipations are incorrect, and who falls into their hands! In general, I do not like medical men; they form the most arrogant and unprincipled of all classes, next to the nobles, and rival the priests (as they used to be, for they are now on quite a different road), and the political economists. And no wonder, for they, too, must have a consciousness of internal untruthfulness, from the contrast between their pretensions and what they really are, and they try to conceal this from themselves by self-conceit. And just as it is very difficult for a statesman not to be corrupted by degrees, unless he is a thoroughly upright man, because the contemplation of the blunders that he often can not help making is all too painful, so the same takes place with the physician, who, besides, depends more than the statesman on reputation, and can not, like him, gloss over his mistakes. That this hatred toward the class does not extend to every individual is, of course, to be understood; why, I even like and esteem individuals among the nobility (of course, I am not speaking of you and such as you), among the priests, and the political economists.

Thus I have tried another medicine, in the shape of some most select reading. I wanted a book that would rouse my imagination and my feelings. So I took up Mirabeau's "Essai sur le Despotisme." Do you still recollect lending it to me thirteen years ago? I remember your copy perfectly, and your pencil marks on the margin, as well as the deep impression it made upon me. It is a sweet dream to call those times into life again! When we are conscious of the difference in our way of reading the same thing at different and distant times, we obtain some help toward the picture of what we then were and now are. Formerly every thing seized hold of me with infinitely greater power; but it remained in my mind too much as an undigested mass, and worked as such; now I can discriminate and test more keenly. This eloquent book, however, stands my tests; the more it is logically investigated, the less will it be accused of declamation. It shows quite convincingly that Mirabeau was perfectly free from the folly which afterward attacked every head like an epidemic—namely, the idea of binding freedom forever to a country by the forms of a constitution. He certainly knew the contrary to be true, and he can not have lost this conviction. Certainly, too, he is innocent of the horrid idea of universal representation, out of which all the mischief has flowed, and which arose in a spirit of imitation that had taken possession of shallow minds, and so-called metaphysicians. For Necker had a shallow mind, but it was German shallowness, which, if it be adorned with outward showiness, wears an appearance of practical solidity to the mass of Frenchmen. That Mirabeau afterward made use of this power is nothing to the purpose; the great man can make use of every thing by subjecting it to himself. I should like, however, to be absolutely certain that he definitely rejected and contemned this folly. Who, after him, would care to say any thing concerning the degeneration of all branches of the executive power under a despotism? Despotism was the sickness which consumed the energies of Prussia; Denmark has long suffered under it; but it would be a folly to take the trouble to describe the yellow fever after Thucydides, and since ages have not taught mankind to profit by his wisdom, it is at least quite superfluous now to delineate the particular symptoms of the disease.

What inimitable sayings! "L'animal que déchire le féroce léopard, admire-t-il la garrure de sa peau ou la variété de ses ruses?" Set in the place of the first word, the subject, the equivalent term l'Allemand—and the deep truth of the saying is gone. The animal knows nothing beyond the impulse of natural feeling, and seeks no false consolation; but our countrymen have no *true* feeling left; not even that of pain or enjoyment. And on this account, I can not conceive what is to become of us. Are we to be apes of apes? I implore the mercy of Heaven to grant us a new revelation; for salvation must come to man from without; our own longings only prepare the way for it.

Mirabeau was indeed a great sinner; he was possessed by a devil, but he had a very great nature, and there is more joy in heaven over one such sinner, than over a hundred just men. He was too high above his nation, like Carnot, the only two great men of the revolution. His eloquence carried away the people, and they fancied that they admired him; just as the loud noise of a full orchestra seizes hold of the common people, who would have remained perfectly indifferent to the music itself, performed on less noisy instruments. Such sinners excite a peculiar kind of veneration in me, though most truly they do not hold the highest place. There is something yet far higher, and over that we can only weep. Mirabeau says, "Si j'ai dit la vérité, pourquoi ma véhémence, en l'exprimant, diminuerait-elle de son prix?" Vehemence of expression is but brilliancy of coloring, and as this is no defect except when the colors are false, why must I find it so often assumed as a proof that I am wrong? Is it true that he who reaches the goal must necessarily go beyond it, because there is a possibility of his doing so? Is an act of atrocity, of injustice, of folly, annihilated because it excites me to passionate indignation? Or must one even take the poor innocent thing under one's protection against its unjust accusers? Here one learns to speak coldly, that is, in general, to hold one's peace; for amidst the praiseworthy and excellent things to be seen here, the stranger feels at last oppressed by the care bestowed on mere outward life, and the utter incapacity for all elevating sentiments. Opinions here are but prejudices, and those on religion perfectly insupportable. Yet the people, as might be expected, are not really pious; just as they have not been really republicans for many generations; but the administration was free, and more than that would not have suited the nation.......

CIX.

TO MADAME HENSLER.

AMSTERDAM, *12th December*, 1808.

In the first place, I must thank you for all the affectionate friendly things in your letter, beginning with the advice to bear lightly disagreeables which can not be avoided. If you have strong shoulders, it is not difficult to bear—but if they have become weak? Besides, you yourself would not bear any thing of this kind lightly. You have many a time borne with folly patiently. I can do so too, and do it conscientiously where a few good qualities make amends; what now annoys me is something different.

......It must be a strange sort of fellow, a true Margites—neither digger nor plowman, nor acquainted with any thing in the world—from whom I could not gain something in a *tête-à-tête* conversation; on the contrary, I think I surpass most in this art, and hence form so many friendships when in a foreign country, because men of almost every class and calling find that they can exchange something with me. But when such a man turns up, and is fastened upon one, so that it is impossible to get rid of him—a thoroughly worthless man—how can one help feeling disgust toward him, however much reflection he may give rise to. And reflection, properly speaking, is not my *forte*: what I perceive, I see with a glance; and it is not till I have reached my aim (where, indeed, I can not fail to do so) that I am able to connect my new point of view with the old one. But on this very account, I am far less able to choose my own course, than the man whose mental progress is the result of deliberation; my powers, whatever they are, and whenever they are present, depend on an external talisman like Samson's strength. On Faith, in the general as well as the special sense, I would gladly write to you, as I can not talk with you, if a hypochondriac could write a letter equivalent to a book. Your Faculty of Divination I would not concede to you, except as it might be a kind of poetry, which is certainly something very high. But Knowledge and Faith are widely different, and both are founded, as it seems to me, on Perception. A third faculty of a quite peculiar kind (and for which we have no word), is the recognition of the incomprehensible—of the impossibility of what is, according to our ideas, most certain, which we meet with, for example, in all natural circles. What I mean will probably not be made clear to you by this awkward expression; it is something, the admission of which, and the constant reference to it, distinguish the seer in nature from the ordinary learned man—something, of which Dolomieu, for example, had a strong feeling, and which must some day throw a new light on all our sciences. Imagination—as the word is commonly used—will be our guide least of all here; more may be gained from the steady gaze, by which we may at last even obtain a glimpse into the regions of knowledge. To me, faith without testimony is impossible. But as far as faith in all personal relations of life is concerned, I believe, by all that is holy! in all that I see to be beautiful, noble, glorious—unalterably and forever! To these belong sympathy, kindness, and self-sacrifice, when the latter forms an abiding trait of the character. But I believe only in the very rarest instances in an unalterable feeling of interest in a person, or subject; for such interest is in its causes and in itself a variable quantity, and may change its direction without any change taking place in the character. Yet I know that I myself possess this kind of constancy—which is no merit in me.

Stein's evil genius has blinded his eyes, and led him on from one false step to another; whether it be, as some say, that he, the unsuspicious, has been entangled in a net of artifice, or, that want of deliberation, and a resolve to break through his bonds, careless of consequences, have led him to the very point to which his enemies wished to allure him. In times of good fortune, it is indeed easy to appear great—nay, even really to act greatly—but in misfortune, very difficult. The greatest man will commit blunders in misfortune, because the want of proportion between his means and his ends progressively increases, and his inward strength is exhausted in fruitless efforts......

CX.

AMSTERDAM, 10*th January*, 1809.

Yesterday I saw Stein's proscription in a Dutch newspaper.* I was quite unprepared for it, as you will have been, and you can fancy the grief and consternation that seized me. But it is a time in which one must lock up one's sorrow within one's own breast, especially in my position, and as far as letters are concerned. I am waiting with a beating heart for to-day's papers, which will perhaps already confirm our worst fears. It is so evident that his evil genius has driven him forward to his fate, that I dare not hope that any effort will be made at Berlin to save him.

......I repeat for your relief the assurance that Stein has never written me a word by which I could be compromised; and you will the more readily believe that I have never written any thing which could even be construed into an expression of sentiments similar to those which caused his ruin, since we conversed together last winter about the position of Germany, and I told you, as I told every one, how indignant I felt at the senseless prating of those who talked of desperate resolves, as of a tragedy. Ever since the Peace of Tilsit, my maxims have been those which Phocion preached to the Athenians of his age, and nowhere have I seen among the declaimers on the other side, a Demosthenes, or even a Hyperides, but many a Diæus. To bear our fate with dignity and wisdom, that the yoke might be lightened, was my doctrine, and I supported it with the advice of the prophet Jeremiah, who spoke and acted very wisely, living, as he did, under King Zedekiah, in the times of Nebuchadnezzar, though he

* The sentence of outlawry against Stein was signed by Napoleon at Madrid 16th December, 1808, but did not reach Berlin till early in January, 1809.

would have given different counsel had he lived under Judas Maccabæus, in the times of Antiochus Epiphanes: "Seek the peace of the city whither I have caused you to be carried away captives; for in the peace thereof shall ye have peace."......

CXI.

TO COUNT ADAM MOLTKE.

AMSTERDAM, 15*th January*, 1809.

......You can imagine how the thought of Stein's proscription tortures me, by raising imaginations which I can neither follow out nor banish from my mind. A faint hope that it may not come to the worst comforts me at times, and encourages me to dismiss the most frightful pictures that present themselves; it would not be the first time that the terror of a sentence of condemnation had been deemed a sufficient punishment. I will form no conjectures on a question which events will have decided before you read this. It is as if there had been a demon at work, leading him on from one delusion to another, now blinding him by hope, now by despair, now by over-security, now by misplaced confidence, till he was brought to the edge of the precipice; and his previous course terrifies me above all, by inspiring the fear that he will plunge into the lowest depths of the abyss before him. I shall never deny him, and never forget him, though he has become estranged from me of late, and has often acted under the influence of a spirit that grieved me, and almost drove me to despair. It was his misfortune that I was separated from him, and this conviction makes me sadder still...... I loved him for his fiery spirit, his rough cordiality, his integrity, his contempt of shams, his clear understanding, the extent of his knowledge, his real enthusiasm, and his penetrating glance; his sharp angles did not hurt me, and his weak points were partially vailed, though not so closely, but that I often suspected them, and sometimes recognized them with dismay. Such as they were, however (I saw them first and very early, in his unaccountable bestowal of confidence on unworthy persons), they rather affected the minister than the man; had we worked together in ordinary times, they would have had no injurious consequences in the business I had to transact, and my connection with him would have been a bright spot in my life. He was never reserved, never enigmatical; he did not receive expressions of warm attachment as a due homage, but welcomed them; he returned them fully, and valued them highly. He seized the whole character at a grasp, and did not pick out this, and that, and the other quality in a man, in order to determine their value and weigh them against others. I shall never forget with what reluctance he took leave of me in Memel: he called me back time after time, said I must not go yet, and after all, we did not suppose it a final parting. At that parting we were truly friends, as truly as persons can become so *after their first youth;* the unions we form then are indeed of a different character from any of later years. He also wrote me very affectionate letters afterward. When he came to Berlin, in the spring, their tone altered; he seemed already to be under foreign influences, his views became distorted; I wrote fiery words in reply, and his old affection came forth again from its disguise. But the length of our separation may have weakened it—or was it the influence that seems to have taken possession of him at that time? Since the spring his letters lost their former tone of familiarity; we retained our business connection with each other, and who knows but that the former ties might have been restored if we had been brought together again? For some mysterious change must have taken place in him during the interval. You know that his successor* and I became good friends while we were colleagues. His character is amiable and very upright; he possesses a feeling heart, more sentiment than passion, an unequal amount of knowledge on many questions, which will hardly admit of being treated separately, too much of the routine of a system, scarcely that penetrating eye, by which a statesman ought to be able to take in all the outward bearings, and inward import of a question with a glance; but the best choice that could be made, and one in which I should rejoice under less hopeless circumstances; though his systematizing, and his slow way of going through every step in a chain of reasoning, often hinder the dispatch of business. However, this will not be of any consequence to me now, as, on many accounts, my retirement from public affairs is rendered desirable, indeed almost necessary. I must at once take measures to prevent injury to my reputation from the ill-success of plans which I know to be impracticable; and I really can not place myself in the dilemma, of either undertaking a responsibility in the guidance of affairs under such hopeless circumstances, or finding myself a mere nullity, or unavailing unit amidst opposing voices of equal weight; consequently I must retire. It is no unimportant step: I feel all that it involves; but even if the end of our State is not so near that, whether a little sooner or later, it will be reduced to its former attitude at Königsberg, perhaps in a still worse place, I assure you it would go hard with me to eat my daily bread in security, as a not absolutely necessary servant of the State, while the country is in such misery. It seems that many would be pleased at my retirement, for intrigues and cabals are not less rife or less malignant, when a state is sunk to the lowest point of degradation. Massenbach's account of Prince Hohenlohe's joy at being named general-in-chief of a disorganized army, that was visibly hastening within a few days to complete destruction, is extremely striking and remarkable.—Altenstein, and probably the King, are perhaps the only ones who would see me depart with regret. Altenstein has less rigid principles with regard to the payment of public servants, than I, who have a more republican belief in the obligation to serve, if we can be of use; my invincible feelings seem to him over-scrupulousness; however, I do not know how he will reconcile his pressing invitations to me to return, with the organization of the new government, which seems to have been formed without any reference to me. D. appears to know more altogether about the cabals against me than I myself, who can only have a presentiment of them; he will probably have told you a good many things too.

And here have I been saying not a little upon subjects to which I only meant to allude.......

Through the circulating library, which is our great resource here, my attention has been accidentally turned once more to French literature, which we foreigners may well take under our protection, since it is now the fashion among the French themselves to decry their own literature, with the exception of the poets of the age of Louis XIV., as the production of hell. Massillon's "Petit Carême," the sublimity and splendor of which you know,

* Altenstein.

(and if you do not know this book, you must read yourself, and may read most of it to Charles, and recommend it to Dora,) induced me to read his "Histoire de la Minorité de Louis XV.;" a book which, in my opinion, is not only the best historical work in the French literature, but is not inferior to any in any other modern language, and may be compared to the ancients. The grace of the style is inimitable; the descriptions are speaking truth; the proportion in the distribution of parts harmonious; the apothegms full of deep significance; and the verdicts passed, those of a great statesman. The judgment which the Bishop of Clermont pronounces upon subjects of finance, might put to shame nearly all the ministers who have no other vocation: but that is the true test of a great man, that from his eminence he can survey all fields. The whole work displays a spirit of elevated purity, the real human sentiments which animate his sermons also, his classical cast of thought, and the truthfulness of a man who is at one with himself—his freedom from all bonds of class and opinion, strong as was his own faith, his love of liberty, his correct appreciation of the duties of this world;—finally, it breathes throughout, the exquisitely beautiful spirit of the "Petit Carême;"—the spirit, which in his Orations, gave rise to that delineation of the times of Louis XIV., which must have made his hearers tremble, as the great man, scarcely guessing their feelings, poured forth his own soul. This description is annexed to the "Histoire." I am certain that, if you ever read it, it was so long ago that your memory can tell you little about it. Take this golden book in hand, beg Dora to read it also, and place it among your books, not beside the writers of his own nation—except perhaps Diderot and Montesquieu—but beside Thucydides and Sallust: if you have it not, lose no time in procuring it. The discovery of such a pearl gives me a day of delight, and you need such days. But do not speak of it to those of your order; Massillon was no friend to that; on the contrary, he abhorred it. The noble who can not bear this, had better not attempt to read him.......

This autumn I have read Schiller's "History of the Thirty Years' War," and, time after time, I have raised my hands in astonishment, not in admiration of the work, O by no means! but in wonder at the possibility that a book like this, which is not even tolerably well-written, and in which the narrative never flows smoothly on, but is ever halting and stumbling, should be allowed to rank as a classical work. Time will assuredly do justice to it, and allow the thing to sink into oblivion.......

CXII.

TO MADAME HENSLER.

AMSTERDAM, *February 26th*, 1809.

......I have made a very interesting acquaintance in Valckenaer,*

* Valckenaer was the son of the celebrated philologist. His literary fame, and still more his opposition to the Orange party, procured him the professorship of Jurisprudence in Utrecht, in 1787. He was one of the deputation who went to Paris to request the assistance of the Convention, in 1795. He remained in connection with the government up to the resignation of King Louis, when he also retired from public life. It is somewhat remarkable, that Niebuhr should have formed so close a friendship with a man so completely identified with the principles of the Revolution. They continued to correspond after Niebuhr left Holland, and a series of his letters to Valckenaer are still in existence, which his friends have made many efforts to procure, but hitherto without success.

who was formerly embassador from Holland to Spain. He is a Frisian, a man of uncommon intellect, and possessing a vivacity, and a power of taking interest in a wide circle of subjects, which are very unusual here. From his father he inherits noble philological attainments, and it is the first time, at least for many years, that I have met with an intellectual man conversant with ancient literature; as familiarly acquainted with Rome and the classics, as, for instance, we Germans, or other nations possessing a literature, are with their own literature and history, and with whom I could converse on a footing of equality. For all the other more eminent philologists I have known, assume an abominable air of initiation which I by no means concede to them. Valckenaer has moved about in the world a great deal, and has another key to the meaning of ancient authors besides grammar, and looks, too, for other things in them besides antiquities and words. Our views are very much alike. He has been a man of much ambition and violent passions, and his life has been full of storms. In his house lives an old poet, also a Frisian, named Van Kooten, who has written charming Latin poems, an achievement, the value of which we must not underrate, when the rare case occurs, that a poetical genius has so completely mastered one of the ancient languages, as to use it with perfect freedom. In such a case it is not mere sport nor affectation, and if a poet, as must happen if he is born in Holland, finds himself forced to choose between a thoroughly plebeian idiom—possessing, however, forms and rules of poetry, which he can not break through without losing the tone, to which he and all his nation have been accustomed from childhood—and an ancient language and forms of poetry, which are indeed absolutely inviolable, and therefore true fetters, but were created by the most exquisite sense of beauty—he will do best service to his genius, I think, by choosing the latter and more difficult course. There still exist a good many composers of Latin verses here, and one passes for a great poet; Van Kooten is, however, the only real poet among them. We Germans are happily not limited to such a choice.......

CXIII.

MELDORF, *4th May*, 1809.

......We have found all our friends here pretty well. My father is not much altered, a little paler, much blinder, and it seems as if his blindness had led him to indulge in melancholy reveries in his hours of solitude, which have impaired his cheerfulness. This disposition to groundless anxiety he had indeed before; it relates principally to the imprudent manner in which his property has been frittered away, about which we strive to set him at rest. It is touching to hear his unjust reproaches of himself, for having neglected different objects in his travels. Thus are we always most apt to censure ourselves, for not having accomplished to the uttermost what lay before our hands, and was the easiest part of our work; while we overlook our neglect of what was more important, but what we had to find out for ourselves. I have always regretted for him, and still regret, that on his return with such an abundant store of observations and discoveries, the worth of which could scarcely have been affected by a few facts more or less, he closed his active life, and did not rather, when equipped with all this knowledge, undertake some learned work. Hence it is, that his spirit has long languished under a sense of indigence, like a man who has given away a fortune, earned with hard labor under a conjunction of circumstances that can not again arise. He does not guess the cause of his inward dissatisfaction; he never did. And woe be to him who should open his eyes to it!

On our journey we found papers, which heightened the painful anticipations with which we had left Nütschau, by the depressing intelligence they contained. Since we have been here, we received along with more recent papers, a letter from our obliging friend, containing the inclosed:*—

The events that have come to pass grieve me deeply, and almost destroy all my hopes. Even if the news of Hiller's victory† be confirmed, that will do little toward retrieving our affairs, for I can hardly believe the possibility of a junction being effected between him and the Grand Duke, if the latter has really crossed the Danube, which he must have done at Ratisbon. After the faults that have been already committed, we can scarcely look for great results, even if this better contingency prove to be the real state of the case. On the other hand, very great misfortunes are possible, if the contrary be true; although it is evident that the organization of the army has been much improved, and probable that the courage and energy of the Austrians answer to the manifestations of their government, and that these last are really, what they always ought to be, the fruit, and the faithful mirror of their internal sentiments.

Victory was evidently so near! And then all had been saved! Then should we have entered on a life which we should not have dragged along as a weary burden. But armies are still intrusted to boys because they are the sons of princes; divisions to generals who have outlived captivity; and he who feels in himself that he could counsel and lead, remains in the background, not only because of a thousand miserable considerations, but because the hour of dissolution is not yet come in which he would press forward! I have, as you will see, guessed the whole of his plan at a hundred leagues distance; that those, who were immediately opposed to him, have not done so is plain. . . . .

Read in Gibbon the history of Majorian; behold a man who surpassed in virtue all the emperors that had sat on the throne of Rome, who yielded to none in talent and valor, who still had at his command a powerful army, small only when compared to that of former times; see how he not merely understood the art of government, how he perceived that he could only help the nation by granting them a due measure of freedom; but even if he had not died early, and under suspicious circumstances, he could have availed nothing against the influences of his age, and for him individually death was a blessing—the highest blessing. He died in the enjoyment of a delusive hope in the possibilities of the future. . . . .

CXIV.

MELDORF, 14*th May*, 1809.

A strong desire to relieve my bitter grief and comfortless affliction, by freely pouring forth my feelings to you, has, day after day, been forced to yield to the pressure of engagements which assail us on every side. . . . .

I am constantly asking myself here, whether we are really living in the

* This inclosure contained an account of the occurrences of the war from the 19th to the 24th April, at Ratisbon, &c.

† Over the Bavarians, under Wrede, at St. Verti, April 24th.

same age of the world that we did formerly, when we calmly reckoned beforehand on the future, or built castles in the air; or whether all before us is not, as it seems to our eyes, Chaos and Night—a universal destruction of all that now exists?

My old father never comprehends, nor dreams, that my outward circumstances are a house of cards. He comforts himself with the idea that we shall want for nothing! For his own sake, I try to prepare him for the contrary, but whenever it comes, it will be a terrible surprise to him.....

Schill's desperate step will, I fear, quite decide the fate of Prussia. It is only a legitimate consequence, and the last for which I would blame the Emperor. For he will say to us: "Either you gave your consent to it, or you did not; if you did, you are my enemies; if you did not, you are no longer a State, because you can no longer control your own subjects."

Is Schill an adventurer, or a great man? In any case he is a fortunate man, even if he fall. It is the first new and unheard-of thing that has been done for many years. The dissolution of all civil bonds and institutions is completed: now must begin either universal death and putrefaction, or the heavings of a new life. But where are its germs?

Which excites our indignation the most: he who applauds the desperate man as he would a rope-dancer, because the spectacle amuses him; or he who chides him for his recklessness?

I can not, in common prudence, set off for Berlin now. Napoleon is probably already in Vienna. Do you not love the Tyrolese? Their leaders are plebeians.

CXV.

NUTSCHAU, *25th July*, 1809.

......The faculty of simple endurance, mere passivity under the pressure of a heavy calamity, this beautiful and noble power, to the practice and development of which you exhort me, is unfortunately more foreign to my disposition, than almost any other kind of power that can be nourished and strengthened by exercise. But be assured that I shall go forward toward the future, not only undaunted, but for the present consoled: even should we be summoned to Königsberg before the consequences of this mischance have had time to develop themselves.

Moltke became still more unwell in Hamburgh, and came on here before us very much indisposed. To-day, thank God, he is beginning to improve.

We are not yet properly settled down here. I will tell you in my next how I get on with my studies, toward which I feel a strong desire attracting me, but which are now rendered difficult from long disuse.

I have no inclination to say much to you about the dreadful decision of this great judgment-day of the world. You know as much about it as I do, and our sentiments are the same.* The sacrifice of the Tyrol drove me to despair; but I was ready to believe it at the first report, it was so exactly like him, so completely in accordance with his system of dragging his victims through the dirt, and making them as contemptible as possible; just as the boa constrictor covers his prey with his slime, to swallow it with the greater ease. But it is a hard task to learn how to live quite without hope; almost harder still to see the hopes that had revived, crushed

* This letter would refer to the armistice of Znaym, concluded between the Archduke Charles and Napoleon, on the 12th of July.

to the earth again. Gallicia, even Terrol and Corunna, were evacuated. Romana had a well-disciplined army of 30,000 men. The armies in Estremadura were united; that from Sicily had most likely already landed in Catalonia, the great expedition to Bayonne or Biscaya was decided on. So completely did salvation hang on the turn of a straw! This is the time when the elect are proved; he who has endured to the end will have a bright evening to his life. But for the present—happy are those who have never withdrawn themselves too far from the calling and work, which can now be to the individual his only consolation! Such feel many things much less acutely than he who has irrevocably bound up his own destiny with political life. Happy, too, are they who have early resigned themselves to trouble; and, like you, have learnt in other ways and former times, to bear the yoke and cross.

In other respects I have no cause for complaint. The last blow has not greatly affected my health, my hopes hung on such a slender thread. The thought of the wounded—of the inhabitants trampled under foot by their conquerors—of the Tyrolese—is more than the heart can bear. And the aspect of the future for all of us, who are now parted, and shall soon be still more widely separated from each other, is indeed very grave.

It is very beautiful here at this season; but it is the first time that we have been here without you, and O how we miss Marie!

CXVI.

NUTSCHAU, 3*d August*, 1809.

You will be anxious to hear from us. The pressing necessity for rest and recreation, which you have too often traced in my looks, may assure you that Moltke's society, the quiet of this place, and the pure country air, would do me good. Many a chord that has been vibrating with sharp and yet sharper pain for years, till its power of endurance was exhausted, rests and slumbers here, where there is neither the fever of constant rumors and news, nor the consuming passions of intercourse with the great world to torment me. I succeed in the attempt to keep myself from the contemplation of things for which there is no consolation, and even from thinking seriously about our own fate, while I withdraw my thoughts from the more remote present, into the narrower circle of the present that surrounds me at this moment. I succeed in reawaking many interests that had long lain dormant, many of my half-forgotten ideas; and the fresh breezy air, the corn-fields, the woods, the meadows, infuse something of their life into me. Though I am still frequently unwell, seldom in good spirits, I yet feel that I am much better here in the open air, than I should be in a town, and that a return of health and enjoyment is not impossible.

However, I fancy that for the present I shall only attain to a negatively better state, which is certainly in comparison, a real good, but is far from being all that is wanted, and will, I fear, scarcely long outlive the external repose which has produced it. I have hardly as yet attained, even for single moments, to that free creative meditation on voluntarily chosen topics, lighted up by the glow of imagination, in which alone I can possess the full measure, and enjoy the satisfaction of all my faculties. Is it that I strive after an element which is not natural to me? The instinct that impels me toward it, can scarcely be an illusion; I should surely find satisfaction in a lower sphere, if that were my appointed place. But my wings are clipped, my limbs are become stiff for want of use, my mental habits have grown rigid, my will refuses to act, is awkward or heedless, while my accustomed mode of life impels the course of my thoughts in an opposite direction.

You will find it pardonable, though not conducive to the attainment of my objects, that the pile of books upon my table is continually increasing. For I have been too long denied the great enjoyment of a library, not to feel manifold temptations to revel in it now; and this, too, has in some respects its advantages. Only in this way, by striking a hundred chords that have lain silent for years, will my memory revive again, and without this revival, many things would before long have been irrecoverably lost to me, which have now so faint an existence in my mind, that I am unable to call them up by a simple effort of the will. I even find it necessary to learn afresh by practice how to read and investigate on learned subjects, and this is the best way in which I can accumulate materials, if I should ever be so fortunate as to produce any thing.

I have been collecting contributions to the subject of my old studies, from Dionysius of Halicarnassus, and pursuing the track of proof for my conviction, that in very early times a mutual acquaintance and traffic subsisted between Rome and Greece: he has also given me some helps toward a survey of the primitive races of western Europe. I have likewise read, with great admiration and respect (and are not these feelings among our most invigorating enjoyments ?) some of Mirabeau's papers on finance, which I had long been seeking in vain to procure. They have reminded me of some of the faults I have myself committed, which I long since recognized, and might have avoided, had I been earlier acquainted with his doctrines ; but not less of the egregious blunders of others, before whose eyes this light was kindled, when they ought to have been mature enough to have profited by it, and whose infatuation was such that they chose rather to grope in darkness ! And this, then, is the vaunted or imagined use of even great writers ! His fatherland was deaf to him, and plunged into the abyss, which he had pointed out with a cry of terror, and the warning of example as well as of truth was lost on other rulers !

I am reading the very remarkable physico-philosophical writings of Baader, which are pervaded by a spirit of the wildest mysticism, and in general are undoubtedly as mischievous as they are effete, by reason of their obscurity. For indubitable as it must be to any one, who can not satisfy himself with definitions and explanations, which are nothing better than reasoning in a circle, that there exists a wisdom and a truth above the sphere of our sciences, a wisdom and truth which bear the same relation to them as the living creature does to its delineation, yet we are none the less incapable of divining truth without these sciences; and the transient forecastings and glimpses, which present themselves to us at times, have their truth and deeper significance only in and through the steady, intelligent keeping in view of the boundaries of science; apart from science they become day-dreams and castles in the air. To excite an interest in these presentiments before the need of them is felt, or the capacity of calling them up exists, is a dangerous gift, and it were to be wished that such views should be revealed in mysteries to the initiated, and to none besides. Just as with views regarding freedom and civil institutions, where the best is remote indeed from the actual, and yet it does not follow that the latter is altogether inadmissible for the time being, or that the former is capable of being put in practice. Nevertheless, I recommend these treatises to you, that is, all those which do not form part of the system of natural philosophy, which appears to me, to say the least, extremely adventurous and dizzy; particularly all respecting subjects whose elucidation can be assisted by profound meditation, elevation of feeling, searching observation, and a pure and warm heart; for all these my mystic possesses. I read Horace also daily; he is my constant companion, and dearer to me than ever.......

CXVII.

HAMBURGH, 29*th August*, 1809.

On the opposite side I wrote you, in the first glow of my feelings, the details of intelligence that will not leave you unmoved, for it relates deeds to which our age was a stranger, and a result which, up to this time, had been denied to the noblest enterprises.*

Whether this ray of light will reach germs which only awaited warmth to burst forth into life, is another question. For my own part, I begin to cherish the encouraging belief that many hearts have grown purer and stronger, through danger and suffering, and that on all sides there lives a spirit, though straitened and repressed, whose power must increase, and produce something far better than that dull, comfortable existence, which B. describes as the golden age of thirty years ago. It was from the insufficiency of this, that the aimless striving after something beyond arose, which, combined with the universal effeminacy, led to the miserable results which he describes as constituting our later condition, and which we have all experienced. If God would take pity on us, I almost believe we might, though with bitter grief and pain, attain to something much better than that former state. We are indeed standing at the parting of two roads, where the most probable among the many possible contingencies is that we shall have to endure the double sorrow of seeing this flame, which has been secretly growing more and more intense, extinguished by oppression. Much indeed would still remain to us in the very consciousness of our loss, and in this instance I entreat you not to listen to the voice of your heart, but to strive against that tendency of your mind to analysis, in which you have more than once sought consolation, when we have been conversing about the misery of our times, present and future. The value of every earthly good and happiness may indeed be explained away by reasoning, just because what makes it good and lovely is not a thing belonging to the region of ideas, and can not be founded on ideas alone; but unless you can completely transfer yourself into Klinger's† cold intellect, it seems to me, that even in the clearest mind this must introduce a false state of feeling, which may indeed suffice for present comfort, but is

* The successes of the Tyrolese, who had in July succeeded in completely establishing their independence, and were at this time governed by the peasant Hofer.

† A poet of the last and present century. In his earlier productions the passions reign supreme; in later years a kind of reaction took place, and he placed stern decision of character and moral energy above all things. The struggles and difficulties of his own life had imparted, moreover, a degree of bitterness to his judgment of others and of the world in general.

not good in itself. Forgive me this warning! It is the only one which I think you may need, on account of your propensity to solve every thing by reasoning. Perhaps, too, I warn you because I envy you this faculty, though I would not wish to make use of it.

In this case, I would fain see you become the advocate among your friends of that which as yet scarcely begins to stir in the bosom of night, but whose existence is certain, for they are far too much inclined to look for and to see salvation in the dead remains of the past. Let them not (I refer particularly to L. Stolberg) regard what still exists on the surface of things, and is the tottering wreck of an age gone by, as the only possession left to us. Let them reflect that it is not the Known, in what remains, that can profit us; that this is every where simply injurious; but the hidden things which must be brought to light, and are here and there forcibly breaking their way; that a single spontaneous stirring is worth more than a thousand oscillating movements of worn-out and decrepit forms. Who could have dreamed that we should see the days of Morgarten and Naefel once more? Who can deny that the Tyrolese have stepped from childhood into manhood since 1790–7–9, 1800, 1805? Who can doubt that the spirit of the Spaniards, the martyr-spirit of the Holy Father, his anathema pronounced at the high altar in the midst of the French soldiery, have elevated the hearts of the Tyrolese; that their example will react upon the Spaniards, teaching them to disregard the prejudices of birth, and rewarding them for their sufferings? For they can not but feel that they themselves have sown this seed-corn. Have you heard the following? When Lannes' adjutant came to Saragossa to summon the city to surrender, he found the assembled junta in the act of going to the cathedral, whither the president requested him to follow them. Two thousand armed men marched in military order into the church, and the envoy asked the president what it meant. "Give the marshal this answer to his summons," replied he, "that these are the sentinels on duty to-day, who have come to hear mass to prepare themselves for death: this is done every day." Were but the right impulse given from above, we should see great things likewise among other nations, in every nation, according to the measure of its capacity for greatness.

I go to Prussia with a heavy heart. Besides, I dread the exhausting effects of the journey, from which I shall have no time to rest, but must enter forthwith upon business that will be troublesome and painful in many ways; I dread the distressing scenes on the road, and the effect of our stay in Königsberg, and the climate there upon my health. But there is no help for it.

I must have left unsaid much that I had wished to say to you. I was introduced to Villers yesterday; we met on both sides with a favorable prepossession. He seems to me to be a truly intellectual and upright man......

CXVIII.

KÖNIGSBERG, 21*st September*, 1809.

You can not have looked more eagerly for tidings from us than we have been wishing to write to you since our departure from Berlin. But during the journey it was not possible to write; we traveled too quickly......

We took the route through Frankfort, Londsberg, and straight across West Prussia to Marienwerder. From the frontiers of Neumark to the

Vistula the old Polish barbarism reigns over this territory, which has scarcely ever, until lately, been trodden by the foot of a stranger. On the Bromberg road every thing had already assumed a German aspect. Here, even in the so-called towns, you scarcely see any thing but walls of planks with gaping chinks, and roofs thatched with brushwood; a look of wretchedness which is not the offspring of poverty alone, but of habitual contentment with a low animal condition. The same mode of life prevails also among the Germans, by whom I found, to my surprise, the whole tract as far as Conitz inhabited. Even the churches are as wretched as the dwelling-houses. The soil is indeed, also, very bad; many of the fields only produce the double of what is sown; and the whole region reminds one of the wildest parts of North America, for the thinly scattered villages, with the fields belonging to them, are only spots of cleared land in the vast forest still inhabited by the wolves and wild boars. The aspect of the country improves immediately on crossing the boundaries of West Prussia, at the point where the rule of the Teutonic knights introduced, four centuries ago, a culture which the Polish sway has never been able entirely to efface. The wilderness I have mentioned belongs to the valley of the Netz. At Neuenburg, and still more at Marienburg, our admiration was excited by the remains of the monuments of those extraordinary men, which are Roman in their grandeur; the churches, and, at the latter place, the castle of the Grand Master of the order, are *chef d'œuvres* of the most beautiful Gothic architecture. In this place we also saw the tombs of these great men, and the barbarism of the late masters of the country, who have turned the principal building of the castle into a magazine. As we approached Marienwerder, we saw the beautiful levels—there, no fens, but an accumulation of rich light soil—a succession of contiguous orchards. Here, the frequent recurrence of newly-repaired houses and fences showed that the ravages of war had been great, but energy and industry had already restored the former appearance of things. In the much more fertile levels of Marienburg, also, the small number of cattle was the only trace left of devastation. But on this side Elbing, the general misery was but too visible; not so much in the remains of ruined houses, or wide tracts of land left untilled—of these I only saw a few unequivocal instances, but by much more frightful tokens, the tattered garments and famished look of the inhabitants, the wretched huts that numbers had erected by the roadside, and from which they came forth as we passed, with looks that bespoke their misery, though they did not complain, but thanked us eagerly for the alms we gave them. By universal testimony, they are a very good set of people here. We found among our friends at Braunsberg the cheerfulness which is inspired by great activity, and much rejoicing over the new corporation—Stein's work, from whom all the towns have received an independent municipal constitution, the worth of which is best appreciated by the citizens of a town like this, which was a free town up to 1772. Our venerable friend, Oestreich, was chosen president by his fellow-citizens, and elected by his native town and *all* the towns in Ermland, as their representative in the Diet—a reward for his many years' faithful and active service which is with justice dear to him. I shall send you some copies of his simple and beautiful speech for the Reventlows, &c., that you may all become better acquainted with the noble character of a man whom we esteem so highly, and who has been the distributor of your alms. It contains, also, a very lucid explanation of this new institution—the only plan that has been carried into execution, out of a universal system of free administration which has been frustrated. In these parts, all classes are exerting themselves to repair the ravages of war. Heiligenbeil, too, with its suburb, is, for the most part, rebuilt; but it is quite otherwise in the more remote districts higher up the Passarge. There, whole villages, and numerous farm-houses (which are here generally built very badly, even on noblemen's estates), have entirely disappeared; and in many which are still partly standing, the population has been almost or altogether exterminated by pillage, hunger, and pestilence. In one of these villages, there is only one girl left out of the whole population. The towns, portions of which are in ashes, are in an equally deserted state, and all the inhabitants of this part of the country are plunged into like poverty. It is generally anticipated that nearly all the landed proprietors will become bankrupt, and that property will entirely change hands; a great calamity, because those who grow rich in times of war and misery, are nearly always the worst members of society. The people do not derive much help from the abundant harvest, because prices are so low, and the freights for export so enormously high. One remarkable phenomenon is the Associations for the Good of the People which have sprung up within the last year. They are composed of all classes, and their object is the restoration of prosperity, by uniting their efforts to improve all hitherto neglected sources of wealth. Where this is carried out in such a spirit as at Braunsberg, it certainly deserves all praise.

I should have much to say to you about ourselves, if I could trust the post. As it is, I can only say this much, that the outward position of the State is discouraging, and its internal condition any thing but admirable.

I find nothing decided respecting my appointment. Violent party-spirit divides my most intimate acquaintance. Some are impelled, by their resentment at Stein's conduct, to utter bitter invectives against him which cut me to the heart. It is absolutely impossible to arrive at any well-founded conviction respecting the grounds of these charges against Stein, and equally so to get a reliable account of the last moments of his official life, and the occurrences that led immediately to the fatal result. Even men of the greatest veracity make statements which are entirely irreconcilable with each other, in many separate particulars.......

CXIX.

KÖNIGSBERG, 28*th September*, 1809.

I wrote to you from Nütschau, that, in spite of Milly's unbelief, I was determined this time to have faith. The result has not justified my hopes. I have had a notable proof that respect and attachment, even when they are accompanied by a kind heart, and, through long intercourse, have assumed the color of friendship, afford a weak pledge for actions, if their possessor is not free from selfishness. However, I should probably soon succeed in opening for myself a fair career of mental activity in this place if tolerable apartments were to be obtained. Besides this, I feel very seriously, and even depressingly, the effects of the last three years, during which my life has been constantly unsettled, and my movements determined by others. Such a life has no inward vitality; it is like a flower plucked from its parent stem—it fades, and leaves no seed behind.

I find every thing here much what I had expected from my former experience. One day slips away after another, without leaving any trace of its existence; there is no earnestness, no steady contemplation: it is like the life of a worldling, who is wasting in a consumption, expecting death and a fearful eternity, and yet shrinks from the pain of turning his thoughts upon himself. This universal tone of feeling (some exceptions of course there are) is to me the most shocking possible, and it gives me an indescribable feeling of oppression to see it prevailing all around me. By the side of this, it is frightful to perceive the general self-complacency, and the opinion of many that every thing possible and needful is being done, that any thing more would produce evil.

Humboldt, the king of letters, I have only seen once as yet. His reception of me was most friendly. I had expected indeed to derive much instruction from his conversation. He asked very kindly after Moltke.

There is much that is very beautiful about Pantheism, in the wider sense of the term, to be found in Schelling's philosophical writings, in his Researches into Freedom.* In reading this treatise I can perfectly enter into his system, but to mould my own mind into it, would be quite impossible. Besides, I shudder at the presumptuous attempt to scale heaven, by piling mountains on mountains, much as I delight in the wide-spread prospect from their heights. This treatise deserves to be widely read; it is clearly written, and full of thought. Its defects are those inseparable from the nature of the rash and fruitless attempt to set limits to the Infinite. Still I have felt myself, for some time past, more strongly attracted than ever I was before to the search after the Real, the Living, and on this account I have enjoyed reading it. In many parts I have recognized, with great pleasure, the inmost convictions of my brightest hours. But I can not ascend to the summit of his philosophy upon his ladder, nor fly upon the wings of others. There are some strong, and almost bitter expressions attacking Schlegel's "Review of Stolberg's Church History," which I also think an unsatisfactory performance, though, on other grounds, I can by no means reconcile myself to this method of interpreting the Old Testament, which is in such direct opposition to my feeling of historical criticism, that it is the greatest obstacle in the way of my faith. If Lord Chatham's letters to his nephew, Thomas Pitt, fall in your way, read them; you will spend a pleasant hour in contemplating the picture they afford of paternal tenderness, and the urbanity of a truly great man. Have you read Goethe's "Benvenuto Cellini?" Though I found fault with you for setting too high a value upon mere power, or cherishing an overweening predilection for it, (I may, however, have been unjust toward you on this point), this man will interest us both equally. Nowhere can you find a more vivid picture of the artist's great era than in this biography, and with mournful feelings do you watch it fading away with the hero, and see him outlive it. There are coarse, and worse than coarse passages in the book, but you will easily avoid them by referring to the table of contents.

I have found a fellow-admirer of the Faust, in Prince Radziwill, and his admiration does not remain as barren as mine. He has set to music all the passages adapted for singing; but though the music is very touching, I can not be persuaded that Gretchen's song at her spinning-wheel is

* Philosophical Researches into the Essence of Human Freedom; published in May, 1809.

a suitable subject for a high style of composition; that is to say, I should prefer something extremely simple. I am quite delighted with his delicate sense of every beauty, though he is no German. I am curious to know whether Villers really, *bonâ fide*, understands and likes the Faust? Vanderbourg has written some great nonsense about it.

In this unprecedented state of the world, individual character assumes a greater distinctness of outline than in any previous age, and a few exhibit a firmness, decision, and truthfulness, such as was, perhaps, rarely to be met with in former times.

I have been studying Davy's "Chemical Discoveries" with great interest. They open to us a hitherto closed sanctuary. My only fear is, that men will again content themselves with standing at the door.

CXX.

KÖNIGSBERG, 11*th December*, 1809.

In our last we said it was not likely you would receive another letter from us dated from this place; but I will not so far yield to the pressure of business and interruptions, as to leave, without bidding you yet another farewell. My old impulse to communicate to you without delay every thing of consequence that concerns us, will not let me wait a day before telling you that this morning my fate has been decided, as I have received my appointment as Privy Councilor of State, and head of the section for the management of the National Debt and Monetary Institutions, in conjunction with L'Abbaye. This double appointment is an anomaly committed at my request, in order to avoid a very injurious division of the public business, and to anticipate and prevent the mortification, which an old and deserving servant of the state might otherwise possibly feel. I receive no increase of salary, because I think it a sin at the present moment to accept more than I absolutely require, though all my colleagues have had their salaries raised 2000 dollars per annum. Since, however, there will now be many fresh sources of expense and new taxes, I shall really be worse paid for my services than I was three years ago; and therefore shall accept with all the better conscience, an official residence now standing empty, which, moreover, M. Von Stein had three years ago destined for my use, together with an addition to my salary of 1000 dollars, which I have never applied for, and now resign entirely. I am sure we shall be able to manage by making use of the interest of our capital.

I have been persuaded for some time, that this would be the issue of affairs with us, and therefore did not hesitate to meet a proposal made to me, by the Carlsruhe cabinet to enter their service as vice-president, with the answer that I expected shortly to receive a permanent appointment, and only in the opposite case could I, or would I, entertain the idea of leaving this country. The picture of the beautiful country, the southern climate, and the milder air, is not without its charms to me; but I long for a permanent position and occupations, and for rest; and I am attached to this government and nation, by the bonds of common sentiments and common sufferings. I should have felt myself a foreigner there; as I shall do, perhaps, in Berlin; for as yet I only feel at home in the land of my youth. I feel at this moment, when all is decided, as a bride might feel, who had given her hand away on well-considered reasons.

Will you believe—I know you will—that the outward show of the post

I have just received has not for a moment attracted or pleased me? I feel that I am free from that ambition, which received its hateful name from the presumed existence of a bad motive—but not from that which springs from the feeling and consciousness of a vocation to action and power; this no one can censure. I commiserate the nation, and I feel a calling to alleviate its misery, even if its greatest evils admit of no remedy. The object of my wishes and plans is to save the poor state-creditors (who are in the greatest extremity and have received no interest for years), without the necessity of imposing fresh burdens upon the nation; to satisfy the most sacred claims of thousands of sufferers; to regulate the provincial debts, so as to relieve the poor inhabitants; and to save the landed proprietors. I trust that the restoration of the paper currency to its full value will be the result of one of the plans I have drawn up. Outward events may frustrate these undertakings at their very commencement; the difficulties which their details present to myself, I feel that I am strong enough to conquer, for the importance of their object inspires energy and power; no one can lay any thing to my charge, and a definite vocation is a fulcrum by which your lever can raise any weight. And even if your enterprise only succeeds to a certain extent, so long as you can not attribute its partial failure to your own indolence, you have a sweet reward—you sleep in peace and your heart is at rest, even amid bitter disappointments and irreparable losses. If I were to talk in this style to others, it might be called boastful and ostentatious; it is not so to you, with whom I am used to talk as with my own heart.

We begin our journey to-morrow by way of Pillau and Dantzic; the best route there is, though it is bad enough......

CXXI.

TO HIS FATHER.

STETTIN, 22*d December*, 1809.

...... I had made up my mind to accept no post, in which the execution of my plans would have been committed into other hands, for I know that these plans are salutary, and I feel an unequivocal vocation to render help to this suffering nation. The administration of finance is not a science that can be learnt by studying a system; it is in reality an art. Many of its rules can not be reduced to the principles of a system, even in the hands of those who have the clearest practical acquaintance with them; besides, there are a hundred arts and knacks connected with its management, which one can only find out for oneself, by actual experiment, and long practice. I am conscious of possessing this art, and venture to say, moreover, that I know very few who are more than bunglers in it. It would be bad, indeed, if I did not possess it, seeing that its acquisition has cost me the best years and the true vocation of my life. While I was in Copenhagen, indeed, I only practiced it as an apprentice; still, I shall always reproach myself that, through my weakness and desire to oblige, the views which I saw to be correct were not carried into effect. It does not silence my conscience on this point, that the structure I wished to rear was overthrown by terrible convulsions, when it had scarcely risen above the ground; for, with really wise institutions, even when their general fabric is shattered by calamity, some detached results remain; an attentive observer sees every where around him, even in common things, traces of the deeds and actions of long-past centuries. The last few years, likewise—weary, bitter years to me, during which I have constantly removed further and further from my earlier sphere—have not been lost as respects my progress in knowledge of this kind; but so much the more binding is the duty of putting in practice what I have learnt, especially considering the urgency of the present distress, in which every alleviation is a blessing. What is there left, too, for myself, but to act so as to have the comfort of this consciousness, since my favorite studies and favorite ideas are lost and gone? . . . . . .

[After giving an account of his colleague, L'Abbaye, and explaining their relative position, he proceeds as follows:]

My first business now, is to mark out and divide our respective departments. In general, my department includes the management of the national debt, home and foreign, the bank-notes or treasury-bonds, the financial arrangements respecting the alienation of the crown lands, the investment of all the cash balances not immediately required, the collection of the outstanding debts due to the exchequer, the salt monopoly, and the banking operations of the state. From the personal confidence with which the minister, Count Dohna, honors me, I shall also exercise a general supervision over the public debts and systems of credit of the separate provinces, and over the private banks, which I propose to establish. The extent of my duties will thus be very great, and unless my health keeps good, I shall scarcely be able to get through them. But with method and a retired life, arranged in all respects with reference to my work, I trust it will be possible to satisfy the demands of my conscience.

I have the great pleasure of finding that the ordinance I drew up respecting the treasury-bonds has made a very favorable impression on the public. They have already risen to 80, and there is no doubt they will be nearly at par in the course of two or three months. This change, which will extend the currency of the country by two or three millions, has been effected by a comparatively slight effort; and I hope that the payment of interest on the exchequer bills will be accomplished in the same way, without adding to the burdens of the nation. I told you in my former letter, dear father, that I was convinced the Königsberg bonds would rise as soon as I was intrusted with the management of the national debt. My expectation was justified; they have risen, in fact, from 64 to 72. This proof of national confidence is to me the most flattering distinction I could have; and it is incredible how much popularity will accomplish in financial matters. If I succeed in being elected at the next renewal of a part of the municipal council of Berlin—the so-called town deputies—I hope to restore the credit of that city, now almost destroyed, by the same plan that I drew up for Königsberg. The new municipal institutions have worked very badly in many places, because the so-called people of rank have refused to take any share in them; but the spirit of these institutions is admirable, and will inevitably purify the mode in which they are carried out. But there must be an example given of a public officer of high standing who does not object to meet operatives and petty citizens as his equals in this connection.

I hope, my dearest father, that neither you, nor any of our friends to whom you may communicate this letter (it will interest Behrens particularly), will think that my expressions savor of ostentation, or making a boast of juggling expedients. None of you can so mistake me, and whoever will believe my word, must believe me when I say, that I would willingly give all this popularity, to go back to the world in which I lived so happily in years gone by. Still, it is happiness to feel that you can alleviate misery, pave the way for what is good, and avert evil. When the heart is heavy, you feel that thus you can lay up joy in secret, and even in heaven. I have made a speculation for my poor Ermlanders, with moneys that would otherwise have lain useless in my coffers, which I hope will bring in upwards of 12,000 dollars. If so, they shall give joy to many a heart that has felt none these three years......

CXXII.

TO MADAME HENSLER.

BERLIN, *27th January*, 1810.

...... The war has hitherto cost the remnant of our State not less than 100,000,000 dollars, and yet in the country parts here things are scarcely worse than in many other places where the ravages of war did not reach; in the little towns things are certainly much worse. I presume you will admit that commerce is a good thing, and the first requisite to the life of any nation. It appears to me that this much has now been palpably demonstrated, that an advanced and complicated social condition, like that in which we live, can only be maintained by establishing mutual relationships between the most remote nations, and that the limitation of commerce would, like the sapping of a main pillar, inevitably occasion the fall of the whole edifice; and also, that commerce is so essentially beneficial, and in accordance with man's nature, that the well-being of each nation is an advantage to all the nations which stand in connection with it......

CXXIII.

BERLIN, *16th February*, 1810.

......I complained to you lately of the numberless hindrances and interruptions which deprive me of all the satisfaction I might otherwise derive from my official occupations. If it were not for these, which render it impossible for me to accomplish what I ought, and would like to do, my official duties would often afford me some gratification; though the ruins amidst which I have to clear a spot, and commence a new edifice, are melancholy enough. As it is, however, the natural connection between thought, action, and consequences, is quite broken, though my efforts are not wholly without success. Things of apparently little importance hinder or absolutely prevent the accomplishment of what is most essential. Another source of grief to me, lies in the spirit in which the administration is carried on, and in the principles of the financial arrangements for the country at large, which are widely different from mine. Frugality, the utmost retrenchment of the public expenditure consistent with the due performance of the state services, and the just claims of individuals—the encouragement of all sources of wealth—the mildest possible taxation according to local and other circumstances—conscientiousness and judgment in the appointment of the subordinate officers of government, combined with a strict superintendence of them—are among the most indispensable conditions of an administration such as we need, which, however, any man must and will fail to carry out, who has not passed through a long course of preparation, and is not possessed of deep and penetrating wisdom.

Besides all this too, I must confess that my sorrow for the sacrifice of my inward life to this miserable finance often wakes up with renewed force. A consciousness how dearly any perfection in this art must be purchased by a man who is fit for something better, is probably the true reason, why so very few honest men have ever made themselves masters of it. This consciousness, with which I was vividly impressed with regard to official life in general, before I had entered on it, did not warn me, when after my entrance, a path opened to me toward finance. For a long time past, I have been almost unable to refresh myself by study, and yet the mind becomes sadly poverty-stricken when filled by no other thoughts than those arising from one monotonous occupation. This estrangement from my true life has now already lasted nearly three years and a half, and time tends ever onward away from the forsaken shore, till return becomes impossible.

As yet I have seen very few of the learned men of this place.

I still consider our future as very precarious—many times I doubt of it altogether; the Dutch loan, however, does something to render it more secure. Poor Holland is often in my mind, and fills me with compassion. I have little doubt, however, that we shall drag along for a time in our present position. And so we trust that nothing in our fate will hinder us from seeing you here this summer, and receiving you—oh, with what joyful hearts!

The Countess Werthern is very weak; her sister has at last been set at liberty in Paris, and is now with her. Stein is said to be in Brünn, and in good spirits. It is said here that negotiations are going on for Hardenberg's recall.

CXXIV.

BERLIN, *27th May*, 1810.

We want sadly to see you just now, that we might forget in your society the miserable position in which we are living. Hardenberg, who can scarcely at present enter the government openly as a minister, exercises, nevertheless, a sort of premiership in private. He is at a country-house about a mile and a half from the city, where he is concocting measures on subjects of which he and his assistants are perfectly ignorant. The present ministry is, in fact, quite set on one side, and is sinking into exhaustion without having resolution to resign.......I have remained firm to my conviction, that we must not use bad means, nor enter into companionship with the wicked, even for good ends; that an honest man even should he possess sufficient skill to fight intriguers with their own weapons, must not do it, and that we must never suffer ourselves to be misled, by the hope of being useful, into doing what we should not be willing to avow openly. I leave the present ministry to defend itself; but being convinced that the actual state of things is injurious, and that the next step will not be an amendment, I have sent a very earnest representation of the state of the country to the King, pointing out its evils, and have requested my dismissal, and, at the same time, my appointment to the chair of history, in the University which will be opened here at Michaelmas.

Milly has been unwell for some days, &c., &c.

CXXV.

TO HIS FATHER.

BERLIN, 3d *June*, 1810.

Amelia has already written to you about my position, as it *ought* to be at present, and since then you will have read an official article on it in the "Hamburgh Correspondent," copied from the Berlin journal. I certainly am not so free from government business as I had wished, but am still connected with the finance department. However, I am no longer personally engaged in the Finance Commission, and the rest will no doubt settle itself in time. If, however, things should continue as they have been for the last week, during which my time has been completely taken up with composing reports on proposed measures, there is but little hope of improvement in my health or return to my studies. I particularly wish to resume the study of Arabic, to which my thoughts have been recalled by Lord Valentia. I have been reminded, too, how unpardonable it was in me to content myself, when in Copenhagen, with merely looking at the Chronicle of Zebid, which, from the contents of one chapter I remember, would doubtless enable us to fill up the gaps in the Abyssinian history of the middle ages, and probably throw light on that of the Mohammedan states. If things should remain quiet, and I am able to make use of the permission granted me to travel for literary purposes, I intend, therefore, as soon as I have revived my Arabic, to go to Copenhagen, in order to examine the Arabic MSS. there, and in particular this Chronicle.

As long, however, as I am occupied with business which must absorb any one who is not accustomed to work superficially, and am obliged to confer and associate so much with people who have no life beyond their official one, so long it is impossible for me to return to science as completely as I should wish. Still, a great step has been made toward the attainment of quiet.

It gives us the greatest pleasure, dearest father, that this termination of affairs does not annoy you, and that it seems as though you, too, would be pleased to see me more decidedly devote myself to letters.......

CXXVI.

TO MADAME HENSLER.

BERLIN, 1st *July*, 1810.

......There are schemes afloat about which I can not be silent. I have risked every thing by venturing to expose their essentially pernicious character, and even though the consequences to myself should be very unpleasant, I have never enjoyed a clearer conviction of having acted rightly and wisely. I am satisfied, that even if I fail in the attempt to stifle them in the birth, they will come into the world only half alive. My opposition, which, I am pleased to find, wins me respect in many quarters, gives others also time and courage to come forward, though I have long stood alone in my efforts to protect the State against their projects. Such opposition has its dangers, and I have not been altogether without uneasiness. Yet I soon recovered my calmness in the consciousness that I stand or fall in a thoroughly good cause, and however things turn out, I shall never recall this time with regret, but rather dwell upon its memory with pleasure.

When this crisis is over, I hope to succeed in abstracting my thoughts from public affairs, and returning to my studies. We are at last expecting the arrival of my library, along with our other effects. When surrounded with my books, a few months will suffice to revive the images that have half faded from my memory, and then I must resume my pen—unless fate should have forever denied me rest, as a punishment for having desired excitement and activity.

You are not far from us now, yet I scarely dare to think of your coming to us as certain and near.

CXXVII.

TO COUNT ADAM MOLTKE.

BERLIN, 3*d July*, 1810.

Dearest Moltke, I feel it to be one of the greatest advantages I derive from my partial liberation from public business, to be able to answer the letter I received from you yesterday. A few weeks earlier, it would have been impossible, from the causes which have overwhelmed me with a greater amount of correspondence than at any previous time since my return from Königsberg, and of a more unpleasant nature. But suffer me to pass over the period that is just closed; it has, however, been one of the darkest, perhaps quite the darkest portion of my life. I was very ill at Königsberg, so ill that the foretaste of intellectual, if not of physical death was on my lips; I sank under the influences of the climate, combined with the bodily exhaustion produced by long-continued exertions of passionate intensity, and the disappointment of all my dearest hopes (allow me to attribute to my body a participation in the operations of my mind); and in this state I was forced to toil at Prussian *Citissime's*, accompanied by ponderous piles of deeds. There was nothing cheering to turn to; every thing excited bitterness and discontent; I was indeed in a new world—in the world of the coldest iron age. When I was only beginning to recover, I traveled hither at the worst season of the year; tried to conceal from myself how ill and exhausted I was; got stupefied with business and new faces; pushed and dragged at the rusty wheels of the machine till my hands were sore, and I was worn out with fatigue; continued constantly unwell; grew worse from time to time, and quite unfit for any sort of exertion: at last I got a little better, but by that time business had accumulated so that I had to work doubly hard till I fell ill again.

When the intrigues began, which have led to the present changes (perhaps not yet ended), I soon got an inkling that they might very likely issue in my release from the yoke of public life.

Your letter of the 25th of April, about the provincial system of credit, did not reach me till the end of May, and then—which quite puzzles me to conceive where it could have come from—bearing an address in a strange hand, and franked through Boitzenburg. You can neither have sent it from Hamburgh nor Kiel by that route. About the matter itself, I can say little in a letter, and nothing in the space of a few lines; for it could only be suitably disposed of in a voluminous report, or a verbal discussion, and for the former I feel by no means inclined just as I have made my escape from business. I think that our system of credit, which reached a much greater extension than people seem to be aware of in your country, and at last kept in circulation mortgage notes to the amount of more than 54,000,000 dollars, has done much injury, by promoting a trade in land, although it has been, and still is, productive of some advantages.......

Pray for free trade, for if you could export your wheat, barley and oats, to foreign countries, you would be saved, just as in that case East Prussia might also recover from the war in the course of a few years.

None of the new works, with which the Leipsic fair has rejoiced your heart, are known to me as yet. With our heavy expenses, we are obliged to be very economical, and I deny myself new books like wine. The new edition of the original text of the "Nibelungen Lied" is the only thing lying before me, and that was sent me by the editor himself. In this form, this wonderful poem can not fail of producing the greatest effect upon you.......

CXXVIII.

TO HIS FATHER.

BERLIN, 21*st* *July*, 1810.

......As Salt appears to be a very judicious and unassuming man, who will not in any way irritate and insult the feelings of the natives, I firmly believe that the embassy may be of the highest benefit to the Abyssinians, since they seem to be peculiarly prepared for the reception of European arts and civilization. The only fear is, that the unseasonable activity of the London Missionary Society, which has disturbed the peace of India, might endanger there also the good understanding which would no doubt subsist at first between them and the English, from their not regarding the latter as Catholic Europeans. The Abyssinians with their lively curiosity, stand nearly on the same level as the Russians did before Peter the Great, and in their beautiful climate, civilization may develop itself with more completeness and nationality than in Russia, where it has been spoilt by a bad model. That England will reap any political advantages, or even any considerable extension of her commerce, is very improbable. She might perhaps enlist some very serviceable soldiers there, but the entire trade of the country itself, and of that part of Africa to which Abyssinia would serve as an approach, can only employ a few ships, at least for many years to come. In the course of a century perhaps a great market may be opened even in these regions, and this may be worthy of consideration in the policy of a state, which may calculate with security on a prolonged existence, unless it be destroyed from within.

No one certainly can deny that England is at this moment rapidly advancing in power and prosperity, but that she is safe from internal convulsions and changes, can not be affirmed with equal certainty. The present ministers are not equal to the exigences of their position, and no internal prosperity can allay the discontent and fermentation arising from this circumstance, which may, too, lead to something much worse than the existing grounds of dissatisfaction, and yet ought not perhaps to be deprived of an outlet for expression. In times of extraordinary internal prosperity and great outward emergency, the absence of great men is almost as ruinous as in times of great calamity, and unquestionably England has never been so poor in great men as she is at the present moment.......

CHAPTER VII.

NIEBUHR'S PROFESSORSHIP IN THE UNIVERSITY OF BERLIN, 1810 TO 1813.

NIEBUHR's relinquishment of office, in 1810, forms an important epoch in his life. He was now thirty-four years of age, and since his twentieth year (with the exception of the sixteen months passed in England and Scotland), had been actively engaged in the public service. During this period he had indeed never lost sight of his philological researches, but he had only been able to devote to them his few hours of leisure ; now, it was to be seen whether he could find satisfaction in the life of a student, after years passed in the midst of the great world, and surrounded by exciting circumstances. How far he had, however, turned these leisure hours to account, may be judged by the following memorandum, found, with many others of a similar kind, among his papers, and written, most probably, in Copenhagen, about 1803.

"Works which I have to complete :

"1. Treatise on Roman Domains.

"2. Translation of El Wakidi.

"3. History of Macedon.

"4. Account of the Roman Constitution at its various Epochs.

"5. History of the Achæan Confederation, of the Wars of the Confederates, and of the Civil Wars of Marius and Sylla.

"6. Constitutions of the Greek States.

"7. Empire of the Caliphs."

No detailed outlines of these, or any of his other literary undertakings, are to be found ; but it must not be inferred that such memoranda contain mere projects, toward whose execution no steps were ever taken. That Niebuhr proposed any such work to himself, was a certain sign that he had read and thought deeply on the subject, but he was able to trust so implicitly to his extraordinary memory, that he never committed any portion of his essays to paper, till the whole was complete in his own mind. His memory was so wonderfully retentive, that he scarcely ever forgot any thing which he had once heard or read, and the facts he knew remained present to him at all times, even in their minutest details.

His wife and his sister once playfully took up Gibbon, and asked him questions from the table of contents, about the most trivial things, by way of testing his memory. They carried on the examination till they were tired, and gave up all hope of even detecting him in a momentary uncertainty, though he was at the same time engaged in writing on some other subject. He was once conversing with a party of Austrian officers about Napoleon's Italian campaigns. Some dispute arose respecting the position of different corps in the battle of Marengo. Niebuhr described exactly how they were placed, and the progress of the action. The officers contradicted him; but on maps being brought he was found to be in the right, and to know more of the details of the conflict than the very officers who had been present. One day, when he was talking with Professor Welcker, of Bonn, the conversation happened to turn on the weather, and Niebuhr quoted the results of barometrical observations in the different years, as far back as 1770, with perfect accuracy.

This power was not a merely mechanical faculty; it was intimately connected with the power of instantaneously seizing on all the relations of any fact placed before him, and with his wonderful imagination; his imagination, however, was that of an historian, not of a poet—it was not creative, but enabled him to form, from the most various, and apparently inadequate sources, distinct and truthful pictures of scenes, actions, and characters. Hence his keen delight in travels; hence, too, his habit of pronouncing judgment on the men of other countries and of past times, with all the warmth of a fellow-countryman and a contemporary.

With his warm affections, and clear-sighted moral sense, it was impossible for him to form such opinions on past or present history, coolly standing aloof, as it were, and regarding the subject with calm superiority; he could not but condemn and despise all that was pernicious and base; he could not but love and reverence, with his whole heart, whatever was noble and beautiful. Such opinions and feelings he expressed with the utmost frankness, sometimes even with vehemence, when prudence would have counseled more guarded language.

It was this same power of entering into the cast of thought and circumstances of others, which led foreigners to find pleasure in his society, and even to form intimate friendships with him, and which enabled him to predict, with remarkable accuracy, what course such and such statesmen would pursue in public affairs. But he was not, in general, fond of analyzing character, especially the characters of those whom he loved. He could not endure to separate off their different qualities, and balance their excellences against their defects; he seized on the whole personality at once. In his friendships he was most warm and constant; though his constitutional irritability of mind and body sometimes betrayed him into expressions which gave pain for the moment, yet no one could be in truth more tender-hearted. He was fully aware of his own uncommon endowments, but his absolute freedom from envy, and his eagerness to recognize and do homage to merit of whatever kind, preserved him from such mean faults as vanity and conceit. He was himself habitually serious, but had a quick sense of the ludicrous, and greatly enjoyed wit and humor in others. Of children he was very fond, and was always a great favorite with them.

The university of Berlin was opened at Michaelmas, 1810. The most distinguished men in nearly all the departments of knowledge had been appointed, among whom Schleiermacher, Savigny, Buttmann, and Heindorff are names well known to English readers. Indeed Berlin, from this time forward, may almost be considered as the centre of the intellectual life of Germany. Niebuhr was, therefore, in a favorable atmosphere for the prosecution of his learned researches, and, in fact, the next three years formed one of the calmest and happiest portions of his life. The political state of the world occupied him less than at almost any former period, partly because he was satisfied that no great improvement in the outward position of Prussia could take place for the present, while he retained the hope that, after a long preparatory night of discipline, a brighter day would yet dawn upon the future; partly because he now lived almost exclusively in the world of letters, and had comparatively little intercourse with political circles.

His first literary production, after his retirement from public life, was a Treatise on the Amphictyons, written in July, 1810.

At the opening of the university, Niebuhr delivered those lectures on Roman History which formed the foundation of his great historical work. He thus describes the mode in which the idea was first suggested to him, in a letter, dated the 31st of August, to Madame Hensler, who had just quitted Berlin after a visit at his house: "We meant to be alone after you had left us, but Spalding dropped in accidentally. He told us that he meant to deliver lectures, in connection with the university, this winter, and urged me to do the same. Nicolovius, to whom I mentioned the subject afterward, was most warmly in favor of it. I would willingly take Spalding's suggestion as a call to the work; but he who announces a series of lectures without any official call to do so, especially when he can not conceal from himself that he should be disappointed if he had not some distinguished auditors, is bound to deliver something of more than ordinary excellence. Now the time for preparation is short, and I could never reconcile myself to patching my work up, and eking out the deficiencies with irrelevant matter. To give a course of lectures upon the whole of a science, or the history of a country, for the instruction of youths, is not a hard task; in most cases, one which simply requires a continued effort of memory; but it is quite another thing when one wishes, and ought to give only a quintessence, to the exclusion of all generally known points. I think I should succeed best at first with an account of the political and civil institutions of the nations of antiquity. You know how much study I have bestowed on these subjects already."

It is evident here that he had not yet decided upon the subject of his lectures, but on September 1st, he writes: "I have determined to give a course of lectures on the History of Rome. Spalding urged me to deliver, instead, a course for young men at first, and afterward a single lecture upon some select theme. I would never have undertaken to write the History of Rome, but to lecture on it is a somewhat less rash undertaking. I shall begin with the primitive state of Italy, and, as far as possible, represent the ancient races, not only from the narrow point of view of their subjugation, but also as they were in themselves, and as they had been in their earlier stages; then, in the Roman History, I shall give an account of the constitution and administration, of which I have a vivid picture before my mind's eye. I should like to bring this history down to the latest era, when the forms developed from the germs of antiquity became utterly extinct, and those of the middle ages took their place." He writes to his father, in October, that he feels very happy in his new, or rather old, sphere of action, and desires its continuance; although there are moments in which he almost reproaches himself for his tranquillity, when he is conscious that he could fulfill certain public duties better than those who are now charged with them. This letter is also a proof that the most intense occupation with a subject like the Roman history, which called every feeling and power into action, could not stifle his interest in other perfectly dissimilar studies, belonging likewise rather to an earlier period of his life; for he relates to his father several facts connected with Bruce's Travels, which had recently come to light through the publication of the journals of the Italian who accompanied him.

Savigny says, of this opening course of lectures:* "Niebuhr himself describes the impression made by his course of lectures on Roman history, in a manner that can not fail of its effect on the mind of any susceptible reader.† Certainly many might be disposed to think that in this letter he overrates the extent of his own success, as we are so apt to do in our own case, even when we are animated by the strongest love of truth; but I can testify that he has rather said too little than too much. Niebuhr was appearing for the first time in the character of an instructor; he had as yet earned no fame as a writer, and thus the esteem and consideration which he certainly already enjoyed, were necessarily limited to the narrower circle of his personal acquaintance. He told me himself at the time, that he had only expected to have students, and a small number of them, as his hearers, and should have been fully satisfied if that had been the case; but in addition to a large audience of the students, they were attended by members of the Academy, professors of the University, public men and officers of all grades, who spread the fame of the lectures abroad, and thus continually attracted fresh hearers. It was the fairest harbinger of the future eminence of the youthful university. This unexpected success re-acted on Niebuhr's susceptible nature, and filled him with fresh inspiration. While he had previously felt a peculiar partiality for this subject of research, his courage and his inclination were now raised to the highest point by this respectful appreciation of his merits, and the daily and familiar intercourse with distinguished scholars.

"His time, at that period, was unceasingly occupied in productive efforts made with youthful energy and joy, and rewarded by a

* In his Essay on Niebuhr, appended to the Lebensnachrichten, vol. iii. p. 143.

† See letter, page 220.

grateful recognition of their value; and it is visible even in these letters, as well as confirmed by many expressions to his friends, that no portion of his life afforded him such high and unmixed enjoyment.

"The mode of his delivery was also remarkable. He had written down his lecture verbatim, and read it off before his hearers. This proceeding, which usually injures the liveliness of the impression, had, in his case, the most animated and powerful effect, such as in general only accompanies an extempore delivery. His hearers felt as if transported into ancient times, when the public reading of new works supplied the place of our printed books, and there was a less extended circulation, but they made a warmer and more personal impression."

The writer of the foregoing extract was one of those to whose intimacy Niebuhr considered himself most deeply indebted for the acquisition of new ideas, and for that sympathy with his own, which was the best stimulus to his creative powers. Von Savigny had already attained a high reputation as a professor of jurisprudence, at Marburg and Landshut, when he was called to Berlin at the opening of the university; but he had not yet published his "History of Roman Law in the Middle Ages," and "System of Roman Law at the Present Day," through which he has since acquired celebrity. Niebuhr has acknowledged his obligations to Savigny, in the preface to his first volume of the "History of Rome." Another of the learned friends to whom he alludes was Nicolovius, who was now employed in Berlin under the minister for ecclesiastical affairs and public instruction.

Schleiermacher, Buttmann, Heindorf, Spalding, and two others, with Niebuhr, instituted a sort of little philological society, the members of which used to meet once a week at each other's houses in turn, to read and correct some classical author. The evenings concluded with a supper, at which the utmost freedom and hilarity prevailed. Buttmann especially was as much distinguished by his sparkling wit as by his learning. Niebuhr's was one of those child-like open natures that can not exist without the unrestrained communication of their thoughts. Probably this impulse to express his ideas, just as they arose, was one of the chief causes which so long withheld him from coming forward as a writer. He threw out all his best thoughts in conversation, and lost, by so doing, the incentive to any further communication of them; meanwhile he retained them with unfading colors in his own mind, by means of his unexampled memory, without needing to write them down, and with this he was satisfied. To this must also be added, that he set before himself an unattainable ideal, which, on objective rather than subjective grounds, he thought it a duty to realize before submitting any production to the world.

Now, however, the success which attended his lectures in the delivery, induced him to extend his researches, and to combine their results so as to render them fit for publication. From this time forward he regarded the writing of his " History of Rome" as the vocation and task of his life.

He was closely occupied during this winter with his lectures, and their preparation for printing, which began as early as May. But he found time to write, besides, a " Treatise on the History of the Scythians and Sarmatians," for the Academy of Science, and at the request of the minister Dohna, drew up a plan for the re-organization of the provincial governments.

By the middle of June, 1811, the printing of the first volume of his history was so far advanced, that he was able to take a long-projected journey to Holstein. The fatigue occasioned by his constant labor in the composition of his History, had begun seriously to affect his health, and rendered a change necessary. He remained among his relations in Holstein till the middle of September. These family meetings were among the most delightful recollections of all who took part in them. After spending the morning in work, Niebuhr devoted the rest of the day to relaxation, entering eagerly into the games of the children, or reading aloud to their parents, on which occasions he used generally to take the comic parts, to the great amusement of his hearers.

On his return to Berlin, he found the first volume of his History ready for publication. In the winter of 1811–12, he continued his lectures, and at the same time prepared the second volume of his History for the press. He attended, this winter, Schleiermacher's lectures on the history of philosophy, and declares in one of his letters that, " he does not think any other university can boast of any thing like them." In December he wrote a treatise for the Academy, on which, however, he himself did not set any great value. The second volume of the " History of Rome," which he composed during this winter, contains the remainder of the lectures that he delivered in the preceding one. According to the plan he had made at this time, the lectures of 1811–12 were to form the third, and a part of the fourth volume. He then expected to be able to bring the History down to the time of Augustus, with the fifth volume—which he afterward found impossible, as his researches extended—and hoped to complete the work in a few years, if he continued to labor at it without interruption.

In February, 1812, he was seriously ill with an inflammation of the chest, and was obliged to discontinue his lectures for some time.

In the spring of this year, the French armies began their march through Prussia, on their way to Moscow. The interest in politics, which had only slumbered for a time in Niebuhr's mind, could not but be roused again by the aspect of affairs, and directed with eager attention to the results of the events that were taking place. On occasion of the passage of one of the bodies of troops, he met with Intendant-general Dumas, whom he had formerly known in Holstein, when he took refuge there after the French Directory had condemned him to be transported to Cayenne. He regarded Dumas as an honorable and intelligent man, whom he should have heartily rejoiced in meeting under different circumstances.

Though the constant arrival and departure of troops occasioned him much disturbance, as soldiers were quartered in his house, he got his second volume ready for the press by May. He wrote several reviews during the summer of 1812, but, with this exception, allowed himself, at length, a little intermission from his labors. These reviews he did not wish to survive him, and he had a similar feeling with regard to all his polemic writings. His opinion was that, though it is necessary to be able to contend for the truth, no unfriendly words ought to be preserved. With regard to his political writings he said, that they might be collected after his death if it seemed advisable.

Meanwhile, the second volume of his Roman History was sent to press. The indifference with which, as he thought, it was received by the public, pained him much; but he persisted in his resolution of continuing the work. The circumstances of that time, when the public attention was universally engrossed by the great transactions taking place in the north of Europe, were necessarily unfavorable to the reception of a work like his.

In October, 1812, he began a course of lectures on Roman antiquities, and went on with them to the end, notwithstanding the excitement occasioned by the frequent passage of troops. He was likewise occupied by the revisal of the third volume of the History, which he intended to have ready for the printer by the beginning of the new year. This plan was frustrated by the important events that ensued, which engaged all his thoughts, and filled his soul with new hopes of deliverance from the French yoke. He was soon involved in the bustle and turmoil of public life.

Niebuhr had hitherto read his lectures gratis; he now took fees for them, which he devoted to the assistance of distressed families, who were naturally at this time more numerous than usual. To have it in his power to afford help wherever he saw anxiety or want, was always a joy to him. He and his wife exercised their benevolence most nobly, both in great things and small, and he often expressed his thankfulness to God for having given him the means to be of service.

During the winter of 1812–13, French troops were constantly passing through Berlin on their way from Russia. Their disasters kindled a ray of hope in every heart; and though the unutterable sufferings of the enemy excited general compassion, the spirit of patriotism rejoiced in the prospect of brighter days. On the evacuation of Berlin by the French, in February, 1813, Niebuhr shared in the national rejoicings, and not less in the enthusiasm displayed in the preparations for the complete re-conquest of freedom. When the Landwehr was called out, he refused to evade serving in it, as he could take no other part in the war. His wish was to act as secretary to the general staff; but if this were not possible, he meant to enter the service as a volunteer with some of his friends. For this purpose he went through the exercises, and when the time came for those of his age to be summoned, sent in his name as a volunteer to the Landwehr. He would have preferred entering a regular regiment, and applied to the King for permission to do so; but this request was refused by him, and he added that he would give him other commissions more suited to his talents.

Niebuhr's friends in Holstein could hardly trust their eyes, when he wrote them word that he was drilling for the army, and that his wife entered with equal enthusiasm into his feelings. The greatness of the object had so inspired Madame Niebuhr, who was usually anxious, even to a morbid extent, at the slightest imaginable peril for the husband in whom she might truly be said to live, that she was willing and ready to bring even her most precious treasure as a sacrifice to her country.

In the mean time, however, that he might at least do something, if only indirectly, for the good cause, Niebuhr established a journal, under the sanction of the Prussian government, entitled the "Prussian Correspondent," the name of which expresses its object. He edited it himself, until he was, after a short time, called to head-quarters. He resumed the editorship several times afterward, but never for long together, because he was so frequently summoned in other directions. During the intervals, when the journal was conducted by other hands, some very bitter articles appeared against Denmark, which excited his strong displeasure, but for which he has nevertheless been much blamed in that country, where it was supposed that he was responsible for their insertion.

Extracts from Niebuhr's Letters from the Summer of 1810 *to the Spring of* 1813.

CXXIX.

TO MADAME HENSLER.

BERLIN, *1st October*, 1810.

Zelter says that Goethe is at work on his biography, and means afterward to continue Wilhelm Meister. Zelter has been studying his Questions upon Music, and declares that he, not being at all musical, not even having learnt music, will yet bring forward a doctrine of acoustics, which is profound, quite novel, and in his opinion convincing. Here, also, he discovers the law of diverging tendencies. Is not this an extraordinary triumph of genius? Goethe has seen the King of Holland, and they are mutually pleased with each other.

I have offered my services to the Minister Dohna, with whom I am, as you know, on a footing of friendship, to organize the affairs of the provinces, but my name is not to be mentioned. I have already finished a considerable part of this work, and given it in. If it should be carried into actual operation, I should hope to feel myself of sufficient use, for my conscience to be easy about the receipt of my salary.

I have been unwell for some time with low fever, but it is going off.

CXXX.

BERLIN, *13th October*, 1810.

We are gradually making our arrangements for a more settled mode of life. My Milly has arranged all my books upon the shelves with much care and industry, which is worth a great deal to me. I buy a good many books at auctions now, so that my library enlarges every week......

Within the last few weeks we have seen Savigny several times. He seems inclined to be very friendly with me, and I fancy we shall get intimate when we have known each other longer. His wife is very lively and pleasing.

I have bought at an auction a bundle of pamphlets written in the sixteenth, and beginning of the seventeenth century. If, in a collection formed so fortuitously, we find many things that are excellent, and none that are positively bad, we can not but conceive a respect for the age that produced them. This collection contains a string of apophthegms, under the title of "New and True Gazette for the year 1620." Our literature has not, since its revival, recovered the truthful and earnest spirit which they breathe, although it has taken a higher flight. What does this profit us? It is now the delight of a few; formerly it was an expression of the national character; and we may justly call the period from Luther to the Thirty Years' War, the golden age of Protestant Germany.

I agree with you, that it is better not to read books in which you make the acquaintance of the devil. I have been reading criminal trials lately, and have seen how judges and accusers have come to look on the most hardened and crafty criminals as objects of interest. But no danger of this kind can arise from reading a poetical work. In general the danger springs from the way in which vices are made to border on virtues, and the two are mingled together in characters, so that you rarely find any one so abandoned as to have no good sides to his character when you look closely into it, and hence you are apt to show him undue indulgence.

Amelia's eyes are again very weak; and you will therefore receive only a short postscript from her, for she can only write by daylight, and it is already some time since dinner. Her cough is rather more tolerable, but not gone.

CXXXI.

BERLIN, *9th November*, 1810.

Milly has already answered your questions about my lectures, while I was at our philological society yesterday, so that I can only glean after her...... She has told you that the number of my hearers was much greater than I had anticipated. But their character, no less than their number, is such as encourages and animates me to pursue my labors with zeal and perseverance. You will feel this when I tell you that Savigny, Schleiermacher, Spalding, Ancillon, Nicolavius, Schmedding, and Süvern were present. In reply to your other question, I must tell you that I am more satisfied with them myself than with any of my former productions; (I have quite remodeled the introduction.) This is, no doubt, partly owing to the universal approbation they call forth, which is a great stimulus and high enjoyment to me. For besides the number and selectness of my audience, the general interest evinced in the lectures exceeds my utmost hopes. My introductory lecture produced as strong an impression as an oration could have done; and all the dry erudition which followed it, in the history of the old Italian tribes, which serves as an introduction to that of Rome, has not driven away even my unlearned hearers. The attention with which Savigny honors me, and his declaration that I am opening a new era for Roman history, naturally stimulate my ardent desire to carry out to the full extent the researches which one is apt to leave half-finished, as soon as one clearly perceives the result to which they tend, in order to turn to something fresh. That it is impossible, with two hours a week, to present the history of Rome in due proportions in the course of a single winter, I am quite aware; and yet I would on no account compress what I have to say; for it is precisely this vivid, life-like representation of a multitude of well-defined objects, which constitutes the excellence of any historical work, that aims to rise above mediocrity. As far as I can, I compose the whole in manuscript in such a way that it may serve as the basis of a work, suited for publication. For I must begin to think of publishing now, because it is while I am delivering my lectures that my best discoveries in ancient history come to light, which, if not published, might probably be forgotten, and lost to the world. In addition to my previous discoveries, which are now all gaining in clearness and certainty, I have already made several new ones, some of which are very important, in the progress of my labors.

Our little philological association will not degenerate. We are reading and emendating Herodotus. I explain the historical, others the grammatical part, and thus we really form a miniature academy.

CXXXII.

BERLIN, *24th November*, 1810.

I advance but slowly with my lectures, and shall have to stop far from the goal; but I discover much that, to me at least, appears interesting; for instance, the cyclical system of the old Italian mode of reckoning the years is new. The Mexican mode of chronology gave me a light upon this point. I have collected a great number of data tending to confirm my long-cherished view, that the West of Europe possessed a primitive and quite peculiar cultivation—a system of science strictly speaking—before it had received any influences from the East. I would rather write to you about things of this kind, than of what we see, and hear, and witness.

I have received a commission which some might think important, but to me appears of very little consequence—to draw up a Constitution for the Academy of Science, in conjunction with Ancillon and some others. I like Savigny very much, and he seems to have a great regard for me too. Our respective studies lead us over the same ground, so that we have much to talk over and exchange with each other. I felt diffident when I first heard that he was among my hearers, but his extraordinary interest in my lectures is the most favorable sentence that could be pronounced on them, as he is certainly better acquainted with their subject than any other of our contemporaries.

7th December.—Since writing the above I have been at work on the Constitution of the Academy, with the view of completely remodeling it. I have also read a paper in the Academy lately. You see that I am fulfilling my engagement to you, and writing more than I read. May all go well with you, and Gretchen speedily recover! . . . . . .

CXXXIII.

BERLIN, *19th March*, 1810.

. . . . . . With a little more quiet my position would be one more completely in accordance with my wishes than I have long ventured even to hope for. There is such real mutual attachment between my acquaintances and myself, and our respective studies give such an inexhaustible interest to conversation, that I now really possess in this respect what I used to feel the want of; for intercourse of this kind is quickening and instructive. The lectures themselves, too, are inspiriting, because they require persevering researches, which I venture to say can not remain unfruitful to me, and they are more exciting than mere literary labors, because I deliver them with the warmth inspired by fresh thoughts and discoveries, and afterward converse with those who have heard them, and to whom they are as new as to myself. This makes the lectures a positive delight to me, and I feel already quite averse to bring them to a close. What I should like would be to have whole days of perfect solitude, and then an interval of intercourse with the persons I really like, but not to remain for so many hours together with them as is customary here. This is the very land of calls and parties. Even our Friday meeting I would sometimes rather be without, though it has always hitherto done me good. It would scarcely be possible to have less frivolity or dullness in a mixed society. Schleiermacher is the most intellectual man among them. The complete absence of jealousy among these scholars is particularly gratifying.

My historical researches seem to me to gain in importance every week, and I hope to solve enigmas in the history and constitution of Rome, which my predecessors have either labored at in vain, or passed over in silence. Much is wanting, indeed, to the formation of a history, and I shall not give my work to the world as such......

CXXXIV.

BERLIN, *in March*, 1811.

......Milly has already written to you about your skepticism with regard to the existence of in-born, incorruptible integrity, unswayed by motives of self-interest. I should be shocked at it, were I not already aware of your holding other similar opinions which belong to the same theory as this. Yet you *can* have no doubts with regard to your own motives; and without asking whether I too may not defy any suspicion of the kind through the whole course of my life—whether self-interest of any sort has ever had charms for me—I will point you to other examples. You yourself are convinced that there is an innate difference in talents, at least in man as he exists in the actual world. Now even granting that this arises solely from organization, and that this organization is from the beginning something external and foreign to the individual, and that its consequences do not affect the spiritual unity of man's nature; still among actual living men one individual is essentially different from another. In one, certain tendencies predominate from the first, in another, opposite ones. This can not be denied by any one. In one man, we see disinterestedness from his earliest childhood; in another, covetousness. In most cases these tendencies may be controlled or suppressed; a large majority of men may become utterly corrupt; but the man who has an innate love of justice, who would scorn to oppress or injure another, will resist the external influences of his condition in life, especially where he might reap a base advantage for himself. It must indeed be admitted, that ambitious pretensions may dazzle and take a firm hold of minds, noble in themselves, but narrow in their views, and we will forgive them for it morally, as laboring under a mischievous delusion. But no moderately honest man can say, "Others shall become poor that I may remain rich;" and whoever says this, to himself or aloud, is not one whit better than a thief.

Who could have the heart to sit as a judge in criminal cases, if he listened to the voice of such sophistry: "Behold! the criminal whom thou art about to condemn—to render wretched for his whole life, if not to deprive of that life—is at bottom no worse than thou. Had he been born and brought up in thy condition, he would sit on thy seat of judgment; and thou, in his place, wouldst have stood before the tribunal to answer for thy crimes!" "No," answers the just man, "I will not deny my sins, nor that I might be rightfully judged by my superior—I might have committed greater faults than have actually occurred—but that I could never have become base I know, as I know my own existence, for it is a part of my existence, which is no mere transcendental, colorless 'I am.'" No one can be further than I am from the proud belief in an absolute freedom of will belonging to all human beings; for the will can be exercised only by means of, and with thought; and can we think as we will—or do we think as it is given to us? Thus, too, I believe only in a limited force of will, to every one according to his kind, and his original peculiar impulses. These impulses may be in some individuals so bad, so decidedly wicked, that in their wickedness, in the lawfulness of exterminating so deformed a creature, lie the right and the duty to inflict the penalty of death in cases which legislators no longer punish with severity. In others, every thing is so undecided and weak, that they can never attain to more than *habits*, with regard to all that is not purely animal; and these habits, even when good, testify to no intrinsic virtue. You may be perfectly right, as far as such persons are concerned, in saying that their disinterestedness—a quality, however, very rare in people of this kind—occupies a place in which other circumstances might have planted covetousness and shameless arrogance. But no one can have less right to extend this verdict to the generality of men than you, whose strong and beautiful soul certainly possessed within itself the capacity for becoming what it is, however we may allow that external circumstances may have helped to enrich it. But circumstances were favorable to you, only as they are to the pine, which possesses within itself the strength to entwine its roots among the rocks, and to spring into the air from the mountain peak.

You have often wounded me, and done me injustice by the assertion that my strictness of judgment is dictated by party feeling. Yet in spite of this condemnation you will hardly accuse me seriously of unwarrantable palliation of faults, which, however, is always presupposed in party opinions; the one never exists without the other. The degree of danger, of injury, of conscious responsibility, may render our judgment of an action milder or severer; the hearer must weigh this, and calculate its worth. It is impossible to feel an equal amount of indignation toward a band of poisoners, or of incendiaries in Turkey, and one in the city where we live; for, in the latter case, the impression which gives rise to our feeling multiplies itself, and a human weakness mixes with it some dim apprehension of personal danger. But I should be a childish novice, unworthy to believe myself capable of writing history—which means, in fact, to depict and pass sentence on the past as if it were the present—or of conducting business, if a thing appeared to me good or bad, according as it came from the east or the west. The financial legislation of Austria, for instance, is evidently dictated, like all her measures, by honorable intentions, and is not intended to favor the nobility, or any other class—any unfairness which may have crept in, is so slight as not to be worth mentioning—yet it is so perverted and ruinous that it has made me almost as angry as the projects of the Notables among us, only with this difference, that anger is much sooner appeased in this case than where selfishness is the root of the evil.

And now something else, as I have still room. Have you ever heard of Goethe's inaugural disputation, and of a theological essay, which he wrote in his youth? I first heard of them lately, and have had the latter in my possession (since Boje's auction) without knowing that it is his. In this he proves, not in jest, but to the full conviction of all truth-loving readers, that it was not the Ten Commandments, but the ten fundamental laws of the distinctive peculiarities of the Israelites, which were inscribed on the tables of the law. This was also the subject of his inaugural disputation, which he wished to publish at Strasburg, where he took his degree. The heads of the University, however, considered it as profane, and denied their permission. The second half of the essay, in which he explains the phrase "to speak with tongues," is very remarkable, because it is quite mystical, and belongs to that strange period of his life in which he was a mystic.......

CXXXV.

BERLIN, 18*th May*, 1811.

......You have no doubt seen Oehlenschläger: what impression has he made upon you? The Danes undoubtedly possess poetical talents, if they were not so deficient in clearness and penetration of mental vision, without which the imagination can never create pure and great conceptions, free from mannerisms, as well as from Oriental phantasms.

I am now approaching the conclusion of my lectures, and the printing is about to commence. I begin it with a thorough consciousness of what is in my book, and of the rank it will hold at some future day; but I am not quite easy as to its immediate reception, partly because I am aware that the execution might and ought to be improved in many respects, partly because no one is allowed to bring forward novelties before our public with impunity, however clearly their correctness may be proved. Then I have already enjoyed, for the most part, the reception given to it by affection, from Savigny and other friends: that of disapprobation is still to come. I have written with such strict conscientiousness—not merely with regard to the praise and blame I have dispensed, but also with respect to the historical researches—that I could die on this book. It certainly will furnish little reading for recreation, and I confess to myself that by the side of many passages successful in point of style, there are others very awkward and stiff. The great merit of the book lies in the criticism of history, and in the light thrown on many insulated points of the constitution, laws, &c. You will understand that I talk to you about my work, because at present I am living wholly in it. You will hear all the less of it when I come to see you. To-day the publisher has sent me Frederick Schlegel's lectures; I have dipped into them here and there, and received a pleasant impression. He incontestably possesses genuine talent, and he has freed himself from that unhappy taste which he formerly did so much to promote.

CXXXVI.

HAMBURGH, 11*th September*, 1811.

...... The president of the court of justice, De Serre,* is spoken of in the highest terms. He is so completely master of the German language that he opened his first sitting with an address in German, which gives the consolatory pledge that all proceedings at law will be carried on in the language of the country. In a party of Germans, a short time since, he defended Klopstock from the attacks of his fellow-townsmen, adding, indignantly, that no one should dare to speak of him who had not a pure heart himself. It appears as if the French courts of justice had, in general, retained all the respectability of the old parliaments.

I have no inclination to write to you of political facts and rumors. Let us know every particular about yourself and your employments. Yesterday the Behrenses also will have left you. I fancy you will have found your house oppressive, and sought the open air. Do not chase away the image of your absent friends, when it rises up with longing before you; do not despise its companionship. But perhaps I do you injustice; and you know how to retain as well as endure the feeling of separation. Give our love to Gretchen, and all our friends. We shall not be able to write to you from Berlin for a week to come.......

CXXXVII.

BERLIN, 5*th October*, 1811.

Milly has told you of the anxiety caused us by the detention of your letter; we have received it to-day by the Russian post. If we were able to write freely, I should have much to tell you worth relating, though it does not immediately concern ourselves. However, it is impossible to be quite silent respecting things on which our fate and external repose depend, even if this letter should be opened. During our absence the public alarm and excitement have been great, but there has been no talk of the departure of the court, or of packing up at the palace, as you were told. Preparations for war have been made, and, as this has been done in imitation of the French, it has excited attention on both sides. As I told you in my last, we found the public mind unexpectedly calmed down, and the report was current that the Emperor had written an autograph letter containing an assurance of his friendly intentions. Now this letter has, in all probability, merely existed in the heads of some who thought themselves bound to keep the public free from uneasiness, even by deceit; this much only is certain, that the Count St. Marsan had an audience of the King, and that in consequence the preparations which were in progress have been suspended. The main question, the maintenance of peace between France and Russia, is still as undecided as before. Some affirm that Austria is engaged in active negotiations, and that the winter will pass over without war. Others draw an entirely opposite inference from

* This Count de Serre became, many years after in Rome, one of Niebuhr's dearest friends. His family had emigrated from France in 1791, when he was sixteen years of age, and settled in Germany. He thus became early acquainted with German literature, and he seems to have had by nature a cast of mind more German than French. He supported himself for some years by keeping a school, till Napoleon made him president of the Court of Appeal in Hamburgh, after that city had been incorporated with France.

circumstances that are known, and from an unprejudiced consideration of circumstances, which we can scarcely expect to be overlooked by him on on whose will the decision depends.

If, however, I do not reckon as confidently as many on a quiet winter, I am not much disturbed about the matter, and freely give myself up to the enjoyment of the quiet that has hitherto been unexpectedly prolonged.

My lectures will recommence at the end of the month, and I must be preparing for them. The journey has certainly put me out a little, but I shall soon get into train again; the being too long engaged with one subject is a more dangerous enemy; both because one's interest may relax, and because one contracts an habitual mode of looking at things, whereby the work loses a part of its distinctness—the worker his susceptibility to new impressions. I shall have to guard against both dangers, particularly at first, for their publication has certainly to me stripped the charm of novelty from the subjects of my history. I shall not hurry the composition of the second volume, that my mind may remain fresh.

This morning we have been to see the Museum of Natural History, which is being formed here under Illiger's direction, and is really a very splendid one. I do not know whether it is my own fault that such collections suggest no pious thoughts to me? The infinite variety of nature is brought too close to one; and in its contemplation the individual vanishes entirely from view; only the species remains, and one asks one's self, why should it be otherwise with man? Besides, the melancholy-looking, as well as the ugly animals give me a very painful impression. Yet I could willingly linger there, and can only console myself for my ignorance, as compared to the learning of naturalists, by reflecting that, after all, they confine themselves so exclusively to the external side of things, that their knowledge would only give one hints for investigation, and but little insight.

I have begun to attend our philological party again. There are two of its members wanting, whom we all miss very much, Spalding and Heindorf.

CXXXVIII.

BERLIN, 1st *November*, 1811.

So Goethe's life has come out, and I shall have it in a few days. It always gives me a melancholy feeling when a great man writes his life. It is already evening with him then, and that he relates how he lived, shows that he no longer lives quite from the root. Else he could never do it. Jacobi's book is not yet out; as far as I know, can indeed hardly be looked for yet. I do not know whether I can rejoice in its appearance. When he was in his prime he felt, very rightly, that the spirit of his philosophy required to be presented in a visible shape, in the picture of a life, just as the philosophy itself does not separate the formal from the real; in an abstract, systematic shape, it will not be like itself.

I enjoy my lectures for their own sake. I should like to deliver several more courses. My audience is much less numerous than it was last winter; there are only about sixty, and among them several officers. I do not know whether I may reckon this as a confirmation of the favorable opinion I have often expressed of this class. There are many elements of good among us striving for life—of a better spirit than existed in happier times. There are heavings under the heavy burden, and though we may have evil days still before us, yet a better time must follow than that which succeeded to the misery of the Thirty Years' War. Nonsense of all kinds has been so brought to the test, and become so powerless, that, at last, sense must necessarily take its place, be it under what form it may.......

Have you heard that Madame de Staël has received an intimation not to hold intercourse with Schlegel? A violent resentment against him reigns at the French court, because it is supposed that it was he who inspired her to praise the German literature. Her praise has done us a bad service in France; for to it is owing the animosity against German literature, which lies at the bottom of the regulations concerning the publishing trade in the new Departments.* The German literature is considered as hostile to the French, as an intellectual power which proudly refuses to the latter the homage due to that of the victorious nation. The French translation of the "Lectures on the Drama," is prohibited; and some consider this as a just punishment of Schlegel for having said he would not indeed use the French language for poetry; but for prose, he would use that which was most widely read.......

CXXXIX.

BERLIN, *16th November*, 1811.

When it came into my head to say to you that autobiography in general was the song of the swan—and Goethe's no exception—I certainly made too sweeping an assertion. With him, at least, youth has been renewed by the contemplation of his youth, and if he should write nothing like it again, he has written nothing like it for a long time past. The picture of his life is inimitably sweet and graceful. I feel sure that we can not differ in our judgment of this book. The number of trifles it relates will not annoy you—you will fancy him narrating, and it is the peculiar charm of the style that you can really feel as if he were telling you the whole. The story of his first love is exquisitely beautiful; no second equal to it can occur in the history, and I should not be sorry if the book were to remain unfinished.

Our life flows on in its uniform course without change. On Friday, I attend my society; four days a week I hear Schleiermacher; two days I lecture myself; we seldom go into company, and visits at our own house take up much less time than they did last winter. I might do a great deal in consequence, but I can not boast.......

......One evening in the week, the Savignys and ourselves generally spend together; and we often spend an evening with one or other of our friends besides—at Prince Radziwill's, for instance.

CXL.

BERLIN, *29th November*, 1811.

......I have been for some time past disturbed by something in Schleiermacher's lectures, which could not come out so plainly in the first

* Publishers in the parts of Germany that were incorporated with France were obliged to submit all books to a censorship before bringing them out, and works containing any passages which could be construed into expressions of hostility to France or French interests, were liable to be prohibited.

part, and certainly enables me to comprehend the unfavorable impression entertained of him by some noble-minded men, which used to give me pain, as I thought it unfounded. Schleiermacher does not content himself with bare notices of the various philosophical teachers; he brings them into connection, and endeavors to trace out the fundamental idea of each of the ancient philosophers. This is as it ought to be; but it is a very difficult and critical matter to pursue such investigations, and requires that you should divest yourself of your own views; the necessity of which he himself inculcated in his introduction most impressively, but which he does not put in practice. It is my firm belief that he acts with perfect honesty in the matter, and that those who dispute his strict integrity in such, or any other cases, do him wrong; nevertheless, he appears to me to be in error. Though he does not indeed always attribute to the ancient philosophers that pantheistic view, which regards matter merely as a phenomenon, and yet calls a Cause of the world external to matter an absurdity, he constantly refers to this view as to the primitive one, from which the various systems gradually departed, although it was only presented originally in poetical works. He also speaks of Anaxagoras, who first taught that Reason was an independent order of the universe, with a distaste, almost amounting to animosity, which has made a very painful impression on me, little as I am inclined to implicit faith. According to him, too, the early Ionian philosophers, the most elevated of all those who clothed their faith in the form of the popular religion, did not act sincerely in so doing. With these drawbacks, I like his lectures *much*—they revive many recollections of the wisdom of the ancients, and contain much which I have never yet read. If we still possessed Herodotus and the earliest philosophers, we should recognize at what an infinite height they stood above Plato and the later philosophers. Schleiermacher probably feels this too, with much more capability of exploring the recesses of the subject than I possess, and yet, on the other hand, there is something in him which repels him from them, and that is what I would rather not have perceived.

When you receive your own copy of my History, give the one you have now to Gretchen.

It may be interesting to see Goethe's opinion of Niebuhr's History of Rome, as expressed in the following letter to him, on receiving a copy of the first part of the work.

FROM GOETHE TO NIEBUHR.

If I have often sinned against my friends and well-wishers by the delay of my answers, I will rather, for this once, be somewhat premature, and thank you, even before I have received your work, for the pleasure you have given me by your letter. You bear a name which I have learnt to honor from my youth up, and of yourself, I have heard from many friends, so much that is amiable, excellent, and distinguished, that I feel as though I already knew you well, and can sincerely assure you that I have a great desire to make your personal acquaintance.

In the mean time, the work which you announce to me will afford me an agreeable and instructive occupation; for what can be more attractive than to find a subject, which has been so often and so variously discussed, placed in a new light, and, as it were, born into a fresh life, by means of new researches? However rarely it has been permitted to me, in the course of my life, to occupy myself with topics which interest me so deeply, I know well how to value those who have the talent and perseverance to undertake such enterprises.

I hope you will accept kindly these hasty thanks, and continue to think of me with friendship.

GOETHE.

JENA, *November 27th*, 1811.

I brought this letter with me from Jena to Weimar, where I found your excellent work awaiting me, and immediately began to read it. Now I have finished it, and should like, before I begin it over again (which is most necessary in order to understand and profit by it), to express my thanks, not merely in general terms as a first impression, but in detail as they have been called forth by the various points in your work. Very probably, however, a considerable time might elapse ere I should be able to do this, and with the best will in the world, I might be forced to detain this sheet still longer. Permit me, therefore, to say no more than that I have felt myself transported to the time of my own visit to Rome, when all around me impressed me perpetually with the want of such researches, while at every step I became too clearly aware how little capable I, no less than others, was of conducting them. Since then, a long time has passed, during which I have continued to turn my attention to these subjects; and your book, which solves so many enigmas at once, is most welcome.

We can now picture to ourselves the condition of Italy before the Roman period, and form a clear idea of the order in which, so to speak, the various strata of population were deposited one above another. Your discrimination of the poetical from the historical element is of inestimable worth, since by it neither is destroyed, but rather for the first time fully confirmed in its true value and dignity; and there is an inexhaustible interest in seeing how the two again coalesce, and exert a mutual influence. It is much to be wished that all similar phenomena in the history of the world may be treated in the same method. Does it need many words to assure you that I have derived the utmost instruction, from your development of the position of the State and of its finances, of its relations to Greece, of the anarchical condition of Rome after the expulsion of the kings—in short, from all and every part. Were I to go into detail, and to speak of your description of Ancus Martius, of your unvailing of the Sibylline books, or to dwell upon the poems of Lucretia and Coriolanus, I should have to write book upon book, and these sheets would never reach the post. Rest assured that you have sent me a noble gift, for which I shall all my life feel grateful to you; that I am looking forward to the continuation with the greatest eagerness, and, in order to render myself worthy of it, am making your first volume thoroughly my own by the most diligent study.

May I ask you to give some attention to the inclosed papers, and especially to procure for me the autograph of your honored father. Recommending myself once more to your kind remembrance and friendly sympathy.

GOETHE.

WEIMAR, *17th December*, 1811.

CXLI.

TO MADAME HENSLER.

BERLIN, *14th January*, 1812.

......I do not take M.'s verdict in bad part. The two great Greek historians are essentially episodical, and if I wrote better than I do, I should, no doubt, place and connect the episodes with more art, but there would certainly be rather more than fewer of them. For do we see a country by merely traveling throught it on the most direct post roads, or by deviating frequently from the route, while keeping to one main direction?......

CXLII.

BERLIN, *28th January*, 1812.

The censure passed by some upon the inequality of my style was not unexpected. I can not trust myself to decide whether it is deserved or not. You are well aware that the style, such as it is, is the unsought-for expression of my thoughts at the moment, and never affected. That inequality is not a fault in itself, and that the simplicity of a chronicle may stand side by side with poetry in the same historical work, I am ready to maintain against any one; for there is much that is only rendered bearable by the greatest simplicity of expression, but with that becomes even good; and then, again, there are parts where the clearness of your inward vision raises your style to what is called poetical. In this sense, Thucydides is unequal, so unequal that, even in ancient times, critics have doubted whether the eighth book was his composition; and how unequal is Demosthenes in one and the same oration! Must not the style naturally follow the change of the subject? Cicero is very uniform; I think not altogether to his praise. For uniformity is the color which the writer lays on; though I allow that a great author *may* have such a perfect command over his subject as to bring even the most dissimilar parts into one ground tone without injury, as Tacitus has done in his *latest* work, the "Annals:" with the modern writers, however, who have attempted this, objective truth is utterly lost. Should I some day, when the first volumes are quite completed, be able to prepare a new edition, I will conscientiously examine whether I have caught the right tone for each passage; I may have failed in this respect, but I can not judge of it at present. However, the judgment of the reader on this point does not trouble me much; few, if I may venture to say so, are familiar with the true antique style, and can enter into its spirit when presented to them under a new form; and as such, in fact, I regard the varying tone of my discourse. Does not Shakspeare give us the most commonplace language in one scene, and, in the next, the highest poetry? Is it possible, for instance, to relate the Bavarian War of Succession, and the struggle of Thermopylæ, with the same cast of expression?

I am not quite satisfied with the few first sheets of the second volume, which are now printed; they are wanting in life and movement. It is a bad thing to be obliged to force oneself to work of this kind; industry we can command, but the state of mind comes from God and from without. Meanwhile, the contents are not bad. I am continually finding confirmations and developments of my fundamental views. In my lectures I have just been relating the story of Pyrrhus with real pleasure; he has always been my favorite hero......*

CXLIII.

BERLIN, *6th March*, 1812.

I thank you for the sympathy expressed by your anxiety about my health, but there is no cause for uneasiness. It is not likely that I shall be really and permanently well before the spring. There is some one ill in every house; nearly all my acquaintances are more or less unwell, low-spirited, and good for nothing. I fear that the traces of my present state will be only too visible in my book......

So Müller's Letters have made as agreeable an impression upon you as they did upon Savigny; but with him this impression has not proved lasting.

I have not seen them yet, because I do not choose to buy them. They will be as remarkable as those to Bonstetten, but I can not blind myself to the fact that, from his earliest youth, Müller's † feelings and opinions were made up. The pure vital breath and freshness of truth are wanting in all his writings. He had an extraordinary talent for assuming a character, and maintaining it with consistency, till he changed it again for another; but, after reading his writings on the Bellum Cimbricum, it would have been clear to me, from now to the day of judgment, that he had no native solidity of character, even had I never seen him. There was no harmony in him, and the sources of his power gradually dried up as he advanced in age. His talents marked him out for a literary man in the narrowest sense of the term; historical criticism was utterly foreign to him; his imagination had no wide range, and the unexampled multitude of facts which he accumulated, remained in reality a lifeless and unorganized mass in his head. Forgive me for this verdict: you will not suspect that I, who am only just coming forward as an historical author, would willingly say any thing in disparagement of the man who enjoys the highest celebrity among us in this department; though he is hardly read at all, and the worthlessness of his "Universal History" is acknowledged even by his admirers......

CXLIV.

BERLIN, *21st April*, 1812.

Again your letter has come a day too late. Though we could not have

* In the latter part of this letter, and in the next, dated 22d February, he gives an account of a serious illness he had about this time.

† Johannes von Müller, the celebrated author of the "Universal History" and the "History of Switzerland," the first German historian who attained literary excellence in the treatment of his subject. The great blot upon his character is his abandonment of his country's cause, and espousing the French interests in the calamitous days of October, 1806. He had drawn up the Prussian manifesto before the battle of Jena, and when the French entered Berlin on the 27th October, he was the first to announce his adhesion to the Emperor Napoleon. When the news of the battles of Jena and Auerstädt reached Berlin, and it was evident that the authorities must remove northward, Niebuhr called on Müller to propose that they should travel together to Stettin. Müller, who had not long before been appointed historiographer, and had just comfortably settled himself and his library in his residence, replied, pointing round to his precious books, "Alas! traveling is out of the question for me; look at these; what can I do?" "The man who can think of his books *now* is a scoundrel!" muttered Niebuhr indignantly, as he turned on his heel.

concluded with certainty, from the delay, that it had been opened, its appearance left no doubt on this point. This must, however, explain and justify to you my silence respecting our hopes and fears, even when they positively concern our own fate. Besides, all my knowledge is confined to mere rumors. The impending stroke is preparing with a most undeniably judicious secrecy. All that I can say—and that is rather based upon calculation than positive testimony—is, that none of the reports about the possible continuance of peace deserve any attention. The armies are collecting from all sides. Such enormous masses of men have never before been brought against each other in the whole course of modern history, indeed never since the Crusades and the migration of races. The long continuance of winter weather may a little delay the opening of the campaign; for in East Prussia they are still using sledges, and when the frost breaks, the state of the roads will prevent any rapid operations for a few weeks.

Dumas is here as Intendant-general of the army. I met him at the Princess Radziwill's and we have since exchanged visits. Nicolovius has invited him and me to dine at his house to-day. He is very friendly, and inquires very particularly after all his friends in Holstein.

And now we will retire from the outward world into our own private one. Milly is constantly unwell without being positively weak. But it pains and alarms me that the physician does not seem to know what measures to take for her relief. Her cough remains just the same in spite of all remedies. I am rather better than for some weeks past.

I have now finished the most difficult part of my book—the Roman law respecting the public lands.

I have felt the death of old Hegewisch deeply. So his fainting fits last summer were the beginning of his gradual decay. People in Germany were no longer just to him. His best writings were forgotten.......

CXLV.

BERLIN, 16*th June*, 1812.

It will be an evil omen to you that Milly's pain in the eyes continues, when you see, on opening this letter, that she has again left me the greater part of the space. It is even so, &c.......

We are reading Wilhelm Meister at present, as fast as my want of practice in reading aloud will permit. I had never before been able to take any pleasure in this book, and was curious to see if it would be different now, as in middle age we are less one-sided than in youth, and can enjoy relative and separate beauties, even when the whole does not make an agreeable or overpowering impression on us. But it is the same as ever with me. Our language possesses, probably, nothing more elaborate or more perfect in style (excepting Klopstock's "Republic of Letters"); in clearness of outline and vividness of coloring, there is nothing to compare with it in our literature; it contains a multitude of acute remarks and magnificent passages; the situations are managed with extreme ingenuity, and all the parts are in admirable keeping; all this I can appreciate now better than formerly. But the unnaturalness of the plot, the violence with which what is beautifully sketched and executed in single groups is brought to bear upon the development, and mysterious conduct of the whole, the impossibilities such a plot involves, and the thorough heartlessness, which even makes one linger with the greater interest by the utterly sensual personages, because they do show something akin to feeling; the villainy or meanness of the heroes, whose portraits nevertheless often amuse us—all this still makes the book revolting to me, and I get disgusted with such a menagerie of tame cattle.

Is it not your feeling, too, that few things leave a more painful impression than for a great spirit to bind its own wings, and seek to excel in the lower regions of art, while renouncing the higher? Goethe is the poet of human passion and human greatness under all their manifestations, and as such he appears in his early poems. Probably, indeed, he might then have made himself master of the whole sphere, to the furthest limits of which he was often involuntarily borne on the wings of spontaneous inward impulse. He neglected to possess himself of this united realm, which perhaps no single intellect had ever ruled with so absolute a sway as might have been his, and the wild and fragmentary character of his youthful productions displeased even himself in his riper years. It was chiefly after he had studied art, during his travels in Italy, that he strove after unity and completeness. His first attempts in this style, and his productions from 1786 to 1790, are quite unworthy of him. They simply display a thoroughly unpoetical, wearisome reality. But he wished to become a master in this style as well as in others, and to do so, he narrowed his mind. To me this is most melancholy. If you study his writings from this time forward, you find in nearly all of them a tameness which is quite unnatural to him. By degrees, there appears some re-awakening of his native and peculiar feelings, particularly with reference to his own inward life, at least in recollection; but the years gone by are lost, and, through them, those also which yet remain to him. I hope that he will find his youth restored by living through his history again in memory. The second part will be certain to come out at Michaelmas. So early as the end of April he went to Carlsbad, to work there in solitude. They expect him back at Weimar this month. We shall not see him now this year, but I shall write to him more at length when I send him my second volume.

The physical sciences had been so exclusively limited to what was visible and demonstrable, that a reaction was inevitable as soon as the one-sidedness of this was perceived; now, when you find it said, in so many words, in printed books, that a dreaming state is higher than a waking one, and that madness is the highest condition of humanity—now the charlatans have done their worst, and the ridicule with which they have covered themselves, will soon put an end to their trade.* The good will then remain, and a considerable interval will elapse before people can return to the old one-sided views. For, in truth, it is ever the fate of modern nations to oscillate between two follies.

Have you seen A. W. Schlegel's noble Essay on the old German poetry, in the January number of the "Deutches Museum?"

I have filled these two pages with the things by which we try to divert our attention from the sorrow impending over all. If I could write to you on this subject, I should have much to say.......

CXLVI.

BERLIN, *27th June*, 1812.

You will have seen from the proclamation of the Emperor Napoleon, that

* This refers to animal magnetism.

the war has actually begun by this time. We know nothing here as yet of the events that have happened.

We have not yet finished "Wilhelm Meister;" the latter part pleases me no better. Mdlle. Klettenberg is alluded to in the "Confessions of a Beautiful Soul."

You will have seen Stein's arrival in Hamburgh from the newspapers. It is said that he is going to St. Petersburg, by invitation of the Emperor.

We are calm and composed, but not cheerful, still less mirthful, for this is a solemn and critical epoch. The war is inflicting no wounds on this part of the country, but all is sick enough, and the bleeding provinces which have to supply the resources of war, will, in time, infect the capital with their fever. The accounts from East Prussia, which had not fully recovered from the last war before this new misery began, are enough to overwhelm one with grief......

CXLVII.

Berlin, *11th July*, 1812.

We have no news whatever from the seat of war; it appears that we shall have to learn them first from the pages of the "Moniteur." We only know that the whole of the northern French army stands on Russian soil. How far the Russians have retreated, whether they make any show of offering resistance on any part of the road between the Niemen and the Dwina, probably no human being here knows. This utter silence respecting events of such prodigious magnitude, heightens the terrors of expectation. Meanwhile, it enables us to concentrate ourselves more entirely on the present, by leaving us leisure for other thoughts and occupations.....

I do not even read any thing requiring exertion at present, but, among other things, I have taken up Klopstock's "Correspondence." I find it very attractive, and still more instructive. The more you study it, the more materials do you find in it for the intellectual history of our nation; and it exhibits the history of Klopstock's mind, with scarcely a break, from the year 1750 onward. In these letters his character appears indescribably amiable, sincere, and spotless, which we certainly knew before to be the case. They give a singular picture of the period in which his youth was passed. Accustomed as we are to great variety and precision of thought, the circle of ideas prevailing then seems to us poor and narrow; each one is occupied about himself; all are, we may almost say, ignorant, contented, nay, even delighted with things that we should with reason pronounce mediocre, and filled with reverence for men who would now be thought commonplace; all of them are so self-important, so convinced that their united works must form a golden age of literature. And for this reason they have all faded and passed away, except Klopstock, who, in his innocence, was far enough from suspecting how little they were his equals. There is something really maidenly about him and the best of his friends, not only in the good sense of the word, but in that which is incompatible with the manly character, particularly in that limitation of their range of thought I have mentioned. From the beginning to the end of his correspondence, you could not perhaps find a single uncommon, or even ingenious idea, nor yet in any of his works, except the "Republic of Letters." It is possible that such ideas, like all abstractions, are only suggested when the mental harmony is somewhat disturbed, and that he would not have retained that deep peace, in which he always lived, if he had attempted to fix his attention voluntarily and exclusively on objects of reflection. But how much higher, how near the ancients he might have stood, if he had done so—if his cultivation had not been so extremely one-sided, and on the whole—to confess the truth—so indolently carried on! I have just been looking at several of the metres he invented, and have made a singular discovery. In the beginning of each piece, as you know, he marks the metre, and, till now, I have always read his verses as he has marked them, and often found them unpleasing, or discovered strophes where the measure was not sustained. But this time I have read them without reference to his divisions, according to the rules of Greek rhythm, with which he was quite unacquainted, and find that they then possess the most beautiful cadence of the old Greek poetry. O that he had but poured into these beautiful forms a corresponding richness of meaning! For it can not be denied that, excepting the lays of his love, his odes do not speak to the heart at all, or only address themselves to a few of its emotions, and never fill and raise the soul as a single verse of a Greek lyric poet has power to do. The character of the women, too, is a remarkable feature of the times of Klopstock's youth. The cultivation of the mind was carried incomparably farther with them, than with nearly all the young women of our days; and this we should scarcely have expected to find in the contemporaries of our grandmothers. It was not, therefore, the work of our native literature, for that first rose into being along with, and under the influence of the love inspired by these charming maidens. For some time after the Thirty Years' War the ladies of Germany, particularly those of the middle classes, were excessively coarse and uneducated, as is proved beyond a doubt by a curious Book of Manners which I have bought this winter. This wonderful alteration must have taken place, therefore, during the eighty years from 1660 to 1740, though we are quite ignorant how and when it began.......

Jacobi is certainly right when he says, that it is only existence in motion which excites our interest in others—ideas as they rise up; nothing that merely rests in their memory affects our feelings toward them. Perhaps it may do so on a first acquaintance, but it soon runs dry, and then such friendship is at an end. We can never grow weary of that sound sense which on all occasions, great or small, answers to every appeal.

CXLVIII.

TO V**

BERLIN, *12th July*, 1812.

......To all that you say against a Church union,* which must end either in the subjection of our Church to the domination of the Catholic, or the destruction of that which is regarded by the latter as its essential excellence, I subscribe with all my heart; as well as to all that you say on the folly of expecting spiritual benefit from the ceremonies of the latter. With equal warmth do I sympathize in your indignation against the pseudo-Mystics; not less against those who are a prey to their own over-excited feelings, than against those who are enacting a revolting and scandalous farce.

* Referring to the wish, then entertained by many pious persons, for such a reform in the Catholic Church, as should enable the Protestant to unite with it.

On the other hand, I must confess that I do not coincide in the views you have expressed in your essay, respecting that which you also call Mysticism, and the philosophy of religion which you recognize as Protestantism. That you may not mistake me, however, and suppose that I lay claim to beliefs and feelings which I do not possess—therefore dare not even seem to possess—I must just simply repeat to you what, if I mistake not, I have said already in the conversation which your friendship has deemed it worth while to remember.

Faith, properly so called, in a much wider sense than religious faith, it is either not given to every nature to possess, or the possibility of its taking root and flourishing, may be annihilated by an inharmonious intellectual life. The soil may be fertile, but the climate ungenial. My intellect early took a skeptical direction. With my whole attention bent upon the real and the historical, eager to comprehend, and to get to the bottom of every thing, I let my thoughts follow the natural association of ideas, without endeavoring to guide them into any particular channel; and in this respect had neither, properly speaking, a truly creative imagination, nor any strong feeling of the need of something beyond the boundaries of experience to satisfy my heart; or perhaps I let both perish for want of nourishment. Altogether, it was very seldom that the consciousness of a thought vanished from my mind in the contemplation of its import and object. To this, unquestionably my natural turn of mind, was added the influence of miserable religious instruction, and of the living study of classical antiquity. Thus, it was in riper years, and through the study of history, that I came back for the first time to the sacred books, which I read in a purely critical spirit, and with the purpose of studying their contents as the groundwork of one of the most remarkable phenomena in the history of the world. This was not a mood in which real faith could spring up, for it was that of the Protestantism of the present day. I needed no Wolfenbüttel Fragments* to discover the discrepancies of the Gospels, and the impossibility of even drawing the outlines of a tenable history of the life of Jesus by such criticism. In the Messianic allusions to the Old Testament, I could recognize no prophecies, and could explain all the passages adduced with perfect ease. But here, as in every historical subject, when I contemplated the immeasurable gulf between the narrative and the facts narrated, this disturbed me no further. He, whose earthly life and sorrows were depicted, had for me a perfectly real existence, and his whole history had the same reality, even if it were not related with literal exactness in any single point. Hence also the fundamental fact of miracles which, according to my conviction, must be conceded, unless we adopt the not merely incomprehensible, but absurd hypothesis, that the Holiest was a deceiver, and his disciples either dupes or liars; and that deceivers had preached a holy religion, in which self-renunciation is every thing, and in which there is nothing tending toward the erection of a priestly rule—nothing that can be acceptable to vicious inclinations. As regards a miracle in the strictest sense, it really only requires an unprejudiced and penetrating study of nature, to see that those related are as far as possible from

* The anonymous fragments on the discrepancies of the Gospel narratives, edited by Lessing while head-librarian at Wolfenbüttel. Lessing was long supposed to have written them himself, but after his death clear proofs were found among his papers that they were from the pen of Reimarus.

absurdity, and a comparison with legends, or the pretended miracles of other religions, to perceive by what a different spirit they are animated.

According to these statements, I might, perhaps, fairly claim to be called a genuine Protestant Christian; to be recognized by a Church, which does not even thrust from her bosom those who make Christ into a cunning political aspirant—a skillful charlatan and juggler—men who, it is to be hoped, will not die without receiving the punishment of indignant universal contempt, and whom you, my respected friend, no doubt likewise despise in your heart, mild as your words are with respect to these blasphemers. Nevertheless, I can not as yet make this claim for myself, nor would Luther recognize it, for I am far from having so firm a faith in these objects, so vivid a certainty of them, as of those of historical experience; they are still only in and among my thoughts—not external to, and above me.

In the sense in which many, and in which you in your paper, use the term Mystics, you can not, in truth, save the Reformers themselves from this name. For are the ideas of incarnation, redemption, divine grace, any thing else than mystical? Mysticism, as I conceive (apart from the follies that usurp the name), is nothing else than the belief, that the pious man, only capable of longing and striving after a state of faith and Christian temper of mind, attains these through a supernatural assistance; and, when he has been made a partaker of them, may receive an illumination of the heart and mind, in a manner inexplicable by logic and psychology. and to them foolishness. Who can deny that this may give rise to the wildest fanaticism? But, on the other hand, who can deny that people the latchet of whose shoes I am not worthy to unloose, have held this belief with unshakable confidence, and that the reflection of their faith shines out in their writings and deeds? This mysticism is certainly capable of taking such various shapes, that one in whom it is a spontaneous growth, and who has not been born in the Catholic Church, can not possibly accommodate his feelings and thoughts to her unity. And yet, that it finds more nourishment in the Catholic Church than in ours, is also undeniable. Let us turn away from the misguided men, who counsel us to restore the piety, of which they have not a conception themselves, by ceremonies and sacrificial rites. But let us not refuse to recognize, that the Catholic Church speaks to the heart in many things where ours is dumb; that we must not judge of her doctrines (her tyrannical hierarchy is another matter) from their degeneration into senseless, heartless, decrepit formalisms; that a genuine mystic, like Fénélon, might develop his spiritual life with the greatest energy within her fold, without running the risk of spiritual pride, and enthusiasm in the bad sense, to which our Protestant mystics are exposed. Confession may be very unnecessary for him who acts sincerely by himself; but so is the sermon, too, for such a one; and after all, is not the latter always destitute of special application for the larger part of the hearers, while the former is quite personal? Confession may be addressed to very unworthy ministers, but are there no preachers of the same stamp? Why is it necessary for us to represent absolution in its most exaggerated form? Do we not absolve ourselves daily, without having confessed ourselves very strictly? And in what a communion of love does the truly pious Catholic stand, through the whole series of blessed spirits and saints up to the person of Christ, who, connected with him by this unbroken line, is therefore more of a mediator to him!

If, therefore, a longing, harassed, pious Protestant, in despair at the deadness of his own Church, and the waxen image which bears her name, should cast a look of love upon the Catholic Church, while concealing her weak points from himself; if he creates an illusion for himself all the more readily because he has probably never seen her priestcraft, or not in its degeneracy—we ought not, I think, to take offense at such a one.

Certainly, we are bound to say to one who goes too far in his admiration, Do not transfer your ideal to that the reality of which you are able to test! See how the spirit, for whose sake alone, you are ready to cling with love to a figure the aspect of which would else terrify you, never penetrated its substance, and show us where it dwells in it now, and say whether necessarily in this form! See how that very tendency toward the Ideal, which has produced many of its peculiarities, when it has vanished, leaves something behind much worse than that which preceded it, as such a tendency always does; how hypocrisy and rant have grown out of asceticism, priestly tyranny out of church discipline, the wildest license from mortification of the flesh! The forms are still there, wherever the Catholic religion exists, but if the spirit have fled from the existing forms, how can you hope to awaken it again through the outward assumption of these very forms?

Is it quite correct that the decline of religion has proceeded from the Catholic countries? A moral turpitude, which is hostile to religion, has undoubtedly always prevailed among the people of Romanic descent, but as a national characteristic, and quite apart, by the side of strict faith in the Church, or blind obedience fancying itself faith. Thus it is still at the present day.

With us, as it appears to me, indifferentism took its rise from indignation at the revolting *Orthodox* party, who persecuted the Mystics, Spener, Franke, &c., in a truly popish spirit, carrying the insolence of priestly claims to an extent that no Capuchin could exceed.* I quite understand how those who lived under their rod of discipline, if they did not become Mystics, should turn aside to free-thinking with bitter hatred. The real Protestant free-thinking, however, which has usurped the territory of the

* Spener and Franke were the principal authors of a revival of religion which took place in the Lutheran Church, in the latter part of the seventeenth century, very similar to that which took place in England, in the eighteenth century, owing to the influence of the Wesleys and Whitefield. The Lutheran church had become as dead and formal, previous to this awakening, as the Church of England in the last century, but there was this great difference between the two reforms: in the dead English Church, morality was preached without those doctrines which touch the heart-springs and give the languid will energy to perform the duties required; in the dead Lutheran Church, dogmas were preached to the neglect of morality and the cultivation of devotional feeling; hence the one reform brought the doctrines of the gospel forward, so prominently as sometimes to throw the inculcations of morality into the background, while the other neglected positive dogmas, in the endeavor to kindle a living flame of devotion in the heart, and to purify the life. The Pietists of Germany were persecuted by the old orthodox party nearly as much as the Methodists in England; but, happily for the Lutheran Church, their opponents did not succeed in excluding them from its pale, as was the case with the enemies of the analogous party in England. Franke was also the founder of the great Orphan House at Halle, still flourishing at the present day.

Church, and would fain continue to bear sway under the name of the vanquished party, appears to me to have been imported entirely from England. The free-masonry which likewise, at the beginning of the eighteenth century, spread first through North Germany, and thence into other parts, may have greatly promoted it in the first instance. Voltaire and the French "*belles-lettres*" philosophy rather aided the former, than had much independent agency, except among the higher classes. In the eighteenth century, however, it was not these, but our middle classes who determined the national turn of thought in Protestant Germany.

You remind the panegyrists of the Catholic Church, with great reason, that the most beautiful hymns have been composed by Protestants. In modern times certainly, at least with very few exceptions. But have not all really exalted and elevating poems of this kind been composed by Mystics? Is there one of them that can find favor among rationalistic theologians, if it be not hacked and remodeled in all directions? Undoubtedly it is a revolting absurdity when people say religion is poetry, for the good meaning which we might put upon the expression, is its imposed, not its natural one. But the root of poetry—feeling and intuition—is certainly also the root of faith.

I often ask myself, what shall we come to? In Catholic countries the clergy is dying out; in a short time men will neither be able nor willing to take orders. Among ourselves we have names, and forms, and a universal dull consciousness that all is not right; every one is ill at ease; we feel like ghosts in a living body. I speak only of the Continent; for in England, I grant, Christianity stands firm as a rock, from the very fact of the innumerable sects ever newly springing up, which testify to the fertility of the soil. But I am perfectly tranquil as to the result. We shall become truer and purer, when every thing has been eliminated, which does not belong to the heart of any of the numerous sects that will then develop themselves. "Offenses must come, but woe be to him by whom they come!" I would not overthrow the dead Church, but if she fall, it will cause me no uneasiness. Let us trust that a comforter will come, a new Light, when we least expect it. All the sorrows of this era will lead on toward the truth, if we are only willing.*

CXLIX.

TO COUNT ADAM MOLTKE.

BERLIN, 15*th August*, 1812.

......Perthes was here a few weeks ago; when you see him he will tell you how comfortable I am at present. How long it will continue so, I leave fearlessly to fate. Things certainly will not *remain* quite so pleasant, not only because external circumstances will almost inevitably stand in the way, but also because my outward position is really *too* enviable. Much is wanting which can not be compensated, but this can not be reckoned as belonging to my outward position; the latter could not possibly be more favorable in any part of Germany, though we live in the midst of a sandy desert, and far away from beautiful objects of any description. You shall allow yourself to be persuaded to carry out the plan you former-

* This letter should be read in connection with those addressed to Madame Hensler, written from Rome, of 7th March, and 1st May, 1818.

ly mentioned, of residing for a time in Berlin. You, who are so fond of interesting society, could not but find this singular colony of intellectual and accomplished men, collected from all parts of Germany, exceedingly attractive, though you would not be equally pleased with what is, strictly speaking, native to the place. Before you receive my letter, Perthes will have sent you, in my name, the second volume of my History. You will see that the work here begins to take the form of a regular history, though the digressions, which you wished away in the first volume, will be found here in equal number. In the third, they will be of little importance. A deep silence still reigns in Germany; I do not know whether it is that people are startled at the new phenomenon; or whether they neither understand the style, nor enter into the mode of thought and treatment. I do not know whether I shall ever have the satisfaction of seeing the public on my side. An author ought not to make advances to the public, but it is very seldom that a great work entirely fails in gaining it over.

I shall hardly finish the third volume during this winter. I had worked myself quite stupid; complete relaxation, and the Pyrmont waters are now, however, refreshing me greatly. But, on the one hand, I must sketch the outline of a course of lectures for the winter, on Roman Antiquities, as bringing my ideas into train for the History; and, on the other, I find change of subject beneficial, and Greece allures me now with charms as strong as those she had for me in my youth. O how would philology be cherished, if people knew the magical delight of living and moving amid the most beautiful scenes of the past! The mere reading is the smallest part of it; the great thing is to feel familiar with Greece and Rome during their most widely different periods! I wish to write history with such vividness—so to replace vague by well-defined images—so to disentangle confused representations, that the name of a Greek of the age of Polybius and Thucydides, or that of a Roman in the times of Cato or Tacitus, should instantly call up in the mind the fundamental idea of their character. May I succeed in my object! There is no want of materials; we can not excuse ourselves on that ground; if we fail, the fault lies wholly in ourselves. I should like to write, in the same way, on the golden age of Greece, then on the rise of the sciences and the decline of poetry, and on the immeasurable gulf between the age of Pericles and that of Demosthenes. I should further like to write a work on ancient literature as a whole, similar to Schlegel's "Lectures on the Drama," (which you, too, of course, think glorious?) on the lost writings, as well as those still extant, from Homer to the Byzantines.

But the Roman history shall not be neglected. What is the most likely to keep me back, is the difficulty of meeting with thoroughly good military maps, without which there is much that it is scarcely possible to describe. Fancy and divination may certainly often hit the mark; but they can not so imperatively demand belief.

What are you working at? You scarcely allude to it, and Perthes knew nothing about it.

Farewell, my dear Moltke. Do not repay me evil for my silence, and accept, with your old affection, Milly's and my own best love to yourself and the boys.

Your faithful NIEBUHR.

CL.

TO MADAME HENSLER.

BERLIN, 19*th August*, 1812.

......As to the aim of Wilhelm Meister, you will probably have somewhat changed your opinion by this time, as I suppose you are near the end of the book. Goethe has certainly written it, in part perhaps designedly, in part unconsciously, as a representation of the stage. The disenchantment of the enthusiast, and his picture of the universal worthlessness of the players, even of those among them who are real artists, are very likely a satire upon himself, as no one ever carried the passion for the stage, and the attempt to cultivate the taste of the players further than Goethe. I have made another conjecture, which I can not indeed verify in a few lines, but it might be established by a comparison of passages differing widely in other respects. It is that he meant to bring forward the following view (at all events in the work as it now stands, for the first sketch of it was made at least as early as 1799, and was, no doubt, quite inartificial), that each will succeed best in his own style, by following out his original tastes, and cultivating them to perfection; that though there are perfectly pure and highly exalted natures, others coarse and superficial, and some even false, all are good of their kind. Further, that it is a folly to regard accidents as judgments, and the circumstances that alter the direction of our life as providential; and finally (toward which much in the "Elective Affinities" also tends), that what we deem our wise resolutions, will usually work much evil to ourselves and others, if they break any link in the natural chain of our destinies. I by no means commend all these views; that they are Goethe's, and contained in this book, I am ready to maintain. Many parts are, no doubt, simply poetical, without any ulterior aim, and the whole would be most likely better if there were more of the same kind.

I am now busily engaged with the Greeks. I think I never appreciated them so keenly before. Moreover, some very crude productions on the subject have given me a great inclination to use up a few sheets, in sketching a survey of the different periods of the intellectual history of the Greeks, from their golden age, to that in which they were in no way superior to ourselves.

Oersted* leaves to-morrow for the Rhine and Paris. I am really very sorry to lose him; I scarcely know another natural philosopher who has so much intellect, and freedom from prejudice and *esprit de corps:* then, too, he keeps within bounds, and never loses himself in arbitrary conjectures. Besides, his character is very estimable; and he parts from me with regret. Thank God it seems as if the dangers which threatened you were passing away.

CLI.

BERLIN, 8*th September*, 1812.

......It interferes much with close study that we have troops always quartered upon us, and that they are perpetually changing.

During this vacation, I have been reviewing all kinds of books, not without a reference to the circumstances of the times. But I have another object, namely, to earn some money for a friend who wants it. I find re-

* The celebrated natural philosopher, and author of Der Geist in der Natur.

viewing no pleasant task; I should like to get hold of books that I could really take pleasure in, and recommend, but I very seldom hit upon such; most of those which come before me are a tissue of shallowness and error, often, too, of gross ignorance, in which I really can not find any thing to praise.

I continue to take the waters, and thereby lose a great deal of time. The time for my lectures, too, is approaching, but that does not alarm me, as I mean to deliver them extempore, and have most of my materials already stored up in my memory. This course will be a very useful one for the young men.

I began reading Plato a short time ago. Theages is still my favorite, of the dialogues that I have read afresh; the declaration of the young man, that he feels himself better and higher, if he is only in the same house with Socrates, and the more so, the nearer he is to him, and the most so, when he can look into his eyes and read his soul, is worth more to me than the most acute dialectics, where you have to toil through ever so many long dialogues, and gain nothing at the end. But such an evidence of emotions which we have experienced, and still experience ourselves, when we think of any of the few great men of our own day, is worth much. I have also been reading a tragedy of Sophocles again, and was glad to find that I was more moved by it than I had ever been before....

CLII.

BERLIN, 2*d October*, 1812.

For the last week past, our slumbering anxieties respecting Denmark have been revived, and in a way that makes it difficult to calm them by unbelief. You say nothing on this subject, perhaps lest we should be alarmed, perhaps for the same reasons which kept us silent, when we knew more about the progress of the war than the papers told us. But it seems almost impossible for the storm to blow over, and whatever may be its issue, it will bring misery and calamity to our poor fatherland. This apprehension lies heavy on my heart, but of course I can not tell you in writing the possibilities I fear. Devastation is now proceeding with fearful strides, from the deserts that are forming in Russia, to the total failure of the crops in Norway. I am not ashamed to confess to the selfishness of affection, and that amid all these horrors, I am thinking with a heavy heart of the misfortune which the paper currency will bring on my nearest and dearest friends......

I have seen here a collection of antique works of art, which is quite unique. It was made by Klaproth, and belongs to him, but he is of such a retiring disposition that its very existence is news to every one to whom I mention it. The collection consists of antique works in glass; some are mosaic, some transparent, some opaque glass of the most exquisite colors. Two singularly-shaped pieces have come from Guinea, where they have been used as sceptre points by the negro princes. There can not be the least doubt that they have traveled thither from Carthage. Klaproth has also some fragments of metal mirrors, where the proportions are precisely those of Herschel's telescope. The Greeks were no artists in chemistry, and the Romans knew absolutely nothing of it; hence it is only through analysis and actual observation that we discover how, *even in these things*, we stand below the ancients. Stranger still; many chemical preparations, colors for instance, were still handed down by tradition, and kept as a secret in the sixteenth century, that are now lost, and seem to have been invaluable. Science is advancing very rapidly now, but she is grown an utter stranger to art.

CLIII.

TO PERTHES.*

October, 1812.

Our dear Nicolovius lost no time in conveying to me the good news he had heard from you. I have not seen him again since then, and do not know whether he is writing to you; if he has not time to do so, I know I may say, in his name as well as our own, how much we are pleased, and wish you and your dear wife joy from the bottom of our hearts. When the little boy is as old as one of us (you or I), and is talking with his gray-haired parents about the evil times when he was born, I trust he will be able to thank Heaven for having lived from his youth in so fresh a period of regeneration, and revival from desolation; and that it will be a better founded prosperity than that which followed the Seven Years' War. You see that I expect good days for you and your wife yet.

Do works of art, if not very expensive, still find a sale in your provinces? (I consider you as sovereign of the publishing trade from the Ems to the Baltic.) There is coming out here, but it has not yet appeared, and the price is not fixed, a very beautiful set of "Studies from the old Italian Masters," (*i.e.* Giotto, Gaddi, and Masaccio), by an artist named Kuhbeil, who is as poor as a rat, has lived upon contemplation and labor in Italy, mended his own shoes, &c. Some of them are from the pieces which the Riepenhausens have copied, but, according to the testimony of eye-witnesses, incomparably more faithful. There are really sublime things among them. Nicolovius takes a great interest in the work. Should you be able to assist its circulation? By-the-by, it is remarkable that, even in France, people are beginning to suspect that this old art was really in spirit the highest, and that while Raphael, who may bear the same relation to these old masters as Sophocles to the earliest lyric poets, rose to the very summit of art—with him likewise, the inspiration of genius departed. When you see a light breaking in upon questions like these, upon which you have made up your own mind in silence for years, it reconciles you to much else that displeases you in your contemporaries. It has given me downright delight to see the Leipsic Catalogue so thin; only two pages of novels! I must confess that it looks very miserable in other respects, too.

* Perthes was one of the largest booksellers and publishers in Germany, a man of uncommon energy, enterprise, and good sense. He was a friend of many of the most distinguished men of his day, and was intimately connected with the Holstein circle, among whom Niebuhr passed his early years, from whom he imbibed much of their peculiar religious tendency. He was a determined opponent of the French rule in Germany, and took so active a part in the insurrection which freed Hamburgh from the French yoke for a short time in 1813, that, on the return of Davoust, he was proscribed. His friendship with Niebuhr began when both were young, and lasted through life, though its continuance was threatened in the winter of 1813–14, because Niebuhr would not concede the honor to the conduct of Hamburgh which Perthes thought it deserved, and, in the "Preussische Correspondent," compared it, in a depreciating style, with the heroism of Prussia. Nicolovius, however, prevented a breach, and from this time they remained in habits of the most friendly intercourse.

The Catalogue you will bring out will not be much calculated to bring our literature into repute among foreigners.

What will become of poor Denmark ?......Are not you, too, startled at the Sicilian constitution ? (The "Hamburgische Correspondent" has, no doubt, given you an account of it.) Don't you see that it is altogether the work of the aristocracy ? It is true that many grievances are cleared away at a stroke, over which travelers have lamented, for the last forty years, as hindrances to prosperity ; and the island may become wealthy ; but how can there be tranquillity ? Every thing will go on seething and fermenting. England sends forth in all directions, probably quite unsuspected by the ministers, a spirit of republicanism, which will make that country as much disliked by all sovereigns and governments, as it is already by their subjects for its conduct with regard to their commercial and manufacturing interests. The emancipation of the Irish Catholics is a crisis in the English Constitution itself, through which the republican portion of their institutions receives increased power, and H—— is certainly quite wrong in asserting that the English will end with an absolute monarchy. They are much more likely to try a republic, unless fate has pre-ordained it otherwise.

CLIV.

TO JACOBI.

BERLIN, *November* 21*st*, 1811.

HONORED JACOBI—How I am to begin the first letter after a silence of many years—how I am to select the most essential particulars from among the thousand things I might say to you—how I am to arrange these most essential points, on which I would fain speak unreservedly, in any kind of order, is an enigma which I can find no means of solving. . . . .

That you have sent me your work, which I received a few days ago from our dear and noble Nicolovius as a gift from you, has afforded me an encouragement, for which, however, I should not have waited before approaching you once more. Perhaps you have already received the first part of my Roman History through Lindner ; at all events it will most probably be in your hands before this letter reaches you. May you accept it with as much kindness and indulgence as I feel gratitude and affection for your gift ; may you be able to connect it with long-past years, the broken thread of which has for me been re-united by this token of remembrance from you !

I still remember most vividly—as it is impossible that you should do—how, in the years of my ardent youth, I sat at your feet, rejoicing in the kindness with which you listened to my dreams of the possibility that I might one day be capable of restoring the history of antiquity, and encouraged me to work toward their realization. I must confess, that you will not find the ideal, which then stood before me, fulfilled in the attempt to transform these dreams into waking realities, which I have at last undertaken, after many, and in some degree wasted years, and with but the remnants of my original powers. Yet I am equally convinced that you will not regard as insignificant my diligent and not quite fruitless researches, nor look on some of their results as mere creations of the brain, though at first they will be so termed by many till they have grown accustomed to the unusual shapes. And if you do find that you may say of the difference between the early ideal and the later reality, that the amphora has been turned into a pot, yet coarse potter's ware can not be dispensed with, and the man who can make no better is sufficiently punished by his incapacity.

To know you, to see and hear you, was one of the highest enjoyments of those few years of my youth, which succeeded a period of frequent depression, and were passed in the intoxication of brilliant day-dreams—in a sort of heaven upon earth. It was not that my youthful vanity was flattered by your kindness—it was a pure and perfectly innocent sentiment. That it was so is proved, perhaps, most incontestably by another sentiment which grew up beside it, and at last, like the lean kine of the seer, swallowed it up, and brought about my separation from you.

I have indeed now no right to make confessions, but here they can not be avoided.

I was born with an inward discord, the existence of which I can trace back to my earliest childhood, though it was afterward much aggravated by an education ill adapted to my nature, or rather, by a mixture of such an education with no education at all. I did not conceal this from you in former days. Had I to choose my own endowments for another life on earth, I would not wish to possess greater facility in taking up impressions from the external world, in retaining and combining them into new forms within an inward world of imagination, full of the most various and animated movement, nor a memory more accurate or more at command (a faculty inseparable from the former), than nature has granted me. Much advantage might have been derived from these gifts in childhood; perhaps, in some pursuits, they might have insured me every success; nay, this result would have arisen spontaneously, had I not been subjected to a kind of education, which could only have been useful to a mind of precisely the opposite description.

Our great seclusion from the world, in a quiet little provincial town, the prohibition, from our earliest years, to pass beyond the house and garden, accustomed me to gather the materials for the insatiable requirements of my childish fancy, not from life and nature, but from books, engravings, and conversation. Thus, my imagination laid no hold on the realities around me, but absorbed into her dominions all that I read—and I read without limit and without aim—while the actual world was impenetrable to my gaze; so that I became almost incapable of apprehending any thing which had not already been apprehended by another—of forming a mental picture of any thing which had not before been shaped into a distinct conception by another. It is true that, in this second-hand world, I was very learned, and could even, at a very early age, pronounce opinions like a grown-up person; but the truth in me and around me was vailed from my eyes—the genuine truth of objective reason. Even when I grew older, and studied antiquity with intense interest, the chief use I made of my knowledge, for a long time, was to give fresh variety and brilliancy to my world of dreams. From the delicacy of my health, and my mother's anxiety about it, I was so much confined to the house that I was like a caged bird, and lost all natural spirit and liveliness, and the true life of childhood, the observations and ideas of which must form the basis of those peculiar to a more developed age, just as the early use of the body is the basis of its after training. No one ever thought of asking what I was doing, and how I did it; and it was not until my thirteenth year, that I received any regular instruction. My friends were satisfied with seeing that I was diligently employed, and that, though I had at first no teaching, I was equal to boys of my age in things for which they had had regular masters, and soon surpassed them when I had the same advantages, while, moreover, I was as well acquainted with a thousand matters, to be learned from books, as a grown-up man. Yet, after a time, I began to grow uneasy; I became aware that, notwithstanding my empire in the air, my life in the actual world was poor and powerless; that the perception of realities alone possesses truth and worth; that on it are founded all imaginative productions which have any value at all, and that there is nothing truly worthy of respect but that depth of mind which makes a man master of truth in its first principle. As soon as I had to enter on the sciences, properly so called, I found myself in a difficulty, and, unfortunately, I took once more the easiest path, and left on one side whatever cost me some trouble to acquire. I was often on the verge of a mental revolution, but it never actually took place; now and then, indeed, I planted my foot on the firm ground, and, when that happened, I made some progress.

When I first became acquainted with you, I was happy, and I was, perhaps, on the way to do what is more difficult than to gain knowledge without help from others, to restore what was distorted in me to its right place. But at a later period, when I left my quiet and healthful position, for a superficial world, which held me with a strong grasp, and confused and deadened my mind—where I was dragged along a path which I had no wish to tread, and which led me further and further from that for which I hopelessly longed; where I was forced to endure applause and praise, at a time when my want of knowledge on essential points, and the superfluous matter with which I had loaded my memory on others, my unsettled, disconnected ideas without true basis, my undisclipined powers without adequately firm habits of work, particularly of self-improvement, rendered me a horror to myself—I was as unhappy as you saw me to be.

However, my eyes were opened to much that had hitherto escaped me, and I was to some degree forced into the actual external world, by my travels beyond the sea, and my residence among a nation distinguished by sober thought and resolute activity, where I was obliged to occupy myself with the objects of practical life, and saw this life ennobled by the perfection to which it was carried, and the invariable adaptation of the means to the end. I then starved out the imaginative side of my nature, and placed myself, as it were, under a course of mental diet, according to which I lived for a long time in absolute dependence on the actual world around me. But this did not bring me into the right path of my true inward activity and development. I felt that I was now, on the other hand, poorer than ever, as regarded what had always possessed the strongest attraction for me, though I seemed to be excluded from it by an insurmountable barrier. For years, I was immersed, as far as my occupations were concerned, in the most prosaic work-a-day life, with the pain and torment of feeling that I grew more used to it every day, of feeling that I was shut out of Paradise, but that the bread I gained by tilling the earth in the sweat of my brow, was not at all distasteful to me, nay that, perhaps, if Paradise were re-opened to me, I should still feel some longing for the spade.

In this mood—amid my then habitual employments—at a time when, as it seemed to me, I never rose above mere mechanical work, and even this was but seldom of a literary kind—I was ashamed to appear before those who belonged to a higher sphere. It had formerly given me pain that you were too kind toward me—a pain arising from the double consciousness that you recognized the roots, though they had brought forth no tree, but only tangled underwood, and were awaiting with friendly indulgence the growth of one of these wild shoots into a tree; and then that you attached overmuch value to what was but outside appearance in me, though an appearance with which I honestly wished to deceive no one; *now*, however, I felt before you and others as Lais before her mirror. Why I felt this most strongly of all toward you, might be said to any one except yourself, not to you, or you would think I sought to regain your favor by flattery. It is true, indeed, that I would fain win it back by soft words—for soft words are the language of love.

Singular circumstances removed me from Copenhagen soon after you had left Holstein. A protecting angel watches over me. Our first entrance into this city was simultaneous with the dissolution of the State to which I had gone over, and now, amidst distress and grief, I went through scenes far more remarkable than any in my whole former life. My position was perpetually fluctuating; I was forced to struggle, to act with foresight, to be cool and resolute. It was a great tragedy, and no longer the tedious drama of my former tame middle-class life. I learnt to stake my all at every step on a pin's head, and fortune was on my side. The wreck on which I had pumped so long was cast on shore, and behold! on this shore I found the home of my youthful aspirations, leisure that I could devote to research and letters, surrounded by highly favorable and very agreeable circumstances.

Can you, and will you, once more extend your hand and your affections to one who has strayed so far? Will you not, at least, receive him again as the Prodigal Son?

I certainly can not say all I should like to say on the subject of your work, as far as I have read and comprehended it, on half a page, &c.

Farewell, dearest Jacobi! May I see you once more, and in such a manner that our meeting may give you pleasure, and I may be better able than in former days, to seize every moment of the fleeting time!

FROM GOETHE TO NIEBUHR ON RECEIVING THE SECOND VOLUME OF HIS HISTORY OF ROME.

When I received your kind letter in Carlsbad, there was nothing I wished for more, than that your second volume had arrived at the same time with your letter; for when there, I am at liberty to devote several days together to one subject, and to what subject could I better devote them than to your work? Now I have been already eight weeks in Weimar, and spent three in Jena, and have rarely been fortunate enough to keep my attention uninterruptedly fixed on one topic even for a few consecutive hours. At the present moment, it is only by making a firm resolution and a determined effort, that I can accomplish this communication with you.

My interest in your labors is undiminished; indeed, it is always on the increase. Suffer me here to speak in general terms, rather than in details! The Past can be made present to the inward eye and imagination, by con temporaneous written monuments, annals, chronicles, documents, memoirs, or whatever else they may be called. These place in our hands an immediate portion of that time itself, which gives us pleasure just as it is, but which we, for the sake of others, or from a hundred various impulses and aims, seek to cast into a new form. We do it, we remould the given materials, and how? As poets, as rhetoricians! This has been done from the earliest times, and these methods of treatment exert great influence; they take possession of the imagination and the feelings, they give food to the mind, strengthen the character, and arouse to action. It is a second world, which has swallowed up the first. Conceive, then, the feelings of men when the second world is destroyed, and the first does not come forth perfect to view!

The critical science which strikes in pieces the accumulations of later ages, and, where it can not wholly restore the original edifice, at least arranges the fragments, and affords glimpses of their mutual relations, is most welcome to all who would fain see events once more as the ancients saw them. But ordinary men of the world have no such wish, and they are right.......

Allow me here to pass over a chasm. Had we lived together; had I had the good fortune to have been acquainted years ago with your investigations, I would have advised you to follow the example of the noble and amiable St. Croix, and to entitle your work, "A Criticism of the Authors who have handed down the Roman History to our times." But to me the book is the book, and, as you know, titles are a modern invention. Accept, therefore, my expression of the pleasure it has given me, to find that your opinions coincide with mine on all essential points concerning the world and its races; accept my thanks for having once more rendered the Roman history a source of enjoyment to me, by conscientiously bringing to light its stationary and retrograde periods. For what man of sense will deny that he has often felt the presence of some error in his picture of those times, when an Iliad of such varied scenes, such an endless succession of glorious heroes, the four thousand Fabii included, achieve so little in four hundred years, that the city, the State, which had just for the first time, after infinite toil, got rid of the Philistines of Veii, is destroyed on the Alia like any little provincial town, so that they have to begin again from the beginning? But when the matter is placed clearly and plainly before us from your point of view, this reflects no discredit, but rather honor upon that people. I must pass to another topic.......

You throw the whole blame of the retrograde movement on the aristocracy, you espouse the side of the plebeians; and this is right and allowable in an impartial investigator, at a period when both have ceased to exist. One more general remark, with which I will conclude. Every state is aristocratic in its commencement; it can only extend its power by means of the masses, which are kept at a distance and kept down, till they obtain equal rights for themselves; from this moment monarchy becomes desirable, and is infallibly introduced, and then many courses—some of progress, some of retrogression—are open to the community. For all three states (state is a stupid word, for nothing stands fixed, and all is changeful), all three relations suffer from Change, which makes a sport of what is right and great, even as of what is bad and mean, that all may be fulfilled.

By what I have written (I look back but for one moment), though it may sound somewhat strange, I hope to convince you that no one can take a deeper interest in your labors than I do, even in their smallest details. Your two volumes—and the third, and its successors when they appear—will always accompany me wherever my varying year may lead, and neither you nor I can foresee the whole extent of my obligations to you; genuine activity of mind is alone refreshing. Mountain and valley never meet, but wandering men may, and why should not I hope to fall in with you somewhere? Let me add to this letter, as I should like to do to every one I send, the *clausula salutaris*, may you see in it cordiality and good intentions, if not insight and adequate comprehension!

With best wishes, GOETHE.

JENA, 23*d November*, 1812.

CLV.

TO MADAME HENSLER.

BERLIN, 11*th December*, 1812.

I willingly recognize Herder's great qualities, and they reappeared in all their vigor as he lay upon his death-bed. During the latter half of his life they had been obscured. This idea has been expressed on one occasion lately, in a very striking manner, but we must look deeper for its cause. Herder was no longer the same man when he ceased to be religious. (That was the case before he published his book on the "Spirit of Hebrew Poetry;" but the most beautiful portions of this work had been written at an earlier period). A discord then arose in his mind which tortured him as long as Hamann lived, and ended, after the death of the latter, in his making poetic-religious quibbles; for the "Discourse on Immortality," the "Essay on St. John," &c., are nothing more. He still desired to maintain a harmony with his earlier tone of expression, and yet he was animated by a different spirit. He was proud, and loved power. See how he treated the elder Spalding even in early life. And his after conduct toward Spalding, the way in which he contrived to get his own letters back from him, was absolutely dishonest. To place himself even on a level with Goethe, without presumption, he ought to have had clearness of intellect; but, on the contrary, he is only effective, and able to produce a really deep impression, where he speaks vaguely and suggestively, and excites emotion; as a philosopher he is commonplace. In his later writings, there is much that is quite intolerable, and the more so because you here and there recognize in their pages, the distorted lineaments of his youthful beauty. Nothing but the memory of his early greatness, and Goethe's own kindly heart, could have made the latter so gentle and forbearing toward Herder, as he remained for many years. Herder hated Kant for having reviewed his "Ideen." He wanted to press Goethe, among others, into the service of his philosophical crusade against Kant, with whose writings Goethe was probably only partially acquainted, and in which he found much that was uncongenial to his nature, though he recognized in them the greatness of their author. You say, Goethe would not have printed this, had Herder or his wife been still living. Certainly not; but it would have been because his whole book is written in such a mild and gentle spirit, and because he would not have chosen to hurt the feelings of a noble-minded woman, or a really extraordinary man; which Herder certainly was, though he was much less in mature years than, I will not say, he promised to be, but actually was, in his youth.......

Epidemic typhus is raging in Königsberg; six physicians have died of it already. The hospitals can no longer contain the sick and wounded, and it is necessary to quarter them in private houses. Heaven knows whether they will be able to manage in any other way here, if the army should encamp on the Vistula. Else we have been remarkably fortunate hitherto. When the town is fully garrisoned, I have to maintain an officer and three privates; but we are frequently without these guests.......

CLVI.

TO PERTHES.

December, 1812.

We are reading the "Nibelungen Lied" with Nicolovius, who is attending Zeuner's lectures upon it; his delight in the poem gives me a permission to indulge mine, undisturbed by the sneers which it has been the fashion to bestow on it among the *beaux esprits*, ever since the golden age of 1780. We are building castles in the air about making the study of the old German language an essential part of philology, and of all scholastic education; about school editions of Ulphilas, King Alfred, Ottfried, &c., school dictionaries, and exercises in old Frankish, Anglo-Saxon, and Gothic; and then, of course, we must have a professorship established for these languages at the University, to which I should like to see the inseparable brothers Grimm appointed. Have you yet got the Hildebrand and Hathubrand?* In them I find the other end of the fallen-in gallery, the opposite end of which I have discovered in antiquity, and from which I shall begin to clear out the rubbish in my third volume.

I sympathize in the pleasure you have received from Goethe's second volume, dear Perthes; I have just received another very friendly letter from him, which attracts me toward him more than ever. But yet I can not help feeling that I would much rather see him a downright heathen poet, than in this priestly vesture (in the objectionable passage) which he does not know how to wear. I stand to my opinion, and appeal again to the similar feeling it excited in N * * *, that Goethe confounds sacraments with ceremonies, and has no proper idea of a sacrament at all, for which certainly no other reason can be given than that which Claudius assumes, and has given. Now it is positively painful to me, that a confused use of terms should be favored in this way, and that the empty praters, of whom there are so many, should be encouraged to pretend that they regard every ceremony to which they happen to take a fancy, as a sacrament, because they have the highest authority on their side. You are very likely already aware that Neander is invited to come to our university. As to Julian, I believe that he was animated partly by a just hatred against Constantine, partly by indignation at the meanness of the priests; and partly, that his highly poetical and princely mind rendered him adverse to the new religion. He looked on the hierarchy only as a means to his end. He must have been unacquainted with antiquity to be able to submit himself at any time to the new order of things.......

* An epic poem, written in the eighth or ninth century, of uncertain authorship.

CLVII.

TO MADAM HENSLER.

BERLIN, *9th January,* 1813.

According to all appearances, our whole position is now very critical; and if we had been plunged suddenly from the unbroken peace in which we lived years ago, into our present circumstances, we should, perhaps, have found it difficult to maintain our cheerfulness and composure. The gentle education of fate gradually accustoms the unarmed citizen, as well as the soldier, to danger, and begets a happy fatalistic levity, a trust that the evil times will not be quite unbearable, and perhaps the cloud will pass over our heads without breaking. We hear nothing like rumors of peace. A circumstance that will increase the general misery is, that the murrain among the cattle is now prevailing in all parts of Poland, and has shown itself in West Prussia and elsewhere on our borders. To keep it out, by laying an embargo, is, under present circumstances, as good as impossible, as there is nothing like a police force in any part of the country. In Königsberg the deaths are over a hundred a week, mostly of typhus fever; the usual average is thirty-five. Dumas was in Elbing a short time since, and has nearly recovered from the fever; but I hear he complains that his memory is much affected by it. However, he will most likely resume his functions. We are expecting Grénier's division here next week, which will necessitate the quartering of a great number of troops upon the inhabitants, probably for a considerable time, even if an army should be collected on the banks of the Oder.

I was interrupted while writing the above, by the intelligence, that so far from the Russians having entered Königsberg peacefully, the above-named division had arrived there on the third, and when our informant left, a battle was being fought before the gates of the city, which is probably, by this time, suffering all the horrors of war.

Milly has a return of her bad cough, which has been much less troublesome; it makes me very uneasy. I am perfectly well, but do not get much work done. I can not keep my thoughts from wandering at such a time. I shall not be able to *finish off* any thing at present, but I must endeavor to turn the time to some account, by collecting materials and performing preliminary tasks.

I am quite of your opinion that an active life of short duration, is far preferable to a lengthened one passed more languidly. . . . . .

CLVIII.

BERLIN, *22d January,* 1813.

I could only give hints about the destruction of the great army when I wrote to you, not describe it in its full magnitude, as we knew it already. Of 400,000 men, exclusive of the Austrians, Saxons, and the corps of Macdonald (which was composed of Prussians and Grandjean's division), who marched into Russia, there have not been collected at the Vistula, from all quarters, 10,000 men sound and able to bear arms.

Our position is critical, and was for some days perilous. The people are in a most excited state; I can not say that this first showed itself since the destruction of the army, for it appeared several times very plainly, even so early as the summer; you will understand that I could not refer to it in my letters. On the Emperor's birthday there was quite a tumultuous outbreak. Of course, during the last few months, it has been impossible for such expressions of feeling to take place; but there have been daily affrays. The people could not be made to refrain from ridiculing and insulting the French, although the city was so strongly garrisoned.

We have received a promise that 2000 of our own troops shall march in on Tuesday. If so, we are safe, and can await in peace the issue of affairs. The Russians may arrive here in a fortnight. Their behavior throughout the country is exemplary. It seems as if their great deeds and great sacrifices had ennobled the whole nation. The peasants are hastening to remove their more valuable property from the country into the city; some, perhaps, for fear of the Cossacks (who often, however, pay ready money), but most, because they hear that the French are laying waste all the plains with fire.

For the last two days, the fugitives from the Vistula have been coming in; a spectacle that I can not describe. This is by far the most memorable epoch of my life; no danger, no difficulties it may involve, could make me wish it erased. These things ought to be witnessed close at hand. And courage comes, one knows not how.

Since the return of the Emperor from Moscow, the universal cry has been, let us free ourselves! The Court has not been able to decide upon any sudden step, but has been negotiating with Austria, with whom we are to maintain a close alliance. Whether this will be possible, when the Russians are in the country, and find themselves supported by public opinion, the event will show. There is a considerable force collected in Silesia: what may be expected of a Prussian army in the cause of France, has been shown by the corps of General York, whose example is decisive on that point.* A corps under General Bülow, consisting of trained soldiers disbanded in winter, is stationed on the marsh near the Oder. The decision of our fate, in all respects, is now closely impending. I have so completely dissolved all connection with the government, that there is, perhaps, only a single man in it who could dream of intrusting any office to me. I do not like to be useless, but our administration is not such as I could work with. On the contrary, I feel more inclined to connect myself with the military service. I have made the only step in my power toward this, by applying for an appointment on the general staff. I will write to you again on Tuesday; but it will be by post, so you will have to draw inferences from hints. Our correspondence will be unavoidably interrupted by the entrance of the Russians, Heaven grant not for long. It is worth while to live through such a period, but one can not yet breathe quite freely.

* The Prussian contingent, under General York, had been cut off from the army of Macdonald, by General Diebitsch, on which York concluded a separate convention with the latter for the safety of his troops, by which his corps, amounting to 15,000 men, were to remain neutral for two months. The King at first disavowed this convention, and conferred the command on General Kleist, but York refused to acknowledge the proclamation to this effect, which appeared in the Gazette, till he was formally superseded by the arrival of his successor, and meanwhile, affairs advanced so rapidly as to change the whole policy of Prussia.

CLIX.

29th January, 1813.

......It was a false report that the French troops were going to occupy the fortresses on the Oder, and that we should have the comfort of a Prussian garrison. We have still an extremely strong French one; also many sick and wounded in the city; a post-office is established in our house.

Dumas was expected here to-day. The French say that he will not remain here, but go to Mayence, where the head-quarters are to be fixed for the present.......

CLX.

BERLIN, *13th February*, 1813.

......The crowd of volunteers, coming to enlist, is as great to-day in front of the Town Hall, as it is before a baker's shop in famine. But to give you an idea of the zeal, with which every body here is pressing forward to inscribe their names in the volunteer rifle detachment, I must tell you this. It is only three days since the formation of this corps was announced, and to-day the post* is going out with nine extra carriages full of the recruits, besides those who go on foot, or by other conveyances. This is naturally, too, only a very small part of those who have enlisted, for the greater part have business to settle and equipments to provide, before they can leave. Among the volunteers are young men of all classes, students from the university and public schools; clerks from warehouses, apothecaries, journeymen from all the trades, middle-aged officers of rank and standing, fathers of families, &c., &c.

CLXI.

TO PERTHES.

February, 1813.

It has just occurred to me that I have never thanked you for your copy of Neander's "Julian." You have not praised it too highly beforehand. The subject is such that the author must either become a favorite with his reader, or make himself positively disagreeable to him. With me he has become a great favorite. I think his views clear, correct, and candid; the whole book is written in a deeply truthful spirit, which is truly refreshing to me, because it is so rare in these days; and I rejoice in the love which the upright and pious historian bears to the noble-hearted man, who was only outwardly in error. For this, however, he has been punished by the anathemas of the stupid zealots, and, as if this thirteen hundred and fifty years of purgatory were not enough, by the mingled delight and contempt, with which he was regarded by the "philosophes du 18me siècle." It is to be hoped, that Neander has now accomplished his salvation, and that he will become as great a favorite with really pious people, as he must have been with your father-in-law,† when he published the Hymn to the Sun, with annotations. Nicolovius has likewise read the book, and approves it highly. We both wish to have Neander here as theological professor. Probably, some time will elapse, before you will have the pleasure

* The diligences in Prussia are a government undertaking, and always termed "post," as well as the carriages, answering to our postchaises, which are termed "extra-post."

† Claudius.

we are now enjoying, for Goethe's second volume has reached us. While it is throughout as masterly a performance as the first, it is perhaps less pleasing; for his loves are certainly no Gretchens; his college life not his childhood; and literature a much less entertaining subject than the old imperial city. It vexes me, too, to read what is a godsend to the promoters of abuses, and can not be sincere in Goethe's mouth, namely, his defense of the Catholic sacraments. I well know what may be said in their favor, but *that* Goethe plainly never thought of saying, and his representations must be offensive to both parties. His account of the development of his own mind, which is evidently quite trustworthy, is inexpressibly striking, so completely irrespective of all the influences of ancient literature, and yet so entirely after the manner of the ancients, by nourishment of the most various kinds drawn directly from the present realities of life, combined with the restless, ever brightly burning fire in his own bosom. Goethe has sent me a very friendly message by a traveler, saying he wishes much to see me, which I shall therefore make arrangements to bring about next year, if God will.

CLXII.

TO MADAME HENSLER.

BERLIN, *6th March*, 1813.

It is a pity that I have only time for a few lines to you to-day; in such haste I can not conclude nor fill up the details of Milly's account; * so you must be satisfied with fragments. The day before yesterday, both Berlin and Frankfort on the Oder were evacuated by the French; they are slowly retreating hence in the direction of Wittenberg. Our festival, the day before yesterday, was overclouded by the burning of the suburbs of Spandau, and they have likewise laid the suburbs of Küstrin in ashes. We shall soon see whether they mean to hold Glogau and Stettin. These towns are, like Spandau, easy to take; but it is different with Küstrin, which can only be dismantled. Winzingerode's corps is pressing forward through Lusatia. The light troops are probably already in Dresden. The electorate of Saxony may become the scene of important events in this war. The Cossacks say they are going to Paris; they have a most original appearance; they bivouac with their horses in the city; about four in the morning they knock at the doors and ask for breakfast. This is a famous time for the children, for they set them on their horses and play with them. Some Calmuck and Baschkir troops have also been here, but few of them have remained in the town. Even the Cossacks point to the latter, as to a kind of extraordinary animal.

You can not picture to yourself the joy of the whole city on their entrance, and they are welcomed in the same way in all parts of the country. Russia and Prussia are like brothers together. I do not yet know what my work will be. To sit idle here is what I can not endure. My health will hardly allow me to serve as a volunteer. I have sent an urgent entreaty to one of the generals, who is a friend of mine, to take me as his secretary in the general staff; but he is trying to get me a higher appointment. Milly, my anxious, tender Milly, is satisfied whatever be my fate. Farewell! Our hearts are with you, whatever befall.

* Of the retreat of the French, the entrance of the Russians, and the universal rejoicings.

CLXIII.

BERLIN, 22*d*, *evening*.

. . . . . . I come from an employment in which you will hardly be able to fancy me engaged—namely, exercising. Even before the departure of the French, I began to go through the exercise in private, but a man can scarcely acquire it without companions. Since the French left, a party of about twenty of us have been exercising in the garden, and we have already got over the most difficult part of the training. When my lectures are concluded, which they will be at the beginning of next week, I shall try to exercise with regular recruits during the morning, and as often as possible practice shooting at a mark. At such a time, it is worth a great deal to be regularly trained to arms, and it may become a matter of absolute necessity; for we are daily expecting the publication of a law on the Landwehr. It is not yet known whether it is the intention of the government merely to have a Landwehr formed, so that it may be called out eventually and joined to the army, in case the enemy should recover ground again, or whether it is intended to fill up and strengthen the regular army with this levy as soon as it is trained. The latter course appears to me by far the best; if the French beat us in the revolutionary war by means of masses, we must beat them now by the combined force of masses, and a regular army, which they did not then possess. It seems settled that, as a preliminary step, the fortieth of the whole population are to be drawn by lot for the militia. Those only who can prove physical incapacity are exempt, together with clergymen and teachers; all other men, between the ages of eighteen and forty-five, must draw lots. From the provisional decree, it seems probable that officials in actual service will be allowed to find substitutes. But as I am not really an acting official, I should certainly be liable to serve; and this being the case, it seems to be the more right and becoming course to come forward voluntarily, that is, to join some of my friends, before the lottery begins, in setting the citizens the example of willing self-devotion. By the end of a month, I hope to be as well drilled as any recruit who is considered to have finished his training. The heavy musket gave me so much trouble at first, that I almost despaired of being able to handle it; but we are able to recover the powers again that we have only lost for want of practice. I am happy to say that my hands are growing horny; for as long as they had a delicate, book-worm's skin, the musket cut into them terribly.

This is certainly a very serious step, if the government are as much in earnest as they ought to be, and since all military ordinances proceed from General Scharnhorst, we may hope that all is really being done that ought to be done, and that the course chosen is the best. But unless the deliverance offered to us by the manifest and wonderful providence of God—after he has chastened us sufficiently for our deeply-rooted sins—find each of us ready to devote his life to its attainment, we can not be saved. We must not expect the army to conquer our freedom for us; we must conquer it for ourselves, under the guidance of our older and more practiced brethren. I mentioned to you, a short time since, my hopes of getting a secretaryship on the general staff. With my small measure of physical power, I should have been a thousand times more useful in that office, than as a private soldier. Since all correspondence, even in our own country, is so fettered, I can not quite understand what should hinder my friend from granting my request, unless it be a false delicacy about placing me in such a position to himself. Perhaps, however, it may seem odd to the King, whose consent is indispensable to my appointment. The friend I have referred to, would like me to enter the ministry, but that is more impossible than ever. Perhaps something unexpected may turn up yet. Idle, or busy about any thing but our liberation, I can not be now. Perhaps I could aid it by editing a newspaper.

Not every action, professing to be dictated by patriotism and enthusiasm for freedom is pure; but none can doubt that there are great sacrifices made from the highest motives. Thus, for instance, a M. Von St. (an officer) has made a present of the whole revenue of his estates to the government, about 3000 thalers; another gives five good working horses, all taken from his farm, to be trained as cavalry horses, 300 measures of corn, maintains a number of baggage-horses, and comes forward himself, with two of his servants, all mounted, to join a troop; a Mr. Von B. (formerly an officer) offers himself, with seven or more men, all mounted and armed at his expense, to serve as privates in a cavalry regiment; a banker here has equipped and horsed, one after another, twenty volunteers; a brass-founder has enlisted with all his apprentices and journeymen, and shut up his shop. In Berlin alone, I hear that 11,000 volunteers have inscribed their names. It is so universal to go with joy that no one can make a boast of it; to betray the contrary feeling would bring disgrace. When the King wanted to leave Potsdam, a levy of horses was required; though the French were masters of the country, every horse was offered without exception. In the same way the so-called *cocked-hats* (trained soldiers, some of whom are on furlough, and the rest disbanded in ordinary times), came forward every where voluntarily; they were collected under the very eyes of the French, and sent off to Silesia. They only asked eagerly, whether it was certain they were to be led against the French, and the officers dared not assure them of it, except by hints. That these armings, and the raising and marching of the volunteers, should take place while the French army was actually occupying the country, is a most singular and notable circumstance. When the cockade was assumed here, the French unquestionably expected an insurrection. It shows the extent of their fear, that they never ventured to arrest any one; for uninterrupted communications were carried on with the Russian troops, and this was known to so many, that the French had, no doubt, full intelligence of it. In case of any emergency, I kept a pair of pistols and a musket loaded in my room. Such times form an admirable education.

I have been with some of my friends to pay my respects to General York. We owe every thing to him; for, had he not decided as he did, the Russians could not have advanced till they had received large reinforcements, and by that time our own country would have been laid waste. York is certainly an excellent General; he inspires absolute confidence. The gratitude, with which he had been received, had dispelled his almost melancholy gravity, and he was very affable. He said he should not have fully justified the affection expressed toward him till he had reached the Rhine; but he knew what he had done, and how different would be the position of affairs, if he had not chosen the Right at the right moment.

You will feel it quite natural that this long letter only speaks of that which fills our souls to the exclusion of all other topics.

What Dutch and German troops are still with the French, will no doubt gradually come over; occurrences of this kind are happening daily. Yesterday, one hundred and fifty Westphalians, who had deserted from Magdeburg, entered our gates with their trumpeter at their head, escorted by Cossacks. I have seen General Dörnberg. He has very pleasing manners.

CLXIV.

TO PERTHES.

March, 1813.

I can quite understand, dear Perthès, your having no leisure to write to me, for we hear that the universal joy at our liberation, has been even more tumultuously expressed in Hamburgh than with us, and, in the first transports of rejoicing, one can hardly write a letter. But, when joy has survived transport—when, blended with the contemplation of those great aims, to which all who break their fetters have pledged their lives, it stimulates all the energies of your soul—then I am sure you will remember your friend also, and anticipate his desire to hear from you.

Our journal of to-day is rich in news: hasten to read it; it will tell you every thing. Who could have dreamt that such days were in store for us, as we have lived through during the last few months—you, within the last month? Only let us now preach to every one—we have no need to recall it to ourselves—that an inactive joy were as despicable as it were ruinous. Neither will you, I am sure, yield to fear, because the path to the mountain-summit of freedom winds up by the edge of a precipice. We must tread it cautiously, with our eyes open; not gazing too frequently into the depths beneath, but ever looking upward, yet not unmindful where we plant our steps. Our deliverance can not remain an incomplete work; it can not go back, if we, in any measure, do that to which we are summoned by every motive.......

I am going to edit a weekly political newspaper here; you shall have the prospectus of it very shortly. You will also receive a few thousand copies of Arndt's classical pamphlet on "Landwehr and Landsturm." I shall write you further particulars about it soon; it is to be distributed gratis from house to house; your senate must take this in charge, and have a new impression of it struck off for distribution. You must also get it translated into Dutch; for we shall soon be able to send it into East Friesland and farther. No house must be without a copy of this paper. To writing, and to serving as a common soldier, am I restricted *at such a time!* Fate has so ordained it.

The excellent "Word of Command" is said to be by our King himself; and it bears the impress of his fine and unsullied character. The personal qualities of our King are a consolation for much besides; I hope that foreigners may learn to appreciate him also. You are taking the best course in allying yourselves with Prussia. Farewell, dear friend, and love me.

CLXV.

TO MADAME HENSLER.

BERLIN, 9*th April*, 1813.

Milly has already told you every thing. Her calm acquiescence in my decision is touching. You know how anxious she always is on my account, but here the strength of her mind is evinced.

The expression of your love is a comfort to me; but do not give way to sadness; all is well, and will be well. It is my fixed determination to take part in the crusade; and if, in a matter of such moment, it is a relief when the decision must be partly left to fate, I have this consolation also; for it is necessary to obtain the King's permission. If, in my case, he annuls the unbecoming distinction made in favor of landowners and officials, I shall have a very simple duty to fulfill. Do not fear for my strength; it will hold out. If the King refuse his consent, I shall take it as a dispensation of Providence, and I shall have satisfied my sense of duty, and saved my honor in the eyes of my conscience. I certainly believe that I can do as much good with my newspaper as with my musket, but on this point no one has a right to judge for himself; our course is simply to take up arms, without caviling as to the usefulness of the post assigned us. And therefore it is my earnest wish, to enter as a musketeer into one of our excellent regiments of the line, where the privates are really as thoroughly respectable as you find it stated, from authentic sources, in my journal. I shall write to you again, as soon as any thing further is settled. Dohna goes to-morrow to join the volunteer corps under his brother-in-law. Be of good courage, as we are!

CHAPTER VIII.

NIEBUHR'S RETURN TO POLITICAL LIFE.—SECOND JOURNEY TO HOLLAND. FROM APRIL, 1813, TO MAY, 1814.

TOWARD the end of April, Niebuhr received a royal summons to repair without delay to Dresden, where the King of Prussia, and the Emperor of Russia, had already arrived. In pursuance of the treaty of Breslau, between the two sovereigns, a central council had been formed, charged with the provisional administration of the German countries reconquered from Napoleon—the execution of treaties with the Princes of Germany respecting the troops, subsidies, and supplies, to be contributed by each—and the appointment of government officers within the provinces under its jurisdiction. Stein, who acted as the representative of Russia, was chairman of this council; Schoen and Niebuhr were associated with him, as the representatives of Prussia. Both had been selected by Stein for the office.

Immediately on his arrival in Dresden, Niebuhr was employed to negotiate with Lord Stewart respecting the subsidies to be advanced by England, and afterward, to draw up a commercial treaty between England and Prussia.

When the defeats of Lützen and Bautzen obliged the allied Sovereigns to retreat to Lusatia, and afterward to Silesia, Niebuhr followed the head-quarters, and witnessed the battle of Bautzen from the distance of a few miles.

The treaty concerning the subsidies was signed on the 14th of June, 1813, after which he remained about two months longer at head-quarters, now stationed in Reichenbach. Hardenberg offered him a temporary mission to London, but he believed that it was more advisable for the interests of Prussia that the treaty on which he was engaged should be brought to a conclusion at head-quarters, and, on his representations, Hardenberg renounced his plan.

In the middle of August, he followed the Sovereigns to Prague. Here he fell ill, and had several relapses, which obliged him to remain there till late in the autumn.

His relations with Stein had been any thing but satisfactory, during these months. The latter was in a delicate position, as the representative of the Russian interests; and, appreciating the necessity of supporting the Emperor Alexander in his undertakings, as the only means through which the deliverance of Germany could be effected, he felt it right, for the time being, to keep his Prussian sympathies somewhat in the background, lest the jealousy of the Russians should be aroused, and he should be supplanted in the Emperor's confidence. Schoen and Niebuhr feared that his German patriotism was cooling, and accused him of unduly favoring the interests of Russia. This gave rise to repeated misunderstandings, which were aggravated by the irritability and petulance of Stein, who was suffering greatly from gout, at the moment when the cares of half Europe were resting on him. Niebuhr, who was by no means of a patient temper, does not seem to have made due allowance for Stein's situation, and the result was a temporary estrangement between the two friends, who, however, at a later period, renewed their intimacy, which was thenceforward only broken by death.

In consequence of these circumstances, Niebuhr returned to Berlin in November, 1813. His joy at the deliverance of Germany was clouded by his sorrow for the misfortunes of Denmark. He and his wife were filled with anxious apprehensions respecting the fate of their friends in Holstein, for they knew that among the troops which occupied that province, there were many animated with a very different spirit, from that which had been roused in the Prussian warriors, by the struggle for their father-land.

About this time, Niebuhr, by official request, drew up a project for the constitution of Holland, which was to be submitted afterward to a commission, for examination. It does not appear whether it was finally turned to any account, but most probably it was not, as some passages, written at the time of the Belgian revolt, express his regret that his counsels had not been adopted, when he proposed a completely separate administration for the two countries. It may seem, at first sight, inconsistent, that one who had so often expressed his contempt for "constitution-mongers" should have attempted to draw up one himself, but it must not be overlooked, that he did so for a nation that already possessed constitutional forms.

In February, 1814, Niebuhr was sent to Holland, to negotiate further arrangements for subsidies with the English commissioners. He set off on the 21st of February, with his wife, who was in very bad health. The weather was extremely severe during their journey, and for a part of the way the roads were almost impassable. The traveling, and the living in rooms imperfectly warmed with open fires, was very injurious to Madame Niebuhr. Her obstinate cough had already awakened anxiety in her friends, but she was naturally of a hopeful disposition, never suspected the impending evil, and used to encourage her husband, when he sometimes expressed apprehensions, by saying, that she had often been worse before, and had recovered.

By the beginning of June, the business had proceeded as far as it could be carried at that time; his wife had meanwhile so far recovered that they were able to take a journey into Brabant.

On his return to Amsterdam, Niebuhr received tidings of the renewed occupation of Holstein, but this did not prevent him from undertaking his proposed journey thither. There he spent his time in the house of his aged father, who had now become both blind and lame. His friends assembled round him, and the time passed happily and too quickly away, for it was impossible not to feel sometimes that such a meeting could never recur. Niebuhr could not hope to see his father again, and his friends saw but too clearly that Madame Niebuhr would never be able to revisit them. She herself was still full of hope, and ready sympathy with all around her, and this seemed to blind her husband to her real danger.

On his return to Berlin, Niebuhr was requested to give the Crown Prince instruction in finance. He was thus brought frequently into contact with the young prince, whom he inspired with a warm and lasting attachment, while the talents and amiability of his royal pupil won his affection in return.

Toward the close of 1814, Niebuhr wrote a pamphlet entitled, "The Rights of Prussia against the Court of Saxony," one of the most spirited and able productions of his pen; the object of which was to refute the libels against Prussia, industriously circulated throughout Germany by the partisans of France and Saxony. It excited great attention, and had a rapid sale. The Prussian government formally expressed their thanks to him for it, and requested him to send a hundred copies to Vienna, and to get it translated into English.

Niebuhr's domestic happiness was clouded over with mournful apprehensions. His wife's symptoms grew more and more alarming, and he could not conceal from himself, that she became weaker after each short interval of improvement. Besides these personal sorrows, he was deeply grieved by the final decision of the Congress of Vienna. The partition of Saxony appeared to him very disadvantageous for that country itself, and the cession of East Friesland to Hanover pained him exceedingly, as destroying the possibility of Prussia's becoming a maritime power. He saw in all the terms of the convention, a prevailing desire to weaken Prussia, and by placing her in opposition to France, to sow the seeds of her dismemberment at some future period.

Napoleon's return from Elba roused him from his melancholy contemplations. Like many other Prussians, his first emotions at the intelligence were rather of joy than of sorrow. He fancied that it would produce instant union between the Allied Powers, and that the influence of Prussia would be increased by the new struggle, in which she would once more have to play a principal part.

But when Napoleon's power established itself without opposition in France, he shuddered at the prospect of the perilous conflict about to be renewed, and the consequences of a protracted war on the prosperity of the country, and the morality and education of its youth.

While oppressed by these domestic and political cares, he received tidings of the death of his father in April, 1815.

Extracts from Niebuhr's Letters from the Spring of 1813 *to May*, 1814.

CLXVI.

TO MADAME HENSLER.

DRESDEN, 3*d May*, 1813.

From my letter to my father, which you will have read at Meldorf, you will have seen that I have been summoned here. I received the order on Monday night at eleven o'clock, and the next day at noon we were in the carriage. Göschen has undertaken the editorship of the journal for a time. Milly is writing to you about our journey. We feared we should not get accommodation here at once, as the Emperor Alexander and our king were here with their retinue; but all was right. We found room in the first hotel we stopped at, and the day before yesterday we were quartered at a private house, where we are living in style.

Negotiations with England respecting subsidies are my immediate employment. I have to act with Baron von Hardenberg and M. von Stein. I had not seen the former since my retirement from office, but his behavior toward me is just what it used to be, and as if our connection had never been interrupted. Stein is unequal (perhaps he is soured by his misfortunes), and hence it is often difficult to deal with him.

Yesterday and to-day, we have been in constant anxious expectation of a battle. Our latest positive intelligence is of the day before yesterday, and then a battle was daily expected. A cannonade was heard in this neighborhood yesterday; we are awaiting with beating hearts the tidings which must soon arrive, unless the cannonade was a delusion, or only proceeded from an unimportant affair. We know that the French army is by no means so small as it was foolishly represented to be; and know that we have an extremely hard struggle before us. The excellence of our army gives us confidence.

As I am busy all the mornings in conferences or at my desk, we have seen little here as yet. We have been once to the Gallery.

The intelligence we have received here from Denmark makes us very uneasy. God grant, that the apparently insurmountable difficulties may admit of a solution.

Goethe had left this place before our arrival, and from the accounts we hear of his political bitterness, his sinister prophecies, and his ill-humor, I am well pleased not to have seen him *now*. I have not yet made acquaintance with any of the residents here.

It vexes one to be living in an occupied country which takes no part in the war. In Berlin, the universal activity and enthusiasm, the warlike preparations, &c., constantly inspired cheerfulness and courage. But the people are German in their hearts, of which we had many touching proofs on our way hither, in the country districts.

God be with us all! Give my love to my father and all our relations.

CLXVII.

NEUMARKT, IN SILESIA, 25*th May*, 1813.

. . . . . . I presume that Behrens has forwarded to you the letter which I wrote him from Liegnitz on the 16th. I shall therefore continue my account from the time when we resolved to return to Görlitz, where the administrative head-quarters had been meanwhile erected. We performed the journey from Liegnitz thither very quickly; passing through a beautiful district, full of towns, whose buildings and environs betrayed their former prosperity, which has now been almost every where destroyed by the wars of 1805-6. But since poverty has universally taken the place of this prosperity, and the cloth and linen manufactures find no sale, nothing but a steadfast hope of better times can keep one from being positively depressed and saddened by the signs of former opulence. Through the greater part of this country the scenery is magnificent, and Milly and I have both said to each other, how much we should like to visit this beautiful Silesia some day with you; but this time I was much too anxious to enjoy it. Görlitz was greatly altered since our former stay there. Then, too, the long market-like main street of the town was thronged with an endless train of wagons, but they were filled with the wounded, who were being carried to the hospitals. Now, there was nothing of this kind, but the town swarmed with the troops quartered there, and the streets and squares were full of Russian equipages, round which the horses were stationed, as in a camp. With some difficulty, we found a place at an hotel where we could put up our carriage and horses, and hired a room at the house of our former hostess, a good-natured citizen's wife. I found that nothing was lost by my absence; for the business which I had been summoned to transact—in which, however, I can not act till others have prepared the way for me—stood exactly at the same point as before my departure from Dresden, and had rather gone backward than forward. I can not now relate to you how I found an opportunity the day after my arrival to bring it, at one stroke, almost to a settlement, and by what unaccountable carelessness this opportunity was lost. We now learnt that the armies had been standing opposite to each other for some days, ready for fighting, and there could be no doubt that the French would soon attack, as they were suffering from want of provisions. The position of the allied army was not above five miles at most from Görlitz, and our situation in this town so insecure, that we could not think too soon of taking precautions for our safety. For, although a bridge of boats had been thrown across the Neisse below the town, in case of a retreat, full half the army, with the baggage, artillery, &c., would still have to take the road through the town, and over the bridge which connects it with the suburb. Upper Lusatia is a mountainous and very beautiful district, and its towns lie on the summits or slopes of hills; thus, Görlitz, properly speaking, consists, like Edinburgh, of only one long and very broad street, stretching along the ridge of a hill, that becomes so narrow and steep, as it slopes down toward the bridge, as to require great care at all times to stop the horses in descending it. It will be long before I shall be able to think of this *défilé* without a shudder. It was easy to foresee that we should remain here till a battle had taken place, and then hundreds would be wanting post-horses at once, if it were necessary to retreat. We were, therefore, obliged to secure our safety by purchasing horses, and engaging a coachman. Thus we made our arrangements, so as to await the last moment with as little danger as the position of the town allowed.

On Wednesday, 19th, the bloody and glorious engagement of Königswartha took place on the right wing of our army. On the following day (20th) at noon, while the corps under Barclay de Tolly, which had gained this advantage in conjunction with that under General York, was still distant from the head-quarters, the main army of the French made an attack upon our whole line, especially on the right wing. This attack was repulsed with great loss to them, and we maintained ourselves every where in the position which we had assumed at the commencement of the fight behind Bautzen. All the disadvantage of the day was on the side of the enemy, except that the disposition of our troops allowed him to take possession of some ground, which our out-posts had occupied before the beginning of the affair. We had taken cannons and made prisoners. General Kleist and his division distinguished themselves above all others. Toward evening, Barclay de Tolly came up with the army. The firing ceased when the darkness came on; but the renewal of the battle next day was inevitable: it re-commenced on the 21st at about four in the morning.*
......Neither in this engagement did we lose a single cannon; but, on the other hand, some of our badly-wounded were left on the field, because the miserable avarice of the Russian soldiers as regards every sort of vehicle, had caused the removal of all the carriages and horses in the neigh-

* Here follows a description of the battle, which, however is sufficiently known from other sources.

borhood, far to the rear of the army. Our loss in dead and wounded was not so great in the three days together, from the 19th to the 21st, as it was in the battle of the 2d. During the retreat next day, a brisk cannonade was kept up, but without effect. In Reichenbach, a skirmish took place with the rear-guard, in which the French cavalry, having ventured too far in advance, lost 400 prisoners. (The left wing had also captured cannons and prisoners on the 21st.) On the following days, likewise, the firing was kept up on both sides, but there was no actual fighting. The sad truth is, however, that the allied army has continued its retreat from Lusatia, across the borders of Silesia. Still we are encouraged by remembering that a new Russian army under General Sacken has already passed through Breslau, and is advancing by forced marches to meet the retreating one; that the reserve battalions will soon arrive, and will fully repair our losses, so that in a few days the allied army is certain to be more numerous than it was before the battle of Bautzen; and that before long we may expect a diversion in our neighborhood from Austria, although, indeed, a general like Napoleon will not suffer himself to be disturbed in his plans by the more remote movements of the larger Austrian army. But if he be forced (as we hope to God he will be) to come to a stand before our iron resistance, our country will still suffer terribly. However, in that case, he must almost inevitably see his army broken to pieces. In this hope, though with mournful hearts, we have traveled to Breslau, where I shall finish this letter, uncertain whither I shall next be summoned.

On Thursday, the firing sounded very near and loud, but we listened to it with great hope, because we had learnt in the morning the victory of the day before: when, on Friday, the sound drew nearer, and became frightfully distinct and violent in the afternoon, we grew very anxious. Stein then advised us to depart. We made our preparations; the carriage was loaded; but we did not like to leave until we had some positive intelligence. Till past eleven at night, I went about from one acquaintance to another, to try if I could learn any thing, but all the accounts I heard were vague and undecided. Still I could guess from them that a retreat was resolved on. Many Russian equipages had left already during the afternoon; and toward night, thick rows of wagons began to defile through the town. We, with some of our friends, had settled that if any decisive intelligence arrived, we were to be called at any hour of the night. About midnight we laid down in our clothes. It had not struck one, when they shouted under our windows that every one was leaving, and we had no wish to linger. The evening before, the coachman we had engaged, frightened at the idea of wandering, heaven knows how far, from his native town, had taken his departure, and we should have been in most terrible perplexity if our own servant had not known how to drive. One of our horses was sick; however, we started, and got through the close ranks of the wagons in the dark without accident, and through the narrow pass I have described above, where we were obliged to drive up close against the side of the street to pass Stadion's equipage. We have seen war in a horrible form; we have passed through bands of pillagers, and crowds of beasants who had flocked together to defend themselves from being plundered. Our good star has not forsaken us. I must conclude, in order to send this letter by post.

CLXVIII.

REICHENBACH, 16*th June*, 1813.

We have at last received two letters from you, which have been sent about from place to place. . . . . .

I think that, while we were still in Dresden, I mentioned to you, that the change in my residence and society was any thing but cheering. At Berlin, the consciousness of the excellent spirit which animated the nation was ever present to us; and yet we were sufficiently removed from the sight of all that is saddening in the actual details of the war. We lived with all the energies of our souls and hearts in action, and each one derived his belief in the immeasurable energy of the nation, from his own inward consciousness. It was this which made us so full of confidence. In Dresden, we were separated from the nation, and its most excellent part, the army, and transported into a circle of fashionable people who were strangers to us, at least there were only a few of our public men among them. Here we saw as exclusively what was commonplace, as at home what was beautiful and good. The few eminent men were, however, among my friends. And of well-digested plans, of creative ideas, of enthusiasm or love, I saw no trace.

It is far from enough, to say that our troops have fought with unexampled heroism; to feel as high a respect for them as they deserve, it must not only be remembered, that they were placed at the absolute command of foreign generals, who have not maintained their previous reputation, and thus have become the victims of their mistakes and unskillfulness; but also that their own superior officers were deficient in experience and sagacity. And as regards the inferior officers, the best of them were often wanting either in experience or cool blood; they have lavished away their lives. But in spite of all this, our comparatively small army, at all times only partially supported by our allies (it is but just to say, however, that whenever Russian divisions have come to an actual engagement, they have fought extremely well, only not with enthusiasm), and opposed to an immensely superior force, has achieved things which would have been held impossible, because each man has fought, as if all depended upon himself alone. Battalions, nearly the whole of whose officers have been shot off or wounded, have fought on with the greatest order. In addition to this, the patience of our troops, their quiet resignation when they have seen the fruits of their exploits surrendered without a cause, their morality, their discipline—not a single instance of excess is named, not one soldier has pillaged on the retreat—is so elevating, that one can not but feel a true reverence for such an army. God knows what will be the fate of Germany and ourselves. If, however, what might be the means of a most glorious deliverance should, through the fault of others, remain ineffectual, the freedom of Germany will close with a glory for Prussia, which will throw Frederick's military greatness into the shade. Would the army be as pure if we had him with us now? I scarcely think so, and yet it might be so, and then we could defy once more the united power of the whole world.

By the unanimous verdict of the army itself, Colonel Von Grollman is one of the first officers it contains, and it shows the spirit which animates our officers, that lieutenant-generals of advanced age, have declared that they would willingly obey him, if the king would intrust him with the command. He and I have long known each other by name, and cherished a mutual respect and affection, but I only became personally acquainted with him three days ago, and I have never before seen such a man. York and Kleist are most noble-minded men, who think of nothing but the general welfare.

On the 2d of May, the French only took a single unwounded Prussian prisoner. In all partial engagements, we, and the Russians also, are certain of victory.

I write unconnectedly to you, because I can only write about the surface of things, and that is of immense extent; if I dared to go to the bottom, I could say all in a few words.

I saw the king at Breslau; he was very gracious, and said it gave him much pleasure to see me again in his service. But I shall soon have arranged the business, for which I was summoned, because there was no one else who understood the matter besides myself; and will there be any thing further thought of afterward? I do not wish for any thing on my own account; that I can say with a safe conscience.

Now I must tell you a little about ourselves. I returned from Schweidnitz the day after I had written to you, and brought the intelligence that a truce had been concluded for twelve hours, and that a longer one was being negotiated.* Our pain on hearing this I will not describe to you. There is much to be urged both for and against an armistice; but only let people ask themselves, without descending to all the details, whether a longer armistice *with such* an enemy *can* be a good thing. It alleviates our apprehensions respecting it, that all we do is in conjunction with Austria, and in accordance with our good understanding with that power; and besides, that our preparation for war will be carried on with all possible zeal and activity. It is a guarantee that our government are in earnest, that the day before yesterday, they signed a treaty of alliance with England, stipulating for subsidies, which are to furnish the means of paying the expenses of the war. The consciousness that I have helped to further this work gives me great joy.

We came hither on the 6th June from Frankenstein. This little town has been quite swarming with human beings for the last ten days. We arrived here some hours before the great body, and hence were able to obtain a very good room in an hotel, which we much prefer to being quartered in a private house. These ten days have been spent in bringing about the treaty, in which verbal negotiations did more than written papers. It is beginning to grow a little quieter here now; the people are dispersing in various directions. The Emperor Alexander has set off for Bohemia today, to have a meeting with his sister. Many think that he will have an interview with the Emperor of Austria; that is hardly probable.......

CLXIX.

TO THE PRINCESS LOUISA.

REICHENBACH, *July 12th.*

Your Royal Highness will be better acquainted than I am with the melancholy situation of our country—discontented, disappointed, and aban-

* The armistice of Pleswitz, concluded for six weeks from June 4th.

doned to ruin, as it seems, by shallow egotists, who doubtless, in their hearts, have despised, from the first, the tokens of inspiration and heroic virtue given by our country, and who will probably end by making these very virtues a ground of accusation against it, and a reason of state for sacrificing and annihilating a nation, because it can not remain immovable and without feeling like a slave, up to the moment when it may please the cabinet to let it loose against those who stand in the way of some temporary advantage. We were very credulous, so far as we placed our trust in men; yet who can repent the wishes that he has cherished?—wishes which might serve as a guide to the government, would they receive counsel.

It is possible that our nation may sink into a condition far beneath its state previous to the war; but no nation has ever done or deserved more to reconquer freedom and happiness. We can not but feel, that it possesses within itself means of victory which far surpassed even the possible dreams of enthusiasts: and, if we are vanquished, that triumph might have been secured by our own resources alone, had our rulers understood how to make use of them; nay, perhaps, it would have been enough to insure success, had we got rid of the men, at whose disposal they have been placed through mistaken trust and complaisance. No one ought to feel more than Stein, the deep sadness which is inspired by the view of our misfortunes; he, however, strives apparently to escape from it, by giving way to fits of ill-temper and even passion, with all who suffer from it as he ought to suffer. In fact, hardly a shadow is left of the old ties which once bound me to him; we can not carry on a connected conversation; we must avoid the topics which most deserve our attention, if I do not wish to draw on myself attacks, which are always unreasonable, and would be unendurable to any one who had not formerly loved him. What makes my relation toward him most embarrassing is, that my path would be much clearer if I allowed matters to come to a complete breach. If one does but make a remark, he instantly contradicts it, and always in a very unsuitable manner, as though it were an absolute absurdity.

I could never have believed, that a time would come when I should go to see him, and be glad not to find him at home. Yet I have still so much tenderness for him left, that I am always touched, when I find him calm and open to a conversation in the least resembling those of the good old times, and I shall bear with him to the end because fate has inflicted wounds upon his heart which he seeks to hide even from himself; and it is precisely this discord in his inner nature which renders him unendurable to others. For the rest, he has changed his opinion of many men and things; at Dresden, he wrote me an insulting note, because I ventured to doubt the honesty of an individual, of whom he now speaks with the greatest contempt. I should not have written all this to your Royal Highness, had I been obliged to intrust this letter to the post, which is very insecure. For the only branch of government carried on with zeal by our present Minister* is the strict watch kept on all persons who are induced to despise him, for abandoning us to the consequences of his own incapacity and indolence, and the crimes of the miserable creatures with whom he has surrounded himself.

* Hardenberg.

CLXX.

TO MADAME HENSLER.

PRAGUE, *7th October*, 1813.

......We were more than two months at Reichenbach. The little town was crowded with human beings. The executive, embassadors, the administration of the army, and a swarm of officers (mostly Russians) filled it to overflowing. The market-place was always heaped with baggage-wagons, beside which the Cossacks bivouacked. There was a continual bustle and noise, and yet, being a time of truce, none of the exciting activity of war.

......I return to the account of our stay at Reichenbach. The armistice and congress of Prague had a disheartening and paralyzing effect upon the minds of all. I was happily of the number of those who (with the exception of a few moments, when appearances were so unfavorable that they irresistibly led us astray,) persevered in believing, that the pressure of circumstances would bring about a result, which many of those at the head of affairs would rather not have seen; and therefore I was not in bad spirits. But it is a miserable condition when you are impelled by every motive to concentrate all your faculties on the consideration of a single point, and yet can perceive nothing distinctly. It is certain that the Russian cabinet, and a party in their army, were inclined to peace;* but the Emperor Alexander was most inflexible, and we owe him many thanks for it. Among ourselves, the peace party was extremely small, and all its activity was confined to pitiful intrigues; the nation, as well as the army, cried loudly for perseverance; the Austrians had advanced far enough, and constantly became more deeply implicated with us; though this much is certain, that their ultimatum would have proved to be none at all, if the Emperor Napoleon would have made the smallest concession.

It was exactly on this blind, arrogant obstinacy that I built my hopes, and on Fate, which is determined to be avenged on him. Nevertheless, when the congress assembled, and so many things came to light, I had no lack of anxieties and fears. We had a numerous circle of society. General Stewart, the English envoy at our court, with whom I had more particularly to negotiate the treaty of alliance and subsidies, has become my friend in the true sense of the word.......Prince Radziwill visited us from time to time. Through him I became acquainted with the young Prince Czartorinsky; and found him to be a most intellectual and highly-cultivated man, filled with sorrow for the fate of his country. A Saxon, Colonel Von Carlowitz, who came to us with General Thieleman, had already pleased me much in Dresden, and I now found his society very agreeable, particularly as he was the only person with whom I could converse on matters unconnected with the present moment, since he possessed a great amount of historical information. Solly was about half the time there. An English Colonel Campbell and I struck up a warm friendship. I was on a very friendly footing with several other Englishmen. Ompteda, the Hanoverian embassador (cousin to the Countess Münster) pleased us much by his warm-hearted honesty. The Russian embassador, Alopæus, is a polished and sagacious man of the world. Arndt we saw but seldom; but

* See Stein's Leben, Book vi., sec. 4. The Court, including the Empress Mother and several of the generals, wanted to force Alexander into making peace.

he is an honest soul, and full of life and warmth.......A great number of officers visited us. While there I became more intimate with our excellent Colonel Grollman, and he exceeded my expectations, which were not slight. He would be the general for Germany. I think he is also attached to me. I love him so that my heart beats whenever I think of him.......M. Von Stein I saw almost daily.

They thought of sending me to England; but under circumstances in which I could do little good. I succeeded in convincing Baron Hardenberg that the idea was ill-advised, and the expense unnecessary. He afterward offered to send me formally as envoy extraordinary, and I expressed my readiness to accept such a mission, but submitted it to his consideration, whether the advantage would be great enough to be worth the expense. (My position there would in other respects be more agreeable than that of any other embassador, because I am personally acquainted with so many men of note.) On my representations, I at length received the reply that Baron Hardenberg thought the mission superfluous for the present. When the conclusion of the armistice was announced, and the head-quarters were removed to Bohemia, we followed also. I staid two days in Landeck, to arrange business with Hardenberg and Stewart. On the 21st we came on to this place.*

If you admired the spirit with which our nation took up arms, your admiration must be heightened now, when you see this spirit living on with undiminished vigor, amid distress, innumerable difficulties, and many disheartening circumstances. Our troops fought like lions. The newly-formed battalions of militia, many of which had scarcely any officers who had seen service, fought like veteran regiments, only with too much fury. ......A nation containing less than 5,000,000, impoverished, torn by internal convulsions for the last seven years, has sent forth more than 250,000 men into the field, with *comparatively* slight assistance from foreign powers; and when has an army ever fought with more heroic valor for their own and the general freedom?

This is acknowledged very warmly here; the brotherly affection and kindness which the inhabitants have shown to the wounded, is probably without a parallel. It is above all praise. The friendship between Prussia and Austria has been restored on a stable foundation, and we may securely trust that the government, as well as the nation, are sincerely desirous of promoting our interests. Austria entered into the war with reluctance, but will unite faithfully and perseveringly with us, in carrying it to a happy conclusion.

CLXXI.

TO PERTHES.

Frankfort on the Oder, *December*, 1813.

......You will, no doubt, easily obtain a promise, guaranteeing the independence of your towns; I think that is among the settled points. I should have been much surprised if you had obtained more, for it appears that the decision of the positive changes to be made, is to be left to some more distant time.

* Here follows an account of an illness which he had in Prague, and a summary of the events of the war.

Your picture of the misfortunes of Hamburgh is terrible, and yet I believe it is not exaggerated in a single feature. Only do not imagine that Hamburgh stands alone in its misery; the condition of Stettin, Dantzic, for example, not to speak of the Spanish towns, is still worse. And who can help it? And what claim can a single city make, to receive assistance from all the rest—from those who have suffered quite as much, and at the same time (you will neither deny it nor misconstrue me) have done infinitely more? With us here in Prussia, likewise, nine-tenths of the landowners, both in town and country, are ruined, and yet they must still go on paying contributions—it can not be otherwise—till they are cut down to the bone. Many, many thousands of our youth, of our men, are shedding their blood, are pining away their lives in hospitals, or in want and wretchedness; what have the Hanse Towns done? I do not reproach them for the passive surrender of the city, but certainly see in it nothing heroic, nothing that lays other states under a moral obligation to make sacrifices in their behalf.......

It is a terrible thing that a city should be ruined for two generations: but how long did Magdeburg lie in ruins and ashes? Is it often that we can give help where we would? Must we not rather be resigned to circumstances? You have enjoyed the advantages of independence: the helplessness of a city, which stands alone as a state, is inseparable from them. In a great state, all may unite to raise up a single ruined city. It has, as such, no national debt. For a single city to have a large national debt, is to have a monster devouring its vitals. Even Holland, although it is little more than an assemblage of towns, can survive a bankruptcy: and perhaps it will be a benefit to the nation. The experiment had been made once already, since the war of 1672, by the permanent reduction of one and a half per cent. in the dividends. With you the case is certainly somewhat different; but you must not fold your hands and say that it is once for all impossible that any of you should live to see the restoration of your old prosperity.......

My poor, poor Holstein! O that you could hasten back, and protect my relations! There seems to be a deliberate intention to turn that land into a desert, because every heart in it is with Germany. My blood boils at this atrocity—which raises the indignation of our real allies and the English—at this arbitrary move to the north, from which none but the French can reap any advantage. That the Cossacks should commit ravages, is a matter of course; but do you really expect it of the Hanseatic soldiers, that they, like all other newly-formed troops, would choose to "indemnify" themselves in this manner? The real Prussians among Lützow's regiments will not wish to indemnify themselves by outrage and cruelty. A Prussian never plunders, even in an enemy's country; Holstein is not an enemy to any German. Are these your Hanseatic citizens, toward whom your heart overflows with affection! If they are really such as you say, if sorrow works thus upon them, so differently from its effect upon the Prussians, let them go to the devil! The French custom-house officers, and all Davoust's crew were also a set of hungry wretches, and wanted to indemnify themselves. I can make sacrifices too, but it does exasperate me, to see all that I love best given up to bands of marauders without any object. God would give me strength, if necessary, to bombard a town that contained my dearest friends, but to see an innocent country abandoned to pillage, to see people, who are among the noblest of their times, reduced to misery, by an unprincipled policy and rapacity—I cry to Heaven for vengeance on it!

CLXXII.

TO MADAME HENSLER.

BERLIN, 21*st December*, 1813.

With what anguished hearts we have looked forward to your letter, you will have seen from the one I wrote you on Saturday. The most fearful images rose up and scared away our sleep, and on waking they returned with all their painful reality. They mingled themselves with our dreams; and in the absence of intelligence, one even transforms the shapes of fancy into data, which heighten one's vague terror. Had you been visited by Prussian troops of the line, we should have been free from apprehensions for your personal safety; but those who came to Holstein from us, were only free corps, raw recruits and strangers, or the dregs of the capital, and the rest were all foreigners, and for the most part such as had reckoned upon booty. And now, letters were received here from the army, giving an account of the devastation of the country; and these were succeeded by the bulletin which left no doubt that Tettenborn had gone to Husum, and little, of his having taken the route through Meldorf.

God be praised, that our apprehensions on *your* account are, to a certain extent, allayed, by learning that the actual horrors of war are no longer probable in the towns; but we are still looking forward with undiminished terror to the probable fate of Husum and Meldorf.

We are assured here, that the conclusion of the peace with Denmark may be regarded as certain, and I have long felt satisfied that it would be brought to pass. This could be foreseen; and, therefore, I was filled with sorrowful indignation by the conviction that Holstein would be made to suffer, solely as a means of compelling the cession of Norway, and would be doubly punished in order to revenge the limitation of the claims brought about by the intervention.

Thus, though our fears for you may be calmed, by finding that you have weathered the storm without sustaining much outward injury, I shall still mourn over the poor country, whose prosperity has been fruitlessly destroyed, like some unhappy victim whose fate it has been to experience only those sorrows which humiliate and enfeeble, and has had no opportunity to make those sacrifices by which individuals and nations are purified and exalted.

Of all the letters you have written since the beginning of July, we have only received one, dated the beginning of October; not even the one sent through Count Bombelles. None of the letters which Count Dohna sent to the head-quarters, with his own dispatches, have reached me. Owing to this uncertainty, I hardly know what to tell you of the months that have passed since our correspondence was interrupted, without repeating what you already know.

When you last saw Berlin, an avalanche was impending over us, whose crushing fall we were expecting from month to month. While it hung over us, it deprived us of air and sun; we could do nothing but resign ourselves to what appeared, to human eyes, our unalterable fate, as men in similar periods of the world had been forced to do, and confine ourselves to the little sphere we could still call our own, till imperious Destiny should step in. It was certainly, indeed, at that time permitted to us to forget the outer world of the present, and to bury ourselves in pleasant studies, and by this distraction of our thoughts, to live as happily as was possible under such circumstances. How all is changed around us now! Never have good will and good ideas ripened so universally into good deeds as with our people. He who had beforehand declared what ought to be done when the time of trial should come, did it now himself (with very few exceptions), and to the fullest extent. The behavior of the women, too, is admirable. There are hundreds, who not only renounce every pleasure, but even a close attention to their households, in order to superintend the hospitals, to cook, to tend the sick, to mend their linen, to procure money and other necessaries, to look after the hired nurses, and keep them up to their duty. Many have already fallen victims to typhus fever. The men can scarcely interfere with the regular course of these occupations, which have assumed quite an organized character.

All that is the spontaneous expression of the national mind, is elevating. The recruits leave their homes with shouts of rejoicing; practice the exercise together out of the hours for training, that they may be able to join the army so much the sooner. And this is not done that they may lead a merry life of excess; the soldier hungers when his host can give him nothing, rather than use violence; he gives his cloak to his captive when he is shivering himself. One can not speak of these things without emotion, without saying to one's self that these people are better than we should be in their place. Our guards are as modest in their requirements as a regiment of militia, and yet they are the finest and bravest troops in the world. The officers are patterns to their soldiors. And all the people of North Germany might be like these, if they could be united, and brought to a common recognition of each other's excellence by seeing it in action. The core is sound here; what is wrong on the outside will be remedied in time from within. The King respects the nation. I am delighted with the Crown Prince. His noble poetical nature is gradually beginning to be recognized by some. He has extraordinary depth of feeling; and he preserves his individuality of character, sometimes without effort, sometimes consciously, among people who do not understand him, and are always blaming him. There is something very uncommon about him; the King calls his strongest feelings into play. He gives promise of great days for Prussia and for Germany—of the fulfillment of all that is yet wanting.

CLXXIII.

BERLIN, *25th January*, 1814.

......The conditions of the treaty of peace suggest more thoughts than can be committed to paper. The cession of Swedish Pomerania will have scarcely been expected by any: the submissiveness of Denmark was to be anticipated. The very first movement against Holstein grieved me so much, because I foresaw how the matter would end; how the energies of the country would be exhausted without any prospect of corresponding good results. The Allies could only permit the Danish war as an episode, and every thing betrays a determination to avoid any crisis by which matters would be brought to a settlement, as if they intentionally husbanded materials for future wars.

With what different feelings from those which filled our minds during the summer, is our attention now directed to the theatre of war? We may now dare to cherish brilliant hopes; and even if, here and there, the tide of our good fortune should turn, we need fear nothing that can affect the decision of our fate. I belong to the small number of those who do not seriously build castles in the air about the advance of the allied armies to Paris: I can not yet feel sure that Napoleon is sufficiently weakened for me to desire it; for if it is to be accomplished merely as a feat of arms, and were not absolutely decisive, it would be most undesirable. The peace is universally believed to be very near; but it can scarcely be so, if the restoration of the frontiers, as they existed before the revolution, be insisted on. We seem to be dreaming when we now take up the maps we used one-and-twenty years ago. I wish that those in whose hands the decision lies, may remember that it is no dream, but that they really have the power in their own hands, as much as our enemies had sixteen months ago. In France, the nation is so weary that the Allies are received as friends. In Savoy, where the custom-house officers have fled, when the people recovered their independence, they shouted *viva!* not to their old Sovereign, but to our King.

We are reading Madame de Staël's work on Germany: we have only just got the first two volumes. These are very unequal in value; the second, which treats of the German drama, and contains translations of several long passages, &c., is very unsatisfactory; and makes most of the chapters in the first, seem all the more excellent by comparison. The chapters on Goethe, North Germany, and Vienna, are extremely good, and even the great mistakes and omissions in some of her accounts prove that the book can not have been written by Schlegel under her name. He can not even have seen it before it was printed. She speaks of Goethe with profound respect, and portrays him with the most delicate accuracy, which does wonderful honor to her sagacity. It is evident that she has guessed him, for all her translations show that she does not half understand the words of his poems. Her attempt to render them into prose (she even tries at the Bride of Corinth) is an utter failure.

St. followed the head-quarters as far as Freyburg, and has now arrived here. I hear from him that, a month ago, they talked in the most decided manner of sending me as a commissioner to Holland; he had been assured that the dispatches were to be sent off to me without delay, and therefore supposed me to be in Amsterdam. I have not heard even a word on the subject. Probably, as soon as I have made arrangements for working regularly again at my newspaper, I shall be called away on a sudden. Since my return, I have only written single articles in it; Arnim has been the editor up to this time, but it is now going into other hands.

Milly is busy to-day making bandages for the hospital, and it affects her weak eyes so much that she can not write. She sends her best love, and will write to you soon.

CLXXIV.

AMSTERDAM, 10*th March*, 1814.

......Our present visit to Amsterdam is very unlike our former residence here six years ago, when the greater part of my time passed in leisure and deep repose, which were extremely beneficial to me. I am now as full of business and engagements, as I ever was in my life; but I hope to have the satisfaction of rendering important services, which will give me a right to return, when the world is once more quiet, to that literary leisure in which, in ordinary times, I fulfill the peculiar vocation of my life. My position here is as agreeable as possible. My English fellow-commissioner, a Chevalier Bergman, is a very polished and clever man, who thoroughly understands the subject; we are already very good friends, and treat each other like fellow-countrymen. Hence my society naturally consists, for the most part, of Englishmen, who treat me with great confidence and cordiality. Their mode of life is certainly something new to me. The day before yesterday, I came home about midnight, from a dinner-party where we had sat at table till eleven o'clock.

On our way hither, we had the sorrow of learning all that had passed in Champagne from the 10th to the 26th.* Our first intelligence was drawn from the French statements respecting England, published in the Dutch newspapers; our next from the account of an Austrian, according to which our armies sustained little less than total defeat, and their retreat was to be continued across the frontiers, and the Rhine; but it was much to be feared, that only a small part of the army would come out of the struggle in good condition. This depressed me terribly. It is certain, too, that it would have come to this, but for the heroic constancy of Blucher's troops. Thank God, the former position of the conflicting powers seems now to be restored. We do not know a syllable respecting our friends in the army, and the battles have been so murderous, that some mournful tidings must be awaiting us. Neither can we shut our eyes to the fact, that the difficulties are greater now, than they would have been a month ago, if Blucher had not been left in the lurch. It has not been Wrede's fault; may God reward him for it! The Russians, too, have always done their duty bravely and honestly. Now, when the Dutch nation is called on to display other virtues than those of the passive and limited kind, which won my admiration six years ago, it certainly does not appear in a favorable point of view, especially to us who have acquired, from what we have witnessed, a standard of virtue, such as was unknown at that time. Heroism is utterly absent; no one will even serve in the army, who is not compelled by poverty to sell his life for the sake of the bounty. It is universally permitted to send substitutes even for the militia, which is not the case with us. The minds of all are simply bent upon the restoration of commerce and trade, and they rely partly on the enlisted soldiers,† partly on foreign troops, for the completion of their deliverance, and the establishment of their independence. On the Lower Rhine, they have a very droll caricature, in which Dutchmen are represented as sitting, with their tea-cups and pipes, in a carriage, drawn by Prussians, Russians, and English, with the words, "Zoo gaat het wel."‡ Unfortunately it is but too correct, Thus, too,

* The successive defeats of Blucher's and the Grand Allied army at Cham paubont, Montmiral, Vauchamps, Nangis, and Montereau.

† The term "enlisted" (*geworben*) has a significance in German which it has not in English, owing to the circumstance, that in Germany all are obliged to serve in the army as they are drawn, no substitutes being permitted, so that the average character of the troops is equal to the average character of the nation: soldiers who enter the army simply for the pay, like so many day-laborers, are looked down upon in Germany, where the term *geworben* always implies a touch of contempt.

‡ So goes it well.

it is really saddening to see their perfect indifference about the constitution, which is to be settled by an Assembly of Notables, who meet a fortnight hence. There is not even the least curiosity as to the tenor of the fundamental laws, which are not known by the public as yet, and therefore I am completely ignorant of the spirit in which they are conceived. If they confer a tolerable amount of freedom, it will be a liberal present on the part of the sovereign, to which he has not been in the least compelled by the public voice.

CLXXV.

AMSTERDAM, *9th April*, 1814.

......May we meet you *all* again with joy! The *when* of this wished-for time we are, indeed, far from being able to fix. It is possible, that I may be able to leave, as soon as the war is ended, at least within a short time after; on the other hand, we may have to stay here for a considerable period longer; it is, indeed, possible, too, that my destination may be changed. But, in fact, when will the war be quite at an end? The conquest of Paris is a very great achievement; the proclamation of Louis XVIII. is also full of significance; and it is possible that a large part of France, where no restraining military force is present, may soon declare for the termination of the revolution by a return to the old dynasty. The reasons are nearly equal for and against the probability of submission on the part of the troops, and especially of the generals. If the snowball begin to roll any where, it may quickly become an avalanche. But probably this is impossible till there has been a victory over Bonaparte, and his army is scattered. Whether he has only from forty to fifty thousand men, or more, is not of much consequence: it is certain that he can not possibly be strong enough to attack the allied armies with success. But will he do it, notwithstanding, in desperation? Or will he make forced marches to his armies in the south, unite them, and attempt to revenge himself on the provinces which have really declared against him with enthusiasm? In former times, when his military eye was so piercing, that one could never doubt of his taking, on the whole, the right course, I should not hesitate in assuming that he would adopt the latter decision. I still expect that he will do so, because the alternative of choice, which has led him into the greatest faults ever since the Russian campaign, both on the Elbe and now on the Marne, is really no longer open to him. His march from Arcis to St. Dizier, on the 22d of last month, is a mistake only comparable to that of General Mack. The oscillating movements to which he was compelled, the necessity of regulating his proceedings by those of the enemy, had evidently paralyzed all the powers of his mind, so that he committed the most obvious blunders. Now he has no longer a choice, and if he attempt to advance toward Paris, it will be plain that God has again smitten him with blindness. But if any stand by him to the last, there will be a fearful combat to sustain with the infuriated tiger, when nothing but death is before his eyes.......

Is the restoration of the Bourbons desirable? As the only possible means of terminating that political system of France, which has desolated the whole of Europe, I think it is. Some sort of constitution must, at any rate, be established. And besides, where a party shows such energy as was displayed at Bordeaux, for instance, and formerly in La Vendée, it becomes the party of freedom. Forms are nothing; the spirit is every thing......

CLXXVI.

AMSTERDAM, 19*th April*, 1814.

......After this account of what more immediately concerns ourselves, I can speak to you of nothing but the extraordinary crisis, whose speedy termination has certainly taken every one by surprise. No one could have expected that Bonaparte would have displayed such pusillanimity; that he would have been as abject in adversity, as he was arrogant so long as there remained a gleam of prosperity. As little could any one have anticipated, that the soldiers would follow the example of defection, set them by an Assembly, which they had always regarded with contempt. Whether it was desirable that things should be brought so very rapidly to a crisis, or whether a slower and more thorough process of fermentation would not have been more wholesome, experience will most likely teach us in a short time. Many impure elements might have been eliminated, if the decision had taken place in the southern departments. As it is, all the persons who were connected with the administration under Bonaparte, remain in office, and we must not, because he has fallen, impute to him alone all the countless crimes of the past government. Bourrienne is high in office; so is Beugnot. That Talleyrand should stand at the head of affairs, no one can blame; for extraordinary talents, and an understanding which throws all the rest of his fellow-countrymen into the shade, give him a claim to this rank. The new constitution is a very sensible production; though the care which the Senators have taken for themselves, is about the greatest piece of effrontery I have ever seen. It will probably afford the French all the freedom of which they are capable at present; and, therefore, I only pass censure with hesitation, even where some essential things seem to have been omitted. All depends now upon whether it is carried out in earnest. If so, we may congratulate Europe on the establishment of civil liberty on a practicable and durable basis, in the centre of the Continent, midway between the senseless anarchy of the Spanish constitution, and the absolute monarchy, which has been introduced here in Holland, under forms which, at first sight, convey the impression that constitutional freedom really exists.

I am not quite easy, however, about the conditions of the peace; not quite satisfied that France will be every where reduced to the boundaries of 1789, boundaries which I should rejoice to see further narrowed by the restoration of Alsace and Lorraine. It has been suggested, that more may be done than to guarantee the old boundaries, and this is always ringing in my ears; then other questions come up about the distribution of the conquered countries; for ourselves, I desire above all things a compact empire in North Germany, as far as it is practicable. I saw last summer, what a world-wide difference there is between Silesia and Bohemia; a difference which certainly did not exist to such an extent, before the former became Prussian territory. And the inhabitants of Westphalia and the Lower Rhine are much more similar to ourselves than those of Silesia. A remarkable age is still before us; the world will not sink back into its old insipidity and sluggishness again for the rest of our lifetime, and the foundation may be laid for better times.

It would be a severe sacrifice to me, to remain long here—long away from Berlin. We are not at all pleased with the state of feeling here There was a short fit of noble enthusiasm in the middle of November; some individuals displayed a fine spirit; but when the few days of excitement were over, the attention of all was absorbed in the enjoyment of the advantages gained. The call of honor found deaf ears, or, rather, it appeared to them a folly. They are now pursuing their wonted avocations, and exhibit the same besotted avarice, and love of ostentation as ever; but in times of universal servitude it was less repulsive.

CLXXVII.

30th April, 1814.

......A young officer, a special favorite of mine, sent me a noble letter after the battle of Laons. Whether he, or any other of my friends in the army, have survived the late bloody engagements, I am utterly ignorant. He is one of nine sons of an old superannuated general; five of them have been officers already, two are still boys, and also destined for the army. Of the seven elder sons, one fell so early as 1807, at Colberg; a second last autumn at Culm; the third, who had been wounded before in Courland, died of his wounds at Dresden; the fourth, my young friend, received a shot in the temples at Lützen, which has much impaired his sight and hearing on that side; the fifth had his arm shot off at Leipsic. Only one was still unwounded, when the seventh joined the army, last new-year's day. My favorite was already in the army in 1807; he left it after the peace, learnt Latin, went to college, became an able jurist, and was afterward companion to a rich young man, for our nobility have ceased to think such a career degrading. Our young noblemen study as hard as others at the gymnasia and universities, particularly since 1807. May God preserve to us all the good we have gained from our misfortunes! When the war broke out, he became an officer again, and is an excellent one. He tells me that, owing to the great privations our troops had to suffer, their hatred of the French at last prevailed over the humanity which the officers preached to them, and which they had long practiced. They were exasperated by the cruelty of the French, who attacked single individuals, murdered the wounded, &c. Our troops had long known that the French would give no provisions even when they could, and had long suffered in patience; but when the Russians pillaged, the hidden stores came to light, which had served the French army in their eternal marches and countermarches, while our people were put off with words, and went hungry. Thus they began to help themselves, and from taking, came to plundering, of which, up to that time there had not been a single instance among our men, during the whole war. He tells me, he could not sleep for grief. Even then, there was still a world-wide difference between the Prussians and the rest of the allied troops; for it must be confessed, that France has suffered a terrible retribution. After the victory of Laons, the field preachers took for their text, "What will it profit a man if he shall gain the whole world and lose his own soul?" and exhorted the men to return to the patience and honesty they had shown till lately. The brave fellows wept bitterly, and promised with a loud voice to do so. On this, General York stepped forward, reminded them of the sacredness of their vow; said he well knew what sufferings and privations they had to bear, but he too, was not on a bed of roses; he had to lie awake with care while they slept; he had always loved them as children, they had been such good children; but for some time past they had given him much sorrow. In this battle they had proved themselves again as *brave* as ever; they ought to be as *good* as they were brave. After this he ordered one man to step forward from each company, spoke to them singly, and took their hand upon it, that they would suffer any thing rather than be guilty of any excesses. The narrative of my young friend is as touching, as these anecdotes are beautiful, and certainly unparalleled since the days of Gustavus Adolphus. I have given Stolberg's son, who has been sent to our army, a letter of recommendation to this officer. If the present spirit lasts, every father would do well to send his son to the army in case of a new war....

I can not persuade myself, that they have reached the goal in France, and that the Bourbons will now sit quietly on the throne, which is what people call governing. If they are to fulfill their promises, and the hopes which the agriculturists and citizens entertain of repairing their losses, they must lower their receipts to a third of those which Bonaparte extorted, during the latter years of his reign, from a population, half as large again as that of old France, and then they will not be able to satisfy the demands of all those who have been paid, not only out of these collective revenues, but at the cost of half Europe. The interests of Bonaparte and of the soldiers were essentially the same; only that for the latter, the extremely unpleasant chance of being shot dead, or maimed for life, was superadded. But this could not be helped; and even if his soldiers murmured, they knew very well that it could not be otherwise without renouncing all that they liked best—reveling at other people's expense, extortion, stealing, and growing rich, tyranny, ostentation, and idleness. If, therefore, you have any wish that France should receive a little more chastisement, and that the Bourbons should not be immoderately favored by undeserved and unexpected good fortune, there is a very tolerable prospect of the fulfillment of your desires.

CLXXVIII.

AMSTERDAM, 17*th May*, 1814.

......Milly fancied herself almost well again when she began to write, but unhappily the cold wintry weather has disagreed with her, and a walk that she took has brought on a relapse.......She sees absolutely no one here, beyond those who come to me on business, and the number of such is not large; neither am I much tempted to extend the circle of my acquaintance. I am not at all comfortable here at present; the people have too little sympathy with us Germans in what lies nearest to our hearts, and the manner in which this nation has stood the hour of trial necessarily influences our feelings toward them. You can have no idea of the universal want of energy. Long subjection has stimulated selfishness to the utmost extent. With many, their chief fear is lest England should insist upon the abolition of the slave-trade by all other states; she herself having discontinued it for the last seven years. "You see," said a planter to me, "it is the same with our negroes in Guiana, as it is with sugar-boilers, glass-workers, &c.—they never grow old at their work. They can not stand it long. And, besides, we only keep two women to five men. My God! at this rate, all the most beautiful countries, where so many hogsheads of sugar might be produced, would be left a desert; and even the old plantations would go to ruin! And if Spain can no longer import negroes, what will become of the mines, which can only be worked by them? Is the gold to stay in the earth?"

CLXXIX.

AMSTERDAM, 28*th May*, 1814.

......The French writers are no longer brilliant, but as superficial as ever. Formerly, they were sometimes profound through their very ingenuity; now, their ignorance and shallowness stand unvailed before the reader. It is very remarkable, too, that a few of these writings, in speaking of the French Revolution, exhibit an ignorance and forgetfulness, equal to that which we are accustomed to see in French historians, when treating of distant countries or ages. I am not alluding here to points with respect to which we can conceive an intentional falsification. This proves how completely every one has banished the past from his memory, instead of making it the subject of reflection. It has passed over them like a fearful storm, of which we only retain a general impression, because it is too painful to realize it afresh. Literature is quite extinct here. If we compare the intellectual condition of North Germany with that of other countries, not merely with that of the French at present, we must feel strongly how right Arndt is, in saying that we are a different and a better people. Our literature, too, may be somewhat in danger at the present time. If we do not look about us now, and collect our thoughts before we write much, it may decline among us also. Our peculiar heritage, learning, had been languishing for some time, and has now received a heavy blow.....

CLXXX.

BRUSSELS, 20*th June*, 1814.*

......The public works which Bonaparte has carried out are certainly astonishing; they prove what can be accomplished by the despotism of one restless man who spares no means to effect his end. His principal works in Holland are the impregnable fortifications on the Helder, which were finished in a year and a half; but it must be remembered that not only were the peasantry for many miles round obliged to send their beasts for statute labor, but that the Spanish prisoners also worked at them by thousands. A great part of the stones used in the construction of the causeway to Utrecht, have been taken from houses which were given up by their possessors, because they could no longer pay the land-tax, and for which the State could not find purchasers at any price. Amsterdam is externally the least changed of the Dutch cities. The houses on the great canals are kept as beautifully as they were formerly: except in the very remote quarters, you see nothing of the decay and desolation which you would expect after a bankruptcy. The appearance of Haarlem is frightful; it is said that three hundred houses have been destroyed there. The country houses have suffered the most, however. The causeway has been carried in a straight line wherever it was possible, and therefore mostly through bare fields; while the old high road wound along the banks of the Vecht among the smiling country-seats and park-like gardens. The most beautiful piece of this charming road has, however, been preserved; it is

* The former part of this letter contains an account of Madame Niebuhr's state of health, which seems by this time to have exhibited signs of consumption; and of the beginning of a little excursion which they made into Brabant.

about two miles from Utrecht, where the road runs between two parks, whose great forest-trees look almost like a wood, through which you catch glimpses of pretty dwellings. Utrecht, which was still a place of some trade when we were here before, because King Louis held his court there, is now evidently sunk into much deeper poverty; its streets swarm with beggars. We staid there a night. The road from thence to Gorcum, close to which little town you cross the Rhine, lies through a very fine alluvial plain; you see many of those little manors, which are as numerous in the province of Utrecht as they are rare in that of Holland. But the dwellings of the peasants exhibit few signs of prosperity. I approached Gorcum with curiosity, because our expectations had been strongly excited last January and February by the capture of this place. For a considerable distance, the ruins of peasants' cottages, and the buildings of the suburbs, gave evidence of the siege. But the fortress itself by no means corresponded to the expectations which its importance had raised. Here, too, we had a proof that Bonaparte scarcely ever thought of preserving important works already in existence, but only of creating something new. Nothing can be more ruinous than the walls; a double row of palisades had been erected as a defense against an assault; there were no outworks, nothing that could stand a regular siege. Every thing seems to depend upon the inundations, which, however, are no protection in winter against a bold enemy, and thus the unaccountable surrender is explained. The city has long been one of the poorest in Holland; if the times had been good, it could hardly have recovered from the floods of 1809; and no repairs seem to have been made yet, since the bombardment last winter. Many of the windows are quite boarded up; broken panes are left unmended; we took our dinner in a room that was in this condition. Our companions at the table-d'hôte were a merchant from Elberfeldt, and a party of Dutch officers, some of whom had served under the French, and still bragged of their campaigns and their quarters in Germany. This Dutch army is a most melancholy affair, destitute of moral dignity, severed from the nation (so much so that in Amsterdam you never see officers in society, and to enter the service is regarded as the last resort for one who is good for nothing else): without even self-respect; and yet the people never dream that such an army is no protection to them—that they must bestir themselves, and train themselves to the use of arms......

CLXXXI.

TO PERTHES.

AMSTERDAM, *June*, 1814.

......I have perceived here, for months past, how the French poison corrupts a nation; what a miserable figure it cuts when its fetters are removed after years of slavery. In Brabant, I have seen still more vividly, how the union with France has so accustomed the people to a yoke which they hated, that they now long to be under it again—can no longer exist otherwise: and I hear it is the same in the Catholic countries on the Rhine. Truly these times have proved the worth of our Protestantism. I can not write more to you to-day. God give you his blessing, and preserve your noble powers!

With old and faithful love, your N.

CLXXXII.

BERLIN, *October* 1814.

If I understand you rightly, I think you are laboring under a misconception as to the Congratulatory Address and its subject.* As no one among the general public could have declared on oath who is its author, so none but He who reads all hearts can tell what the religion of this writer may be, and whether you, or any one else is entitled to envy him his religion or not. At least those Independents of the seventeenth century, wrote just in the same manner about introducing the precepts of men into the worship of God —nay they wrote, spoke, and acted under the influence of the most fanatical hatred; and for my own part I would quite as soon wish for the religion of Milton, or even of Vane, as for that of Jansenius. If you believe that we should gain any thing by adopting the Catholic form of worship, we will not contest the point; though I thought we had agreed, in conversation, that a more efficacious form of worship could never be called into existence, until the church herself had sprung up afresh from the ashes, and had acquired numbers and consistency by her own internal development. To me and others, this writer appears to aim at the same point. Were he known, I should like to put him to the question, whether he is speaking of a church founded on faith and conviction, or whether by a church he only means an ecclesiastical State; but as this is impossible I can say nothing, and must believe the best.......

It is not the Pope, but the imposition of a creed, which the true lover of freedom fears; for no one individual can undertake to hold the same creed unchanged throughout his life, and no two can believe exactly alike, unless they choke themselves with words. And where do we now see the stirrings of aspiration and faith? In Protestant or Catholic Germany?...

CLXXXIII.

TO MADAME HENSLER.

BERLIN, 1*st November*, 1814.

......We arrived here at twelve last night. We called on Nicolovius and the Göschens as early as we could this morning, and I went to Ancillon to learn what was meant by the announcement that I was to give lessons to the Crown Prince. I found that these lessons could only occupy two hours a week, as mathematics, military science, &c., would fill up the remainder of his mornings. I am required to teach finance; but I have reserved to myself the liberty to connect other subjects with that. Savigny is also to give lessons to the prince for two hours a week;—a general survey of jurisprudence.......

The aspect of Berlin is quite changed since last winter. The great majority of those you see in the streets and squares are men; you meet soldiers in all directions, and it is quite curious to see the multitude of orders and decorations. All who took part in the war wear medals; and many are now going about with military decorations, whose dress shows that they have returned to the miserable life of a day-laborer.

* There were some at this time, who wished to introduce into the German Protestant Church, a liturgy more similar to that of the Church of England. Perthès was in favor of it; Niebuhr thought it unadvisable, if not springing spontaneously from the hearts of the people.

It seems no longer doubtful, that the unhappy consequences of neglecting the favorable opportunity which presented itself in April, will make themselves felt in our relations with France. It is not known whether Talleyrand has really left; but the communications with him have certainly been broken off. As a warlike spirit is universal in France, I can not conceive how it is, that while all allow that a new war with France is inevitable sooner or later, scarcely any one sees that it is just as likely to break out now as at any other time. People fancy that the French have laid down their arms, and that is quite a mistake.......

CLXXXIV.

BERLIN, *17th December* 1814.

......The mysterious course of public affairs still seems to threaten danger. Nothing more is really known since my last letter. That scarcely anybody feels anxiety, proves nothing at all. It is certain that France is arming, and is raising a large force; and the grounds on which people conclude that the Bourbons would not venture upon a war, are only valid, in case we may assume that they will not allow themselves to be forced into it. The Duke de Berri is quite on the side of the army, and I believe that he leads his father; for in this way, Dupont's dismissal, and Soult's appointment may be accounted for. I do not like our position; still, when one sees in what good spirits our protectors and heroes are, one is ashamed to be gloomy. The army is my constant consolation and delight—all the members of it whom I meet, are ready to open their hearts to me. In other respects, the aspect of Europe is not encouraging. In England, the want of genius becomes daily more visible. I have had an idea of trying to work upon public opinion there, in favor of my beloved Prussia (in nineteen-twentieths of the people it is with us already); but it is a delicate thing to do, when one is so imperfectly acquainted with the relations of the two cabinets. My vexation on this subject is not my only uneasiness with regard to England. Now and then, indeed, a bright gleam appears; as, for instance, the intended introduction of the trial by jury into Scotland, to the same extent that it exists in England, from which we may hope that in all repects, Scotland will gradually be brought to the enjoyment of the same freedom as England, which she is far from possessing as yet.

I have already, several times, wanted to sit down and tell you, how much pleasure I receive from my lessons to the Crown Prince; but interruptions, or work have prevented my doing so. I rejoice when the day comes to go to him. He is attentive, inquiring, full of interest—all the noble gifts with which nature has so richly endowed him, unfold themselves to me in the course of these lessons. We often wander from our reading into conversation, but not into idle talk, and it is no waste of time. His gayety of disposition does not render him less earnest; and his feelings are as deep, as his fancy is playful. He seeks instruction and counsel from others, without surrendering himself to the authority of any. I have never seen a youth with a finer nature. He knows, too, how much I am attached to him; that I see in his looks; and the cause of my affection, that it is not his external position which attracts me. It is one of his dearest castles in the air (how it is to be accomplished he does not know), to be the ruler of Greece, in order to wander among the ruins, dream, and excavate. When I hear him it revives my old castles in the air. "If we should be at Athens some day," I said to him, "make me your professor of Greek history, your keeper of the monuments, and director of the excavations!" "No, not keeper; you shall not have that title; I mean to make the excavations myself, but you shall be present."

In my next, I will give you some answer to the problems which Hume has not solved for you. I willingly recognize Hume's great qualities, and his decided superiority to Gibbon; but, in the earlier times, he overlooks many more things of the kind you have noticed; and in later periods, he does not enter into the mental wants of the men whom he accounts fools and rebels. But this is equally the case with Gibbon.

CLXXXV.

BERLIN, 30*th December*, 1814.

.....Our anxiety as to the state of feeling in the countries between the Rhine and the Maas, seem to be groundless. The manufacturers there have found a compensation for the loss of the French market—the source of their prosperity since the re-union—more quickly than could have been expected; the free trade by sea opens Italy to them, and they have more orders than they can execute. They are not likely, therefore, to want for worldly prosperity; but these districts, parts of which are, moreover, pure Walloon, need a spiritual regeneration. God grant that if these become ours, we may do as much for the souls of their inhabitants, as King Frederick did for the material welfare of Silesia! In Saxony, too, we should undoubtedly make very rapid progress in winning the hearts of the people, if we came forward to them with thorough cordiality. Oh, how I should like to receive some commission, by which I might leave a good work of this kind, and a memory behind me!......All Italy is in a ferment, and Murat, no doubt, is on the watch for an outbreak. He would be a sad deliverer! But, in one way or other, that country will certainly be formed into a single realm, in the course of one or a few generations. The dreams of early youth are strange. Something of this kind took supreme possession of my mind in the visions of my early life, and the separation of Sicily, as the first spot where a free constitution could take root, came before me in those dreams. When once the Congress is over, we shall again be able to read the future. Up to this time many things are still left undecided. But I firmly believe that Italy will yet fetch her works of art back from Paris, and that France will one day be dismembered......

CLXXXVI.

BERLIN, 14*th January*, 1815.

My pamphlet* comes out to-day, and I am sending a packet of copies off to you. Now that this little work is finished I hope it will please you. I must observe that it was composed as for an oration before an assembly, and flowed straight from my heart, and hence it must be read like a speech. Any one who should read it to himself, or aloud, without modulating his voice, in a uniform tone, like a treatise that is merely concerned with ideas, would probably be as much puzzled with it, as the ordinary reader is with

* "Preussen's Recht gegen den sächsischen Hof." The Right of Prussia against the Court of Saxony.

Greek orations (I do not mean to institute a comparison here), particularly those in Thucydides, before he has learnt to read with the ear. Do not misunderstand me. I am well aware, that I by no means belong to the great masters of oratory in writing; but I also know, what most of our authors do not in the least know and consider, that the old prose writers wrote as if they were speaking to an audience; while among us, prose is invariably written for the eye alone, at least only for the ear in case of an easy narrative. This is why my style is found so strange and unusual, and hence punctuation is so difficult to me, for I ought to have many more signs in order to indicate my exact intention. In fact, with all that the writer composes as if he were speaking, the character of the movement, and the time, ought to be marked, as in music, for the ordinary reader. Among the many good hopes which I cherish for the future, one is, that we may some day attain a good prose, in which that which I at least feel, may be perfectly expressed. If I had found some guidance, and had not wearied myself with some things while neglecting others, I might have reached it myself. As it is, that is out of the question. I break off to take a copy of my tract to old Blucher.

......Not to leave your historical questions quite unanswered a second time, I reply to your first, that in the middle ages, England stood in the same relation to the manufacturing districts of the Netherlands—where agriculture did not begin to flourish till after the decline of their textile productions in the fifteenth century—which the countries on the Baltic now occupy toward England. It fed their great cities with its corn: and then, too, the export of raw wool was an extremely profitable trade. The country also possessed ships and fisheries. At the same time, the nation was very frugal, and all, with the exception of persons connected with the court, clothed themselves in home-made stuffs; and hence it is no wonder that so much gold was coined there at such an early period.

I do not feel myself quite clear about the position of Lorenzo de Medici. I know the offices he filled, but that does not suffice to account for his power. He is no favorite of mine.

I shall soon set about the continuation of my great work, and have made all sorts of discoveries. Farewell.

CLXXXVII.

Berlin, *18th February*, 1815.

I am very gloomy, and you will easily enter into my feelings. Ever since Monday, it has been known that the Congress at Vienna had come to an agreement respecting the partition of territory, and the day before yesterday, their decisions were published here, so far as they relate to Prussia. My feeling is one of mingled sorrow and indignation at our enemies. I strongly fear that we shall give up East Friesland, and other territory besides, to Hanover; so that that state, which has not made the slightest effort against France, will be enlarged by one-half. We are robbed of old subjects, and shall be left in a worse position than we were in 1805.

To England herself, this extension of Hanover, and her permanent implication in the affairs of the Continent through Belgium, is most disadvantageous. I waver between the impulse to give vent to my dissatisfaction, and the voice within that tells me to cease dwelling upon painful subjects, and to return with all my thoughts to my studies; especially as my health is suffering from the constant renewal of mortification, while I can not really accomplish any thing, in the sphere of actions and decisions, by speaking or writing. France has managed every thing very cleverly for herself. How soon will she succeed in regaining the left bank of the Rhine? If we had defied her, the cowards would soon have given way, and even if it had come to a war, it would indeed have been a struggle for life or death, but we should have conquered in the end......

CLXXXVIII.

BERLIN, *March*, 1815.

......You, too, will find that although the number of my acquaintance has much increased, there is far less of youthful life, activity, and variety in our social intercourse, than there was five years ago. We live in a much more retired way, on account of the rise of prices, and the disbursements which we regard as a matter of duty, and see much less company at home; and then, too, every body is grown older. This winter has every where destroyed cheerfulness, just as the war had already suspended people's interest in their own business. When times were at the worst, men turned once for all from the fruitless contemplation of the public misery, and thought of themselves and their own affairs; during the struggle, these were forgotten, and their whole souls were occupied with the public fate—and with hope. The general excitement now existing must be calmed down, before people can be quite themselves again.

Milly will have told you of her resolution to try magnetism. She is better since its use, and free from cough in the evenings, when she used to be particularly troubled with it; she sleeps better, &c. God grant that this may be a *real* progress: it had need be so, for she is terribly reduced. She has not had the least touch of magnetic sleep as yet......

The return of Napoleon has drawn forth the most vehement expressions of delight from many here; this may surprise you, but you will be able to understand it on reflection. The King of Saxony and Maria Louisa knew of his departure from Elba, two days earlier than the allied sovereigns.

CLXXXIX.

BERLIN, 1*st April*.

You want above all things full particulars of Milly's state. In the first place, I beg you, in Milly's name as well as my own, to lay aside all your fears as to the irritating effect of magnetism; on the contrary, she is, in fact, in a much less irritable state now, than before she began to try it. Besides you must not confound the effects of Puisegur's magnetism with the wand, with those of a soothing manipulation. She almost always feels decidedly better than usual after the manipulation, and, imperfectly as I can practice it, she feels quite soothed after I have magnetized her, as well as I can, before going to bed, inclined to sleep, and as soon as she lies down she falls into a quiet, unbroken slumber; whereas before she often laid awake till morning.*

If we had believed that Bonaparte would be received so completely without opposition, most undoubtedly, no one here would have rejoiced at

* Here follows a further description of her symptoms in detail, which were such as must be any thing but consoling to an unprejudiced person.

his landing. What the right-minded among us hoped for, was, that we should seize this opportunity to save East Friesland, the loss of which I, even more than most others, feel to be a terrible grievance. But even this seems to have been left undone, and therefore his return is an unmitigated calamity, and no one can see what the end will be. I look forward to this new war with a heavy heart. However, we must keep up our spirits as well as we can. Our youth and our rural population go to meet the enemy with great alacrity. Some of the principal towns, where people have speculated largely in paper-money, are in a dreadfully depressed state. In a few weeks, hostilities will be in full operation; in all probability a second advance on Paris will be attempted; I doubt whether the attempt will not be made rashly and prematurely; meanwhile, whatever betide, to lose heart would be the very worst thing we could do. It is, indeed, lamentable that a still larger portion of our youth should be cut off, and the rest most likely be left to a great extent uneducated; it seems inevitable that a great decline of science should take place in consequence; and moreover, it is not favorable to the hope of civil freedom, that the whole nation should be converted into practiced warriors. But we must take every period as it is, and seek to make of it what its peculiar characteristics allow.

The Crown Prince has lately given me a keepsake; it is a cut glass, which belonged to Frederick William I., whom I have held up to his respect, but whose harshness revolts him.

Our young friend Chr. Stolberg will, of course, return to his regiment. He is a thoroughly good youth.

CXC.

BERLIN, 2*d May*, 1815.

So far Milly had written last Saturday. Since then, Frederica's letter, with its sad news, has reached us. How unexpected it was, you can hardly imagine; for I scarcely doubted that the quiet life of my dear old father might be prolonged for years to come, so that we might look forward to seeing him again next year, if Milly's health permitted the journey. I can not help reproaching myself for this want of all foreboding of his death; for I think that if I had thought of him as often as I ought, some presentiment of his approaching release must have visited me; and on the very day of his death I do not remember to have once thought of him. Oh that I had been with him in these last days! What would I give that it had been possible! If he had been less unexacting in all the relationships of life, less thoroughly unselfish, less easily satisfied, he would often have felt hurt that, partly owing to my faults and impatience, partly to his misunderstanding me in early life, I gave him so few active proofs of love and tenderness. That this was not a source of pain to him, that his son was a joy to him notwithstanding, does not excuse me. When the time is gone by, in which it is possible to atone for acts of neglect, they begin to press heavily on the heart. And I owed it to my noble-minded father, to return and to reward his honest love, though in many cases it mistook the way to its end. If omissions of this kind can in any way be atoned for on the other side of the grave, it shall at least be my endeavor to atone for them there.

My sister has not yet written, and Frederica gives us so few particulars, that we hardly know any thing about his last days. From his bodily state I fear—and should be so glad to think otherwise—that his death must have been attended with great pain. His soul was no doubt at peace, and departed without reluctance or fear.

It is a great comfort to me that we are much alone, and have few interruptions at present. To me, my father's death is like cutting off a part of my existence, little as it can influence the facts of my life at my age, and so separated as we were from each other.

Oh that Milly's health were more encouraging! I would so gladly say any thing to cheer you about her, but I dare not tell you what is not true. I *can not* perceive that she is improving. She varies very much, and there are days when she feels easy and well. We make no further progress with magnetism. I wish so earnestly that she would take Heim's medicines, but she will not hear of it. That all her present illness is the result of that unhappy expedition up the Wertha Hills, becomes clearer and clearer to me. May God help us. I trust it will be practicable for you to come to us.

How can I conclude this letter without thanking you once more, and praying for a blessing on you, for all the love that you have shown to my father; for all the comfort and pleasure your society afforded him after his fall, and for the love and tenderness that he received from you during our visit. It would make you still dearer to me, if any thing could do so.

May Heaven reward Gloyer, too, for all that he has done for one that was a stranger to him!

Farewell! Gretchen has most likely already gone back to her friends; if not, give our best love to her.

CHAPTER IX.

NIEBUHR'S RESIDENCE IN BERLIN UP TO JULY, 1816.

In the spring of 1815, Madame Niebuhr's state of health altered for the worse, with a rapidity which revealed the full extent of her danger. Madame Hensler, on hearing of it, hastened to Berlin, and shared in Niebuhr's cares and fatigues. Her sister lingered till the 21st of June, when she died in the arms of her husband. He had never spoken to her of her approaching death, much as he longed to receive her parting wishes, because the physician forbade all excitement. Once only, a few days before her death, as he was holding her in his arms, he asked her if there was no pleasure that he could give her—nothing that he could do for her sake; she replied, with a look of unutterable love, "You shall finish your History whether I live or die." This request was ever present to his mind, and he regarded its fulfillment as a sacred duty, though years elapsed before he was able to resume his work.

Madame Niebuhr's death was an unspeakable bereavement to her husband. Their early marriage—the perfect harmony of their sentiments and tastes—the perils and anxieties they had shared during the war—the passionate interest with which they both regarded political events—even their childlessness, had bound them so closely together, that they had scarcely a thought or a wish apart from each other. It is a proof of the high character of her mind, that she was fully capable of appreciating her husband's intellect, and of entering into all the topics which interested him. He was in the habit of conversing with her on the subjects of his researches, and consulting her even on his political relations. Such a union can exist only once in a life-time, because a common history furnishes a deep ground of sympathy, such as nothing else can replace. Thus Niebuhr felt, throughout the remainder of his life, the inadequacy of any other companionship to supply the place of that which he had lost, tenderly as he was attached to his second wife. The depth of his affliction was proportioned to the happiness he had enjoyed; still he recognized the duty of striving to endure his pain with fortitude, and devoting his life and powers to the service of others.

A few weeks after his wife's death, the government proposed to send him as embassador to Rome, in order to negotiate a Concordat with the Pope. Under other circumstances, this proposal would have given him the greatest gratification, as affording him the opportunity of carrying out his long-cherished wish of visiting the scenes of his History; but now he shrank from the utter isolation from his friends which it would involve. He however accepted it, as a matter of duty. According to the plan first proposed, he was to leave Berlin the same autumn, but his departure was unavoidably postponed; first, on account of the preliminaries which had to be arranged before he could take his instructions with him, and then, because Hardenberg wished to make him a member of a Commission to draw up the Constitution. The appointment of this Commission was, however, afterward given up, or at least indefinitely postponed.

Madame Hensler had remained with Niebuhr for some time after his wife's death. He accompanied her on her return, in order to take leave of his friends before their long separation. He strongly wished that she should accompany him to Rome. Much as Madame Hensler loved him, she at first felt reluctant to part with her home and friends, but at length acceded, and promised to come to him, in the spring, with her adopted daughter, Margaret Hensler, a niece of her husband.

Meanwhile, Niebuhr passed his solitary winter in a state of extreme depression, and his health suffered so much, that he some times suspected he had caught his wife's disorder. Yet he seems to have accomplished an extraordinary amount of work. He, indeed, found it impossible to return to his Roman History; it revived too many painful recollections; and while he could force himself to industry, he could not command the productive energy, which seldom exists in the absence of happiness and vigor. But he studied the canon law, as a preparation for his mission—prepared, in conjunction with Heindorf and Buttmann, an edition of the Fronto, discovered by the Abbé Mai—continued his lessons to the Crown Prince—wrote a preface to M. Von Vincke's Essay on the Internal Administration of Great Britain—an Essay on Fronto, containing a description of Marcus Antoninus and his age, and another on the Geography of Herodotus—drew up a memorial on the freedom of the press, at the request of Hardenberg—and wrote an answer to a pamphlet on Secret Associations, by Professor Schmalz, the Rector of the University. This pamphlet was entitled "Correction of a Passage in Venturini's Chronicle for the year 1808." It was, however, in fact, an attack on the Tugendbund, in which, moreover, Schmalz attributed unworthy motives to the sacrifices that Prussia had made in order to throw off the French yoke, and tried to prove that secret societies, of a treasonable character, were still in existence and activity. Schleiermacher, Friedrich Förster, Koppe, and Krug, as well as Niebuhr, entered the lists against him, and the controversy was waged with great vehemence, till a royal edict appeared in 1816, forbidding the further discussion of the subject under heavy penalties. Besides these various occupations, we find Niebuhr also endeavoring to restore the tone of his mind, and invigorate his health by riding lessons, walks, and visits to his friends, but with little success.

After the arrival of Madame Hensler and her niece in April, 1816, his health improved, and his grief assumed more the character of a quiet melancholy. About this time he wrote the life of his father—a model of biography, lively, truthful, and affectionate. His departure for Rome, which had been fixed for April, was again postponed till July, because his instructions were not ready. Meanwhile, the presence of Madame Hensler and her niece gradually cheered him; the former was as closely acquainted with his inward and outward life as his Amelia had been; Margaret Hensler soothed him with her gentle attentions, and gave him peculiar pleasure with her sweet singing. After some time he engaged himself to her, and married her before he left Berlin.

Niebuhr's young wife was well aware that his heart still clung too strongly to the past, for him to be susceptible of positive happiness; she sympathized with his feelings, and trusted that time would restore him to a brighter frame of mind. She was of a noble, affectionate disposition. She could not, indeed, though a cultivated woman, enter into her husband's deeper researches and political ideas, as fully as his first wife had done, but she had strong practical sense, and was devoted to him. Unfortunately for both, her constitution was almost as delicate as that of Amelia.

Niebuhr and his wife wished that Madame Hensler should still accompany them, but she felt that it was best to leave the newly-married pair alone; and felt besides, that it was a somewhat hazardous experiment to transplant herself in middle-life into a foreign country and an untried position, when no longer called to do so by the duties of friendship. She, therefore, firmly withstood their pressing entreaties to accompany them, and returned to Kiel.

Extracts from Niebuhr's Letters from August, 1815, *to July,* 1816.

CXCI.

TO MADAME HENSLER.

BERLIN, *5th August*, 1815.*

This date would be a sufficient token that I have reached the end of my journey, to you, and to our brothers and sisters, who will most likely be at your house, when this reaches you, expecting to hear some tidings of the poor friend who has left them. Indeed, I can not write much more for weariness, from which, owing to the heat of the weather, added to the depression produced by my loneliness, I am suffering much more now, than on the more fatiguing journey to Lubec with you.

I arrived here to-day at noon, and found no letters. I feel extremely exhausted. This is only temporary, but shall I never cease to feel the void, the desolation in my home, which now crushes and deadens my heart? I doubt if these feelings will yield even to the most strenuous occupation. Time will show. I had the same sort of feelings once before, eighteen years ago, when I returned to Copenhagen after my engagement with Milly, and after I had spent so long a time with you; I conquered them then, but it was a terrible struggle. However, I must do as well as I can. On the journey, my eyes often filled with tears, but the constant onward motion did me good, though it was through a very tame country. Now, I sit before the objects which ought to cheer the mind by giving it full occupation, as a sick man, who loathes food, sits before a table which has been carefully spread with all that would please his palate, were he in health.

God reward you for your presence when Milly died, and for staying with me afterward! If you could have remained here longer, if you were here now, I should feel differently; but it could not be, and perhaps it is best as it is. You have again left me a treasure in your remembrance. Oh, that I were not so thirsting for conversation, or, rather, for sympathy; that I can not get used to having no creature with whom I can talk of the past! Only to have a child, like little Sophy, with me that I loved, would be worth more to me now than the most intellectual society. But it is needless to paint to you the feeling of loneliness with which I sit within these dreary walls. It was by the same road that I came to Prussia with Milly; for the most part, the same by which we returned last autumn; I entered the city by the same gate, drove along the same streets. I was so unused to live alone that it made me quite dependent. My inward consciousness refuses to believe that I am alone, even more now, than when you were still here, and I could have the consolation of speaking of my sorrow with you. When I awake from sleep, for the first moment I can not believe in

* Written on his return from Lubec.

my solitude. You know how, when the news of victory first came,* and every time fresh tidings of advance were brought us, I always used to turn round, as if I could still go to her bedside and tell her about it. I feel as if Milly or you *must* be near and within reach, as you always have been in past times, for me to tell you all that is in my thoughts.

There is, indeed, no need to cherish and feed these feelings to render them lasting; but to try to repress them would seem to me a sin, and a renunciation of the only means of communication by which I can reach Milly, and afford her the one blessing which was indispensable to her in life. But the difficulty will be to combine the emotion which arises from this, with the firmness, without which I should be more liable than ever to sink under my grief.

A thousand, thousand thanks to you for all your boundless and unspeakable love and faithfulness, and you must say the same to our brothers and sisters, for the love which they have shown me both face to face and in their letters. I feel sure you will write the day after to-morrow; that you will not wait to receive this. How could such formality be possible between us? I quite reckon upon receiving a letter from you on Friday—the first to me alone for sixteen years; and I shall count the days till it comes. Beg Behrens, and Lene, and Freddy to write very often to me also. My sister will do it without reminding. They all know how dear they and their letters are to me. I want to know how traveling agrees with Cartheuser, and what he is going to do.

My journey was not attended with any personal inconveniences. With several of the postillions I chatted very sociably; in this way one learns a great deal; and even among this class, friendliness goes further than large fees without it; at least with many. The one from Ratzeburg was quite sorry that he could not drive me further; he, and one of those in Mecklenburg, had been robbed of their hard-earned savings by the French. He gave the Danes a good character; there were bad men, indeed, every where, but at Ratzeburg they had mostly sided with the inhabitants, and protected them against the French; they were not to be complained of. How is that beautiful country disfigured! Almost all the wood in the valley in which the city is situated, has been cut down during the war. I have heard much, which I can well believe, of the bitter poverty left behind, after those calamitous times have passed away; of the heavy contributions levied on the inhabitants of Mecklenburg; of the gradual drying up of all sources of trade. With us, too, things are bad enough, but the people bear their burdens cheerfully; in the Marches every one is in good spirits, and things look encouraging, at least for the agricultural population.

I will now go out and make one or two calls.

Farewell! Of course I shall write again soon, and will always write when I want to lighten my heart. With a little use, I could sit at the table before the sofa, and silently converse with Milly and you; but that would be a short road to insanity.

CXCII.

BERLIN, 17*th August*, 1815.

The quiet melancholy which you desire for me, I seldom enjoy. I am, indeed, sufficiently alone, but my mind is in sad confusion. Every thing

* The entrance of the Allies into Paris.

around me jars upon my feelings, like a false note. The mornings are my least desolate times, because I rise late, and go to sleep late, generally with some fever, so that I awake weary and stupefied. I am the freshest about the middle of the day. The alterations which the servants have made in the arrangements of the furniture during my absence, are the following...... My only wish would be, never to leave this dwelling, for here I always feel as if Milly were still alive and with me, and often as if I saw and heard her busy about her household duties, or other things. At first, I only saw her as she was during her illness, sitting, or lying down, but now, as she used to be in former times. You are just as present to me. When I go out, something impels me home again, and makes me feel as I used to do, when Milly was uneasy if I did not come home again as soon as possible.

Evening.—Schmedding has just left me. I have had some hours of consoling conversation with him. The Reimers are at Magdeburg, and at the Göschens the swarm of dear little children unavoidably disturbs conversation; else neither of these families is among the number of those who shun all allusion to the only subject which it relieves me to speak of. You must not fancy that I should not enjoy conversation on scientific subjects even now, but this is not started, and what is said is not congenial to me. With Schmedding I talked a good deal about my future vocation, and not a little of Milly and you. You have left a strong impression on him, too, and he sees that your accompanying me would be the only blessing I could still enjoy. He himself was very much affected, and I was able to give way to my feelings with him.

The constant rain, together with my great lassitude, and the distance, have prevented my visiting the cemetery as yet, to see how far the workmen have got on. For God's sake do not take it for negligence! On Sunday morning, I shall go to the mason, whom it is not easy to find at any other time, and on Monday, to the foundry. I can not yet say, therefore, when I can lay the beloved corpse in its cool bed. I should like to do it on my birthday, and I hope to be able to manage it.

You long to see Milly, if only for a moment! The promises that you would fain give her, she has already received by words and deeds from you, and taken with her into eternity. I dare not cherish the wish that you express; for I feel as if it might very possibly be granted to me, and would cost me my reason.

I can occupy myself, thank heaven! and if I could only stay here in quiet, all would be well. At least, I am reading records, and have also begun canon law.

Rauch will in no case go direct to Rome. I shall, therefore, still be much obliged to you to write to Lund, and offer him to travel with me free of expense. If I do not go yet, he can stay with me as a visitor till we set off.

CXCIII.

BERLIN, *8th September*, 1815.

I often busy myself with plans for profiting, to the utmost extent, by the advantages Rome presents: I should certainly need some assistants in order to do so. Perhaps it is true, as people say, that in the clearer and brighter atmosphere there, one can work incomparably harder than here;

it had need be so, if I am to get my History written, in addition to performing the duties of my office, and studying the city and its treasures. I must, by degrees, search through all the manuscripts of the Vatican; by so doing I can scarcely fail of making some discoveries. I think I have a trace, which will not disappoint my hope of digging up a treasure, in an almost unknown Greek poet. I shall also look for palimpsests among the parchments in the archives, as well as those in the library. But all this enlarges the sphere of my researches so indefinitely, that my goal seems quite to have receded out of sight.

...... Heindorf has drawn my attention to the fragments of Heyne's autobiography contained in Heeren's; I recommend you to read them also. It is quite another question, whether or not Heyne, who afterward tried to grasp much more than he could retain, and accepted, as his due, the exaggerated admiration and false fame that was offered to him, was a distinguished philologist; and this praise must be denied him. But the picture of his character, of his struggles under difficulties, and of his mind, which is given by these biographical fragments, as well as the poems prefixed to the work, deserves all respect.

CXCIV.

BERLIN, 15*th September*, 1815.

For some time past, I have been very unwell; but it was, perhaps, nothing more than a cold, though I had pains in my chest. At last it turned to influenza, which obliged me to take to my bed. However, I have remained true to my resolution, not to yield to effeminacy again, and yesterday I went out. I rejoice in this heavenly weather and lose the painful sense of solitude; you like a beautiful autumn better than the summer, and Milly liked it too. We once enjoyed a most exquisitely beautiful autumn in Copenhagen; we took long walks in all directions, without regard to distance, and this afforded Milly the full enjoyment of what was to her the highest gratification. That was in the times when we lived as yet in perfect seclusion, when there were many, many days on which we had not a single caller, and whole periods passed away without our, or even my making a visit. I had a dim feeling that it was best for us both; Milly was less satisfied; and yet the storms and billows of the world have been too much for her strength. Heindorf's stay with me has cheered me in another way. It is refreshing to feel that the pleasure of seeing one, can give animation and cheerfulness to a friend from whom one has long been separated. You know how soothing this consciousness is, and how I have, more than once, renewed my youth in your society. Heindorf has done the same among his friends here, of whom I am one of the dearest to him, and I do not care whether others be still dearer to him or not. . . . .

Reserve, the silence of profound meditation, complete absorption in one's own thoughts, are easily recognized and must be honored; but where there is great talkativeness in general, and it is only when the conversation turns upon what is known to be the real vocation of the man, that it ceases to flow freely, there must be other causes than those I have mentioned; the man's heart is not in his calling, he does not live in it. Or, what comes to the same thing, he has not worked out results, which he cherishes, and with which he holds converse. Now this has been accomplished by Heindorf, to a wonderful extent, with regard to grammatical rules, and all that belongs to the narrower sphere of philology, so that he can form positive decisions, for which he can always instantly assign his reasons, where others have only a dim feeling. That he has elaborated his philological system, by unwearied assiduity, in spite of constant ill-health from his childhood up; that he has never allowed himself to be stopped in his progress by sickness; that he thinks nothing of all his knowledge and acquirements, and knows no greater happiness than the admiration and love of those whom he rates above himself; that he even sets little value upon his peculiar department of philology compared to others; that friendship and kindness are his sole enjoyments—all this makes him one of the most lovable persons among the literary men of my acquaintance. I am somewhat proud of his dedicating the most perfect of his writings to me, and inwardly rejoice that the one, with which he has connected my name, is that which, he says, will certainly endure, and has been written for posterity.

To give him some pleasure during his stay with us, I invited his friends to meet him at a dinner in the Thiergarten the day before yesterday, and asked Nicolovius and Rauch, (who spoil no society) as well. It was the first party that I had really enjoyed for many months. One is tempted indeed to reproach oneself afterward, but yet it is right perhaps to change the current of one's thoughts. In former times too, I have reproached myself for it, if I enjoyed myself in a party which Milly did not share, and I preferred staying away on such occasions, because Milly never had, or would have, any pleasure for herself alone, so that she had much fewer enjoyments than I, and I would not suffer that. In general, too, she preferred my refusing invitations without her; but after her illness assumed a serious character, she altered in this respect, and wished me to go into society, for the sake of change of scene and amusement. However, at that time, it would have been unbearable to me.

There are many things which become indispensable to us, when we are accustomed to them; and if you are conscious of being able to fill more than one vocation, you can not repress the impulse to embrace more than one. Indeed, you feel that you wrong the cause, as well as yourself, if you renounce either of them. This is my feeling now with regard to the highest spheres of statesmanship. Unhappily we always learn wisdom too late, and I shudder when I look at the years that lie behind me, and the age I have already reached. But this terror is nothing to my bitter remorse for faults and oversights on higher matters—the remembrance of which would soon overwhelm me, if I dwelt upon it, and yet, not to drive it from me, seems the only possible atonement for them. If there be another and a real atonement—for what destroys the energies, and makes life useless, can not be the right one—oh, how thankful I should be to any one who would announce it to me!

Your welcome letter has again done me much good.

CXCV.

TO PERTHES.

BERLIN, *September*, 1815.

I thank you for the interest you take in my mission, which is at least highly probable, though not absolutely and irrevocably fixed. My heart can scarcely be light or joyful, when I am bidding farewell to my country, most probably for the whole of the short portion yet remaining to my life; but certainly for so long a time, that if I return, it will be to live as a stranger in my own land, with changed feelings, and with habits that can not be altered at an advanced age. Especially as the work which is the calling of my life, the Roman History, however the reverse may seem evident, can not by any means be so well composed there as here. Finally, I must renounce the tasks that the times continually set before us, and in the performance of which, I have a most distinct inward call to co-operate. Now, if the embassador to Rome were but the mediator of wise and wholesome measures—but he is only the instrument of what he is ordered to undertake; and how little that will be in harmony with my views I can already perceive. For the true welfare of the Catholic church in our State, such a spokesman can do nothing at all—since the ecclesiastical authorities of the Papacy are obstinately bent upon keeping the Church under their own jurisdiction, and the deep inward degeneracy of the Catholic clergy is not less prejudicial to it, than the many perverse and mischievous views held by Protestant statesmen.

Many form an idea of this office, which is quite at variance with the reality, and then congratulate me on a mission, which would indeed be glorious, if the attributes they assume, really belonged to it.

As regards philology alone, unquestionably my stay there can not be useless. But I should have accomplished much more, could I have kept strictly to the unconditional furlough granted me in the first instance. The embassador is nailed down to Rome, and Rome does not contain the twentieth part of the literary and historical treasures of Italy which would reward the labor of bringing them to light; these are scattered over the whole country. But it is ordained that every thing good must be spoilt.

CXCVI.

TO PROFESSOR BRANDIS.

BERLIN, *26th September*, 1815.

You have applied to me, dear friend, on a matter in which you need counsel and assistance, and you apologize for it with a bashfulness which proves that in this amiable, but self-tormenting weakness, you are the same as of old, just as you are in all other points, but especially—and of this no one will ever doubt—in your sentiments toward your friends. I wish you could know, *to your shame*, not only how interesting your letter is to me, but how full of melancholy pleasure, for it recalls vividly to my mind that time when you were with us in Berlin, as companion to my sister-in-law. The recollection of that time is indeed a melancholy pleasure to me, which you, too, could not willingly forget. It was the epoch at which I reached the quiet and secure haven of literary leisure, after passing through the storms that had convulsed society; when a period of contentment and happiness began which aroused all the inmost powers of my being, and rendered me capable of enterprises which I had long despaired of undertaking. Now, all is night around me; I have lost *all* which then made me rich, and taught me the true value of my riches; yet there are moments of strength, when the memory of the past is a source not of torture, but of consolation. I thank you too most sincerely for the confidence you place in me; for when a man has found that all his confidence in others has been abused, and that there is no firm rock on which he can build, and yet is conscious that he is himself faithful and trustworthy, he feels deep gratitude toward those who do him justice and trust him.

It is very right and reasonable that you should wish to come to Prussia. That State in North Germany, which gladly receives every German and regards him, when he has once entered her service, in the same light as a native citizen, is the true Germany; and it is comparatively of little consequence whether it may cause some inconvenience to other neighboring States, which persist in their isolation, in the face of God's providence and the general welfare, or even whether temporary and accidental defects may exist in its administration. They are but the moles in the face of the beloved one; I would not exchange our nation for ancient Rome itself. In Denmark you, as a German, can never breathe freely, can never feel that you have a father-land. Therefore you are right, and in the path of duty, to leave it, even if philology, and the other liberal branches of knowledge, were in a better condition there than is actually the case. I hope that the time will come, when the facility with which Germans make themselves at home in foreign countries will no longer form a trait in the national character, and rejoice over every instance I meet with. But the sudden progress which science and letters have made in Germany, renders it impossible for the philologist to find a fitting sphere beyond its limits, and this consciousness oppresses me when I look forward to my removal to Italy. Antiquity in walls and stones is but the shadow of antiquity; the spirit lives in the ancient writings.

I thank you most cordially for your friendly wishes concerning my future fate. God will not let it become too hard to bear. He, who has long been the spoilt child of fortune, feels indeed bitter pain when he finds himself stripped of all his possessions and beggared; but he, too, learns to endure.

I hope that a very dear friend of mine, an excellent officer of our army, will join me in Rome as soon as he can obtain leave of absence, and so I shall not be quite alone and forsaken in the strange country, of which I have an indescribable dread. Besides such isolated instances of faithfulness, and love which truly deserve the name, we have a source of joy and strength, such as we never knew before, in the social and patriotic feelings that have prevailed in Germany since 1813, and we know it is not a delusion which we are cherishing in our hearts.

CXCVII.

TO MADAME HENSLER.

30th September, 1815.

The funeral has had to be put off again; the grave was not ready. Else I should have snatched myself from my bed, and—perhaps God would have blessed me for it with a shorter illness. Thus, I have been obliged to give up the hope of having the whole finished in the course of this week. So I shall bury my beloved Amelia on Sunday, the 8th of October. It is the anniversary of our arrival here, and of a completely new period of our lives, full of joy and sorrow.

I had written so far, when I fell into a state of insensibility, from which I was only recovered with difficulty, and then fell asleep. I wanted to give you further particulars of the requests I have to make of you. So now I am really seriously ill, which I promised to let you know of.......

CXCVIII.

BERLIN, *9th October*, 1815.

At last I have reached the goal, and laid the corpse of our beloved one in its resting-place. It was yesterday afternoon at five o'clock; the very hour at which we entered Berlin nine years ago; it was just growing dark then as we turned into our lodging; as it was now when I returned alone to my desolate room.

In the morning I attended service in St. Mary's church, where a very good man preached, and prepared myself with a still heart for the bitter way. Nicolovius and Göschen, who knew of it, came in the afternoon to accompany me. May God reward them for it, as well as for all the love and sympathy they show me! We found every thing ready, and the coffin was lowered. When it had been let down, I sat on the planks, and was able to weep bitterly, and to pray from the bottom of my heart. God knows that I would gladly have rested in the grave, and that I looked with sorrowful longing on the empty space which, I feel assured, will never receive my corpse.

In the evening I was quite alone again, and sufficiently composed to set about some necessary work. I felt more satisfied, as if I had laid my Milly in her bed.

I will send you the occasional paper by the first opportunity;* and with it a catalogue of the works of art that have been recaptured and are now exhibiting. The Dantzic Last Judgment is a miracle of art, perhaps the highest specimen of its kind.

CXCIX.

BERLIN, *15th October*, 1815.

N.† left me an hour ago.—I have had a long conversation with him. First about myself; and then about my business in Rome, and what is to be done for the Catholic Church.—I told him, that all such measures as might really raise the church from her terrible state of internal decay, lay entirely within the sphere of the legislature and the government, so much so, that if they fail to do their part, no formal regulations to which the assent of the Romish court would be necessary, could avail any thing, but must remain utterly fruitless. The measures most necessary to be adopted at home, are to make a suitable provision for the payment of the clergy in the Rhine provinces, West Prussia and Posen, as in these countries the church lands have been confiscated; (on the other side of the Rhine the salary of the parochial clergy has only amounted to 130 dollars per annum since the concordat;) to raise the character of the instruction in schools of every grade; to establish good Catholic universities (in which, however, we are met by the insuperable difficulty, that in that church knowledge and talents are now so extremely seldom combined with piety—you can find the one or the other, but scarcely ever the two in union), and to choose eminent men for the cathedral chapters, which would secure the election

* The preface to Von Vincke's work on "The Internal Administration of Great Britain."

† No doubt, Nicolovius.

of such for bishops, and, where the choice of the bishops falls immediately to the crown, to appoint only men of high character. Moreover, all decisions relating to the better regulation of the Catholic Church to which the assent of the Pope is necessary, ought to emanate from this place, and to be dispatched to the embassador in a finished state. The latter would never be authorized to remonstrate against them : this would be to overstep the duties of his position. I told him that if the proposals were reasonable it would require very little skill to get them accepted; if they were unreasonable it might still be possible to carry them through; but who would suffer himself to be an instrument in such a work? With respect to many things of which the people here fancy the attainment possible, they should recall H's* words : "The angel Gabriel could not bring them to pass at Rome. The negotiations there might be divided into two classes, such as could be very easily transacted, and such as could not be transacted at all." I said, too, that skillful negotiation with Italians, patient preparation, silent observation of character in order to find out how to work upon it, were not my forte, and besides it was long since I had had any practice of the kind. If, indeed, men awoke once more to great aims, and great endeavors, if one could embrace all around one with affection as in 1813, then in truth my powers of mind might also re-awaken; but here there was nothing great either to be done or sacrificed, nor yet to be obtained in a straightforward way by simple skill. As to resisting the encroachments of Rome, it was needless to preach to any one on that subject; every one would do that who had not sold his heart to the priestly party.

Yesterday I was too sad to write to you. I tried to distract my thought by paying the Dohnas a visit, and I got something better than amusement by it. They were both very friendly and showed much feeling; and I was able to talk about my Milly. Believe me, it pains me more than any thing, that no one enters at all into conversation with me on this subject. Every one is silent when I speak of her. I am indeed not quite well, and still rather feverish; but in a tender and calm state of feeling. For some time my sufferings were great; you know in general, from my letters, my condition from time to time. As it frequently passed into painful nervous excitement, this will explain and excuse to you the irritability which has frequently appeared in them. My natural disposition is gentle—as it was when you first knew me; my irritability has come on much later in life. I miss two things in my Milly :—the life with her, and her love. But this is not all; I also miss the indescribable energy which she imparted to me in a far higher degree than I was aware of. The grave is now in order. Would to God, that it might one day receive me, when I had fallen peacefully asleep in the consciousness of having fulfilled my true vocation.

CC.

BERLIN, 12*th December*, 1815.

Your letter has been a great comfort to me. I feel much more satisfied, in the prospect of living with you. What I shall still feel the loss of, and enjoyed when I had my Milly with me, we will mourn over together. I only hope that now you will be able to come with an easy mind. I dread these last days for you, and the parting from those who have always known what they possessed in you. I shall be a debtor to all of them. . . . . .

* Probably W. Von Humboldt, who had been embassador in Rome.

My mind will be opened to the enjoyment of the treasures of Rome, and the beginning of a completely new life may, perhaps, make me young again. I am very glad that our circle of intercourse will be small; it promises me a life of close application to study.

A very unsatisfactory tone of feeling prevails here, as is the case, perhaps, throughout Germany. The interest in literature is so much on the decline (indeed it is weaker now than during and after the fever of the French Revolution), and our bright visions so fade away one after another, that we can not help perceiving that the noblest opportunities of attaining a permanently higher intellectual standing for the nation have been thrown away or abused; and we have reason to fear that an age of mediocrity is before us. Great injury must inevitably result from so large a part of our youth having taken the field for a second time; they are nearly all snatched away from their studies. The first war did them no harm, but that was conducted in a different spirit from the present one. The regiments of the line have given way to excesses, and what is still worse, many officers have acquired a taste for Paris. The noble path of life is terribly narrow. I have very few hearers as yet.

As Gretchen herself has some apprehensions, do not persuade her to come with us. Only I should be so glad if you could have some companion, who could be like a daughter to you. If you could but have little Sophy or Louisa.

Since the weather has become so severe, I often vividly recall the time that I spent with Milly in Bordesholm, in the winter of 1800—a golden age for her and for me.

Pray take Christmas presents to the dear children at Meldorf in my name; and choose something pretty for our friends at Husum.

CCI.

Berlin, 23*d December*, 1815.

......On Tuesday, Hardenberg sent for me, and fixed to have an interview with me the next day; the result of which is, that he has appointed me one of the Royal Commissioners to take part in the deliberations on the Constitution. This will necessitate an indefinite postponement of our journey, for a considerable time will probably elapse before the delegates to the assembly are even named, much more before they arrive in Berlin. This may not take place, perhaps, till the end of January, and then we know by experience how slowly business advances in an assembly the members of which are totally unused to deliberations in common. So, though Hardenberg himself fancies that the work might be finished by the end of March, or at furthest in April, we can not at all reckon upon this being the case, and, in fact, it is impossible to fix any time for the termination of our labors...... I do not know whether I shall find any sympathy with my views among my fellow-members of the assembly, but I feel as if I should have missed an essential calling of my life, if I had had no share in the drawing up of the Constitution. We can not expect that this work will result in the establishment of thoroughly mature and wise institutions at the present moment. It can only be a beginning and a germ, to be gradually developed by time and circumstances. But if this opportunity can be seized to carry through even a few good laws, they may have lasting consequences. It will be a satisfaction to you also, that I have received this commission; and when I said, at first, that it was not quite welcome to me personally, that was only in reference to its lengthening my separation from you......

I have got the Servian national songs, and shall translate them where it is possible; they are very beautiful. This season carries my thoughts back to the past very much. It was a time that Milly always enjoyed so much. Oh, how willingly would I give my whole life for one year with her! Even if it were a life most rich in pleasures and prosperity. Yet a life rich in activity and usefulness I should not dare to sacrifice even at that price, and she would not wish it. May she watch over me (as you will too, with her spirit), and at last receive me to herself in peace.

CCII.

BERLIN, *16th January*, 1816.

A stranger has brought me a collection of modern Greek songs. I send you a translation I have made of one of them. Perhaps it will draw tears from you, as it did from me. The modern Greeks believe that the soul does not part from the body till the form of the latter is destroyed by corruption. A child speaks thus from its grave to its mother:

"Beyond the rocky mountain peak, that rises high and frowning,
Its summit wrapped in floating clouds, its steep glens dim and misty,
There grows the herb forgetfulness, beside the still cold fountain.
The mother-ewe eats of the herb, and then forgets her yeanling;
My mother, pluck the soothing herb, and then forget thy darling."
The Mother. "A thousand times I'll pluck the herb, but I forget thee never."*

In another song, which begins—

"Thou fiery-red carnation, thou purple hyacinth,"

the soul of the child, whose body is decaying, takes leave of the flowers which are planted on his grave, and asks them to bend down their heads to receive a kiss, and transmit it to his parents. Another relates how Charon, now the dæmon of death, passes on his horse through the village, with the host of dead after him, the little ones hanging to the saddle; the poet entreats him to stop by the cool spring, that the souls may speak one word to their loved ones, and the children play with the flowers! He denies it: they would not be willing to leave it again. Many illustrate the praises of heroes, who are, it must be allowed, only captains of robber bands, but what men! You soon become accustomed to the rhythm, and exclaim with delight, that it is poetry not beneath the poetry of old Greece!......

CCIII.

BERLIN, *20th January*, 1816.

......Some one preached to me lately that I should do this, and that; take up my history, &c. I answered, happy is the man who has succeeded in convincing himself that the simple act of willing can enable himself and

* "Jenseits vom steilen Felsgebirg, das hoch dort ragt und düster,
—Die Scheitel decken Wolken ihm, und Nebel füllt die Klüfte—
Da wächst am stillen kalten Quell, Vergessenheit das Kräutlein.
Das Kräutlein pflückt das Mutterschaaf, vergisst sodann der Lämmer.
Das Kräutlein pflück', mein Mütterchen, vergiss sodann des Kleinen."
Die Mutter. "Ich pflück' es mir wohl tausendmal, vergesse Dein doch nimmer!"

others to do every thing. If so, how superfluous are all intellectual gifts! We need only exert our will, and we are competent, not merely, as all the world has believed hitherto, to tasks requiring research and industry, but to produce works of genius. And this under all circumstances! It is not true, therefore, that genius is unfolded by outward circumstances, as plants and flowers are by spring-tide and summer, and that there are times and cases when genius can no more exist than the violet can blow in the autumn: it is not true, that in the age of Alexander there were no great poets, because there could be none then. From this truth, we may soar upward in a straight line to the regions in which Fichte seemed to us weaklings to rave, and look forward to the time when the will may suffice to make the rocks bear fruit, and the glaciers bring forth corn. We may spare ourselves all sympathy with our sick and weak brother; it is his own fault if he does not choose to be healthy.......

CCIV.

BERLIN, 30*th January*, 1816.

......Since [reading my treatise last Wednesday in the Academy] I have been busied in preparing the Fronto for the press. Heindorf and Buttmann take part in the critical revision of it, but by far the largest and most difficult task falls to my share. The Milanese editor has put together the loose leaves (which are quite unconnected, only legible in parts, and altogether form only a small portion of the whole work), without the slightest regard to their natural order, and printed them in such a manner, that you can not see where one fragment begins and another ends. I have been obliged to reduce this chaos to the fragments of which it is composed in the first instance, and must next bring together the parts which are immediately connected, or only separated by fragments which are lost. It is a work of great labor, but for which I have a peculiar talent, so that if I did not undertake it, centuries might perhaps elapse before the poor dismembered thing would find any one to put its limbs in their places again.......

You ask after my cough. I really can not say when it began; but I have been suffering from colds ever since the beginning of December, because I am obliged to go out in all weathers; to dinner, to the Crown Prince, to the riding-school, and when I want to escape from solitude; and then generally I have to walk long distances. About a fortnight ago, my cough was really very bad; now it is of no consequence, only it is constantly irritated by the dust, and damp, and draught, at the riding-school, so that I have been sometimes afraid I must give up this pursuit. This would be a pity, for I have conquered the greatest difficulty; I have lost my awkwardness, and am told that I have much improved in agility. I feel safe and bold on horseback. If I remain a part of the summer here, I shall attend the shooting-gallery, and perhaps the fencing-school. When my cough was at the worst, it was a welcome thought to me that perhaps it might be a legacy from my beloved Milly; the best gift she could leave behind with me.

A thousand thanks for your tender and sympathizing letter. But you do not know, you did not see, and can not understand, how a work such as my History arises, and can alone arise—in love and joy only, not in affliction, anguish, and bereavement.

CCV.

BERLIN, *10th February*, 1816.

......My author himself is a miserable hero, but the letters are extremely attractive, especially the youthful letters of Marcus Antoninus, which throw much light upon his inward history. What an angel do we find here too! But he likewise appears to have fallen in his later years under thes way of a woman, who has much more resemblance to Marie Antoinette, than poor Louis to Marcus Antoninus; and this book makes it clearer, and more comprehensible, how it should have been possible for the rule of this heavenly man to promote and hasten the dissolution and corruption of the State.

I have heard nothing more about the plague in Italy; but I feel we must not at all conclude from this that the report of it was false......

CCVI.

BERLIN, *20th February*, 1816.

I no longer doubt that we shall go to Italy, unless the plague prove an obstacle, in which case I should have great scruples about it, and, if you went with me, feel very anxious. There are certainly other considerations against it, with regard to Gretchen, which press heavily on my heart. I have foretold the spreading of the pestilence to Italy ever since the autumn, as many can bear me witness; it is not from any prophetic gift of mine, but on very natural grounds. It attacked Venetian Dalmatia a year ago, from which it had, up to that time, been excluded by quarantine regulations. It has also penetrated into Austrian Croatia, and is raging in Corfu. Hence we had reason to fear that it would advance from the Adriatic Sea over Italy. Besides, I hold to my assertion, that under certain circumstances—when Death is hungry—it overpowers all the obstacles which in ordinary times bar its progress. That such is the case at present, we may conclude from the fact that it has reached Corfu and Croatia, where all possible precautions have been observed, and up to this time successfully.

Flight might not be found quite so practicable; if a place is really threatened, no one is allowed to pass thence to the neighboring districts. But I think that the spread or cessation of the epidemic must be decided before we enter Lombardy, and, if God permit, we may wait in the Venetian Alps to see what turn things will take......

CCVII.

BERLIN, *27th February*, 1816.

Although here, as well as abroad, they keep to the system of leaving the public in the dark respecting the pestilence, things come to light from time to time, from which the danger seems to grow more and more decided. The plague does not simply slay its victims and depopulate countries; it eats away the moral energies as well, and often quite destroys them; thus, as I have shown in my last public lecture before the Academy, the sudden and complete degeneracy of the Roman world from the time of Marcus Antoninus onward, may be referred to the Oriental plague which then entered Europe for the first time; just as, six hundred years earlier, the plague, which was strictly speaking a yellow fever, coincides too exactly with the termination of the ideal period of antiquity, not to be regarded as a cause of it. In such epidemics the best individuals always die, and the rest degenerate morally. Times of pestilence are always those in which the animal and the devilish in human nature assume prominence. Neither need we be superstitious or even pious, to regard great pestilences as something more than a conflict of the physical with the human history of the earth: I fear my conviction that it indicates the victory of the negative and destructive of the two contending principles, would be thought terribly Manichæan and impious.

CCVIII.

BERLIN, *29th June*, 1816.*

I had so much to say to you, I do not know what I can and will say. I therefore intend to write very little to you to-day, and to wait for your letter. I may still receive it here; and I hope that you will reckon upon it, as it is settled that Brandis is to come to us here.†

My thoughts have traveled with you; you have arrived by this time. We still mean to depart at the time fixed with Brandis.......

Heindorf died last Sunday without being sensible of his approaching end. His friends will now have to look after his seven orphans. My position will allow me to take my share. Why was I never able to promise it to him? Yet he no doubt relied on his friend.‡

In the evening after you had left us, when your carriage went out of sight and I returned home, I felt very sad. Gretchen's spirits were quite overcome by the parting, and I recovered myself in trying to console her.

God grant that you may be happy! You need only wish for me the enjoyment of tolerable health; for as it is now I can never get on. All will rejoice to have you back again. Rejoice with them; but remain to to me what you have been.

Give our best love to all our friends.

CCIX.

BERLIN, *6th July*, 1816.

Your confidence that I should become more tranquil, has not quite deceived you; I am so on the whole. Gretchen does all in her power to promote it. She enters thoroughly and kindly into my state of feeling. She keeps herself constantly employed, and has shown the greatest method and judgment in the arrangements and preparations for our removal and packing up, which she has executed with indefatigable energy. She says indeed, when she sees me sad, that it would depress her terribly if she did not hope that I should recover my spirits again in time.

I do not despair of my mental powers. I derive much benefit from

* This was the first letter Niebuhr wrote after his parting from Madame Hensler, and her return home.

† Brandis accompanied Madame Hensler on her return to Holstein.

‡ In an earlier letter, Niebuhr says: "One of the sons is my godchild. I shall provide for him." For several years after Heindorf's death, his family received a considerable sum of money regularly every year, without being able to discover whence it came. In process of time, as their circumstances improved, it ceased, and it was only after many years that Niebuhr was found to be the author of this assistance, in addition to the other friendly offices he rendered them.

simple warm baths; they have already given a more healthy tone to my nerves. Gretchen has stood the fatigues of packing very well. Her chest is quite free from oppression, and she has little pain in her side.

Our departure is positively fixed for the thirteenth. I shall not take my instructions with me; it would take too long to wait for them as I had intended, and so I shall travel forward at once. Hardenberg has promised to send them after me.

We shall most likely take the most direct route. The two months and a half from now to the end of September is so short, that we must curtail our stay wherever we can, in order to stop long enough at the important places to make some use of them. I have no answer from Goethe; his wife is dead.

You will write as often to me as you have time and ability. Pray write by the next post to Nuremberg, and a week later to Munich. I shall probably stay more than a week in Munich.

I look forward to the journey with great pleasure—as much as I can now feel. Gretchen also enjoys the prospect.

The sorting and arranging of my old papers has again excited my sad feelings. Many of them you will one day read, not without emotion; some merit to be preserved. However, I do not now think that my death is near. Love to our friends. I shall write you one more letter home. God bless you. Farewell.

CCX.

BERLIN, *20th July*, 1816.

Your anxiously expected letter, in which and from which I hoped to take a blessing with me on my journey, has never arrived. Perhaps you have been persuaded to remain at Husum. If so, ten or twelve days will elapse before I find your letter at Nuremberg.

I am so tired and exhausted that even if you were actually here I could scarcely say any thing rational to you. My audience with the King was on Wednesday, and not till then could we make definite preparations for the journey. The next day, my Milly's birthday, I wanted to celebrate here; that is, at her grave.

I can not describe the feelings with which I leave this place. I often forget my sorrows, but I can not yet be happy. The general aspect of political affairs also weighs heavily on my mind.

The Crown Prince has taken a very affectionate leave of me, and shed tears at parting. All the other princes are likewise cordial and friendly.

People in general express sincere regret at my leaving, and hope that I shall return with official advancement; which I, whose judgment is unwarped, do not at all expect.

The best piece of news I have to tell you is, that Gretchen's health is much improved.

I must conclude. God bless you richly a thousandfold. If possible I shall write a few lines to you daily during our journey.

CHAPTER X.

NIEBUHR'S MISSION IN ROME. FROM 1816 TO 1823.

FROM this time forward, Niebuhr was so entirely removed from the friends of his earlier life, that few facts respecting his outward history are to be obtained excepting from his own letters. These, however, succeed each other in such an almost unbroken series, that they require but few connecting links, and therefore there is little occasion to regret the absence of other sources of information. But, while his letters give a very complete picture of his personal circumstances and occupations, it must always be borne in mind, that most of them were written under great restraint with regard to the expression of opinion upon outward events, on account of the surveillance exercised at the post-offices of the countries through which they passed. He often had to deny himself the utterance of a sentiment altogether, for fear of the total suppression of the letter.

Niebuhr quitted Berlin in July. His friend, Dr. Brandis (now Professor of Philosophy in Bonn), accompanied him as Secretary of Legation. He had made the choice of his secretary a condition of his accepting the mission, and in the first instance had offered the post to Professor Dahlman, who however declined it, having just accepted the office of Representative to the nobles and prelates of Schleswig-Holstein.

Niebuhr first visited Munich, where he staid a week, partly to look through the MSS. of the Royal Library, partly to see his aged friend, Jacobi. Thence he proceeded to Innspruck, and visited the memorable scenes of the Tyrolese war. The next place at which he made any stay was Verona, where likewise he explored the manuscript treasures contained in the library, and made his famous discovery of the Institutes of Gaius. He spent a short time at Venice, Bologna, and Florence, and reached Rome on the 7th of October.

Niebuhr had sent his books by sea to Leghorn. He soon learnt that the ship had been wrecked at Calais, and was for several months in uncertainty respecting their fate. As no books were allowed to be taken out of the public libraries, he was for a considerable time deprived of the means of pursuing his studies, and this, joined to the ill-health which seized both him and his wife almost immediately on their entrance into Italy, and the, to him, unaccustomed privation of all intellectual intercourse, account for the tone of depression which prevails in his earlier letters from Rome. In spite of these disadvantages, however, he turned his time to account, as far as possible, by visiting the library of the Vatican, and in November discovered the fragments of Cicero's orations, and some of Livy, Seneca, and Hyginus; after which he occupied himself assiduously with their correction and preparation for the press. Their publication, however, was from many causes delayed for several years.

Niebuhr's relations with the court of Rome assumed a very satisfactory aspect from the first. A mutual liking sprang up between him and the excellent Pope Pius VII., and he was on terms of personal friendship with Cardinal Gonsalvi, the prime minister and secretary of state, of whose character as a statesman Niebuhr had a high opinion. During the earlier years of his residence in Rome, Niebuhr had merely to dispatch the current business with the Papal court, as the instructions for his special mission, which Hardenberg had promised to send after him in a few weeks, did not arrive for four years.

His intercourse in Rome, beyond that which he enjoyed with Brandis and Bunsen, with the latter of whom he soon formed an intimate friendship, was chiefly confined to Germans and English, though he had likewise several acquaintances among the French. Among the Italians there were very few whose conversation afforded him any pleasure, owing to their entirely opposite cast of mind, though there were a few of the higher ecclesiastics who formed exceptions. Niebuhr associated much with the young artists who were then studying in Rome, and laying the foundation of the present German school of historical painting. Among them he was particularly intimate with Cornelius, Platner, Overbeck, and the two Schadows. He made their acquaintance on the anniversary of the battle of Leipsic, eight days after his arrival. The artists celebrated the day by a dinner, to which they invited Niebuhr and Brandis. Niebuhr sat between Thorwaldsen and Cornelius, who both instantly inspired him with the strongest interest, and he made an equally favorable impression on them. Niebuhr always took a lively interest in art, particularly in paintings, and his judgment was considered, by those most competent to form an opinion, remarkably correct, though he had no practical acquaintance with any branch of art.

Letters written in 1816.

CCX.

TO MADAME HENSLER.

MUNICH, 13*th August*, 1816.

Gretchen has, I think, furnished you with the thread of our journey as far as Ratisbon. From Meiningen I sent you the history of our adventures and calamities on the road through the forest of Thuringia. We saw nothing of that town; it rained in torrents, and if the brother of our old Heim had not lived so near, I should not even have visited him. From him I heard that the duchy contains 54,000 inhabitants; not much could be said about its wealth; but the people help themselves through, which is, perhaps, what is most to be wished for. The weather cleared up as we started, and the valley of the Werra, through which we were hastening, on an excellent high road, appeared in all its beauty. The roads, from this neighborhood till beyond Wurzburg, were extremely good; they seemed to be made of the basalt of the hills near Wurzburg and Fulda. The little towns in the Wurzburg district are not pretty, though they are probably more prosperous than those on the Saal, as the land is very fertile and rich. The country is beautiful, and thickly dotted with villages of some size. At Wurzburg we stopped for twenty-four hours. The city is certainly very well situated; part of it lies on the opposite side of the river, at the foot of the hill, on which are the Marienburg, and a place of pilgrimage. This hill produces the Stein wine, and it stretches so far into the country that it affords to a wide district the enjoyment of its delicious products, of which Brandis and I partook. The bridge is adorned, like that of Prague, with statues of saints, single and in groups; altogether Wurzburg swarms with Christian statues—all bad, all mannered, and tasteless. The cathedral is new, and so are the paintings, which are worthless; many of the buildings are large and handsome, and show that the city was once the seat of a Chapter composed of a proud and rich aristocracy. We—which, in such cases, always means Brandis and myself—hunted out Professor Goldmayer—found him not at home; he had received my card, however, and came to me at the hotel. I found in him not merely courtesy, which is shown by what I have just said, but a simple, obliging, straightforward, upright man, with nothing unprotestant, that is, no stifling of his genuine German nature about him. This seems to be the case with the rest of the Wurzburg scholars, and their political ideas appear to be quite satisfactory. The librarian showed me what I wished to see, the MSS., among which are some of very great antiquity; one was of the kind for which I am looking out,* but the obliterated writing was nothing but an old Latin translation of the Bible, written probably in the fourth or fifth century. I wasted several hours, that evening and the following morning, in carefully looking over these works, to me quite useless. But I had

* *i. e.* Palimpsests.

pleasure in examining the works of art which I found among them, the exquisitely carved ivory tablets which ornament their covers, and must be at least as old as the eleventh century. They really must be regarded as specimens of alto-relievo, of which ancient art would not need to be ashamed. Copies from it they may be, for some of the figures are in unmistakable Roman costume. Similar carvings are to be found among the illuminated MSS. of the Munich library, some with Greek, others with Latin inscriptions, the letters of which are so accurately formed that it is impossible to ascribe them to Constantinople.

Our road brought us through a district where the different territories were formerly curiously intermingled, for the most part belonging to Bayreuth or Anspach, and I thought I could still distinctly recognize the difference of religion and of their former political relations. We caught sight at once of the whole extent of Nuremberg, with its castles and its high steeples. The city is much smaller than I had expected from its ancient population, which, calculating from 4000 yearly births, must have amounted, in the fifteenth century, to more than 100,000 souls. It lies on hills. Nearly all the names of the streets have been changed since the change of the government. Two churches had been already pulled down because they wanted repairs; one was sold, as we heard, for five hundred florins, for the sake of its building materials. The price of houses is unusually low. A house for a family of the ordinary middle class may be had for five hundred florins; a very handsome one, which in Berlin would probably cost from sixty to eighty thousand dollars, may be had here for ten thousand florins. Yet the city appears by no means so empty and deserted as you might anticipate from this, and trade is reviving; orders have unexpectedly arrived from America. The debts of the city, amounting to 9,500,000 florins, have been made over to the Bavarian government, with a reduction of one half in the rate of interest. The municipal constitution has been quite abrogated; the city is governed by a royal commissioner; a town-council has been nominated, but it does not assemble. But the Bavarians have hopes, from the express words of a law promulgated last year, that, in the larger cities, magistrates will be again appointed, to whom the management of the fiscal matters of the communes, and even the administration of justice and the police will be restored. Magistrates have been already conceded to the smaller towns. In consequence of all these changes the Town Hall is useless and empty, or, at least, appropriated to other purposes. The old decorations and emblems have been carried away; a screen of finely-executed brass-work, which stood in the council-hall, has been sold, &c. Those churches, the preservation of which seemed necessary for the wants of the city, have been suffered to keep their immense treasures of art untouched. You are not prepared to see so many sacred relics of antiquity in a Protestant city; the appearance of the place is quite Catholic; nay, to judge by the present state of the Catholic Churches, it might be maintained that the works of art would have been far better preserved if the Reformation had become universal, supposing it to be carried out with as much moderation as at Nuremberg. St. Sebald's and St. Lawrence's have grown rich in old paintings through a custom which I never met with elsewhere; on the death of a citizen of consideration, a painting was hung up in the church to his memory, to which a tablet bearing the date of his death was affixed, but which had no other personal reference to the deceased, rarely even to his patron saint. These pictures are shockingly neglected; they are regarded as the property of the family who presented them to the church. There is one extremely beautiful painting in St. Lawrence's, ascribed, like every thing else in Nuremberg of unknown origin, to Albert Durer, but it is much older. But the most beautiful painting of all was actually discovered by Brandis; it was painted before 1450, to judge by another picture near it, which is provided with a date. Brandis had climbed on to an old stone altar to look at another picture, also of great merit, when he suddenly became aware that there was one far superior, hanging on a column behind, of which you caught sight through an arch. To get near it we were obliged to send for the key of the clerestory—it was worth the trouble. It is an altar picture with wings; in the background is Christ, very youthful, and with a crown on his head, engaged in crowning the Holy Virgin who is also represented in very early youth. Its beauty is hardly to be surpassed. Of the works of Hans Kulmbach, hitherto an unknown artist to me, I could give you no account, unless I had written every day. There is a gallery in the castle, in two halls, which contains some very respectable and very ancient pictures, and some masterpieces by Michael Wohlgemuth. I never knew what he really was till I came there. There are eight large figures of saints, which are splendid, all of course on a gold ground, the handling vigorous and delicate, the coloring brilliant. A Last Judgment of his leaves me scarcely a doubt that he was the painter of the Dantzic picture; nothing else can explain the likeness between the portrait figures. We could only see the very ancient imperial chapel, said to date from the Emperor Conrad, through a window. An old lime-tree stands in the court-yard, hollow, and scarcely to be called alive; the saying goes that it was planted by St. Cunigunda, the consort of Henry II., whose memory is still poetically preserved by monuments, not only in Nuremberg, but also in Bamberg, Merseburg, and Ratisbon. From the halls of this castle I overlooked the country where Gustavus Adolphus was encamped within his lines, in the summer of 1632; Wallenstein was opposite to him; I could trace the circuit of the lines of the great Swedish monarch; a large portion of them is still existing. The Frauenholz collection at the Town Hall, which is brought together for sale, contains some magnificent things. There I saw for the first time an important work of Martin Schoen. I also visited the town library with Brandis; but there was nothing of value in the whole collection of MSS.; the most interesting thing was a globe on which Cuba is represented as a continent, and there is a greater confusion in the northern part of Europe, that is, in Norway and Sweden, than in our maps of America a hundred years ago. Among the people whom I saw in Nuremberg, where the Museum renders it very easy to see people and hear them speak, the most attractive and important to me was Seebeck, Goethe's friend and fellow-laborer in optics. Hegel was not at home when I called, but immediately returned my visit, and staid a long time. To *you*, dear Dora, I may venture to say—and you will see no danger in it for me—that I have met universally with a very distinguished reception. This does not make me vain; it humbles me; I often say myself, they might spare their trouble; they only see my corpse and ghost. Twenty years ago, when older men made me feel my distance, they did me wrong; I was conscious that I had something in me which merited affection and welcome. Nay even I might have felt this but a few years ago deeply! We ought to have spent at least another day in Nuremberg; there was yet much to see, and I was still quite unacquainted with the citizens, who have retained somewhat of their former remarkable character; it would have been amusing, too, to have seen with our own eyes the relics of the Guild of the Master-singers and of the Fruit-bearing Society.* We left on Sunday afternoon. We slept at Neumarkt, where the Archduke Charles first defeated the French in 1796. As we did not expect to find the means of conveyance always ready, we had sent a circular to the post-masters as far as Ratisbon—a very unnecessary precaution, and here, it seems, a very unusual one, except with persons of high rank. In Neumarkt, when we drove up to the post-house (in Franconia and Bavaria it is usual to sleep at the post-houses), we found every thing in commotion, and the house full of lights; the landlady lighted us up-stairs, offered us a ready-prepared supper, enumerated her wines, which, after all, turned out not very good; but the beds were arranged and decked in the best style. Müller remarked, but we did not know it till after our departure, that on the door of the room was written in white chalk, "For their Royal Highnesses;" and the landlady asked the next morning when she knocked at our door (we did not hear it), "Are your Royal Highnesses still asleep? Then every thing shall be quiet in the house." Neumarkt is not a bad-looking little place. The Upper Palatinate is moderately fertile. Toward Ratisbon, on approaching the Nab, the scenery becomes picturesque, and the view from the heights, where you first catch sight of Ratisbon and the Danube, is glorious. The whole country, on both sides of the river, is full of historical associations of the years since 1809, with the heights above Hof, whence the Austrians were obliged to set that unhappy town on fire with their shot in order to cover their retreat, and southward the walls and fields in the neighborhood. I had not expected to see Hof so completely rebuilt! I have already written to you about its noble bridge, and the incomparable view we had from our windows. The second pride of the old city is her cathedral, and in particular its most original, rich, and splendid façade. It is imperfect, and the interior is interesting only from its beautiful architecture. A strange tradition, which the sacristan told us, but which we had already heard from a working man, says, that a pupil of the master who built the cathedral, constructed the bridge in league with Satan; hence he had finished his work the first, in despair at which the master threw himself from one of the pinnacles of the church. Ratisbon has not a very ancient appearance, which may be explained from the circumstance that, for the last 150 years, the embassadors were the chief persons in the city, and though they were not permitted to possess any houses in their own name, they bought and built under the name of some other person. The old corporation was quite Lutheran: this fact, in the midst of Bavaria, and where the majority of the inhabitants are Catholics, is a very curious historical phenomenon, which, I confess, ought not to be an enigma to me, as its solution must be to be found in history. The once noble library of St. Emmeran, and even the town library, have

* This society was founded in 1617, for promoting the purity of the German language. At their meetings the members of the society laid aside their own names, and took that of some plant, or fruit. It was open to men of all ranks, but always had some sovereign prince at its head. It lasted sixty-three years.

lost their MSS., which have been brought here. Had I been aware of this, and believed the assertion that we could reach Landshut in eight hours, I should have remained there only one day. From Ratisbon, passing over the battle-field of Eckmühl, you enter a very rich country; the roads are the most beautiful in the world, and they ought not to be otherwise, for in all Bavaria, south of the Danube, the gravel is inexhaustible, and every where close at hand, so that it only needs to be dug up; it is nowhere necessary to break stones as in other countries. Still the country can not be called beautiful, except in the neighborhood of Landshut. At Freysing there are some beautiful meadows by the water, which seem to be kept with great care, but from whence to Munich it is a steppe without trees. We reached Landshut too early to make it a halting-place, and arrived in Munich the following day at noon. Traveling here is incredibly rapid. It was the 8th of August on which we arrived.

I will not begin here to tell you about Munich. We go to the Jacobi's every day. Schelling is not here, but in the country, working at the "Ages of the World." . . . . . .

CCXI.

TO NICOLOVIUS.

MUNICH, *17th August*, 1816.

I have written to you twice on my journey, my dear friend; the first letter from Erfurt has, no doubt, been punctually forwarded, because I informed the postmaster that, among other things, I had represented his complaints of the badness of the roads; the second, from Nuremberg, a mere note, has most likely also reached you, as it was intrusted to the care of a friend. Since both contained things requiring an answer, and you are as exemplarily conscientious about correspondence as I am hardened in sin (at least, often seem so), I almost fear that your reply has been stranded somewhere, which would be a bad beginning for my exile.

We have traveled very slowly. We were obliged to go round by Gotha, because we knew that the route by Coburg was quite impassable, and did not know that there was a road through Kahla and Schleiz, which certainly could not be worse than the one we have chosen, with a circuit of not less than from twelve to fifteen German miles. We staid one day at Wurzburg, two at Nuremberg (unhappily not longer), one-and-a-half at Ratisbon. We arrived here ten days ago, and have been prevailed upon by Jacobi's kind entreaties to stay longer than we had intended; so we shall not start again till the day after to-morrow.

I go hence southward with a heavy heart on all accounts. In all human probability, I shall never return along this road; and even if cheerfulness be not to me a treasure irrecoverably lost, I could not look back with cheerfulness from the summits of the Alps upon my poor Germany. Tranquil as every thing seems here, the various rumors of warlike preparations, which appear in the newspapers, renew the feelings I have before experienced on the eve of the outbreak of storms in the political world. I sigh for peace, and can not think of the possibility of its disturbance without inexpressible repugnance; so much so, that I grow indignant, or at least vexed, with the "Allgemeine Zeitung," and other circulators of these reports, innocently as they may have related what they have heard. If these fears accompany me to Italy, what will become of my enjoyment of antiquity and of the country?

Another reason of the sadness with which I quit Munich is the parting with Jacobi; we are certainly parting for the last time. It is not easy to describe his state to you as vividly as I could wish. His heart is still young; his intellect is only occasionally such as we have known it formerly. He is more inclined to narrate than to pour forth fresh thoughts, as he used to do; but his judgment is still acute and unwarped when subjects are presented clearly before his mind. He himself is evidently sensible that his life is an after-summer, when the unclouded sun only shines warmly during the noon-tide hours, and can call no new vegetation into life; and he feels this with a melancholy which is more touching to his younger friend than to himself. Roth is invaluable to him as a companion and inseparable friend; he does more than enliven Jacobi's existence, he is essential to it; he deserves the warmest thanks of all Jacobi's friends for his faithful and indefatigable endeavors to entertain him, and make up for the partial loss of sight by reading aloud, &c. I find the sisters unaltered. But their society would not supply sufficient materials for his mental life, to keep him tolerably happy; and without Roth I do not know how he could get on at all here, as much that is new, and rich in significance to me, and in which I could find sufficient materials of enjoyment, must be quite indifferent to him.

If there is the least truth in the common saying, you must all have had as great a ringing in your ears for the last few days as if we had been constantly touching the most sonorous English glasses to your health.......

My stay here has done me a great deal of good. The spiritual magnetism whose power I have often experienced, but to which I thought I had lost all susceptibility, has exerted itself once more, and the state of soul-sickness from which I have so long suffered is much relieved.......

I have every where met with the most friendly and courteous reception, and could have staid some time longer here with pleasure. I have been much interested by several persons whose acquaintance I have made, as well as by the immensely rich scientific and artistic collections. Director Naumayer, to whom I was introduced at Jacobi's, a man who has, perhaps, never crossed the frontiers of his native country, seems to me one of the most worthy and intelligent men I have ever seen. I have got some very instructive details, from intelligent Catholics residing here, about the convents and their church. Sailer* himself said, at Landshut, the convents must have gone to ruin, even if they had not been suppressed; and a very ingenuous young man gave us the sad history of his education in a Norbertine convent, such as makes me shudder when I recall it. The reading of a German book, Gellert's Fables in the "casus in terminis," was punished with stripes by virtue of a law recently introduced.

I am told that here, likewise, among the youth, there is a mysticizing, well-meaning, but very wrong-headed party forming. I saw the superb collection of casts in company with one of these young men, among the rest the Colossus of Monte Cavallo, which is shown here in a new building, with the advantage of varied artificial lights. After a long silence, my

* He was at this time professor at the University at Landshut, but was afterward made a bishop. His truly evangelical piety and tolerance toward Protestants caused him to be looked upon as half a heretic himself for many years His simplicity of character, and genuine child-like piety interested Niebuh deeply.

companion covered his eyes with his hands, and exclaimed quite seriously, "To me that is horrible." "Horrible?" I asked; "I should have said magnificent." "Horrible," he continued; "I seem to see the very incarnation of the spirit of heathenism." Now, as I have no such horror of this kind of heathenism, I feel angry with such vagaries, which are only fit to stand in De Groot's Annual. Our age knows nothing but reactions and leaps from one extreme to another. Among such people Winkelmann is regarded as a fool.

Travelers, who have lived some time at Rome, tell me I shall be able to hire a furnished house there without difficulty. I am very glad of this, as I shall thus be able to settle myself gradually, without going to too great an expense the first year. As this is the case, I shall give up going round by Leghorn, and thus gain time either for the journey or to arrive the sooner in Rome.

Be so kind, dear Nicolovius, as to give my best remembrances to Savigny and all other friends. I wish we had some little certainty of our letters reaching their destination. I have heard here that at least a third of the correspondence to Italy through the ——* post-offices is suppressed.

Tell Savigny, too, that I no longer despair of continuing my History. I am reading Livy again on the journey, and have learnt to see many things in him that had escaped me previously. Why should I not also confess that the manner in which I have found my History read and known along the whole course of my journey, particularly in South Germany, has helped to stimulate me to resume it?

Gretchen sends her kind regards to you. Farewell, and maintain your friendship for me.

Your faithful NIEBUHR.

CCXII.

TO MADAME HENSLER.

MERAN, IN THE VALLEY OF THE ADIGE.
26th August, 1816.

We left Munich on the 19th. . . . . It is so cold here, that the people say there are not five days in the year when they do not light a fire. Unfortunately we could gain no information at all as to the height of this district above the sea, but it certainly can not be as high as Innspruck. These Bavarian mountaineers agree with the Tyrolese in asserting that the cold has much increased within the last few years. The lake here† was formerly always open in winter: for the last few years it has been completely frozen over every season; in the Tyrol the glaciers are enlarging, and the frost is gradually killing the Indian corn. The Tyrolese, however, do not consider the change for the worse as permanent, but as periodical; they say the glaciers grow during one seven years, and diminish during the next.

From the Wallensee to Mittenwald, the last Bavarian village, the road constantly ascends, passing through wild and barren tracts, where the Isar falls noisily down from rock to rock. The only thing that attracted me at Mittenwald was the church-yard. Instead of the grassy hillock at the foot of each cross,‡ there is an open black chest in the form of a coffin,

* Austrian.

† The Wallensee.

‡ The cross which in Catholic countries is always placed at the head of each grave.

and filled with earth. Flowers are planted in this earth, or scattered over it. On the boards at the side are inscriptions, for the most part in very bad verse, but full of feeling. . . . .

The fortress in the Scharnitz lies in ruins, just as it was left after it was razed by Ney in 1805. It would be an exceedingly strong pass if the avenues to it were watched and guarded. The heaps of rubbish formed by the ruins of the old walls, the tokens and the effects of the dreadful havoc the war has made, in the shells of the burnt-down houses, the miserable poverty, the swarms of beggars, made a most painful impression upon us, on our first entrance into long-expected Tyrol. We were equally disappointed at Seefeld, the first place where we stopped for the night. The devastations of the war were every where visible; the walls, indeed, are indestructible. The people of these parts are ugly. The whole scene changes as you descend the mountain toward the valley of the Inn. Clouds gathered and dispersed, adorning rather than concealing the view; and when a ravine opened toward the valley, and I caught sight of the mountains in all their beauty, lying before us and around us, and the rich valley, with its magnificent stream, can you doubt that my first thought was of you and our Amelia? You have to drive in a zig-zag, with the hind wheels locked, for at least an hour, from the top of the mountain down to Market Zirl, the first stage in the valley of the Inn. Here, too, the ravages of war were still frightfully visible. Brandis and I had descended on foot, and had made some acquaintances by the time the carriage came up. The people were very obliging and sociable, and told us their history; the son, who was now on the mountains hunting, had served as an officer in the war of insurrection; the old man showed us the places, one by one, where the enemy's soldiers had been shot down by the peasants in his house, and the marks of the balls; and gave us some account of his flight to the Alps with his family, and how his wife died there. From Zirl, the high road to Innspruck runs beneath the steep and lofty rock of the Martinswand, doubly celebrated, for the legend, that on its summit the Emperor Maximilian I. lost himself while hunting, and took refuge when exhausted in a cave (visible from the wood), from which an angel led him down; and for the story, that when the Tyrolese drove the Bavarians out of the country in 1703, they made a furious onslaught on their retreating foes at this spot, and would have slain the Elector Maximilian Emanuel, had not his general sacrificed his own life for him by assuming the place of honor, and thus deceiving the unerring marksmen. This valley of the Inn is a most favored and lovely plain, with a level surface, and a rich and productive soil, in the highest state of cultivation. Maize, or Indian corn, is every where cultivated, and considered the most profitable species of grain, for when the crop is good, a yoke of land, or 6000 square feet, will yield a harvest worth 150 florins.

The kindly courtesy of the Tyrolese was shown even in the behavior of the men who asked for and examined our passports at the frontier. I can assure you, that among the many Tyrolese to whom I have spoken, I have not found one uncivil or immoderate in his demands; and I repeat this declaration once more, because some who have, in other respects, done justice to this noble people, still charge them with avarice. In more than one instance, where persons might certainly have thought a fee due to them, they have gone away without it, or taken it as a present; not one has either by words or looks murmured at receiving too little. Innspruck is pleasantly situated; the town is not large; it contains some six hundred houses, and ten thousand inhabitants. From our windows at the hotel, we looked out on the beautiful bridge, and the mountain range on the other side of the river. Hofer had occupied the same rooms when he entered the town for the first time. Hence the house contained many relics of him; he had presented the hostess with a horn snuff-box; some of his proclamations, accompanied by some not badly-drawn scenes from the great war, were framed and glazed, and hung round the room. As soon as we had dined, Brandis and I put ourselves under the guidance of a man who had served as a rifleman in the revolt from the very beginning, to visit and survey the hill Isel, which has been immortalized by three hard-fought combats in the principal epochs of the insurrection. Our guide was, as to station, what would be called a common man, and the influence of this would have made him a bad companion, if he had not belonged to a free people; but his conversation and manners were such, that we heartily congratulated ourselves upon his society. It seems to help these people to a correct and unembarrassed sense of their relation to a traveler, when they hear with what profound veneration he speaks of the host of Sand,* who is the hero of their idolatry, but whose earlier life was passed in as humble a position as their own, and whose humility did not forsake him when he rose to be Regent of the whole country, for he never considered himself as the superior of any other Tyrolese peasant. From this guide I learnt at every spot what had happened there. He afterward conducted me past the waterfall of Wiltau to the old castle of Amras, from whose turrets a wide prospect over the lovely valley and the lofty mountains rewards the not inconsiderable labor of the ascent, though all the curiosities and treasures which it formerly contained have been either removed or are, like the picture-gallery, closed.

I suppose I need not tell you who Speckbacher is? Speckbacher's son was taken prisoner in the war, and educated in a division of the cadet school, because the King took an interest in him; for he is a boy of extraordinary talent, and his letters to his father are as beautiful in thought, and refined in language, as any youth of his age could write. We did not see the boy himself at Munich, but Brandis, who is indefatigable in profiting by every opportunity of seeing things, and gaining information that the journey affords, applied to his tutor, and obtained from him a letter of introduction for us to the father. Equipped with this, we set out on Thursday, all three in a mountain car. Speckbacher lives at Rinn, in the mountains above Hall; the way thither is over almost impassable mountain roads. I send this letter off unfinished (from Trent), because the post is going out.

The narrative, which is here broken off, has been supplied to the translator verbally by Professor Brandis.

* Sand was the name of a little hamlet on the Brenner where Hofer was the innkeeper. He commonly went by the name of the *Sandwirth*, or host of Sand. Almost all the innkeepers had been officers in the war, and they were generally very intelligent men. Niebuhr always used to question them about the war, and received a great deal of valuable information from them, especially from the host at Pfunz, the pass between the Inn and Adige valleys, whom he found also well versed in the local history of the country.

Niebuhr and Brandis were obliged to leave the carriage at some distance from the house, so that Madame Niebuhr was not able to accompany them in their visit. When they knocked at the door, it was opened by a tall, spare, haggard-looking man, with flashing black eyes and aquiline features, who, in answer to their inquiries, replied that he was Speckbacher himself, and begged to know who his visitors were. When Niebuhr told him that he was the embassador from Prussia to Rome, the astonishment of the simple peasant was extreme, that such grand personages should have come out of their way to visit him, and he was about to kiss Niebuhr's hand, but Niebuhr drew it back, exclaiming, "No, it is I who ought to kiss your hand," fell on his neck and embraced him, and they were friends directly. Speckbacher began to make apologies that he could give them no better entertainment; his wife and daughters were out reaping, and he was alone in the house, and had nothing to set before his honored guests. "Never mind, we only want to see you; sit down and tell us about the war." He then related the events in which he had been engaged; and took them out to show them the stable where he had been concealed by his faithful servant, Zoppel, for more than a month, in a hole dug in the ground and covered with hay. After the peace of Vienna* he fled to the mountains, and was for a long time concealed in a cavern among snow and ice, but at length the winter became too severe, and he left his hiding-place and took refuge in the stable of his own house, where he remained while the enemy were searching for him in every direction, and a considerable number of Bavarian soldiers were actually quartered in his house. Not even his wife knew of his being in the neighborhood. Zoppel could only bring him food at night, and sometimes not even then, when there were soldiers about.

During the struggle, he sent his wife and children up the mountains for safety. His eldest child, a boy of ten years old, could not be induced to stay quietly there, but after several ineffectual attempts succeeded in reaching his father. When Speckbacher found that it was impossible to persuade the boy to go back again, he agreed to keep him with him. In the last battle fought before the peace of Vienna, Speckbacher was defeated, and escaped with difficulty; his boy was separated from him, and taken prisoner by the Bavarians. When they asked him where his father was, the child undauntedly replied, in the Tyrolese patois, "Boer Ferkel schiesse." (Gone to shoot the Bavarian pigs).

To the disgrace of the Austrian government, the only reward Speckbacher received for his services was the rank of a major in the militia, to which a small pension was attached. It was proposed to send him an order, but even this was prevented by the court party, who could not endure that a peasant should be thus distinguished. The Emperor sent him, instead, a large gold medal, which Speckbacher showed with great delight to Niebuhr, exclaiming, "See how gracious the Emperor has been to me!" Niebuhr had to bite his lips to repress his indignation that this should be the sole honor this heroic patriot had to exhibit, but Speckbacher himself was perfectly contented. He had only one wish ungratified, namely, to receive a rosary that had been blessed by Pope Pius VII. He had written to Vienna to make this request, but "it was very natural," he said, "that those great lords should have had no time to attend to a request from an insignificant peasant like him, and he had never received any answer."

* By which on the 14th of Oct., 1809, the Austrians ceded the Tyrol to Bavaria.

The first business Niebuhr transacted with the Pope was to lay Speckbacher's wish before him, and, in a few days after his arrival in Rome, he had the pleasure of forwarding to Speckbacher a splendid rosary, as a gift from his Holiness. Speckbacher returned a letter of thanks to the Pope, together with his portrait, painted by another peasant, a most frightful thing.

One of the interesting personages the Niebuhrs met with at Innspruck, was an old fruitwoman who kept a stall in the street. In the war she had sold all her goods, bought provisions, and followed the army, supplying the soldiers for nothing as long as her means held out, when, as was frequently the case, they were unable to pay. Madame Niebuhr was so touched by her tale, that she took off a gold necklace and hung it round the old woman's neck as a keepsake.

In traveling along the valley of the Lower Inn, in the neighborhood of Landsberg, they came to a pass where the Tyrolese who were coming to attack Innspruck, had stopped the Bavarian troops, by means of a singular contrivance. The road was overhung by rugged mountains; the Tyrolese had dislodged huge masses of rock, which they bound together with ropes so as to keep them from rolling down; they held the ropes tightly in silence till the first company of Bavarians was immediately below them, when, exclaiming "In the name of the Holy Trinity!" all loosed their hold, and the ponderous missiles rushed down on the heads of the soldiers beneath, crushing nearly a whole company, and effectually barring the road for those who followed, while the Tyrolese descended the hill-side with their guns, and shot them down from behind trees and rocks till few of them remained.

CCXIII.

TO SAVIGNY.

VENICE, *4th September*, 1816.

Except at some rare seasons of cheerfulness and mental activity, it has always been a peculiarity of my first letters to my friends after taking leave of them, that a considerable portion of space is occupied with an apologetic explanation of my delay in writing; and this firstling of my correspondence with you, will form no exception to the rule. However, I will restrict myself to informing you, that I am quite aware I owe you such an apology, and if you will forgive me without requiring it at my hands, it will be an act of generosity on your part. As, even amidst the wonders of this magnificent city, my mind is not bright and unclouded enough to allow me to write playfully, and yet I do not like to relate in a grave tone the ideas which occurred to me in a merry mood, I have felt as if I had no right to appear before you with a letter, till I had some discovery in the shape of a juridical "ineditum" to present you with. But I hasten, at all events, to satisfy the curiosity which the sight of the uncial letters on the inclosed sheets, will probably have excited in you the moment you opened this letter; particularly as these inclosures are the reason for my taking advantage of the earliest opportunity to write to you from this place.

The Cathedral of Verona possesses a library extremely rich in very old Latin parchments. Fortunately for it, about the middle of the eighteenth century, a thoroughly learned prebendary—a rare phenomenon even there—Gian Jacopo de Dionigi by name, examined and arranged the whole of its contents; and some time after, Antonio Mazzotti, a very honest and industrious librarian, made an excellent catalogue of them. This catalogue, however, has not helped me to my discovery, concerning the subject of which, it does not contain a syllable. The first thing that fell into my hands, on opening the chest containing the manuscripts, was a very thin little volume of extremely ancient single and double leaves of parchment, which, according to the title page, were collected from among dirt and rubbish by the said Dionigi in 1758. Most of them are biblical fragments, from perhaps the sixth to the eleventh century, and a note, by the hand of their diligent collector, exhibits their contents. But almost instantly I espied among them two fragments of quite a different kind, whose nature he did not understand, and of which he has therefore omitted all notice.* . . . . . . I have only copied this fragment that nothing might be overlooked. But now comes the main piece of news I have to announce to you: namely, that there is preserved at Verona, as much of Ulpian as would fill a small octavo volume; of which, however, I was only able to copy a single leaf by way of a specimen and attestation, which I herewith transmit to you for publication.

I had already begun when at Wurzburg, to look out for palimpsests, and had hit upon one there almost immediately (which Ogg has described); but it only consisted of fragments from the "Itala." At Munich I looked through all the old Latin parchments, and could only detect among them a single palimpsest: that, too, was merely a biblical text, under St. Jerome and Gennadius "De Vitis." At Verona my lucky star was again in the ascendant, for I found the Codex 13, containing the Epistles of St. Jerome, a pretty thick quarto volume of the ninth century, which is a complete palimpsest, except about a fifth part of the leaves, which are new. Some of the part written over is of a theological, but by far the greater portion of a juridical nature. It is written by the same hand as the fragment of Gaius, from which we may conclude that the cathedral chapter, or the church at Verona, was once in possession of several works on jurisprudence, which the ecclesiastics afterward used up; and that it had these books before Justinian's time, and under King Theodoric. My transcript is as exact a representation of the original as it was possible to make, without tracing it through transparent paper. Single words here and there, of a yellowish color, could be made out where the lines did not exactly coincide, from which the nature of the contents could be gathered, but it would be impossible to make any thing of it without the aid of chemistry. The best re-agents were not to be procured at Verona. I was obliged hastily to prepare for myself an infusion of gall-nuts, which, imperfect as it was, produced so much effect as to allow us to hope for full success with better means.

Now, dear Savigny, here lies a treasure waiting for your hands to dig it up; a bait that shall lure you over the Alps to us. Or will you give the necessary instructions to Cramer that he may set to work? Or will you persuade some one else to come?

You will never suffer this discovery, which is exactly what you have been wishing for so ardently, to be lost for want of some one to make use of it. But whoever comes, let him not depend merely upon his own eyes. Let him bring with him the best chemical re-agents to bring out the writing, and also a good magnifying glass. Now I think I fairly deserve your best wishes, that I may discover something for myself also. There is nothing here in the library of St. Mark. The republic had no library before

* Here follows a description of the fragments.

Bessarion's time, and this Greek collected no ancient Latin manuscripts; the oldest is of the eleventh century. Of Justinian's works on jurisprudence, Verona possesses only the Code with a new gloss. I will write you word of all I meet with here another time.

And now I hand over to you the raw materials that I have collected. If you publish my transcripts, I only bind you to this, that you do not give them to the world without your notes and explanations. Make such extracts from this letter as may be advisable; to which I must add, that the obliging way in which the prebendaries permitted the library to be opened for me, deserves the highest praise; and also the patience of the Custos Archiprète Eucherio, who, with the greatest kindness, gave up his mornings and evenings to me whenever I desired it. If you put the affair into your Journal, let there be twenty extra copies printed, and I will let you know hereafter what is to be done with them. I can not tell you any thing about the journey to-day, for an Albanian from Scutari, whose acquaintance I have made, will be waiting for me in the Turkish coffee-house. A Greek is our guest to-day at dinner. Thus immeasurably, almost oppressively, rich in objects of interest do I find the progress of our journey, but my mind is vailed in deepest night. Gretchen often causes me great anxiety. She does not bear the traveling well, and can derive little enjoyment from it......

We had a delightful journey through the Austrian Tyrol. Your friend Salvotti received us very kindly. We both send our kindest regards to you and all our friends. I have written three times to Nicolovius. I beg you will address your next to me at Rome, for you must answer this letter, dear Savigny. Mai has made a fresh discovery, something from Dion. Halic.; it is not known here yet what it is, but it is said to be from the History; that would be in my way. Farewell, my dear friend, and remember me.

P.S. The fragments of Dion. Halic. have come to nothing. They are excerpts from some other historian, that hardly contain a single new fact. I will make a report upon them shortly to the Academy. Here there is nothing to be found except a leaf from a MS. of the Code of the eleventh century, with inscription and subscription. I have collated them for you. The variations are considerable. To-morrow we go to Padua. Yet once more farewell, dearest friend. Have mercy, and write!

CCXIV.

TO MADAME HENSLER.

FLORENCE, 24*th September*, 1816.

I have not even been able to write a diary for you, during my journey. I will now tell you a few facts of a general nature. My pre-conceived opinion of the scholars and higher classes in Italy has proved perfectly correct, as I was convinced would be the case, because I possessed sufficient data to form an accurate idea of them. I have always allowed the existence of individual exceptions as regards erudition, but, even in these cases, there is not that cultivation of the whole man which we demand and deem indispensable. I have become acquainted with two or three literary men of real ability; but, in the first place, they are old men, who have only a few years longer to live; and, when they are gone, Italy will be, as they say themselves, in a state of barbarism; and, in the second, they are like statues wrought to be placed in a frieze on the wall; the side turned toward you is of finished beauty, the other, unhewn stone. They are much what our scholars may have been sixty or eighty years ago. No one feels himself a citizen. Not only are the people destitute of hope, they have not even wishes respecting the affairs of the world, except as they concern their several cabinets; and all the springs of great and noble thoughts and feelings are choked up. I have met with one noble-minded and agreeable young man, who unites depth of feeling and profound melancholy about the state of the world, with a very poetical mind, and a considerable amount of scholarship, though not such as would come up to our standard. He is not, however, a native of Italy, but a Greek from Corfu. He has promised to come to Rome, and a visit from him would be worth much to me.

The three genuine and intellectual scholars of my acquaintance, Morelli, Garatoni, and Fontana, are all ecclesiastics; they are, however, only ecclesiastics by profession; for I have not found in them the slightest trace either of a belief in the dogmas of Catholicism, or of the pietism which you meet with in Germany. When an Italian has once ceased to be a slave of the Church, he never seems to trouble his head about such matters at all. Metaphysical speculations are utterly foreign to his nature, as they were to the old Romans. Hence the vacuity of mind which has become general since the suppression of freedom, except in the case of those who find a sphere of action in writing literary and historical memoirs. Their public men are immeasurably behind the Germans in knowledge and cultivation. Perhaps there may be more of this found, here and there, among the advocates, but the physical philosophers are the most reflective class. In Rome, it is solely among the clergy that I expect to find men with whom I can hold intercourse.

The common people are, on the whole, better than I expected. At Padua and Venice you can not help feeling a real attachment for them, and for the burghers; they are earnest, honest, and intelligent, indeed even kind. Their soft and graceful dialect, warm and caressing, makes it a pleasure to talk to them. The lowest Venetian is polite and decorous. In this respect, as in others, there is as great a difference between the Italian towns as if they were inhabited by different races. The shameless rapacity of the innkeepers and postillions is disgusting; and it is very unpleasant to be obliged to beat down all the tradespeople, not excepting the booksellers. But they are rather avaricious than deceitful in their dealings. The day before yesterday, I went with Brandis to visit the ancient Fiesole, situated on the hill about half a German mile from hence; the peasants there did not differ in their manners from Germans, and did not even seem to expect money from us......

As I anticipated, I certainly see and inquire into much that other travelers have not seen or inquired into; but, on this very account, I have seen less than most of what every one sees. About the landed interest, tenure of land, husbandry, the right of boundaries, I have already learned much that will be of great use in my researches into antiquity; and therefore, as I am only just beginning my inquiries on these subjects, I hope to obtain rich spoils. It also contributes greatly to a vivid conception of historical events, when you can survey their scene for yourself, and, if you can traverse it frequently in different directions, you can not but gain very important assistance. I am indefatigable in making inquiries of all kinds, and shall continue to be so. But one can not help feeling indignant with those who visited this land twenty or thirty years ago, for it is incredible how many relics of antiquity have been lost or destroyed since then. Still, there are a thousand traces of past ages to be found if you look for them; there are very many connected with husbandry. The stone coffins at Verona, of the middle ages, are quite Etruscan in their form. I have found in an old Etruscan temple wall that has been dug up at Fiesole, a similar style of dressing the stones to that of the exterior walls of the Florentine palaces of the fourteenth and fifteenth centuries. (The peasants of Fiesole can distinguish perfectly between Roman and Etruscan masonry.)

Be assured that I shall not forget the work to which I feel myself most sacredly pledged; but, to enrich my store of materials for it, I must often turn aside into by-ways and examine every path that presents itself. Besides, a residence in a foreign country involves the necessity of making myself thoroughly acquainted with its language and literature, and attempting to gain an accurate knowledge of its topography. Here again, I feel how greatly my memory has suffered, how much escapes me nowadays. It used to be an amazing assistance to my memory that I repeated every thing I read or thought to my Milly, who received it with interest and life, and presented it again to me in new points of view.

It will take some time for my constitution to adapt itself to the climate. I have many inconveniences to suffer; I can not drink the wines, and am always catching cold. But Gretchen suffers far more. She was very well till we got to Erfurt, but from thence onward she has been constantly getting worse. At Munich she revived, but as we came along the valley of the Adige, toward the south she grew more and more indisposed. Her eyes are also very weak. She derives scarcely any pleasure from the journey, because she is obliged to sit so much alone (and now ill) at home; but she bears this with touching gentleness and resignation.

We hear news from Rome of the rise of prices of all kinds, especially in the rent of furnished apartments, occasioned by the concourse of foreigners, so that we shall most likely be obliged to furnish next spring. The ship in which our goods were embarked, has been wrecked at Calais. Under the best circumstances, it will be long before we receive any of our things.

I have already seen a great deal of the works of art here. My preference for the old masters, up to the time of Raphael, has been decidedly confirmed. Giovanni Bellini, who was my favorite eight years ago, has become so again at Venice. And we have seen also some really wonderful productions of Francia at Bologna. Masaccio, Mantegna, Vivarini, and Carpaccio, can be studied only in Italy. Of Giotto's works I have already seen a great number, and have now got a complete idea of the history of art in Italy. The direction of our journey by way of Nuremberg and Munich has been of great advantage to me in this respect. In the fourteenth century Giotto leans to the antique; his school departs from it again. Masaccio soars at once on high. After him art sinks again; and, during the first sixty years of the fifteenth century, the Germans stand high above the Italians. Then the other scale descends. After the time of Raphael and Durer, the *spirit* was dead on both sides of the Alps; but the *art* survived in Italy. In architecture, the Italians of the middle ages are not to be compared to the Germans. In the plastic arts they excel them.

The day after to-morrow we proceed on our journey. When we arrive in Rome depends on circumstances. If I should find any thing in the Chapter libraries of Arezzo and Perugia, I shall halt there. But, at all events, we shall certainly be at Rome long before the answer to this letter can arrive. Do not deny me this refreshment. Our love to all our relations and friends. Farewell! God bless you!

CCXV.

ROME, *7th October*, 1816.

......It was with solemn feelings that this morning, from the barren heights of the moory Campagna, I caught sight first of the cupola of St. Peter's, and then of the view of the city from the bridge, where all the majesty of her buildings and her history seems to lie spread out before the eye of the stranger; and afterward entered by the Porta del Popolo. I have already wandered through a part of the city, and visited the most famous of the ruins. My presentiment of the emotions with which I should behold them has proved quite correct. Nothing about them is new to me; as a child I lay so often, for hours together, before the pictures I gave you as a keepsake, that their images were even at that early time as distinctly impressed upon my mind as if I had actually seen them: then, besides, it repels me that all the remains are those of the imperial times, and it is impossible for an architectural work of art to speak to the feelings, if considered as isolated, and without connection with other ideas. But the influence of the completely modern part of all that here surrounds you, and intrudes itself upon your attention, is most disturbing; the glaringly bad taste of the churches of the last two hundred and fifty years; the utter want of solemnity in all that meets the eye. In Petrarch's time, all must have made a profound impression of grandeur and magnificence on those who were susceptible to it; indeed, much that but a short time since spoke to the sense of poetry, has now been destroyed by the clearing out of the rubbish from the Forum and the Colosseum. Now, their walls and columns stand stripped and naked, corroded by time, despoiled of the luxuriant and wild vegetation which once flourished among the ruined stones. The extent of Rome, too, appears small to a traveler; still, the distance from the Vatican, where I hope to find my chief pleasures, must be further than from the last house which Milly and I occupied, to the Konigsthor at Berlin, which, in rain and the hot sun, is not an agreeable prospect. This library is closed now, and will remain so for the whole of this month, so that I must school myself into patience. In Florence, however, I attained a high degree of probability that the Greek poet—in the possibility of finding whom I have always believed for the last five-and-twenty years—really exists there, and has only failed to attract notice owing to the carelessness of those into whose hands he has fallen. If this treasure should really be reserved for me I shall not have come hither in vain.

......But when one sees this favored land, to which our most fruitful districts are barren; sees how, at Terni, two harvests of grain are reaped from the soil in one year—one of wheat in June, and the maize soon after it in October; how this goes on year after year, and the wheat yields fifteen fold; when one sees how there is, strictly speaking, no peasant class at all here; how the very happiest places are those where the peasant only has to give up half the produce, and not where, as for many miles round Rome, all husbandry is performed by day-laborers under the enormously rich nobles; when you see the swarms of beggars who assure you, with looks that bear witness to their assertions, that they have not tasted bread to-day; when you hear what numbers have died of hunger; * it does indeed raise bitter feelings. It has become perfectly clear to me how this misery arose in the imperial times, and has been rendered permanent by the German conquerors, who have in no respect made themselves benefactors to Italy.

CCXVI.

TO SAVIGNY.

ROME, *17th October*, 1816.

If a letter which I wrote you from Venice arrived punctually, dear Savigny (of which, however, I do not feel at all confident), and found you at Berlin, I am certain that you must have written to me; for my discoveries at Verona were, I should think, almost enough to induce you to order post-horses on the spot, and set out for Italy yourself; and I conjured and supplicated you to let me hear from you.

Just now, however, I will neither torment myself because the wished-for letter seems to loiter on the road—although it would be doubly painful to me if my packet and its inclosures should not have come to hand—nor yet postpone this second letter till I know something certain about it.

We arrived in Rome ten days ago, and removed, the day before yesterday, into the apartments which we have taken for the winter; the innumerable calls are over except a few, and we have made our acquaintance in the circle of my official intercourse. We are now able to survey our position and prospects. Do not make an outcry when I say that these are any thing but agreeable; and beg others who may hear this from you, not to do so either. Were I a young man of twenty or thirty, coming hither as an independent traveler, with a mind free from care, and the prospect of returning home sooner or later, perhaps I should find this place to my liking, though I would not take my oath of it. But now, what is permanent presses me down with its leaden weight, and what is transitory has no charms for me. Only one utterly unacquainted with facts could suppose, that the life of an embassador here in Rome could be free from restraint and interruption; but it were really a pardonable mistake to imagine it somewhat less fettered than it is; for that, as such, I should be obliged to observe all courtly formalities toward the Spanish court of Charles IV., of the Queen, and the Prince of the Peace, and even to the Queen of Etruria, I confess I did not dream; but so it is. I foresaw, of course, that I must unavoidably hold frequent intercourse with my colleagues, and gradually learn to adapt my conduct to the claims and dictates of their

* It ought to be noticed, that the year in which Niebuhr went to Italy was a famine year, and that this operated greatly in heightening the unfavorable character of Niebuhr's first impressions of the country in general, though his opinion of the moral and intellectual condition of the higher classes remained unchanged. Professor Brandis related to the translator, how at Vicenza they were positively driven out of the amphitheatre by the crowd of beggars that surrounded them, and at Venice were unable to sleep at all the first night, from the cries and shrieks of the starving crowd assembled under their windows, and calling for bread.

opinions. Then for any foreigner, except a single man living independently of others, Rome has become extravagantly, nay frightfully, dear. Furniture is only to be procured at this moment at quite unreasonable prices, and we have been thankful to hire a very small suite of furnished apartments for the winter, at fifty scudi a month. We have not yet engaged a cook; one has applied, and asks eighteen scudi a month wages, and two scudi (nearly three thalers) a day for providing dinner for us three, with Müller and himself. Without a written agreement, nothing can be done. A hired carriage costs at least sixty-five scudi a month. The extra charges for lights, drink-money, &c., are endless. Do not, however, ascribe it to the influence of these unpleasing prospects, or of my vexation at foreseeing how miserably the time I need for the completion of a work which was begun, and can only be continued in quiet and retirement, will have to be frittered away, when I further confess to you that the sight of Rome has by no means made a cheering or elevating impression upon me. This it can not have on any one who really sees what really exists.

The aspect of Venice and Florence appeared to me grand and pleasing; in both, the images and monuments of the times of their greatness still remain visible and tangible. Venice is to me the grandest thing I have ever seen, and I liked every thing connected with it. Its inhabitants pleased me, too; their manners are mild and noble, and they have all an expression of grave, quiet sadness, that spoke to my inmost heart. In Florence every street is historical, and so are hundreds of the buildings. I have traced the circuit of the Roman colony, and of the walls after their extension, step by step; visited Dante's house; read manuscripts written by Machiavelli and Benvenuto Cellini; seen the tombs in Santa Croce and San Lorenzo. In both these cities there still exist unbounded treasures of genuine art—*i. e.* up to Raphael's death. Rome has no right to its name; at most it should only be called New Rome (like New York). Not one single street here goes in the same direction as the old one; it is an entirely foreign vegetation that has grown up on a part of the old soil, as insignificant and thoroughly modern in its style as possible, without nationality, without history; it is very characteristic, that the really ancient, and the modern city lie almost side-by-side. The abominable rage for building in the sixteenth and seventeenth centuries has called into existence a multitude of churches and edifices which any unprejudiced observer must allow to be mean and tasteless, and removed or built up every ancient structure.

There are nowhere any remains of any thing that it was possible to remove. The ruins all date from the times of the Emperors, and he who can get up an enthusiasm about them, must at least rank Martial and Sophocles together. In pictures, Rome (except the Vatican) is poor, compared to those two cities; Bolognese manufactures, and others still worse, I do not take into the account. St. Peter's, the Sixtine Chapel, and the Loggie are certainly splendid;* but even St. Peter's is disfigured internally by the wretched statues and decorations; and who, indeed, would deny that even Rome has its glories? The statues I must acquire a taste for by degrees; the doors of the Baptistry, particularly the ornamental work

* In another letter he says, "The Last Judgment I do not yet understand. The statues by Michael Angelo at Florence I prefer to those of antiquity. The Perseus of Benvenuto seems to me, on the contrary, mediocre."

round their edges, which was not designed by Ghiberti, but by Giotto, take my fancy more than all the bas-reliefs. Science is utterly extinct here; of philologists there is none worthy the name, except the aged de Rossi, who is near his end. The people are apathetic, and truly if they ever were remarkable in any way for personal appearance, they must have strangely altered. In all Italy (with a few exceptions at Venice) we have not seen one handsome face, most certainly not one here; but much more positive ugliness than in Germany. Moreover, what as yet seems to us quite unaccountable, there is nothing like song to be heard, either of human voices or birds' throats; only a horrible screeching every now and then.

This, then, is the country and the place in which my life is to be passed! It is but a poor amends that I can get from libraries, and yet my only hope is from the Vatican. That we may be crossed in every way, this is closed till the 5th of November, and to have it opened sooner is out of the question; in other respects, all possible facilities have been promised me by the Pope himself, Cardinal Gonsalvi, Monsignor Testa, and the Prefect of the Library, Monsignor Baldi: this last is now engaged in printing, at his own cost, a work on which he has expended 600 scudi, without hope of receiving any compensation for it. It is on seventeen passages in the Old Testament, in which he has found the cross mentioned by name. A manuscript collection of inscriptions has been bequeathed to the Vatican by Marini, which can not be printed for want of funds. About that I shall write some day to the Academy. Should I find nothing in the Vatican, I shall be dreadfully disappointed. But I will still hope for something there. It is only open three hours a day, and shut on Thursdays and all the innumerable Catholic festivals; and it just now happens that our meetings for conference have been altered from Thursday to some other day, so that in general there will only be three days a week, at most, in which I can work there. Of living antiquities I can expect none at Rome, as all the estates are "latifundia," without peasants. At Terni I found the old art of land-surveying still extant; I rode along what was probably an ancient "limes," found the "rigor" and the "V Pedes," and the coals and bricks under the "termini." Unfortunately there was no "acclimensore" in the town (as the people now call the occupation). I shall go there again if I live till next autumn. It is a charming place. There are at least fifty houses in the town—among them one very large—which date from the Roman times, and which have never yet been observed or described by any traveler.* Several of the churches are Roman private houses. If one could but discover in Rome any thing like this! I long inexpressibly to have it for my burial-place. Every thing is ancient in Terni and its neighborhood; even the mode of preparing the wine. Oh, to have been in Italy 500 years ago!

Since my own literary life is brought to a close with this mission, I endeavor at least to make myself useful to my friends, as far as it may still lie in my power. Your commissions, dear Savigny, have not escaped my memory. First at Bologna; Ridolfi has been removed thence to Padua, where I have twice been without knowing this. Your book has been forwarded to him through that philological miracle, Mezzofanti. The catalogue of documents I left with the Canon Londi, as it would have required full eight days merely to copy it. This Canon and Schiassi, the Keeper of

* There was, too, an old bridge at Terni, also of Roman architecture, which particularly interested Niebuhr.

the Archives, have promised to get a copy made for me. I obtained a similar promise at Florence from Villani and Bandini, on behalf of the Chapter; for as I made it my chief object there to examine the Laurentian library as thoroughly as possible for palimpsests (the search proved fruitless, as also in the Marcian library), time failed me there also. I had great difficulty in discovering the MSS. of Bologninus. They were found at last in a chest.

CCXVII.

TO MADAME HENSLER.

ROME, 30*th October*, 1816.

It makes me very uneasy that I have still no answer from Savigny to my announcement of the discovery I made at Verona. The letters to me must be detained somewhere on the road, for you would never *all* keep silence to me and Gretchen in this manner.

It is extremely depressing while we can receive no sympathy in conversation, to be deprived of all communication by which my mind can be roused into life. I shall never be able to feel at home here. Any thing from Germany, even a leaf from the "Allgemeine Zeitung" is the most welcome acquisition to me in this foreign land.

I have indeed some German fellow-countrymen here; but it is with them as I expected. Among the artists, the two whose conversation I find the most agreeable, are Cornelius and Wilhelm Schadow. The latter is particularly refined and intellectual; but he is unfortunately a convert to Catholicism. Overbeck, to whom he yields precedence as an artist, and whose physiognomy is very prepossessing, is taciturn and melancholy. Rome is a terrible place for any one who is melancholy, because it contains no living present to relieve the sense of sadness; the present is revolting, and in what exists, there is not the slightest trace of antiquity to be recognized; there are not even any remains of the Church of the middle ages. It does no good (to me especially) to be thrown back upon works of art and nothing but works of art. My colleagues are tolerably agreeable people. Among the Italians you seek in vain for even *interesting* conversation, although this would be far from sufficient for me now. There is only one man of talent and mental activity here, at least among the philologers and historians—an old ex-Jesuit on the borders of the grave; and he repeats the verdict which I have already heard from the lips of the few old men in whom I have become acquainted with the relics of a more intellectual age; "l'Italia è spenta: è un corpo morto;" and I find it so. Cardinal Gonsalvi is an intellectual man, and would be really distinguished among any ministers of any court. I have found some intelligent men among the prelates, but we Germans and they find each other's society devoid of stimulating influence; many of our thoughts may be mirrored in each other's minds, but pass away and exert no living power. The aged and venerable Pope received me with remarkable kindness and affability; I staid to dinner with his chaplain, and it was about the brightest day I have spent since my arrival. So far from there being any truth in the absurd rumor, that the court of Rome had protested against me personally, it turns out that they have looked forward to my coming with great pleasure, and certainly no Catholic embassador can boast of a more distinguished and friendly reception.......

It is a real misfortune that our goods, consequently my books, have not arrived yet. We are still without tidings of them, and the captain who could make shipwreck at Calais in the middle of summer, would need a miracle to get safely to Leghorn at this season. Besides, there are Barbary pirates cruising off the Portuguese coasts, who plunder every vessel they come near. I wish I had followed my own plan, and sent the books, at least, over land. If they are lost, it would be impossible to replace them in Italy. But I bow in resignation to every calamity of this kind. Only it is very sad that with them I should lose every means of study and employment, for no book is lent out of the libraries here under any conditions whatever; and so how can I undertake any learned work? The libraries are open five days a week, for three hours each day, and of these five days, two are those of the ministerial conferences. However, as I said, my murmuring spirit is broken; perhaps just because one only desires passionately when one is full of life. All other things may turn out as they will, if only God protect and preserve to me my dearest treasure. Farewell!

CCXVIII.

Rome, *20th November*, 1816.

......Brandis is a very agreeable inmate, and sympathizes with me on every occasion.

I have found in the Vatican a manuscript full of treasures from the Roman literature, and am working busily at it. I have discovered fragments of the lost parts of Cicero's Oration for Fonteius, and probably also the conclusion of that for Tullius. I shall have these fragments printed here, together with some passages in the fragment of Livy which their first editors could not read, as soon as the indescribably laborious work is finished, in order that it may gain me access to more of the same kind. I think I can also recognize long passages from Cicero's lost philosophical writings; if I prove to be right, I should like to sell them in England for a good price, by way of earning some money for our young artists. Among these, there are some really excellent young men, who are languishing for the means of cultivating their talents, and are at the same time hard put to it for daily bread. I should like to get enough money to set a few of them to paint a fresco in the Library. Some of the ecclesiastical officials reject all fees; these I shall also lay aside for this object. Cornelius is the most intellectual of them. Overbeck and Wilhelm Schadow are amiable men and very clever artists, notwithstanding their proselytizing spirit.......

I am zealously performing my official duties. Unhappily I am still without instructions on all the important points, though I have urgently entreated that they may be sent me. The moment is favorable; besides, the people here are well disposed toward me, and I think I shall be able to come to arrangements with them.......

23d.......I am glad too to hear that the German artists here call me the German minister. People from all parts of Germany who have no ambassador here, come to me as the representative of their respective countries.......

CCXIX.

Rome, *7th December*, 1816.

Thank Heaven, my books have arrived at Leghorn; though no doubt it will be a long while before I shall get them here. I hope, with their assistance, to return to occupations that can fill my mind. It gives me great pain to think that my History must remain unfinished; that my Milly's only request will be left unfulfilled. Oh that I could fulfill it! But what I could do now would be too unlike the former part. From the general account which I have received of the review, mentioned also in your letter, it does not vex me much; it would do so, perhaps, if I read it. They may say what they will about the matter; I am as certain of the correctness of my views as I am of my own existence, and that I have discovered the solution of the enigma. It is not the love of conjecture that has impelled me, but the necessity of understanding, and the faculty of guessing and divining. For many points, still more numerous and express proofs might be produced, than those I have brought forward. He who presumes to pronounce a judgment on this subject without knowing more than the current opinions on it, has really no voice at all in the matter. Further, it is not to be expected that every one, or even that many, should have that faculty of immediate intuition which would enable them to partake in my immovable conviction, for which I should be ready to die. Mortifications do not annoy me now as they used to do; but still it is melancholy that the love and appreciation of literature is so declining in Germany. This I may say without arrogance, that he who refuses respect to my History, deserves none himself......

CCXX.

Rome, *Christmas Eve*, 1816.

Now, at the dead of night, as Gretchen has gone to sleep, and all is silent in the house, I will sit down to answer your two dear affectionate letters.

You will not misunderstand and misinterpret me for having suffered a week to elapse after receiving your former letter before replying to it. My eyes will not allow me to write late at night, though until now I have been able to read then without difficulty. I have perceived this change with alarm for the last month past; it is probably the effect of having worked too hard at deciphering writing more than half obliterated. Perhaps it will give way when this murderous work for the eyes is finished, which is not the case yet.

If reflection, when it has become too one-sided, and too domineering over a deeply feeling heart, is apt to lead us into errors in our treatment of others, it gives us, on the other hand, the power of looking every thing in the face, of supporting the most dreadful prospect, and maintaining our equanimity; but he who has neglected to cultivate this power, and always lived exclusively in imagination and direct perception, with these faculties nourished by an interchange of every thought and feeling with another, is, when a great calamity befalls him, robbed of his whole wealth, and incapable of replacing it.

......My first impression of the city remains unchanged. Brandis, too, finds nothing Elysian here. Neither the city, nor its inhabitants, so far as it is inhabited, have any charms for me. The magnificent prospects toward the surrounding mountains from some of the eminences would delight you. I still find the ruins of the imperial times uncongenial to my taste; there is wonderfully little that is truly beautiful. The frescoes of Raphael and Michael Angelo, and some ancient statues, are all that is really living in Rome. I often ascend the Capitoline Hill to look at Marcus Aurelius and his horse, and I have not been able to refrain from caressing the lions of basalt. You can not stand on the Aventine or the Palatine without grave thoughts, but standing on the spot brings me very little nearer to the image of past ages.

Among the present living occupants of Rome, our German artists alone have any worth in them; and in their society, as far as their sphere reaches, you may sometimes transport yourself for a few hours into a better world. Cornelius you know, from his illustrations to the "Nibelungen Lied." They are incomparably surpassed by those to the Faust, which have been already engraved. Cornelius is an entirely self-educated man. His taste in art is quite for the sublime, the simple, and grand. We are constantly becoming more intimate, and may already call ourselves friends. He has an excellent wife, a native of Rome, who I hope will be of service to Gretchen when she needs a friend. He is very poor, because he works for his conscience and his own satisfaction, and purchasers who would or could measure their remuneration by the same standard are not to be found. I can not afford to give the artists work, but I am glad to be able to help them as a friend when their necessities are pressing. Another frequent visitor of ours is Platner, who has been made a painter by an unlucky accident, whereas nature intended him for a scholar and historian. He is still poorer than Cornelius; his wife is very like Mrs. Reimer. The Tyrolese Koch, whom you will have heard of as a landscape painter, is a friend of theirs, an eccentric, petulant man, full of just thoughts and bitter sarcasms. With these three we can thoroughly harmonize, though Platner is Saxon in his politics, and only attracted to me by personal liking; Koch, however, has such an antipathy to Hackert and to the Propylæa, and Goethe's Winckelmann, that he even speaks absurdly and spitefully against Goethe himself. I like Overbeck and the two Schadows much, and they are estimable both as artists and as men; but the Catholicism of Overbeck and one of the Schadows excludes entirely many topics of conversation. Rauch was here for some time. Thorwaldsen estimates the representation infinitely higher than the thought, and maintains that a work which is false in conception, but correct in drawing, is still the work of a master; while, on the contrary, a picture having the noblest idea, if in any respect erroneous in drawing, or imperfect in coloring, is only that of a learner. There are no learned men among the foreigners here at present, except my old tutor and friend, Playfair, of Edinburgh. Bunsen is here, however, and for him one must feel the highest esteem, but he is much engaged with an Englishman to whom he gives instruction.

You want to know my way of life. Whenever the library is open, and no conference with the Secretary of State stands in the way, I go, if the weather is tolerable, to the Vatican. There I am still occupied upon a manuscript in which I have found lost fragments of Cicero's Orations, a part of the fragment of Livy, which the earlier editors have not been able to make out, and other fragments of Seneca and Hyginus. The printing of these things will soon begin; I shall dedicate them to the Pope, for whom I still retain the reverence I felt at a distance. I often go to the Forum, where they have excavated an interesting spot. More distant walks can seldom be undertaken at this season of the year. When Gretchen feels inclined we take a drive. Three times a week, my Italian master comes, who is, however, a very bad one. Every Tuesday, there is a large dinner-party at the French embassador's, which, as it always consists of the same persons, gets more tiresome every time......

1817.

About this time, A. W. Schlegel's attack upon Niebuhr's History came out in the Jena "Litteratur Zeitung," and other unfavorable reviews of it appeared in the Heidelberg "Jahrbücher," which vexed Niebuhr all the more, as, owing to his absence, he was unable to defend his work as he would have wished. A much more serious annoyance was caused him by a statement which appeared in the "Alte Freimuthige," from the pen of Gottlieb Merkel, accusing him of having torn the fragments of the Gaius, which he had sent to Savigny, out of books belonging to the Cathedral Chapter at Verona, and carried them off. Niebuhr caused a judicial investigation to be instituted, the result of which was that Merkel was condemned to "six months' imprisonment, or a fine of 500 dollars, for a libel against the Privy Councilor Niebuhr."

In April, 1817, his wife bore him a son after long and severe suffering. This event gave him the keenest delight, and it was the first thing that dispelled the cloud of melancholy which had hung over him ever since his first wife's death. He had never had any anxious wishes for children in his first marriage, but now his heart yearned toward the child that was born to him with the whole fervor of his deep affections.

During the summer of this year Niebuhr, with his family and Brandis, spent some time at Frascati, where he translated an essay on the Poor and Pauperism that had appeared in the "Quarterly Review," and had greatly excited his interest. He occupied what leisure he had from the duties of his office this year, in studying the history of Greece and of Asia, from the time of Philip of Macedon to their conquest by the Romans, in order, as he himself expressed it, "to obtain a sharply-outlined picture of the period when Greek and Roman history first begin to run parallel to each other without coming into contact, up to that in which they at last coalesce." These studies were interrupted by a lingering illness, his recovery from which was long doubtful. It was, however, remarkable that even during his illness his mind felt clearer and brighter than for two years previously. While still confined to his bed he was able to study, and was conscious of the revival of that faculty of divination and happy combination, the loss of which had so often depressed him. From this time forward, a brighter era in Niebuhr's life begins, notwithstanding his settled dislike of the nation among whom his lot was cast. He was, however, long unfit for any bodily exertion.

On his return to Rome, in October, he found Professor Bekker, of Berlin, who had been sent with Professor Goeschen, by the Academy of Sciences, to follow out Niebuhr's discovery of the Institutes of Gaius. Niebuhr invited Bekker to become his guest during the ensuing months which he intended to spend at Rome, and found in his society the opportunity of conversing on the subjects of his studies, the want of which he had hitherto felt so painfully since his arrival there. He now renewed his investigations in connection with Roman history.

Many foreigners visited Rome during this winter, among whom were the Crown Prince of Bavaria, Lord Colchester, and Lord Lansdowne; with the two latter, Niebuhr formed a sincere and lasting friendship.

Letters written in 1817.

CCXXI.

TO MADAME HENSLER.

Rome, 1*st January*, 1817.

My first employment this day shall be to write to you. Till this time two years, the close of the old year was generally a happy and joyous time: my Milly made it a festival for us at home, at least, and we used to enter on the new year reading and talking together; frequently, with a spoken recollection of you—at any rate, with a silent one; for she clung to you with the warmest, tenderest love. She so often spoke of you with affection; she longed so to have you with her, though she was so happy in her love, that she could endure your absence.

How delightful were those eves of the new year, and of Christmas while we lived at Copenhagen, and before we had been drawn into the whirlpool of politics! But how delightful they were too at Berlin, although on the whole the destruction of our quiet, unconscious, individual life, had issued in a new, perhaps more brilliant, but less blessed epoch of our existence.

I try to employ myself; but it is to little purpose, for I find it is still as ever the case with me, that I can only work with success when I linger with pleasure over my occupations. My powers are still further paralyzed by the disagreeable and deadening effect of the fashionable parties which are very numerous at this season. Then, too, the parties here are more insipid and and annoying than any I have ever been in before. I have formed the intention of, at least, revising and correcting the Roman History, if I can not finish it; I sit faithfully enough for hours together before my books, but memory and sagacity will not serve me as formerly; vague recollections of things I have read, and of the existence of relations dawn upon my mind, but refuse to let me grasp them, or to assume a distinct shape.

I have many times before felt what it is to be in a foreign land; I felt it least of all in England;—in Holland more, after the first interest was exhausted, but never as I do here in Italy; here you can never learn to feel at home. There is no possibility of intimacy with those around you—that is, with the Italians—no possibility of growing attached to them through common interests or feelings. No object of science or of occupation brings you together. If we could but let each other entirely alone, it would not be so bad; for we are not at a loss for society and friends, but that is impossible. I must keep up an intercourse with them. Every one is titled; every one has a certain rank; the noble and beautiful alone has neither rank nor existence. All the topics which occupy us in Germany are foreign to them, have no existence for them; their thoughts are not directed to any object or aim.

I have other anxieties, relating to my father-land, that is, my adopted one. There are rumors of war abroad, and they only give weight to a long-cherished presentiment of mine. I have long feared a coalition against Prussia. I can not bear to think out the details of the calamities which such an occurrence may and almost certainly must entail, of which, the least would be a progress toward barbarism and slavery. In such times, it is no happiness to become a father, and a heavy misfortune to be at a distance from one's own country. The impossibility of holding any affectionate or interesting intercourse with the natives of this country, is a great obstacle to progress in their language. Another hindrance is, that while all my anticipations regarding the miserable condition of Rome, in a moral point of view, have been fulfilled to the uttermost, I find the difference between the wretched language that is current, and the beautiful old language of the literature, far greater than I had ever supposed it to be. The more modern writings are such as no one could peruse with care; it is hardly possible to run through them, still less to appropriate their language; but neither can you obtain a perfect mastery over the old classical language, for the new which you are constantly hearing, mixes itself up with it, and corrupts it. In Florence it still lives, but like a learned language, in the pens of many, and in the mouths of a few cultivated men. I felt there that I could render myself a complete master of it; but here it is so badly spoken, that it is impossible for me, at least with my present capabilities, to acquire it. I have begun to read Guicciardini aloud during the evenings; his fullness and power of vivid description render him most admirable as an historian. Further, we do not get on with our reading together as I could wish.......

CCXXII.

TO JACOBI.

Rome, 11*th January*, 1817.

......I am making some effort to purchase the tomb of the Scipios. It is a characteristic trait of this modern Rome, that when this unique and venerable monument of antiquity was discovered in 1780, the bones of Scipio, which were in a state of perfect preservation, were torn from their stony couch and thrown away! When people try to console you for the passing away of the old Roman times, by saying that modern Rome has become Christian and Catholic, I can not help quoting Lucan's consolation for the civil wars, that all this blood had not flowed in vain, for else Nero could never have reigned.

However, among the artists here, the pious and believing are by far the most eminent men, and there are some of them highly deserving of respect; but no place seems to me so fitted to confirm one in Lutheranism as this; unless, indeed, you are in close intercourse with the Pope, for whom your personal veneration increases with your knowledge of him.......

Have I told you that I have found our Indian numerals in use in a Greek MS., which must certainly be older than the seventh century?

Goethe's Travels have only just made their appearance here, and I am reading them much as the Man in the Moon might read Schröter's Selenographical Fragments. But it is too wide a subject for me to enter upon it now. I had so much to discuss with you and Roth! among other things, the French Electoral Law, which I am quite full of at present, so much so, that I have begun a pamphlet on the subject, which will probably, however, be left unfinished.*

CCXXIII.

TO MADAME HENSLER.

ROME, *15th January*, 1817.

......Gretchen is not at all well.......But how much, to her as well as to me, hangs on the life of this child, which will very likely be your inheritance if Gretchen and I go before you. I know that you will tend and educate our child with the warm love of a mother.

I certainly look forward with gladness to the birth of this child. In case it should be a boy, I am already preparing myself to educate him. I should try to familiarize him very early with the ancient languages by making him repeat sentences after me, and relating stories to him in them, in order that he might not have too much to learn afterward, nor yet read too much at too early an age, but receive his education after the fashion of the ancients. I think I should know how to educate a boy, but not a girl; I should be in danger of making her too learned. In Montaigne's times, the sons of learned men acquired Greek and Latin by conversation, like a modern language. I would relate innumerable stories to the boy, as my father did to me; but by degrees mix up more and more of Greek and Latin in them, so that he would be forced to learn those languages in order to understand the stories. If it is a boy, he shall have the name which my Milly would have given to hers; that of my father and of yours.......If it is [a girl] it shall have Amelia's name and yours, and your united blessing.

Brandis feels the effects of our troubles—I fear of the climate too..... For the rest, you know how much I am attached to him, and how I value

* This fragment is contained in a volume of his smaller writings, published in 1842, p. 471.

his society. A purer heart, a more noble and unselfish disposition than his, there can not exist; and these derive a rare worth from his refined intellect, and his quick appreciation of all elevated ideas.......

CCXXIV.

TO NICOLOVIUS.

ROME, 22*d January*, 1817.

I have been ill for some time, dear Nicolovius: I was so for several weeks before I would give way; but at last I was forced to take to my bed. Now I am enjoying the refreshing feeling of recovery. While it lasts, I will clear off, without further delay, the heavily-accumulated debt of answer to your kind and consolatory letter. It is better that my reply has been put off so long, for such a black cloud hung over my mental horizon, that any thing I could have written in that state would only have given you pain.

The physical cause of my illness was the changeable weather, The winter has been on the whole mild up to this time (and if nature is in any respect what she was in ancient times, spring must begin A.D. VIII. *Idus Febr.*), and pleasant from its dryness. No snow has fallen in the city, and the Triton has only had a beard one morning at most; but the Tramontane gives you cold much sooner than a snow storm, and the excessively rapid changes of temperature are more than my constitution can stand, particularly since I am frequently obliged to wear full court dress, and then to come from before an immense open fire down the exposed staircases through an icy-cold sea of air. Then, too, the very quality of the winds here has quite altered since the ancient times; which has, I think, never yet been remarked. The Aquilo, or Greco, no longer blows from the N.N.E., but from the N.E., and the Scirocco, or Vulturnus, was formerly dry and not very disagreeable: thus, too, I do not doubt that the character of the Libuccio and Ostro has changed much for the worse, though in the main they are what they used to be. Do you see that I am already becoming a Roman of the present day? for the prevailing wind, and the price of oil, and the size of the *pagnotti*,* are the main ideas that occupy their minds; in fact, what can and dare we poor wretches think about besides? So in order to complete the information, which you have a right to expect from a Roman of the present day, I beg to announce to you that a *fogliette* of oil costs from two-and-twenty to four-and-twenty *bajocchi*; in your time it will not have cost more than seven or eight at most. Some aged men among the natives remember when an insurrection was near breaking out, because it rose from two and a half to four *bajocchi*. The price would have risen to forty with us, as the forestallers and regraters set no bounds to their audacity, but that a counter-speculation was set on foot. Meanwhile, that forestalling is an honest trade, to which the State can offer no opposition; and that by these high prices and their profits, large capitals are created, which contribute much more to the increase of the national wealth than the pennies trickling through the poor man's purse for his daily wants —has been proved to satisfaction by political economy, for which science there is unfortunately no gallows, because it was only in the schools of the rhetoricians that one could bring forward an accusation of *inscripti maleficii*.

* Penny rolls.

Our forefathers, however, would have drowned the teachers of this wisdom, and my old Romans would have banished them still more rigorously than the Greek sophists, or at least would have ordered them to cease from their *ludus impudentiæ*. At Castelmaggiore, in Sabina, sixty-two human beings have already died of hunger, as I have been assured by a parish priest, who seems to be an intelligent and honest man; this is the state of things every where among the mountains. As for ourselves, we are, indeed, in no danger of starvation, but I am obliged to renounce all indulgences in order to make both ends meet; can buy neither books nor works of art; and must quietly put up with having it said that we do not live suitably to our station.

I have written about Titel...... I wish my recommendations of our much more eminent young painters may also be successful. I have no need to press this matter further upon *your* attention; and if there are great difficulties with regard to it, I am only making your heart heavy. There are two ways in which something really useful, and conducive to the dignity of Prussia might be accomplished; the one would do honor to the government; the other at any rate to the public. Either let the government summon some of the most distinguished artists to Berlin, and commission them to execute some great work in fresco—say, in the cathedral (to which the King would perhaps be most inclined), or in the University, or some other public building. Or, if the ministry will not listen to this, let a subscription be raised if possible among the wealthy for the same object, to which end you must go out into the highways and hedges and invite them to come in, where people are beggars only in a spiritual point of view, and their scrip is full. I have written to Savigny about a similar notion.* I think that the Princess William might be interested in this matter, and if necessary I would write to her about it. You have probably not yet seen the Faust of Cornelius—have you? It has, or will far surpass your expectations. Cornelius is a very high-minded, intellectual, and amiable man; a Catholic by birth, but so little a zealot, that when we were talking with him about his favorite idea of painting a Last Judgment, though he refused our request that Luther might be translated into the heavenly glory, on the plea that he dared not do that, he said that he should be represented as holding up the Bible to the devil, and the latter as retreating at the sight of it. I fancy Stolberg would approve of this too in the depths of his heart—don't you? I recommend the two Schadows strongly to the notice of the government. As for William, I fear that he is exerting himself beyond his strength and will not live long; but you must not let his father know more of this than is necessary to induce him to moderate his demands upon his son. Both the brothers are extremely industrious, and like all our eminent young men, of irreproachable morality. Rudolph is beginning to acquire celebrity, and there is some prospect of his receiving important commissions from Englishmen. If so, it would be a terrible pity that he should not remain here for some years to come; for it is only through such labors, by producing great and numerous works, that the artist can truly develop himself. If obstacles of this kind should prevent him from obeying the dictates of his father, those who are in Berlin must excuse his conduct to the old man: in this

* This is interesting as being the first suggestion from which the Art Unions, now so numerous in Germany, took their rise.

case I have promised to claim your mediation, dear Nicolovius, and you would do a good work if you could prepare the old man for it beforehand.

There are two others besides, in whose behalf I shall boldly apply to the Home Office—the two Rhinelanders, Gau the architect, and the painter Moseler, who received stipends from the provisional government. I must earnestly entreat that these may be continued to them. Gau is a real genius, and has begun to make most important discoveries respecting ancient architecture; he has made drawings at Pompeii, which inspire much more confidence in their accuracy than those of Maizoy; here in Rome, he has made observations from the summit of the Capitol, which have suggested some very important ideas with regard to the ancient ground-plan of the city—for instance, that there are fragments of two plans of completely different proportions; he has also discovered the Ulpian Basilicæ; and further, recently, that the arch of Janus is constructed out of fragments of the so-called Temple of the Sun. He is extremely industrious, and it would be a thousand pities if he were obliged to leave Italy just at present. Unless I am much deceived, we may expect great things from him. Moseler is at work on copies from the old Cologne school of painters, which Wenner is bringing out at Frankfort with an historical introduction, which has the great merit of dispelling, by its impartial and acute investigation, the mist that even the Boisserées have thrown over the supposed early period of art in that city. His results, unlike theirs, are in harmony with what is known from other historical sources, and therefore it is to be hoped that, after their publication, we shall hear no more of a school of art at Cologne under the Byzantine Emperors, or even dating back to the Roman times. But it is of great moment, to enable him to form a connected history of art from the earliest times, that he should see Tuscany and Venice.......What are they doing about the University on the Lower Rhine? I wish some appointment there could be found for our friend Platner, who is not great as a painter, but has a real vocation for literature. If it were possible to establish there, or in any other university, a professorship of Italian literature and history, and the history of Italian art, that would be the post best suited to his talents, and he would fill it with great honor to himself. He has begun to prepare an edition of Vasari, and would be quite capable of writing an excellent commentary upon Dante, if the publishers would condescend to patronize him. Unless my memory deceive me, he was not named according to his merits at Berlin. He is a particularly noble-minded man.

Be so kind as to return my kind regards to L. Stolberg, with the assurance that I should not fail for want of "going piano," even if the utter absence of all instructions did not render it impossible to advance a step forward. This is a misery for which I can not console myself, because a conjunction in every respect favorable is thereby lost to us. The Pope is ready, nay, offers to do all that is reasonable; he could not have expressed himself more clearly on this subject, than he did to me, a short time since, in a long conversation. We are regarded with favor in a political point of view, and as for myself personally I certainly do not stand in the way of the business. The dedication to the Pope of the Ciceronian fragments I have discovered here (I sent him the MS. a week ago), has greatly pleased the kind-hearted old man; and the government are really more obliging to me in regard to public business than I could have ventured to hope; for they have gone so far as to receive from a Protestant embassador, the filling up of incomplete clerical certificates. Still, I ask, if I am to have no other vocation than that of negotiating dispensations; is it at all worth while that my life and real calling should be thus sacrificed? With me, dearest Nicolovius, the inward life is burnt out, and my body too is exhausted. I lived through the spirit, and that is fallen asleep.

That the Cathedral Chapter of Cologne should extend its jurisdiction beyond the Rhine, is certainly out of the question, so long as the new bishopric of Aix-la-Chapelle stands in the way, and this gives a great deal to do in the way of negotiation; but if Cologne were created into an archbishopric, all difficulties would be removed; assuming, that is, that the government would endow the Cathedral Chapter and bishoprics, as Bavaria has done, which really does not involve an extravagant expenditure, and allow the Chapter to elect their own bishops. I have made a report upon the Bavarian Concordat to the foreign department, and hope that your department will learn the contents of my report upon ecclesiastical matters. Oh that you had it in your power to get my instructions forwarded to me!

I am still occupied upon the same codex; some extremely trivial leaves from Seneca, which are dreadfully illegible, but unhappily have never been printed, are costing me many valuable hours now, and will probably cost my eyes a great part of their power. I hope the dedication to the Pope will open the private closets, and then it seems impossible but that something should be brought to light. But Rome affords me no help toward my History. This Rome is a *Codex rescriptus*, where Cato's Origines have been erased, and a "Diario di Roma"* written over them. It is particularly unfortunate that one can not get to the mountains, but that is quite impossible, on account of the banditti. We can not even venture as far as Palestrina, or Cori.

Since your time, every thing must have changed beyond recognition. This I am assured, too, is the case by those who have long lived here. The inhabitants of Trastevere are as tame as all the rest; as ugly as all the rest; they all steal along in silence and melancholy; the sound of song is nowhere heard. I have not seen a merry face since I have been here.

I deeply sympathize in what you tell me of Göschen's anxieties. Oh if it were but possible to be of any help to one's friends under such calamities! . . . . . .

CCXXV.

TO MADAME HENSLER.

ROME, *7th February*, 1817.

. . . . . . To-day, at eight o'clock, begins the wild buffoonery of the Carnival, to us a melancholy spectacle. It is a question whether even the Romans will enact it with any real gayety of heart. Probably they did so as long as their easy life still resembled that of children in the holidays, but all merriment is strange to them now. A people of utterly vacant mind is capable of childish enjoyment as long as it has outward comforts,

* A miserable little daily paper at Rome.

but when a period of agitation and calamity comes, when its playthings are broken, and it has to go hungry, it must inevitably become heavy and stupid. The difference between my expectation and that of those who had seen Rome many years ago, consisted in my having a distinct conception of this change. There is scarcely any thing more repulsive than a fool without mirth. I can well understand how it was that Nicolovius and others, in the gayety of their own youth, should have delighted in these merry fools. They should come and see them now! Every countenance is careworn, even those that are not emaciated by hunger. All is so changed here, that even the far-famed gesticulation and grimace of the Italians have almost entirely vanished. The people are kept in order by the iron rigor of the police; the cavaletto—the machine on which those who infringe the police regulations are whipped—is almost permanent. You certainly hear of no murders committed within the city, and it may be, that when a people is condemned to live in such an indescribable state of physical and political misery, nothing but this iron discipline can enable us of the upper classes to live in safety. But what a state of things! You can not venture to go where this coercion can not also reach, and in Tivoli, a highly respectable man was murdered, a few weeks ago, in his own house by masked robbers. Latium, on the other side of Frascati and Albano, is quite inaccessible to me; and yet it is that spot which would above all things have rendered my residence here valuable to my History.

Certainly the country and the climate are beautiful. The fertility of the soil is inconceivable, and I should think that seven *jugers* might well suffice for a household. But the rank soil exhales death, and even the laborers are obliged to forsake the vineyards in summer. This has been a winter such as can scarcely be remembered, so mild and dry, but too dry for the crops. No snow at all has fallen in the city; but the high mountains in the Sabina are adorned with it. That snow can be beautiful, is incomprehensible to the Romans, *è pur cosa brutta*. By this time, however, it is melting away. In the gardens, every thing is sprouting and growing green, as it does with us in the end of April; and it is as warm; the birds are singing and chirping. It is said that in Florence the distress is still greater than with us, and that people are dying of hunger daily in that city.......

The editing of my little work takes up a great deal of my time. The fragments will be accompanied by an introduction and notes, besides a long essay. I possess Latin words and idioms in abundance, and of the best kind; the language is like a living one to me, so that if it were possible for the old Romans to rise again, in a few months I could speak it like a native, as fluently as I do English; yet I am not safe from the critics, for I know how liable one is, even in a modern language, to commit faults here and there, which those who are watching for them are quite able to perceive, even when they are by no means masters of the language themselves. Now we must see if there are any MSS. of a different kind to be found. This is very uncertain, and even if some old treasures should still exist here, the hitting upon them is a matter of chance, and a good many artifices are necessary before you can gain access to them. I have quite won the hearts of the people at the Library: I have earned this respect and good-will by notices of a few of their detached MSS. The worst is, however, that what I seek is not marked in any catalogue, but can only be discovered by personal researches.......Gretchen is too ill to write to you herself.......

CCXXVI.

TO SAVIGNY.

ROME, *16th February*, 1817.

......The old Greeks were pretty near the mark, when they pictured our coasts, *i. e.* those of Italy, as the land of Cimmerian darkness, and fabled Apollo as wandering between Delphi and the noble Hyperboreans. It has already come to this with me, that I feel I am growing as superficial and ignorant as a modern Italian, and look up to all that you could send me with sorrowful humility; the genuine native Italians would indeed have to look up to it from the depths; those here, I mean, for whom I always feel angry that there is no other name than the shamefully profaned one of Romans; for the old men at Venice, Bologna, and Florence said indeed with bleeding hearts, that all was over with their nation and their literature, and that their departed greatness was but an agonizing remembrance.......

I rejoice in your plenitude of life, which is such an utter contrast to my stagnation. But I will pain you no longer by speaking of this, for I know that your love for your absent friend remains unchanged; I know how thoroughly you realize my present situation, and how deeply you sympathize with me. I will only tell you about myself and all of us what will give you pleasure, and speak of you. Your traveler delivered your packet faithfully, and it is long since any thing has so delighted and interested me. I give you special thanks on my own account for your masterly essay on the advocates of legislative novelties, which is as just in thought as it is powerfully written. My Cassandra-spirit says indeed, Alas, it will be of no avail! We are absolutely powerless to turn the broad shallow current of the spirit of the age into a deeper channel. But it is in itself a noble thing to sacrifice yourself by unwearied exertions; and more meritorious to scoop out in the mud a bed for the stream, than to sustain a sublime conflict with wild torrents. I can not help thoughts of this kind; it is not because my own little barrel runs thick, but because every where things are on the lees, that I despair of the age and of posterity. Brandis will suffer no censure to be passed on the generation of his contemporaries; he himself and Bunsen have, from their own character, a right to challenge respect for their generation. I am well aware too, how many excellent young men you and I have come in contact with, and my dear young artists are miles above those who have hitherto borne the name. But it is not only true of the legislation of states, that the virtue of the nation can do no more than modify the errors of their rulers; the same thing holds good also with regard to the legislation of opinion and sentiment in such difficult times. If the road were but in some measure traced out and leveled for us, oh then the danger would not be so urgent! But nothing is further from the fact; and even if we were willing to allow that our country is richer in young men of ability and moral worth, now that our poetical age is over, than in the times of our fathers, our hopes for the future would not be thereby assured, if, as is undeniable, the problem of this generation is a hundred times more difficult of solution. We want a new creation, and in what respect are we prepared for this work? I see the jacobinical spirit that pervades our political writings, and, at the same time, I know for certain that thousands of our youths, without any bad intentions, never see any thing else. It is one of my troubles here, that I see nothing but the "Allgemeine Zeitung;" some German paper is a mental aliment I can not deny myself; but this is bread from which you are obliged to scrap off the dirt. Does not the most senseless Westphalian and Rhine-league spirit display itself in the most arrogant manner in that journal, especially in all that relates to France? I take a great interest in the proceedings in France; I read the "Journal des Débats" from beginning to end every post-day, though there is not a creature here (except the French embassador) with whom I can talk of it. I do not wish to rate these proceedings too highly, but in my opinion it is saying a great deal too little in their favor, to pronounce that we should manage things much worse in Germany. But this by the way. There we have a ministry which I rate incomparably above any other in Europe, in point of intelligence, ability, and good intentions; a ministry honestly attached to the throne and to freedom; supported by a party adverse to all revolutions; opposed by a party who find themselves exactly in the position of the Tories under George I. and George II.—a faction whose heart is set upon a counter revolution which can not take place, and who therefore constitute the most wholesome check possible upon all really revolutionary tendencies.

With regard to the cause of which you are the only true advocate, I have heard from Bunsen, and see with my own eyes, that the opposite party have an enormous majority. This is the case here too. A new code is to be drawn up. The French had annulled all the municipal constitutions. It must be confessed their diversity was carried to a great extent. Morelli, who made a collection of them in the library of St. Mark, brought together more than three hundred, and many were still wanting. Almost every city had gradually formed its own civil law, and this may partially explain the great rarity of MSS. of the Justinian Code. These repealed constitutions are to remain repealed, and the fundamental decree for the Papal States, of the 6th of July in last year, promises a new three-fold code of laws, while there is beyond a question infinitely less capability for such a work here even than in Germany; in fact, absolute incapacity with no individual exceptions. In the mean time, some general principles are promulgated. "What serves as the standard of law in the mean time?" I asked the president of a High Court of Appeal. "That is a great difficulty certainly," he replied; "the old Roman Code in two thick volumes *forse lo conosce?*" —An advocate sighed yet more deeply: "un libro grosso cosi! bisogna, facchini per portarlo, he, he, he!" This advocate has composed a preliminary treatise on criminal law, which is by itself three inches thick; for the Italians, with their utterly vacant minds, delight in native and foreign verbiage without ideas. Only a pregnant solid style is distasteful to them. He completely proves his vocation according to one of the criteria which you lay down, namely, he speaks in a pamphlet of the barbarity of the old Roman laws on debt. These belonged to the *jus prætoriale* which was the work of *capriccio.* Even the Twelve Tables did not alleviate the barbarity of the abominable *jus prætoriale.* Appius Claudius, the decemvir, was himself a prætor, and there lies the root of the matter.

We are very grateful to you for Goethe's Life. It no longer, indeed, reveals to us the golden and silver ages described in the first volume, but a very iron age, where even his joys and delights are a fit of intoxication, which the spectator neither can, nor desires to share; a strange, to me for the most part incomprehensible kind of delirium, in which he often neglects what is most glorious; and what does he not admire? In many respects he was doubtless infected by the spirit of his age, and in this way his mention of the Gallery of the Caracci in the Farnese palace, of the Bolognese school in general, and even of the St. Petronilla of Guercino, must be explained. I remember taking pleasure myself in Guercino, and even in Guido, but my liking for them had passed away before I could venture to express an opinion on such subjects. Our friends here are orthodox. But I could never have spoken coldly of Francesco Francia, and at the same time enthusiastically of Domenichino. The modern Bolognese themselves are, indeed, just the same. The Canon Schiassi was obliging enough to take me into chapels not generally visited, where wonderful master-pieces of Francia lie forgotten, but he smiled at my Transalpine folly. It seems to me to be the same with Goethe himself as with many others, who affect connoisseurship on subjects for which all true feeling is denied them. I am inclined to think that Goethe is utterly destitute of susceptibility to impressions from the fine arts; that is, that he has no inward, native insight, which reveals to him what is really beautiful independently of the taste of the age, still less in opposition to it; or if he ever possessed this gift as a young man at Strasburg, he lost it during the unhappy period—passed over without notice in his narrative—of his court life at Weimar, before his Italian journey, and has never recovered it; witness his "Winckelmann and his Century," "Hackert's Life," the "Propylæa," the "Æsthetic Problems" and "Essays on Art" in the "Litteratur-Zeitung," not to speak of his "Rhein und Main." This is one thing; another is, the whole tone of his mind during his travels and residence in Italy, which is most remarkable, and would alone have rendered this description of his journey more interesting to us than any thing else you could have sent us; but is it not enough to make one weep? To treat a whole nation and a whole country simply as a means of recreation for one's self; to see nothing in the wide world and nature, but the innumerable trappings and decorations of one's own miserable life; to survey all moral and intellectual greatness, all that speaks to the heart, where it still exists, with an air of patronizing superiority; or, where it has been crushed and overpowered by folly and corruption to find amusement in the comic side of the latter—is to me absolutely revolting; perhaps more so to me personally, than I can reasonably expect it to be to others, but I think it ought to excite sentiments similar in kind, if not in degree, in every breast. I am well aware that I go into the opposite extreme; that my politico-historical turn of mind can find full satisfaction in things for which Goethe has no taste, and that I could live contentedly without feeling the want of art, not only amidst the glorious scenery of the Tyrol, but on moor or heath, where I was surrounded by a free peasantry, who had a history. But truth, though it always lies between two extremes, does not always lie in the middle. Goethe too, in his early life, belonged rather to the Rome of the fifth century of the city than to that of the Cæsars—rather to the Florence of Dante and Boccaccio than to that of Ferdinand the Third—rather to the Germany of Luther and Durer than to that of the eighteenth century—nay, he belonged wholly to the earlier period when he wrote "Faust" and "Götz," and his Songs. What evil genius inspired him with the notion of doing justice to the eighteenth century as well? From these "Travels in Italy" sprang the "Grosscophta" and those other productions, in which all that was holy and great in his nature is shrouded from view. To return to the question, I maintain, that it is absolutely impossible for a genuine and correct taste for art to exist apart from historical feeling, because the arts are inseparable; that historical feeling will manifest itself wherever there is a true taste for art, without any erudition, as is the case, for instance, with Cornelius; that even Carlo Maratta and Mengs are not without relative beauties, corresponding to the times in which they lived; only they possess no intrinsic value, and form part of an absolutely bad whole. Were I still "qualis Præneste sub alta," I would say much more on this topic.

When I recall the enthusiasm of Nicolovius for Italy, and compare it with the delirium of this book, how wide is the interval between the two! I think that Nicolovius saw much in too fair a light, but the earth and the sky enchanted him, and he delighted to his very heart in the *naïveté* of the people, which at that time had not yet ceased to exist; he was sincerely in love with all around him.

Goethe likes Venice; yet, in the procession of the Doge and the Senate, he sees—not the image of her ancient grandeur, of her countless great and wise men, but simply a theatrical spectacle. But, throughout, it is curious to remark, how he generally leaves the finest objects unvisited, or if he sees them, only places them in the second rank. Thus at Padua, for instance, he has not seen the Chapel of the Annunziata, where you ought to linger for whole days, but is highly pleased with the wide, marshy Piazza della Valle, garnished with statues so miserable, that they might have stood in St. Peter's; at Venice, he does not see San Giovanni e Paolo, which contains Vivarini's master-pieces, and the tombs of the heroes, with inscriptions that speak to the inmost heart, nor yet the urn of the general who was flayed in Candia; nor San Giobbe, which was then standing in all its glory. But altogether, how incredibly little he has seen in Venice, can only be appreciated by one who has been there himself. Yet, even those who have had this privilege, will be disappointed to hear nothing of the Ducal Palace, and the true marvels of the Place of St. Mark. Of Florence I will say nothing, not even wonder how any one could hasten through it in such a way, nor yet of his omitting to see the water-fall of Terni. I say all this merely to prove my assertion that he has beheld without love.

Italy was then quite another country; now she is despoiled and sick. I can enter into the feelings of those who saw her, when they were not made miserable by the sight of mortal anguish, of wounds that can not heal. I, had I seen her then, would doubtless have shared the transports of those who did behold her in the gladness of their youth; though even then my transport would have been mingled with sadness.......

I broke off on the previous page, having continued my letter yesterday (17th). I broke off, because the merriment of our assembled friends was resounding from Brandis's room, and we did not want to shorten our evening unnecessarily. Cornelius of Dusseldorf, Platner from Leipzig, Koch from the Tyrol, Overbeck from Lübec, Moseler from Coblentz, and William Schadow from Berlin, were assembled in Brandis's apartment with Bunsen. In different ways and degrees we are attached to them all, and think them all men of talent. Their society is the only pleasure we derive from human beings here, and they have already performed much in their art, and promise more for the future. I believe confidently that we are on the eve of a new era of art in Germany, similar to the sudden bloom of our literature in the eighteenth century; and that it only needs a little encouragement on the part of our governments to render us the participants of this beautiful development. Cornelius and Plàtner are, strictly speaking, intimate family friends, and so are their wives. Roman women, of the good burgher class, are great favorites with Gretchen. The women of this class are here incomparably superior to the men, just because they have a natural vocation, and show great zeal in fulfilling its duties; these two are agreeable and sincerely kind-hearted. Mrs. Platner is very like Mrs. Reimer, which is a great recommendation to us. Next to these, Koch and Moseler are our most intimate friends.

In the morning I had been to Cornelius and William Schadow with the joyful intelligence that Schukman's letter gave hopes of the fulfillment of their ardent wish to paint the interior of a church. If this should be brought to pass, it is indispensable that their labors should be shared by their inseparable friend, Overbeck, for both of them do homage to his genius, and regard him as the highest artist among their contemporaries. For my own part, I must confess that the genius of Cornelius appears to me even superior in fertility, while his power of drawing is certainly more wonderful. My good news has set them all in motion, and they came to spend a merry evening with us. They were followed by their friend and fellow artist, Ruschweyh, from Mecklenburg, the eminent engraver, who is likewise a very intelligent and estimable man.

We were all in high spirits, and amused ourselves with making fun of Platner, who has something of the Leipzig politeness still about him, which we are determined to dispel by fair means or foul, and he is therefore undergoing a regular course of strict moral diet, and is carefully watched if the least symptom of his old complaint betrays itself. Koch, who has a most thorough enjoyment of life, was chuckling with delight over a somewhat coarse allegorical representation of our ministerial and government politics, which he had introduced, after the manner of Shakspeare's comic scenes, above, in the foreground of a picture of Hofer setting out on his enterprise, which he is painting for the Minister Stein. In one part a hissing snake was darting on the Tyrolese—"That means the traitors who robbed the country of its freedom at Vienna." Then there are frogs decorated with orders, and a centipede, which is his particular favorite—"Those are the useless government officers." In one corner of the foreground lies the jaw-bone of an ass—"That is for me to fight the Philistines with." After looking at this, we went on with our reading, where we had broken off. Koch always falls asleep over the reading, unless it is something to make one's hair stand on end; so he slept quietly in the corner of the sofa. When we came to the passage, where Goethe describes how the dead are summoned forth after the curtain has fallen, Cornelius called to him—"Koch, the curtains have fallen with you too!" He started, and rubbed his eyes—"What is the matter?"

Cornelius is a most thorough enthusiast for Goethe, perhaps none more so; at least no man has owed so much of his inspiration to Goethe. He has a warm heart, and a fertile and profound intellect. At every spirited, life-like description, his face lighted up with pleasure, but directly that was over, resumed its expression of sadness and regret. The passage about the gondolier songs found an echo in all our hearts and from every mouth. But when we closed the book for the night, and we men still stood talking it over after Gretchen had gone to bed, before we sat down to our frugal supper, he broke silence to say, how deeply it grieved him that Goethe should have looked on Italy thus; that either his heart must have been pulseless during that period—that rich warm heart must have been frozen up—or else he must have instantly stifled all emotion, so completely to keep himself aloof from the sublime, so completely to divest himself of respect for the venerable. As for Palladio, we were all agreed that those of our party who had been in Venice, had neither at Vicenza, nor at St. Justina at Padua, nor in San Giorgio and the other churches built by him in Venice, seen any thing that we could call chaste and really beautiful, and that it was quite inconceivable how he, who had been the first to do honor to the manes of Erwin von Steinbach—he, who had probably directly or indirectly reawakened in all our souls the sense of the beautiful, should have seen in the works of Palladio sublime antiques, and never so much as named the Cathedral of Ratisbon; that the cause of this phenomenon must perhaps be sought in an unfortunate mood, and obstinate steeling of his heart against the sense of power in the works of others, in order proudly to hold every thing he saw, as it were, in his grasp—to treat it as his absolute property, and to depreciate it when it pleased him; and we all lifted up our voices and lamented over that fatal court life at Weimar where Samson was shorn of his locks.

All, however, will allow that very many things must make an entirely opposite impression according as they are read on this or the other side of the Alps; and hence also, we trust that our friends will allow themselves to believe, that if they, like us, had seen the objects he describes with their own eyes, they might regard in the same light as we do, those detached points which they now see with the eyes of this magical writer, whose very brilliancy (and this is what gives the edge to our sorrow) probably conceals something from their view.

To one whose views always rest upon an essentially historical basis, Goethe and his works are so entirely a part of history, that every detail which helps to throw light upon his own personal history, whether painful, or inspiriting like the story of his youth, is in the highest degree interesting. Do not therefore call me a renegade, dear Savigny; I have not forgiven him Sesenheim either; but if you read parts of this letter to any of my friends, for all of whom it is intended, take great care what you say to our friend Madame Göschen lest she should be angry with me.

...... The artists in Rome are divided, by a broad line of demarkation, into two parties, the one consisting of our friends and their adherents, the other of the united phalanx of those who sit around the burning bush on the Blocksberg. At their head stand the R.,* fellows who know the world, who ingratiate themselves with the foreigners, and to whom our academical colleague, Goliath,† pays all respect. This set intrigue, and lie, and backbite; they intend there shall not be light, come what will. The former are exemplary in their life: the latter display the old licentiousness which characterized the German artists at Rome thirty years ago.

* Riepenhausens. † Hirt.

Happily, at the present moment, the more talented of the new-comers range themselves on the side of the former; the latter, too, are not wanting in recruits. It is significant, however, that some foreigners, and even Italians, are beginning to pay attention to the works of our friends. The Marchese Massimi has commissioned Cornelius and Overbeck to paint two apartments in a villa, and will pay them handsomely. Cornelius means to paint a series of subjects from Dante—Overbeck from Tasso.

......I shall cost you a good deal in postage, dear Savigny, but I will make amends for it by sending you essays from time to time for your journal.*

With regard to myself, I have often had thoughts of death this winter, and Gretchen too, I think. Brandis still more frequently for me. I have no strength at all, and have grown excessively thin; my memory has suffered much, which is natural when you have ceased to take a hearty pleasure in any thing. Only what the mind drinks in with eagerness becomes thoroughly our own, so as to form part of our life. God help us!

The carnival mountebanks are bellowing under our window, though it is a little retired street. I have only once gone to see the horse-racing, where the barbarity with which the horses are treated is revolting, and there is nothing to be seen but a horse which springs from his master and rushes wildly away. The masks are a wretched buffoonery; dull caricatures; wit is nowhere to be seen or heard. Of course we have not once attended the masked balls.

We have taken a house to ourselves from the 1st of June. It is a very beautiful place. Houses are the only cheap article in this terribly, incredibly dear city; where, moreover, the prices of every thing required in housekeeping have risen one-third since our arrival. For fifteen rooms on the ground floor, most of them large, besides bedrooms, and six above, we are only to pay 300 scudi, about 440 dollars Prussian currency; in addition to these, there are a coach-house and stables and a lovely garden. Nicolovius will remember the theatre of Marcellus, in which the Savelli family built a palace. My house is the half of it. It has stood empty a considerable time, because the drive into the court-yard (the interior of the ancient theatre) rises like the slope of a mountain upon the heaps of rubbish; although the road has been cut in a zig-zag, it is still a break-neck affair. There is another entrance from the Piazza Montenara, where a flight of seventy-three steps leads up to the same story I have mentioned; the entrance hall of which is on a level with the top of the carriage way through the court-yard. The apartments in which we shall live, are those over the colonnade of Ionic pillars forming the third story of the ancient theatre, and some, on a level with them, which have been built out like wings on the rubbish of the ruins. These inclose a little quadrangular garden, which is indeed very small, only about eighty or ninety feet long, and scarcely so broad, but so delightful! It contains three fountains—an abundance of flowers; there are orange trees on the walls between the windows, jessamine under the windows. We mean to plant a vine besides. From this story, you ascend forty steps, or more, higher, where I mean to have my own study, and there are most cheerful little rooms, from which you have a prospect over the whole country beyond the Tiber, Monte Mario, and St. Peter's, and can see over San Pietro in Montorio, indeed almost as

* Zeitschrift für historische Rechtswissenschaft.

far as the Aventine. It would, I think, be possible besides to erect a loggia upon the roof (for which I shall save money from other things), that we may have a view over the Capitol, Forum, Palatine, Colosseum, and all the inhabited parts of the city. You may fancy the immense height of the walls of the old theatre, when I tell you that it lies in the valley between the Capitol and the island. You see, dear friend, that there is plenty of room for you, according to our promise, if you will keep your promise of paying us a visit. I am quite delighted with this dwelling, though I had some scruples in hiring it, on account of the great expense of furniture, and the probability that my life may not be of long duration. We are all longing to remove into it; but my wife must have quite recovered her strength before she can look after the necessary arrangements, for which I should be absolutely unfit. Gretchen is very clever in beating down and bargaining with these people, who overcharge their customers shamefully. She can converse with them about all the things of daily life, which I am utterly unable to do.

It is time to turn now to our literary business.......

My constant indisposition has hitherto prevented me from putting the finishing strokes to the manuscript of my *inedita.* I have been obliged to supply many passages, which have been cut out of the fragment of the *Rabiriana*—I hope with success—one passage only is doubtful. To the *Fonteiana*, I have subjoined the evidences of the Romans having used double entry in book-keeping.......

And now, as the Italians say, *voglio levarli l'incommodo!* that is to say, I take my leave of you. What a monster of a letter! Best love from us both to you and your wife. Remember me to all my friends; it is needless to name them. Give my special thanks to Roeder for his letter, which I shall answer shortly. Farewell!

CCXXVII.

TO MADAME HENSLER.

ROME, *8th March*, 1817.

......The day before yesterday was one of my Milly's festivals, which she never neglected to celebrate. It was the day on which I visited her and your parents from Meldorf, before I went to Copenhagen. It was indeed a happy day. How inexpressibly happy I was at that period, how cradled in the lap of fortune! I clung with such warm, unreserved attachment to you and your family, and your friends. Your father received me so kindly, Milly with such frank sweetness: I was so light-hearted, was conscious of all my powers, looked out into the world with curiosity and bright expectations. The day before yesterday was a very lovely day here; the almond-trees are in full bloom, and the peach-blossom is out; with the violets, which have been plentiful ever since December, you can now pluck hyacinths in the deserted gardens;—the air is like summer. On that day, the earth was covered with frozen snow; and though the sun shone clear, there was an icy wind; but what has north or south to do in the least with real happiness or even cheerfulness?

I expected not to see Schönborn again. There, too, has a fine character been rendered almost useless by the force of circumstances; there was more in the heart of the tree than ever appeared in its foliage and blossoms....

CCXXVIII.

ROME, 2*d April*, 1817.

The trial is over, and a fine and healthy little boy is born to us; but it has been a terrible trial.......

The boy weighs nearly nine German pounds, is fat and large, has red cheeks, yellow hair, and blue eyes. How Gretchen rejoices in the possession of her darling child, after all her sufferings, you can well imagine. She is very much exhausted, but very happy. She sends you a thousand kisses. She received and read your welcome letter during her two-and-thirty hours of suffering. Her patience was indescribable. In my terrible anxiety I prayed most earnestly, and entreated my Milly, too, for help. I comforted Gretchen with telling her that Milly would send help. When she was at the worst, and she leant her weary head against me, almost dying, she sighed out—"Oh, can not Amelia send me a blessing?"

I have already told you what our boy's name is to be; but he shall have a Roman one in addition, either Marcus or Lucius, by which he will be called. You have the first claim to be his sponsor; Behrens is one of course, Savigny—his guardian if I die—likewise, and Nicolovius. Should Playfair return, we shall beg him to perform the ceremony of baptism, as he was formerly a clergyman.

I had so much to say to you on this occasion from the very depths of my heart, but I am not calm enough. Besides, I am quite exhausted by sleepless nights, anxiety, and fatigue. Your heart will tell you all. I can not say any thing in answer to your letter to-day. You shall have tidings of us punctually.

Farewell. Give our love and the news to all our friends.

CCXXIX.

30*th April.*

I was absolutely unable to write to you on the last post-day.

The child is full of health; he looks briskly about him, and already begins to take notice. I can handle it very well; and it becomes quiet with me directly.

I am thinking a great deal about his education. I told you, a little while ago, how I intended to teach him the ancient languages very early, by practice. I wish the child to believe all that is told him; and I now think you right in an assertion, which I have formerly disputed, that it is better to tell children no tales, but to keep to the poets. But while I shall repeat and read the old poets to him in such a way, that he will undoubtingly take the gods and heroes for historical beings, I shall tell him, at the same time, that the ancients had only an imperfect knowledge of the true God, and that these gods were overthrown when Christ came into the world. He shall believe in the letter of the Old and New Testaments, and I shall nurture in him, from his infancy, a firm faith in all that I have lost, or feel uncertain about. He shall learn to perceive and to observe, and thus grow familiar with Nature, and nourish his imagination.

CCXXX.

ROME, 18*th May*, 1817.

......Gretchen still does not gain ground as I could wish, and my everlasting feverish colds are continually returning.

On Friday, the baby was christened by the name I told you. I stood proxy for you, Brandis, Bunsen, Platner, Cornelius, Schadow, and Overbeck, for Savigny, Behrens, Jacobi, Schön, and Nicolovius. Madame Von Pobnheim was his other godmother. An English clergyman performed the ceremony according to the solemn ritual of the Established Church. I was deeply affected, and repeated the vows for my child with my whole heart. Even the Catholics who were present could not help confessing the sublimity of this liturgy. The baptism was followed by a prayer for and with the mother, which is repeated kneeling. I held the child in your name.

He is coming on famously. It often gives me a melancholy feeling, when, in the evening he stretches out his arms toward the light, and makes us carry him to the window, where he gazes up into the sky with a fixed, bright, serious look; then the recollection comes over me, of how Milly, too, gazed up into the sky the last time that we took her out. I thank Heaven that I can at least shed tears over this remembrance.

With my old friend, Playfair, I have renewed the times of my youth, and am glad to find that there are some in Scotland who still retain an affectionate remembrance of me. The dear old man and I parted with heavy hearts. The Marquis of Lansdowne regrets that I am not embassador in London. I harmonize very well with the English nation, and am sure that I should soon feel at home among them. How I miss writing to my father now, when I meet with people from distant countries, and ask them questions! I have made the acquaintance of an intelligent priest from the neighborhood of Nineveh, an Abyssinian; and of an Englishman who has lived for twenty years in the wilds of North America.

CCXXXI.

FRASCATI, *20th June*, 1817.

I have spent yesterday and last night in thinking of my Milly, and this day, too, is sacred to these recollections.* I saw her a few days ago in a dream. She seemed as if returning to me after a long separation. I felt uncertain, as one so often does in dreams, whether she was still living on this earth, or only appeared on it for a transient visit; she greeted me as if after a long absence, asked hastily after the child, and took it in her arms.

Happy are those who can cherish such a hallowing remembrance as that of the departure of my Milly, with pious faith, trusting for a brighter and eternal spring. Such a faith can not be acquired by one's own efforts. Oh, that it may one day be my portion! Not that I am a materialist; you know well that no one can be further from that than I am; but the *possibility* of an existence, of which we can form no distinct conception, is not enough for me, does not help me; other and opposite possibilities always present themselves. I well know what is that faith which deserves the name, and recognize it as the highest good. But it would only be possible to me to attain it through supernatural communication, or wonders and signs beheld with my own eyes: it is one thing to respect, and not to reject, quite another really to *believe*, as in one's own existence.

What I hear and see among our acquaintance often leads my thoughts to the subject I have mentioned—faith, and its true nature. Several of them have a very earnest belief, though their belief is of very different shades; there are others, who fully imagine they possess religion, yet to

* Amelia's birth-day.

whom one can scarcely attribute more than a self-delusive assumption of it. I associate chiefly, indeed almost exclusively, with the artists who belong to the religious party, because those who either are decidedly pious or who strive after piety, are by far the noblest and best men, and also the most intellectual, and this gives me an opportunity of hearing a good deal on such subjects. Cornelius alone seems to have grown up from childhood, with uniform and lasting habits and convictions, which are as rooted in him as the facts of his experience; and his Catholicism is at bottom nothing more than the creed of the old Protestants. This he owes to the training he received from a pious and by no means bigoted mother, and to his completely unlearned education, in which the Bible (though in a Catholic family) was his only book. The case appears to me very different with those who are born in the Catholic faith, and have grown up in indifference. Of those who have been converted to this religion, O——* is an enthusiast, and quite illiberal; he is a very amiable man, and endowed with a magnificent imagination, but incapable by nature of standing alone, and by no means so clear-headed as he is poetical. He bends easily and naturally under the yoke which another of our intimate friends, who has taken the same false step, has constantly to impose upon himself afresh, because it slips off him.† Another, who is in the Roman college, I hope to bring back to Germany, and to see converted to Protestantism; he is a Jew, baptized on full conviction, who had taken a violent disgust to the modern teachers among the German Protestants, but finds every thing here so revolting, that he has been almost driven into insanity by his despair.‡ Mournful as is the absurdity of going over to the Catholic religion, it may be accounted for, on the part of our young friends, in a manner which does them no discredit; but strikingly shows how entirely many of the Protestant clergy have departed from all positive faith, and done violence to their conscience; for if those who had the teaching of these youths had instructed them in the doctrines of Luther, they would certainly never thus have gone astray. It was because they missed, in what they had been accustomed to regard as religion in their homes, that, without which religion is mere ballast, and found it, in words at least, at Rome, that they have been seduced into adopting all the follies of Rome as well. If my position did not forbid it, I should like to exhibit to the world the present state of the church here; it might, perhaps, be of use. I have become acquainted with one very remarkable man, a peasant from Trèves, who came to Rome to get absolution from the Pope for some scruples, but has met with a very contemptuous reception. From his example, it is very clear that the Romish clergy are quite right with their views in prohibiting the reading of the Bible; for, by diligently reading the Scriptures, he had become nothing else than a very warm old Protestant pietist, without, however, being aware of it himself. He insisted boldly that the Bible alone was the source of faith, and that differences of belief could not affect eternal happiness. He had some similarity with Jacob Boehme in the style of his mental culture, which was quite uncommon, and in the persecutions he had undergone; was like him an enthusiast, and not free from the proud humility of the pietists, though only infected with this to a slight degree. I felt a great respect for him personally, and I hope to save him from further persecution. His history and character seem to belong to quite a

* Overbeck. † Platner. ‡ Dr. Wolff.

different age. His case has made me think it probable that if the Protestant clergy still retained a positive belief, and the Bible were circulated in Catholic Germany, a second Reformation would not be at all impossible.

I told you before that Gretchen was ill; I trust that it is not a fever, but your hopes that her health would improve after her confinement have been by no means fulfilled. We came hither from the city, because I wanted to spend these few days quite without interruption......

CCXXXII.

ROME, 12*th July*, 1817.

Your welcome letter has quite relieved my anxiety respecting your health.

It has been very hot for the last few days, but in our noble spacious rooms I bear the heat better than I expected. Besides, we have both of us improved in health, and therefore in spirits, for some time past. Our sweet, healthy, lively baby has also had its share in this change for the better. I delight in giving myself up to my joy and pride in him, nurse him a great deal, play with him, and am rewarded by his smiles and fondness for me. But his mother is still the favorite, and I willingly yield her the privilege; it is her recompense for her unspeakable sufferings.

I wrote to you, a short time since, about my little work, the translation of an English Essay.* I have always taken a great interest in all relating to these simple duties of humanity. I thank Heaven I have often had it in my power to give help and relief, and this is still my greatest pleasure. If I could choose my sphere of action now, it would be that of the most simple and direct efforts of this kind. Since I can not, I rejoice in all that others are doing in this way. I have little faith in the introduction of freer institutions, still less that they could lead to good results, while nations and their ideas remain what they are. Our evils could only be removed by a total change in our mode of life and habits, by the discipline of our morals and manners, by an increase of general comfort, and by the greater simplicity of our whole life. It is to me so pitiful and disgusting that men should quarrel about the law-giving, while they are indifferent about the laws themselves, which are the only end of the legislation; and I find no other better object than this among any of those who write on such subjects; the high-sounding phrases of liberty disgust me: not that my heart does not beat for liberty, more warmly perhaps than any of theirs who so mistake her true nature; but their worship of her is exactly like a Roman Catholic service. If a single one of these writers would but go his way, and, at the sacrifice of his leisure and comfort, teach children, hold out consolation and a helping hand to the poor man where he can do no more; if he would strive by his advice and influence to obtain land for the cotter, property for the peasant; if he would first divest himself of the prejudices to which he is a slave; if, in these and other ways, men would begin to combine for humble and laborious objects which no government could hinder, we should have something on which to rest our hope. But so long as I see no public spirit, no public virtue, no self-discipline—so long as I see nothing, even among the better class, but the idolatry of wealth (as regards the commonwealth, if not for themselves), and the delusive notion that you can produce a work out of all materials alike—that figures kneaded out of clay can endure like those hewn out of marble—so

* An Article in the Quarterly Review, on the Poor. Vol. xv. p. 187.

long, if I were a ruler, should I give little satisfaction to the clamorous, and excite a terrible outcry because I would not, with them, begin to build from the upper story downward. How gladdening is it to see the humane efforts made by such numbers in England for really good objects, for the prosperity and education of the people! The observations on these subjects, contained in the article I have mentioned, are as if written from my inmost heart, and this *first* attack upon the Mammon system is so entirely what I have thought, and in part already said, that I should like to diffuse it as widely as possible. I should like to add many ideas of my own to it. In my earliest youth the longing desire arose within me to spend my life exclusively within the precincts of a narrow circle, teaching and laboring; would to God it had been my fate!

CCXXXIII.

FRASCATI, 20*th September*, 1817.

As the direction of this letter will have calmed your worst fears on my account, I will begin at once with the announcement that I am decidedly improving. I am indeed still writing to you from my bed, to which I am confined for the greater part of the day, and I am not secure from the chance of a relapse, but my state is very different from what it was a week ago. Then, I scarcely expected to write to you to-day, or only in order to prepare you for my departure. I thank God that the issue has been otherwise. How it would have grieved and shaken you! This severe illness seems to have done me good mentally. The inclination to study and work has once more awakened, and many ideas which I could never recall before, have returned with full distinctness as I lay upon my silent sick bed. God grant that it may last! I shall do all in my power to promote it. My weakness is still far too great to allow of my converting the desire to work into actual work. Else I feel as if I might yet be able to redeem my promise to Milly (to continue the History), and to meet her eye without fear.

During most of the time, I have regarded my death as quite certain, and often thought it near. I felt it sad to die thus in a foreign land, but I was indescribably calm, and quite peaceful in the prospect of another life. My Milly with her love would have embraced me with joy. I more than once chose the day on which I wished to die, and hesitated between the 8th and 9th of October; the first, the day of our (Milly's and my) arrival at Berlin; the second, that on which I laid her in her grave; where I shall never have the ardently-desired blessing of resting by her side.

By this time, the thought of death has nearly forsaken me; though I do not see how I am to recover fully; particularly as the physicians here know no tonic but quinine, which I can not take at all.

......If I recover, I mean, in the first place, to write a treatise on the constitution of the Greek provinces and cities of the Roman Empire, up to the time of the later emperors; and another to prove that an oration attributed to Dion is not his work. The former will conduct at its close to an investigation into the constitution of the Christian communities. From a passage in Origen, I am persuaded that they were formed on the model of the political communities, and must therefore have differed in the Eastern and Western churches, which throws quite a new light upon the subject. I have also collected some decisive proofs, principally from the style, that the author of the African war is not that of the Alexandrian. Questions of Latin philology have been long attracting me, and I hope, if I live, that I may yet become a proficient in this branch of learning. In pursuing these studies, I have a view also to the instruction of my Marcus. I hope to get practice in speaking from Bekker, whose coming is a very joyful prospect to me in a philological point of view.

My poor Gretchen suffers doubly through my illness; both mentally and physically. Marcus is a very lovely child, large, fat, full of life and very sociable. Brandis's kindness, judgment, and amiability are not to be exceeded.

CCXXXIV.

ROME, 18*th October*, 1817

......Bekker's arrival has given me great pleasure; it is agreeable at once to give and to receive. I shall spend a great part of the evenings in grammatical and critical readings with him. We mutually know what we are worth, and in what respects one excels the other, while neither regards the superiority of the other with envy. It is a satisfaction too, especially when your own heart has been torn with sorrow, to feel that you are to a distinguished man, what few can be, and some even of these do not choose to be. Bekker has been rudely, and even cruelly kept down and oppressed from his childhood upward; and it has made him morose and reserved; with us he is already beginning to expand, is becoming open and confidential. He had beforehand told others in Berlin, that I was the only person with whom he could become so. He lives with us, but dines out of the house.......

CCXXXV.

ROME, 13*th December*, 1817.

......Rome is altogether an unhealthy place. The proportion of deaths to births is as three to two, and frequently still more unfavorable. It is worthy of notice that this was not the case under the French. One of the physicians here accounts for this by the superiority of their sanatory regulations. At that time, the children were obliged to be vaccinated. Last year 940 died of the small-pox. At that time, there were workhouses; now, the paupers are put into filthy dens, where they are thinned by contagious disorders, and die of hunger.

I have taken up a study which bears directly on the Roman history: I am traversing the desert of the ancient Latin scholiasts. I did not expect much from it, but I have found things of quite unhoped-for importance, particularly relating to ecclesiastical law, and the daily life of ancient times. It will very likely be possible to sketch a tolerably complete picture of both, though the separate features are still for the most part unconnected. I should like to re-write many passages in my first volume, by which the whole could gain much in force and precision.

I have still less idea how any improvement is to be brought about in religious than in civil affairs; unless we have a new revelation. A religion in which people can not stand firmly on their feet, but must hold on by their hands while their feet are suspended in the air, can not long maintain itself.

The coarse proceedings on the Wartburg, mingled as they are with religious comedy, have deeply distressed me. They exhibit our youth as empty, self-conceited and vulgar. Freedom is quite impossible when the youth of a country are devoid of reverence and modesty. If I wrote according to the dictates of my heart, they would burn me also in effigy, and yet I know that all the *genuine* republicans of all ages would subscribe to my doctrines.......

CCXXXVI.

TO SAVIGNY

ROME, 26*th December*, 1817.

The great difference between this and the previous winter, and which, in truth, far outweighs every thing else, is the possession of our darling Marcuccio. The child retains his perfect health and beauty; is always lively, always sociable, and favored by nature.

I am sadly pinched for want of books, now that the *inclination* to continue my History has re-awakened during my illness and recovery; my *courage* to attempt the work is still far from adequate. I have been studying the Macedonian history (in its widest sense) subsequent to Alexander; and though it is impossible to restore the whole structure of this history from the miserable fragments yet remaining, I have attained a subjective, intuitive view after my fashion, of the *vita publica et privata*, both of this kingdom and of Greece, during the period for which we have no continuous narratives, so that I think I should be capable of delineating it, when I came to the epoch where the transmarine policy of Rome commences. These investigations introduced me to that extremely interesting arch-rogue, Josephus, whose writings are a mine of treasure for Macedonia, Syria, and Egypt; from him, I went on to researches into the Jewish constitution under the second temple (the Sanhedrin); and as I was reading the old Testament (with which, in our German version, I believe myself to have been more minutely acquainted, for many years past, than ninety-nine out of a hundred theologians) afresh very assiduously during my illness, I was compelled unawares by my critical good or evil genius, as the case may be, to observe, not only the very remarkable character of the Mosaic institutions, but also the difference of authorship in one and the same biblical book, the date of their composition, and the totally mistaken views prevailing—so far, at least, as I am acquainted with the various opinions on this subject—with regard to the history of the Hebrew literature, &c., &c. These are investigations, however, which to be carried out to distinct and positive results, would require a knowledge of the innumerable notoriously worthless writings on these points, and the few sensible works of whose existence I am aware, (or believe in out of charity), as well as an array of oriental philology, which I am too old, and moreover, just now, too much occupied with Marcuccio to acquire. Besides, I should probably give offense to some whom I would least wish to offend, and what is worse, please people of a different stamp. For the former would be quite wrong in taking offense at me. I might possess a much firmer and more lively faith (I only know an historical one) than from the circumstances of my mental history is now possible for me in this world, and yet hold at the same time my present critical views.......

1818.

THE events which took place in Germany and France during the latter half of 1817, recalled Niebuhr's attention to political affairs. During 1816–17, France had been thrown into great agitation, by the success of the ultra-Royalist party in obtaining the disbanding of the Imperial army, the banishment of persons connected with the Revolution, the re-enactment of the laws prohibiting divorce, &c.; and it was rumored that they contemplated nothing less than the restoration of landed property to its original owners. Toward the close of 1817, the Moderate party had come into office, but met with very partial success in their efforts to calm the storm that had been raised. In Germany, what was called the gymnastic *régime* had been in vogue since 1815. A large portion of the professors of the universities, and government officers, and nearly all the young men, wished to advance with rapid steps along the path of reform; and, as one means to this end, organized the youths in the schools and universities into associations, called Burschenschafts, for the promotion of their views.

They also laid great stress upon physical training, which should enable each individual personally to struggle for the good cause, and gymnastic exercises occupied a considerable portion of the hours spent in the schools. There was, however, a strong party who wished to suppress—by violent means if needful—the development of all popular institutions, and bring things back to the old condition existing before the Revolution. The Tricentenary of the Reformation was celebrated in 1817 throughout Germany, on the 18th of October, the anniversary of the battle of Leipsic, so that the festival was at once a commemoration of the religious and political liberation of the country, and naturally gave rise to contemplations of the present, and anticipations of the future. The Burschenschaft of Jena resolved to celebrate the day by a procession to the Wartburg, the fortress where Luther had been confined, to which they invited delegates from all the German universities, excepting those of Austria. They were accompanied by the authorities of Eisenach and four of the most celebrated professors of Jena—Fries, Oken, Kieser, and Schweitzer. In the first instance, moderate speeches, exhorting to patriotism and virtue, were delivered, and the assembly broke up and returned to Eisenach, where after dinner a service was held in the church. In the evening, however, when they formed a torch-light procession to the Wartburg, to kindle the so-called October Fire (the bonfire still customary on the 18th of October), much more excited speeches were made; and, at last, when most had already left the mountain, a Berlin student appeared with a bundle of books and papers, and exclaimed—"As once Luther, by the burning of the papal bull, gave the signal for the separation from the Romish chair, so shall a signal be given here by devoting to the flames the writings branded with the contempt of the German nation for their un-German tendencies, and their opposition to the spirit of the age." And amid the applause of the spectators, various works of an anti-liberal and reactionary character were thrown into the fire, together with an Austrian corporal's stick, a Hessian pig-tail, and a Prussian military sash, after which Charles Follen's celebrated "Grosses Lied" was sung. Unhappily, several of the works thus anathematized were the productions of men high in the Prussian service, Von Kamptz, Ancillon, and Schmalz; and since rumor, as usual, greatly exaggerated the occurrences, the governments of Berlin and Vienna took up the matter, caused the ringleaders in the affair to be arrested, and instituted inquiries, which lasted for a long time, on the supposition that a revolutionary conspiracy had been formed; but it was finally proved that there was no ground for such an idea. Niebuhr, as will be seen from his letters, agreed with neither of the contending parties.*

This festival also gave rise to many theological productions, and others were called forth by the speech of the King of Prussia on the occasion, whose recommendation of a union of the Protestant Confessions was the first germ of the efforts that finally issued in the fusion of the Lutheran and Reformed Churches throughout the greater part of Prussia. Previous to this date, there had been in many sincerely pious Protestants, who were disgusted with the rationalism that widely prevailed in their own church, a disposition to fraternize with the Catholics, and a hope that something like a compromise might be brought about. But the spirit of controversy evoked by this celebrated festival, and the revival of the order of the Jesuits by the Pope, widened the existing religious

* See his letters of 13th December, 1817, and 10th of January, 1818.

differences of every kind, and produced much bitterness between the Catholics and Protestants.

The strong interest which these circumstances excited in Niebuhr, suggested to him the idea of delineating the moral and intellectual history of Germany since the Thirty Years' War, but the impossibility of procuring the necessary materials in Rome prevented the execution of this project.

Incitements to research in other directions were not wanting, and, among other things, he discovered in the course of the summer the key to the Oscan tongue, and succeeded in partially deciphering an inscription in that language.

In July, his second child, a daughter, was born.

In the autumn, he had to regret a serious loss, in the departure of Dr. Brandis, whose health was much injured by the climate of Italy, and who, besides, wished to devote himself exclusively to those philosophical researches which have since raised him to so eminent a position among the scholars of Germany. He was succeeded as Secretary of Legation by M. Bunsen, who, however, as he was already married, did not reside in Niebuhr's house.

During this winter Niebuhr obtained the appointment of a Protestant clergyman to the embassy—a circumstance which afforded him much satisfaction.

Letters written in 1818.

CCXXXVII.

TO MADAME HENSLER.

ROME, 10*th January*, 1818.

. . . . . .I was frightened at the prospect of composing my third volume, and the disproportion of my present powers to the work, although there are many interesting materials for it.

I have become indifferent to the reception of the earlier parts; probably I should not be so if by straining all my powers I had brought forth another from my inmost soul. Would it be well if I were so? No, I am convinced that this philosophical equanimity is real death, and that the most vehement emotions, as they have ever been the companions of all greatness and beauty, are also necessary to their existence. Without this storm, the mind will not sail over the floods, though it may sink in them, and now perhaps generally does sink. I also look forward at the turn of the year, with gloomy forebodings, to the age that is before ns. I see nowhere any encouraging signs: if there are deficiencies among the rulers, there are quite as many among the governed. It is utterly impossible to deny that our youth are, on the whole, declining in cultivation, and becoming coarse and barbarously indolent. Under the gymnastic *régime* there must inevitably be an end of science and literature; and, indeed, of all that is noble, quiet, and beautiful.

Did I tell you that my correspondence with Stein has been renewed by a friendly letter from him containing commissions? Stein is very melancholy and hopeless.

In France, there is a dreadful fermentation, which will probably lead to fresh calamities. It is but too certain, that the French also will not find the right path again, at least not for a long time to come; but they have gained much in intelligence, and you not unfrequently hear thoughts from them, more sound and weighty than any which reach us from Germany. The Germans seem to be reeling in a beer revel.

We have scarcely joined at all in society hitherto, but that will not do any longer. We are settled in our house, and must now, from time to time, give large parties. One is awaiting us to-morrow. With the French envoy I am most intimate. I am very friendly with the old Bavarian embassador, but he is quite decrepit.

CCXXXVIII.

ROME, *7th March*, 1818.

Your last letter, written out of the regular course, was a refreshment to me such as I have not had for a long time.

It has always given me a sufficiently fearful idea of the sufferings of hell, to conceive of them as consisting in a full perception (devoid of all consolation, all delusion, all intermission), of the whole misery into which we have been plunged by sin—of all the consequences that have sprung from it, and all the happiness of which we have deprived ourselves.

Yesterday was always a festival to me from 1798 to 1815; that is, ever since my visit to your parents and Milly in Heide. The day of my visit, and indeed that last winter that I spent in Kiel, in constant intercourse with you, was one of the brightest spots in my life. My Milly always kept the day, sometimes by giving me little presents, always with conversation, and a holiday dress. Her first word on waking in the morning was to remind me of it. I believe that I often dream both of her and you; but my former vivid consciousness of my dreams has passed away, along with my vivacity in all other respects. Fate has, however, granted me the festival of this day by permitting me to see both you and Milly in my dreams, in which you were both so lively, so affectionate, so really present to me, that I awoke, and even in awaking still retained a sense of the old happy days......

I have received Harms's Theses,* and Falck's article on them. They

* Harms's "Ninety-five Theses" were among the numerous theological publications that appeared on occasion of the Tricentenary of the Reformation. They were directed against the rationalistic tendencies of the age, and maintained the old orthodox Lutheran doctrines of the utter corruption of human nature, and the necessity of a correct creed to salvation, in all their strictness. The Theses made a great sensation, and called forth numerous answers, to which Harms replied in a "Defense of the Theses" and a pamphlet entitled "Demonstratration of the Worthlessness of the Religion of Reason." Harms is still preaching with all his wonted vigor, and influence upon the minds of his hearers, in Kiel, at the age of seventy-three (1851). Although he has been blind for the last two years, he has lately published a Letter against the Kirchen Zeitung, edited by Hengstenberg, vindicating the one hundred pastors who have been expelled from Schleswig-Holstein by the tyrannical Danish government.

have occasioned me much thought. I wrote an essay on them, but it is too bitter. We should soon come to an understanding with each other about them by word of mouth. I agree with Harms in all that he says about the irreligiousness of a system of morals on an independent basis; and further, in his aversion to a Christianity which is none, and I even approve of his personalities against many of your Holstein theologians. But I consider his limitation of genuine Christianity to the symbolical books,* and his zeal against the union of the Protestant churches, as an error. All who are acquainted with church history know, that no system of doctrine respecting redemption, hereditary sin, grace, &c., existed for at least the first two centuries after Christ; that on these points, opinions and teaching were unfettered, and that those were never considered as heretics who simply accepted the Creed (the so-called Symbolum Apostolicum), kept in communion with the Church, and were subject to her discipline. Now certainly this test would be amply sufficient to exclude those hypocritical pastors who only nominally belong to the Church; for such *can not* accept this Confession of Faith. This Creed, together with a simple faith in the contents of the New Testament as the revealed word of God, is at once sufficient and indispensable; but I do not see why we should desire to impose any further yoke. The orthodox divines of the seventeenth and eighteenth centuries subscribed to the symbolical books with a fullness of conviction which we can not possess now, because they are a systematic body of doctrine, and the systems of one century are uncongenial with the mental habits of another. But it was this party which persecuted the most pious men of those times—Paul Gerhard, Franke, and Spener. If the golden age of Christian liberty subsisted within the limits I have mentioned, why must we now have slavery?

Next, as to the union of the Churches.† I should say that one must be a Eutychian to lay any stress upon the dogma of consubstantiation. A pietist, for whom I have a great regard, delights in the idea of union; for, he says, "That of which I am convinced is, that the Lord's Supper is a promised and miraculous means of conveying strength and sanctification, but all that simply concerns verbal interpretation is very unimportant to me; and the form of the ceremony, and the theological doctrine respecting it, are as indifferent to me, as it was to the blind man whether his eyes were touched with clay and spittle, or with any thing else. But it is not indifferent to me whether we Protestants remain divided or not, considering our present position between an active mysticism and Catholicism. But for our divisions, the whole of Germany would have become Protestant, and the misfortune of the Thirty Years' War would never have taken place." Luther's position was very different from ours, and the use of historical insight is to show us clearly how a thing may be wise at one time which is not so at another. After all, the most difficult matter is to walk in humility, and to govern one's self.

* The Augsburg Confession of Faith, in the Lutheran Church, to which Harms belonged; the Catechisms of Heidelberg and Dordrecht for the Reformed Church. Since the union of the Lutheran and Reformed Churches in Prussia and most other German States, the symbolical books include all these catechisms

† The union of the Lutheran and Reformed Churches.

CCXXXIX.

ROME, 27*th March*, 1818.

...... There are more here who decidedly like me than who are opposed to me. The Pope and Cardinal Gonsalvi treat me with real cordiality, which is of great importance in a place where every thing is decided by personal feeling. Thus, if I had available instructions, I should soon be able to conclude all the requisite arrangements with the greatest advantage to the State and the nation. It weighs heavily upon my mind that it is not in my power to accomplish this, but that I am only putting the State to a large and useless expense; with your strict principles you will quite enter into my feelings. I can give you proofs that I do not deceive myself; my mediation in the case of Geneva has so far prevailed that its affairs will be brought to a successful issue, as soon as a preliminary form has been gone through by the Genevese government; and if the deputies of Berne and Lucerne take the course I have advised, as they have expressed a wish to do, they also will infallibly obtain their object in spite of all the difficulties in the way, which their governments have regarded as almost insuperable. The people here are convinced of the perfect honesty of my intentions, and perceive at the same time that I will not suffer myself to be imposed upon. An Italian despises those whom he deceives; but when he can not succeed in deceiving a man, he respects him, and, if he finds him well-intentioned, conceives an attachment for him after his fashion.......

Every now and then, I make a fresh attempt to write upon these subjects,* and then lay down my pen again, when I consider, that although there have been instances in which political pamphlets have led to the adoption of the measures recommended in them, in a free State, there is scarcely any example, under a monarchy, of a minister having carried out any measures proposed in a recent pamphlet. However, I know that no republican can ever have loved his nation more ardently than I love Prussia.

A tendency toward reformation is at work in the Catholic Church in Germany. A German is here now, who is a sincerely pious man, and is leaving Rome in a state of indignation. I often converse with him about the convulsion that is inevitable, but must proceed from below. He and others like him have chosen the motto of St. Augustine as their watchword: Unity in essentials, liberty in the rest, and brotherly love. It will be seen that this alone can help us.

CCXL.

ROME, 11*th April*, 1818.

Bunsen is a very clear-headed and estimable man. Hardenberg has promised me to appoint him successor to Brandis. I am very glad of it: on my own account, because I like him; for his sake and the State's, because he has a decided talent for public life, and will distinguish himself. Brandis is still undecided as to his plans. It seems likely that he will receive an appointment in the university on the Rhine, which may probably be established next autumn. His father's book upon Magnetism is on the way—one hears nothing on such subjects here. An extraordinary case of miraculous cure, which happened during the early part of my stay here, made a great noise. Perhaps we ought not to attempt to give a

* Political and ecclesiastical relations in Prussia.

philosophical account of such occurrences, but to content ourselves with observing them, and attempting to form a general conjecture as to the direction of the forces which produce them. An absolute denial of so many instances, still seems to me unwarrantable.

The religion prevailing here is an abomination to an unprejudiced person. A Chaldean, a man of great ability, who had applied to me for money to get a Bible printed here in his native language, under the censorship of the Propaganda, will probably be banished from Rome. I had hoped to obtain from England, America, Russia, and our King the money required for this undertaking, and for the erection of a printing-press with which he wanted to print other works at home afterward. This enterprise, to which I expected to have been able to contribute, is one of the things with which I had often consoled myself in moments of melancholy.*

Cornelius has made an agreement with the Crown Prince of Bavaria, and we shall lose him. I am quite grieved at it.

The child is fair and flourishing. He is growing very fond of me, and begins to have little endearing ways. He kisses my hand without being bid.

CCXLI.

Rome, 1*st May*, 1818.

The state of the air is indescribably oppressive. Every body here believes that there has been an earthquake somewhere. The sirocco prevails uninterruptedly; the sky has been dark and cloudy, the air like a furnace, and every one has felt wretched and ill. At such times you are fit for nothing.

With regard to Harms's Theses, let us, in the first place, settle the points on which we agree with each other and with Harms. In my opinion, he is not a Protestant Christian, who does not receive the historical facts of Christ's earthly life, in their literal acceptation, with all their miracles, as equally authentic with any event recorded in history, and whose belief in them is not as firm and tranquil as his belief in the latter; who has not the most absolute faith in the articles of the Apostles' Creed, taken in their grammatical sense; who does not consider every doctrine and every precept of the New Testament as undoubted divine revelation, in the sense of the Christians of the first century, who knew nothing of a Theopneustia. Moreover, a Christianity after the fashion of the modern philosophers and pantheists, without a personal God, without immortality, without human individuality, without historical faith, is no Christianity at all to me; though it may be a very intellectual, very ingenious philosophy. I have often said, that I do not know what to do with a metaphysical God, and that I will have none but the God of the Bible, who is heart to heart with us.

Let him who can, bring the God of metaphysics into harmony with the God of the Bible; and he who can accomplish this, will be authorized to write symbolical books that shall be a law to all ages. He who grants the absolute impossibility of solving the main problem, which can only be approached by asymptotes, will not grieve over the inevitable consequence, our possessing no *system* of religion. Many passages in the Bible admit of various interpretations; are these made a matter of controversy among

* This Chaldean was afterward banished (along with Dr. Wolff) for having accepted assistance from the Bible Society in carrying out his scheme.

pious people? There is a remarkable and noble passage on this point in Tertullian, who nevertheless was a true zealot.

People have aimed at bringing religion into an absolute system in imitation of the scholastic philosophy, and in behoof of church government. In so far as the sense is plain, well and good. But where it is doubtful—and that is the very point at issue—who is to decide? The Catholic Church is not left without a decision; she claims to have a tradition, and she asserts an immediate miraculous influence of the Holy Spirit upon the decisions of councils and popes. We have seen what this has led to, and Luther has saved us from that misery. Luther himself took his stand on tradition. He sketched no new outline; he only cleansed the besmeared picture from what, according to his notion of the original, he recognized as defacing additions. Hence sprang, for instance, his doctrine of the Eucharist. The Christianity, the faith that was within him, not that which stood before him, and was external to him, was the material on which he labored. He always, consciously or unconsciously, took his stand on tradition. Not till after him, came the Reasons of the Orthodox, who wanted to set up a system. In the eyes of these Pharisees, all profound feeling, all glowing devotion, was an abomination.

It has been said with great truth, that the bull *Unigenitus* led to, and is responsible for the overthrow of religion in France; and he who really knows the history of Germany knows the injury which orthodoxy has done to the Protestant religion. It is only an indirect consequence of it, that its obnoxiousness has occasioned the defection of numbers to the Romish Church: for, if you oppose authority by authority, it must be confessed that that of the councils is of greater weight than that of a society of doctors and pastors; we have always left this objection of the Catholics unanswered.

In the symbolical books, there are doctrines respecting plenary inspiration, and the connection of the Old and New Testaments, which can never come into force again; and how much else is contained in them, of which the early church knew nothing! Let any one only try whether the standard which I require be a small matter or a great one; and let no one secretly substitute for it, the permission to explain religion into a human doctrine, and its historical facts, according to the rules of ordinary occurrences; seeing that I demand precisely the reverse.

The matter will remain without practical influence on legislative measures. It can have none, and the controversy will die away, when people have once fairly got to hating each other. Then something else will come up.—You speak of the morbid tendency to innovation in our times: I abhor and mourn over it with you, but the controversy, of which we have been speaking, is in truth one form of it. When the novel part of any question has been quite worn threadbare, people turn to the old, which has then become new again; and thus the ball is thrown backward and forward. It is the same in politics and in literature. How many changes of fashions have I not witnessed already, and I may say witnessed without changing my own position! In my youth I beheld the former theological "*enlightenment*" (with disgust, indeed, although from a distance), during which every adherent of the old belief was an object of contempt. Oh that men would build up! Nothing *can* come of constraint and command in these matters. Oh that men strove, in simplicity of heart, and in union with those likeminded to themselves, to attain true, fruit-bearing faith, piety, and love!

Do not fancy me unqualified to give my voice on this subject. I know that I am qualified, by possessing a fully adequate knowledge of the history of the church, and even of her system, of which I know more perhaps than you give me credit for. Here, where it is of importance to guard young men against the seductions of the Catholic priests, I have ample inducement to turn my attention to theology.

So you think my unfavorable remarks on the Italians too severe. Believe me, the longer I live here, the more they are confirmed. I have become acquainted with one exception (and how should there not be some such?), a man of great talent, upright and honorable—the painter and restorer, Palmaroli; and his history and own testimony are again a confirmation of all I have said. Persecuted with a refinement of malice by envy, neglected and slighted by the government, all his efforts have been a struggle to produce works of art, and to save magnificent old paintings. This man says that his heart expands only in the society of Germans.

CCXLII.

TO NICOLOVIUS.

ROME, *6th June*, 1818.

......I will send you by Rauch a pamphlet that has been published here, intended expressly for the conversion of the young Germans. If Schmieder comes, he must bring Luther's works for me (or send them by sea), and the writings against Popery. It can not be expressed how disgusting these proceedings become the more you see of them. At this moment, the proselyters have S——,* one of the ablest young artists, on their bait. Dear Nicolovius, the whole life that the artists lead here is worse than useless; it is essentially injurious. They are in a completely false position; they associate as equals with people of rank—they get a distorted view of all the relations of the world, and grow vain and prejudiced. For Heaven's sake, do not dream of allowing any of them to stay here too long. It is only in a diversified civil society, comprising a variety of classes, that an artist can remain a healthy-minded man, unless he be a miracle, like Cornelius. That Cornelius is a healthy-minded man, I will give you a proof. The evening after Bunsen's child was baptized, we and several more were at his house. Bunsen lives in the upper part of the Palazzo Cafarelli, and over the Palatine; as we were standing, after midnight, on the *loggia*, we saw Jupiter sparkling as if he were looking down on his Tarpeian rock. We were drinking healths. I said to Thorwaldsen, "Let us drink to old Jupiter!" "With my *whole* heart," he replied, with a voice full of emotion. Some were startled: Cornelius touched our glasses and drank it.......

CCXLIII.

TO MADAME HENSLER.

ROME, *20th June*, 1818.

......The negotiations at Frankfort are spoiling every thing. They

* Schadow.

imagine themselves able to make a reformation in the church, because they have a hankering after novelty, and never dream that such undertakings can only succeed when hearts are lifted up in their behalf, as in Luther's time, whereas, they themselves have no feeling about the matter; and, indeed, no one can have any feeling in connection with the mere ordering of external relations. They may perhaps be instruments of good, but their way is as false as Luther's was correct......

I shall write to you again next week. I could not let this day pass without a letter. Read the soul of its writer. In those old times too we clung to each other. May we be restored to each other in another life!

CCXLIV.

TO SAVIGNY.

ROME, 20*th June*, 1818.

......Brandis and Bekker are going to Florence the day after to-morrow, and Cornelius will leave at the latest in autumn; it is uncertain whether for Munich or Düsseldorf.

The proselytizing spirit here is at last causing complete divisions among us. No one can have judged these absurd proceedings more leniently in insulated cases than myself, or with more kindness and endeavor to enter into the weaknesses and peculiar circumstances of individuals. But when these men take high ground, and seek right and left to make proselytes; when, not satisfied with kind indulgence, they attempt to make their ignorance and narrow-mindedness pass current for a higher insight, it does, and it ought to make one indignant at heart. A little hand-book, by one Abbé Martin, has appeared here, which is full of the most scandalous lies respecting Luther, and the shallowest defense of Popery, and attacks upon us, and it is put into the hands of every young man on his arrival.

The proof sheets of the Gaius have thrilled me like an electric spark. If Göschen is not inclined to the revision at present, he need not be afraid to put it off for a time. In a good mood he can do it admirably, and it *must* be done admirably. Be sure to send me all the proof sheets as they are printed. What does the postage signify? It was once intended that I should receive a copy in small writing on fine paper; if there is such a copy made, be so good as to give it to Beneke, to be forwarded to me. I should much like to append some emendations, not so much for the public, as for your consideration and use, if you can turn them to any.

The mention of the privileges of the Flamen Dialis in this proof sheet, has accidentally (as is generally the case) thrown a light in upon my mind. Why did he emerge from the paternal authority without *capitis diminutio;* why were his relations in so many ways strange and abnormal? Because his inauguration was a kind of *arrogatio*, whereby he entered the *gens* of the gods, at any rate became their client. I find the proofs extremely interesting. They appear to be extracted from the part which has been twice written over, and I bow in wonder before the skill of Göschen and Hollweg. The double rescription proves the inadequacy of our palæographical definitions. Such a chance is inconceivable, as that the remnants of the half-effaced MS. should have been left untouched for centuries, then taken up, then erased again, and then by accident used for the same purpose over again. But unquestionably this was the true state of the case; the transcriber began to write the Epistles of St. Jerome in large uncial characters; it struck him afterward that this would make the book too cumbrous, so he erased what he had done and wrote in italics. Or perhaps the calligrapher who could write the uncial characters died, or removed, so that they were obliged to take another. The character in the codex of the Gaius is the base of the Anglo-Saxon; consequently this was in use so early as the seventh century. I much wish this opportunity may be embraced to give a brief elucidation of the affinity of these characters....

What do you say to the Bavarian constitution? what a *mauvaise plaisanterie effrontée!* Particularly the law on the freedom of the press. That on ecclesiastical relations is sensible and praiseworthy; but how does it agree with the Concordat?

I wish there were any form in which I could write about politics; and that we were not so certain that to print any opinions would be in itself a reason for the adoption of contrary measures. The government order respecting Coblentz has pained me to the heart. Görres' pamphlet is the best thing of the kind that I have read from his pen, and much better than we could have expected.* It shows a capacity for sound views. If I were in Berlin, I would write what alone is true, and no one should be able to take exception to it. There, too, I could write the history of the moral and intellectual changes of our nation since the Thirty Years' War, the key to all else; here, naturally, I can write nothing.

......You will receive through Rauch the copy of Ulpian that has been collated by Brandis. There has been scarcely any thing to alter in it.

CCXLV.

TO JACOBI.

26th June, 1818.

Roth's letter, (rich in cheering news of you), and your own, to both of which I intend this as an answer, found me recovering from a severe illness, a state such as you know and have described; one which comes near to a rejuvenescence, and, like youth, opens the whole soul to all that speaks to the heart and the intellect.

......The spring began here a day earlier than Pliny has fixed for its commencement, namely on the 6th of February; the air was soft and refreshing, but there were no leaves nor singing birds. This was followed by cold, and heavy showers, and now all at once it is as hot as in the dog-days. Even in the early morning, you have scarcely any sense of coolness in rooms where the windows have been open all night. Still, every thing is bearable when the sirocco does not blow. But, in April, there were days when we all, Gretchen, Brandis, Bekker, and myself, lay half dead each in our own

* Görres, who was at this time decidedly liberal in his views, and edited the "Rheinische Merkur" with great ability, presented an address, on occasion of the visit of Hardenberg to Coblentz in the spring of 1818, praying for various political reforms, which was followed by other addresses of the same nature from Mayence, Treves, &c. Hardenberg held out hopes of their wishes being attended to; but the King was highly incensed that the people should take upon themselves to dictate the measures necessary to be adopted, instead of waiting to see what reforms he thought fit to grant them; and Görres, who had taken the lead in the matter, found it necessary to retire to Frankfort. Several other expressions will be found in the following letters of Niebuhr referring to these proceedings.

room. It can not have been so in ancient times, or it would not have been an honor to the Romans to have overlooked that the habitable world began with the Alps.

About the Italians you will have heard R.'s* testimony, and we Protestants can leave it to him to paint the clergy and the state of religion in this country. In fact, we are all cold and dead compared to his indignation. His society has been a great pleasure to us all, even to our reserved friend Bekker, who in general turns pale at the very thought of Popery, and finds me far too indulgent. With an enthusiast so full of heart as R., you can get on; between such a luxuriance of fancy, and the unshackled reason, there is much such an analogy as subsists between science and art; while, on the contrary, the slavish subjection to the Church is ghastly death. The most superficial prophet of so-called enlightenment can not have a more sincere aversion to enthusiasm than the Roman priesthood; and, in fact, their superstition bears no trace of it. Little as the admirers of Italy care for my words, I know that I am perfectly correct in saying, that even among the laity you can not discover a vestige of piety. The life of the Italian is little more than an animal one, and he is not much better than an ape endowed with speech. There is nowhere a spark of originality or truthfulness. Slavery and misery have even extinguished all acute susceptibility to sensual enjoyments, and there is, I am sure, no people on the face of the earth more thoroughly *ennuyé*, and oppressed with a sense of their own existence, than the Romans.

Their whole life is a vegetation, and when we who live here, recall the apologies made by a partiality which even excuses their indolence, it is impossible to repress a feeling of indignation. While whole families, not to speak of the servants, sleep round the charcoal pans in winter, and often get suffocated out of pure idleness, the nobles carry on *conversazioni* which are not much better, and in which, besides, most are neither speakers nor listeners. The universal knavishness and love of pilfering are also the effect of laziness; people must eat and cover themselves; and this must be made possible without interruption to their laziness.

The present government have undertaken the task of introducing tolerable civil security by police, in the midst of ever-increasing wickedness and degradation—a system of constraint and terror that may impose fetters upon the wild passions of the animal man.

They never so much as think of securing at least his physical comfort; he may sink into deeper and deeper misery, but he shall fear blows and the galleys more than he cares for his own instincts. Surrounded by an omnipresent espionage of police, conscious how he himself would be ready to accuse and betray any other man for a certain reward, Dread shall be his supreme deity. In the metropolis, this has succeeded to astonishment, and crimes of violence upon the person are rarer than in other capitals. The cavaletto, or flogging machine, is nearly permanent, and during the carnival literally so. The police regulations for the carnival, for the theatres which are open then, and for all public festivities, sound revolting, and they are carried into execution. There is no criminal code at all, but the punishments are quite arbitrary. One of the most scandalous crimes is punished very mildly, why? . . . . . .

* Ringseis, a physician who had accompanied the Crown Prince of Bavaria to Rome, and was a zealous and pious Catholic.

The execrable Cardinal Ruffo* is dead, and an historical character, who is not inferior to any commissioner of the Convention, relates, chuckling with delight, what his Calabrians did with the towns, and even the convents, *that had been jacobinical.* Even the murder of a wife is very leniently punished. I have extracted the *casus in terminis* from the lists of sentences, because no one will believe what I say on these points. The effect of this severity, however, is seen in the absolute lifelessness of the common people. The nobles, who have nothing to fear, are equally apathetic from their utter inaction, and the gratification to satiety of the lowest desires.

Dear Jacobi, I could not venture to say openly to our German patriots, what I do not hesitate to write to my government, that the overthrow of Bonaparte's rule has been the greatest calamity to Rome, and the restoration of the old government the greatest sin against the nation. They could no longer proceed in their old careless routine; they were forced either to adopt wiser or more ruinous measures, and the former course was impossible.

God knows whither their present course is tending, since there is no prospect of reform and alleviation. Did not Woldemar,† who lived in a golden age compared to the present, declare that he knew not how a change was to come without a deluge or a miracle. The Jeremiades on the misery of Rome under Bonaparte are the stupid twaddle of ignorant artists. To extirpate priestcraft, such as it was and is, was a necessary amputation, and, *on the whole,* it was performed—my friends may cry out against me as they will—with discretion, forbearance, and moderation; the people were employed and cared for. The population of the city was suddenly diminished, but those who remained would soon have found themselves much better off, and all things would have been brought into a natural course. The number of births increased rapidly, the priests were no longer able to command or permit abortion; the number of deaths diminished incredibly. The conscription was disliked, but was wholesome for the people; a French regiment was a school of honor and morality to an Italian, as much as it is of corruption to a German. Some life was awakened among the higher classes; they began to take some interest in things, and very much, perhaps all that is possible, would be gained for the Romans if they were to recover animation. There were a pretty good number of criminals executed without the attendance of a priest, consequently condemned to eternal damnation; while now, in the opinion of the common people, every criminal who is executed goes fully absolved into heaven. The officials set the Romans a pattern of liberality and conscientiousness, and the *fournisseurs* were models of strict integrity and humanity, to the managers of hospitals. All this you will not misunderstand.

It must be confessed that fiscal avarice, and the idolatry of so-called property, stood in the way of a radical reform. It would have been necessary to compel the great nobles to give heritable leases on their estates, and to divide the ecclesiastical property *viritim;* and this indeed would never have been done. The imposts are heavier now than in 1813.

What it must be, to an honorable and public-spirited man, to live among such a people, I leave you to imagine. It is an utterly false idea to suppose that any relics of antiquity have been preserved in manners, customs, &c.; in the country there may be some isolated instances of the

* He had been the leader of the counter-revolution in Naples.

† Woldemar was the title of a novel written many years previously by Jacobi.

kind; but you can not penetrate into the interior on account of the robbers. To you I may venture to say, without disparagement to my interest in the works of our German artists, that I am sickened of art as I should be of sweetmeats instead of bread. But there is no one here, particularly since Brandis and Bekker have left, with whom I can converse upon the subjects that lie nearest to my heart, mutually giving and receiving information. Colonel Fischer, one of the deputies from Berne, made a transient exception, which was invaluable to me. Still I could, if need be, do without learned conversations; but to have no one with whom I can hold a rational conversation upon the affairs which concern mankind in general, upon the events occurring in England, Germany, and France, is positive death. Whether the Disputa, or the Heliodor, be the more perfectly painted, &c., &c., leaves me not only indifferent, but in the long run becomes insupportably tedious. Besides, it is not improving to be always limited to talking on subjects that you understand imperfectly, and on which you are always obliged to take a very inferior position to the persons with whom you converse, without any fault of your own.

However, this is not the only evil in our German society. Our young artists are not uncontaminated by their contemporaries; without learning, without reflection, they are extremely dogmatical, and, on all points, quite look down on those who are not of their confraternity. Some who are here exhibit astonishingly fine talents, and no one perhaps is more zealous than myself in furthering their development. Truly a new day has dawned upon art, and Goethe has sinned greatly in denying the fact. To speak without a ridiculous modesty, my mission, in other respects so useless, has in this probably been of most essential service. Your Crown Prince may do more; but his stay here has so far done more harm than good. He has made the young men arrogant, and turned their heads; their prudent friend no longer satisfies them, because he does not worship them, and places art, in the usual narrow sense of the word, far below wisdom, and that art of which it is the embodiment.......

Your countryman Cornelius, who will bring you a letter in a few months, makes a glorious exception among our artists: he is the Goethe of the painters, and has in every respect an open and powerful intellect, free from all limitation.

Your Constitution is an important event. It will give you an idea of Rome, when I tell you that no one has any thing to say about it; the name of a constitution is enough for the Germans, and more especially the *freedom of the press*. I do not ask for a perfectly unconditional freedom of the press, but where such a law exists I would still avail myself of the proffered advantage of the censorship for my security. This law appears to me the least good of the whole series, and that on religious institutions the best.

In your Constitution it is very remarkable what trouble has been taken to find business for the Estates to perform. They are only auditors of accounts with greater solemnity. Meanwhile, I congratulate you sincerely; though I would rather have had something different and better. For as I adhere to the principles of Möser and Fievée,* I care little for a worshipful *assemblée legislative*, unless it be— but that would lead me too far.

* This refers to their advocacy of communal and municipal freedom. Fievée's letters on the history of the French Legislative Assembly, in 1815 and 1816, had just come out. In his general principles, Fievée trod in the footsteps of Turgot.

It frets me to be out of Germany, and therefore unable to say any thing about important national questions, on which Görres, to my astonishment, has come pretty near the truth. In this long letter, I will not enlarge upon the various details of your elective forms, in which I am sorry not to see all the former imperial towns represented separately, as is the case with the mediatized princes. On the whole, however, every amelioration gives me pleasure, even if it is imperfect.

Farewell, dear friend. Give our kindest remembrance to Roth and your sisters. Gretchen and I kiss your fatherly hand.

CCXLVI.

TO SAVIGNY.

ROME, *1st September*, 1818.

I must have already told you more than once, dearest Savigny, that your letters operate upon me like blood upon spectres, whom it nourishes. The time and space, that separate me from a better life, disappear for the moment; images and recollections rise up with vividness, and thoughts, which there has been nothing in the dead vacuum of Hades to excite, form themselves once more into shape. This simile is more elegant, and, at all events, more worthy of your letter than another, which has perhaps still more truth with regard to myself. I might compare myself to a dead frog, in which movements that bear the resemblance of life are produced by the touch of metal.

Be that as it may, your letters instantly excite in me a desire to answer them, and when I received, about three weeks ago, yours of the end of July, I replied to it immediately; but the intense heat which had prevailed almost without intermission for nearly two months, and had been rendered unusually intolerable by a constant sirocco, had had such a depressing effect upon me, that I did not like to send you my grumbling epistle, and I became still less willing to do so, after it had once been laid aside that it might be replaced by another. This latter was never written, owing to very sad circumstances. You know already that Gretchen has been confined again.......probably, also, that the child was very delicate. Added to this, the summer months are very trying here for children. We know the style of the medical treatment at Rome. The child would certainly have been lost, had not a young physician from Berlin been here, and adopted reasonable measures. The infant has certainly now made some progress toward recovery, but is still far from well, and its possession is an extremely precarious blessing.

Gretchen's health has received a severe shock, owing to the anxiety from which she has scarcely been free for a day since the birth of the child, and her unspeakable anguish since it became seriously ill.......

I was not made ill by the excessive heat, because I constantly vegetated in-doors; but I was very much exhausted, and the sudden change of temperature brought on an attack of dysentery, which has been removed, however, by instant attention. Marcus alone has stood the heat with unabated vigor, and never felt the change of weather in the least. He is such a happy, sprightly child; always full of mirth and laughter. Probably his overflowing health is the reason that his teeth are developed so slowly. His making no attempt to speak yet, may partly result from his being able to make himself understood about every thing, partly from the mixture of the two languages which he hears buzzing about him. Every body loves him, from the women, to an old Franciscan of Ragusa, who often pays us a friendly visit; and his nurse, who has no very warm attachment to her own children, tells her fellow-servants that she weeps when she thinks how soon she shall have to leave him. The happy time is now not far distant, when he will be able to listen to stories; and this will make Rome and my life here tolerable to me, even if I should be compelled to renounce entirely a wider sphere of action. The more disordered the state of the world, the more needful is education; in an age that is growing old and decrepit, a simple world of ideas must be created for the child, in which its mind may grow up strong and unclouded. A clear understanding can least of all be dispensed with, when the confusion of ideas and half-truths is greatest; it is exactly at such a time, that principles, which have been early implanted and carefully watched over, so as to gain all the strength of a prejudice, confer extraordinary power, both over the world within and that without. He who begins his course thus armed, fights with a weapon which is wanting to those around him. Moreover, the mass of things to be learnt, which oppresses and confuses the brain when you have no guidance, may be wonderfully simplified by a teacher, and yet the child may be fed on marrow instead of dry bones. It will be a great blessing for the child, if the King's promise is fulfilled, that a chaplain to the embassy here should be appointed.......

The difficulty of governing in these times is immense. Superficial opinions have diffused themselves on all sides, and acquired authority. No change in the forms can give birth to a higher wisdom, the rarity and impotence of which is the worst disease of our age. In the rest of Germany, things are no better, and in most parts still worse than in Prussia, though the malice of our enemies has the craft to avert censure from themselves and direct it on us. The Bavarian constitution is a genuine child of the age; hence it will be extolled far and wide.

The Austrian administration of finance has been unvailed to the initiated, by the invaluable documentary evidence set forth by its panegyrists.

As I have often told you, I can execute no learned work here. Neither have I been able to avail myself of the Library this winter, because the only two librarians who were obliging and knew where books were to be found, have been occupied in replacing books, that had been collected and ranged in new mahogany cases with splendid plate-glass fronts, for a few hours, by express command, that the Pope might have the satisfaction of surveying them. Then, too, I did not begin to keep a carriage till March, and I live about two miles from the Library. Now Mai is coming here, and then every thing of the kind is out of the question.......

Do you know that I have some prospect of becoming a citoyen de Genève? And that I have earned this title by my services? If I do, I must certainly write something one of these days with all my titles and dignities after my name. We have had a Swiss embassy here, whose intellectual head, Colonel Fischer of Berne, was one of the most sagacious, noble-minded and estimable men whom I know. He and I became great friends, and his departure pained me as if we had lived together for years. I find that I have still got a frightful quantity to tell you, and have neither space nor time left. To-morrow (I am ending this on the 4th), we are going to Genzano, where we shall live under the same roof with Madame von Schlegel. Curious! Our little one is rather better; the country air will very likely benefit her and her mother. What a pity it is that we can scarcely stir beyond the walls of the towns for fear of the banditti! I mean to observe the mode of husbandry there. The peasants are not so bad, if the poor creatures had but a little property. But the barons and the clergy have swallowed up every thing; so late as 1590, the inhabitants of Aricia were lords of a great number of small estates in the valley (though the Savelli had already got many of them into their own hands by confiscation); at that time there came a dreadful famine, and these barons took every thing the people had, in exchange for corn, which they sold to them at the rate of *forty* piastres for the *rubbio*, which in ordinary years now costs *ten*. There's a sacred right of property for you! The peasant women, whom we know most of, are honest people and capable of attachment; only their avarice must be gratified, which, however, happily is possible. But the higher classes, the clergy, the so-called citizens—no, dear Savigny, you can form no idea of such a pack of vagabonds. Farewell! Our hearty love to you and your wife.

Yours, NIEBUHR.

CCXLVII.

TO MADAME HENSLER.

ROME, 1*st September*, 1818.

We are going into the country to-morrow for a month, to Genzano, a very pleasant place above the beautiful Lake of Nemi, where the shade and fine trees make the country very charming to us Germans, when we compare it to the bare desert about Rome.......

It is a subject of great satisfaction to me, that the King has acceded to my proposal that a chaplain to the embassy should be appointed, and that the choice will most likely fall on a very excellent young clergyman from Saxony, a great friend of K. Roeder's. According to the testimony of Professor Heubner, he must be all that one could wish in a teacher of religion for our child. It is my most ardent wish that Marcus may be sincerely and earnestly pious. I can not inspire him with this piety; but I can and will support the clergyman. His heart shall be raised to God as soon as he is capable of a sentiment; and his childish feelings shall be expressed in prayers and hymns; all the religious practices that have fallen into disuse in our age, shall be a necessity and a law to him.

Hemsterhuis says, that, even as a golden age subsisted in the unconscious innocent contentedness of man, favored by nature like a child by a mother, so must the race by manifold wanderings arrive at a state of clear understanding, in which man will cultivate and govern the desert for himself. I by no means share in this dream, but for the individual it is possible, as regards the understanding and intellect, if instruction is brought to the aid of natural talent. That intensity of conviction and of feeling on which all else depends, may be attained by cultivation. But whether a strong-minded and clear-thinking man may not find himself continually more and more a stranger and an outcast among his contemporaries, is another question; for the age on the whole is declining intellectually.

You know, perhaps, that Savigny and I have taken up the idea of the continuance of the Roman municipal institutions under the barbarians; I have definitively discovered their transition into the republican institutions of the middle ages, and am certain that I have found the key which will enable us to understand the old German civil liberty and equality.

In the country, I shall occupy myself with agriculture, in order fully to understand that of the Romans. I shall also try how far it is possible to get toward the old Latin cities in the opposite range of hills; *i. e.* if the robbers are not too near; for, though less numerous, they are worse than ever. Their chief is as if maddened, since his whole family has been murdered. Now, he murders every one he can get hold of, and the government has set a price upon his head, and promised a pardon to any one who may deliver him up, in the hope of seducing some one of his comrades to do so. Every thing that occurs betokens a horrible degeneracy of the whole nation.

CCXLVIII.

TO SAVIGNY.

ROME, 1*st October*, 1818.

We have already returned to town, dear Savigny, contented with having, by our visit to the country, avoided the pestilence of September, which, this year, has certainly been sufficiently antique in its character. It is a very expensive affair to stay in the country during October; for all who have contrived to remain in Rome during the unhealthy months, when you are condemned to utter idleness by the heat and the weight of the air, stream out into the country as soon as the atmosphere begins to cool, and the vegetation to revive. By this time, it often begins to be very cold among the hills, but in Rome it is a mild after-summer; while through the summer, the air on the mountains is temperate and elastic. It is not even the vintage which attracts the people; to their taste, the theatre in Rome is more interesting. But such is, once for all, the established usage, and when a number of people are thus crowded together in small places, equipages and dress attract more attention. In spite of the threatening cold, I left Genzano with reluctance. It afforded me a thousand times more enjoyment than the oppressive city. I should have liked extremely to see the vintage, and the wine-pressing, but it was too expensive for us, after all the disbursements of the summer.......

It is no easy task to German parents to bring up children here; you must have them almost constantly with you, for it were better to see them dead than that they should grow up like the people around them. No one can fully appreciate this without personal experience, and I beg you will not shake your head at what I say. If you were only here a week, as a resident, and as the father of a family, you would see what is the state of a people without reason and conscience, in whom all selfish impulses are let loose. The only difference is, whether these impulses are kindly or malignant, and whether they can be brought into some degree of equilibrium and harmony among themselves. You see here what the human being becomes under the combined influences of a wretched superstition, and utter incapacity for piety; in Naples, by all accounts, matters are still worse, because the people are by nature more passionate and more malignant. The character of the passions there, and what you see of them here, is as unpoetical as possible, they rise to savage fury in the twinkling of an eye. Confession, and absolution, and indulgences may work well among a conscientious and deep-hearted people like the Tyrolese. Here, they open the door to utter abasement. All this seems the strangest to me, when one looks back to the old Romans, who were governed by a religion of the strictest veracity, fidelity, and honesty. If it should ever be in my power to continue my History, I shall venture to demonstrate how this religion, which was something quite different from Stoicism, was the foundation on which the greatness of the old republican time was reared, and how the whole life of the constitution depended on it. It was not the splendid *balance des pouvoirs*, but that the balance was suspended among a virtuous people.

...... Your explanation of the unfriendly feeling toward us, which is so prevalent, and which I perceive only too distinctly among the young Germans in Rome, is, to a certain extent, incontestably correct. But you must also take other causes into the account, to which your benevolence will hardly attach sufficient importance, but which nevertheless exist. In small States it is not so much a *fear* of the mightier State belonging to the same nation, as wounded vanity. Ever since he lost his simple greatness of character, the German has been by nature fond of slander and detraction, by no means candid, and still less loving. For some time after our war of liberation, they were forced to be silent, and respect us: but respect is, to a German, a terribly oppressive feeling. I think it possible that, at that time, great men might have founded an enduring respect for us. Let us remember how Athens saved the liberties of Greece in the Persian war, and that Thebes, &c., betrayed her. The moral condition of Athens was not much more praiseworthy than that of the other States; still we know now, after the lapse of two thousand years, that Athens had a very different intrinsic value from them, notwithstanding the Cleons and Hyperboluses. But envy excited hatred and ingratitude toward Athens, and the cowards and traitors were the genuine Greeks.

CCXLIX.

TO MADAME HENSLER.

ROME, 7*th November*, 1818.

...... We have had a busy season of court festivities, which I have been obliged to attend—a wearisome kind of life to me. Still there were occasionally some beautiful spectacles, and if the aspect of political affairs were different, one could feel some amusement as a looker-on at such a festival, in spite of its emptiness. But when the people are wasting away with famine, when the money that is squandered is taken from the necessitous, when dissatisfaction or apathy reign every where, you feel indescribably melancholy at an entertainment, where you do not even see a single happy face.

One plague of the winter is the ever-increasing swarm of travelers of rank. I have a number of them on my hands just now.

The proselytizing tract of the French ecclesiastic is not in the book shops. If I can get you one copy you will have enough of it; for it will not bear a second reading; it is a shallow thing. I think you are correct in saying that Stolberg's life of St. Vincent would better serve the purpose of these proselytizers, because in that, words and example speak to the heart; for truly not even an uninstructed man will allow himself to be caught by controversial writings; and if Secker's work against Catholicism be put into his hands, he has not the shadow of an excuse. But if such a beautiful picture, which, though a true representation of the individual, is completely defective as applied to the class, had an undue influence on an ardent mind, you ought to refer such an one to the biographies of pious Protestants—of Franke, Paul Gerhard, and so many others, who are certainly not inferior, in point of self-sacrifice, energy, and warmth, to those isolated instances of saints with human feelings in the Romish Church. There is one Italian whom I should like you to know, Paul Sarpi, who, while acting as a lay-brother in a monastery, was a genuine Protestant. You will easily be able to procure an account of him. One appeared as a pamphlet about ten years ago, by Ferdinand Delbrück, and is said to be very well written. I have read an Italian life of him lately, written by a Venetian, his contemporary. If any one wishes to know how the Papists behave, when they want to disseminate opinions respecting those who think differently from themselves, let him read in this book the reports spread by the Court of Rome about the death of this saint, and the infamous lies about Luther in Bellarmine's Catechism.

1819.

Niebuhr had now been more than two years in Rome, yet the instructions, that were to form the basis of his negotiations with the Papal Court, were still delayed. He was further annoyed by rumors—which, however, were not realized—that the Prussian government intended to associate Bartholdy, the consul at Florence, with him in the negotiation. Niebuhr was decided to take his leave should this prove to be the case.

In this, and the following years of his residence in Rome, Niebuhr passed the months of May, September, and October, at Tivoli or Albano. His principal literary production this year was an Essay on the Historical Advantages to be derived from the Armenian Version of the Chronicle of Eusebius, occasioned by the recent publication of the Armenian version, discovered in the convent of St. Lazarus, at Venice, and edited under the auspices of Mai. This Essay was written for the Academy of Sciences in Berlin. He also edited the Fragments of Livy, which he had only delayed so long because he did not choose to submit his work to the censorship of a Dominican, from the necessity of which his high position did not exempt him, while it would have given offense in Rome to have published it elsewhere. He now waived this objection, because he feared that Mai who was just appointed librarian at the Vatican, would publish a bad edition of them, if not forestalled by a better. They appeared in the spring of 1820.

In July, partial instructions at length arrived, but the general ones were still kept back, which vexed him all the more as he was now beginning seriously to think of returning to Germany, on account of his wife's ill health, and extreme dislike to Italy. For his own part, his health had been better, after the first year, than at any former period of his hife.

Letters written in 1819.

CCL.

TO MADAME HENSLER.

ROME, 14*th April*, 1819.

You are decidedly against Gretchen's traveling without me, and consider such a separation as a voluntary renunciation and slighting of the nearest relationships. I should think it as wrong as you do, unless it were justified by the weightiest reasons, and you may well conceive that I could not suffer Gretchen and the children to travel alone, without the greatest anxiety, or be separated from them without a great sacrifice on my part. But her state of health is not only very unsatisfactory in general; she is unquestionably threatened with amaurosis. In fact, the effects of this climate on a nervous constitution are something of which you can form no idea out of Italy, and of which a person utterly ignorant of medicine, who has personally seen and observed them, has a much clearer comprehension than the greatest physician can have who has never visited Italy. Would the father of our Brandis ever have believed that traveling in the mountains could be beneficial to his son? And again, others who also are suffering from chest disorders, would be destroyed by living at the height of 600 feet above the sea; while others die in a few weeks in the sea air of Naples, to which they have been ordered by German and English physicians, to keep off consumption. The physician who accompanies Prince Metternich on his travels, a very clear-headed and well-informed man, finds himself quite at sea in all the cases that come under his notice here. The number of Germans who suffer from mental disorders in Rome, is at least from ten to twenty times greater than in Germany among persons of the same rank, and occupied by the same classes of ideas. In one house, which is always let to Germans, five occupants in succession have become insane within the last sixteen years. In another country how can you form the slightest conception of the effects of the smells, or the sirocco? It is utterly impossible; and therefore you are unable to estimate the effect of this climate upon a delicate constitution, from your knowledge of that constitution in your own country; hence it is that natives and foreigners unite in urging a removal from Italy, as soon as a foreigner finds his health declining. For my own part, I have ransomed my health with a year of suffering, and now I should never think of changing my residence on my own account; only I find, as all others do without exception, that one can get through incomparably less work here than in Germany.

16*th*. I laid my sheets aside yesterday to dress for one of the court parties that are taking place almost daily here just now. You can easily conceive with what heart I can be there, when I leave my invalid in a solitude which she can not enliven by any employment, but can only brood over her own sad thoughts and fears.

I shudder at what we see and hear of things in Germany. Kotzebue's murder, what an utterly insane act! Is the perception of what is right and wrong, lawful and atrocious, really so perverted in Germany, that voices can be raised in defense of such a deed? And even putting that aside, can the men be blind to the consequences of a deed so pregnant with calamity? Are they become so short-sighted? Can not they foresee the impression that it will produce on the governments? Yet it is almost impossible to say this to the deluded men without being regarded as a blockhead, and proscribed.

CCLI.

TIVOLI, 21*st May*, 1819.

......There would be many advantages in passing the summer here; but Gretchen can not get baths; the walks (with the most glorious prospects) are without shade; and I should be obliged to leave her alone some days in every week, which would be very dull for her, as she can employ herself so little.

Bernstorf gives me a furlough of six or eight weeks. His letter is very friendly.

The inhabitants of Tivoli are the most most arrant beggars on the face of the earth. They beg with laughing faces, attack the stranger, and abuse him violently if he gives them nothing. I have made the acquaintance of the richest man in the place; he is a usurer and a miser. The priests here seem to be certainly not better than the rest. I have met with one man, however, who is a fresh proof that the Italians might be raised, if they could be made small proprietors. He is a yeoman, who inherited from his father a house, a vineyard, and an olive-garden, but with debts far exceeding the market-price of his possessions; for small estates fetch such low prices, that the produce of a single year will often reach the half, or more, of the market-price; the land requires so much labor, that he who cultivates it by hired laborers can scarcely make both ends meet, in spite of the extraordinary proportion which the prices of products bear to the price of land here.

This honest man has so far extricated himself, by extraordinary industry and energy, that he has now only a few hundred dollars still owing of his debts, and can look forward to the time when he shall have worked them all off. "When I had earned a hundred dollars by the harvest," said he, "I was obliged to give up eighty, and wept with my children." He mortgaged his olive-garden for ten years to a usurer, who takes the whole produce, which, in good years, is equal to the capital lent, and receives besides ten per cent., which the poor fellow has to get from his other pieces of land. What a state of society! And believe me, that, at most, I do not know more than one Roman who would be shocked at such facts as these. If the man can not pay the two hundred dollars next year, his vineyard will be forfeited. If it is at all within my power I shall lend him the money. Wherever you find hereditary farmers, or small proprietors, there you also find industry and honesty. I believe that a man who would employ a large fortune in establishing small freeholds, might put an end to robbery in the mountain districts. The Italians are still, as in the time of the Romans, adapted simply and solely for agriculture. They are as little a poetical nation as the old Romans were; on the contrary, they are prosaic, and not even lively, as the Germans are in some districts. No nation can be less musical; they have only a ritornel melody, which is most unpleasant, and no national songs at all. The wisdom of the old Romans is strikingly displayed, among other things, with respect to the size of the separate estates, which was determined by law. Seven jugers are amply sufficient to feed and clothe a large family. On this extent they can perform all the tillage themselves, of which much more is needed than with us. The corn requires weeding. This work occupies the whole year, and there is no winter month when there is nothing to do in the fields. A larger estate is no benefit to an Italian, and he who lets his piece of land, and lives without work is a lost man, as well as the poor fellow who can get no work. The mere day-laborer is also in a pitiable condition, and this class are, for the most part, a bad set; but it is from destitution. The great farmers hire them by the job, and, in order to save a little, many of them work themselves to death: in the summer, at least, the hospitals are always crowded with them. The rich learn nothing, and take no interest in any thing. There is no, strictly speaking, burgher class at all; and nothing is rarer than to find artisans who understand their trade and are industrious. The priests are generally very poor and incredibly wicked. In Rome there are parish priests who go about begging. The monks are certainly nearly all good for nothing, though I know one very estimable Franciscan. Learning and literature are at a lower ebb than perhaps in any other country. The devotion is merely external, and this has very much diminished. I have been assured by Italians themselves that the younger people have scarcely any faith at all. From the greatest to the least, all unite in hating and despising the government; but at Rome there are none, or very few, who cling, as so many in the other parts of Italy do, to the very pardonable chimera of the unity of Italy. I was conversing here with an intelligent landowner about the city and the inhabitants, and he drew a frightful picture of one after another of the most influential men, which had, however, quite an air of truth. As he had previously been blaming the government—unhappily with only too much justice—I asked him how any good could be done then, if those who would come into power on the fall of the priestly domination were so bad? He acknowledged that no amelioration at all could be anticipated. The small holdings are swallowed up year by year, and thus the number of vagabonds in the towns is constantly increasing.

If one could but penetrate further into the retreats of the agricultural population! It is only among them that any addition to our knowledge of antiquity could be obtained.

Bunsen and his wife have been with us about ten days. He and I have been visiting ruins that no stranger has ever visited before, and which are very remarkable.

CCLII.

TO NICOLOVIUS.

ROME, 3*d July*, 1819.

From Schmeider's official letter and mine, you will see, dear Nicolovius, that our evangelical worship has been happily commenced, and truly "in God's name." The 27th of June will be a notable day henceforward in church history; for what Protestant worship there had been in Rome previously, was destitute of all spiritual power.

That ours will prosper under such an excellent clergyman is certain. I think I have always known what a genuine pastor must be, who should in our days raise up a church, and infuse into her a new life, but I had never seen such a one till we became acquainted with Schmieder. I can not tell you how we all love and reverence him.

It will not occasion offense; I spoke to the Pope after the first Sunday, when he had, no doubt, been informed of all that passed, and he was as friendly as ever; I had a favor to request for a friend of mine from the Secretary of State, but he declined saying any thing to the Pope about it, and told me that I had better apply to him myself, he would certainly not refuse me; and he did not.

The *prêtraille* do, indeed, cavil much at our burial-ground. The most perplexing circumstance to us will be, if apostates should want to return to us; one has announced his intention of doing so already; you may rely upon it that we shall act with due forethought and circumspection.

I only wish that Schmieder had his wife with him. As he will receive 200 dollars increase of salary, and the congregation can do something for him, she must come. He is so made to be happy and to confer happiness, that he ought not to be subjected to this cruel separation. We shall do what we can toward the expenses of traveling and removal; as I shall now remain here till next March, I shall be able to spare something toward it. But the 200 hundred dollars may be regarded as certain if his wife comes.

I earnestly entreat an answer by return of post if possible. I can not tell you how I long for freedom. Here I have been too long compelled to be on friendly terms with despicable men, for the sake of the service, and the relations which it involves; and I grow more and more acutely sensible that these gentlemen despise all that is good in me, and despise me myself on account of the evil that is not in me.......

CCLIII.

TO MADAME HENSLER.

ROME, 17*th July*, 1819.

......You will be glad to hear that I have gained courage and energy to undertake an historical work of some magnitude, and that I have nearly brought it to a conclusion. Namely, I have made a collection of the previously unknown facts and dates occurring in the fragments of the Armenian translation of the Chronicles of Eusebius, which have been recently discovered, and collated them with others already known, but frequently very obscure. By this process, the history of the earliest periods of the Babylonian empire, that of the Assyrian empire, and that of the Macedonian dynasties after Alexander, will in many parts gain considerably in clearness and extent. The light thus thrown on many points, completes the refutation of those who maintain that Herodotus only knew history as an assemblage of unconnected legends, and had no definitely arranged chronological outline before his eyes; the new facts furnish the greater part of the materials necessary for a work on all the races and states standing in connection with Rome—a work which can not be incorporated into the continuation of the Roman History, but must be present to my thoughts in a distinct shape. I do not so completely despair of this continuation, since I have found that I *can* write, and in a much more impressive style than in better times, although very slowly. But it is terribly laborious to write here, because you not only have to go to the public library for every book which you do not yourself possess, but have to contend with the indolence of the Italians, as soon as you require several books in order to look out single scattered passages. Until lately, I had very seldom had occasion to visit the library where the printed philological works are generally to be found, and the regular librarian does not know who I am; hence, he has lately treated me with great ill-humor for giving him so much trouble. The librarians are Dominicans one of the most repulsive of the monastic orders.......

Schmieder lives and boards with us, and will continue to do so until his wife comes, which will probably be in the autumn. It is my earnest wish that this noble-minded man may enjoy the happiness which he deserves. I have at last received partial instructions. I fear, however, that the Pope is near his end, and then it will be again impossible to do any thing. In that case, the instructions could not be executed in their present form, and I have in the first place to report this to my government.

CCLIV.

ROME, 13*th August*, 1819.

No intelligence has reached me since the unhappy occurrences in Berlin.*

Here we have only very confused accounts of the arrests, and the search after papers. The seizure of Reimer's † will have made you uneasy on my account also. Not that you would think me capable for a moment of harboring criminal designs against the State, or rash ones against the existing ministry. But you will fancy the possibility of strong expressions of vexation. It will set you at ease when I tell you that I have not written to Reimer at all for more than a year, that I have at no time written frequently to him, and that my letters were always short and of no political importance. Neither my wishes nor my hopes were in unison with his.

To Schleiermacher and Arndt I have never written.‡ I am ready to take oath that, according to my full belief, not one of these three is connected with any thing that could be reasonably called a secret association, still less a conspiracy. Reimer may have used unwarrantable expressions, and has made himself bitter enemies by his never-ending squabbles with the censorship.

* This refers to the investigations which were set on foot after the murder of Kotzebue, by Sand, to discover the revolutionary conspiracy with which his deed was supposed to be connected. It was afterward fully proved that he had acted under the impulse of maddened fanaticism without any external instigation; but the government, at this time, fancied that the whole Burschenschaft was a secret association which aimed at the overthrow of the existing authorities, and, therefore, all those who were in any way connected with it were called to account.

† Reimer was a publisher in Berlin, and an intimate friend of Niebuhr's.

‡ Schleiermacher's papers were soon restored to him; but Arndt was less fortunate. He was suspended from his professorship, and his papers were detained for several years.

Schleiermacher may have said unsuitable things on unsuitable occasions, but he has never been an advocate of revolution any more than Arndt, and I remember his saying to my Milly and me, when all these ideas were first beginning to ferment, that he shuddered to think of them. As far as his papers are concerned, I am quite easy about him. I am less so about Reimer's; I fear misinterpretation (firmly as I am convinced of his innocence), because he often formed connections for a time with hot-headed men, till he perceived that there was nothing to be done with them. Still, nothing can be brought to light worthy the name of a crime. His credit may, however, be seriously injured by such an affair and such an interruption to his business.

Whether there exists any sort of conspiracy among the young men, I do not know; it does not seem to me impossible; at all events there is a fanatical political sect, which is more dangerous than a conspiracy, because it has roots that can not be destroyed except by plowing up the soil itself —a course not to be expected of governments which have allowed the evil to grow up under their own eyes, without counteracting it by wisdom and virtue. And this would have been possible. In 1814, the ground was cleared and ready to bear fruit; but no seed was sown, and so of course weeds shot up in rank luxuriance. Nothing can exonerate those who neglected their duty at that time from the blame of these results. Then, love dwelt in every heart, and all were ready to welcome whatever was noble and good. Now, the tone of public feeling has degenerated, and God knows how it is to be raised. To me, our democrats are as hateful as lackeys aping the ways of a despot.

CCLV.

ROME, 28*th August*, 1819.

Since I wrote to you this day week, your missing letter has come to hand, after a week's delay. Even the communications which I have received from the ecclesiastical authorities, have been opened without ceremony and detained on the road, of which I have made bitter complaints to my minister. I conjecture that it takes place at Frankfort.

You say that a life in Germany would now afford me little that was cheering, and I, too, clearly perceive this. In fact, I should unquestionably remain here in spite of all that I risk by doing so (about which I wrote to you), if there were any hope that Gretchen's health could be re-established, or even improve in this country. Whether this will be the case in Germany, we do not know, but we must make the experiment. I believe that you yourself will pronounce me in the right, if, after a full consideration of all the reasons against this step, I decide to take it as a duty toward my poor Gretchen. Indeed I assure you that I could not do it without great sacrifices on my part, consequently am in no danger of being seduced by inclination. I have gained access here to papers which are preserved in a building where you can not work in winter; believe me, I should resign them very unwillingly, and all the more so, as it may be anticipated that, since they have lain there for eighty years untroubled, they may probably remain unnoticed forever, unless I profit by them. They are critical collections of extracts from manuscripts of Cicero's Orations, with the criticism of which I have been busily engaged ever since the winter, and of which with these aids I should be able to publish regular edition. I have acquired a taste for critical researches into language, which formerly I was far from possessing.

The aspect of things in Germany is certainly in every respect unfriendly and discouraging. You can not unite with any party, and a man of clear and correct views finds enemies on every side. I really look upon it as a blessing that I am not in Berlin at this moment; that is, if the unhappy circumstances which have occurred there could not have been averted, of which, however, I am not so fully convinced, if I could have taken a part in public affairs. Unfortunately our men do not perceive that in this case no coercive measures can avail; indeed nothing can do good but a government whose wisdom and virtue should put the deluded to shame, and win over and appease the universities. My dispatches have often given me an opportunity of expressing my views respecting the inward disease of all States; and while no man can find so much as a pretext for denouncing me as an adherent of revolutionary sentiments, I have openly expressed my sense of the deficiencies of our government.

I have sought to make it intelligible that they are presuming and seeking for a conspiracy where there is a sect. The latter is perhaps more dangerous than the former, but it can not be crushed, even if composed of men of a different stamp from those who took part in this hazardous enterprise among us; a crusade against them is as fruitless as against a religious sect. Much has been done in ignorance; did the governments take the right course, they would rule over loving subjects, and a few fiery heads, such as always exist, would find no materials on which to work. Now, when the sect has acquired firmness and consistency, the only prudent course is to soothe them by adopting wise and good measures, neither yielding to them, nor yet directly irritating them. There has never yet been a sect which did not contain some grain of truth, and this grain is what we must seek to appropriate; if we do so, the residuum of folly and perverseness will fall to pieces of itself before a firm yet kind opposition; but if you attack it, just as it stands, you often find it invincible, and at all events place yourself in a very dangerous position. I do not by this mean to deny that there may be some actual plotters behind the scenes; but the number of such can not be great, and they will no doubt know how to keep themselves concealed.

I am again throwing myself with full energy into all kinds of occupation, and to a certain extent with success. In fact by this means I grow calmer, and more able to forget the annihilation of all bright visions in the social world. I have finished my treatise on the historical acquisitions afforded by the Chronicles of Eusebius, which, among other things, contains the account of a whole period of the history of the Seleucidæ. It has almost grown into a small book.

This is a very unhealthy season. Thank God we keep free from the prevailing distempers. The numerous cases of sickness keep our dear, active Schmieder fully employed. There are many German artisans here, particularly from Switzerland, with their wives and families. Their misery at such a time is inconceivable, and hitherto they have often taken these poor creatures into the hospitals, and when there, if they refused to change their religion, have left them for days together without attention or food. The establishment of our Church will remove a part of this misery; it will procure the means of help, and the poor will know to whom they may look for assistance. I can not say too much of Schmieder's conduct in this, as in every other work. I feel much more happy in my own mind since he has been here. You see in him what genuine piety in any form makes of a noble spirit.......

CCLVI.

ROME, 17*th September*, 1819.

I did not write to you this day week, because I was ill, and did not know whether it might not become serious; but I have been restored by prompt remedies.

I do not know whether you have heard that a pamphlet has appeared in Paris, upon the so-called secret associations in France, which is written in a very good spirit, but, to judge from the extracts in the newspapers, contains many errors and inaccuracies, as to matters of fact. My name is mentioned in it, but with respect. Although, however, it does not speak of me as belonging to the *Tugendbund*, it is very unpleasant to me to find it stated, that, in 1813, Gneisenau, Humboldt, and I gave our approbation to the principles of this society. Now as I can stake my life upon it that I never was connected with any association, and malicious persons could easily take occasion from it to represent my former declarations as falsehoods, I felt much tempted to insert a letter on the subject in the French newspapers. I gave up the idea afterward, because the ill-intentioned, who have always some misinterpretation at hand, would immediately have said that I sought to exculpate myself through fear, and because, in my position, I can not openly express my feelings about the state of affairs.

And besides, even if I had not been held back by my position as a servant of the State, other obstacles would have been in the way. Much as I disapprove of the course that has been taken, I could not publicly acquit many of my friends of having acted so that appearances were against them, nor of cherishing very perverted, although not guilty sentiments.

This opens a mournful prospect for me if I return to Germany. A sober man among drunkards is in a horrible position. Now my convictions are still the same as those which I expressed many years ago, and by which I drew down upon myself such absurd and venomous attacks from the Liberal party—that the change of forms which is necessary, and would save us, can not properly affect the sovereignty, but only the administration; that the evils from which we are suffering, so far as they are the work of the executive power, are not connected so exclusively with the persons of those who are now in office, but that we should be certain to experience the same again, or others, after the introduction of any representative system whatever; that the source of our maladies lies in our national manners and tone of thought. Each man wants to govern, and thinks he can do it extempore; if you doubt his capacity, he feels himself insulted. But no one is ready to bear burdens for the community. Every where men make the most unreserved claims to a comfortable life at the cost of the State; and this is, in fact, with most the source of their desire for change, coupled, however, with a different and far more innocent motive, namely, such a long familiarity with scenes of violent change and excitement, that their minds have grown habituated to them......

CCLVII.

TIVOLI, *1st October*, 1819.

To-day I have some news to tell you, which is of no slight importance to me. I have received an official announcement that my instructions are about to be sent off. This renders it nearly impossible for me to carry out my proposal of requesting my recall in December. Had I not to consider Gretchen's health, it might and would give me much gratification to find myself at last engaged on more important business; for a life in Germany to me would now be scarcely the shadow of my old life there. I look upon myself as one forgotten in my own country; while here, the Pope and the Cabinet show me the most marked respect, kindness, and confidence. My health has improved; my powers have been refreshed by the work I have just gone through; and I am ready at least to make an attempt to resume my History. If this attempt should not prove as successful as formerly, it will not be wholly fruitless; and I shall have eased my conscience by the endeavor to fulfill a sacred duty toward my Milly. I have no fear of finding myself unable to conduct the negotiation well and skillfully; but now comes one great drawback; people in Germany make such absurd demands on the results of such a negotiation, that it is utterly impossible to satisfy them; and when the affair is brought to the only practicable conclusion, I shall be decried without mercy. They imagine that if we only set to work in the right way, we might succeed in driving the Roman Court to renounce its principles and its pretensions, and to leave the bishops so free that they could regulate the Church according to their own pleasure; and that, failing in this, the governments ought to break off all connection with Rome, and take the whole settlement of the Church into their own hands. But such people do not reflect that only a very small party among the Catholics would agree to such a course; and that in many districts, particularly in the Rhenish provinces and Westphalia, nothing would so infallibly excite discontent and disaffection among the King's subjects as this compulsory emancipation; for, though, doubtless, there would be no lack of persons willing to undertake the office of bishops, yet as such bishops would be schismatic, all true Catholics would consider every rite performed by them, or by any priest consecrated by them, as unlawful, nay, criminal. But, however difficult it may be to content both parties, this negotiation is indispensable; and if it be at last brought to a happy conclusion, so many evils will be obviated, that from this higher motive I shall derive satisfaction from it, though it may occasion much that is unpleasant for me.

But Gretchen's health! . . . . . .

CCLVIII.

ROME, *20th October*, 1819.

We returned to town again on Saturday, and it was well we did, for the autumn rain has been pouring down in torrents ever since. The severe and premature cold weather almost spoiled our stay on the slopes of the Apennines. Gretchen has been obliged to give up the grape cure. The children grew quite robust there. Amelia has at last taken courage to go alone; she speaks much earlier than Marcus. The dear fellow is not at all jealous, and readily gives way to his sister; he fondles her with intense delight, and calls her *Amà mia!* He is a remarkably good child.

The Carlsbad decrees* have made a most mischievous impression on the Germans here, who are mostly young men, and many of them possessed by wild dogmas; from this we may easily gather the effect they will produce in Germany. A favorable impression they can not make on any unbiased mind. It is equally severe and unjust to have recourse to severe and coercive measures against a sect, which your very violence converts into a party, without in the least reforming your own proceedings, without redressing a single real grievance. How utterly without love, without patriotism, without joy—how full of discontent and grudge must life be, where this is the relation between the subjects and the governments! Our rulers do not perceive that Prussia can only subsist upon a moral and spiritual basis. I know very well whose spiritual children the democrats are; I know that you can not allay the wild clamor, however well you govern, unless you do them the favor of adopting their senseless plans; but they would be detached from the people at large, if the latter found that they were governed wisely and well.

1820.

In July, 1820, Niebuhr at last received his instructions, after having waited for them four years. They arrived at a moment very unpropitious for negotiation, for the revolution in Naples broke out on the 7th of July, and it was rumored that on the 17th, a similar rising was to take place at Rome, in accordance with a plan previously concerted with the insurgents of Naples. The expectation of an Austrian intervention prevented the revolt in Rome from coming to a head, but it could not secure the inhabitants from the risk of a sudden incursion of the bands of robbers who

* During the agitation occasioned by Kotzebue's murder and the investigations to which it gave rise, Metternich and Hardenberg agreed to fill up the chasms left in the Act of Confederation of 1815, and, for this purpose, to hold ministerial conferences at Carlsbad, to which plenipotentiaries from all the German states were invited. The conferences began toward the end of July. Their results were communicated to the Frankfort Diet, and the measures based upon them were all brought in and accepted unanimously in one day. They consisted—

I. Of the appointment of a commission to watch over the execution of the decrees of the Diet, which were to supersede the existing authorities in any German state, in case of an opposition on the part of the latter.

II. Measures were to be taken to watch over the universities, and put down any indication of a revolutionary spirit among either the students or the professors,

III. A rigid censorship of the press was to be established.

IV. The appointment of a Central Committee for the investigation of all democratic attempts was decreed. This committee sat at Mayence, and had power to cause the arrest of persons on suspicion, in any part of Germany, and have them brought to Mayence, and detained there as long as might be found necessary.

had been collected and organized in large bodies by the Neapolitan Carbonari. There were very few troops in Rome, and none whose fidelity could be relied on.

Under these painful circumstances Madame Niebuhr was confined of a daughter on the 9th of August.

Niebuhr's position was very trying, as he could neither leave Rome so long as the Pope remained there, nor send his wife and children away without him, while, in the city, they lived in constant fear of being attacked by brigands and plundered, or carried off as hostages. At the same time, it was necessary to proceed with the negotiations, for which, however, the Roman government had little attention to spare at such a moment. This state of anxiety lasted till the arrival of the Austrians in the February following.

During this autumn, Niebuhr was also involved in some very unpleasant literary disputes. His edition of the fragments he had discovered in the Vatican in 1816, had come out in May. About the same time, a Codex was discovered by Peyron in Turin, which confirmed the arrangement of the fragments of Cicero's Oration for Scaurus, to which Niebuhr had been led by his own study of them. The Abbé Mai, who could not forgive Niebuhr for having found so many defects in his edition of Fronto, and of the Armenian Eusebius, and regarded him with envy as a fortunate rival in the path of discovery, accused him in a public journal of having learnt from the Turin MS. what he had put forth as an original conjecture. Niebuhr was about to publish an indignant defense, when Mai was persuaded by his friends, who represented to him the consequences of his proceeding, to retract and apologize for his statement in the same journal. On this Niebuhr agreed to take no further notice of the matter. The same charge was, however, repeated, and in a much more malignant manner, soon after, in the "Bibliotheca Italiana." This he could not leave unanswered, and therefore printed a pamphlet in which he refuted the statement by the clearest proofs. In January 1821, Niebuhr received a letter from Peyron, stating, that though he had discovered the fragments in question in the previous March, he had not found the key to their arrangement, which was the subject of the accusation, until September; consequently, not until three months after Niebuhr's edition had been in print. Peyron announced his intention of inserting this letter in a Roman journal; the permission to do so was at first refused out of consideration to Mai, but Niebuhr succeeded at length in extorting it from the government, which he would hardly have accomplished but for his official position.

In spite of the unsettled state of political affairs, the concourse of foreigners at Rome, in the winter of 1820, was unusually large. Prince Henry of Prussia, Prince Christian of Denmark, and the Crown Prince of Bavaria, with many other distinguished personages, spent the winter there. This rendered it necessary for Niebuhr to enter into society so much more than he had done hitherto, that he was scarcely able to carry on his studies at all. He had, however, the great pleasure of receiving a visit from Stein and his two daughters in December, and conversing once more with the great statesman upon the political topics that still lay nearest to his heart.

Letters written in 1820.

CCLIX.

TO MADAME HENSLER.

ROME, 1*st January*, 1820.

I can not allow the coincidence of the New Year and the post-day to pass without sending you a greeting, although it must be very short; for to us this New Year begins like the last, with a severe illness of Gretchen's. She bears it with admirable patience, but it is a great calamity to us all. I do not think that she is in any danger, but what a life it is that she leads, and for me too? And what comfort have the poor children of their mother?

Thus our immediate prospects on entering the New Year, are but gloomy; gloomy like our sky, in which the sun has seldom appeared for the last three months. As concerns the world at large, I shut my eyes to the future. I have never deviated from the straight path since the times have grown so difficult any more than I did previously, and I shall continue to walk in it with unswerving footsteps. So long as two months ago, I expressed my sentiments directly and openly to the King, on occasion of the well-known circular;* I wrote unreservedly to the minister when the first arrests took place; since then I have expressed myself with equal freedom to the Crown Prince—I, whom the revolutionists, no doubt call an enemy of freedom. And I shall continue to act with the same openness, and leave the consequences in God's hand.......

I must conclude, because my Marcus, who has been waiting patiently for nearly an hour, is now begging me with tears to come and play with him. Let me commend my dear angel children to your affection.

CCLX.

ROME, 22*d January*, 1820.

......The deadening influence of the climate of modern Rome is not common to many places in Italy, but wherever there is a similar climate,

* A circular, by which the different embassadors were called upon to state their views with regard to the general political condition of Germany.

wherever this sirocco prevails, you see the same intellectual results. I will not remind you of the fact that Rome remained quite barbarous up to the fifteenth century, but the stagnation of mind, and the incapacity for all deeper insight and classical thought, which has displayed itself in later times, is by no means to be ascribed exclusively, or even chiefly to the government and its form. From that time to this, Rome has produced no poet, no great author of any description, not even artists, with one exception; only one great philologist, and he has written no connected work of magnitude. Pisa has just such a climate as Rome, and, while at Florence the human mind was exhibiting the greatest activity and life in every direction, no man of intellect has arisen at Pisa, and all the great works of art, which the wealth of that city has called into existence, have been executed by foreigners.......

I think you will not hear without interest, that the republic of Geneva has sent me the freedom of the city. With a good deal of trouble, I had succeeded in obtaining a papal decree separating the Catholic community of Geneva from the diocese of Chambery, and transferring it to the bishopric of Freiburg, in spite of the violent opposition of the court of Turin. Trifling and insignificant as the matter must appear to those unacquainted with the circumstances, you would not easily find, even among the most intricate negotiations, one beset with greater difficulties. This title of citizenship gives me quite a different sort of pleasure from any honor that could flatter my vanity; though we shall all probably think very differently now of him who gave celebrity to the title *citoyen de Genève*, from what we did thirty years ago. They also offered me a present of 8000 francs, which I declined on the spot. Do not let us question whether this decision might not possibly arise from an impure motive, instead of, as I think, from a pure and disinterested sentiment of honor; I really only know that it seemed to me unbecoming to accept such a recompense and to sell my services. You, who know me so thoroughly, will believe me when I say this.

What do people say now to the state of things in France? I have the sheets still by me, in which I exposed the absurdities and inevitable consequences of the electoral law, and experience has justified every one of my predictions.

If you can find a German translation of the History of the Revolution in Naples, in 1799, read it. From that, you will see with your own eyes, what hopeless ruin is brought about by the want of sound practical sense, even in good men, who have been embittered by a bad government and are filled with chimeras. I know nothing more excellent of its kind.

Snow has lain on the ground for two days. Such an occurrence puts the Romans beside themselves. All the schools, libraries, &c. are closed. Marcus is full of glee at this strange sight, and plays with it, as the children do with us.

CCLXI.

ROME, *5th February*, 1820.

The detention of your letter beyond the limits of the long-past interval of delay assigned, is not only a subject of regret to me this time, but, coupled with the unceremonious opening of your last, it makes me uneasy on several accounts. In the first place, I fear lest those whose office it is to inspect letters at Frankfort, should suppress yours entirely, of which there have been instances; in the next, that by twisting the sense they may use it as a *corpus delicti*. Let us, however, be rather more cautious in the exposition of our feelings and views, and thus avoid, for God's sake, the interruption of a correspondence without which I can not live.

......[After repeating his reasons for leaving Rome, he thus proceeds:]

I hope that you too will see that I could not act otherwise. I am well aware of what I sacrifice if I go; my health has improved, &c. Do not fancy either, that I imagine that in another climate, and under different personal relations, my intellect would once more become what it was. That depended upon other conditions. I am now a lopped tree, which may put forth green boughs again, but whose glory has departed with its spreading branches.

That I look forward to the decision with an anxious and heavy heart, you will conceive. And besides that, there are so many other things to make me feel anxious and sad. A storm seems gathering on the frontiers of Germany; and though I have rejoiced that in France a man had found the place which Nature called him to occupy, and have hoped it would be possible to arrest the spirit of Revolution which an ambitious man had called up, in order to keep the reins of a power for which he had no vocation, a short time longer in his hands; I fear now that the destroying fates will triumph in that country. And, however deeply we must abhor the tyranny in Spain, no immediate redemption can be expected from a revolt, followed by the proclamation of the most senseless constitution that was ever hatched, but only misery and civil war.

I am an anti-revolutionist, and from principle; but I am so likewise from my antipathy to revolutionary ideas, which would be in themselves repugnant to me, such as they are when conceived in shallow brains, even if they led to no results whatever. At the same time, however, I hope you will give me credit for the most decided hatred to despotism, though I would not attempt, nor do I think it possible, to counteract it by evoking the demon of revolution. Dreaming will do no good; we must think; and we must rather resign ourselves to an evil, than wish the gates of hell to open upon us. But believe me, I am not so unfair as to condemn those who merely dream, and wish this in their dreams, though I could weep tears of blood that such errors should be possible. I know that noble minds may be thus led astray; but when the confusions they excite deprive us all of the modicum of liberty still left to us, I have a right to be indignant. I am not now referring to the bad men who form the ringleaders; they are morally criminal; wisdom would not treat them as politically criminal, even if some among them are so, on which I will not decide, for if you touch them, you make martyrs of them. The only salvation would be to rule with conscientiousness, virtue, and love; and by this means the goal would infallibly be reached; and on our side, to become better, more virtuous, and more contented. No government could succeed, in the long run, in carrying out pernicious measures against a strong people, inspired by good and noble sentiments, and fulfilling its duties faithfully and conscientiously. To wish to bring about a better state of things by revolutions, which generally owe their origin to the base motives of their leaders, and in which bad means are invariably resorted to, is to pay homage to the jesuitical maxim, that it is lawful to make use of bad means to accomplish a (supposed) good object. I shall adhere to these principles, although I foresee that malice will persuade folly, on the one side, that I am a revolutionist, on the other hand, that I am a foe to freedom. Strange! that I am not misunderstood in France and England, where I am daily becoming better known.

Not to conceal from you the good qualities of Rome, I must tell you that the spring is already so far advanced, that at this moment, some hours after sunset, a knot of the common people are singing under the windows of my room (in which I have no fire) with the guitar: the Carnival has begun, and does impart some vivacity to these inanimate Italians.

I am very tender-hearted to-day; I have had an affecting dream, which transported me to past times with such vividness, that their scenes have been floating before me all day with a half reality.......

CCLXII.

ROME, *25th March*, 1820.

This time, too, the apprehensions aroused by the non-arrival of your dear affectionate letter have been happily dispelled.

I could wish that our authorities would make it a maxim, as much as possible, to promote the sons of landed proprietors in the army in preference to others. This is not a question of the possession, or absence, of noble birth, but of a particular species of fixed and independent property. For people who possess a fixed and independent income, the army is a worthy occupation, which they may resign without becoming a burden on the State, and then live with dignity in the country. It is in this way, and by filling offices like those of the Justices of the Peace in England, that the *gentry* becomes respectable; with a genuine *gentry* all depends upon these characteristics, not upon what we generally understand by the term nobility. The war has left us far too many young officers without property, many of whom have been withdrawn from other professions. The great point is, that each should have a fixed mode of life, an appropriate calling; so that the people at large may not wander from the manifold paths of human activity, and throw themselves on the one road of governing. On questions respecting the State, and the highest subjects of this high art—for which there is a peculiar talent, and an aptitude for cultivation just as much as for the other arts, and which is just as rare as other talents—dogmas are now enunciated with an arrogance, and a superficiality which must provoke, or grieve all men of penetration. People praise and decry without knowledge of mankind, without insight into political science, without understanding the aims, the means, or the difficulties of their rulers.

That people should form a correct judgment respecting persons and circumstances with which they never come in contact, no one can demand; but we have a right to demand, that those who have not the means of seeing to the bottom, should express their opinions modestly. Under the terror of wild revolutions, all Europe is congealing into an iron despotism, and Germany is drifting toward foreign servitude.

Spain, likewise! For King Ferdinand no punishment can be too severe;* but remember my prophecy; the constitution, if really carried out, can not subsist six months: such a monster of anarchy! A great part of the coun-

* A military insurrection in the January of this year had proved successful, and Ferdinand had been compelled to swear to the constitution of the Cortes.

try, nay, whole provinces, have not the least wish for it; and, in this instance, too, no higher wisdom has been recognized than the idol of smooth uniformity, to which millions are required to sacrifice their feelings and their freedom! In such a case, nothing but a military government can exist, and even under such a rule one leader must contend with another, until one gains the victory, and in his turn comes to be overthrown.

We are tending toward that condition in the Roman Empire, when absolute sovereigns reigned without hereditary succession. Our hereditary monarchies are a blessing, which will be recognized when it is lost. Not that every hereditary dynasty is so—in Spain, for instance, it has greatly sinned. But that any sudden catastrophe is the greatest misfortune, I feel with the fullest conviction.

CCLXIII.

Rome, *6th May*, 1820.

I think you, too, would allow that one could hardly find a better and more amiable child than Marcus. He wins all hearts—his openness, his joyous sensibility, and the absence of all disagreeable ways, give every body a steady liking for him. His little outbreaks of self-will, which never go so far as ill-temper, and the reproofs for them, which he receives with tears, are always followed by remarkably good behavior. He is quite free from the ugly fault of covetousness. He daily shows indications of a good heart, which make me love him more and more. I trust that he will grow up a very simple character, without show and pretension. May God preserve his present fine and noble nature! I have not seen in him a single "spirituel" trait, and it may be, perhaps, that my father may in all respects live over again in him. He will have very good abilities for learning and retaining. He knows his letters. He does not yet take much interest in stories; but all the more in seeing things, and when I walk with him I tell him the names of every thing, of buildings, &c. His perceptive powers are excellent. Thus, for instance, he distinguishes marble from travertine very correctly, and the latter often from peperine. The less lively his imagination is, so far, the less need I hesitate in reading the poets aloud to him, as soon as he likes to hear them. On this account, however, it is a pity that he is so backward in German, and that there is no readable Homer in Italian; else it must familiarize a child much more with the ancient poets, and bring them nearer to him, to be able to show him the statues in the museums. I shall for the present direct the whole course of his instruction mostly to visible and living objects.

You ask about Spain, and I think I can give you a very decided answer. The constitution deserves all the evil that is said of it, and is as wretched and shallow a piece of parchment, as has seen the light any where, since it has been the fashion for people to employ their odd hours in framing constitutions; not to mention the fact, that it renders it impossible to retain America, whose share in the representation, even taking only the white population into account, is, in every point of view, so disproportionately small, that it remains practically without any part in the government, and is, moreover, absolutely compelled to protest against the uniformity of legislation. So, too, the Cortes of 1810 drove the Americans to rebellion, and the greatest atrocities took place under their government in Mexico, while their fall brought Mexico into subjection again, just because they had been hated to the last degree. The equalization of all the Spanish provinces of the peninsula is an absurdity, and as great an injustice toward Biscay, as were the violent measures which the Directory adopted to compel the Swiss to unity. Since the supreme power is placed without limitation in the hands of a hundred and eighty men, who are chosen on no other grounds, at least at present, than their political fanaticism, and for speeches which sound magnificent to fools, nothing can be more certain than that the proceedings of such an assembly will be marked by a total want of wisdom, and the most arbitrary exercise of power. This would be the case, even if they found no opposition; but they will find opposition, and excite it; in the first place, from the provinces which find their privileges attacked, like Biscay, and from those which desire something quite different—namely, a federative republic, like Catalonia and Galicia; in the second place, from the chiefs of the army, who have already, in 1813, refused to obey an imperious and ridiculous assembly, and who, with some isolated exceptions, do not trouble themselves in the least about the constitution, but only care to get power into their own hands. If these parties should rise against each other, the now insignificant faction of the king, and the much more powerful one of the clergy, would mingle in the strife—gain nothing for themselves, but make confusion worse confounded.

The Spaniards, with the exception of the Catalonians, who differ little from the French, are divided into two classes, which are as different as any two nations; the people, especially the inhabitants of the country, and the country towns, which, at least up to the time of the war, had remained nearly what they were four centuries ago; and the educated ranks, whose mental cultivation is entirely French. I am reading just now a survey of the Castilian poetry by Quintana, their most celebrated author, and it is really disgusting to see not only how entirely destitute he is of all feeling for the magnificence and genius of the Spanish literature, but how his own language is crammed with Gallicisms, so that his book, translated literally into French, would read like an original work, but one below the average of mediocrity. The Spaniards have never understood either how to obey or to command; certainly not how to govern, except as despots; not only in the revolutionary war, but throughout the whole course of their old history, nothing has been accomplished by masses of men, but always by detached bands. They are the only nation whom you can call, in its essence—the common people—truly poetical; the cultivated classes have quite lost this beautiful characteristic, and have not acquired in its stead those qualities which can not spring up where that exists. Pride has always been the distinguishing feature of the Spaniards; in the very heat of the revolutionary war, many generals were faithless to the common cause (although the number of actual traitors was extremely small), because they were too proud to take an inferior position. Hatred is much more common among them than love and friendship; the slightest offense converts friends into deadly enemies. These are no elements of freedom. Were it not for the compact power of France, I would wish nothing better for Spain than that she might become a federative State, since the monarchy has once for all been trifled away: only, without some special good fortune, I hardly think that such a State could sustain the first severe shock, and maintain itself till the people had become habituated to it. If King Ferdinand's conduct had not been quite so unbearable, a sudden convulsion in favor of absolute monarchy would have been very possible, such as took place in 1814, when there were universal rejoicings over the fall of the Cortes (for the truth of this fact is quite certain); but he has acted too insanely.

One good trait of the Spaniards is integrity in money matters, and not a single accusation has ever been brought against the Cortes in this respect. How different is it here in Italy! What is to become of Italy, if a revolution break out, one can not even imagine. Thoroughly bad as the government of the priests is, I declare with full conviction, that if the power were to fall into the hands of other classes here, the state of affairs would be incomparably worse.

During the last few days, I have been reading with great interest a quite forgotten, though printed pamphlet of the year 1420, entitled, "A Project for the Peloponnesus;" it furnishes a remarkable instance of how men look to revolutionary changes in the legislature for real help, in times of utter national decay, when in fact no resource remains, and improvement from such a quarter is a sheer impossibility. It contains the fundamental ideas of the French economists from the pen of a Byzantine scholar......

CCLXIV.

ROME, 25*th June*, 1820.

......I have been obliged to begin an entirely new and different life here from my earlier one, and this is a miserable thing. Perhaps I am better than you ever knew me; more patient, more self-sacrificing, freer from selfishness, more reasonable. If so, I owe it to having children to train, and to my duties toward the children and my poor Gretchen.

With regard to my political views and convictions, I have the repose of that unshakable conviction which results from the immediate intuition of the truth; and opposite opinions do not irritate me, because they can not perplex me for a moment. All comes to pass just as I had long ago foreseen and foretold, and all that I now foresee will also come to pass. There are men whom I have never seen, with whom I could act in perfect concert, because what they say and think is as if it came from my inmost soul. Such an one is the minister de Serre, who saw as I did three years ago, then allowed himself to be led astray by yielding his conviction to that of his friends; whose heart is broken for his error; and who now presents, perhaps, the most tragic spectacle in Europe, that of a man who is sacrificing his life to atone for an error, although it is too late to remedy it, and that which is intended as a remedy is still an evil, though certainly of infinitely less magnitude. A year and a half ago, I said to a friend of de Serre, "Your friend will soon wish to buy back the words he has uttered with his life, but I can not therefore cease to love and revere him."

The night before last, I read through a thick packet of pamphlets from Spain. What empty bombast, what miserable twaddling, what a dark night without a ray of hope! In Spain, there are perhaps many well-intentioned persons on the revolutionary side; hundreds of thousands are exasperated, and with justice. On the other side, there is, perhaps, nothing healthy and good; but the shallowness and incapacity of the well-meaning among the revolutionists throws their game into the hands of the rogues among them, and is in itself enough to ruin every thing. They will strive after a republic with uniformity and despotism, and it will end with a military dictatorship. In the ministry, a second party have already attained the height of reputation, and even these are already beginning to decline.

......I have had a literary pleasure in reading the Provençal Troubadours which have come out in France. They display a beauty such as I had never dreamed of. They are far above their reputation. The new poems of Lamartine are also beautiful. We can get nothing here from Germany, and for new books I am almost entirely limited to French literature.

CCLXV.

ROME, 28*th July*, 1820.

Three weeks ago, I wrote you in haste the news of the revolution that had suddenly broken out in Naples, and a fortnight ago, I sent you an equally hurried letter, saying that we are anticipating similar occurrences here. My silence will have made you uneasy, but it was impossible to write.......

Our fear that a revolution would break out here also, was no chimera. A plan, intended to put the people into a ferment, was fortunately discovered and frustrated, and, by a still greater piece of good fortune, the leaders of the Neapolitan revolution, who had previously formed conspiracies through the whole of Italy as they found opportunity, had grown shy of carrying on proceedings which might draw down a storm on their own heads, while they might otherwise hope to remain undisturbed. Hence they rejected the proposals of the Roman malcontents, though they had stirred up a revolt at Beneventum and Pontecorvo only a week before. These circumstances give us some security; though security is not the right word, for any accident may cause the tempest to burst here too. The populace is extremely ill affected toward the government, and after all the changes that have taken place in the world, and in men's minds, an ecclesiastical government can scarcely have any stability in itself.

The army can not be relied on; if it were not for that, we might sleep in peace, weak as it is in numbers; for without an external impulse which would justify our worst fears, the population of Rome will certainly not stir.

But things can not remain quiet for any length of time, if the revolutionary party in Naples should maintain themselves in power, or if, as appearances betoken, the agitation there should resolve itself into a wild anarchy.

In the first case, the present authorities of Naples would gain courage, in which they are very deficient at present; in the second, bands of men would force their way over the frontiers.

The Neapolitan revolution, accomplished apparently with such unanimity, and without acts of violence, as great pains are taken to report, may appear a very splendid affair at a distance, but seen near, it is a dreadful and melancholy occurrence. Not that the former government was good, and worthy of respect—far from it; it was superficial and foolish; not tyrannical, but the taxes it imposed were very burdensome.

The revolution has been effected, on the one hand, by ambitious officers, on the other, by the lodges of the Carbonari, who are in every respect the wildest and most execrable class of Jacobins. The two parties have worked side by side and together, but not for the same end. The most widely differing views prevail in the different provinces. Apulia, for instance, and others, want to secede, and form separate republics. This is, at bottom, the characteristic tendency of the Italians now, as in the middle ages. The idea of unity exists in some large towns among the very small class of educated persons, and those who hope to get higher and more lucrative posts in a larger State. It is espoused by the army. At the present moment, not a creature pays the taxes in the Neapolitan territory, and the State is obliged to pay not only the soldiers, but also the thousands of Carbonari who have enlisted in the ranks.

Among the new ministers, there is one whom I know well by reputation, and to some extent personally, Count Zurlo,* an excellent man, whom the King ought to have called in long ago; but already the Carbonari are calling for his head, and very likely he will have to be sacrificed. They are endeavoring, at Naples, to arm the most respectable citizens, and to turn the armed Carbonari out of the city. If they succeed in both attempts, and if General Pepe will lower the insolence of his tone, the government may maintain itself for a time till the Cortes assemble, when, indeed, the confusion of Babel will certainly commence. Meanwhile, however, they are risking the defection of most of the provinces.

We know as yet very few details of the horrors of Palermo.† The people at Naples seek to draw a vail over them. So much is certain, that the massacres lasted five days; the troops fired upon the people; the soldiers were fired on from the houses, and even the nuns poured boiling water on them. National hatred and party hatred have had free scope. According to the smallest estimate, three thousand persons have perished. Seven hundred galley-slaves were let loose to assist in the attack on the soldiers. These united themselves afterward with the dregs of the populace in committing all imaginable atrocities. The Prince della Cattolia, a man of great beneficence, was murdered, and his head and limbs carried about on pikes. All the gates were shut, and there was no bread left in the town. It is conjectured, that the soldiers who were taken prisoners have died of hunger. This is revolution for you!

And we should have had just such scenes to expect here, where, besides the other prisoners, and the innumerable criminals who go about at large, eight hundred are shut up in houses of correction; and there is no army, nor national guard, that can be depended on. The most frightful case of all would be if the revolution here broke out among the populace, who would instantly begin to plunder. A military revolution passes over quietly, as far as private individuals are concerned.

The Carbonari in Naples would have arrested and murdered all the Sicilians of rank. Some of them the government has been obliged to send to a fortress, in order to save their lives.

At Benevento, murders have been committed out of sheer wantonness. This, too, would never have reached our ears, but that Benevento is a Papal town. The proclamations issued by those who are in authority there,

* He had been minister under Murat.

† The Sicilians did not trust the new constitutional government, and wished for the independence of Sicily. Their resistance continued for some time.

show them to be fellows of the lowest class; their chief had been previously in the galleys.

Under such circumstances, one can think of nothing else, and must be heavy-hearted. Then, too, there is the fear, which is becoming very general, that through the anarchy prevailing in Naples, the plague may be allowed to spread from Majorca to Italy. It is raging to a fearful extent in that island; whole villages have been depopulated, and the houses destroyed since by fire. But the *cordon* has been broken, and thus the whole island is probably infected.

It was most intensely hot weather here till Sunday evening, 30° Reaumur, in the sun up to 45°; and we have had no rain for two months. Either from this, or accidentally, or from incendiarism, some woods have caught fire; more than two square German miles, containing 25,000 olive trees, vineyards, &c., have been laid in ashes.

Under such circumstances, I have to conduct a negotiation, the issue of which would be problematical, even if every thing were quiet; for which no one here has now any attention to spare, and at which I am nevertheless obliged to work as arduously, under the burden of the oppressive heat, as if we could look forward to a long and secure future. I have succeeded very well with the principal part of the business, but I have worked myself almost ill with it.

......Moltke went to Naples some time since. Charles seems to be a noble-minded youth.

CCLXVI.

ROME, 23*d September*, 1820.

You will ascribe it to the disturbances and my interruptions that I did not write last week.

Gretchen will tell you with her own hand about herself and our little Lucia. Amelia, sweet child, grows more and more affectionate in her ways. Marcus is always a source of joy to us. His nature is thoroughly good, and his faculties become more and more harmonious as they develop themselves. He has a very quick understanding.......

You inquire the origin of the Carbonari. They were originally nothing more than a development of freemasonry, and it might perhaps be said that all the freemasons in Italy are Carbonari, or Guelphs, or Adolphs, &c., though the converse would not hold good; for the derived associations have attained a much wider extent than the parent society. When the French invaded Italy in 1796, and occupied Rome in 1798, Naples in 1799, the revolution had been prepared in the lodges of the freemasons, and, with a few exceptions, all the freemasons declared for it. The generation who were then growing up, without affection for any thing, striving only after commotion, still harbored under the French rule a longing for ferment and change, while the elder generation, especially those whom we term cultivated people, attached themselves with joy to the government of Bonaparte, whose legislation afforded them the realization of all that according to their system they demanded as that without which there can be no salvation; viz.: new codes of law, equal inheritance, the removal of all corporations, convents, &c.; some of which measures were wholesome, some injudicious, and some vitally pernicious. When the name Carbonari came into use, I do not know; but the class already existed in the provinces under Murat. They did not, however, attain much importance till afterward, when they were joined by the party of Murat, which certainly was a curious amalgamation. They have the greatest variety of objects, from the unity of all Italy under a Bonapartean, to her dissolution into a federative republic. Of course, by far the majority of them simply follow their leaders blindfold, and large numbers have no object, that is, they only desire anarchy. The tendency to a federative republic prevails, however, to the greatest extent among those who have the most practical truth in their views, as it does in Spain and Portugal, which the revolutionists would divide into seven republics. To this the armies are opposed, except in so far as their chiefs may influence them on the condition of becoming presidents themselves. The conspiracy lately discovered at Naples to murder the ministers, shows what we have to expect when the parliament shall be assembled. There are numbers of the clergy among the Carbonari, especially monks, who lost their taste for a conventual life during the secularization; they have many members, too, among the inferior nobility. A part of the higher nobles were with them also at first, attracted by the promise of an aristocratic constitution.

Our baby will be christened to-morrow in our chapel. She will be called Lucia Dorothea Elizabeth. Freddy, Cornelius, the Göschens, and the Bunsens are her sponsors.

CCLXVII.

ROME, *14th October*, 1820.

The time of terror is still deferred from day to day; the danger of contagion and of an internal explosion is dispelled by the assembling of the Austrian troops, but that of an invasion, which should throw every thing into anarchy, is still as threatening as before; and, in such a case, one must either remain, or if flight were still possible, leave all one's possessions behind. Most people are careless enough to entertain no further apprehensions, because the invasion has been delayed beyond all expectation. Now it is certainly true that the Neapolitans, if they have good counsel among them, and remember the events of the war between 1798 and 1815, must halt their army on their own frontier, where they can take up very advantageous positions. But this would not prevent a corps of Carbonari, with their followers, from coming here, as soon as the Austrians advance from the opposite side, and such an incursion is naturally much worse than the entrance of a tolerably disciplined army. One great thing is, that fugitives from hence would find it very difficult, if not impossible, to leave in a hurry, because hundreds of carriages would quit the city at once, and not more than twenty post horses are provided at any stage; eighty could not possibly be mustered, for no horses are used in agriculture here, not to mention that the first four or five stages are in a desert. We must console ourselves with thinking that we might be still worse off. The Sardinian embassador, a man whom I like much, has seven children and a very aged father in his house; the latter is so weak that he can not bear the motion of a carriage, and has to be carried in a litter.

Will the Neapolitans offer a vigorous resistance? The army certainly will not; according to all appearances it will present in the field nothing but scenes of disgraceful cowardice; it is certain that the soldiers have already displayed timidity. So too the Palermitans behaved miserably in the field. In Naples itself, a similar resistance may be offered to that in Palermo, where horrors occurred over which it is sought to draw a vail. The upper classes had fled from the city, and the lowest populace certainly fought with an heroic fury. This class, however, took far more interest in the matter than the corresponding class in Naples; for although every one is now enrolling himself among the Carbonari, it is only done in order to obtain recommendations, favors, or impunity for crimes. There will be no lack of assassinations, and shots from behind hedges.

The leaders reckoned on an insurrection in France, or they would not have ventured so far. They are a thoroughly bad set, but we must not refuse to admit that in the capital the cause has been joined by men of talent, of whom there is not in general such a deficiency in Naples as in Rome.

God only knows what the issue will be; tragic it must be in any case. The bloodlessness of this last revolution is a delusive appearance. Blood enough has flowed in Sicily alone, and many single murders have occurred in Naples, but have been hushed up. In Spain, too, eight-and-twenty have been condemned to death at one time, and in many towns, fights have taken place which have been accompanied with loss of life; those executions are but the commencement. Paladini and his accomplices, who have been arrested at Naples, intended to assassinate the ministers. For the rest, in Spain civil war is inevitable; whole districts are opposed to the new order of things; whole provinces wish, on the contrary, for a federative republic, and on the third and following days, Riego and his companions intended to murder the King and Prince Carlos, and to depose the ministers; and at the same time, another revolutionary party planned to take advantage of the indignation excited by these machinations to put an end to the Cortes, and overthrow those same ministers. All hope of founding a system of order and law is lost in this horrible confusion. If the revolution take root, one can only look for a military rule, or, after long, unspeakable conflicts and misery, for a republic on the American footing, which is, in truth, the most unprofitable and distasteful to all the wants of our heart and intellect that can be imagined. All higher individuality, nay, all true private life disappears, where only low political interests are the ruling topic, and barbarism draws close upon us.

It is impossible but that the coquetting with Catholicism, which is now in fashion among a certain class, should come to an end; it is altogether too untruthful and revolting a comedy. Here, in Italy, faith in the Church has so completely died out, that the mummy would fall into dust at the first hard blow. But what will replace it, God knows, since there is not a human throb in the heart of these people, and not a want is felt beyond those of the animal nature. It is just the same among the educated classes in Spain, where religion is regarded as an insupportable yoke.

Some time ago, you called the present rapid spread of dishonesty, a consequence of the extinction of religion. I do not know whether the generation which we saw around us in our youth still retained, in general, much religion; they too, for the most part, had grown up in an age when the old respect for religion no longer subsisted. But they had grown up with habits of peaceable endurance, of economy, and moderation in their requirements, and were still imbued with the old maxims of integrity and honor, which must not be ascribed entirely to religious belief, but in great measure to their condition as citizens. When every one makes claims to a higher standing than he possesses, not from a correct comparison of himself with others and a consciousness of his true worth, but from ambition and unfounded presumption;—when all sense of duty is extinguished, and all family feeling vanishes;—when men are no longer intent upon laying a foundation for their children's future fortunes, but want to live luxuriously in show and splendor, the course of things must be what it is; and the unhappy generation who have been neglected by their parents, and grown up under the deadening influence of constant dissipation and amusement, sink into crime and barbarism. You can scarcely see a sadder sight than a great part of the youths in this city; they are, without exception, warm (so-called) friends of freedom; for freedom means with them to know nothing, and to learn nothing, and yet to be puffed up with conceit, and to do whatever their hearts lust after. Among the elder men, there is a poor sort of learning; still it is a sort, and gained by real work, though of a stupid kind. The younger men are much duller still. Old truths have become something quite foreign, and of new truths there is not even a germ, so that nothing but crude force can take effect—this alone has any truth to them.

The people can no longer afford to pay the taxes, and if an army make a revolution, unopposed by the people because they find their state unbearable, the first thing will be, that the soldiers will insist on an increase of their pay, as has taken place in Spain and Naples. The end may be, that the troops divide the land among themselves in districts, and give rise to a new feudalism.

I have brought my negotiation to a conclusion, with the exception of a few unimportant points on which a decision has to come from Berlin, and I may say a brilliant conclusion. Bernstorf* recognizes this warmly.

With regard to myself, I have no plans at all at present, and leave every thing to Providence. On Marcus's account I should now prefer staying here for another twelvemonth.......

CCLXVIII.

Rome, 28*th October*, 1820.

The month is drawing to a close without any calamity having overtaken us; and that is more than I, or probably you, had expected. Among the Roman populace itself, the fear of foreign troops has long since quenched all disposition to rash attempts; and, in Naples, the power of the Government, who expect nothing but great calamities from a war, is just now sufficient to restrain the madmen who expected all the advantages of plunder from an irruption into the neighboring country, without great peril, because they could run out again in time. Meanwhile the decisive event is approaching, and can hardly be delayed so long as a fortnight; and for this interval we must pray God for his merciful protection.

The annulling of the capitulation of Palermo, will have given your quick sense of justice a standard by which to judge of these revolutionists. The Sicilians demanded nothing more than their established right of a separate government—like Holstein from Denmark; and the decree that every town, great or small, should have an equal vote, was the most decisive refutation of the charge, that Palermo wanted the sovereignty of the island

* The Minister of Foreign Affairs.

for herself. Will this perfidious canceling of the articles of capitulation be also called in Germany a brave and splendid deed, as so many of a similar kind in the French Revolution have been? The interior of Sicily is still in full revolt, in which, moreover, the whole population takes part; while in Naples it is a mere fragment of the nation that takes any interest in the new *régime*, from which people neither expect a lightening of their burdens, nor the removal of any real grievance.

Stein is to arrive here in December—a meeting which I never expected. I have already received several letters from him, written in a mild and friendly tone. My only fear is, that the disorder in his eyes will have made him peevish; else, what would I not give, to see any one here with whom I could converse on the subjects that refresh my heart!

......Have any little pieces and fragments, written in his glorious youthful period, come to light in the new edition of Goethe? Any fragments of the Wandering Jew, or his Mahomet? Or the deified Demon of the Woods.

CCLXIX.

ROME, 11*th November*, 1820.

The post has brought me no letter from you, and now, all letters are opened.

You will perhaps have seen from the newspapers, that the Neapolitan government has given notice to the Roman, that their troops will advance as soon as the Austrians do so. No fault can reasonably be found with this. But thus the critical moment for us is at hand. Remain, the embassadors can not, if the Pope goes away, who, on his part, must not wait the arrival of revolutionary troops, and run the risk of being carried off. How desperate the chances of escape are, I have already told you. Our property must, in any case, be left at stake. The insubordination and want of discipline that already exists among the Neapolitan troops is unparalleled. By way of doing all that is possible, I have taken a trustworthy Piedmontese into my service, who must look after my things as far as he can.

The Neapolitan parliament are acting in the most senseless manner; their financial measures are wretched. Two motions alone display intelligence and insight, both made by Sicilians; one is for the repeal of the dues on consumption which appertain to the communes on feudal estates; the other, for the transfer of conventual estates to the parishes, and their division into small, hereditary farms. Both motions violate strict justice, but they would produce a salutary effect. That is not the case with such as spring from a wild revolutionary spirit. For instance, in Spain, two-thirds of the landed property are being brought into the market almost at one moment, because all the ecclesiastical estates, valued at 5000 milliards of francs, are to be sold, and the half of all entailed estates is made salable from the present time. By this measure, the value of all other estates is annihilated, as has been the case for some years past in Sicily, where, before the revolution broke out, estates to the value of 20,000,000 piastres were offered for sale, and not a single purchaser could be found. The State is about to sell the Church property by auction; and has declared that it will not pay interest upon its bonds, nor recognize them in any other way than by receiving them in payment at these sales. These bonds are, for the most part, the old paper currency, bearing interest, which came into the hands of the stockjobbers long ago, some of it at from 5 to 6 per cent. Large sums are in the hands of foreign stockjobbers, and such will now become purchasers, or let others buy for them. What a class of large landed proprietors will be thus created! As a sacrifice to the idol of uniformity, a general law respecting the corn trade has been made, of which the consequence is, that in Gallicia, which does not produce half the corn it consumes, prices have already doubled, because the entrance of foreign grain is prohibited till the average price of the whole country has reached a certain height; but now, as high roads and conveyances are wanting, and as the corn from the interior must be brought four hundred miles on mules before it reaches the coast, a famine must prevail in the northern provinces, till the prices there make that average when reckoned together with the extremely low prices in New Castile. And is such a government and legislation praiseworthy, and the harbinger of prosperity and freedom? But where revolutionists have the upper hand, such blundering and pernicious measures will never be absent. They must occur, because this party neither possess a general knowledge of the capabilities of a country, nor understand governing, and the inevitable consequences of this are measures that defeat their own end, and laws that bring calamity in their train. Smuggling and highway robbery are now carried on to an unexampled extent in Spain; this is acknowledged even by the liberal journals of Madrid. The worst enemies of the liberals could not say worse of them than they say of each other—that is, those who want places say of those who have them. All are asking for rewards, places, pensions. The year can scarcely end without a crisis.

In Naples, a week ago, all the troops were ordered out during two whole nights, cannons planted, &c. To prevent a counter revolution? Nothing of the kind—the police had had a desperate smuggler arrested. But as the fellow was master of a lodge of the Vendita, the Carbonari united to release him by force from the prison, and assassinate the ministers.

Whether the new electoral law in France will be sufficient to prevent shameless anarchy from obtaining a legitimate organ in the State, I do not know; experience alone can decide this point; but that without an alteration of the mischievous one that preceded it, a revolution would infallibly have occurred at the New Year, I was quite convinced, when it was still doubtful whether the new ministry would decide upon bringing in such a measure.

I have now seriously set about the continuation of my History; far more to distract my mind from its gloomy apprehensions respecting the state of public affairs, than in the hope of satisfying myself with what I write. I have already told you of the difficulties under which I labor with regard to it. I have likewise taken up the political writings of Plato again. No doubt I have often confessed to you already that I find little congeniality with him, and that the mixture of profundity and sophistry, of elevated thought and aimless oddity, in this tedious labyrinth torments me; and that the consolation that there exists an inner doctrine of which we see only the outward husk, does not satisfy me. It is, to say the least, a capricious whim to give us, not that doctrine, but a form at which we have a right to cavil. Meanwhile, I am seeking to divine this hidden meaning; and I have an episode in my mind in which I shall make use of it, either before or after the first Punic war, in order to exhibit the manners, the religion, and the jurisprudence of the earliest times of Rome. I shall afterward give the judgment which Plato and Aristotle, or their disciples, would, according to their own principles, have pronounced on Rome as it then was, if they had known it.

I have been induced to write down my ideas respecting a more effectual regulation of the universities. Essential improvements in them may be easily indicated.......

CCLXX.

ROME, *16th December*, 1820.

......You will have seen by the papers that the sovereigns have invited the King of Naples to a conference at Laybach. What ensued thereupon at Naples is briefly as follows. The ministers, with the exception of two Carbonari, Ricciardi and de Thomasis, were convinced of the mischievous effects of the revolution. This was above all the case with Count Zurlo, a very eminent man; he therefore induced the King and the majority of the ministers to issue a proclamation, whereby the King declared that he would grant a modified constitution, guaranteeing every thing that could be reasonably desired. He expected support; he has found himself mistaken. All have shown themselves cowards; and his colleagues have been impeached by the jacobinical ministers. Count Zurlo is charged with high treason, and is probably ruined. The King has left Naples, and war is inevitable.

Amidst these alarming prospects, this winter has been to me the least quiet that I have passed here. Prince Henry of Prussia, and the Princes of Denmark and Bavaria are here. All this gives occasion to parties and invitations from which I can not excuse myself; and the dinners always cost me the time from four to nine o'clock. M. Von Stein arrived here also last week.......

1821.

THE Austrians entered Rome, on their march to put down the Neapolitan constitution, in February, 1821. The doubts that were felt respecting their success were soon dispelled, by the unexampled cowardice of the Neapolitans, who fled at the first attack.

In the same month, Hardenberg, who was attending the conference at Laybach, unexpectedly came to Rome, and, during his short stay, the negotiations with the Papal government were brought to a satisfactory issue. The terms of the treaty were already settled before his arrival; nothing was wanting but its ratification. Niebuhr readily gave up the credit in the eyes of the world of having accomplished this transaction, for the sake of forwarding the business itself, and proposed, of his own accord, that Hardenberg should undertake the conclusion of the treaty.

It was stated in many public journals, that Niebuhr had spent four years in fruitless negotiations ; while Hardenberg found means to conclude a treaty in a few days. But whoever wrote or believed this can hardly have been acquainted with the nature of the negotiations, which included the entire regulation of the relations between the State and the Church of Rome, or they would surely not have supposed that subjects of such magnitude, and on which so many conflicting opinions and interests had to be consulted, could be settled in the course of a few days. Neither was it generally known that Niebuhr had waited nearly four years for his instructions, and it was forgotten that the negotiations were carried on at a time of extraordinary difficulty. It is rather to be wondered that they should have been accomplished at all at such a time, and Niebuhr himself always ascribed it to the personal friendship of the Pope and Cardinal Gonsalvi. He says, in one of his letters, "I have purchased this termination of the business with the sacrifice of personal considerations, and resigned the appearance of having had the honor to accomplish it. The minister of ecclesiastical affairs, however, knows and acknowledges that it is no slight matter to have achieved within eight months, what other embassadors have been working at in vain for four years. And at what a moment were our negotiations carried on !"

Niebuhr took an active part in the Topographical Description of Rome, undertaken by Bunsen and Brandis, in conjunction with Cotta. The work was executed by Platner, Bunsen, and some others. Niebuhr sketched the plan of the work, and promised a chapter, giving a general account of the topography of ancient Rome; but in the progress of the work, his assistance was claimed to a greater extent than he had foreseen, especially in all that related to antiquities.

Letters written in 1821.

CCLXXI.

TO MADAME HENSLER.

ROME, *10th February*, 1821.

I have only a few moments to write, but I must use them to tell you that, up to this time, no misfortune has befallen us, though the tidings that the Austrians had crossed the Po, arrived here so early as Tuesday, and must have reached Naples by Wednesday morning. According to this account, they might have been across the frontiers by this time. We can not infer any thing as to our safety, from the fact that nothing has yet taken place; but if another week pass over quietly, we are saved.

We are not decided whether to fly to Civita Vecchia, if the Pope goes thither, or to stay here for the sake of our children and property.

If regular troops come, I think we shall stay, but if mere rabble, we must certainly endeavor to escape. We hear that three French ships are coming to Civita Vecchia, on board which we shall be able to embark.

The Austrians can not be before our gates, at the earliest, sooner than the 22d instant. How we long now for the days to pass over! And thus life speeds away!

I gave Stein a beautiful entertainment yesterday, in which the singers of the Pope's chapel performed ancient music.

I have been much cheered by receiving a letter from old Peyron, at Turin, which he means to publish himself, and in which he not only quite takes my part, but attests that he did not discover the point in question till September, &c.*

CCLXXII.

ROME, *17th March*, 1821.

It must be three weeks since I last wrote to you. Even then, our immediate apprehensions and fears had been removed; only it hardly seemed possible that the war in Naples should not, at least to some extent, be carried on with the savage fury of a war of opinion; and as the means of attack would in that case be insufficient, we could not feel quite easy respecting our position. Never have more brilliant speeches been made than at Naples; the foreigners, especially the young men who had listened to the orations, were quite carried away, and saw in these Polichinellos the heroes of antiquity risen again. I, and all others who knew the Italians, made, indeed, great deductions, and thought very lightly of the moral worth of those who delivered these splendid orations; but still we fancied it possible that the sectarian organization in particular might have enkindled a fanaticism, which the extraordinarily ill-judged proceedings on the other side could not fail greatly to promote. That the whole had been such a mere miserable piece of lies and mouthing, no one ever dreamed. Even the official reports do not place the matter in so strong a light as truth deserves. In the engagement of Rieti, each side may have lost, perhaps, from fifty to seventy men. As the Austrians were very weak, they were not even able to pursue the enemy; and after this affair the whole army of General Pepe dispersed so completely, that only a part of two regiments which had not been in the engagement, but stood at some distance, threw themselves into Pescara; Pepe himself arrived at Castel Saegro on the 11th, without a single soldier. Between Rieti and Aquila there are three formidable passes, Borghetto, Antrodoco, and Madonna di Grotta, where a handful of men could arrest an army. These were left so completely undefended, that the Austrians had only one man wounded, and their opponents not more. The Neapolitans help themselves with their Italian untruthfulness, and are not ashamed nor afraid to say in their journals, that

* Referring to the dispute with Mai.

Antrodoco was taken by superior numbers, after a most heroic resistance. To-morrow, or at furthest the day after, the other army on the Garigliano will be attacked. It is already much weakened by desertion, at least, compared to what it ought to be to resist the attacking army, and all accounts agree in stating that the soldiers will not fight, and that the militia are only waiting for an opportunity to disband and run home. The corps, of which we may assume that they consist of Carbonari, those, for instance, under Avellino and Salerno, show themselves just as cowardly, and desert just as much as the rest; indeed, they were the first to set the example. Those with the high-sounding names—the Sacred Squadron, the modern Fabii, the three hundred Bruttii, who had entreated the privilege of occupying the posts of greatest danger, have never made their appearance at all, but have completely dispersed themselves.

One trait more. The robbers, who a short time since carried off the boys belonging to the Seminarium at Terracina, and murdered two of them in cold blood, after having received three thousand piastres for their ransom, have been pardoned, and formed into a corps; their chief had made it an indispensable condition that the regimental band should conduct him from Fondi, and this has been done. Between Aquila and Rieti, the Neapolitan troops have plundered every thing in their own country, not only in their flight, but also on the march home.

A very different event from the miserable Neapolitan revolution, which ten thousand men could have put down in September (even now only five battalions have been under fire), is the revolt in Piedmont, which we learnt yesterday, just when we thought that the termination of the first farce had secured our safety for the remainder of our stay here. The Piedmontese are a brave and estimable people, but fearfully passionate, and we can not conceal from ourselves that this incident may lead to incalculable consequences. The Austrians were only prevented by an accident from opening the campaign a week sooner; had they done so (since the result would no doubt have been the same), one might wager any thing that the conspirators in Piedmont would have relinquished their enterprise. God knows what it will come to now!

When you see the blind political faith of young men, in other respects well meaning and intelligent, you can not help perceiving that with this generation wisdom itself could not succeed in averting a revolution. But the course along which their blindness impels them is one, at the end of which, as has been truly said by M. Von Stein, the Jews will be the ruling class, the husbandman a clown, and the artisan a bungler; where all ties will be dissolved, and the sword alone will be the ultimate authority; but for poor Germany, it will be the sword of the foreigners, who will divide her.

The time is gradually approaching, when the strangers would forsake Rome and we should have quiet, if revolution and war were not raging around us. Still, I will not despair of being able to return afterward to quiet and my salutary studies. At all events, the festivities and parties are leaving off, with which we occupied ourselves at a time when every one ought to retire into the most solemn silence. Stein will probably remain here another month. All his old affection for me has re-awakened, and mine was easily revived, so that we are on a footing of cordial friendship. Old age becomes him well, and I can only think of him with tender sadness; it is most likely the last time that we shall see each other, and I thank God that we have met thus.

The children are well and good. Marcus seemed for a time inclined to be delicate. Perhaps I worked his head too hard: I have relaxed a little in this respect. The difficulties of reading are overcome; and if the love of reading awakens later in him than in me, I shall not consider it any misfortune to him.

Gretchen suffers again from time to time with her eyes, and does so at the present moment. How are all your people? I think of them with anxiety. God protect you!

You will most likely have learnt from the journals that the Chancellor of State has arrived here, accompanied by officers of his department. I only heard of it two days before his arrival. I have given him a splendid entertainment, which I dare say he would very willingly have dispensed with; but if it had not been done all the world would have censured me. Thus are we obliged to plague each other, out of conventionalism and politeness! He will leave again in four or five days. Bartholdy was in Naples, but has been summoned.

I have heard from Sch——, who accompanies Hardenberg, that the clergyman at Sesenheim was his uncle, and had four daughters; the unhappy, but universally beloved, Frederike died a few years ago. Her brother, a respectable clergyman, is also dead. She lived to see the publication of Goethe's life; whether she read it, he does not know.

CCLXXIII.

TO NICOLOVIUS.

ROME, 28*th March*, 1821.

Dearest friend, embrace me; the negotiation is concluded, concluded with success, and now we are proceeding to draw up the bull, which I hope will be issued in a month. May Heaven only guide the thoughts of Monsignor M. by a right lively representation of the more or less costly snuff-box that awaits him, and direct both our pens, so that no outcry may be raised against the bull at the last moment! You will learn every thing through Count Bernstorf.

Hardenberg's journey hither has really been a blessing; it cost me nothing more than the sacrifice of allowing him to take the credit of having brought the affair to a settlement. And as he will thereby be bound to its execution and results, I incited Cardinal Gonsalvi to speak to him in my presence, as if it were his work, and to express it in his note.

Now, when the matter has to be carried out, your ministry can do much; and I have assured the Pope that he may rely upon honest intentions.

Only above all make haste with all your proposals respecting appointments. That the Roman cabinet have accepted so long a delay is a brilliant proof of the confidence which they place in our good-will.

Your letter, my dear friend, belongs to the rewards which Heaven has accorded to my efforts. I thank you a thousand times for it in my own and Gretchen's name. But I always stand in such deep self-abasement before your humility, and your over-estimate of me. What am I? a decayed wreck. If it were not for the children I should sigh, my God, when wilt thou break it up!

However, I rejoice in the success of my undertaking. I began it without any hope of attaining my end. Now we are the first in the field.

How long I shall remain here, as my presence will soon be no longer necessary (I allow to myself that it has been useful, that with the same instructions the business might have foundered), who can tell? For now I can take my leave with a good conscience, if I meet with any new *dégoûts*. I have begged the Chancellor—and I think it will tally with your wishes—to have a large picture painted by the very eminent artist, Philip Veit, as a present to the cathedral of Cologne, on occasion of the restoration of the Archbishopric. I should propose to Veit, as a subject, either the presentation of the relics of the Three Kings to the deputies of Cologne by the Emperor Frederick Barbarossa, after the taking of Milan, or the Vision of Count William of Jülich.

I can not give any orders for pictures now, for I give all that I can spare to my poor dear S.* How I should like to see him a bishop!

As soon as the bull has been dispatched, I shall hasten to Naples. At present, you can have an Austrian escort for the whole distance, and General Frimont will no doubt, in case of necessity, open every thing that would otherwise be inaccessible to me, with his grenadiers.

The issue of events at Naples has exhibited the baseness of these Italians in its proper colors. Their sole moral incentive is vanity, and vanity is not bullet-proof.

It would be different in Spain, and yet even there you might demolish every thing with thirty thousand men.

We have disgraceful contemporaries. Our poor children! We rejoice heartily as your true friends in all the good news that you tell us of your family, and mourn in sympathy with our dear friends the Göschens.

Accept love yourself from Gretchen, and give our united kind regards to your family and all friends. Excuse haste, and embrace me once more.

Your faithful Niebuhr.

CCLXXIV.

TO MADAME HENSLER.

Rome, *7th April*, 1821.

It grieved me much not to write to you last week, but it was impossible. Happily, you could not have made yourself anxious about us for some time past. But I should so have liked to have written to you, because I was full of joy at having concluded my important negotiations on ecclesiastical affairs; concluded, not so but that there is much to do in carrying out details, but still so far that we have come to an agreement on all essential points, and only some quite unforeseen circumstance, such as, for instance, the death of the Pope before the completion of the bulls, could interfere with the matter.

Now since we must assume that good may arise from this settlement—and at least it is certain that the prolongation of the present state of things would involve actual evil—it would have been very painful to me if I had not been able to accomplish this business. And how often, and for how many reasons this seemed likely!

It contributes to improve my position as regards the social annoyances which I have to suffer even now from the impertinence of a few fools, that

* Schmieder.

the Emperor of Austria has presented me with the grand cross of the Leo pold Order. You know that probably there are not many who care less about these things than myself, and that I know what is true honor. Would to God that I had never been placed in any position where this is insufficient! But I have been drifted into another sphere, and am compelled to live among people, to whom all that would have secured me due appreciation among the highest class, counts for nothing; who, in fact, rather deem my learning and studies unbecoming my position, and a thing to be pardoned. In this place I have gradually worked my way up to influence and consideration, and have not often occasion to feel the want of it; still indications are now and then given, and were formerly much more frequently perceptible, of contempt for my station and plain name, which will be put an end to by such marks of distinction. Had not Count Blacas,* who is regarded in Germany as the most extreme aristocrat, displayed the most friendly feeling toward me from the very beginning of my residence here, and treated me quite as his equal, my position in these circles as a commoner would have been much more unpleasant even than it has been.

Stein has given me his portrait. It is a drawing, and very like him. He much preferred my house to any other during his stay here. Old age has made him very amiable. May his remaining years be happy! When he bid Marcus good-night yesterday evening, he kissed and stroked him; I remember that his own children only used to kiss his hand. Thank God that I shall part from him with this remembrance! To-morrow, I shall accompany him at his request as far as Tivoli.

Marcus is losing his robust appearance; he has no signs of ill-health; still it makes me uneasy.

The editor of the "Independente," one of the most violent Neapolitan journals, is now contractor for the Austrian army. Thus do these fellows change their colors when they see any advantage to be gained by it. . . . . .

CCLXXV.

ROME, 28*th April*, 1821.

Last week I received your letter, in which you speak of the anxiety that the Piedmontese insurrection has caused you on our account. Your care for us has touched me deeply.

The occurrences in Piedmont appear to us of importance, only because we know that they owe their origin to the leaders of the Left in France, and that there was a wish to make the experiment of a revolution in France itself. The plans for such an event had been so completely worked out, that in a letter from Madrid of the 24th of March, which has been delayed on the road and has only just been communicated to me, it is stated that this revolution has been arranged with the knowledge and sympathy of the heads of the Cortes, and in particular of the Count Toreno, and would break out in a few days, if it had not broken out already.

For the rest, I should have expected that the Piedmontese would have shown firmness in the execution of their rash enterprise; but although the conspirators were numerous, considered as such, they formed an infinitely small part of the nation, which did not expect any good from the hands of dissolute and frivolous young officers, nor from any of these ambitious men.

* The French embassador.

Thus these good-for-nothing fellows have brought an inexpressible calamity on their country, in the shape of foreign occupation, and the exchange of a narrow-minded but honest and well-intentioned king, for a prince who will not govern mildly. Who would have thought that we should live to see those revolts of arrogant soldiers, who, after giving away thrones, fled, or practiced some new treachery, which characterize the worst periods of ancient history, and were hitherto unknown in recent times?

The Spanish ships which took on board the fugitives from Naples, have landed them at Ischia, probably because they had no money. In Spain, the minister of finance has detected the greatest dishonesty in his predecessor, and the deficit is estimated at 28,000,000 piastres! And this is the minister of finance on account of whose removal, with his colleagues, the Cortes wished to excite a new revolution, and may perhaps do it yet!

It is true that in most places it is only evil in conflict with evil, but that evil which establishes its empire with the utmost tyranny, and founds its right on false pretensions to moral and intellectual eminence, is far more hateful to me, because far more pernicious, than that which takes its stand, almost stupidly and without thought, on possession, and for the rest, interferes with no one else in his possessions. The quiet of summer is now approaching, and the crowd of foreigners is dispersing. Stein is gone to Naples.......

CCLXXVI.

Albano, 11*th May*, 1821.

......I have formed a very interesting acquaintance with Lord Colchester; indeed, it has come to that mutual feeling of attachment which the acquaintanceships formed in later life seldom exceed. With me he threw off his usual silence and reserve. He earnestly wishes that I might come to London as embassador; but even if this could be brought about, I feel that the whole mode of life involved by such a vocation is injurious to me.

I think I have never told you, that in the beginning of the winter, the celebrated Countess of Albany, Alfieri's friend, born Princess Stolberg, was here; she is intellectual enough to make it worth one's while to become acquainted with her. What has reminded me of it is, that the Pretender, her husband, once fitted up and lived in the house which we are now occupying at Albano. After I had seen her, I made a good many inquiries about her, and certainly learnt much that justifies what we are so often compelled to feel, namely, that eminent and varied talents by no means always coincide with moral worth. Her husband abandoned himself to drinking, because she drove him to despair by her infatuation for Alfieri; and she did not even remain faithful to Alfieri to the last, although she has erected a magnificent monument to his memory with the ostentation of the widow of a celebrated man. Though very old now, you may still call her beautiful.......

CCLXXVII.

Rome, 11*th August*, 1821.

This time I have long remained in your debt for your last dear letter, and yet it is long since any letter has rejoiced me so much.

The children are my delight, and when one has seen them in danger, one's anxiety lasts long after the danger is over. Marcus has not indeed got rid of his complaint, and the least trifle aggravates it; still he has much improved, and is gaining flesh. Our Amelia has been threatened with an attack of dysentery lately, but the danger has been averted. Amelia, too, clings to us now much more than she did, and is growing a very sweet child; her obstinacy is gradually giving way, and she is learning to obey without ill-humor. We do not tease her with lessons yet, and it will be a great difficulty with her, too; she is so lively and volatile. Marcus could learn any thing if he did not prefer any kind of motion to sitting still. We talk German with him a good deal now, and he understands every thing. Lucia runs alone, and is very quick. She is very fond of her brother.

Certainly, my attention, too, is fixed upon Greece. I curse Ypsilanti's enterprise, which has sacrificed the lives of thousands in vain, and abandoned many to a still worse fate. God grant that the Emperor Alexander may fulfill his noble idea of taking nothing for himself, but founding an independent State there, against whose existence no one could have the face to raise an opposition. Meanwhile, there is only one form under which the Greeks and the other tribes can have a national existence—that of antiquity and the middle ages, a sovereign whose powers are undefined, but who allows each tribe and each community to do what they think best with respect to their internal affairs, on condition that they perform fixed services in war, and pay certain imposts. It would be a most important and advantageous revolution for Europe. Millions could settle in the waste lands of the most highly-favored countries, and the emigration now turned toward America, and lost to Europe, might create a new source of strength to the latter. Who knows how far into the interior Asia might not become European in time?

CCLXXVIII.

ROME, 16*th August*, 1821.

I only write to you to-day to impart my consolation to you. If I can think of any thing besides my boy, it is the reports from the Archipelago. We have as yet no certainty that the report of the naval battle before Mitylene is true; but the accounts of it from Corfu are of a character that renders it credible. If so, though these Greek mariners, taken singly, are nothing better than pirates, and no one who loves his life will embark in a ship of Hydra with any tempting property, I respect them notwithstanding, and begin to expect something from them. The deed must prove the man. It was the Dutch corsairs, accustomed to plunder friend and foe, who, in 1572, took Briel, and founded the republic. A Greek republic is a chimera, but a State may very likely spring up there; and my imagination pursues the endless developments of the events which may result from the dissolution of the Turkish empire, and the opening of Asia Minor and Syria to European colonization. Only I do not see how a nation like the Greeks will allow themselves to be governed. If you attempt to make them European, they will become absolutely worthless. I imagine German colonies in Bithynia, &c.

CCLXXIX.

TO NICOLOVIUS.

ROME, 15*th September*, 1821.

I give you my special thanks for the first volume of Hamann's* writings. O that I may not have to receive the rest in this den! You can not imagine how painfully we lonely and forsaken creatures feel the want of any one with whom we can hold a conversation; how often, of a Sunday evening for instance, we are reminded that we are in Tomi, and sigh, Oh, if we could but have the Göschens, Nicolovius, or Savigny with us for an evening! Hamann's writings make me feel the want of you with tenfold acuteness, though one evening would not be sufficient to say all we should have to say about them. He who looks on every thing from a historical point of view, finds himself in a former and remarkable world as he reads them. It is another question—and one which before I was acquainted with these writings, I had not expected to find myself forced to ask—whether their publication is likely to prove beneficial—I mean with a public such as ours is at the present day. For the moment, a certain coquetting with pietism seems to be in fashion with a considerable number of the younger generation—not altogether from hypocrisy and vanity, but with very few from inward and honest feeling. Our age demands glaring colors and shrill sounds, now of one kind, now of another. This fashion will not last long, but the moment is unfavorable for the appearance of any thing that gives it authority, because people do not understand such a work. But my anxiety extends beyond the present moment; I fear lest the generation, who can not in the least understand Hamann and the times in which he flourished, should take lasting offense at this representation of a rude and shaggy form. I had not read the biography, when I expressed the wish that it might appear as it was; and never dreamed of the publication of a correspondence such as that with Lindner. I confess to you that I would now give much, that any one who was competent—you above all—should have worked up the two, the biography and the letters, into a single life of Hamann, by which means much that must now be misunderstood by nine hundred and ninety-nine out of a thousand, would have been rendered intelligible, and much that is painful would have been avoided. Few will know how Hamann—evidently from his very childhood—grew up and took root in the poetical pietism then prevailing at Königsberg; and how in the crisis that took place in him in London, *such* a religion might rise even to fanaticism and fierceness, without the slightest admixture of affectation, and should remain the permanent key-note of his soul. Does it displease you, my friend, that I say *even to fierceness?* I confess to you that this is my feeling with regard to his connection with the Behrens family, and for my justification let me tell you, that Gretchen's feelings recoil from it no

* Hamann was a celebrated and profound, but obscure writer on theological and philosophical subjects, of the last century, and an opponent of Kant; he was born, and spent the great part of his life in Königsberg, and was an intimate friend of Herder and Jacobi, on the former of whom, especially, he exercised great influence in early life. The character of his theology is sufficiently apparent from Niebuhr's letters. His detached Essays and Letters have been collected and published by Roth, 1821–1825. He never wrote any comprehensive work. To characterize at once his almost prophetical insight, and the obscurity of his style, he was called the Magus of the North.

less than my own. This renunciation of all gratitude, these despotic pretensions, this excessive petulance, appear to us merely other phases of the demoniacal nature which appears in such a fearful shape in G., indeed, still more frightful, because the conscience of the man who has abandoned himself to these impulses, approves his conduct and confirms him in it. I turn now to another consideration. If all extraordinary persons were exhibited to the very recesses of their soul, by the publication of their correspondence, they would be as it were on a footing of equality, and one might let one after another appear, without lowering any relatively. As it is, this is not the case; indeed, I say, God be thanked that it is not! It is not well that the world should see into the inmost soul of every man, and both the world and history would be unendurable if it could. There are garments of the soul which you should no more strip off than those of the body; and a biography that vails nothing is neither right nor wholesome.

In one respect, at least, this history when understood clearly, and in its details is useful—that it teaches us how even the greatest and most exalted spirits of our human race are ignorant how accidentally their eye has assumed the form through which they see, while from the extreme intensity of their consciousness, they authoritatively demand that every one shall see as they do. He who has not recognized this quite distinctly and in many instances, may be subjugated by the presence of a mighty intellect, that casts the most intense passion into a given form; and the immediate contemplation of the daily intellectual life of a powerful man, has all the injurious effect upon an immature mind, of novel-reading upon a weak girl. The most captivating novels are those which are wholly or mostly written in the form of letters. It is these which stir the emotions, and historical composition which deserves the name, speaks in discourses; it is not the actions, but the speeches and the thought, which touch our hearts. If I had the energy which I have not, I would, if only by way of proof, relate what might inflame the imagination in the most dangerous way, so that it should not move you; and then again, sway the imagination of my readers so that they should espouse the party of Marius or Sulla; so that they should not scruple at the bloodshed, but have the guilt of all that flowed upon their consciences.......

CCLXXX.

TO MADAME HENSLER.

ROME, *29th September*, 1821.

Your last letter affected me deeply in more than one way. When we can no longer attain, or no longer endure a life of exciting emotion and action, the only thing left us to wish for is peace and quiet. This applies to me personally, as well as to public life at the present day.

I meant to write to you a short time ago about Hamann's works, and the impression they made upon me. Hitherto our feelings have harmonized, or if not at first, have, with very rare exceptions, been brought into harmony when we have explained ourselves. I was anxious to know whether our inward agreement would be interrupted on this remarkable occasion. I hope not. You will doubtless have read his writings. Now, I ask you, do you sympathize with them? Are you glad to possess them?

Much about Hamann has been made clearer to me. I understand now the origin of the first, and perhaps the most remarkable of his writings, of which I before knew nothing. But it was not enough for me to perceive that the original mould of his mind was that of a giant, who had survived a perished race, and lived on in an utterly different age of the world? It was indeed necessary to know something of that earlier race, and to understand how it lived in the pietism, which, in Königsberg, more than any where else, had acquired a strong and living power over men; the traces and traditions of which we see in Hippel's writings, and amidst whose influences Hamann too grew up.

But what do we gain by the publishing of his life and letters? Or, rather, how much do we not lose by the dispersion of the mist that concealed the personality of this mysterious man? We see a young man, whose aspirations and struggles the present generation will not be able to understand nor even to divine, giving a loose to his inclinations, neglecting, in the most careless and unconscientious manner, his obligations toward his unselfish and loving friends, swimming with the stream of his passions, and when at last, the difficulties of his desperate position recall his earlier pietistic feelings, yet not led back by them in the least to his duties toward his fellow-creatures. We see him, on his return, despising the same friends in his spiritual pride, accepting their benefits while hating and condemning them, yet still reserving the privilege of returning to them, whenever necessity may drive him to such a course. Apart from all the unhappy influences which this book may and will exercise over perverted minds, allowing that such temporary effects are not to be taken into account (which I am less willing to concede the older I become, and the longer and more attentively I regard the varied forms which perverted views assume), how does he appear to us? As a man possessed by a demon, who believes himself called to rule despotically. From his earliest childhood, he had been accustomed to this pietistic interpretation of the Bible, to look on it as a handbook for every event of life; in moments when his whole nature had been overwhelmed by distress, difficulty, and remorse, it had seized hold of his mind with a force which influenced his whole life; but this supposed sanctification had no effect on his actions. The correctness of these views of the Scriptures is not affected in the slightest degree, practically or historically, by this Life. God grant that no one may assert that it is! His mind was beyond all question one of the deepest and most powerful that Germany ever produced, and his sayings, clothed in the language which had become a second nature to him, assumed the coloring and mystery of oracles. The unfettered mind, which is neither frightened nor enslaved by formulas, extracts the living power from these oracular sayings, without regard to their form, which it is absolutely impossible for any man fully to accept, unless he has a peculiar cast of thought, and has been brought up in a peculiar atmosphere. Now, however, it is made clear to us, that Hamann himself regarded this form as the true essence, and thus we have become vitally estranged from him. No one perhaps can fully comprehend how fearful this pietism is, who has not often been forced to hear that all human virtues are damnable, nay, are even dangerous, and that the most sinful human being who has true faith in Christ's redemption, stands infinitely nearer to the Saviour, than the man who is, according to human ideas, the noblest and most virtuous, but without that self-loathing.

I maintain that, as a general rule, the letters which lay bare the inmost being of an extraordinary, but not saintlike man, should never be published. For his sake they ought not to be given to the world, because it is not good nor just to exhibit one isolated soul naked, while the immense majority are not so; nor for the sake of others, because what is concealed by the relations of life ought not to be laid bare. Why was not his life written as it might have been told?

The most remarkable part of the book to me is that passage from St. Augustine, which I must either have passed over, or not yet comprehended, when I read the Confessions. I would recommend it to the consideration of those who would restore the Church by means of outward formulas. Let them reflect why it was, that the most profound among all the Fathers wished so to express himself on matters of doctrine, that every man might find his own belief, if it were not an utterly false one, in his words.

I have now begun to teach Marcus Latin by conversation, and he learns very well......

CCLXXXI.

ROME, *29th December*, 1821.

For the sixth time we are ending our year at Rome. Meanwhile time exercises his power, and without ceasing to be, and to feel ourselves strangers in this place, we are also becoming estranged from our own country. Thus life passes away, and one feels that it passes miserably; and yet I can not agree with the pious persons who call life a miserable thing in itself. I know, on the contrary, that it becomes miserable only through our own follies, faults, and weaknesses; and that a life wrought into beauty and harmony is a blessing possible not merely in dreams......During this winter my health has not been worth much, though I could not exactly call myself ill. I want the refreshment of sympathy, without which I always feel exhausted, and can not be really healthy, and which in itself is a sufficient recompense to me for some degree of physical indisposition.

......It gives me very great pleasure that you agree with me as to the publication of Hamann's letters. It struck me, too, how deeply-rooted the acquaintanceships of his youth must have been. At that time there was nothing in Germany but oak trees and creepers; now there are only half-grown trees, blown awry by the winds.

1822.

IN February, 1822, Niebuhr's wife bore him a third daughter. Since the chief object of his mission was now attained, and the health of his wife rather grew worse than better, he determined to request his recall. The Minister of his department advised him, however, in the first instance, only to ask for a year's furlough, and thus to leave the way open for his return, if he should think it desirable at the end of that time. And certainly, as far as he was personally concerned, he might probably have remained many years longer in Rome, as is shown by his letters of the preceding year. He had become acclimatized, and accustomed to the mode of life in Rome, and now looked forward to a time of greater repose, in which he might devote himself with zeal to his studies. For, however far his course of life might seem to carry him from his own peculiar pursuits, he always retained his old partiality for them, and anticipated some future time when he might return to them. His high views of their true principles and method may be seen from a letter, inserted at the close of the extracts belonging to this year, and entitled—"A letter to a young man who wished to devote himself to Philology." It was written in the course of this summer, and addressed to a young friend of his, whom he believed to be pursuing an erroneous path.

In August, 1822, Niebuhr had to engage in a very unpleasant contest on behalf of the Protestants living in Rome. A blindly fanatical, priestly party, was bent on the demolition of the Protestant burial-ground. Niebuhr felt himself bound to resist this outrage to the feelings of his fellow-worshipers with all his might, and to assist his friend Lord Colchester, who shared his efforts in the cause. He spent part of this summer in Albano, and made a little excursion besides to Tivoli, with Chevalier Bunsen and M. Lieber, whom, on his return from Greece, he had engaged as tutor to his son.

In November, the King of Prussia paid a short visit to Rome, with a small retinue. Niebuhr and Baron Alexander von Humboldt accompanied him to the most celebrated spots in the city and its neighborhood. Several of Niebuhr's old friends were in the King's suite, so that he had the satisfaction of renewing his intercourse with them for a short interval.

He also derived much enjoyment this winter from the society of Messrs. Pertz and Bluhme, who had been sent to Rome to prosecute researches into ancient MSS., and were able to enter into the literary subjects which engaged Niebuhr's attention.

Meanwhile, Niebuhr sent in a request, agreeably to the advice of the Minister for Foreign Affairs, that he might either be recalled, or receive leave of absence in the following spring. The latter was granted him, and he thankfully accepted it, although he was persuaded that his wife's state of health, as well as his views with regard to their son, would prevent him from ever returning to Rome. The child's attachment to the place was so great, as to make his father fear that if he remained longer there, he would never feel at home in Germany. This consideration, joined to the difficulty of educating him in Rome in the manner he wished and intended, had a great influence upon Niebuhr's decision not to return thither. Indeed, after he became a father, Niebuhr considered the training of his children, especially of his son, as the most imperative duty of his life, to which all other considerations, except that of very evident and important service to his country, ought to be subordinated. In ordinary times, he placed private duties above public ones. No one, who has read his life thus far, will suspect him of undervaluing the latter.

Before leaving Italy Niebuhr wished to see Naples, and to take leave of his friend De Serre, who was now embassador at that court. As the time of his departure drew near, Niebuhr felt how much it cost him to forsake Rome. There was, indeed, much in his circumstances that did not harmonize with his peculiar tastes; but, on the other hand, he felt that he was giving up an independent, and in many respects advantageous position, and entering on a period of uncertainty.

Thus, but for the sake of his family, he would not have quitted Rome for ever. His friends and children exclaim with sorrow, "Oh that he had remained, and then perhaps he would yet be spared to us!"

Letters written in 1822.

CCLXXXII.

TO MADAME HENSLER.

ROME, 19*th January*, 1822.

......We have daily proofs of Marcus's noble nature; still I am well aware that this affords us no guarantee unless it be guided with the most watchful care. I trust he will never turn out a conceited, shallow fool, nor a man who is himself contented with superficiality, and assumes an appearance to throw dust in the eyes of others. I could never be consoled, if I were one day to see him go out into the world as an arrogant young collegian, or an empty blockhead and shallow prater, or as a vain fool seeking to make himself of importance, not by real ability, but by means of unwarranted pretensions or affectation, which is the case with so many of our young people nowadays. Either they are puffed up with conceit, and want to make reforms, and think themselves qualified to pronounce on all subjects, and look down on people the latchet of whose shoe they are not worthy to unloose; or if they do not belong to this party, they know nothing, learn nothing, can not set about any thing with earnestness and capability, and assume the show of refinement—of course only on the outside—and think that if they can but shine in their own opinion, and in the empty assemblies of fashionable life, they will have gained all they need, and are perfectly prepared to take a standing in the world. I succeed with teaching as well as I could have ventured to hope. He already knows no inconsiderable number of Latin words, and he understands grammar so well that I can now set him to learn parts of the conjugations without their teasing him like dead matter; he divines many of the forms, from his own feeling. I am reading with him selected chapters from Hygin's Mythologicum—a book which, perhaps, it is not easy to use for this purpose, and which yet is more suited to it than any other, from the absence of formal periods, and the interest of the narrative. For German, I write fragments of the Greek mythology for him. I began with the history of the Argonauts; I have now got to the history of Hercules. I give every thing in a very free and picturesque style, so that it is as exciting as poetry to him; and, in fact, he reads it with such delight that we are often interrupted by his cries of joy. The child is quite devoted to me; but this educating costs me a great deal of time. However, I have had my share of life, and I shall consider it as a reward for my labors if this young life be as fully and richly developed as lies within my power.

Unexpected thoughts often escape him. Two days ago he was sitting beside me, and began—"Father, the ancients believed in the old gods; but still they believed also in the true God. The old gods were just like men."......

CCLXXXIII.

Rome, *6th April*, 1822.

Again your longed-for letter has failed to reach me.......

Marcus is reading Diodati's beautiful (Protestant) Bible (the Gospels), and he reads it with lively interest. He draws very carefully.

I spoke to you, a little while ago, of the ill-fated men who are returning in shoals from Greece. Till now, my intercourse with them has been almost confined to one individual, who is a very well-intentioned youth, a Rhinelander, who had served in the Landwehr. He and a few Saxons curse the pamphlets, and all the rest of the rhodomontade, which had deluded them into the idea, that a Greek army of 30,000 men was in the field, and only required to be officered, &c. They found no army, and instead of receiving any pay, were obliged to sell every thing they had for the necessaries of life. Their presence was not all desired, and they might thank God if they could but find means to get back again. My acquaintances confess that I told them all this beforehand; thus, for instance, that, by Greek soldiers, they must only understand associated bands of Klephthi (robbers), who would be joined in certain cases by the peasantry;—by their commanders, bandit chieftains, who would be equally avaricious and bloodthirsty, to whom it was absurd to offer their services, except for the artillery; who absolutely could not afford to pay a single man, and who would distrust every body. Nevertheless, I wish them, from my heart, every blessing and success. One must be a fool to expect virtuous heroism from them, and a cold politician of the present day to surrender them to extermination.

CCLXXXIV.

TO SAVIGNY.

ROME, 23*d May*, 1822.

Your work,* my friend, was a real refreshment to me; somewhat such as it would be to see you here, where I have none of the interchange of thought, to which I had been so habituated, and on which I am so dependent. In this respect, believe me, you could not have a duller life in the most stupid little country town, than I lead here, leaving Bunsen out of the question. That I read your book immediately, from beginning to end, and some parts of it repeatedly, it is needless to say; and yet I must say it; and likewise, that it answers my expectations, and that I honor you all the more for it, because I could not write any thing like it myself. I can not honor any man for writing what I could have written myself—only appreciate him, and allow that he is not less than I am. Understand me, this is no pride; so far from it, it is my honest feeling that a man is little enough if he can do no more than I, since I feel how infinitely more I could do if I had acquired more correct notions of facts when I possessed my full powers, and if I had not wasted my opportunities so dreadfully. You have opened quite a new world to me, and I believe to all your readers, by your account of academical institutions in the Middle Ages; for this very reason I have nothing to say to you on that subject, but turn to other topics which are not so foreign to me.† . . . . . .

It is possible that I may have written something like this to you years ago, but I think scarcely in so distinct a form. The union was effected every where in Italy in an extremely rough and unskillful manner; with much more dexterity in many of the German Imperial towns, where the relations [between the orders] were precisely the same; and, besides, the German nobles were much more honorable and obedient to the laws than the Italian ones, who allowed themselves the most criminal license, while the burgher class were also a worthless set. For Italy has been an infernal pool, from the Middle Ages to the present time, as it was from the Empire to the Middle Ages. It is a strange thing how any one can get up any enthusiasm for the Italian republics. Read Varchi's History (which, by the way, is one of the most picturesque, consequently most perfect, in existence; so that the reader, particularly if he have visited Florence, forgets every thing around him, and can live the whole day through among those of whom he is reading), and you will find it conceivable how Fr. Guicciardini should have made those Machiavellian projects to render the revival of the republic impossible, which make our hair stand on end. It is nevertheless true that it was Satan and Beelzebub striving together; that this does not make the cause of the Medici a good one, and shall not prevent us from honoring Francisco Ferrucci.

Let me always write down these digressions as if we were talking together, and remember my fondness for entering into the views of all parties, and being guided by none, not even in history.

* Savigny's "History of Jurisprudence during the Middle Ages,"—his principal work.

† The portion here omitted treats of the constitution of the towns in Germany and Italy in the Middle Ages, and the gradual fusion and organization of the various elements of which their population was composed.

In passing, I must also tell you, or rather repeat to you, that I entirely defend Machiavelli's "Principe," taken in its full and literal acceptation, even as he certainly wrote it in the bitterest earnest. How much is there, which we may not say aloud, for fear of being stoned by the stupid good people! There are times in which every individual must be sacred to us; others, in which we can and ought only to treat men in masses; all depends upon a true understanding of the times. A hundred years sooner, Cæsar would have been a criminal; when he lived he was forced to govern. To talk of freedom in Italy, in our days, is what none but a fool or a villain could do; and I know nothing more miserable than Alfieri's affected panegyric of Trajan. Tacitus lived like a stranger in his century, but, with all the aspirations of his heart, it could never occur to him to wish for any thing beyond a tolerable present. I see that it is as usual with me, when I let my pen take its own course in writing to you. For how many days could we talk without coming to an end of what we had to say!* . . . . . .

Of the old Roman constitution, it is plain that Cicero had only the most confused conceptions; he never troubles himself in the least to trace its development.

It is only a piece of good luck that no passages occur which the blockheads could seize as express evidence in favor of the old trivial opinions, in order to refute me with authority. Hence the interest of the book is confined to its other aspects. In the first place, the style and language are exquisitely beautiful; and then, too, the fundamental political idea is remarkable. I can not believe that Cicero wrote without any immediate reference to his own times—that he was merely stringing phrases together without any practical application. If I am right, we see that what he wished for, as the only safeguard for freedom in that unhappy age, was the sovereignty of one individual for life, with a division of the powers as they had existed in the old constitution (or as he had conceived them to exist there); not the elevation of a family to an hereditary kingship. The factious power of the so-called *optimates*, between whom and the demagogues men had then but a mournful choice, he estimates at its true value, in a very remarkable passage. I believe most decidedly that the work had an elevated practical significance, which is obscure only because the lost books were the most important part of the work. Unfortunately the idea was impracticable, because Pompey and Cæsar were both living at once, and it was needful that Destiny should be fulfilled, as it always must be fulfilled, when decay has proceeded so far. The yearly elections were, at that period, a constant renewal of misery, and had no longer any result but that of gratifying the ambition of many; their original import was lost, and could not be restored. What is your opinion about it, my friend? I should like, if I had opportunity, to translate these fragments, to fill up the chasms with supplements in the translation (to do it in Latin would be an impertinence), and to append notes to it.

After I have said so much to you upon learned matters, perhaps I may turn to our personal concerns. With regard to these, the constant indisposition and increasing weakness of my wife is the darkest side of the picture. The children leave us nothing to wish for. They have just got over

* Here followed an account of the books of Cicero's "De Republica," discovered by Mai.

the hooping-cough; my wife had paid her debt to it in her childhood, but I was also attacked by it, and have not yet recovered my strength. That under these circumstances, I have not been able to carry on any continuous study, you will readily imagine. I am so weak that I can bear very little exertion. The climate, too, makes one indolent.

We have lived much alone for some time past. In Cornelius we lost a friend whose society we enjoyed and valued.

Your friend is certain of a cordial reception. But we can not supply what travelers often desire. We give no dinners, and there are no *soirées* at our house, where they can find society assembled. Hence travelers find great fault with me, and it is seldom that any come to me who enjoy me as I am. But then it is the right people who do so; for instance, Lord Colchester and De Serre. Between the last and myself a downright passion has sprung up.*

CCLXXXV.

TO MADAME HENSLER.

ROME, *7th June*, 1822.

......De Serre has been here,† and we have been very intimate with each other, and lament that we can not live together. I could form a friendship with him such as I have not formed for many years. In mind and heart he is entirely what I had pictured to myself; he is one of the rarest and noblest human beings that I have ever met with. We have expressed our sentiments to each other with perfect openness respecting all that deeply occupies the intellect of man; about the past and the future, about Germany and France. Nationality is no barrier between us; he is a perfect master of our language, though he prefers talking in French, because I speak it more easily than he does German. He is thoroughly acquainted with our literature; pronounces, for instance, exactly the same verdict as we do upon Goethe's writings at the different periods of his life. While an admirer of his youthful writings, "Wilhelm Meister," and others of a similar stamp are distressing to him. He suits a court about as well as I do, except that having better spirits, he more easily adapts himself to every thing. Our political convictions are essentially quite identical.

A young man has lately arrived here, a M. Lieber, of Berlin, who went to Greece as a volunteer, and has returned, partly that he might not die of starvation, partly because he found the boundless corruption of the Moreans,

* In a later letter, Niebuhr writes as follows about him: "I conducted De Serre about the Forum here, and our conversation led us from the topography to the history of Rome—a conversation which would have been impossible with any man less resembling the ancient orators, and which could not have been equally delightful, even with him, in any other place. He understood every thing, as I placed before him with a vividness with which I was inspired by his sympathy, the progress of the constitution, the manners, and religion through succeeding centuries, and justified the Gracchi, Marius, and Sulla. He asked me if I had sufficient affection for him, to write this down for his use, and this I intend to do without any learned demonstration. It may, at all events, help to supply the place of a continuation of the History. He said, 'You must write, bearing it in mind that I am not learned.' I replied, 'You are neither more nor less learned than Demosthenes, and I love you like him.'"

† He had been one of the French ministers at the Congress of Verona, which opened in October of this year.

and, withal, their cowardice insufferable. His veracity is unquestionable, and the horror which his narrations inspire is not to be described. All this has plunged him into deep melancholy; for he has a very noble heart. He has deeply moved and interested us, and we are trying to cheer his spirits by friendly treatment, and to banish from his thoughts the infernal scenes which he has witnessed. He is one of the youths of the noble period of 1813 (when he served in the army, and was wounded), who lost themselves in visions, the elements of which they drew from their own hearts; and this terrible contrast between his experience and all that he had imagined—all that impelled him into distant lands, has broken his heart. He is now here in a state of destitution; I shall at all events give him aid; but I mean to propose to him, in the first instance, to come to us, and assist me in instructing Marcus, and in my literary labors. He was arrested during the unhappy investigations of 1819, but dismissed as innocent.

CCLXXXVI.

ROME, 22*d June*, 1822.

I can only write to you briefly to-day. I returned from Tivoli yesterday, very much fatigued, and have many letters to send off.

For this year past, I had not spent a single day beyond the walls of Rome, and felt the need of breathing a little fresh air.......I have been obliged, however, to leave Cornelia and the rest of the children behind. Marcus, Bunsen, and Lieber accompanied me.

Lieber has now taken up his abode with us. I can intrust Marcus to his care with confidence, and the child, too, is already fond of him. I hope to rescue the young man from utter dejection, and to convince him that just as his experience in Greece taught him the visionary nature of his wishes and expectations, so he would have made the same discovery in any other nation where the masses are liberated from all forms; but that the Noble and Beautiful are not a dream, and will never be wholly wanting in the world, however terrible may be its condition. A young man of warm feelings must be convinced of this truth, before you can attempt to prove to him that the evil which prevails so widely could not be found among the rulers unless it existed in the multitude; that change of form can bring no deliverance unless the individual can be first improved.

I am called away, as a very estimable young man, Dr. Pertz, has come to take leave of me, and I can not let him depart without a blessing.

There is a small circle of men with whom I could spend my life, and wish that we could come to know each other. And if ever a human being existed so persuaded of the correctness and truth of his view of the world that he could stake his life upon it, I am that man. I know that I see truly as I know that I exist.

Amelia has begun to write and to sew. She can read most things without spelling.

CCLXXXVII.

TO THE COUNT DE SERRE.

ROME, 24*th June*, 1822.

When I had the pleasure and honor of seeing your Excellency in Rome, I asked your permission to recommend to your protection a young German scholar, engaged in interesting researches, for which the libraries and archives of the kingdom of Naples contain ample materials—materials which, it is to be feared, will remain inaccessible to him, unless some powerful patronage remove the obstacles which the national ignorance, indolence, and vanity, oppose to the labors of foreign scholars in Italy. This young scholar is M. Pertz, who will have the honor of delivering this letter into your hand. The task which has brought him into Italy is the great enterprise conceived by my friend, Baron von Stein, of publishing a complete edition, corrected from the best MSS. of the "Scriptores Rerum Germanicarum," from the earliest times to the thirteenth century; authors whose writings are only now extant in very incomplete collections, formed without any care. It is thought desirable to add to this collection inedited documents belonging to our national history, and selected with discrimination from the infinite number which the archives contain.

M. Pertz combines all the knowledge and the talents required for so vast and difficult a work; but his best recommendations are his moral qualities, to which he joins much intelligence and a very sound judgment. In an age which I regard as the commencement of the literary decline of my nation, we may congratulate ourselves on numbering among our young scholars a man like him.

At Naples and at La Cava, his inquiries will be principally directed to the history of the Lombards, and that of the princes of the house of Suabia; I am sure, M. le Comte, that though a Frenchman and an embassador of France, you will not regard Charles I. of Anjou with any predilection, and that you will neither refuse your esteem to the emperor Frederic II., nor your sympathy to his unfortunate grandson.

I had the honor of conversing with you, M. le Comte, on the state of England; if I find sufficient leisure to finish an essay on this subject, written in German, and a safe opportunity of sending it to Naples, allow me to submit it to you.

May the air of Naples produce a salutary and lasting effect upon your health, and invigorate the powers which you will need, sooner or later, for the salvation of your country and of Europe, whose safety depends upon the peaceable settlement of your institutions. It is one of my most earnest wishes that you may recover fully, and I entreat you attentively to watch over the effect upon your health of the air you are now breathing.

It may have appeared singular to you, M. le Comte, that a stranger should have displayed an almost passionate veneration and attachment for you—sentiments with which the simple observation of your public life, and the study of the principles which you have developed, have sufficed to inspire an individual, who had never had the advantage of knowing you personally. But I venture to flatter myself that you will find nothing ridiculous in it, and that you will not disdain the idea of an invisible political church, dispersed among all nations, nor the sentiment which embraces political principles, and directs itself toward those who, unhappily in such small numbers, establish and defend them nobly and courageously. It is this sentiment which I shall ever entertain toward you, M. le Comte, and to the expression of which I will not add any conventional courtesies.

NIEBUHR.

The *Concordia* of M. Schlegel, for which you asked me, no longer appears.

CCXXXVIII.

EXTRACT FROM A LETTER TO A YOUNG MAN WHO WISHED TO DEVOTE HIMSELF TO PHILOLOGY.

Written in the Summer of 1822.

When your dear mother wrote me word that you showed a decided inclination to philological studies, I expressed my pleasure in hearing of it, and earnestly entreated her and your father not to interfere with this inclination, by forming other plans for your future life. I think I told her, that as philology is the introduction to all other studies, he who devotes himself to this science during his school years with as much zeal as if it were to form the exclusive vocation of his life, prepares himself for any other that he may choose at the university; and, in the second place, I am so fond of philology myself that I could not select for a youth so near and dear to me as you are any other vocation in preference. There is no pursuit more tranquil and more cheering; none which, from the occupations it involves, and the duties it imposes, is more calculated to preserve peace of heart and of conscience; and how often have I lamented that I forsook it, and entered upon a life of turmoil, that will probably leave me little chance of lasting repose even in approaching old age. The office of an instructor of youth, especially, is a most honorable one, and one of the happiest callings in life to a noble heart, despite all the evils which mar its ideal beauty: it was once the object of my voluntary choice, and it would have been well for me if I had been suffered to pursue it unhindered. I am quite conscious that now, having passed my active life in so wide a sphere, I should be spoiled for it; but I would wish any one for whom I have such a hearty and sincere regard as for you, that he might not thus spoil himself, nor long to quit the tranquillity and security of the narrow circle, in which I, like you, passed my youth.

Your dear mother told me that you wished to lay one of your productions before me, in order to give me a proof of your industry, and to enable me to judge of your progress. I begged her to encourage you to do so, not only in order to give you and yours a proof of the sincere interest I take in you, but also because pre-eminently in philology I am sufficiently acquainted with the object to be aimed at, and the paths that lead to it, as well as the wrong roads which one is apt to mistake for them, to be able to fortify one, who had been fortunate enough to find the right road, in his resolution not to leave it, and to have no hesitation in warning one who is in danger of going astray, and telling him whither he is tending if he do not change his course. I myself have made my way for the most part without a guide, and wandered through many a thorny thicket, unfortunately in opposition to the too gentle hints of those who might have led me. Thanks to God and my good fortune, I have never lost sight of my aim. and have always found the right road again, but I should have come much nearer to my goal, and with much less toil and pain, if any one had shown me the way. I am well aware that it was principally out of tenderness to me that this was not done, and probably, too, some did not like the trouble of making themselves intelligible to a boy at the self-willed age. I know, too, that I should not have relished advice which was not in accordance with my inclination; but if it had come from one qualified to give it, I should certainly have taken it to heart, and it would have been worth much to me now if I had received it; even though it had been harsh, and wounded me to the quick.

I can say with truth, and do so with pleasure, that your production is an honorable testimony to your industry, and that it rejoices me to see how much you have done and learnt in the more than six years since we last saw each other. I see that you have read much, and with attention and love of knowledge. But I must now frankly beg you, in the first place, to examine your Latin, and convince yourself that you are deficient in this particular. I will not reproach you with a few grammatical errors. Upon this point, I am quite of the opinion of my late friend, Spalding, who was least of all impatient of such faults in the school, if their indication had the effect of gradually eradicating them. It is a much more serious defect that you have more than once left a period unfinished; that you use words in an incorrect sense; that your style is inflated and unequal; that your metaphors are illogical.* . . . . . .

You do not write simply enough to express without pretension a thought that is clear to your own mind. That you can not give richness and roundness to your style, is no subject for blame; for though there have been some, especially in former times, who by the particularly fortunate guidance given to a peculiar talent, have been able to do this at your age, such perfection is, as a rule, out of the question. Fullness and maturity of expression presuppose a maturity of soul which can only arrive in the progress of its development. But what we always can and always ought to do, is not to strive after the semblance of more than we can perform, and to think and express ourselves with straightforwardness and correctness. So on this point accept a wholesome rule from me. When you write Latin essays, think out what you mean to say with the greatest distinctness of which you are capable, and clothe it in the most unassuming language. Study the manner in which great authors have formed their periods, and exercise yourself frequently in forming detached sentences upon their model; translate passages so as to break up the periods, and endeavor to restore them when you re-translate the passage into the original. This is an exercise in which you do not need the help of your teacher; do it simply as a preparatory discipline for the use of a riper time. When you write, examine scrupulously whether your language is of one color. I do not care whether you adopt that of Cicero and Livy, or that of Tacitus and Quintilian; but one age you must select, else the result will be a motley texture, as offensive to a real philologist as if one were to blend the German of 1650 with that of 1800. Try to acquire the art of connecting the sentences, without which all pretended Latin is a downright torture to the reader. And, above all, look sharply after your metaphors; all that are not absolutely faultless are insufferable, and for this very reason it is, that Latin is such a capital school for the formation of a good style; and next to Latin, French, for that also can not endure any thing illogical, about which the Germans are so fatally indifferent in their own language.

You did quite right not to send the two skeleton essays you mention, for it is impossible that you should write any thing sensible upon their subjects.

We can not write separate treatises before we have a vivid conception

* Here follow examples from the Essay, which could interest none but the person to whom the letter was addressed.

and an accurate knowledge of the whole of which their subject forms a part, and before we have an adequate acquaintance with the relations of this single part to other classes of facts. Another principle is, that we must advance from the particular to the universal classes of facts, in order really to understand a complex whole. And here we do not need to follow a systematic order, but may yield to accidental impulses, provided that we proceed with circumspection, and do not overlook the chasms which still exist between the separate portions. I began the actual study of ancient history with Polybius, and was earlier intimate with the age of Cleomenes than with that of Pericles; but I knew that my knowledge was objectively a slight fragment, and that I must have learnt infinitely more, before I could even dream of working up materials that were scattered through many ages, with which I was very imperfectly acquainted, and which had a multitude of relations of which I had no proper conception whatever. I worked on and on, and, when I can, I still work daily, in order to attain a vivid conception of antiquity. You have undertaken to write about the Roman colonies, and their influence upon the State. But it is quite impossible that you can have even a half correct idea of the Roman colonies; and to speak about their influence on the State, you ought not only to have an insight into the Roman constitution, and an intimate acquaintance with the Roman history, but also to understand politics and the history of politics, all of which is as yet absolutely impossible. While I say this to you, I add, that at your age none of us, who have a right to call ourselves philologists, could have written upon this subject; nay, not even Grotius or Scaliger, or Salmasius, who became excellent grammarians at a much earlier age than any of us. The second subject you have mentioned is a still less suitable one for you. You must know enough of antiquity to be aware that the philosophy of youth consisted, up to a much riper age than yours, in silent listening, in the endeavor to understand and to learn. You can not properly know the facts, far less propound a generalization, not to say a philosophic one, of facts which are quite insulated, and for the most part problematical. Learning, my dear young friend, conscientious learning—a constant effort to test and augment our knowledge—that is our theoretical vocation for life, and especially that of the young who are so fortunate as to be able to surrender themselves, freely, to the charms of the new intellectual world opened to them in books. He who writes a treatise, let him say what he will, claims to teach, and no one can teach without a degree of wisdom, which is the compensation God gives us, if we strive after it, for the departing bliss of youth. A wise youth is a monster. Further, let none say that he undertakes such compositions for his own sake, in order to explore a particular subject. He who does it with this view makes a mistake, and injures himself. Let him write down in a fragmentary form what he has thought out; but let him not sit down to write, in the hope that thoughts will come by writing. He who attempts to bring into a well-rounded whole, that which can not even have the shadow of completeness, either internal or external, runs the very greatest risk of contenting himself with semblance and superficialness, and contracting a most injurious facility in bad writing. It is well for the young tree that, planted in a rich soil and good situation, is held in a right direction by a careful hand, and forms solid wood! If its growth is hastened by over-watering, and it is weak and flexible, exposed to the fury of the winds, without shelter and prop, its wood becomes porous, and its trunk crooked for its whole life.

Antiquity may be compared to an immeasurable city of ruins, of which there is not even a ground-plan extant; in which each one must find his way for himself, and learn to understand the whole from the parts—the parts from a careful comparison and study, and a due consideration of their relation to the whole. If one possessing only a smattering of architectural knowledge, utterly ignorant of hydrostatics, having scarcely seen the greater part of the ruins of Rome, and nothing beyond Rome—if such a one should undertake to write about the ruins of the aqueducts, he would produce much such a work as a mere student writing a dissertation on some branch of antiquities.

You have therefore done very wisely to choose instead an exegetical treatise. But I must remark that a student ought to keep within his own sphere; that is, let him not believe that he can contribute any thing to the elucidation of a work which has been commentated on by masters.

Exegesis is the fruit of finished study. From the stores of a comprehensive acquaintance with the language and the subjects treated of, it adds to our knowledge of both; it is nothing else than the expression of the meaning as it has been understood, if not by contemporaries, yet at least by people of somewhat later times, to whom the fleeting allusions of the moment were already lost, and it requires a mature and thoroughly cultivated understanding, as well as an infinity of individual observations. The student's part is to show that he has understood the meaning rightly, and to extract the essential points from the commentators, with a statement whence he has derived them.

What I would above all things impress upon you, my dear friend, is to open your heart to a sincere veneration for excellence. It is the best endowment of a youthful mind, and its surest guide.

I must now say a few words to you respecting the style of your composition. It is too bombastic, and you often use inapplicable metaphors. Do not suppose that I am so unreasonable as to require a finished style; I would as little require this of you as of any one at your age; I only warn you against mannerism. All writing should be nothing but the symbol of the thought and speech. You must either write as if really delivering a continuous discourse, in which your genuine thoughts are accurately and fully expressed, or as you would speak if called upon to do so by circumstances in which, indeed, you are not actually placed in real life, but conceive yourself to be, as an author. Every thing must be based upon thought, and the thought must shape the structure of the language. To be able to do this, we must apply our study of language, enrich the memory with a copious store of words and phrases, whether in the mother tongue, or in foreign languages, living or dead; sharply define the terms of the former for ourselves, use the latter in their proper sense, and fix their limitation. Exercises in composition for boys and youths ought to have no other object than the development of their thoughts, the enrichment and refining of their language. If our thoughts do not satisfy us, if we turn and twist in the consciousness of our poverty, writing will become a horrible labor to us, and we shall hardly maintain our courage. This was my case at your age, and for long after. There was no one to enter into my distress, and give the help which can so easily be given at the transition age from boyhood to youth. This difficulty we do not feel if we adopt a fixed style, for then we have the external shape, which is not to be obtained when we work from within outwards; or at least we believe that we have it, and probably find others who suffer themselves to be deceived by the semblance; not indeed those who understand the matter. But with an assumed style you lose all truth, and by degrees all capability of producing any thing of value and originality. In order to give an appearance of fullness, the whole is nothing but a hollow form; all your own thoughts become distorted and worthless; you rank yourself among those whom you fancy you resemble in appearance, and you are in reality nothing, and sink down to the lowest class of imitators.

With some facility in seizing on external features, it must be very easy to obtain the mastery of an assumed style, but extremely difficult to shake it off when you have once had the misfortune to be entangled in it. The difficulty of developing and presenting our thoughts is by no means diminished, when we have obtained a clear insight into our subject, while we have at the same time to struggle against a bad habit, and it is seldom that any one can sustain this double conflict. It will require heroic efforts to break yourself of such a habit, if you have long persevered in it. Hence I call upon you all the more earnestly to forsake this path utterly, and most carefully to avoid it for the future. To an assumed style belong all verbose and unmeaning expositions, with a false claim to a deep insight into the mind of the poet.

But, above all things, we must preserve our truthfulness in science so pure, that we must eschew absolutely every false appearance—that we must not write the very smallest thing as certain, of which we are not fully convinced—that when we have to express a conjecture, we must strenuously endeavor to exhibit the precise degree of probability we attach to it. If we do not ourselves indicate our own errors where possible—even such as it is unlikely that any one will ever discover—if, when we lay down our pen, we can not say in the sight of God, "upon strict examination, I have not knowingly written any thing that is not true, and have never deceived either regarding myself or others; I have not exhibited my most inveterate opponent in any light which I could not justify upon my death-bed;"—if we can not do this, then study and literature render us unrighteous and sinful.

In this respect I am conscious that I make no requirements from others, which a superior intelligence reading my soul could accuse me of not having fulfilled. It was this conscientiousness, combined with the perception of what we may and ought to attain in philology, if we wish to come before the public, that made me so shy of publishing for long after I had reached manhood. Often called upon to do so by my dearest friends, not without reproaches, I felt that my hour was not yet come, which certainly, had my life taken a different course, might have come seveıal years earlier.

I am so strict in this respect, that I strongly disapprove of the quite customary practice of quoting at second-hand, after verifying the quotations, without naming where we have found them, and never allow myself to do so, tedious as the double reference may be. Whenever I quote a passage without remark, I have found it myself. He who acts otherwise gives himself the appearance of greater reading than he possesses.

I would not blame others who are less strict, if I may assume that it is really perfectly indifferent to them whether or not people suppose them to be more profoundly learned than they really are; or if they say beforehand, as some do, that of course most of the citations are borrowed. But of a young man I require, absolutely and without indulgence, were it only as an exercise of virtue, the most scrupulous truthfulness in literary as in all other matters, that it may become a part of his very nature, or rather that the truthfulness which God has implanted in his nature may remain there. With this weapon alone can we fight our way through the world. The hour in which my Marcus should tell an untruth, or give himself the semblance of a merit that he did not possess, would make me very unhappy; it would be the fall in paradise.

I come now to another part of my business in giving you counsel. I wish you had less pleasure in satires, not excepting those of Horace. Turn to the works which elevate the heart—in which you contemplate great men and great events, and live in a higher world; turn away from those which represent the mean and contemptible side of ordinary circumstances and degenerate days. They are not suitable for the young, who in ancient times would not have been suffered to have them in their hands. Homer, Æschylus, Sophocles, Pindar, these are the poets for youth; these are they on which the great men of antiquity were nourished, and which, as long as literature illumines the world, will ennoble for life the youthful soul that is filled with them. Horace's odes may also benefit the young as a standard style formed upon the Greek model, and it is a pity that a contempt for them has spread, which is only allowable and not arrogant in the case of a very small number of masters in philology. In the "Sermones" Horace is original and more pithy, but he who can understand them must read them with melancholy; a beneficial effect they can never have. We see a noble-minded man, who, from inclination and reflection, tries to make himself comfortable in an unhappy period, and has surrendered himself to a bad philosophy, which does not prevent his remaining honorable, but leads him to take a low view of things. His morality is based solely upon the principle of the Fitting, the Becoming, the Reasonable; nay, he declares the Wholesome (to use the most favorable expression) to be the source of the idea of Right. Wickedness is distasteful to him, and excites him—not to anger, but to a gentle reproof. That feeling for virtue which impels us to persecute vice, and which we find not only in Tacitus, but also in Juvenal—in the latter with frightful severity—seems to have no place in his mind. Juvenal, however, with the exception of a few fragments, you ought to leave absolutely untouched for the present, and you lose nothing by it; for if you are allowed to read him, it does harm at your age to dwell on the contemplation of vice, instead of pondering noble thoughts. On the poets I have mentioned, and on Herodotus, Thucydides, Demosthenes, Plutarch, Cicero, Livy, Cæsar, Sallust, Tacitus, among prose writers, I earnestly entreat you to fix your attention, and to confine yourself exclusively to them. Do not read them in order to make æsthetic reflections upon them, but in order to drink in their spirit, and to fill your soul with their thoughts—in order to gain that by reading, which you would have gained by reverently listening to the discourses of great men. This is the philology which does the soul good; and learned investigations, even when we have got so far as to be able to make them, always occupy an inferior place. We must be fully masters of grammar (in the ancient sense); we must acquire every branch of antiquarian knowledge as far as lies in our power; but even if we can make the most brilliant emendations, and explain the most difficult passages at sight, all this is nothing, and mere sleight of hand, if we do not acquire the wisdom and spiritual energy of the great men of antiquity—think and feel like them.

For the study of language, I recommend to you especially Demosthenes and Cicero. Select, in the former, the Oration "pro Coronâ;" in the latter, the "pro Cluentio," and read them with all the thoughtfulness of which you are capable: then go through them so that you could give account of every word and every phrase; draw a sketch of their argument; try to get a clear idea of all the historical circumstances, and to bring them into order. This will give you an immense amount of labor, and from it you will learn how little we can know, and, consequently, you do know. Apply then to your tutor, not in order to surprise him with unexpectedly difficult problems; for there are—in the Cluentiana, for instance—difficulties with regard to facts which the profoundest student can only solve by hypotheses which do not present themselves immediately to any scholar; but that he may be so kind as to consult and think over the passages on which you have exhausted your powers and resources. In the Cluentiana, develop the system of indictment. Make collections of words and expressions, especially epithets with their substantives, and the original sense of the figurative expressions. Translate; after a few weeks turn your translation back again into the original language.

Besides this grammatical work, read those great authors one after the other with greater freedom; but after having finished a book or a section, recall what you have read by an act of memory, and indicate the contents with the greatest brevity. Then besides, write down expressions and phrases that particularly occur to you; so too you ought to write down every new word immediately, and read over the list at night.

Let critics and emendators alone for the present. The time will come when you will be able to read them with profit. The artist must first learn to draw, before he begins to use colors, and he must know how to handle the ordinary colors, before he decides for or against the use of transparent tints. About writing I have spoken to you already. Do not read all that comes to hand, even of ancient authors; there are plenty of bad ones among them. Æolus only permitted the one wind to blow that was to waft Ulysses to his destination, and bound the rest; unchained, and blowing all at once, they caused him endless wanderings.

Study history after a double mode, according to the persons and according to the states. Make systematic surveys frequently.

The advice that I give you, I should give to every one in your place. The censure I should have to give to very many. Do not suppose that I am unaware of this, and that I do not joyfully give you full credit for your industry.

The study which I require of you makes very little show, advances slowly, and it will perhaps depress you to see a long series of years before you, exclusively devoted to acquirement. But, my dear fellow, truly to learn and to acquire, is the true good of theoretical life, and our lifetime is not so short. But long as it may be, we have ever to go on learning. Thank God that it is so!

And now, may God bless your labors, and give you the right disposition, that you may carry them on to your own welfare and happiness, to the joy of your parents, and of all of us who have your virtue and respectability sincerely at heart.

1823.

In March, 1823, Niebuhr and his family went to Naples, where they spent five weeks in examining the remarkable places in its neighborhood, and he explored the public libraries. At the Royal Library, he undertook the revision of a Manuscript, in his opinion very important—that of the grammarian, Charisius. His leisure hours were spent with De Serre, with whom he contracted a friendship such as is rarely formed in later life, and carried on a regular correspondence up to De Serre's death.

On leaving Naples, Niebuhr returned to Rome, visited for the last time, with his son, the scenes and spots that were dearest to him, and then, after a sorrowful parting with Chevalier and Madame Bunsen, and a few of his younger friends, set out on his journey to Florence, whence he proceeded, by way of Bologna, Verona, and Ferrara, to St. Gall.

Here he passed some weeks, partly to recruit his health, and partly to examine the MSS. in the celebrated library of that place. He found that most of them were of a theological character; but, among the exceptions, he discovered the Panegyric of Merobaudes, which he revised and prepared for publication during his stay there. From St. Gall, he went to Heidelberg, to visit two of his earliest friends—the aged Voss, and Thibaut, his companion at college. He next visited Bonn, in order to see Professor Brandis, and, after remaining there some time, determined to select it as his place of residence until it should be finally decided whether or not he returned to Rome.

Letters written in 1823.

CCLXXXIX.

TO COUNT ADAM MOLTKE.

Rome, *8th February*, 1823.

My dear Friend—You must ascribe my long silence simply and solely to awkwardness. As I did not immediately answer the letter by which you offered me an opportunity of renewing our correspondence, after your visit to Rome, I have been waiting all this long time for some other occasion on which I could begin writing to you. But, though I am sufficiently inclined in general to self-reproach, I think I may be forgiven in this instance for not having answered your letter immediately. Every thing came on us at once; my wife's confinement, &c., the effects of which lasted long afterward; the negotiations on ecclesiastical affairs; and the Neapolitan insurrection and Punchinello-revolution, which threatened us here with an unpleasant farce. Then followed such a winter of perpetual society and dissipation as I never underwent before; in short, so much time passed over without my fulfilling the duty which a kind Heaven had pointed out, that I was at last too much ashamed to write.

The particular reason of my writing to you at last, my dear old friend, is as follows: Dora mentions the betrothal of your Charles as an event about which she has already written to us, but this is a mistake. I know nothing more than the bare fact, but it is enough to make me greet you again, and wish you and your Charles every blessing; and I doubt not, nay, I have the fullest confidence, that this decision for his life will be so fortunate, that his friend may rejoice over it with his father. May God grant it, and preserve his paths from the thorns on which you have been forced to tread! Our youth fell in a time of illusions and hopes; the youth of the present age, who are kept close to realities almost as *our* fathers were, have a right to demand other compensations from Fate.

That I never once made use of your residence in Rome to unite the present with departed days, is one of the things—there are not few of them—for which I can never be consoled, which will embitter the retrospect of my life in my last hour. It was as though a spell lay upon me; I felt that it would be enough to utter one word; once to give vent to the emotions of the heart in tears. But I could not unclose my lips to speak that word. The past could not rise again from its grave, and I felt as though it would have shaken the foundations of that present which it is now the duty of my life to preserve and develop.

When you had left, I would gladly have hastened after you, and spent one day more with you, at whatever cost. Thus I suffered under a torturing constraint, which still rends my heart whenever I think of that time which might have refreshed and strengthened me, as far as is still possible for me. My mind is like a nation that has passed through a revolution, and now must proceed in a new order, as the old order is irrecoverably destroyed. I economize the little still left out of my old treasures, recognizing now how inexpressibly valuable was what I once possessed; and with what the new time has brought me, I teach myself to fulfill my duties, and take the relations of life as they come.

My position here has one essential defect, that I can not satisfy the requirements of those who have no possible claim upon me but through my official station; that I can not afford to keep open house for idle travelers, and would rather bear their anger at my doing nothing, than their contempt for what I might offer. Rome has become the chief place of amusement for the collective idleness of Europe, and even if the ministry would give me the means of undertaking a *rôle* in this dissipation, it would be terrible to waste one's time upon it.

This consideration makes it less difficult for me to resign my present office, although we have but a very uncertain future before us, and I will not deny that the prospect of returning to Germany gives me some uneasiness. But Gretchen's feelings are the deciding point; she feels that the air here is poison to her, and so there was nothing more to consider.

Our chief care is to find a place where I may spend the remaining years of my life without the necessity of a further change. Other things being nearly equal, we shall certainly choose to settle as far as possible from the Russian frontier.

My Marcus is a boy of excellent capacities; his education amid antiquity has been perfectly successful. The old world is to him the true and real one; the modern only something accidental. This will undoubtedly render some bitter discoveries necessary in the future. Ancient history and mythology are as familiar to him as to a Roman boy eighteen hundred years ago, and he is burning with sympathy and sheds tears for the heroes of the Trojan time, over the literal Latin translation of the Odyssey which to us seems so miserable. He looks forward confidently to climbing Parnassus, and seeing Jupiter and the old gods there, of whom I told him the modern Greek tradition, that they have taken refuge on the summit of the mountain.

When you were here, my friend, we spoke often, as you will remember, of De Serre; it is the happiest result of my residence in this city, that *he* has been here, and that we have become intimate friends. As the ancients wrote to and for an individual, I mean to write for him a short compendious narrative of the Roman History through all its centuries. Is De Serre still called a thorough-going servant of despotism by the German liberals? There are cabinets in which he is held to be a mad poetical visionary, and no doubt a revolutionist.

Farewell, my dear friend, and if you have not quite effaced me from your memory, write to me about your Charles.......

Your old friend,

NIEBUHR.

CCXC.

TO COUNT DE SERRE.

ROME, *9th February*, 1823.

M. LE COMTE—I shall profit by a perfectly safe opportunity to send you some reflections on the state of England. You will receive them with kindness, but I do not recommend them the less to your indulgence.*

On that country I have a right to form an opinion; I have a right to except against that of the English, and to criticise it, as much as if the question related to my own country, and the opinion of my fellow-countrymen respecting its state, for I know England as well as if I had been born there. I was taught the language in my earliest childhood, and from the age of ten years I was in the constant habit of reading the English journals; my father sent me there to finish my studies, and to become acquainted with the political and civil life of a free people, as well as to study rural economy, commerce, the application of chemistry to the arts, and lastly, finance. With introductions from him (who, though little known at home, was the object of universal respect in England), to the most

* This Essay, entitled "Ueber England's Zukunft," is published in Niebuhr's "Nachgelassene Schriften," p. 426.

eminent men of that country, I was as if naturalized there; and, after having quitted it, I continued to watch with the same interest the minutest details of its circumstances, and have followed its moral, political, and financial history, for the last twenty years, with an attention which even such events as those of 1806 and 1813 have rarely sufficed to diminish. And the more I occupied all my leisure moments with researches into the history of the institutions and laws of the nations of antiquity, the more I was led to turn my attention to the history of England, among those states, where the free institutions of the middle ages have maintained themselves for a more or less lengthened period, and where even important changes—as, for instance, in the tenure of property—have been brought to pass in the course of their natural development. Lastly, I have more especially devoted my attention to the finance of England, on account of a work, the idea of which I conceived some years ago; namely, a history of the finances of all European states from the peace of 1783, preceded by a picture of their condition at that epoch, and terminated by a statement of the results.

I beg, M. le Comte, that you will simply consider this explanation as a statement of the circumstances which make me feel myself entitled to discuss, without presumption, the questions treated of in my little essay.

In reasoning, on the future, I have asked myself, What should I do in Mr. Canning's place, *with his principles and his character?* Will you be one of those who would now accuse me of attributing reckless audacity to him with injustice? I think not.

It was by similar chains of reasonings, that I always used to divine the projects of Napoleon, and even the plans of his campaigns.

England must choose between two futures. Has she the will and the power to adopt a manly and virtuous policy? Then she will occupy herself with the moral reformation of society; she will renounce the project of domineering over and weakening the Continent of Europe; and she will leave the growth of the America of the North in the hands of Providence: she may deplore a war with Spain, but she will not give a mortal blow to the restoration in France. Is she willing to brave the greatest dangers, confident that she can surmount them, and to found an empire such as no power may dare to attack? Then she will adopt precisely the course which I have traced out.

In writing for you, M. le Comte, I have thought it unnecessary to add to my prophecies the restrictions, if *such or such an event happen*, by which on other occasions one is obliged to guard against the taunt, often little merited, of having predicted events which are not realized. Unforeseen accidents may arrest Mr. Canning in his career; for myself, I simply say that he will arrive at the results which I have indicated, if, as every thing leads us to believe, he is able to advance without restraint.

Have you ever read in Germany a paper of Lessing's, which alarms pious persons, but which is none the less worthy of a profound philosopher, "*die Erziehung des Menschengeschlechts?*" * There is in that paper a sentence of the deepest significance: "The enthusiast," he says, "and the philosopher are frequently only at variance as to the epoch in the future at which they place the accomplishment of their efforts. The enthusiast does not recognize the slowness of the pace of time. An event not imme-

* The Education of the Human Race.

diately connected with the time in which he lives is to him a nullity." Do not attribute to me the idea that the defects, which as I think are eating into the vital principle of England, threaten her existence in our times, or those of our children. My views would admit of development to a very much greater extent with regard to Ireland and other points; but these rapidly sketched pages would then extend into a volume.

During the few weeks yet remaining of our stay in Rome, I shall have absolutely no time to write you the essay on Roman history for which you asked me. It shall be my occupation at Baden-Baden. I feel warmly grateful to you for having asked me for it. The ancients wrote for the friend to whom they dedicated a book; this gives marked characteristics to what is written; this enables one to dispense with precautions against the misapprehensions of such and such readers. It is an inestimable advantage to me that you understand our language so well; in writing, for the future, I shall fancy that I am speaking to you. Atticus wrote an abstract of the history of Rome for the use of his friend Cicero; may I not recall this example on my own behalf?......

Society here is about to abandon itself to amusements during the carnival. There is something fearful in these pitiable amusements at a moment when all our lives are in the balance. What a despicable generation is this of ours! I even prefer the Greeks of Constantinople, quarreling about their theological disputes, to our contemporaries, who require diversions for their *ennui*, who flock to balls on the eve of a universal crisis, which is teaching us all *how precious was the time by which we neglected to profit.* For my own part, I share in the feelings of a dying man who reproaches himself for not having employed his life well. Lent and its silence will be a relief to me. I have just bought a copy of Leonardo da Vinci.

......As you do me the honor of allowing me to plan your Italian library, I would warmly recommend to you the Florentine History of Varchi, if you can find a complete copy of it; almost all are mutilated. In reading this author, I have seen that we may be incredibly circumstantial, and yet rivet the attention. It will make you acquainted with a great man—Ferrucci—of whom there are so few!......

CCXCI.

Rome, 25*th February*, 1823.

......I have sent word to Cardinal Gonsalvi that you wish to be informed of the state of his health. Your interest in him has given him the most lively pleasure, and he sends you his sincere acknowledgments. Alas! I have no agreeable news to give you on this subject...... It appears to me certain that the seat of the disease is the œsophagus, and that the nerves of the ganglion are attacked. I am not aware whether you think it allowable to believe in animal magnetism, but for my part I have faith in it, and I believe that if cure were possible in this case, it must be sought in this remedy......

I have read with terror the speeches in the English parliament. I regret that I did not take notes of the number of the "*Espectador*," a journal in which M. de St. Miguel wrote at that time, in which last year his Britannic Majesty, now the ally of Don Miguel, was accused of having poisoned his daughter, his wife, and Napoleon!

I shudder when I think of the future. The infatuated men have brought us to the point of having put England, and the English ministry, at the head of the revolutionary party. There are some ministers who ought to follow the example of Lord Londonderry......

CCXCII.

TO MADAME HENSLER.

NAPLES, *8th April*, 1823.

We have been here a week, and, as is always the case with a season of great enjoyment, the time slips away very quickly, and it makes me sad to think that a quarter of that which we can spend here is already over. It is years certainly since I spent such happy days. In this elastic atmosphere you feel elastic; the sense of weight and lassitude which diffuses itself through your whole body in Rome, at least if you remain long there without a break, vanishes in Naples. I believe it was not without reason, and not merely for the sake of the scenery, that the old Romans regularly visited their country houses and the shores of this bay. Sky, earth, and sea, compose a whole which certainly far transcends my expectations; and in De Serre's society I have all that my heart and intellect have so long and sorely missed, and there is a friendship between our families which already extends even to the children. I really feel several years younger, and able to work hard without a laborious effort.

We arrived here on Marcus's birth-day. The whole journey had been a festival to him, and it was a deep joy to us to perceive his open susceptibilities to all these new impressions. We felt how much he had developed and improved during the past year, on comparing him with his former self. It is an inestimable advantage for him that we have remained here so long, for, in his own way, he enjoys every thing, antiquities and nature, like a grown person, and with all the bliss of childhood superadded. No, I do not think that any one ever had a happier childhood! The night before his birthday, we slept at a little place called St. Agata; we had stopped at mid-day at Mola (it was a most beautiful day), to feast our eyes on the bay and the prospect toward Gaeta. The boy was intoxicated with delight, and his ecstasy kept his soul awake to the last second, when his body was long since quite tired out. When he was in bed, he clung round his mother's neck, and said in German, "Mother, how *very* happy I am that God has given me such a good father and mother, and such good sisters!" My heart was very tender, and I could not help begging his pardon, because I once punished him severely for a piece of mischief which Lucia had done, and not he, but we were compelled to believe that he was the culprit, and was trying to screen himself by a lie; I said that I had been unjust to him: "No, father, that you never were!" he answered with the greatest warmth......

A manuscript which I must collate, at least in all the important passages, in order to be justified in editing a work which has been printed from very bad copies of the same, takes up much of my time which might be spent more pleasantly; but I think I ought not to lose this opportunity, as it is scarcely probable that any one else will be found to undertake a task which has been left undone for three centuries. The people here are very obliging; and when I have finished this task, I mean to embrace the unexpected offer of permission to read the *fac-similes* of the Herculanean papyrus-rolls, the proof sheets of which have been already printed from copper-plates, but which are not yet published.

Of the knavery of the people we had a strong proof, in the sum they asked for unloading our carriage, else they can not be worse than those we have left, and their vivacity is a strong recommendation to them compared with the lifeless indolence of the Romans. It certainly tends to make one judge them more favorably that we have lived so many years in Italy, and have long since ceased to make the demands, the non-fulfillment of which plunges any foreigner into despair, who can not indemnify himself by a general enthusiasm. At Terracina you begin to meet with southern scenery and southern productions; the oranges at Rome are sour, and we have often remarked that we had never eaten such bad ones in Germany; the Sicilian ones here certainly possess a perfection such as they never retain when brought across the sea to the north. But the difference of the climate is shown most strikingly by the fact, that it is advisable here when the sun has shone into a room, to open the window in the evening in order not to suffer from the sultry air during the night; while it was only a few days before we left Rome, that we could do altogether without a fire, and most likely should not have given it up so soon except in prospect of the journey.......

CCXCIII.

NAPLES, 29*th April*, 1823.

......I have seen a great deal of De Serre, and this short period of uninterrupted intimate intercourse has so perfected our friendship as to secure its steady duration, even if we should never meet again. I revere him more than ever, from seeing him in all the relations of life, and I now say, as an eye-witness, what I was convinced of before, from the picture which I had formed of him to myself, that his character is as perfectly virtuous and as spotless in its purity, as he is great as a man, and rare as a genius.

His family is certainly one of the happiest on the face of the earth; a lively and sensible wife who admires her husband, and is proud of him, whom he loves very tenderly; his children are the objects of his warmest affection. All who belong to the embassy belong to the family, and even the servants who have come here with them, seem rather to be in the position of faithful retainers than domestics. The interior of the family has no more the tone of the fashionable world than belongs to his position as a representative of his country, and this tone appears only when his official position is in question, which is very seldom; at other times his mode of life, notwithstanding the size of the establishment, and the elegance of the apartments, is quite that of a commoner, and you enter into all the arrangements and feelings of the family quite as you would with people of our class. De Serre's long residence in Germany, particularly in his youth, during the emigration, his intimate acquaintance with our language and literature, his taste for them, the many vicissitudes through which he has passed, the necessity of earning his bread as an advocate after his return, have certainly brought to extraordinary perfection, one of the rarest spirits that nature has ever created. Conscious of his powers, all his external gifts of fortune are to him neither a possession of value, nor a fetter.

We see each other daily, and often more than once in the day; we have made excursions together as far as the weather would permit, and farther.......

CCXCIV.

TO COUNT DE SERRE.

ROME, 18*th March*, 1823.

......The new Chancellor of the Exchequer proves himself incomparably superior to his predecessor, the inept Mr. Vansittart, so extolled in the semi-official pamphlet which appeared last year. His financial statement deserves full confidence, with one correction, which is, however, very essential; namely, the following:

I adopt his estimate of the receipts, as they would be if no duties had been repealed, at 52,200,000*l*. Deducting the amount of these duties, we shall have rather under 50,000,000*l*.; but I do not doubt that the revenues will reach this amount, or perhaps rather more.

He has, however, no right to add to these receipts the 4,850,000*l*. due from the Trustees of Half-pay and Pensions, because these Commissioners will only have this money by borrowing it; which reduces the real surplus to 150,000*l*., and annihilates the Sinking Fund. I need hardly remind you that I do not regard this as a great evil for England.

Such is the reality which I can vouch for; and I suspect that the very imperfect manner in which these discussions are reported in the English journals, conceals a result still less favorable. I do not find in the statement of expenses the 2,050,000*l*., which, with the 2,800,000*l*. constitutes the 4,850,000*l*. to be advanced by the Trustees of Half-pay and Pensions. Now I attribute this omission simply to the ignorance of those who report the Parliamentary debates in the journals. The new minister has wished to make a sensation to inspire Europe with admiration, but I can scarcely bring myself to believe that he has been guilty of a piece of low cunning, such as the ministers of absolute monarchs not unfrequently indulge in. Still, it seems evident to me that this sum ought to be added to the expenses, and then the balance would stand as follows:

Total expenses without the sum to be borrowed on annuities for the Pension List	£49,852,786
Sum to be borrowed in order to pay the Pension List .	2,050,000
	£51,902,786
Total receipts, after the suppression of the duties, which will be paid however for the first half year. .	50,000,000
From which will result a deficit of	£1,902,786

You will smile at my saying that this budget merits all confidence, when I nevertheless destroy its results. I ought to have said that all the facts are exact; but that the calculations should be corrected.*

What the minister says respecting the reforms and retrenchments made

* The actual receipts of the year 1823, including £4,678,000 derived from the Trustees of the Naval and Military Pensions, amounted to £57,672,999, the actual expenditure to £50,962,014.

in the administration, admits of no doubt, and does great honor to the government.

There is, however, nothing alarming in this deficit, even if it should not disappear before the more ample information which I shall endeavor to obtain from London itself; it will simply force the government to adopt at last the only existing course by which the finances of England can be saved; namely, to change the system of taxation entirely, in the manner which I have indicated.* The opinions of Mr. Ricardo and Lord Somers prove that the most correct thinkers in England are beginning to have a glimpse of its necessity, its indispensable necessity. The repeal of taxes avails nothing, and is not the effect of abundance in the finances; it is the effect of an inevitable necessity, and ought to be compensated by a property tax.

The budget altogether is not a financial, but a political matter. Hence I can not conceive how it is, that, out of England, people do not examine it, nor test the calculations.

This would frustrate the policy of the English minister; but the refutation ought not to exaggerate any thing.

An infinity of facts have come to my knowledge lately, and confirm what I have written upon England. Thus a landowner declares that he would be content to sell for £21,000, an estate for which he paid £72,000 in 1810.

Have you heard, M. le Comte, that Count Munster had informed the Hanoverian envoys, that the King of England, as King of Hanover, entirely approves the resolutions of Verona; and that he is even convinced that Europe would fall a prey to revolution if the allied powers displayed less energy? It is evident that they fear a continental war, which might endanger Hanover.

The French post of to-day will bring you deplorable news! So the men who now exclude a colleague,† without being authorized to do so, by a regulation which is undoubtedly too indulgent, but which is the law, are in part the same who rejected your proposition for increasing the authority of the president.

M. Wicar had promised me to call at last on the picture-dealer to-day, to examine the Filippo Lippi; I do not know if he has kept his promise; he has not come to inform me of the result. The picture-dealer, whom I requested to be at home to receive Wicar, has sent me word that Wicar is his enemy; I hope it has not come to poniards.

I rejoice in your acquisitions in pictures. What a pity it is that the riches of Italy are almost exhausted!

I, too, can not help believing that there are affinities between the convulsions of the physical world, and those of the moral order of things. I venture to predict that, in twenty or thirty years, a terrible plague will

* In the Essay "Ueber England's Zukunft."

† During the debates in the French Chamber of Deputies on the proposed war with Spain, in order to suppress the Constitution and restore Absolutism, M. Manuel, deputy for La Vendée, was excluded from the Chamber, by a vote of the ultra-royalist majority, for having used the expression, "You wish to save the life of Ferdinand, and forget that the Stuarts were overthrown because they sought the aid of France—that Louis the Sixteenth's head fell, because foreigners mixed themselves in the cause of France." These words were declared to be a defense of regicide, although Manuel explained that he had used them with the contrary intention.

devastate Europe. In three or four hundred years, it will be possible to calculate the increase or diminution of the human race, and the change in the maximum of heat and cold, &c.

Au revoir, Count, if the communications of Wicar do not occasion you another letter, before my departure. Meanwhile, permit me to assure you once more of the unchangeable devotion of my heart.

NIEBUHR.

CCXCV.*

The reduction of the rate of interest on the State debt is extremely facilitated by the existence of another stock, to which it is desirable to reduce it.

If none such exist, the fund-holder will estimate the indemnity which is due to him, in proportion to the interest; he will consider himself injured if you do not offer him 125 of nominal capital for 100, when you wish to reduce the five per cent. to four per cent.

If more than one kind of stock exists, at different rates of interest, their respective prices will have fixed themselves in very different proportions, for they are regulated by two efficients of unlike nature; namely, the annual product as an investment, and the expectation of a rise when it may be desirable to part with them. Moreover, experience proves that in all cases, State bonds bearing a smaller interest, fetch a higher price in proportion than those bearing higher interest. Thus, before 1780, the Dutch bonds at two-and-a-half per cent. fetched one hundred and eight per cent., those at three per cent. only from one hundred and ten to one hundred and twelve. It is superfluous to cite the example of the English and American funds.

Up to the financial operations of Mr. Pelham, England had alleviated the burden of her public debt by arbitrary reductions, after the example of Holland, of the various states of Italy, of Spain, not to speak of France, the only one which it is usual to decry as an act characterized by violence. Mr. Pelham found himself obliged to obtain a semblance of voluntary assent on the part of the stock-holders; but the great difficulty found in carrying out Sir John Barnard's plan, arose from the absence of a regulating stock, bearing interest below four per cent. For this reason, it was necessary to wait till the funds had risen much above par, and even then to expose themselves to the risk of failure.

Mr. Pitt did all that he could to augment the mass of the five per cents., in order that his successors might one day have it in their power to diminish the burden of the debt very sensibly; it was in order to render this operation feasible that he made so much effort to give importance to the four per cents. Through pusillanimity Mr. Vansittart did not accomplish till 1822, what he might have done in 1818.

If there existed in France a stock at four per cent., as well as the five per cents., it is indubitable that the latter being at ninety per cent., the four per cents would be at seventy-eight or eighty, instead of seventy-two. The foreigner, speculating in the French funds, would prefer them to those of which the price would be more nearly at par, for his imagination would represent to him a profit of a quarter instead of that of a ninth: the amount of this stock would be more limited than that of the five per cents.,

* This paper bears no date, but it seems to be in its place here, although it may possibly have been written somewhat earlier.

which would necessarily produce a more considerable rise than the investment of the same sum; finally, small capitals would be invested in it to a greater extent.

I could have wished that the opportunity had been embraced of creating a stock at five per cent., when the treasury sold the twelve and a half millions of stock, or else when the reimbursement took place.

Undoubtedly this operation could not have been accomplished without making up your mind to some loss, since the exchequer ought to have the whole sum reimbursed, which it had expended in the purchase of the stock that it had been necessary to realize. But I am inclined to think—so far as one has a right to form an opinion at such a distance—that this loss would not have been very considerable: at any rate, there would have been no need to create fifteen millions, instead of twelve and a half, to obtain the same sum. I believe that the commissioners might have gradually drawn out the four per cents. on the Exchange, and the five per cents. would have risen more than they have done, and that they might have had the satisfaction of ending by investing a part of the four per cents. at the same price at which the grand negotiation was concluded.

You will pardon a foreigner the quaint expression, that there exists a species of emulation between the different kinds of public funds of the same nature, which impels them all forward when they are inclined to rise. Without a stock at four per cent., that at five per cent. would with difficulty rise above par, and till it should have exceeded par, a reduction of the interest of the debt could produce no result of sufficient importance.

In no wise personally interested that this measure should be some day carried out with success, and before long, it being in fact rather contrary to my interest, since I am not at all inclined to sell what I possess in the five per cents., it is for the interest of Europe in general, that I desire to see those brilliant ameliorations effected in France, which will insure gratitude and respect to the government.

CCXCVI.

ROME, *9th May*, 1823.

My beloved and revered friend, this letter to you is the first I have written since my arrival in this city, now almost become a home to me. Yours had arrived here before we had completed our tedious journey, and was the first I read after that of a friend of my youth, who, for a period of almost thirty years, has guided my life like a guardian angel, and who now stands before me and above me like a departed spirit in a better world; a friend who has awakened in me the best powers of my heart and mind, and roused them to action.

I have no words to tell you, how heartily I love you, and how acutely I miss your presence and your society. They could be only words of passion, which I can no longer utter. The time spent with you and yours, was the happiest that we have passed in Italy, and, through you, Naples will remain a hallowed spot in our memory as long as we live. Any real blessing we have once enjoyed is, in its best part, imperishable; and for old age, on the borders of which I stand, there can remain but little beside recollections. Still I fancy if I could live with you, I should grow young again instead of growing old.

I have learnt to know you as a husband and father; and my affection for you has found new and rich food; my wife and children cling to you and yours with that cordiality, without which the friendship of two men who are fathers of families must always remain imperfect. I esteem you happy in your household blessings, and congratulate myself that I have no reason to envy you in that respect. I constantly think of your wife with esteem, and with the pleasure which her bright, energetic, graceful ways inspire, and which is heightened by all that surrounds her; your children dwell in my heart as if they were of my own kindred.

My wife, who had been accustomed to frank sociability, had for years painfully felt the want of it here. She found it in your house, and if she gained strength in Naples, it was certainly much less owing to the air and the neighborhood of the sea, which she had been used to from her childhood, than to you and your dear wife. Marcus will never forget you, and the thought of your approval or disapproval will, I trust, ever remain with him, as it is now, a powerful incentive to good. As he grows older, and able to understand it, he will hear more and more of you, and the love with which he clings to you, is a holy sentiment whose preservation will be one of my first cares. He and the little ones remember your children with childish friendship, and your wife with gratitude and love.

We all pray that God's richest blessings may accompany you and your family, and the pious lips of the innocent children only echo the voice of their hearts. We pray that all the happiness you possess may be preserved to you; that you may have a vocation worthy of your noble mind, and receive a blessing in this vocation! These sentiments are our thanks for all your love and kindness, and for the happy time that we owe to you.

Hearty thanks for your letters, with which your father-land will be no foreign land to us. To your relations and friends I shall be able to speak of you out of the fullness of my heart; here I can not, excepting with a few young friends.......

CCXCVII.

ROME, *9th May*, 1823.

My revered friend, I shall try a commercial route to announce to you some tidings, which are in every point of view important to you.

It seems an understood thing that the King of Naples will remain at Vienna during the whole of this summer; or rather, it is said here, that this is quite certain.

But what I have to tell you now will sound to you quite incredible; and yet on closer consideration you will find it very probable.

It has been represented to your ministry, and they perceive themselves, that it might probably be impossible to get possession of the person of the King of Spain while hunting, and that yet the Junta could not supply the place of the monarch for any length of time. It has therefore been proposed to allow King Ferdinand of Naples, as his uncle, to be nominated to the regency, but with the condition that he shall appoint a substitute. He will hardly choose the Duke of Angoulême as his delegate. The nomination is to take place when the Junta is installed at Madrid; and it is positively asserted that this city will be occupied on the 28th.* Immediately upon this, the Count Brunetti will come forward in his capacity of Austrian embassador.

* The Duke of Angouleme entered Madrid on the 24th of April.

The objects of all this are as clear as day.

Two Spanish privateers have appeared before Civita Vecchia. This has suspended all the shipments of corn to Marseilles, which had just begun with fair prospects.

I say nothing to you about the proclamation of the Junta. You probably know that Eguia is a decrepit, avaricious general, without any personal weight. Of the other two I know nothing.

Give me to understand whether this letter reaches your hands uninjured. If you are sure of it, write to me when you find it necessary to be quite secure of secresy, under cover of a Neapolitan firm to ——, at Rome, or if I have left Italy, in the same way to St. Gall, addressed to ——.

The new Austrian postal regulations, to which the unpardonable detention of the correspondence at Bologna has certainly afforded a justification, place the whole correspondence of Italy under police *surveillance*. As regards the speedy dispatch of letters to Germany this is evidently an advantage; but even the letters to Parma must go *by way of Mantua*.

With all my heart your friend.

CCXCVIII.

TO MADAME HENSLER.

Rome, 11*th May*, 1823.

It goes to my very heart to think that this is the last letter I shall write to you from Rome. We live now like travelers in another house, quite in a different quarter. Yesterday I went with Marcus to our old home, which the owner is having altered and newly arranged for himself. It was like visiting a tomb. During the most gloomy times of our sojourn here, this house has always seemed cheerful to me. The side entrance is close to the remains of the semicircle of the theatre, once so magnificent. The house itself is built upon the ruin. You ascend a high and narrow flight of steps, enter a lofty, dimly-lighted ante-chamber, and turning to the right, find yourself in an apartment, from which the different parts of the dwelling-house recede at right angles, inclosing a garden on the same level, as both the house and the garden stand on arches and fragments that formed the first story of the colossal ruin. Here, all that we saw of Rome was the point of a single cupola, and we heard no sound, but the fall of a fountain in the garden. The owner is having every thing altered; the whole court was crowded with beasts of burden bringing building materials; our sitting-room was full of workmen, who were employed on one side in building up the windows, and on the other in breaking through the walls, in order to change the windows into glass doors, opening on the garden. The marble steps beneath the windows, on which all the children had played in their turns, were already broken up—fruit-pieces, painted in fresco, which had been a constant source of delight to them, were knocked away—where they had so often played and wept, there was no sound but the pick-ax of the workmen;—that garden, the centre of the whole abode, where we had so often walked up and down, unless the weather were extraordinarily unfavorable, was now desolate and as still as death—most of the rooms were shut up, and of one or two only could we obtain a glimpse by peeping through shutters or keyholes. The sight of what we had lost had made our hearts heavy: this scene of destruction and the death-like silence lacerated them. Marcus has both tender and deep feelings; he was affected as I was. The demolition had even extended to the paintings on the ceiling, in which the stories of Paradise and the patriarchal times were represented, though not by a master's hand, still greatly to the delight of the children, whose eyes were constantly attracted thither by the beautiful effects of color. They were already bespattered with whitewash, and as they had long been partially injured, while the poverty-stricken owner (who has lately made a rich match) allowed his princely dwelling to fall to decay, they were now destined to destruction. We went round in silence, and I told my boy, that as we wished to visit the Aventine once more, we would afterward return to gather a few flowers for the last time in our beloved garden. We continued our walk in silence and sadness; the boy, who always tries to conceal sorrow, complained that he was tired, and that his feet hurt him; we sat down on an old wall, and he crept close to me. Even running down a path, along which I had often led him, hardly seemed to comfort him; he took leave of the river, the "pons Sublicius," the island. "Yet I am not so sorry as you are, papa," he said, "for I shall see it all again when I grow up." We went back to the desolate house, and gathered flowers from the plants and creepers which had belonged to us for six years, and among which the children had grown up. I reminded myself that even if we had not left Rome, we should not have been able to remain more than a few days longer in this unequaled abode, and could not have saved it from destruction. Still, it was with heavy hearts, hardly restraining our tears, and but little consoled by the parting greetings which my boy gave to the different buildings we passed, that we returned to our present house. Do not let this make you think Marcus too sensitive, dearest Dora; nothing can be farther from the truth. For God's sake, do not fancy him affected, or acting a part; every thing comes from his heart. But the ruins, and the city, with its neighborhood, form his world. Do not either take me for sentimental, because it seemed to me as though I were parting from a friend when I stood before the statue of Marcus Aurelius, as the countenance was lit up and animated by the brightest rays of the evening sun. I feel very depressed. I leave this place with sorrow, because I know that I leave many true advantages behind me which can not be replaced, and do not know what awaits me in my own country, whither I return as a stranger, and may probably have a bitter life before me....... Farewell; a long and gloomy period to us both lies behind me, and seems now but a short dark night. May God bless you; may He give Gretchen health, may He preserve and develop the dear children! May He give me energy and wisdom to make use of the evening of my life.......

CCXCIX.

TO THE COUNT DE SERRE.

FLORENCE, 22*d May*, 1823.

MY MOST REVEREND FRIEND—I shall put numbers to my letters that you may know and inform me whether, and when any of them are suppressed. I beg you to do the same.......

We have again been delighted with the waterfall of Terni, and admired Assisi for the first time. I think you did not see this town of your great saint, and the noble buildings called into existence by the influence of a great and holy poor man on an age susceptible to such influence. Pray do not choose any other route, on your return, than that which will conduct you to Terni and Assisi. Near Narni you will see some grand scenery, and if you can spare half an hour, visit the Bridge of Augustus, one of the greatest Roman works; in Umbria, you will be delighted with the excellence of the husbandry. At Arezzo, I recommend the Cathedral to your attention, for the sake of its extraordinarily beautiful painted glass. When you come to the Lake of Thrasimenus, picture to yourself (what no historian mentions in this way, but is, notwithstanding, certainly true) that Hannibal, when the Romans were awaiting him near Rimini, on the only high road then opened—that which passed through Rimini and Foligno—forced his way from Lucca into Etruria, through the lower valley of the Arno, then a morass; and, while the Roman army hastened in terror through the most difficult passes of the Apennines toward Arezzo, in order to gain the high road to Rome, he turned to the right, and, passing by Cortona, marched on Chiusi along the *western* bank of the lake; the Romans then advanced along the high road by forced marches toward Perugia; but Hannibal faced round, and took the defile of Passignano, just as Davoust placed himself in our rear at Kösen, on the unhappy 14th of October. Hannibal, however, extended his right wing so far along the heights, that he engaged the heads of the Roman columns in the defile, at the same time that he pushed back their whole line toward the lake.

I do not know whether the unfortunate General Vaudoncourt—in whom I fancy your country has had no slight loss—has taken this view; no previous writer has; and that is why I write this to you against your journey home. Vaudoncourt's work, though printed at Milan, was not to be got at Rome! I expect that one of Bonaparte's generals will have perceived, what the scholars have not dreamt of, that Hannibal's course before the battle of Trevia, was exactly that of Bonaparte before Marengo; namely, that he crossed the Po below Piacenza, and cut the Roman army off from the road to Rome; the Po and the fortresses were behind him; therefore, utter destruction was his doom if he were beaten; but he knew that he should be victorious.

Here in Tuscany, the traveler is gladdened by the general aspect of prosperity and cheerfulness; the people appear to be in exactly the condition most agreeable to their true mode of life and natural feelings. Their moral superiority to the Romans strikes you immediately, still more so their piety, from its contrast to the total absence of it in Rome. You must not take it ill of us Protestants, if, after seven years' residence in Rome (though the people there often go to church every day), we regard this virtue as quite extinct among the Italians, because it is absolutely so in the Papal city. We were much edified here on Whit Tuesday by the real devotion of an immense multitude. It is, I think, easy to explain why it should be precisely at Rome that religious observances are now simply a wearisome task-work.

To him, however, who knows the history of Florence, it is painful to feel how insignificant are the descendants of great forefathers, and how, even the monuments themselves would decay and be utterly demolished, if most of them were not built as if for eternity. Since we were here seven years ago, the façades of several old palaces have been polished up with the chisel and whitewashed! The hotel at which we are staying, and which I highly recommend to you (Madame Hubert, in the Borgo

Santi Apostoli), was the palace of the family Acciaiuoli, whose lion, carved in stone, is still to be seen over the doors: this family, now almost extinct, numbered, from the thirteenth century onwards, great men of every kind among its members. They are every where destroying the old decorations of the houses, removing the pictures, and, instead of leaving the walls covered with paintings, among which there are always some master-pieces, having them daubed over with common landscapes by decoration painters. One family, Orlandini, did so with their villa quite lately, and gave the decorators paintings by way of payment, among which, there was a portrait from *Raphael's hand*, which some favorite of fortune bought of the equally ignorant house-painter for 300 scudi. This is the talk among the amateurs. An intelligent German, who has lived here for a considerable time, says, that since he has been here, thirteen whole galleries have been sold, without including the small collections.......

Literature and science seem to have reached their lowest ebb. During the seventeenth century, the Florentines still lived in the evening twilight of their brilliant day; they were still full of real love for the old time, the material creations of which, as well as all civil forms which did not affect the sovereignty, yet existed, and made that time quite present to them; they regarded themselves as citizens of the first city of Europe. During the former half of the eighteenth century, the country sank into poverty, and the inhabitants lost their acuteness and activity of mind; then followed a wise government, which restored prosperity to the country, but abrogated all the long-descended forms as trammels, and did not, like the Medicean, link itself on to the old times. The city began to understand that it was only a small part of Europe; a literary sect strove against the evidence of this, and, without a spark of the intellect of the old Florentines, wanted to retain the position of their heirs, and rejected every thing that had not passed away; they could see no value in any thing unless it had ceased to exist. It seems to me, that there are ultras in every branch of human affairs, and in every age, when a discord arises between the old and the new. Another party, to which all men of the world attached themselves, seized on the ridiculous side of the former, became cosmopolitan, and found a source of satisfaction in the common welfare of Europe, while evading the obligation of accomplishing any thing themselves. Thus every thing has gone to decay.

The aforesaid literary aristocracy has at last become quite democratic, and is just now engaged in collecting from the mouth of the porters and maid-servants, as the possessors of the treasures of the old language, the idioms which they desire to impose upon the writers of Italy. Does not this union between *that* aristocracy which only consists in pretensions, and the proletarians from whom alone it has nothing to fear, exist also in political history? I have found it in that of Rome.

During the few days that we were in Rome it was impossible to read through the documents laid before Parliament. Very likely they will have ceased to be topics of conversation by the time that I shall have leisure to read them in any place where they can be procured, and my hasty survey of the debates was enough to make me think, like you, that Canning is playing a miserable part; the assumptions, on the strength of which he went to such rash lengths in his expressions at the opening of Parliament, have not been confirmed, and therefore, his system has been altered. I am further certain, that even the English Cabinet would have seen no occurrence so unwillingly as the introduction of guarantees by France; from this fear they are, I should think, quite delivered. The declaration of the Junta might, however, have very hazardous consequences, or on the other hand, very favorable ones, if they adroitly agreed to recognize the interest due on the English demands, which they must do some time, and made it payable.

The course of the military movements in Spain, so far, is exactly what might be expected in such a state of decay and moral degradation. I know, indeed, nothing since the head-quarters were fixed in Burgos. The mention of fevers gave me anxiety, and I feel grieved that up to this time, as far as we can see, none but the clergy and the proletarians have come forward actively in favor of the counter-revolution; there is no mention of the higher classes of the laity. Thus appearances seem to point toward a repetition of the system which was so unfortunately adopted at Naples after 1799. After all, such a decay as that by which Spain falls to pieces at the first blow, is a terrible sight! So rotten has Europe become through revolution! The aspect of this is so threatening for us all, that one can not really abandon one's self to exultation at the exposure of the vaunts of the Liberals. The disease must constantly gain ground.

I can well conceive that the population of France must be increasing at an enormous rate, as ours with 12,000,000 under so much less favorable circumstances, is increasing at the rate of more than 150,000 a year. We are all weighed down by the impossibility of emigration on a large scale. However, we shall infallibly be one day visited by fearful pestilences, which will again produce a receding tide in the number of human beings, as in the fourteenth century; when, at all events, the greater part of Italy and Germany were much more thickly peopled than they are even now.......

CCC.

TO MADAME HENSLER.

St. Gall, *16th June*, 1823.

......We have found the Tyrolese as warm-hearted and lovable as on our journey hither; I think there can be no doubt that the true, noble part of the German character has nowhere been so distinctly preserved as among this simple primitive people. We found now, as before, the most sincere desire to oblige. At Innspruck, I made the acquaintance of a merchant, who was a member of the municipal administration, and was in all respects what one could wish a citizen to be. These people scarcely read even the meagre journal that appears in their country; they think of nothing but their immediate calling and their duties; and the few who have heard a vague rumor that there is such thing as liberalism in the world, are quite anti-liberal. As regards their own condition, they would strongly wish that most things should remain in the old track; but they resign themselves quietly and cheerfully to what can not be helped, and alleviate the pressure of the times by frugality and contentedness. The communes are now obliged to redeem the heavy communal debts by very high rates; they set themselves manfully to the work, and rejoice that they can look forward to an end of it. The peculiar Tyrolese character, cast of features, and costume, do not extend quite to the Arlberg. Before you reach the latter, you meet with that curious mode of building houses entirely of wood, which is common in Switzerland. The language, too, gradually changes into the Swabian Swiss. The race is quite different from the Tyrolese, namely, Swabian; while the latter are Bavarians. The Tyrolese have no gardens and no bee-hives, while both are common in the Vorarlberg and among the Swabian Swiss.......

The little town of Rheinek is old-fashioned and extremely cheerful-looking; else the general aspect of Switzerland betrays a surprising amount of poverty, even among the inhabitants of the beautiful districts I have described,* and their dwellings, quite unlike the villages in the Vorarlberg, which, nevertheless, unquestionably pay much higher taxes. But Switzerland is overpeopled beyond endurance, and this evil is constantly increasing; a man, whose word may be trusted, says, that in the Canton of Appenzell, out of five families, scarcely one has a house of its own and a plot of ground. The appearance of the children is by no means so blooming as in the Vorarlberg and the Tyrol; neither do the grown people look so robust or so cheerful. While, in the Tyrol, a stranger is not charged more than a native, and the traveling journeyman, for instance, will not ask you for any thing, or if they do, it is incredibly little, and demanded with embarrassment, it is notorious how the Swiss cheat travelers, and try to suck the very blood out of them. The Tyrolese seem stanch Catholics; but their superabundant belief is only a light outer garment, which does not conceal the essence of true piety. It is no obtusely superstitious people that affix such proverbs to their houses as the following, which I have recollected:

"We build us houses large and strong,
Where we're but guests, nor tarry long,
Careless a mansion to secure,
Which might for evermore endure."

"This house is mine, and yet not mine,
If thou com'st next it is not thine,
And if a third should take our place,
He'll still be in the self-same case,
The fourth too, men will bear away
Whose is the house then, can you say?"

"He who will build beside the way,
Must little care what people say;
But if he show his skill and art,
His work itself will take his part."†

---

* A thick forest of fruit-trees, among which the houses were scattered separately at some distance from the road.

† In the original:

"Wir bauen Häuser gross und fest,
Darin wir nur seyn fremde Gäst:
Und da wir sollen ewig seyn
Da bauen wir gar wenig ein."

"Das Haus ist mein, und doch nicht mein.
Der nach mir kommt, ist auch nicht sein;
Und wird's dem Dritten übergeben,
So wird's ihm eben so ergehen.
Den Vierten trägt man auch hinaus;
Ei, sagt mir doch! wess ist das Haus?"

"Wer da bauet an der Gassen,
Der muss die Leute reden lassen.
Doch hat er seine Kunst erprobt,
Alsdann das Werk den Meister lobt."

CCCI.

TO COUNT DE SERRE.

ST. GALL, 30*th June*, 1823.

Your consolatory letter, my revered and beloved friend, reached us a few hours after I had taken mine to the post. We have thanked God from our hearts that he has averted the peril that threatened you so fearfully. May He secure to you the possession of the sweet child by bracing her feeble powers, and grant you and yours the joy of living blessings!

I thank you heartily for having calmed our anxieties; still worse, and apparently later tidings, than those contained in your first letter, had reached us from Rome, so that we had scarcely any hope left. Besides, for a long time past, I have ceased to possess the faculty of hope, strictly speaking. I thank you with equal warmth for all the rest of your letter.

We are not able as yet to say positively how long we shall remain here; I can not exactly calculate how long it will take me to get through the work that the library presents. The interesting discoveries I have made here, are fragments of a panegyric in prose, and another in verse, on the great Ætius, who defeated Attila at Chalons. Scarcely any contemporary writings have been preserved from this period, which immediately preceded the fall of the Western Empire, and our knowledge of it is extremely scanty; on this account, these relics possess great interest, and also because they bring to light many facts that were previously quite unknown. They have also a still stronger interest for me, because they establish a circumstance of which I had long been certain, and had said so, but found few disposed to believe me; namely, that in this horrible fifth century there was much intellect, much more than in the preceding one. During the long cheerless apathy of the Roman Empire, all intellect had died out; people did not trouble themselves about the border war that was attended with no danger, and were only occupied with the lowest sensual enjoyments. The irruption of the Barbarians placed the existence of each individual at stake; through sheer self-love men learned that they had a father-land. Isolated great men appeared, and awakened genuine admiration; these panegyrics, in prose and verse, have been inspired by such sentiments. Religion filled men's hearts and thoughts; and the death-struggle of the old religion (of which my fragments contain an unexpected example), at least fired the imagination. Another interesting discovery, of quite a different kind, in some leaves, written at the latest in the sixth century, belonging to a liturgy much earlier than any of those extant; morning devotions of a very ancient date, that seem to belong to the *Stationes*, referred to at the beginning of the third century—extremely simple and venerable prayers. I am copying them for a good and learned monk, as a token of gratitude for his friendship; he can not read the defaced writing, but he will be able to edit them with much more knowledge of the subject than I. Besides these, I have a Latin Grammarian to copy out, who adds several words, not occurring elsewhere, to our stock of pure Latinity. This is a tedious job, and I wish some one else were here to do it; however, there is no one else here.

From hence we go to Zürich, where I also intend to look at the MSS., and shall perhaps find something. I wonder if our stay there will be more agreeable than here? I do not believe it will, except that the Lake of

Zürich affords a very different prospect from the uninteresting valley in which this town is situated, and the view we have from the heights here, where the shapeless outlines of the nearer and remoter mountains appear to form but one range. The cheerless part of the business lies in the dispositions of the people. The Revolution has dispelled all illusions; it was the fruit of the tree of knowledge that brought death in the day in which it was eaten.

For here every thing dates from 1803 and 1814. Men between thirty and forty years of age, who belong to the government, have not an idea what the constitution was before 1798. The dissatisfaction and discomfort which are every where blighting all happiness, exist here, quite as much as in those monarchies which are the farthest removed from fancied perfection—but no one seems to ask the reason of it. Is it not clear, however, that any constitution must produce miserable results, which calls far too great a number from the midst of absolute mediocrity, to power and a conspicuous station? In this new canton, numbering about 130,000 souls, among whom the inhabitants of the little capital (amounting to 8000) hold the same relation as those of any metropolis to the provincials, nine individuals are to be found for the Little Council and the government; then, further, the judges of a Court of Appeal, 150 deputies for the Legislative Council, a dozen under-prefects, more than forty mayors, a dozen courts of justice, besides municipalities, &c. Civil and criminal codes are formed, laws compiled, innumerable resolutions and enactments passed. Such a system can inspire no respect.

......The ferment in Ireland is, perhaps, the most unmistakable symptom of the sickness that has spread through the whole *body of society* in Europe, from which the spirit of civil union has more or less taken its departure. Sooner or later the constitution will have to be annulled in Ireland.

The revolution in Chili is very unfortunate. The wisdom of the dictator, O'Higgins, was incontestably proved by the instructions he gave to the envoy whom he dispatched to Rome. I should rather look upon the recovery of Spanish America as easy than impossible, if your government can venture to afford assistance to Spain. But that would, perhaps, be too dangerous a step.

CCCII.

FRANKFORT, 17*th August*, 1823.

......I thank you with my whole heart for your faithful and wise counsel about our future: but you are quite wrong in apologizing for it. I will write you a full answer as soon as we have found a place where I can have a room besides the nursery to write in. We hope for this at Bonn, where we shal. arrive in four or five days from now.

Up to this time, Heidelberg is the only place where I have enjoyed myself since we left the Tyrol. No doubt you know the town; it is impossible for an inland place to be more finely situated. I could not tear myself away from it, and remained there day after day. I saw again there a friend of my youth. I had looked forward with some dread to the meeting, because he has been involved in an acrimonious literary contest with Savigny, who is my nearest and dearest friend; and also because thirty years ago he was a fanatical admirer of the Revolution. I found that his misunderstanding with Savigny had terminated reasonably, and that his views of the world were as sensible as possible: such conversions are, however, rare among us. But there is a feud between him and an aged man, of great celebrity in our literature, Voss, the translator of Homer, with whom I have remained on terms of friendship from my childhood up, in spite of a thousand circumstances calculated to disturb it, and upon whom I can not turn my back, now that he is in his seventy-second year; and it is impossible to remain neutral between them, else we should probably have decided on stopping at Heidelberg.

My noble friend, since you take so much interest in the account of my journey, I have still much to tell you; and this shall be my first employment at Bonn, as afterward you will be my Muse of history. I have seen and experienced some remarkable things, of which I will certainly send you an account by post.

Please God, the Spanish war is approaching its termination; and yet I see no other end for it than absolute despotism, on the whole, with extensive provincial privileges. I rejoice in your successes; this is clear, that success has been never less abused than by your noble prince and your army. But shall I not also tell you that now, since we have become so closely bound together, I sympathize in all that relates to your father-land, as if it concerned myself, while I had already regarded it with very different feelings from my former ones, ever since you had appeared as a pure light in the firmament of your political world; that is, ever since the advent of freedom in connection with royalty, and your own appearance on the political stage?

We are on our way now to visit Savigny, while he is at a watering-place. I wish, both for his sake and yours, that you knew each other. My wife unites with me in best greetings to yourself, your wife, and the dear children; Marcus keeps both parents and children in his faithful heart. It is a pity that the interruptions of the journey encourage his indolence.......

CCCIII.

TO MADAME HENSLER.

FRANKFORT, 18*th August*, 1823.

......The stream* was full and the spectacle grand; still the rocks between which it forces its way, have an uncouth shape, and one should visit the place before one goes to Italy, not after one has seen the purely beautiful forms of the Velino and the Arno at Tivoli. The Swiss mountains in general have a painfully rude and mis-shapen aspect, from their jagged, quite inharmonic forms; the Tyrolese mountains are much more beautiful, and so are the mountains near Heidelberg, which are really not inferior to the graceful outlines of the most beautiful Italian mountains; they only want the coloring and the sky.

The promised beauties of the valley of the Neckar did not show themselves till about a [German] mile before Heidelberg, when indeed they far exceeded my expectation, and would have exceeded it, even if every thing since we left the Tyrol had not been so far below my conceptions. The scene was so lovely that I left the carriage, with Marcus, and went on foot to the town. It was evening, and we did not visit our acquaintance till

* The falls of the Rhine at Schaffhausen.

the next morning; Thibaut was gone into the country, his wife at church. We set off, not without some uneasiness, on the long walk to Voss's Garden. His reception was not cordial, and not unfriendly in its shy way; painful subjects were not touched upon, and I could soon see my way so as to avoid them. On subsequent occasions Voss often alluded to his position toward Thibaut, but never so directly as to make it unavoidable for me to understand him, and reply to him. Not till the fourth day did he speak of his attack upon Stolberg, when he brought me his last publication,* not his first. I warded off all explanation, and it went no further. To my great astonishment he judges very correctly with respect to the rest of the Wessenbergians.† He is not disinclined to believe that the youth are led astray by their instructors, because philology has been very badly treated by the Liberals. Any one who has watched the course of history, as I have done, during the last seven years, in Western and Southern Europe, must be roused to indignation by the lies of the Neckar Journal, which guides public opinion here. But the most exasperating thing is the Napoleonism of South Germany.

Voss did not look in the least aged since 1803; he is perfectly unchanged in body and mind; his wife is weak and infirm. Fearing that we might probably find it difficult to get on with him, we only expressed the intention of remaining a single day. But as every thing seemed likely to go on more smoothly than we could have expected, and the neighborhood was more beautiful than we could hope to see it again, we lingered day after day, and did not leave till Friday, instead of Monday. We divided all this time between the Vosses and the Thibauts. I have found Thibaut very unprejudiced, and very sound in his views upon all general subjects; friendly, and open. His children are admirably brought up, and the eldest boy has a singularly noble and amiable disposition. Our children were as if in heaven in his exquisitely beautiful garden, and their loveliness won all hearts; Marcus was quite admired for his ability and acuteness. One evening the children were there alone, and Marcus delighted every body by the sharpness of his answers, combined with his perfectly childlike manners.

I have made the acquaintance of one truly excellent man there, the historian Schlosser (from Jever). This I see, that my History has now acquired an authority which no attacks can shake. I staid a day at Darmstadt, and looked through the MSS., which contain nothing of consequence. We are staying a day and a half here in Frankfort, to have the opportunity of writing some letters in a hotel where we are not packed quite so closely together. I have only one old acquaintance here, for whom a few hours will suffice; in those, however, I shall gain much information from him. The embassadors I mean to ignore.......

* "Wie F. L. Stolberg unfrei geworden ist."

† Wessenberg was a liberal Catholic ecclesiastic, who wished for a reform in the Catholic Church, and had many followers in Germany. Niebuhr believed him to be a well-intentioned, but superficial man, quite unfit to play the part of a reformer.

CHAPTER XI.

NIEBUHR'S RESIDENCE IN BONN, FROM AUGUST, 1823, TO JANUARY, 1831.

1823, 1824.

NIEBUHR had scarcely arrived in Bonn when Steinacker's attack on him in his edition of Cicero "De Republicâ," fell into his hands, which wounded him more deeply than it probably would have done at another time, because it embittered his return to his own country. It gave rise to two pamphlets in his own defense on Niebuhr's part. For himself, the controversy had, however, one favorable result; for while engaged in investigating the points in dispute, he suddenly perceived the solution of a difficulty which had been the chief cause of his delay in continuing the History of Rome. This discovery decided him to resume the work, which had been so long laid aside, and he received it as a happy omen that the day on which he formed this resolution was the anniversary of his betrothal with his first wife, to whom he had promised on her death-bed that he would finish his great work.

In September, 1823, he paid a visit to M. Von Stein at Nassau, but postponed his intended journey to Berlin on account of the absence of the Crown Prince. On his return, he set to work on his Roman History, at which he labored with such assiduity, that he completed the half of the third volume in the course of the winter, except its final revision. Indisposition afterward interrupted his studies. He then began to revise the two former volumes for a second edition (the first being out of print), in which he wished to embody the results of his maturer researches. He would have preferred to finish the sketch of the third volume at once, but the alterations necessary in the two earlier volumes occupied him so deeply that they withdrew his thoughts from the later portion.

His studies were again interrupted in the spring by his wife's confinement with a second son, and afterward by his journey to

Berlin, before which, however, he found time to prepare a new edition of Merobaudes for publication.

In May, 1824, he went to Berlin, visiting M. Von Stein on his way. There he presented himself to the King, saw the Crown Prince, with whom he renewed his former friendship, and greatly enjoyed the meeting with his friends. But his happiness was soon disturbed by tidings from home: all his four younger children were taken ill in succession, and the infant died on the 4th of June, after severe suffering. Niebuhr, however, experienced at this time a circumstance which often occurs in human life—that a greater calamity helps to lift us above smaller evils, and quickens our sense of the blessings still left to us. The death of the child raised him above other crosses and cares, and turned his thoughts to that which he still possessed, but might also lose. The recollection of the advantages he had enjoyed in Rome, and the uncertainty which hung over his future prospects, had hitherto frequently exercised a very depressing influence on him. He now resolved to request a definite release from his duties as embassador, and, after repeated applications, at length obtained it, with a provisional salary equal in amount to what he had received before he left Berlin. He thus at last obtained leisure to devote himself to the studies which he had always regarded as his true vocation. He had now decided to settle in Bonn, but the course of his employments was interrupted by a summons to Berlin, to attend the sittings of the Council of State during the ensuing winter. He therefore returned to Berlin toward the end of November, and spent the winter principally in working with two Commissions, appointed by the Council of State to deliberate on the erection of a National Bank, and the tenure of land among the Westphalian peasantry.

The death of De Serre, in the autumn of 1824, affected him deeply. Madame de Serre wished that he should write her husband's life, and invited him to come to Paris in order to examine the documents which she could not send him. It was Niebuhr's full intention to raise this monument to the memory of his friend, but various circumstances hindered his visit to France, and at length his own sudden death frustrated the design.

Letters from September, 1823, *to May*, 1825.

CCCIV.

TO MADAME HENSLER.

BONN, 10*th September*, 1823.

I get constantly more and more ill at ease the longer this existence without a present and a future continues; all that comes under my notice makes an unfavorable impression on me. Wherever you go, you hear nothing but dissensions and quarrels, without being able to sympathize with any party. The feuds between the various factions and *nuances* among the Catholics for instance, naturally strike me in this way, as also their discussions with the Protestants. The people know that I understand the points in question, and am logically fair. I know very well too, what is logical, just, and true; but in such disputes I can not take any kind of interest. It is the same with every thing. Literature seems to me as good as dead, the moral condition of the nation mournful, according to the accounts I hear from persons of the most opposite tendencies, some of whom are far from finding offensiveness offensive. Frivolity, a striving after ease and leisure, and the want of a proper sense of duty pervade the whole of society. In these pursuits our nation cuts a very awkward figure, as Jacobi prophesied more than forty years ago.

I find myself greeted here with a malicious and rancorous literary attack, by people whose waters I never thought to trouble. And so this then is my reception to the bosom of my father-land!

We must give up our journey to Paris; there are too many difficulties in the way. I shall, therefore, leave for Berlin the day after to-morrow, and visit M. von Stein in my way thither; he has repeatedly invited me, and loss of time and extra distance must not be taken into the account in visiting a man so far advanced in years.

......Brandis has received us with his old heartiness and warmth. Another acquaintance of ours is a Catholic Professor of Theology, who staid for some time in our house at Rome—Dr. Scholz—as thoroughly good a man as Brandis. A Protestant theologian, named Nitsch, seems a man of extremely distinguished talent.

CCCV.

TO COUNT DE SERRE.

BONN, 8*th October*, 1823.

......Such an affront as the pamphlet I have alluded to could not be left unnoticed in the face of our reading (and only reading) nation; I began an answer to it, and five times without success. A last attempt pleased me better, though it is by no means what I could have produced in the best years of my youth. But while engaged on it, a light unexpectedly broke in upon my mind, illustrating a point in the Roman history, of whose elucidation I had despaired for twelve years. This consoled me, and inspired me with fresh vigor. It happened that this light related to the great change in the *comitia*, as regards *the electoral law*, and I now gained a complete insight into its import, which I had previously misunderstood to a great extent, as most others have done entirely; namely, I saw that its tendency was to bring the elections under the influence of the landed proprietors and hereditary citizens, without excluding the trades and the citizens not possessing an ancestry. You were constantly in my mind while I was writing; and my heart beat, when I discovered who the great Roman was, who once effected what you too have accomplished; and as a reward for his work, was surnamed Maximus by his nation, a title which five consulates and triumphs had not been sufficient to procure for him.

It so happened that I gained this new light on the anniversary of my betrothal to my late wife, whose last wish was that I should finish my History; and the coincidence kindled my courage to undertake the continuation which had been so long delayed. Thus my life is no longer without a vocation, and my melancholy, therefore, is vanquished. Do you know what has made me recognize most clearly all that you are to me? That in my dejection, I longed inexpressibly to see you, and no less when serenity was restored to my overclouded mind. Do not understand me as setting any value upon the little essay that you are expecting and shall have; the execution of the great work will not interfere with it......

The inclosed is the first of a series of communications respecting the state of Germany, the continuation of which you shall receive from time to time.* God bless you and yours, my only late-found friend! May He keep and defend you! My wife and children unite with me in hearty love to you and your dear family.

CCCVI.

TO MADAME HENSLER.

Bonn, 29*th October*, 1823.

......I have now worked through a very difficult chapter in the History. I have no lack of ideas, but I feel that I have grown old and drier than I should be under other circumstances; outward things disturb me, even the dear interruptions caused by the children. It is but too certain that there is a perfection in authorship unattainable, except where the author has no children, or acts as if he had none; which God forbid! Another great difficulty arises from the absence of my own library.

We have made an excursion to Cologne, which has not disappointed my expectations, but in many respects exceeded them; although the city is ugly, and has been despoiled of most of its works of art. The prebends, who were never reduced to actual want, sold many of the treasures during their emigration, and even a part of the golden shrine that contains the pretended relics of the Three Holy Kings—the jewels as well as the gold plate. A mere accident saved the greater part of them from destruction. Such was the conduct of the men who made an outcry about sacrilege, because they had been driven, it must be confessed very unjustly, from their benefices!

It is cheering to see the universal prosperity in the Prussian Rhenish provinces, which proves that the government has at least the merit of pressing very lightly on the people. You see improvements making in all directions, and fresh land brought under tillage wherever it is capable of it. I hear that this is particularly the case along the Moselle, where the wines have reached a higher price than has ever been known before.

* The paper alluded to is on the political condition of Switzerland, and is published in the Lebensnachrichten, vol. iii. p. 423.

The population of Cologne has increased by 8000; for centuries houses have been pulled down; now new ones are building, and it is said that rents have risen to double their former amount. The same change is taking place to a still greater extent here, at Düsseldorf, at Coblentz, and at every town you hear of.

But for the difference of religion, the people would soon be reconciled to their new rulers, because they are really well off; but unhappily the Rhenish Catholics are either, on the one hand, free-thinkers and Jacobins, or, on the other, bigots, who can feel no attachment to a heretical sovereign.

The government really makes incredible efforts for public instruction, and quite without regard to expense; but the priests look upon all these institutions with jealousy and mistrust, although the government, which committed some errors at first, now wisely avoids every thing which could really give them occasion for uneasiness.

If you compare the state of these provinces with the aspect of things in Baden, Würtemberg, Darmstadt, where impoverishment and misery every where betray themselves, you feel how much better off the people are *under present circnmstances* in great States than in small ones. Moreover, you are often reminded how much fewer blunders are made in a large State than in a small one; because, as soon as you go beyond the limits of a city, the problem of the government is always the same; and supposing, in both cases, the same want of skill in the choice of competent persons, yet in small States the number of such is necessarily so much smaller, and there is less chance of their appointment by a fortunate accident.

The Catholic religion, such as it is in these parts, is called, even by orthodox Catholics, benighted heathenism. For example, on processions to a place in this neighborhood, a fellow dances on a tight rope, with a banner in his hand, to the sound of Turkish music, as soon as the Litany is over. These absurd exhibitions were forbidden under the French rule; they have been allowed to creep into use again by the mildness of our government, and I myself, were I in authority, should fear to act tyrannically in forbidding them. The clergy is constantly sinking into deeper ignorance; the Vicar-general promotes fellows who have been to no school whatever, and refuses to receive those who have studied at the University. What is to become of the Catholic religion God knows! It *may* re-establish itself in *the same way* that it did after the suppression of the Reformation, and then the ignorance prevailing in the Catholic countries of Germany will become still denser. But this proves, above all things, how powerless Protestantism is nowadays.

Events in Spain are turning out, step for step, just as I expected; among other things, the fall and banishment of the noblest men, such as the Marquis de las Amarillas, who, after having in vain endeavored to induce the King to give guarantees against the renewal of his tyranny, remained in the palace on the night of the 7th of July, in order to die with the royal family, if a 10th of August followed; not to speak of the proscription of the noble-hearted Valdes, who did indeed pursue a phantom in his attachment to the Constitution, but whose whole conduct had been without a spot for four years, and who had prevented the shedding of blood after the 7th of July, at the peril of his own life. I have foreseen all this, and yet my wishes have been on the side of the result which has actually ensued. We have witnessed a strange issue of affairs, which must force us to look with profound contempt upon our age; it has been for years impossible to hope for a happy issue, *because the revolutionists* have rendered that out of the question. Of the two extreme results, the actual seems to me the preferable one, though a shocking abuse will be made of it every where. As a member of the middle class, for the sake of my son, the consolidation of a decaying aristocracy is a subject of regret; but with us, in Germany, it can never become so loathsome as Liberalism. The burning fever of the Revolution has spent itself, like a pestilence that at last vanishes spontaneously. A very unintellectual period will come now, but we shall have repose, and be able to return to the quiet life of our grandfathers, who were not, however, threatened like ourselves with subjugation by barbarians.

I recognize and duly estimate the force of your reasons, dear Dora, against resigning my post at Rome; but you can not understand how impossible it would be to take Gretchen back there, since her health is certainly much better in the air of Germany, and, above all, she has so great a dislike to the life we led in Italy.......

CCCVII.

Bonn, 11*th December*, 1823.

...... I turn to answer one part of your letter. It must certainly be owing to some carelessness in expressing myself, that you could suppose I meant to say any thing to the disadvantage of the Germans as compared with the Italians. God forbid! What I mean is, that I ought to have an adequate compensation for what I give up in point of health and comfort, and the variety of interesting objects of contemplation, if I am not to feel that I have lost by the exchange. The case is different with any one who has retained his youthful connections in Germany. I come back to a world in which the opposing parties are impelled and guided by vague sentiments and heated passions, and all alike have adopted their opinions on the authority of newspapers, periodicals, and the Conversations-Lexicon; and in these authorities they put such faith, that they anathematize every one who has more insight than themselves. I would just as soon talk about religion with a bigoted Catholic peasant, as converse with such people about the weightiest concerns of the world. Such wisdom I may dare to despise, when three men, of three such different nations, and each of them the first, or among the first men of their own nation, as M. Von Stein, M. de Serre, and Lord Colchester, give me credit for a profound knowledge of the material and intellectual condition of the leading states of Europe, ask me for my opinion, and take my verdict on matters as an authority, while in these trivial circles every one is wiser than I.

Although I grant you that the state of affairs in Germany might be much more cheering, if the governments were better, you must also concede to me that these governments are a part of the nation; so much so that the difficulty would not be so much to find one man with right views, but how such a one would form a ministry; and supposing he accomplished this, where would he find his subordinate officials, and members of the provincial governments. There is the great difficulty. It is easy to say that you must set bounds to arbitrary power by Chambers and municipalities; I say so too, for it is true; only no effectual assistance is to be hoped from them. For instance, I have always opposed the system of regulating public instruction throughout the monarchy by the central government, and wished that the schools should again, as formerly, be placed under the superintendence of the clergy and local authorities. But then we are met by examples which show how much worse things are where this is the case; not only here, where the Catholic priests aim at excluding the laity of their own church from the schools, or in Coblentz, where men who wore the red cap during the Revolution, and carried the goddess of Reason about, having now turned devotees, though remaining as arrant Jacobins as ever in politics, are straining every nerve to displace or worry to death the upright, learned *Catholic* Director of the Gymnasium —but even in Berlin itself, where the civic authorities, and very respectable men among them, openly avow the wish (and actively exert themselves to further it in the Gymnasium which is under their jurisdiction) to depress the study of philology, and to make instruction in the so-called useful branches of knowledge predominant. The nobility cherish oligarchical pretensions, and yet will on no account consent to strengthen the basis of their order; our order does not know what it wants. Had the men in whose hands the decision lay, attempted to erect a constitution among us in 1816, every thing would have gone to pieces by now. Our gymnastic heroes would have managed no better. I have never ceased to mourn over the persecutions which were set on foot at that time; but if a terrible Fate has decreed that these severities should have been committed, or that we should have continued on the path we were then treading, and suffered the whole youth of the country to be turned into madmen and savages, at all events the least of two bitter evils has befallen us. What fellows they were who then excited universal sympathy as martyrs! Very many of them have veered round to the opposite extreme. The better members of this sect had learnt nothing, and made at least as extravagant claims to be supported by the State, as you could find among any young scions of nobility. I can nowhere see solid ground; and truly I am not alone in my dark forebodings. With the most irreproachable intentions, and sincerely thinking to benefit the agricultural population, they are ruining the whole peasant class by giving them power to sell, to cut up, and to mortgage their land; and every thing is tending in the same direction. The lowest and most superficial views have become universally prevalent; and whether ministries or Chambers have to decide upon measures, you obtain the same results. Men are not ill-intentioned; but in all the German states that are not stationary, the tendency of the legislation is, according to the saying of a distinguished man, to bring our nation to the level of the Italians: in the towns, half-skilled artisans and petty tradesmen; in the country, miserable tenants-at-will, and day laborers. With an agricultural population like that of Wurtemburg, can you ask for freedom?

Believe me, dearest Dora, these are not prejudices. I have studied the history of the legislation of many nations, through a series of centuries, and hence I know where we are standing, and whither we are going. In our nation there are men as excellent, both in mind and heart, as are to be found any where, and such as many nations, the Italians for instance, do not possess at all, or very rarely. Here is Brandis, Nitzsch (an extraordinary man), and several others among the professors in Bonn, are worthy of all honor. One of the most distinguished, whom I should probably never have heard of, in his retired corner, if he had not sent me some essays through M. Von Stein, is a Dr. Schulze, in Hamm, unquestionably a real historical genius, and moreover an admirable writer: so too I became acquainted with Pertz and Bluhme when in Rome. But sound sense and sound morality are not general among us, as they were with our forefathers. In the pettiest towns there are billiards and clubs, and family life exists no longer. The Revolution is vanquished, and whoever now fears revolts, sees phantoms; but as to what will come next, I have no presentiment of good.

M. Von Stein has invited us all warmly and repeatedly to his house. At this time of the year it is impossible to take all the children; but I shall go myself alone to Nassau for two or three days. He warns us touchingly to remember his age, and that if we do not see each other as often as possible our meeting may soon become impossible forever. He has become quite gentle, and his behavior toward me has a sort of fatherly tenderness. I believe that he has much to bear......

CCCVIII.

BONN, *6th January*, 1824.

Marcus has had a violent attack of influenza. The child was obliged to keep his bed two days: I remarked, altogether, that the physician here had returned to the old precautionary measures. This will therefore probably be the present fashion in medicine, with which I am very well satisfied if it only lasts. That medical art consists in fashion is indeed nothing new: we may thank God when no desperate systems happen to be in vogue. Marcus was very good and amiable during his illness; he is certainly a much better child than I was, though I may have been, perhaps, more easy to educate. Göschen teases him too much with learning hymns by rote. I have no objection at all to learning by rote, particularly as the boy finds a difficulty in it, while all his recollections of principles and observations are ineffaceable. I wish, I strive with all my heart, that he may grow up with the most absolute faith in religion, yet so that his faith may not be an outward adhesion that must fall away from him afterward, when his reason comes into play, but, that from his earliest years *the way may be prepared* for the union of faith and reason. I should therefore quite approve hymns, but that the number of those adapted to a child not yet seven years old is so small; for where they can present no idea to his mind, the difficult sentences are a torment to him. To a happy child, hymns deploring the misery of human life are without meaning; so, likewise to a good child, are those expressing self-accusation and contrition. In all departments of education, it is certainly a main point not to come to any thing too early, and that holds good here as well as in learning. I am succeeding admirably in exercising the powers of his mind, by efforts exactly proportioned to them, so that I can say with confidence, that he has not a single thought beyond his age, none that is not quite suitable to a child; and yet he often delights us with the originality of his ideas. I always oblige him to reflect, and to set himself right within his own sphere. It was not departing from it that he asked, during his illness, "in Latin there are already five tenses; but what tense of a verb is that when you want to express that you are on the point of doing something? It can not be the present tense, but yet it is not the future, is it?" From a boy with a decided taste for grammar, which displays itself in the great eas with which he now learns the forms already familiar to him in reading, such a speech is no more a sign of precocity, than the discovery of a mathematical proposition was in Pascal, that born mathematician......

CCCIX.

TO COUNT DE SERRE.

BONN, *4th February*, 1824.

......England will, without a doubt, lower her old four per cent. funds during the present session; the amount of this stock is not very large, but this step will prepare the way for a similar operation with the three per cents. next year, by which the national burdens will be very considerably lightened. But, in order to effect this, peace is necessary, and I venture to hope that, after the experiment in Spain, your government has renounced all idea of attempting to recover America. Posterity will pronounce a woe upon those through whom Spanish America was rent away, and could not again be brought into subjection. I, however, do not see in these countries seminaries and models of the democratic republic; but I see that a portion of them will be converted into negro States, like St. Domingo; the rest will be dissolved, and become a prey to the greatest anarchy, unless a dictator arise. It is now too late to prevent this; and it is England that will have the greatest reason to repent her conduct, since North America must immediately obtain the superiority, and she will infallibly lose her West Indian possessions. What a fatal confusion reigns there already! If it is really true that the resolutions of Parliament respecting the treatment of the negroes, have raised a ferment among the latter, it would follow that you must tolerate the greatest atrocities on the part of those who are under your authority, if they are resolved to persevere in their commission, and if their opposition to your reforms would produce still greater calamities. Is not this a much more difficult case of clashing duties than that of the casuists, where it is a question of saving life? The regulations which the parliament has not even commanded, but simply recommended, do not at all affect political rights; have not even a remote reference to emancipation, but solely to moral enormities, the abolition of which has been fruitlessly recommended by the government in private. In these islands, the white population will be exterminated, if at any time the power of the mother country should be insufficient to suppress a general outbreak; in the Spanish colonies, the whites will be merged in the colored population; in many countries, the Spanish language, which is even now very little spoken by the creoles, will die out; entirely new nations will arise, but they will be barbarous.

My country will owe me no slight thanks if I have excited your interest in it, my beloved friend. Your remarks upon the projected provincial Chambers are full of weight: would to Heaven that you lived among us, and could make them practically influential. You remind me how it was recognized in France, before the Revolution, that it would be impossible to govern, if the whole kingdom had consisted of provinces each possessing Chambers. Has not this principle a still wider application, and is it not always impossible to govern without despotism, where no diversity of rights exists—rights appertaining to provinces or classes? So, again, there is a period when this diversity can not be maintained, because it has ceased to exist in practice. It seems to me that we have committed a great error in making the provinces too large. Had the old provinces been left as they were and not thrown together, a sufficient number of people, of sound understanding and upright character, would have been found in them, who would have managed their domestic affairs unassumingly and well; but in our Westphalia, people assemble from such distant parts that they are strangers to each other, and get upon general topics, because the one knows nothing of the municipal affairs of the other, and takes no interest in them; in fact, the very man who best feels where, as we say, the shoe pinches, is frequently outvoted by the rest, if, as is very often the case, the majority of the other counties are not concerned in the question under discussion. But it is the least of my fears that the ministers will prevent the project from coming into effectual operation at all, by giving the Chambers nothing to deliberate on but trifles. It is worthy of note, how nearly all who have had to do with the scheme, while really any thing but liberal themselves, yet secretly believe that none but liberal ideas are sensible; and, from fear of seeming unenlightened, take steps which even popular opinion would not call for, if they would do something better. In all parts of our territory, except the country on this side of the Rhine, we possess manorial estates, and with them the means of forming an order of nobles, and an excellent criterion for selecting the members of it, viz., the possession of such an estate, coupled either with an hereditary and unforfeited nobility, or with the attainment of a certain grade in the military or civil service. Formerly, the possessor of a manor was only eligible to the Diet when of noble descent, and because this was preposterous (thus, for example, in one of the Saxon circles, there is only a single proprietor of noble descent remaining), they have now gone to the other extreme, and make the simple fact of possession the sole condition. At the same time, the nobility, who are deeply encumbered, are selling one estate after another, and the new proprietors are generally men of the lowest extraction. Well, the nobles are now remonstrating against this in provinces where they have on the whole maintained their ground, as in Münster, for instance; and what do they demand? The old law; that none but noblemen by birth or creation, shall be eligible to the Chambers. Now every grand duke will grant patents of nobility on the payment of fees, and, in consequence, a commoner who prides himself upon the honor of his class, will not allow himself to be ennobled. Thus I should be excluded; every contractor in Darmstadt or Carlsruhe, who is willing to spend a few thousand florins for it, would be admissible. Had I been able to make my voice heard, when I made the assertion, in attestation of which I adduced evidence from the President Hénault, that this was formerly the case in France, and supported it by obvious proofs, that thus alone a self-renewing order of nobles could exist, the public would have been delighted. As it is, they are more displeased that the aristocracy should exist as an order, than pleased that it should have been divested of all moral significance. One hopeless circumstance is the despotic influence exercised by revolutionary ideas among us Germans, wherever absolute power can avail itself of them for its own purposes. In Westphalia and in other parts, we have in the entailed freeholds an hereditary yeomanry, in whom, wherever they exist, we possess a highly respectable peasantry aristocracy, wealthy enough to give their younger sons a good education, with the consciousness of an honorable descent and a youth not depressed by poverty, and thus to add respectable members to the middle class, especially to the clergy of both confessions. But wherever the Code Napoleon has been introduced, its adherents, who have gained the public ear by assuming to be the representatives of public opinion, insist upon the divisibility of landed property. They had already surreptitiously obtained a confirmation of the French and Westphalian ordinances; and though this is suspended, Heaven knows how the matter will be decided at last. Yet people have before their eyes the example of other German countries, where this cursed divisibility has existed for centuries, and the whole agricultural population are beggars. In the district of Montabaur, now belonging to Nassau, no deputy can be chosen for the Diet, because it does not contain a single elector. The qualification for an elector consists in paying *one* florin land-tax. This sounds incredible, but my informant lives close to the district, and has known that part of the country from his infancy.

Here on the Rhine, the larger estates are entirely disappearing, and the smaller ones are constantly divided and subdivided; and what a class are the peasantry! An estate which is considered one of the largest was sold lately for about 85,000 francs. Manufacturers, advocates, &c., buy plots of land and farm them out, so that in the neighborhood of the towns the peasant proprietors are vanishing, as in Italy. The agriculturists, excepting the vine-growers, are suffering severely from the low prices; yet their condition is incomparably better than in Suabia and in Holstein, where a manor, which I know, was sold lately for a quarter of what the deceased possessor expended on its purchase twenty-five years ago, and in real improvements; in a village belonging to it, every peasant is bankrupt. One great difficulty, is the really frightful increase of population, to which people are now beginning to turn their attention after having long childishly rejoiced in it. You will scarcely believe that with us in Prussia, where the population does not yet amount to eleven millions, it is increasing at the rate of more than 200,000 a year. In these parts, however, you see new houses springing up in great number; I hear the Moselle districts are particularly flourishing in this respect, in consequence of the increased protective duties on foreign wines; that new houses are building in all directions, and fresh land brought under cultivation, but in other parts of Germany this is not the case. Our manufacturers are maintaining their ground better than I expected; in many articles in which twenty years ago the English manufactures quite predominated, they no longer compete with our own; for instance, in broadcloth, other kinds of woolen goods, and leather; the demand for foreign iron-wares is constantly diminishing. The misfortune is that the manufacturers over-produce, and then the necessity of selling makes them vulnerable to every accident. As the price of the raw material falls, the manufacturer is obliged to reduce the prices of the articles manufactured when it was higher. The number of paupers is increasing immensely. Cologne has recovered itself to an extraordinary extent since 1814; houses have more than doubled in value, the population has greatly increased, but one learns with horror that out of 55,000 inhabitants, there are 20,000 in the receipt of alms. What will be the position of Europe within a century?

I turn from statistics to a subject which indeed our statists do not overlook in their tables—namely, literature. Poetry is quite at an end. Nothing but novels—precisely what we can not write—are written now; their favorite scene at present is Greece. Of philosophy people seem to have had enough at present, and during the lull, a few here and there are actively prosecuting really profound researches into the Greek philosophers, and coming to perceive that speculation has been exhausted in its results. The study of Roman jurisprudence is carried on with great vigor. Some excellent and many monstrous works have seen the light, in consequence of the shock which I have given to the criticism of ancient history. One book that I should rejoice to see in your hands is Menzel's History of the period from 1786 to 1815, of which the first part has just appeared. It is pervaded by the soundest views, the most thorough contempt for the miserable wisdom of the revolutionists, and such a correct tact in discovering truth, that one is astonished to see a professor in Breslau able to pass judgment upon facts as if he lived in the busy scene of action. Unfortunately the book has been written too hastily, as is usually the case with us, namely, while the printing is in progress, and hence it is wanting in finish. It is far superior to another work, the latter half of which relates to a portion of the same period, F. C. Schlosser's History of the Eighteenth Century. I am acquainted with the author of the latter; he is a most upright man, and his moral sense is pure; hence he abhors and despises the Revolution in reality: but he fell in with Guizot at Paris, nay with Grégoire and it has led him into ugly inconsistencies here and there. For this reason a translation of his work is coming out in Paris. Out of a hundred of those who speak on such matters in Germany, you would hardly find one who would not regard Liberalism as the lesser of two evils, and hardly five who would not regard it as absolutely excellent. Manuel's portrait has hung beside that of Mina in all the print-shops, but he seems at last to be forgotten for a time.

In the Frankfort reading-room, there are two copies of the "Constitutionnel," and the people quarrel who shall get it first. Here the police prohibit that paper, and foolishly enough admit the "Courier," which it is scarcely possible to see the first day, while it is very seldom that any one takes up the "Journal des Debats." The "Allgemeine Zeitung" has drawn in its claws a little after very serious threats, still it often gives vent to its spite. An Ultra journal has been set on foot here, which is injured by the contemptible character of its editor (he was an agent of King Christophe, at Hayti, to hire artisans), and an affectation of bigoted Catholicism; but some very remarkable documents appear in its pages, and some very unpleasant truths for the opposite faction. All such writers, however, carp at your Richelieu ministry. † †, in the "Allgemeine Zeitung," who now swears by the present ministry, will probably in two months adore those whose opposition he has hitherto, on many occasions, gently blamed.

For what place do you stand? You will easily fancy that I am as much interested about that as about the general results of the election; though my wish is, that you may remain in peace under your lofty blue sky. But is this my real wish? I will not be too sure about it, for when we are considering where we shall live for the future, as it will most likely not be in Berlin, there is, in fact, only one reason that decides us to take up our abode here; it is the desire to settle at no impassable distance from you—a thought that pierces my heart when Berlin is talked about, and makes it almost impossible for me to think of living there. If you retire into your province, we shall be quite near each other; and even if you live in the capital, you will no doubt sometimes visit Lorraine. And as nothing binds me to Bonn, we might perhaps settle at Treves, if you lived at Metz. I shall never forget your saying in your last letter, that you and your wife felt the want of my presence in your afflictions.* I can not tell you how deeply I thank you for it. How we miss you!......

CCCX.

BONN, 29*th March*, 1824.

......I think I understand you that the 12th was your birthday. We celebrated it quite in private, and Marcus entreated, in his childish prayers, that you and yours may receive every blessing, and for us—that we may see you again. Tell me, dear friend, whether I was wrong in the day, though a factual error about the date would be of no more consequence, than a mistake as to the historical object of your worship......
I can not write to you any more to-day, as I have charge of the children, and the hour is come at which I am to give my eldest little girl a lesson......

I can not obtain a certainty with respect to my future position. You will agree, that I must have a very strong party feeling when I say that, in spite of these circumstances, I *am rejoiced* to hear of the reduction of the rate of interest in France, though it affects the greater part of my fortune, provided that the emigrants, &c., are to receive some compensation.......

CCCXI.

TO MADAME NIEBUHR.

BERLIN, 18*th May*, 1824.

I arrived here on Sunday, with which ends the first act of this drama. It was still broad daylight when I arrived, and I would much rather have got in at a later hour. I went the same evening to Savigny, where I found old acquaintances assembled at tea. You can imagine, my Gretchen, how the meeting with friends and acquaintance, and the sight of Berlin with all its painful recollections, agitated my heart.......

As to the essential part of our concerns, I have received as yet, simply a recommendation to return to Rome, to which I replied, that the same reasons which necessitated the abandonment of my post there forbade my return; that my grounds for this step were well known, and were not founded in self-interest or ambition. So much was clear, that Count Bernstorf would willingly consent to granting my leave of absence, but this would be a mere postponement of the decision, which would not be of any use. In the afternoon I saw the Crown Prince; his reception of me was most cordial. I was with him three hours, and he invited me to spend some time with him regularly every afternoon.

I have dined with the King to-day: his reception of me was gracious.....

As you will easily imagine, I am every where assailed by persuasions to remain here.......

The attempts to embellish the city do not please me, but I have not

* De Serre had lost his mother and a child during this year.

yet seen any of the country houses, which may, perhaps, show more taste. I do not at all like the theatre, nor the guardhouse with its Doric portico. The Potsdam gate has been pulled down, and is to be replaced in a lighter style, by no means such as befits a large city, the capital of a military State.......

CCCXII.

BERLIN, 21*st May*, 1824.

......Would to God you were here, that I might have the comfort of talking over things and deliberating, if our fate is to be decided now. What with the dizzy whirl of gayety, and my complete solitude when at home—where such innumerable recollections crowd in upon me, that I seem like a spectre to myself—my mind is not less overclouded than *this side* of my outward life.

The Crown Prince has improved beyond description. His heart remains what it ever was, and his mind is enriched by an extensive knowledge of facts. Prince William appears equally warm-hearted and good. In truth, the man who is not satisfied with these Princes must make unwarrantable demands upon the world. Both received me as cordially as if I had been a friend of their own rank. The circle of my acquaintance is very large, indeed, much larger than I was aware of till now; hence, my time is split up in a way that distracts and confuses me. But I am received with the greatest kindness and cordiality both by my old friends and by those of recent date. I find nearly all (not Roeder, who is very fortunate) grown old, and most of them stout.

There is much less life and gayety among them than formerly; on the other hand, show and luxury have increased.

Now I think, my dear wife, that this last circumstance decides the question of our removal to Berlin; unless, contrary to all probability, a moral obligation should compel it. But really I see no reason why we should settle here; for, although my heart beats when I think of the Crown Prince—though some friends and the places which awaken melancholy recollections (for instance, the Thiergarten, where I long to go) are dear to me—though the Library would be a great advantage, and I might have much refreshing intercourse; yet, I feel at every step that all which belongs to my former life has passed away, and that you and the children alone make up my world; a world for which I had a precious setting in the lovely, the glorious sky that encircled us with its brightness and beauty: and then, too, De Serre's presence! I miss these blessings now, but in weighing the considerations that present themselves with regard to the choice of our abode, I must look to it that my leisure and repose of mind are not destroyed.......

The changes in the city are in some parts very great, but in general it is a mere dressing up. The shops have increased very much, and betray a fearful amount of luxury.......

CCCXIII.

BERLIN, 30*th May*, 1824.

......You have misunderstood one sentence in my letter, dear wife. If I merely spoke of you and the children in expressing my hopes for the future, I did not mean that I expected none but positively gloomy days for myself, but that it is only with and through you all, that serenity and cheerfulness can be diffused over the evening of my life. My youthful life, which had up to that time been one connected whole, ended with my fortieth year, and the roots which had nourished it were cut away. A new life had to grow up. I am now limited to this new state of existence for the remainder of my days with you and the children.

Meanwhile, you may be *quite* satisfied, my dear wife, that all will go on *much* better if we can but have a settled future to look forward to, with an income sufficient for our wants. If, in addition to this, I can find full occupation, and God preserves us from severe misfortunes, and continues to me my mental powers, you may be sure that I shall recognize thankfully what I possess.

I need only look at many other families to be conscious what I have in my wife and children, and I assure you that I feel myself much less deteriorated by the influences of time than most of my acquaintance. May God preserve me from living so completely under the influence of the world as many do here; whatever may be the contrast between their life and mine in point of splendor. The elasticity of the intellect is destroyed but too easily by splendor and dissipation; particularly when one mixes with people of very different stations.

I should like to have sent you a copy of my application to Bernstorf, but I have not time. I have reminded him that the embassadorship was granted me unasked, and how the King had given me a promise, to which I limited my requests.

How could I think of returning to Rome, dearest wife, when you say you are "trying to familiarize yourself with the thought of it," and beg me to "forget you in the matter!" What stronger expression of your dislike to Rome could I quote to Count Bernstorf? And what must I be, if in the knowledge of your feelings on the subject, I would decide in opposition to them? But do not suppose, my darling Gretchen, that I did not know them to their full extent before you wrote.......

I always receive messages to you from many friends. At Madame Von Savigny's, I met his sister Bettina several times. A few days ago she threatened to pay me a visit in my room. I shall, of course, anticipate her.

Give my love and kisses from me to the dear children, and tell me all you can about them. Every trifle that happens with you interests me. Little Charles's paleness makes me almost more uneasy than any thing.

CCCXIV.

TO MADAME HENSLER.

BERLIN, 31*st May*, 1824.

Here the recollections of former times rise up like ghosts before me at every step; in the Thiergarten, where there is not a path that does not remind me of the past, it is sometimes almost more than I can bear, and yet I can not help going there again and again. It is so distinctly before my eyes, how we used to walk there in 1810, Amelia, and you, and I; how in the autumn after, and in the following winter, and spring and summer, when I was full of life and energy, and my history was daily growing beneath my hands, I found recreation and refreshment there in Amelia's society: so too, in 1812 and 1813, in the intense political excitement in which every other feeling was merged; and then came afterward, those heart-rending drives with my dying wife, &c.

My sorrow is seldom relieved by tears.

When I pass the house where my highest happiness departed, a shudder runs through me. A very worthy man lives there, a M. Von Schönberg, who would be happy to see me, but I can not enter the house.

Savigny, Nicolovius, Eichhorn, and other friends, are what they were to me. I saw Göschen in Göttingen. He is a true pattern of self-sacrifice for his family.

My Lucia is very ill, my angel child! If the worst were possible! I at a distance, my poor Gretchen alone in her grief!

CCCXV.

TO MADAME NIEBUHR.

Berlin, *1st June*, 1824.

......Your letter reached me, darling wife, as I had written these words. I tore it open with a strange sudden feeling of anguish. You can tell how I am since. The violence of my anguish is proportioned to the strength of my previous security. My Lucia, my beloved child! It is like another pang to me, and yet a consolation that the child has seemed to cling to me so lately. I can not realize the idea of losing her. And I do not despair yet; but I shall await the post with torturing anxiety. If you want me, I shall hasten to you. Every thing else must be put aside if I must come to you, comfort you, help you to bear up.

May God grant us quiet! How thankful I will be for all that I have often hitherto not esteemed at its true value!

The present position of our affairs does indeed require my presence, but it is not absolutely necessary. Sympathy would induce Count Bernstorf to hasten the decision as much as he can. The Crown Prince too, and President Von Schönberg would do all in their power to further it.

Be quite easy on this subject, therefore, if you want me. With all this it will be a hard task for me to-day to accompany Count B. to Tegel. Madame Von Humboldt was sympathizing just as she used to be at Rome, and sends her hearty love to you. Count B. was extremely friendly and communicative.

God reward the dear children for comforting you.......

CCCXVI.

TO COUNT DE SERRE.

Berlin, *6th June*, 1824.

My Dear Friend—My long silence after the receipt of the last letter you wrote me in the past year, deprives me of all right to complain of fate if I obtain no letters from you—these precious blessings of my later years. Therefore I will not murmur, but I have long been sad at hearing nothing at all of you, and now I begin to be anxious. Three cases are possible; my two letters, or one from you may have been lost; you may not have liked to write with a heavy heart; lastly, some circumstance may have robbed me of your friendship. Of these three cases, the first would be bearable; the second, God forbid; the third, I can not even picture to myself. I know, that at a great distance misrepresentations and perversions of facts may sever the most perfect friendships; but I know also that you have given me your friendship as fully as I have devoted mine to you. I know that all the arts of hell could as little induce me to believe any thing against you as against my wife. I know that if you could have seen all the thoughts that have passed through my mind since we have known each other—nay, since I first loved you, before we met—there might be many of them that would need all your indulgence toward human weakness; but none relating to yourself that would be inconsistent with our friendship—none that could make me unworthy of this blessing. But dispel my fears, dear friend; I have no scruple in imploring you only just to tell me that you are unchanged toward me, and how you are. I trust, in God, that you have no bad news to give me.

As it is possible that my letters, I. and II., may never have reached you, I will at any rate repeat here, that in the first, I asked you conditionally, to stand godfather to my expected child; and in the second, that in anticipation of your consent, I had united our new-born infant to you in this bond. His birth freed us from great anxieties on his mother's account. ...... But while I am thus writing to you, I am uncertain whether we still possess him, for since I left the Rhine, the baby and Lucia have both been attacked with inflammatory colds, which are epidemic there, in consequence of the horrible weather; Lucia has recovered—at least her mother thinks so—but when she last wrote, the infant lay so ill that she had scarcely any hope of him; and was suffering so dreadfully, that his mother prayed to God for his release, unless he should completely recover. This sorrow she has had to bear separated from me, and without the consolation of sympathy and help from any female friend. My anxiety about her and the children, especially my favorite Lucia, I am forced to endure amidst the bustle of the metropolis, where I am endeavoring to obtain the decision of our fate, which I found it impossible to accomplish through letters. But I am looking forward now with a beating heart to a probably decisive letter, and shall try to divert my thoughts by writing to you.

This journey to Berlin is a new and decisive step in our life, of which it is worth while to give an account to a friend. All my letters representing that I could not return to Rome on account of my wife, whether it was owing to her absolute incapability of enduring the climate, or to a home-sickness that made every thing insupportable to her; that my mission had only been intended as a temporary one, and that I had an express promise under the King's hand, that after the completion of the treaty I should return to resume my former position; all these letters remained without any answer at all, and it was only indirectly that Count Bernstorf gave me to understand that I had better come here to submit my application myself. The Crown Prince also insisted on my coming to Berlin from different motives. It was almost unendurable to come here as a solicitant in order to hear anew the exhortations already repeated to weariness, to do what I should so gladly do if I *could*—return to Rome; and to be obliged still to repeat the same answer, and to be reduced to beg for, as an uncertain and special favor, a right assured to me by the royal word, and the fulfillment of which places me in a less favorable position than any of those who formerly stood on a level with me. But the period of my furlough had expired, and what else could I do, as I could get no written answer? As to the result of my visit, I can not well say any thing till the King's decision is before me.

The investigations connected with the disturbances of the past years are still proceeding, and the dispositions of several young men, above all those of Witt Döring,* who is now in captivity at Bayreuth, seem to prove, that about the time of Sand's assassination, there was really a sort of conspiracy on foot among the students and those immediately connected with them, led by the so-called captains, the spirit and aims of which were seditious and mischievous, though in many cases varnished over with a show of piety, &c.; but their incapacity for any thing except to commit single acts of assassination, was evidently as great as the criminality of their delusion. No one can discover the slightest indication that this conspiracy ever extended into the army, or into the other classes of society; it seems to have been confined to wicked and foolish students' vagaries.

What sort of a figure shall we make in history, when the government of a great kingdom, supported by an army of whose fidelity there is not even a suspicion, fears such an enemy, while in France, the government are taking advantage of victory to demonstrate their security by pardoning open rebels!

Throughout Germany the political fever seems almost to have ceased, though it certainly must have run very high some years ago. Each has given up his particular castle in the air, and if all Greece were to experience the fate of Chios, it would only produce a transient effervescence. I can not properly make out with what people now seek to replace the want of some powerful excitement; they have not returned to the old quiet family life. The churches are well attended; and, as far as you can judge from outward appearances, there seems to be much piety; external irreligion has really disappeared, and since the exaggerations of a few sectaries are not countenanced by the government, they do not call forth any re-action. Unhappily, irritation frequently arises between Catholics and Protestants, for which some priests among the former, and officials among the latter, are equally in fault. In legislation the most shallow liberal principles prevail among the different ministries, and even among the most able of the men high in office. Do not think it a contradiction that I speak of the shallowness of the principles of those to whom I allow the possession of more than common ability in administration. Since I have been here, I have met once more a friend of high political standing, who unites to unspotted integrity and extraordinary talent in the conduct of all kinds of business, an obstinate persistence in revolutionary principles, though he is a decided monarchist; an inflexibility in his opinions, and contempt for all that contradicts them, which drive an old acquaintance, of a directly opposite way of thinking, to despair. Formerly we often agreed negatively. A great void is felt by all, which leads to amusements

* This Witt Döring was a hot-headed and unstable character, who had, when a member of the Burschenschaft committed acts of violence in spite of the remonstrances of his fellow members. When he was afterward imprisoned, finding that the stream set against his party, or perhaps in a fit of repentance at his really unjustifiable conduct, he turned round, and by his exaggerated confessions led the government to arrest many of his associates, who were thus brought into undeserved misfortune. He afterward accepted office under the Austrian government.

without pleasure. Luxury, such as was unknown even before 1806, pervades all classes, and the booksellers state, that owing to this, though every thing except houses has become so much cheaper, and the public salaries have been raised, yet that scholars, and people of the classes who receive a liberal education, do not buy more books than during the time when the country was under the yoke of Napoleon; a time to which good men look back with regret, because then community of feelings, an intense interest in the general welfare, and noble determination reigned in every breast. The landed proprietors are universally complaining, yet if they were not so deeply in debt, their position would be far from desperate in the manufacturing provinces, and in those where they have skill enough to avail themselves of other productions besides corn. Manufacturers are making more progress than is confessed, and both our own and the French manufactured goods are competing with the English as they never did before. The average physical well-being is undoubtedly raised; and even where the proprietors are not prospering, the workmen and day-laborers are only so much the better off. The prices of all manufactured articles have fallen so amazingly, that stuffs which were consumed exclusively among the richer classes only eight years ago, are now within reach of quite the lower orders. But one species of luxury opens the way to every other, and such as you see here is intolerably unsuitable in a State like ours. Stock-jobbing has found its way here, too; and if we go on in our present course, among us, too, even the women will soon begin to take an interest in the exchanges. It seems as if this sort of gambling helped to relieve the want of some violent mental excitement, which politics do not afford. Contentment exists *nowhere*. This is not only true of Berlin, but also of the smallest and most flourishing provinces. It surprised me to hear from an excellent man in Brunswick, that the people acknowledge this to themselves; while he recognized expressly how impossible it is for us to esteem ourselves happy as a nation, because of our mental and moral deficiencies. At most, he said it was but a North American prosperity; in fact, the people did not wish for more.

I am concluding this letter on the eleventh. Meanwhile, I have received news of the death of my youngest child; the mother has borne his sufferings and his loss with a heroic and heavenly spirit. May God spare us any fresh calamity and support the poor mother till I return, and help her to endure. It has not been the child's fate to have the happiness of growing up in a peculiar relationship to you, my dear friend. God protect you from the repetition of a similar misfortune. I long to hear from you, embrace you in thought, and send my hearty greetings to your noble-minded wife and the dear children, who will by this time be scarcely able to recollect us. Write to me at Bonn.

With my whole heart your friend.

CCCXVII.

TO MADAME NIEBUHR.

BERLIN, *9th June*, 1824.

Presentiments are nothing! I had drawn hopes from the conclusion of your last letter that almost amounted to confidence. Hence, I broke open your letter with less anxiety. I thank God, my beloved wife, that he has given and preserved to you the strength of heart which has enabled you to endure this terrible time with such fortitude.

Even the day before yesterday my first impulse was to hasten to you; how much more so now that I know you are sitting by the corpse of our beloved little one, with a heart heavy with tears! But as our fate will now most likely be decided in the course of a few days, it would be thought a piece of madness on my part, if I left without having taken leave of the King and thanked him, in order to gain a day or two. So I can not yet fix the time of my departure.

Let us consult together upon our future plan of life with perfect openness and tender confidence. I have learnt to appreciate you, and your whole worth thoroughly, my Gretchen, and this misfortune has brought us nearer to each other, and perfected my love for you more than any happiness could have done. And therefore we will take this affliction as another blessing from God's hand.

All that you tell me of the grief of our two elder children is a consolation to me. I press each and all of them to my faithful heart.

Give my best remembrances to Brandis. I am buying little presents for the children, but with what a weight at my heart! I feel as though I had lost all security that they were still mine!

CCCXVIII.

TO MADAME HENSLER.

BONN, 2*d September*, 1824.

......I thank you for your sympathy with me about De Serre's death. It is an immense loss for me, no man was so dear to me; no human being esteemed me so highly. He had no secrets from me, and I was more to him than all the world besides, beyond his own family. Under the succession of heavy blows that fell upon him and his wife during the past year, their sigh was, if only Niebuhr was here! He has departed to God, and his warm affection for me he has carried with him, and his family look upon me as a kinsman, the more so, as most of their relations have been unfaithful to them. Our age has not seen a more brilliant or powerful genius. I purpose to write his life if the family can supply me with data for some periods of it. I possess many from his own accounts to myself. His life would be the history of France since 1814: I have courage enough to write it, though it will not even be the liberals who will make the greatest outcry against my work. What bound De Serre and myself so indissolubly together was, that our views harmonized so completely from the very centre of our being, that each could read into the soul of the other, and no clashing of opinion could ever arise between us. He had the purest soul, and the most loving heart on earth. Why have you never known him? Farewell.

CCCXIX.

BERLIN, 14*th December*, 1824.

That my taking a part in the deliberations of the Council of State can be productive of any good, is a delusion springing from my dear Prince's affection for me. Moreover, I come to the subjects now under discussion without local knowledge, and they relate to a measure so completely spoiled long ago by earlier laws, that there would be little hope of effecting any improvement, even if I were better prepared. Many, in other respects, intelligent people do not know the consequences of their own votes, and in a mixed assembly you can not call their attention to them, or else you lose other votes. Thus some voted yesterday against the claims of the poor cotters to right of common, from a misunderstanding, over which I could have wept; and some aristocrats had the humanity to vote in their favor. Thus, too, I am certain not to succeed in carrying motions for the rescue and maintenance of the peasant order, though important voices among the aristocracy will be on my side.

The Bank project does not come under discussion in the Council of State, but is referred to special conferences. It has not yet been communicated to me, I expect it to-day or to-morrow. It is a great satisfaction to know that one is separated from one's family for real reasons, not imaginary ones, for about the Bank I certainly have a voice, and very few people here have one.

I see no prospect of returning home in less than two or three months from this time; I shall not know when I may seriously begin to think about it, till the Bank business is ended, which can not be dragged on to an interminable length like other things, as the bankers demand a decision.

I have met with little of a cheering kind here, excepting the disposition of the Crown Prince. I shun society and decline all evening assemblies, except formal presentations, which can not be avoided. My old connections are broken up on all sides, and I do not know how we should make a place for ourselves here, even if we had a superfluity of wealth.

There are some good souls, especially among the nobility and at court, who see me again with a sort of superstitious hope; but I tell them myself, that though their hopes touch my heart, they are illusory, and will not be justified. Such expressions *give me no pleasure*, just because they rest upon a delusion.

How Gretchen will get through this winter God knows! Her companion does not come till the middle of March......

CCCXX.

TO MADAME NIEBUHR.

BERLIN *Christmas evening*, 1824.

......I was at Buttmann's on Sunday evening. Dr. Waagen, who has written upon Van Eyck was there. Of all the people who have written upon the history of art, he appears to me to have incomparably the most clear and acute mind, and he really comes to practical results that solve questions which I had hitherto laid before all other historians of art in vain. Rauch, too, is in a delightful state of activity.......

CCCXXI.

BERLIN, 5*th January*, 1825.

......I had just begun, the night before last, to re-arrange what I had written at first about the Bank scheme, in order to bring it into a definite shape, when a note came from Count L——, to request that I would now proceed to draw up my remarks. I now set about the work with redoubled zeal. I had concluded my scrutiny, I had tested all the separate points, and was clear about them; all I had to do (the arrangement I had also settled in thought) was to write. I finished writing it last night, and as I had got the address of a copyist I was saved this labor. But I had afterward a long job to do for the next sitting of the Council of State. Savigny is appointed to make a report upon the same subject. I wish his health may not give way. It is not good just now, and he is quite overladen with work. He has frequent returns of violent pain in the head. He is going on with his History, delivering his lectures, and added to these, there is the work for the Council of State, and the Court of Revision. It is too much for one man's shoulders; and then there is his infirm health.

Thinking about the Bank scheme really puts me into a sort of feverish state. I believe it to be fraught with ruin, and yet see that there is danger of its passing; there are so many and such important persons interested in it. The speculators must have some sort of security of its success, for even now, promissory notes for shares in the Bank are selling on the Exchange, which certainly is mere gambling; still it shows how eager people are in this game. The consequences would show afterward that I had been in the right, but then it would be too late. I write to you about this business, my Gretchen, because my head is full of it; and you must, at least, share my interests, and know what I am busied with, although you can not enter into the subject. Besides, its importance will help to reconcile you to the absence of your husband.

CCCXXII.

BERLIN, 10*th January*, 1825.

......I have sent in my report, and have received since, a written answer, with many fair words about the "importance of my observations," "the value of such a report," &c. I do not know if I am right, but I fancy that all this conceals a rejection of my services in this matter. Well, I must be contented with having done my part. The result does not depend upon me. Still, it will be difficult to submit to it when I have such decided opinions, and know that I understand the matter. All who were interested in the projects of the share-brokers, and all who reckon on places and salaries connected with the Bank will become my enemies; this I can not help, any more than that others will blame me who have no such aims, but have allowed themselves to be deluded.

I have got a letter from M. Von Stein. He calls it criminal if I spare myself on your account and the children's; he dreams that I could confer important benefits on the State, from which I withdraw myself in an unconscientious way, from selfish motives, &c. I will send a mild answer to the noble old man, but not before all is decided; then I will show him that I am capable of acting fearlessly; but he shall not delude me with his pictures of the imagination. For the rest, the letter expresses much affection, and a high esteem for me. Happy are they who live in obscurity and quiet!

Yesterday there was a dinner at Count Lottum's, a ball and supper in the evening at the Brockhausens'; I went away before supper. I am going to dine with Humboldt to-day, to have a conversation with him about Champollion's work on the hieroglyphics. You very seldom get conversations of this kind here. These discoveries are the most brilliant of our age, and one can not rejoice in them too much; they, too, confirm Herodotus......

CCCXXIII.

BERLIN, 1*st February*, 1825.

As Amsterdam is nearer to Bonn than to Berlin, you will have had the pleasure of learning the safe arrival of the ship from Leghorn, laden with our goods, earlier than I, dearest wife. I have really rejoiced greatly to hear of it, for I looked upon the ship as lost, and I am not ashamed to confess, that next to your present of the She-wolf and Zurlo's vase, our dear Marcus's pebbles are my greatest subject of joy. It has often gone to my heart to think that the darling child should lose these treasures. I only hope that the injury to the pictures will prove inconsiderable.

After this joyful news, and a walk along old accustomed ways and paths, I should write to you in excellent spirits, if the aspect of affairs were but better...... They are hastening to the goal, and seem to have assured themselves of a majority. As soon as I can know positively that it is so, I think of writing to the King and conjuring him for the last time to listen to my warning, and to grant me leave to explain my views to him by word of mouth. How the King will take this, it is impossible to foresee. Certainly not ungraciously, unless others prejudice him against me; else, it must be confessed, all hope of court favor is over. If he did, such a reward for long-tried fidelity and integrity would grieve me, but it would not injure me, and as soon as I can sing with Paul Gerhard—

"Nun geht frisch drauf, es geht nach Haus;
Ihr Rösslein regt die Beine;"

the time will have come when the innocent gayety of our children, and the approach of the spring, will enable us to drive these gloomy subjects from our minds.

Now to other things.—Dear Savigny is very unwell again...... I will write to M. Von Stein. Let us look upon the dear noble old man as a father, and receive what he says in that light; he means it all kindly, and if he comes, show him every kindness you can, dear Gretchen. His petulance is really almost his only fault: and you are obliged to bear mine, which certainly is of *another kind*, but I do not know whether it is any better on that account......

CCCXXIV.

BERLIN, 29*th January*, 1825.

......It is an old maxim, to let the log lie when you can not lift it. But when you find yourself unable to avert a coming evil, when you see the object frustrated on which you have expended your best powers from the purest motives, you draw back at last, and cease to interfere, but leave things to take their own course, and, for your own part, only try to think no more about them: and this is a most unhappy result; for that love for the general welfare which makes us forget ourselves, has a purifying and ennobling influence. I have said to many persons, "If you would speak out, and make known what you say is your conviction, without considering whether it would give offense or not, such a weight of opinion would be formed, that the project would inevitably founder." But then, they excuse themselves by saying it would be presumption, &c. Things look rather better than when I last wrote. They are talking of proposing another scheme; which would perhaps be less pernicious, and just on that account can not succeed in passing; it would not allow sufficient profits to share-broking......

CCCXXV.

BERLIN, *8th February*, 1825.

......When I have finished my business here, I shall enter a new epoch of my life with a firm step; and with our dear children, above all with my better self Marcus, and in home pleasures, particularly those which our garden will give us, for which a strong taste and desire have awakened in me, I trust we shall lead not merely a life of serene resignation, but of bright happiness. We will make little excursions too. The impression of the scenery and ruins of Heidelberg, stands quite apart from all that I have seen in Germany, except the Tyrol; we will go there again before long.

While one translation of my History is already begun, a second translator has applied to me. At the same time, the Duke of Broglie is writing a treatise on its contents. On the other hand, a pamphlet has appeared at Warsaw, in which I am called a Radical of the Cato-street school (where Thistlewood and his accomplices, who wanted to murder the ministers, used to assemble), and it is said that Sand's mind was formed by my lectures! What nonsense! This comes from a certain Zinserling, who printed a eulogy of Jerome Bonaparte, in 1814. The late Christian Stolberg threatened to horsewhip him for it, and he bolted. He had had an appointment in the Westphalian police.

CCCXXVI.

BERLIN, *16th February*, 1825.

......The pay for the attendance in the Council is so large that I do not use it all. It seemed to me dishonorable to take more than I wanted; but I am told that it would be considered unbecoming to decline it. So I will apply the surplus to assist those who have suffered in Dithmarsh by the floods. You would, no doubt, approve of my doing so, if I could consult you. I will send the money to Dora, that she may see that is divided so as to be a real benefit, not among too many.

If our things have not been shipwrecked in the Texel, I shall buy some more plate; else the money must go to replace what we have lost.

Give my kind remembrances to Brandis. I often talk of him with poor Cousins: to whom people are extremely polite now.......

CCCXXVII.

BERLIN, *21st February*, 1825.

......Yesterday, on my little Cornelia's birthday, my thoughts were more than usually with you. The weather was beautiful, and I hope you took a drive to Godesberg. I went with Perthes to dine at the Reimers'. Not until to-day did I think of the arrival of the Cossacks on this day in 1813. Thus do we forget! You are no doubt right in thinking that it is wiser not to give the children so many presents as I send them in my impatience....... 23d.—There was much that cheered me in your letter. First, that your companion is really an assistance to you; next, that you have found time to take up Italian again with my sweet little Amelia.

This reminds me that I must in future devote a few hours every week to reading the Italian Grammar with Marcus. Then, too, I am glad that we seem likely to be able to hire the garden in the first place. Do not you think, too, that as soon as we can be quite certain of remaining in Bonn, which can scarcely indeed be any longer considered as doubtful, we might as well buy the garden of Dr. V. at his price? I do not properly understand myself what it is that gives me such a downright passionate longing to possess this garden; it is as if I had a certainty that we shall spend many happy days there with the children. Give me commissions to buy seeds for you. With the sad state of corn cultivation, it may even become a public service to introduce the culture of vegetables that have been hitherto neglected. One can distribute seeds; in this way a demand for them gradually arises, and from the demand cultivation. From next autumn, we can begin to raise fruit trees. What pleasure I have often received, when a child, from the blossoming and fruit-bearing trees in my father's garden!

May it not be our duty to follow a noble example, though at considerable cost to ourselves? You have, no doubt, heard that several persons in Paris, of right feeling, but of quite opposite opinions on other points, have joined together to assist Greece, and among other things are trying to raise ten or twelve millions of francs as a loan. If the Greek government can procure a tolerable sum of money now, we may hope that it will be able to put down the rebels, and break their power entirely; and perhaps even win over the Turkish pashas.

The Crown Prince has given me some volumes of Piranesi, of which he has a double set.......

I am just about to take the step at which I hinted lately in a few words to you. I hope that upon mature consideration you will approve of it. This step is, to send in a letter to the ministry of Public Instruction, requesting that if I should wish to deliver lectures at Bonn, I may be permitted to do so without the formality, which in my case would be unsuitable, of an examination by the other professors of my faculty. I do not thereby take upon myself any obligation, but I mean to act as if I did. This kind of work satisfies my sense of honor, and my need of a sphere of active usefulness; it will keep my mind fresher, to be thus daily stimulated to intellectual communication; and further, it will also give me a reasonable ground for declining frequent journeys hither, as I can not then frequently interrupt my lectures. And will not the lectures be their own reward? In many respects, too, it would remind me of the happy time that I passed after resolving to deliver lectures in 1810. Then, as now, after protracted wanderings, I regained my books and tranquillity. I think I should choose the History of Greece, in the first instance, and only lecture this time till about July, and then make a tour with you. A new existence has now been created for us; and I feel it to be of inexpressible importance to keep fast hold of it, not to begin afresh again and again.

CCCXXVIII.

BERLIN, *2d March*, 1825.

......The wind was very high last night. At every gust I think of the poor dwellers in the marshes. Vinche* is such a thoroughly excellent

* He was at this time President of Westphalia.

man! He has written to the King, asking permission to make a collection for the East Frieslanders, and requesting a donation from his Majesty himself in aid of his former subjects. The King has given 3000 dollars, and a permission for the subscription. I have contributed twenty-five dollars to begin with, and think we can give a second subscription of the same amount. These lowlanders are like kinsmen to me, and it grieves me deeply that East Friesland should be separated from our monarchy. I think very highly of this race. Vinche goes on all occasions so straight to the point, without questioning and fear of consequences; he is so mild of heart, and yet so open and straightforward, and so thoroughly loyal. He has become still dearer to me than he ever was before.......

I have just been reading in Cicero a maxim of some worldly-minded Greek philosophers, which he finds detestable; that in friendship we should never forget that we may cease to be friends. With the noblest class of human beings this is certainly detestable, and wherever there is a warm, mutual attachment. But in other cases it has really a good meaning. You ought to be cautious in your acquaintanceship how you overstep the bounds of friendly good-will, unless you are absolutely certain that your connection can not be interrupted and broken off on one side or the other. This occurred to me in reading what you tell me.

Did you notice again in Marcus's letter a hint of his desire to learn Greek?

CCCXXIX.

BERLIN, 18*th March*, 1825.

It gives a peculiar satisfaction to read what is frequently asserted at the present day, that the rate of mortality is much diminished as compared to former times. Formerly I refused to believe in it, because it is certainly hard to understand. Now that I have children I am too much interested in the question not to believe it.

I sent off my letter to the King yesterday. As I wrote the date at the end, my father's birthday, I felt quite clear that he would have disapproved of this step had he been living. Entirely without ambition for himself he would have wished me to yield in all points not involving a positive violation of my conscience, rather than give up the possibility of attaining a brilliant position. The remembrance of this has not, however, in the least confused my perceptions, the propriety of my step admits of no doubt. I have requested the King's permission to leave in either of two cases, first, that if the commission communicate the bill to me I may leave as soon as I have made my report to the King; secondly, that if I hear that they have sent in their report at once to the King, as soon as my connection with the commission is dissolved. I think that the King will grant this without difficulty. But I have further said that I regard it as my duty to lay before His Majesty a final expression of my opinions on the project, and predictions of its consequences.

I dined to-day with the Crown Prince as usual after the Council of State, and was some time alone with him afterward.......

The English newspaper is a sort of luxury,* but it is not a mere luxury; and it is always a pity to break off any study in which you have acquired a certain degree of proficiency. Thus, I am very sorry not to have carried

* Niebuhr had commissioned his wife to order an English newspaper, saying, "If I quite leave off reading English papers, I shall lose my knowledge of England."

on Persian and Arabic....... Tell Brandis that Cousins is on very intimate terms with Hegel, which is indeed owing to Hegel's interposition in his favor during his captivity. Still it is somewhat extraordinary. Ask Brandis if he ever, when in Paris, heard such strange expressions as the following fall from him, that the gradual formation of Christianity had commenced from the earliest ages, but that Judaism was not its historical source. That Christ himself knew very little of Christianity; the system was completed in the seventh and following centuries: that the Reformers were quite in error in desiring to go back to the first centuries, in which religion had not yet attained its maturity: that Hegel perceived this, but that the rest of us did not, &c. In this way these gentlemen may come to a compromise with Catholicism. Such cloudly utterances from a Frenchman disgust me. Among us Germans they are not quite unheard-of.

CCCXXX.

BERLIN, 22*d March*, 1825.

......I too like to think of Bonn as our future place of abode, and am persuaded that we could not have a better lot. I mean to try to enter into the local interests of the place. By so doing you identify yourself more closely with the inhabitants. Besides, it is a necessity of my nature to concern myself with the weal and woe of those who belong to the same community as myself.

I rejoice in the idea that our garden will furnish us with an occupation that is neither literary, political, nor administrative; that sort of interest which has been so completely out of my reach ever since my childhood, and had become so foreign to me, that I did not believe I should ever be so happy as to experience it again. It is a great blessing that my health continues so remarkably good; although it is the case with me as with sickly children who attain to a permanent state of health; I feel myself much less intellectual than at the period when every impression made itself felt through my whole nature physical as well as moral.

Marcus's affectionate disposition shows itself in his expressions about Göschen and Lieber in his letters. I can not imagine how he should have recollected Lieber's birthday.

It had been said that Lieber was to be released on his father's birthday,* but nothing has come of it. Such carelessness in leaving a good man to languish in fetters makes me indignant, though no cruelty is intended.......

CCCXXXI.

BERLIN, 2*d April*.

......I wrote to poor Lieber, and he has sent me an answer that has touched me deeply. The poor fellow is quite broken-hearted, I wish I could find time to make an excursion to Köpenick and comfort him. Perhaps I shall be able on Monday.†

I am glad to hear that the people will receive my lectures kindly, only they must not carry their kindness too far. It is my earnest wish that more of the professors, &c. should attend the course.......

* He had been arrested on suspicion of belonging to a secret association.

† In the following letter, dated 6th, Niebuhr says, "I visited poor Lieber yesterday, in the Bastile of Köpenick, oh my God!"

CCCXXXII.

BERLIN, *11th April* 1824.

This morning I have at last finished my final application to the King. To write thus for the fourth time about the same thing, and each time to have to answer the same objections over again is very wearying; you can not invent new arguments when you have once exhausted the subject in your representations. You can only try to put it in new points of view from which it may appear somewhat clearer, more self-evident.......

I have yet to write to Schuckenan for poor Lieber. In the evening I shall take leave of the dear Crown Prince.

1825–1831.

WE now enter on the last, and for posterity, the most important section of Niebuhr's life, if we except, perhaps, the three years of his professorship in Berlin. From his letters it has been seen already that he had determined to deliver lectures at the University, though holding no official appointment there. His freedom from other occupations and cares, enabled him at last seriously to undertake the accomplishment of his promise to his Amelia, and continue his Roman History. He returned to the vocation, which had in his youth floated before him as the true ideal of his life, namely, the position of a public instructor; and found ample opportunity to redeem the vow he had made in his early years, to extend guidance and assistance to any young men who might hereafter encounter the same intellectual difficulties through which he had had to wend his own way.

Niebuhr commenced his lectures with a course on the History of Greece after the battle of Chæronea, and had a numerous audience. This course was followed by others on Roman Antiquities, in the winter of 1825, repeated in 1827; Ancient History, in the summer of 1826; Ancient Ethnography and Geography, in the winter of 1827; the History of Rome to the Fall of the Empire, in the winter of 1828; the History of the last Forty Years, and of Rome under the Emperors, in the summer of 1829; and a second course of Roman History, in the summer of 1830.

We have seen that, at Berlin, Niebuhr delivered his lectures verbatim from written notes. At Bonn, on the contrary, his only preparation consisted in meditating for a short time on the subject of his lecture, and referring to authorities for their data when he found it necessary, and he brought no written notes with him to the lecture-room. His success in imparting his ideas varied greatly at different times, as it depended almost entirely on his mental and physical condition at the moment. He always felt a certain difficulty in expressing himself. He grasped his subject as a whole, and it was not easy to him to retrace the steps by which he had arrived at his results. Hence his style was harsh and often disjointed; and yet he possessed a species of eloquence whose value is of a high order—that of making the expression the exact reflection of the thought—that of embodying each separate idea in an adequate but not redundant form. The discourse was no dry impersonal statement of facts and arguments, or even opinions; the whole man, with his conceptions, feelings, moral sentiments, nay passions too, was mirrored forth in it. Hence Niebuhr not merely informed and stimulated the minds of his hearers, but attracted their affections. That he did this in an eminent degree, was not indeed owing to his lectures alone, but also to his kind and generous conduct. All who deserved it were sure of his sympathy and assistance, whether oppressed by intellectual difficulties, or pecuniary cares. During the first year he delivered his lectures gratis; afterward, on its being represented to him that this would be injurious to other professors, who could not afford to do the same, he consented to take fees, but employed them in assisting poor scholars and founding prizes. He often, however, still remitted the fee privately, when he perceived that a young man could not well afford it, and never took any from friends.

But those who were admitted to his domestic circle were the class most deeply indebted to him. His interest in all subjects of scientific or moral importance was always lively; and it was impossible to be in his company without deriving some accession of knowledge and incentive to good. From his associates he only required a warm and pure heart, and a sincere love of knowledge, with a freedom from affectation or arrogance. Where he found these, he willingly adapted himself to the wants and capacities of his companions; would receive objections mildly, and take pains to answer them even when urged by mere youths, and weigh carefully every new idea presented to him. He was fond of society, and while his great irritability not seldom gave rise to misunderstandings and contemporary estrangement in the circle of his acquaintance, there were some friends with whom he always remained on terms of unbroken intimacy; among whom may be named Professors Brandis, Arndt, Nitzsch, Bleek, Näke, Welker, and Hollweg. He enjoyed wit in others, and in his lighter moods racy and pointed sayings escaped him not unfrequently.

His intercourse was not confined to the literary circles. In all the civil affairs of the town and neighborhood, he took an active interest from principle as well as inclination, for he considered a man as no good citizen who refused to take his share of the public business of the neighborhood in which he lived. The loss which left so great a blank in the world of letters, was also deeply regretted by his fellow-townsmen of Bonn.

Niebuhr's mode of life at Bonn was very regular, and his habits simple. He hated show and unnecessary luxury in domestic life. He loved art in her proper place, but could not bear to see her degraded into the mere minister of outward ease. His life in his own family showed the erroneousness of the assertion that a thorough devotion to learning is inconsistent with the claims of family affection. He liked to hear of all the little household occurrences, and his sympathy was as ready for the little sorrows of his children as for the misfortunes of a nation. He was in the habit of rising at seven in the morning, and retiring at eleven. At the simple one o'clock dinner he generally conversed cheerfully upon the contents of the newspapers which he had just looked through. The conversation was usually continued during the walk which he took immediately afterward. The building of a house, or the planting of a garden had always an attraction for him, and he used to watch the measuring of a wall, or the breaking open of an entrance with the same species of interest with which he observed the development of a political organization. They drank tea at eight o'clock, when any of his acquaintance was always welcome. But during the hours spent in his library his whole being was absorbed in his studies, and hence he got through an immense amount of work in an incredibly short time.

The principal epochs of his life, from 1823 to the beginning of 1830, were marked by the works in which he was engaged. In October, 1825, he began to work again regularly at the History of Rome. It was his intention to finish the outline of the third volume up to the end of the first Punic war, and to conclude it with three treatises on the primitive metrical art of the Romans, on their religion, and on their ancient manners and customs. He thought it impossible to attempt the final revision and publication of the third volume till the two former ones were finished, on account of the references to them. This plan he did not live to carry out; it was reserved to the friendship of his disciple and friend, Professor Classen, to revise the manuscript of Niebuhr's third volume for the press. The second edition of the first volume was finished in the summer of 1826, exactly as Niebuhr completed his fiftieth year. It had cost him great labor, for he had thought it necessary to alter the arrangement so considerably, and to rewrite so many passages, that it was substantially a new work. His literary conscientiousness led him not seldom to sacrifice favorite passages because they did not quite correspond to his riper convictions, or disturbed the symmetry of the proportions. But above all, he was most careful to express the exact degree of confidence which he felt with regard to each of his assertions.

The reception which his work met with, not only in Germany, where half the copies of the new edition were ordered before the last sheets had left the press, but also in foreign countries, caused him great delight. Even from Boston, U. S., he received an enthusiastic review of his History and an academical diploma, a most unexpected honor to him as coming from that quarter. Various applications were made to him by booksellers and literary men in France and England who were desirous of obtaining his sanction and assistance in the translation of the work. The latter he readily granted, sometimes at the cost of considerable interruption to his other occupations. Niebuhr was not easily satisfied; the care with which he wrote rendered it the more annoying to him when the exact sense and color of his thoughts had not been preserved, or when, in the attempt to do so, the genius of a foreign language was violated, and thus the impressions which he wished to produce destroyed. He, however, considered the translation executed by Messrs. Thirlwall and Hare, at the cost of the University of Cambridge, a more perfectly successful attempt than he had even thought possible.

About this time, Niebuhr undertook the joint editorship, with Brandis and Hasse, of the "Rheinische Museum," a periodical for jurisprudence, philology, and the history of philosophy.

In February, 1826, he established, with Brandis and a few others, a philological society, similar to that which had afforded him so many pleasant hours in Berlin in the years 1810 and 1811. During this year, he was much depressed by the defeat of the Greeks, whose struggle he had watched with his usual ardent sympathy in human welfare, and also by the death of his friend Voss, the last of his friends belonging to the former generation. On the other hand, he was reminded of all that he still possessed in his friends by the visits of M. von Stein, Professor Falk, M. Pertz from Hanover, and several others. Most of the foreigners who came to Bonn visited him. He had, in particular, so many connections with England, that scarcely any Englishman of note came unprovided with letters of introduction to him. The number of these casual visitors caused him serious interruption to his studies. In this year, the present King of Prussia, then Crown Prince, visited the Rhine repeatedly. His presence was always a source of real gratification to Niebuhr, who still preserved the affection for him, and high esteem for his character, which he had formed when the Prince was his pupil in Berlin.

The winter of 1826–27 was passed in laborious and cheerful application to his studies. He succeeded in obtaining a dispensation from attendance on the sittings of the Council of State, but, at the request of this body, prepared a report for the Westphalian Chambers on the establishment of a projected Bank. In the beginning of the year 1827, he commenced the revision of the second volume of the Roman History, and soon found that it would be necessary entirely to re-write this portion also, containing the period down to the decemviral constitution. In addition to this work he drew up a prospectus for a new edition of the Byzantine historians for the publisher Weber in Bonn, of which he edited the Agathias himself, besides superintending the progress of the whole undertaking. Niebuhr always rejoiced in being able to further such schemes, both for the sake of the literary objects which he thus promoted, and because it gave him the opportunity of exciting and aiding others to similar pursuits. In a short time a third edition of the first volume was required; in this he had comparatively little to alter, but here also he made additions, particularly with respect to the history of the primitive races, of Alba, the Luceres, the election of consuls, &c. It was printed in the autumn of this year. Toward the end of the summer, Professor Twesten, of Kiel, paid a visit to Niebuhr, accompanied by his wife, who was a cousin of Madame Niebuhr, and had been one of her earliest friends. Twesten had also been a pupil of Niebuhr's in Berlin, and one in whom he had always felt a particular interest. Excepting his sister, who had visited him in 1825, he had seen none of his relations since 1816. This was the first renewal of personal intercourse with them, and gave rise in his mind to the resolution of taking a journey to Holstein. Up to this time he seems to have dreaded the impression which the recollection of former times would make upon him, but after he had once decided on the journey he eagerly rejoiced in the prospect of revisiting the home of his youth, and thus linking together the present and the past.

In the winter of 1827–28, M. Classen, of Hamburgh (now Professor in Lubeck), entered Niebuhr's family as tutor to Marcus, and a very warm friendship rapidly sprang up between him and Niebuhr. In letters to his intimate friends Niebuhr often expresses his satisfaction in having secured such a tutor for Marcus, and his own pleasure in Classen's society. Classen continued to reside in the family till the death of Niebuhr; he watched over his dying bed, and superintended the education of his orphan son with the utmost care and affection. It was Classen too who prepared the third volume of the History of Rome for the press, which Niebuhr left in a half-finished state. In the spring of 1828, Niebuhr had the great pleasure of receiving a visit from his friend and successor in Rome, Chevalier Bunsen.

The increasing ill-health of Madame Niebuhr during this winter, threatened to put a stop to the projected journey to Holstein, but she improved as the spring advanced, and in May the whole family set out for Kiel. There they passed the summer in the house of Madame Hensler, and surrounded by their friends, whom they had not seen for twelve years. The time was spent in happy social intercourse and excursions into the beautiful scenery of that part of Holstein. On such occasions, Niebuhr was always the centre of a group of children, who had soon discovered the willingness with which he entered into all their amusements, and his inability to refuse them any gratification. One fortnight he devoted to a visit to Copenhagen, in company with his son and Twesten. He was gratified by the evident signs of increasing wealth in his country, but the growing luxury and love of amusement disturbed him. He writes—"Every one must allow that the population of Holstein equals that of any province of Germany in cultivation and intelligence, though it is subject to many disadvantages from its position on the outer edge of literary Germany. What struck me most, in my last visit to Kiel, is the sort of Viennese life I remarked there, *ou l'on s'acquitte consciencieusement du devoir qu'on s'est imposé de s'amuser.*"

The following account of the last year of Niebuhr's life is from the pen of his friend Professor Classen, from whose essay on "Niebuhr's life and sphere of action in Bonn"* many of the facts in the former part of this section are derived.

"The peace of Niebuhr's life in Bonn was broken by the storms of the year 1830; first came the personal calamity that his new house, in the arrangement of which he had taken so much pleasure, was burnt down in the night of the 6th of February; and before order and comfort could be created afresh from the ruins of his domestic existence, the news arrived of the second French revolution. The former misfortune affected him deeply, for he found his dearest happiness in the peace and order of home; but his noble nature was beautifully displayed on the night of the fire. As soon as he had recovered from the first fearful shock, and had seen his wife and children safe in the house of a kind neighbor, he compared the weight of this blow to other events of his life, and said, sadly, but with composure, to a friend, 'It is indeed a misfortune, but I do not feel nearly so overcome and depressed as I did in the night after the battle of Bautzen, when I was near head-quarters, and believed the cause of my country to be, if not lost, in the most imminent peril. If only the manuscript of the second volume of my Roman History is found again, I can get over every thing else; and, at the worst, I feel I have still power enough left to replace my History, and will set to work again with God's help in a few days.' He conversed thus for some hours with noble calmness, while watching the flames as they devoured their rich booty. Once only he inquired anxiously after the fate of the She-wolf, a beautiful cast of the well-known group in the Capitol, which had been given him by his wife, and always stood in his library; and he expressed the strongest desire that it might be saved; he had always liked to consider it as the guardian genius of the house. Some of his younger friends hurried into the burning house, reached the room, and with much difficulty

* Lebensnachrichten, vol. iii. p. 283.

brought away the heavy cast; but in the hasty descent of the staircase, it was knocked in several places, and reached the bottom in ruins. Niebuhr buried the fragments with melancholy feelings in his garden.

"For the first few days after the fire, the sight of the desolation it had caused rendered his regret more poignant than it had been in the first moment. He was especially grieved by the destruction, as he feared, of his library; for all his books had been thrown out of the windows of the second story in a heap on the snow and mud of the street, and had not been placed under shelter till the morning. It cost him many days' labor to look through what was saved, and bring it into order; but tnere was great rejoicing when here and there a precious treasure was found again which had been looked on as lost; and the re-appearance of the longed-for manuscript of the second volume was greeted with hearty cheers: only a few sheets written out ready for the press were missing, the sketch of the whole had been preserved entire. It was scarcely less than miraculous that his loss in books turned out after all to be very slight; many indeed were more or less injured. Many papers and letters were gone, among the rest his correspondence with his father.

"A new house was soon taken, while the other one was rebuilt on an enlarged scale. In the prospect of a speedy change Niebuhr endured the inconvenience of the new and necessarily hasty household arrangements with unruffled cheerfulness; still he could not feel quite at ease in them, and the recollection of his misfortune, combined with his fears for its effects on his beloved wife, rendered him no doubt more than usually susceptible to gloomy impressions. It was in this mood that he first heard the news of the Three Days of July, news which would have affected him most profoundly under whatever circumstances they had first reached him. Few of his contemporaries took such deep and constant interest in all the events of the day—few had the same power of appreciating all their bearings and consequences. In such a mind as his, this was naturally not the result of fluctuating curiosity, nor the want of a passing amusement, but of a thorough comprehension of the antecedents and tendencies of his age, as far as such can be possessed by one individual. And he now saw himself most bitterly deceived—disappointed in all his hopes and expectations; he had never given the court party credit for such blindness, nor believed the people of Paris capable of such resistance, whether it may have been the consequence of momentary excitement, or of a concerted plan. Enough—the revolution had taken place, and brought in its train many violent changes, while it threatened to spread the sphere of its activity to other countries. But however much he might be distracted and saddened, during the five months in which he was still a spectator of the world's history, by the feverish convulsions of the age, and yet more by the strife of opinions as to their real significance, he never failed to recognize with perfect clearness and distinctness in the universal confusion, which evil was in truth the lesser; never wavered in his attachment to his country and his king, but exerted himself on every opportunity to awaken and invigorate the patriotism of those around him.

The last political occurrence in which Niebuhr was strongly interested was the trial of the ministers of Charles the Tenth; it was indirectly the cause of his death. He read the reports in the French journals with eager attention; and as these newspapers were much in request at that time, from the universal interest felt in their contents, he did not in general go to the public reading-rooms, where he was accustomed to see the papers daily, until the evening. On Christmas Eve and the following day, he was in better health and spirits than for a long time, but on the evening of the 25th of December, he spent a long time waiting and reading in the hot news-room, without taking off his thick fur cloak, and then returned home through the bitter frosty night air, heated in mind and body. Still full of the impression made on him by the papers, he went straight to Classen's room, and exclaimed, "That is true eloquence! You must read Sauzet's speech; he alone declares the true state of the case; that this is no question of law, but an open battle between hostile powers! Sauzet must be no common man! But," he added immediately, "I have taken a severe chill, I must go to bed." And from the couch which he then sought, he never rose again, except for one hour, two days afterward, when he was forced to return to it quickly, with warning symptoms of his approaching end.

His illness lasted a week, and was pronounced, on the fourth day, to be a decided attack of inflammation on the lungs. His hopes sank at first, but rose with his increasing danger and weakness; even on the morning of the last day he said, "I can still recover." Two days before, his faithful wife, who had exerted herself beyond her strength in nursing him, fell ill and was obliged to leave him. He then turned his face to the wall, and exclaimed, with the most painful presentiment, "Hapless house! To lose father and mother at once!" And to the children he said, "Pray to God, children! He alone can help us!" And his attendants saw that he himself was seeking comfort and strength in silent prayer. But when his hopes of life revived, his active and powerful mind soon demanded its wonted occupation. The studies that had been dearest to him through life, remained so in death; his love to them was proved to be pure and genuine, by its unwavering perseverance to the last. While he was on his sick-bed, Classen read aloud to him for hours the Greek text of the Jewish History of Josephus, and he followed the sense with such ease and attention, that he suggested several emendations in the text at the moment; this may be called an unimportant circumstance, but it always appeared to us one of the most wonderful proofs of his mental powers. The last scientific work in which he was able to testify his interest, was the description of Rome by Bunsen and his friends, which had just been sent to him; the preface to the first volume was read aloud to him, and called forth expressions of pleasure and approbation. He also asked for light reading to pass the time, but our attempts to satisfy him were unsuccessful. A friend proposed the "Briefe eines Verstorbenen," which was then making a sensation; but he declined it, saying he feared that its levity would jar upon his feelings. One of Cooper's novels was recommended to him, and aroused his ridicule by its extraordinary verbiage: he was much amused by an experiment which he proposed, and which consisted in taking one sentence at hap-hazard on each page; a mode of reading which did little violence to the connection of the story. The "Kolnische Zeitung" was read aloud to him up to the last day, with extracts from the French and other journals. He asked for them expressly, only twelve hours before his death, and gave his opinion half in jest about the change of ministry in Paris. But on the afternoon of the 1st of January, 1831, he sank into a dreamy slumber; once on awakening, he said that pleasant images floated before him in sleep: now and then he spoke French in his dreams, probably he felt himself in the presence of his departed friend De Serre. As the night gathered, consciousness gradually disappeared, he woke up once more about midnight, when the last remedy was administered; he recognized in it a medicine of doubtful operation, never resorted to but in extreme cases, and said in a faint voice, "What essential substance is this? Am I so far gone?" These were his last words; he sank back on his pillow, and within an hour his noble heart had ceased to beat.

Niebuhr's wife died nine days after him, on the 11th of the same month, about the same hour of the night. She died, in fact, of a broken heart, though her disease was, like his, an inflammation of the chest. She could shed no tears, though she longed for them, and prayed God to send them; once her eyes grew moist, when his picture was brought to her at her own request, but they dried again, and her heavy heart was not relieved. She had her children often with her, particularly her son, and gave them her parting counsels. And so her loving and pure soul went home to God. Both rest in one grave, over which the present King of Prussia has erected a monument to the memory of his former instructor and counselor. The children were placed under the care of Madame Hensler, at Kiel.

Letters from May, 1825, *to December*, 1830.

CCCXXXIII.

TO MADAME HENSLER.

BONN, 12*th May*, 1825.

......I have begun the course of lectures I announced, and succeed very well in delivering them extempore, by which the labor I have undertaken will be comparatively inconsiderable; in fact, I am quite certain that I shall be able henceforward to continue the Roman History at the same time with my lectures, and to give my Marcus lessons for at least an hour and a half each day. Yesterday 298 persons inscribed their names as hearers; there were not, indeed, so many present, because there was literally not room for them in the Lecture-hall; many stood, and the windows had to be taken out that we might not be suffocated. This throng may very likely, nay, will almost certainly, diminish by degrees; still, it is quite clear that the young men receive my course with real gratitude as a friendly gift, and that many of the Professors regard me as a welcome fellow-worker; the citizens also seem pleased that I have chosen to live among them.

The purchase-deed of our garden will be signed in a few days, and if we can find a house for sale in the neighborhood of the garden, that suits us, or that can be made suitable by a few additions, we shall certainly take advantage of it. Bad as the state of the world is in many respects, it is still an inestimable advantage to be able to recover energy and inclination to settle yourself, and make purchases for the rest of one's life; and in our own house, under our own trees, we shall be contented to let alone what we can not alter, and what would not be improved by most of those who want to alter it. You likewise can remember the time before the commotions of the world had banished the quiet of private domestic life; when the laying out of a garden and the success of a plantation was an important event to the head of a household and his friends. I have still a very lively recollection of those tranquil days, and how they passed away so entirely that I did not believe they would ever return during our lifetime. But they seem to have returned as it were in the progress of convalescence. I am far from being the only one who is more interested in the question, whether and how our town shall and can be enlarged, and the neighborhood improved, than in the affairs of the world;—if only they would not exterminate the Greeks!

Our garden occupies an old bastion and part of a curtain, so that it seems to be on a hill, and has a view of the Sieben Gebirge, and the range of the so-called Vorgebirge, and the magnificent Poppelsdorf Allée. It is full of beautiful fruit-trees and vines, which are the more valuable here, as the grapes ripen well and early if the season is tolerable, and the aspect favorable, and good grapes are rarely to be had in the market. From being laid out on a bastion, the lines of division in the garden have acquired a certain peculiarity which could hardly have been obtained by art. We are about to replace dead trees by new ones, and are tranquilly planting what will take years before it will produce any thing. Why have you not enjoyed this heavenly spring in our garden, dear Dora?......

CCCXXXIV.

12th June, 1825.

......I continue to receive encouragement in my lectures......The attentive investigation of the history of these obscure periods is interesting to myself, and profitable as a preparation for the period of the Roman History when that of Macedon falls into it. Indeed when I have finished the third volume, and revised the first, I think I should like, by way of change, to dictate the history of Greece, which I am now delivering, in quite a different form, not as a learned work. The course of lectures which I mean to deliver this winter on Roman Antiquities, will be useful to me in the revision of my history. Whether it will also be useful to my auditors to any great extent I do not know; but my trouble will certainly not be quite lost. The young man who gives Marcus lessons, and is our companion at table, is one of those who receive what I say with affectionate interest; and according to his testimony there are many who do so among the great number of young philologists, who are rising up here on all sides, where a few years ago, out of a hundred thousand souls, there was not one who understood Greek. I have defended Demosthenes upon full conviction, as warmly as if the question concerned a living man, and the young men listened to me with evident sympathy. I never before saw Demosthenes' greatness and excellence in such a striking light. The University here is much decried abroad, as if we lived under Heaven knows what tyranny of the police, and as if the young men were turning Catholics by shoals. Both reports are quite untrue; no one meets with any molestation unless he commit some great extravagance; and there is no danger of conversion to Catholicism except when a young man falls in love in a proselyting family. But there are very few such......

CCCXXXV.

BONN, *20th October*, 1825.

I have been ill since I wrote to you. It was a rheumatic pleurisy, fortunately not violent, but I was quite confined to my bed for four days.

You ask after the continuation of my History, dearest Dora. I should have resumed it this summer—the lectures would not have interfered with it to any extent—but Gretchen's journey to the baths stood in the way; I was obliged to devote myself more than usual to the children who were left behind. On this account I was unable to set to work, and I have only begun the continuation during the present month. The lectures this winter will be no hindrance to me, still the work will advance but slowly. I am satisfied on the whole with what I have done latterly. Life is stirring among the heap of dry bones, and I feel while writing the history as if I were borrowing it from some newly-discovered old records. I may, however, very likely be censured for going too much into details. Another circumstance will give still more occasion for blame. In the first half of the unprinted volume I invented a speech; I have now composed a second, and the outline of one in reply to it. I know beforehand all the cavils that will be made against this; but I know as well as any one what is essential to a living representation of the past, and that it is not possible to enter into the way in which decisive resolutions are formed in critical moments, unless the reader can look into the souls of those who conceive or influence the decision, not through the help of common-places, but by means of a thorough insight into all the special circumstances of the case. Such speeches as those, of which Thucydides has given us the highest model, are truly the lamps of history; I grant that a man must be bold, and free from superstitious scrupulosity, to invent them for periods concerning which only scanty fragments of facts are left. The ancient historians have too often treated moral and political common-places in this form, and such passages are indeed absolutely worthless. When I have finished the first Punic war, I shall write three essays for the same volume upon the earliest metrical art of the Romans, on their religion, and on their ancient manners and customs; and then I shall proceed, not without trembling, to the revision of the first volume. The materials for additions are extremely rich; and as I now see clearly what I only divined or had a presentiment of when I wrote it, I shall be obliged to take it to pieces almost throughout, and erect the old portions, combined with new ones, into a more extensive structure. I shall thank God if I live to finish at least this much of my task, for then I shall have accomplished the restoration of a history that was almost universally misunderstood, even so early as 1800 years ago. The taking of Alexandria by Augustus is the limit to which I propose to bring it down; this I still hope to reach.......

CCCXXXVI.

TO PERTHES.

BONN, *7th March*, 1826.

......I wish, dear Perthes, that you knew any one who had as extensive a knowledge of the history of commerce during the past century as my late friend Büsch, that you might prevail upon him to write the history of commerce and finance during the last hundred and fifty years. I know a great deal about it myself in a fragmentary way, but not connectedly. Besides, even for those who have not that strong interest in monetary affairs which I am not ashamed of confessing, they form as essential a part of the world's history as the history of epidemics. Before 1721, no universal commercial crisis had been known; they are now become more and more frequent, and it is enough to make one shudder to think of the future, when a chain of credit-giving establishments will extend through the whole of Spanish America, as well as through the United States. Truly the independence of these States opens an abyss; the natural arrangement would have been that Europe should have traded with these countries through the medium of an emporium such as Cadiz. However, of what use is it to know this? The old order of things is fast passing away through the fault of those who were its rightful heads, and who would have been the first gainers by it, if they had known how to maintain it. The counter-revolution in France opens gloomy prospects to Germany likewise. In our provinces the oligarchy have carried out their plans respecting the elections by deceiving the Government, and are aiming at Jesuitism and the like. If Russia were out of the question one need feel less anxiety about the matter; for that party can not obtain any present success.

You are quite right in maintaining that neither the gymnastic nor the Mennonite *régime* can conduce to a real and noble respect for the laws. I believe that every system of training which inspires heathen or Christian arrogance, and leads people to consider themselves as privileged individuals, has an equally corrupting effect.

How is your series of histories proceeding? Shall you carry it out? My wife is again very sickly; the children, too, are not free from indisposition. As for myself, since I have at least twenty years to live (for it is not the fashion here to die before seventy), I am striving to make up in creative labors and enjoyment of life, for what I have lost in both during the best years of my life.

CCCXXXVII.

TO MADAME HENSLER.

BONN, 19*th March*, 1826.

I have now concluded my lectures with the reward of very decisive approbation. The lectures close very early here, and I with a few others have continued them some days after the courses of the regular professors had concluded, and have had a respectable though much diminished audience. The numbers had kept up, in general, during the winter beyond my expectation. Brandis, D'Alton, and several other professors were among my hearers. My lectures were received with uncommon interest among the students, although they are accustomed here, in general, to dictation, and require it; and their expressions of thanks and attachment quite surprised me. One young man, as I gave him his certificate, put into my hand, with great embarrassment, a letter of thanks; seized my hand, and said he could never thank me enough, I had awakened a new life in him. Most of those who have been thus aroused are Catholics, on whom a new life is indeed breaking, through the study of the sciences, from which they have been so long excluded, and I trust they will diffuse it over a wide sphere. Their abilities, moreover, as well as their dispositions, are of a very encouraging character. It is certainly incontestable that philology now stands many degrees higher than it did thirty years ago. The knowledge, which then distinguished the few who possessed it, is now become common property.

The idea of standing at the head of a school will not allure me; on this point I know myself; though with the present state of party feeling in Germany, it is almost necessary as a matter of self-defense; and if our disciples and adherents enter the lists with our opponents, we need not hold them back. I have met with some cases of this kind already among persons who are strangers to me. The revision of the first volume involves immense labor.......

CCCXXXVIII.

BONN, 24*th April*, 1826.

......I have been much affected by the death of old Voss. He was the last remaining one of the elder generation with whom the memories of my childhood and youth were bound up: I felt myself still young, so long as I knew, and might yet see, one living person whom I had seen as a boy, and to whom, as a youth, I had looked up with affection. It was not without some anxiety that I went to visit him on my journey hither three years ago. Christiana had more than once written me word, that he had inquired if I had not turned Catholic! And this, be it remarked, after I had set up a Protestant chapel in my house! I felt angry at such a suspicion, besides, the Stolberg affair had left a deep wound behind, as was the case with you too. But the memory of old times prevailed, and I found that it was necessary with him too, not to overlook the palliating circumstances—that there were excuses for much that had passed after the first step. I felt as much affection as ever for my aged friend, whose freshness of mind had something uncommonly venerable about it. I have written to him several times since, and his answers were very cordial. The last time I wrote to him was on his birthday, and those about him tell me that this was almost the last lively gratification that he enjoyed. He intended to pay us a visit this summer, and this project was almost the last thing of which he spoke. I should have gone to see him in the holidays if he had lived. He had already fallen asleep when I fixed my intentions.

Events have justified his predictions in many things about which he was not, properly speaking, in the right, and still less a prophet. A league such as he believed in, was a fevered dream; but things are happening now, and others are impending, which are exactly what he indicated as the work of this assumed league. It requires much historical experience and resignation to retain one's equanimity in spite of all that is passing before our eyes; the influence of the bigoted, monkish, in fact, downright jesuitical party among the Catholics, in matters of public instruction, is most sad. I could, perhaps, bring on a crisis if I were to write on the subject, but the result is too uncertain. This is a more dangerous business than the alleged favoritism shown toward the hereditary aristocracy, which may produce ill effects for a generation, but can not have any permanent consequences. It is indeed clear, I think, that the commoner is regarded by the nobleman with a dislike such as has not existed before for the last forty years. The misfortune is, that this feeling enfeebles the whole of Germany, and particularly our class, which is the sinews of the country.

France is also growing very weary, and there, where the political volcano seems to have spent itself, the priests are creating fresh elements of combustion. . . . . .

I went to Elberfeldt by the diligence last week, and returned by way of Düsseldorf, where I visited the "Tanten Jacobi." * It did me good, only it was not enough. Elberfeldt is, as you probably know, the seat of the Protestant fanatics. I heard such a sermon! it happened to be the general fast-day. But I was told there was another which would have given us something still more outrageous.

The men of business there are clever and energetic. It is a real pleasure to see how new firms and new enterprises are constantly coming into existence, just as in England. The whole duchy of Berg presents this cheerful aspect. New roads are making in all directions, and rows of houses springing up along them. Manufactures are in a most flourishing condition.

CCCXXXIX.

BONN, 21*st May*, 1826.

. . . . . . The horrible fate of Missolonghi almost deadens my feelings both to immediate and more distant objects of interest. Without attaching full credence to the reports of success, I had lulled myself into security, and the blow came upon me this time quite unexpectedly. I can not divert my thoughts from it. Marcus, who is only just beginning to turn his attention to political events, is quite broken-hearted. He wanted to employ his savings'-box for the subscription, and, uniting the ideas of a child with the earnestness of a man, he proposed to melt his leaden soldiers into bullets. From the time that the first rumor of the lamentable disaster had reached us, he could not bear to look at the map of Turkey. Amelia studies maps with him, and gets him to tell her about the places; *this* map he imploringly refused to tell her about; and when she innocently laughed at him for it, he threw himself on my breast, sobbing bitterly. Alas, what hope is now left! The heroes are gone, the Suliots are exterminated, and how horrible to think of the women and children in the power of these barbarians. What can the too long delayed assistance avail now? England has played a detestable part. My old affection for her is well-nigh extinguished. And yet when England is fallen, who knows but what we may bitterly feel the want of her hereafter?

My whole attention is fixed on the proceedings of the Catholics. It seems to me unquestionable that a bold faction among them are secretly aiming to bring on a religious war. In France, the priests have been directing all their efforts for the last ten years to the attainment of physical power, and they have already succeeded in recovering their hold on the populace; and this while they had no means of constraint at their disposal. The prospect that we Protestants may need a Russian Gustavus Adolphus to defend us is frightful. I was relating to Marcus yesterday the history of the religious wars and their horrors. I was glad to see that he distinguished between the bad Catholics and the good ones, such as our friends, who would never have acted so; and also that he did not understand at all how Protestants could persecute. He thought that would be impossible, for they knew that the Catholics were in error, and you could not hate

* The sisters of the philosopher Jacobi.

a person for being mistaken. Our Catholic friends are, indeed, only separated from ourselves by forms; while treated as heretics by the fanatics, they are quite intimate with us, and the most intelligent man among them said to me yesterday, "Superstition is, after all, much more detestable and mischievous than unbelief." . . . . . .

CCCXL.

BONN, 21*st June*, 1826.

The printing of the first volume in the new edition has at last commenced, and will now advance steadily. . . . . .

My French translator was here the end of last week. At all events, he understands German perfectly, and goes to work with great enthusiasm. According to his testimony, expectation is universally excited about it in France, and the publisher is so certain of a brilliant reception, that he will print at least two thousand copies. Such a celebrity among foreign nations is very agreeable to the natural man, philosophize about it as you please; and I least of all make pretensions to be a saint in this respect, or even a philosopher.

Fifteen years ago I had no idea of the possibility of appearing as an author, although I had a very distinct feeling of the worthlessness of that which called itself ancient history; and when I began my lectures at Berlin, under the animating influence of your presence, I never dreamt that they could become the basis of an enduring work. When I see how the ideas which began to dawn upon me in the course of the lectures, have gradually become as clear as day; how the chaos has been resolved into distinct facts—nay, separate details, it is astonishing even to myself. But it really borders upon a miraculous intervention of Providence, that so many remarkable things have been brought to light within the last few years, which were indispensable to the determination of certain points.

My Frenchman gave me a good deal of interesting information respecting the internal condition of his country, agreeing with what an attentive reader may gather from the journals. The pretensions of the priests, who are for the most part utterly uneducated men from the lowest classes, have produced an exasperation against them, which has called forth a party capable of setting them at defiance, notwithstanding the patronage of the King. It is singular how the various parties unite in their common opposition to the clergy, so that people who thought themselves unalterably embittered against each other in politics five years ago, are now quite reconciled. This, indeed, has been only rendered possible by the fact that, thank God, the revolutionary plans of the liberals have been frustrated. For I quite understand how, in France, men whose views fully harmonize with my own, can become reconciled to those whose earlier follies have wrought such indescribable calamity. I have just the same feelings; I would not only send my respects to Royer-Collard, but if Fox were living, should be happy to make his acquaintance.

The sentiments of the English, as a nation, with regard to the Greek cause are undisguisedly bad. An Austrian is not answerable for the acts of his government, but the English are answerable for uttering no expression of commiseration, no cry for help, when there was nothing to prevent them. It is quite different in France; there, tones have resounded in the public journals that have issued from the depths of the heart, and find an echo in the inmost heart of the reader. Have you read Tiedge's poem, "The Struggle of the Greeks with Barbarism?" I should never have thought him capable of producing such a work; faulty as the verses are, considered merely as poetry. The conception is terribly beautiful. But I can not understand how it is that the excitement should not be much greater and more universal in Germany. One sickens at the specious show of feeling, and the faint-hearted apathy of men whom you must allow to pass for well-meaning persons. The personal feeling of our King is very evident and very honorable to him.

CCCXLI.

BONN, 16*th July*, 1826.

......This time fifteen years I made a pause in the composition of my History—during our journey to Holstein. That was indeed, dear Dora, as you call it, the blossoming time of my life. And yet, if it were not winter around me, there were yet within me a time of bloom, if not of spring or summer. I do not feel at all old yet in mind; my life is prolonged by love and happiness, and puts forth fresh shoots. My knowledge has increased greatly in variety and extent since that time; but I should never have undertaken the work, had I then had the accumulation of materials which it now costs me weary labor to organize.

I can not say that I could ever repent my resolution to take up our abode here, since I have once for all given up a more agreeable and attractive life; which I confess I must not allow myself to look back upon, else my heart swells and my eyes moisten. And yet, it may be best so, for in this degenerate state of politics, my position there would have become very difficult. Ten years hence, I may very likely be able to make another journey across the Alps. My spirits rise at this castle in the air, and Marcus is delighted. We had a visit yesterday from Wilhelm Voss, whom I had not seen since 1811, and like much better now, than in his youthful days, one-and-twenty years ago, when he was a Bonapartist at the time of our disaster at Ulm. He had with him the proof sheets of the second part of the "Anti-symbolik," containing an extremely pleasing autobiography of his father's youth—the first fifteen years of his life—but also a fuller recapitulation of the quarrel with Heyne than has ever yet appeared; unspeakably painful. I had intended to write a very short essay indicating what Voss had been to the nation and to literature, and to append to it a few apologetic pages on the origin of the ill-feeling in this affair; which now I can not do.

The sisters Jacobi were here a month with their nephew, the president. They had with them the correspondence of Goethe with their brother, which is a great curiosity. These letters show Goethe in an unexpectedly favorable light; they exhibit a large heart, and strong deep emotions. Jacobi's letters are constrained, artificial, and labored; it gives me pain to say this. In the first period of their acquaintance, before Goethe goes to Weimar, he notices this on one occasion; he wishes for his friend a growth in love, and thereby in simplicity and productive power.

How sad it is, on the contrary, to see the idolatry which Goethe suffers to be paid to him now, about which you too have probably seen the elegantly-printed book!

The sisters Jacobi bear a grudge against Goethe; more especially, as it appears, on account of the "Goldsmith of Ephesus," the conclusion of which it must be granted, is unintelligible, but certainly not intended as they take it; and on account of his description of his stay at Pempelfort,* in 1792.

You think that universal sympathy must overpower the governments? Alas! you do not understand the matter, and do not know the extent of our political paralysis. In England there has not been the remotest expression of feeling as in France; the proclamation which prevented the departure of the ship lying ready equipped, caused the destruction of Missolonghi, and it has not been censured in any opposition paper. Hence I blame that nation beyond all others. Unhappily the feeling among us in Germany is very superficial; and we must be more ashamed of the levity which has allowed us so soon to forget the dreadful end of Missolonghi, than rejoiced at the liberality previously shown.......

CCCXLII.

TO SAVIGNY.

BONN, *6th August*, 1826.

Our government must give us credit for a high opinion of the importance of our thoughts and words, my old friend, when they set a price upon our letters, exceeding that of many small books. I am any thing but parsimonious, but I should write four or five times as many letters, if it were not for the high postage, which makes a single letter cost as much as four printed sheets, on the composition and revision of which you have exerted every power of your mind. However, it is not merely, or chiefly, the opportunity of sending you a few lines—lines, for the time of long, though rare letters, has vanished years ago—but an ardent desire to say a word of affection to you on your journey. May it be blessed to you! I trust it will, for I have myself found health in Italy, which I had thought denied to me forever. God grant that you may find it so likewise! So you are taking the same route which I did just ten years ago. You will know how to enjoy its pleasures, which I foolishly threw away like a froward child. It is easier for you also; for what did I hope for then? How much was there to which I was obliged to resign myself! You can overlook what is foolish and what is bad; as I should now overlook it myself. Go with your heart and all your senses open to the earthly paradise, to Naples above all, and shut your eyes to every thing of which you have a presentiment that it would irritate you.......

Where shall I send you the new edition of my first volume? the revision of which is nearly completed, but the printing advances slowly. I wish you may read it when perfectly at leisure, and that it may satisfy you. It is immensely enhanced in value: much of the new part is, I think, well written; much has been sacrificed, even where I have not been able to replace what has been omitted with any thing equally good; some portions which my friends will miss; but nothing is left which I could not have written in its present form with full conviction. What has become of that time, fifteen years ago, when my daring creations filled me with happiness and delighted you? I do not feel old yet; I feel much clearer in my mind, and much richer in knowledge, but not, as then, fruitful in com-

* Jacobi's residence.

binations and inventions. I long to have finished the revision, that I may proceed to the third volume. It is wearisome to write what you know already, and have brought into a clear point of view. From my childhood, among the divine attributes, that of preserving has always seemed to me extremely *ennuyant;* as an employment almost beneath an angel, and hence we can not wonder that affairs do not proceed particularly well.

I am acting as if a leave-taking were before me, when we jest because our heart is heavy. My heart is very heavy, my old friend! and yet I hope your journey will do you good. A passionate longing to be across the Alps again, still seizes upon me when the birds take their flight thither; and how much more when it is a friend! Why did you not come when I was there? Why have I not been allowed to be your guide there? I press you to my heart, and give you my blessing. My wife sends her love.

Give my greetings to the statue of Marcus Aurelius, and the lions under the Capitol, and my old Teatro di Marcello, and the Gulf of Naples, and —every thing.

Yet again, God bless your journey to you.

Your old NIEBUHR.

CCCXLIII.

TO PERTHES.

BONN, 29*th January*, 1827.

......You say, dear Perthes, that you stand toward the Catholics as east to north. You are quite right in so standing. But that is toward the Catholics as they were in the wholesome period of their depression, when the question was one of difference of opinion, and nothing further. But now all the old evils have awakened to full activity; all the priestcraft, all, even the most gigantic plans for conquest and subjugation; and there is no doubt that they are secretly aiming at and working toward a religious war, and all that tends to bring it on. Therefore, my dear friend, we must now be much on our guard, and look closely to it that we do not serve as tools to these people; I thank God that he has removed Stolberg in time, for he would not have been a match for their artifices. Whoever lives in a Catholic part of Germany, must remark that, with few exceptions, the scholars, the citizens, &c., are what they are among ourselves, but that a curse of stupidity, of vulgarity, or both, seems to rest upon the clergy, and that the proselytizers, and warriors of the holy militia, are true children of the devil.

CCCXLIV.

TO MADAME HENSLER.

BONN, 4*th March*, 1827.

......I have received a friendly letter from old Stein, in which he only contends that I was wrong in assuming that the oligarchy are secretly preparing to assert boundless pretensions; on this point he allows himself to be imposed upon. From our King I have received a letter of thanks which will serve me as a shield, if the oligarchy should raise an outcry.

Several persons in Paris have sent me friendly salutations and invitations to go there. I think of doing so in about two years, and still hope to make fresh discoveries of importance in the library.......

CCCXLV.

BONN, 26*th April*, 1827.

Your affectionate letter arrived here, dear Dora, during my absence. The machine had nearly come to a stand-still, and I felt the necessity of shaking it so strongly, that I no longer delayed availing myself of the facilities afforded by the diligences on these excellent roads, but set off last Tuesday week to Coblentz and Treves, and reached home again last Sunday. The direction of my journey was chosen, in fact, in order to induce Brandis to accompany me; he needed motion and change still more than myself, and Treves was the first place he could decide upon going to. The old Roman city with its ruins, and the relics of antiquity discovered there, had long attracted me; but I had not liked to go there without Gretchen and the children. I do not repent of having made this excursion; the physical object seems fully attained; I feel once more bright and active. I had got so absorbed in intricate inquiries, connected with my work, that I could not drive them out of my thoughts for a moment, and yet was unable to take a comprehensive view of them.

The road from Bonn to Coblentz, which I have now traveled many times, is so beautiful that one can never tire of it, and can delight in it even when the vegetation is still very backward, as it was when I left home; from Coblentz to Treves, the road crosses the hills which connect the Eifel with the Hündsrück ranges, a tiresome road through a bleak and barren district, where even the woods are still without leaves. The situation of Treves itself is strikingly beautiful; the ruins are very extensive, and highly interesting to the antiquary, as they afford an illustration of the great difference that prevailed between the style of architecture in Rome and the provinces at the same period. There, as in nearly all parts of our Rhenish provinces, the prosperity is cheering; handsome new houses are springing up in the city, and roads are repairing which have been forsaken ever since the seventeenth century, and were only to be traced by the garden walls. On the other bank of the river, cottage after cottage is built on the rock against the face of the magnificent hill; so rich is the country becoming through the increased consumption of its wines, which were formerly little esteemed, and now find a sale in all districts of the kingdom. The inhabitants are a lively and very friendly race. I have made myself quite popular in this country; I find myself received every where with the greatest kindness. One of our fellow-travelers in the diligence would not resign the office of my *cicerone* (he was a citizen) though some intelligent tutors at the Gymnasium were waiting to act as my guides. On our journey home, an inhabitant of Treves said, "It was a blessing for Catholic Germany to have a Protestant government, so that the priests could not go on as they were doing in France.

On my return, I set about a long-delayed work, the thorough arrangement of my papers, collecting and putting together those belonging to the various epochs of my life, which were still for the most part in confusion, separating those written at Berlin, at Rome, and since we have been here. It awakened many and very sad emotions. I had shrunk from these feelings, and therefore postponed the work; now it is over. Notwithstanding the age which I have reached, I have won the power of looking forward, and feel still youthful in that respect. When I think of what I have lost irrevocably, it makes my heart beat, and brings the tears into my eyes; I repress them. The great work of my life, so far as it has advanced, inspires me with courage and firmness. I know that my life has not been spent in vain, that I can do more now than before my journey to Italy. I think seriously of visiting Italy again when Marcus has reached his twentieth year, and can delight myself in the idea like a child.

A letter came from Goethe during my absence; an article that he has written for the next number of "Kunst und Alterthum," with a little accompanying note, in which he calls it the *passionate* expression of his emotions in reading my book, which he imparts to the author, because "such a work may have the happiest effects in kindling and confirming our faith in truth and simplicity." Such words are worth much to me, and to you also, dear Dora.......

The following is the article referred to by Niebuhr:

NIEBUHR'S ROMAN HISTORY.

It may appear presumptuous if I venture to state that I have read this important work through from beginning to end in a few days, evenings, and nights, and have a second time derived the greatest advantage from it. But this assertion of mine will be explained, and receive some credit, when I say at the same time that I had already devoted the greatest attention to the first edition, and had sought to make myself master of the facts, no less than of the method of this work.

When we witness the want of true criticism in so many departments of learning, even in this enlightened century, we are rejoiced to have placed before our eyes a model which makes us comprehend what criticism really is. And if the orator must aver with threefold emphasis, that the beginning, middle, and end of his art, is to give a false color to all things, in this work, on the contrary, we perceive that the living, active love of truth has guided the writer through the labyrinth. He does not, properly speaking, proceed on his own former assertions; he rather turns the same criticism against himself which he had formerly employed against ancient authors, and thus wins a double triumph for truth. For this is her glorious nature, that wherever she may appear, she opens our eyes and heart, and gives us courage to look around in the same manner on the fields in which we ourselves have to work, and to draw in the reviving breath of renewed faith.

I honestly confess that many details may have escaped me in my hasty perusal, but I foresee that the high import of the whole will ever unfold itself before me with deeper significance.

Meanwhile, I have drawn from its perusal refreshment and encouragement. On the one hand, I can once more take genuine delight in every honest endeavor, and, on the other, while I do not exactly suffer myself to be irritated by the reigning errors and misapprehensions in science, particularly the logical development of false premises, and the distortion of truth by covert fallacies, yet I can make war with a certain indignation on every species of obscurantism, which unhappily changes its mask with the peculiar characteristic of each individual, and diligently conceals with its manifold vails the pure ray of delight, and the fertility of truth, even from healthy eyes.

The above has been lying since the 8th of February among many other unfinished papers; no use could be made of it, for it does not, properly speaking, say any thing about the book which called forth this burst of feeling; it only expresses with passionate force the condition of my heart and mind at that moment. Yet I now resolve, as I am about to send a little gift on my own part to the esteemed author of that work, to communicate to him a copy of it, in confidence, for it may be of consequence to him to see what effect his peculiar labors have on the general mind; the noblest effect, that while they impart knowledge, they also encourage and animate our faith in truth and simplicity.

WEIMAR, *4th April*, 1827.

This sheet was meant to accompany the last number of "Kunst und Alterthum," but as the completion of that number has been delayed, it shall serve as its forerunner, and recommend me to your continued kind remembrance. With faithful sympathy. GOETHE.

WEIMAR, *15th April*, 1827.

CCCXLVI.

TO SAVIGNY.

BONN, *29th April*, 1827.

......Instead of myself you shall at all events have my work....... Now that so long a time has elapsed since the book saw the light, I can not write about it with the same warmth as on its first appearance; the charm of novelty goes far even with what proceeds from our own hand, and we grow indifferent to the children of our mind, however dear to us, when we have emancipated them, and dismissed them from the parental home. Let it, therefore, speak for itself; you will come forward to meet it with kindness. A more affectionate reception my writings on Roman history can not find in my own family than from you; there is only one thing which I fear with you, that your affection may cause you to regret that the imperfect work, which will be dearer to you from its origin in, and connection with that period in the life of both of us to which no other can ever approach, has been destroyed to make way for a more perfect production. It is possible that your tenderness for the work, which took its rise under the animating influence of your friendship, and the instruction I derived from your conversation, when my indolence and want of literary skill would have forever prevented my acquiring it from books, may have made you too indulgent to its defects, and given you a distaste to what announces itself as an improvement. I know this sort of affection which loves its object just as much in its relations and bearings as in itself, which deems the indistinct aspirations of youth toward something higher than we can perhaps ever attain, dearer than the proportion which a riper age maintains between its powers and its aims: the new St. Paul's may be much more beautiful, and yet I may look upon the old structure with regret in spite of all its faults. I trust, however, you will believe that I could not help forming a different judgment, and not suffer regret to mingle with the conviction which you have doubtless formed, that the contents of the book have gained immensely in value; that its principles are now immovably fixed for all ages. I do not hesitate to say, that the discovery of no ancient historian could have taught the world so much as my work; and that all that may hereafter come to light from ancient and uncorrupted sources, will only tend to confirm or develop the principle I have advanced. This is the case with Dio Cassius, of whom I have discovered that he has copied the earlier history directly from Fabius. How happy it would make me for you to read my book on the ruins of Rome, if your health and spirits allow you to do so.

The revision of this volume has occupied me unremittingly for more than a year, nearly all of which I have passed in better spirits than I could ever have believed would fall to my lot, since my youth was over, which even in times of intense happiness was not strictly speaking cheerful. And as my wife enjoyed very tolerable health during the last summer and the beginning of the winter, we had passed a very happy period, something like that which I enjoyed in 1810 and 1811.......

You will have heard of the edition of the Byzantine historians, which I am superintending. It is a great delight to me to be able thus to infuse some life into our literary doings; to give employment to young philologists; to give extension, activity, and perfection to typography; to contribute my mite to the increase of general prosperity.......

When shall we meet again, my dear, dear friend? I supplicate Heaven that you may be as completely regenerated after a year's sojourn in Italy as I was; meanwhile, when you return to this side of the Alps, you must spare yourself and allow yourself recreation. To spare yourself, it will be necessary for you to take long holidays; and you will best find recreation with the friend who is the nearest to you in all higher points of view, as you are to him. So, in 1828, you must spend more than a few passing days with us.

I conjure you, as I have done for years, to tear yourself from all disturbing and irritating circumstances. I could fain entreat you to remove to our university, but in that case tell me beforehand that I may purchase houses, since the price of students' apartments would certainly rise 30 per cent. Or cast away all the burdens of official obligation, and settle among us, and deliver open lectures as I do, and then we shall both forget that we have grown older since 1810. If my wife were here she would unite her entreaties to mine, as well as her greetings to you and yours. I embrace you with tenderness, my beloved friend. God grant that you may soon recover completely, and that we may meet again.

Your old NIEBUHR.

CCCXLVII.

TO MADAME HENSLER.

1st July, 1827.

In the second volume the first half has been revised, and the period up to the decemviral legislation is entirely new. I have no lack of materials, indeed it is one of my finest achievements, that from the notices relating to these forty years, I have brought out a history worthy of full reliance, although it deviates essentially from the statements of our historians. But I have now quite lost the state of feeling in which I wrote the first volume; the collectedness and quiet in which you can take a vivid survey of the result of your meditations, and adapt your mode of representation to it. May it return! I have often lost and recovered this power; but at my age it will not do for me to be too long without it. I have lost too this summer that feeling of happiness and contentment which gave me last year such a thorough enjoyment of life as I had never hoped to regain. There are several external circumstances to trouble me. In the first place, Gretchen's health. . . . . .

A very intelligent Englishman, who visited me a few weeks ago, looked forward to a very gloomy future for his country. There is a fearful and ever-widening gulf between the wealthy and the indigent classes; they are two hostile nations; poor Ireland is indeed a nation by herself, and her sufferings such as perhaps never can be remedied.

There is certainly great prosperity here, and were the government what it ought to be, our State would be rich in blessings. Wherever you look you see increasing comfort, and active enterprise crowned with success. The advantages of belonging to a great State are innumerable; what a contrast to our condition is presented by the misery in Nassau, Darmstadt, Rhenish Bavaria. The people see clearly, and they say it too in the district of Mayence, that in small States representative forms have no effect but to increase expense. In those parts the people actually refuse to elect members.

One book containing much nonsense but many correct statements of fact is Sidon's Letters on North America. If there are any who have not yet forgotten the childish hopes which some years ago provoked many even to insolence toward the more experienced, let them read in this book, from the pen of a man who fancies himself describing an enviable condition of society, the barbarism prevailing in the United States. It also presents a vivid picture of the Germans in North America.

Have you the new edition of Goethe? The Helena will leave a painful impression on your mind as on mine. How could Goethe hatch such a thing? But among the smaller poems, which have never appeared before, to my knowledge, there are some very charming verses; there are also some songs written in his golden youth, and printed now for the first time, or revived after having long slumbered in oblivion, for instance, the Wanderer's Storm Song. . . . . . .

CCCXLVIII.

TO SAVIGNY.

BONN, 14*th September*, 1827.

. . . . . . During this interval in which I have been incapable of nobler tasks, I have occupied myself with superintending a new edition of the Byzantine authors. Nothing can seem a madder enterprise than to announce the undertaking of a new edition of this library of writings when I am midway in the execution of the Roman History, the business of my life; but here too fortune has waited upon valor. Volunteers are coming forward on every side, to range themselves under my banner, and take the parts that I shall assign to them. The greatest readiness is evinced to aid me with communications, and in particular from Holland and France I have received presents of copies, &c., which are sent to me with expressions of cordiality that I am not ashamed to call touching. I have myself corrected the text of Agathias; several are undertaking to revise authors; copies of *inedita*, collections, come to me from all quarters: *fervet opus;*

the activity is splendid. It has hitherto occasioned me an enormous amount of work in bringing me into correspondences with all parts of the world. The most difficult part by far, nay, all the difficulties, except a few of little importance, are overcome, and I am now once more devoted to my history. Is it not a great thing that a publisher and a philosopher should be able to accomplish in six years from hence at furthest, a work that was but partially carried out in sixty years under the auspices and with the munificent aid of Louis XIV.? But as to the practicability of the scheme, thereby hangs a tale which is not altogether a subject of satisfaction. You must know there is now springing up in Germany a class who buy great books without intending to read them. For a long time we were too honest to do this, and hence, after the devil, in God's service, had put an end to the convents, which formerly used to buy ponderous works, and lay them on their shelves, to lead a useless existence like those monks themselves—works of this magnitude could not be disposed of. At present, new books, which are only bought by readers, meet with ill success, except *Scottiand* and *Claurenciana*. Collections, on the contrary, are sure of purchasers. The *petite maitresse* buys the complete works of Van der Velde, &c., the rich man, my Byzantine Historians, &c.

The Museum has been parted in two; Brandis and I have kept the philological part alone. If you have any thing to communicate, send it to us, even if it should belong to the province of jurisprudence. Between us it is almost ludicrous to mention the fee, two Friedrich d'ors.

Your old NIEBUHR.

CCCXLIX.

TO MADAME HENSLER.

BONN, *4th November*, 1827.

Since I last wrote to you, dear Dora, some time has passed like the summer, in a whirl of bustle through the visits of travelers; it seems to have come to an end now, at least, for the present.......

I beg you will let me know of all the passages which you and Twesten have marked as wanting in clearness of conception or style; it will be a real service. On one account I am sorry that the new edition is appearing so early; the English translation will be injured by it. I have received nine proof sheets of this; and it is more successful than I could ever have ventured to hope for. It is all that I could wish: the apprehension and the reproduction of my meaning are alike vivid: nothing has been sacrificed to the language and national taste; every shade of the German thought has been preserved, without violating the English language. The outward dress is very handsome; this is an honor accorded to the work by the University of Cambridge. I am assured on all sides that it will be well received; not a few copies of the German edition have been sold in England, and the work has also made some political sensation.......

CCCL.

BONN, *2d December*, 1827.

I must see how I get through the winter. The printing of the new edition of the first part is proceeding rapidly: the emendations affect no main points, although they are not unimportant; still they involve labor and meditation; and correcting the press takes up a good deal of time. I have, besides, to correct the press for the edition of Agathias which I have prepared myself. It is my intention to have the printing of the second volume finished before setting out on our journey, but I am sorry to say, I have not yet advanced far enough with the manuscript to feel sure that I shall be able to accomplish this. Unfortunately, the period up to the Decemvirate was the most difficult portion of the whole work, and I had not thought this out beforehand in my own head as I had the fundamental institutions of the State. I have at last made it perfectly clear to myself, but the style is still languid and dry. This list, however, by no means includes all the tasks to the execution of which I am either pledged or challenged in such a way that I can not decline them; not to speak of the lectures, which seldom require more than a preliminary meditation, and arrangement of my topics. I long for the holidays of next summer, which, however, I shall not be able to spend quite in idleness. I promised Bekker to revise Polybius with him, sooner or later. Now I can not put this off any longer with propriety, since the Excerpts from the Vatican have appeared, and as I mean to devote to it my solitude at the Baths of Nurndorf, and a few hours in Holstein. Next winter I hope to proceed with fresh vigor to the revision of the third volume, and afterward to the continuation.

Heaven grant that I may make at least some considerable advance toward the later periods even if I do not reach the goal I have fixed for myself, before all youthful fire is quite extinguished in me, and the tranquillity is broken in which we can now work! The completion of the work is scarcely to be expected, though from the fourth volume onward, the labor will be incomparably less; for but little research is required after that period, and I am so familiar with the events, that except a very few corrections from memory, I could relate them as if I had been an eye-witness. So that in this part of my work, the main thing will be, to secure a bright mood for the sake of the style.

It is very improbable that the repose which we have now enjoyed in these western countries for the last twelve years will be long preserved to us. It is evident that a breach has been made in the wall of the edifice, how long its fall will be delayed depends upon accident. Who can wish that this or that event should happen? We have all, of course, rejoiced over the battle of Navarino; you in Holstein, as well as we in Bonn; but it is the joy of revenge, for it has not alleviated past calamities. The opportunity of rescuing what was still left in the Morea has been lost, partly owing to Pharisaic scrupulosity, partly owing to Canning's delays on the score of the treaty. To us, who are in her neighborhood, France is even more interesting than to those at a distance. If the liberals had conquered in the elections, the choice would have lain between a violent counter-revolution, or a liberal ministry. I believe that the court could have carried the former through. But such a victory would have been a very bad thing for Catholic districts like ours, where the clergy, encouraged by irrational partisans, are continually advancing in their pretensions. On the other hand, a liberal administration would have still worse consequences for us; the journals were already talking about the "disgraceful limitation of France by boundaries which were not her natural ones." They all secretly cherish the idea of breaking out, and extending their sway to the

Rhine; and on this point aristocrats and liberals would unite willingly in the end. Bunsen has arrived in Berlin, and writes that he shall begin his journey back to Rome by way of Bonn, about the middle of this month. Savigny's letters are very gloomy; he is still suffering as much as ever. From another quarter I hear that his approbation of the Roman History is undiminished.

The course of lectures that I am delivering this winter can attract none but lovers of knowledge—or those who wish to be such. It is on Ancient Geography and Ethnography. Still above eighty have inscribed their names, and I should think there are as many present.

CCCLI.

BONN, 30*th December*, 1827.

Gretchen's severe illness has brought great commotion and affliction into the whole household.......

The unintelligible sentence that I sent you a short time since about politics in France, means this: if the liberals carry the day, the French will forthwith overstep their frontiers; and further, every coalition which may overthrow the ministry, without adopting an entirely different political system, will also take this course, in order to appease the nation for leaving other things on their present footing. But if the priestly party get the upper hand uncontrolled, which would be quite the most probable result of Villèle's fall, the prevalent spirit will be that of the League—that which heralded in the Thirty Years' War, a spirit which is now cherished and promoted by many Catholics.

The irrational precipitation of the French priests may, perhaps, spoil their game; it has already alienated from them the higher ranks, who were long favorable to their cause; the middle classes are almost entirely against them; in many provinces a great portion of the common people also: but in others, indeed in many, they completely sway the multitude. For this very reason, many of the nobility regard them as democratic, in fact, jacobinical; and not unjustly.

It is the most senseless proceeding in the world, to aim at Villèle's overthrow, since the King, if he alters the ministry, will throw himself quite into the hands of the priests. Some individuals among the liberals perceive this, as did one who was here a few months ago; but in general the French party-men are incurably irrational.

Farewell, dearest Dora. Gretchen and the children send their love to you.

CCCLII.

BONN, 14*th March*, 1828.

...... I do not know what to think of the East. Nothing hardly can be saved, and they will fight among themselves for the possession of the soil. Woe to those who did nothing in 1821! I abhor those who defend and justify the Turks, and yet I tremble at the consequences of the war. There are periods in which something much better than happiness and security of life is attainable, but I fear that is not the case in our present age. England's rapidly accelerating decline is a very remarkable and mournful phenomenon; it is a mortal sickness for which there is no remedy. I liken the English of the present day to the Romans of the third century after Christ. The course of things in France is quite contrary to my expectations. It is possible that the Left may create disturbances again, if the new elections render them independent of that fraction of the Right led by Agier; but it is also possible that new parties may be formed, as was the case in England under the House of Hanover, which may really keep themselves within constitutional limits. If so, France will become conscious of her power, and woe to poor, divided, decaying Germany!

Portalis appeared to be a respectable man at Rome; but I should never have expected to see him a Minister of State. However, I sent him my sincere congratulations a short time ago; and a few days after, expressed to some other good friends of mine, my regret at his retirement from office.

I have bought lately, at auctions, the original edition of Woldemar (1779), and the Kunstgarten;* it is very interesting to compare both with the later editions. Both has added an extraordinarily beautiful passage as an appendix to the latest edition of the works, on the fruitlessness of the efforts of good men, where the evil principle has the upper hand. Further, it is very remarkable to see how Jacobi shared the optimistic hopes so general in 1779; and to notice, when he renounced them subsequently, the turn which he gave to what he had said on the subject.

CCCLIII.

BONN, 20*th April*, 1828.

I form no conjectures as to what may happen; do not know whether the peace of Germany is immediately threatened or not; no one writes to me about such things, and I generally banish them almost wholly from my mind. But sooner or later, a war is impending over us in Germany as surely as over other countries. A war in which one can not heartily espouse either side for the sake of an idea, but only so far as it affects our own weal or woe—a war whose issue must be in every way most lamentable. The cause of the unhappy Greeks, and the paradise which might have been redeemed from barbarism, is no longer in reality the question, since we have allowed them to be almost exterminated; and new conquests for Russia are a mournful business! Woe to those who did not perceive seven years ago, and did not choose to perceive, that they ought to take advantage of the Emperor Alexander's yielding temper, to found a new Christian empire in the East, without extending neighboring powers; who did not see that such a State would be a much stronger bulwark against Russia than these miserable Turks! As regards Prussia there is no fear that we shall incur the shame of drawing our sword for the Turks.

I should have many good hopes for France, if the election had not called such utterly irrational and extreme liberals into the position of leaders, that it must come to bending or breaking between the Throne and the Chambers. It is sad that people always insist on extreme men, while by far the greater number of those who exercise a vote would gain their real aims much better, by means of sensible people. Very few now seriously wish for any thing essentially bad or dangerous—the case was quite different even so late as five or seven years ago—but it is very easy to impel the majority of the Assembly to extremely senseless and alarming steps, and this may provoke the court to a *coup-d'état*. If they had suspended the constitution a year ago, they would have been playing a hazardous game, but it might have succeeded had they acted consistently—for instance,

* Another novel by Jacobi.

decidedly abolished the freedom of the press. There would have been no danger unless a regiment rebelled, and that was highly improbable. Now, the experiment would be incomparably more hazardous, and yet the extravagancies of the liberals may cause it to be tried, though very few of them desire a revolution.

Have I then really forgotten to tell you that I agreed with one of the booksellers here, a year ago, to collect my smaller writings? I am glad that you approve of it. The political ones will be excluded; they may be revived again after my death: also the polemical ones, which need not be preserved at all. One must be able to contend upon occasion, but controversy should evaporate like a spoken word. It is thus with the orators in the free states, it should be thus in the republic of letters. Neither shall the review of Heeren be reprinted. Have I told you, then, that I have received copies of the English translation of the History? It is not absolutely free from faults; with respect to which, it is singular that they do not occur in really difficult passages, but in perfectly clear ones, so that they can only have arisen from inattention: but these are trifles; on the whole the work is masterly, and a perfectly genuine representation of the original. Then, too, it has such a beautiful exterior. The language is changing; many expressions in this translation, and in other examples of the higher literature, are quite new and unprecedented.

The English pay so much attention now to the literature of the Continent, that two rival foreign reviews appear at once, and compete with each other. In one of them there is a review of my History, as friendly, but not as discerning as I could wish. Were my old affection for England unchanged, it would give me intense pleasure to stand in such high estimation there. My principles, which I announce with the most absolute conviction of their truth, are adopted there without reservation, and will take root too firmly to be extirpated. But my heart has become estranged from England; the period of her glory has passed away; and the shamefulness with which not alone the ministry, but the nation side with the Turks, the unscrupulous practice of usury, and the exclusive idolatry of gain disgust me; and the whole moral condition of the nation is degenerating, although, to a great extent, this is as much its misfortune as its fault. I could fain be younger that I might witness the issue of many things: for instance, with regard to England, whither it will lead, that year by year so many thousands of starving Irish come over, and augment the number of paupers, and that the middle class, between wealth and abject poverty, is becoming quite extinct.

Yesterday I finished the correction of the third edition. It has received an extension of forty pages, through the addition of a number of results and corroborative facts scattered over the whole; I have taken pains also to remove whatever instances I found of obscurity or ambiguity. As this is now certainly the last revision to which reference can be made in the second volume, and as 1000 copies have again been printed, I am certain of five years' rest from it. There is to be a larger impression of the second volume, the editing of which will occupy me during the winter. God grant that I may be able to work at it with a cheerful mind! With the Byzantines I shall really have no more trouble by that time: I am upon the point of finishing the last piece of work connected with them that falls to my share—it is, I think, a successful attempt. Henceforward I shall merely have to distribute the parts: I reckon much on Marcus's tutor, Classen, who is daily becoming more attached to us, and is a genuine disciple after my own heart.

CCCLIV.

TO MADAME NIEBUHR.

NURNDORF, *6th June*, 1828.

You may be perfectly easy about me; the intolerable dullness of the existence here involves no dangers, though it really exceeds all conception. The background of my thoughts is the separation from you, and that is in itself enough to drive such a social being as myself to despair. I already know every path in the promenades and wood, and every road in the neighborhood. I am incapable of reflection and study, and promise you not to attempt it. It is quite too great an exertion even to read Rehberg's writings, which mostly treat of speculative philosophy. It has come to this with me, that I have sent for a novel by Cooper, the American Walter Scott—(N.B.—Translated!)—from the circulating library, in the so-called bookseller's shop here.

Rehberg's collected writings incontestably belong to the most important works in our language. The composition of this volume—the weaving of minor essays and papers of a philosophical description, in the narrow and wider sense of the word, into an account of his views and external relations, during the period in Germany up to 1804 (the period of his youth), is a most original and happy idea, and it is executed in a masterly style. The perspicuity and accuracy with which he describes the connecting and mediating parties is particularly admirable. This will form an introduction to many portions that will find their place in the succeeding volumes. Our respective paths are quite divergent: he is as essentially speculative as I am contemplative and individualizing; over many speculations of most brilliant acuteness I can only smile as the most unimportant thing in the world; still, thank God, I can admire what it is not permitted me to do. His historical surveys do not correspond to the truth, and contain as many errors as principles. Our judgment of Diderot is equally dissimilar; the strictly poetical element is also, I fancy, a foreign region to him. I should care almost more to know him personally and discuss matters with him, than to know Goethe.......

CCCLV.

NURNDORF, *Monday*, *16th June*, 1828.

Since Friday the weather has changed. Pertz and Hartman came to call on me; and after they had continued their journey at six o'clock in the evening, I could not make up my mind to come in from the open air, it was so heavenly. Not a breath was stirring, and there was not a trace of clouds in the whole expanse of sky; but the air was laden with the aromatic perfume of the white acacia and wild jessamine. The honeysuckle is out of bloom. It was the first gala Sunday, the first day on which there was dancing. I wandered about in the avenues, turned into the ball-room from time to time, and then took more distant field-paths: I could not resolve to go in till the sun had set for the third time into a purple glow. Then I wanted to begin a letter to you, my beloved Gretchen; but I was too weary, and soon comforted myself with the reflection that to-day, before post-time, I should have taken thirteen of my baths!

I can give you a very good account of myself. Pertz found me yesterday much altered for the better during the eight days that have elapsed. The day before yesterday I found and plucked the first beautiful forget-me-not; I wanted to send them to you to-day, but they are not dry enough yet.......

CCCLVI.

COPENHAGEN, 19*th July*, 1828.

We arrived here yesterday after as good a passage as possible, my dear wife. Touchhammer and Michelsen were at the landing-place, and helped in the difficulties of disembarkation, getting on shore, &c.......

The empty harbor, the deserted Holm, made a painful impression on me; Marcus compared the eagerness of the porters who seized upon the luggage, with Naples; and certainly the urgency of the beggars reminds you of the worst scenes of the kind in Italy. On the other hand, the cutting wind here makes you feel that you are in an Arctic climate; one perceives a great difference even in comparing it with Kiel; you would fancy Copenhagen as much north of Kiel, as Kiel is in truth and perceptibly, north of Bonn. The eastern part of the city is so still, that it reminds me of the fairy tale where the people are all spell-bound to one point for ages. From the Zoll-bude to the Neumarkt, every thing looks exactly as if I had only left it yesterday, only gone to decay a little here and there. Christiansburg, on the contrary, far exceeds my expectation. The Frauen-Kirche, which has been restored, looks better, too, than I had supposed it would. The parts left uninjured in the northern and western parts of the city, have, I think, improved in appearance.

Schimmelman is at Seelust; and they say at his house that he will be sure to be found there to-morrow, so I shall go there if I receive no express message to the contrary.......

Later. I went to Seelust on Sunday. Schimmelman is quite infirm with age,* and the warmth of his heart seems to be extinguished as well as the light of his intellect. He seems, too, only to retain old circumstances in his memory, and although he knows the positions which I have occupied, to look upon me still as his old dependent. He knew nothing of my Roman History, though I had sent him a copy of my first edition, which proves how much his memory has suffered.

Most of those whom I meet here are very cordial and kind. I think I never spoke Danish so well—I am still received as a fellow-countryman every where.

CCCLVII.

TO SAVIGNY.

BONN, 28*th November*, 1828.

With this you will receive your copy of my smaller writings, dear Savigny.

I have on all sides the most cheering accounts of your health. Thank God! I am not one to doubt what I earnestly wish for, because I am absolutely unable to conceive the possibility of homœopathy. If I were told

* He was at this time eighty-one years of age. He had, moreover, never quite forgiven Niebuhr for exchanging the Danish for the Prussian service.

you had been cured by an amulet, I should not fret myself about the danger of superstition, but thank God that you had recovered by whatever means. Arndt will have told you about us. So far my wife has been tolerably well; my complaint has returned, but is bearable. I sit at my writing, but it does not flow yet. Is my day gone by? or will my intellect brighten again? Our life gets more and more secluded and quiet, as the people come to see that I am really in earnest in retiring from the great world, and can no longer either help or injure them. I am, however, perfectly contented with the idea of living here, and I hope to remain faithful to the wisdom I have earned, and to take life easily. I hear to my great joy that you are doing so, too, and are writing. The Leipsic catalogue confirms what I had already heard, that a new edition of your "Berüf," * with additions, has appeared. What do you say to Rehberg's writings? Is not the framework which fastens the whole together, a master-piece? I am lecturing on Roman History; this time, my lectures do not consist of analyses and researches, but results, and sound as if an ancient author had been discovered, whose writings yielded precisely all that I wanted to bring forward. I hope to bring the History quite to a conclusion. If I should ever see you, I hope to hear from you that you have received my new editions as favorably as the first bold attempt.

Farewell, my dearest friend, my wife and I send our hearty love to you and yours. Your NIEBUHR.

In England, the first edition of the translation, consisting of a thousand copies, is already out of print, and my translators are about to translate my third edition. In England, my results triumph without opposition.

CCCLVIII.

TO MADAME HENSLER.

BONN, *January*, 1829.

......In Holstein, too, I have often been vexed when whatever the government did was censured. The people have no filial piety and no father-land. The true citizen loves his country so well, that he can not revile, or scoff at those who are at the helm of affairs, even when they guide it unskillfully—so well that even if those with whom he is at enmity come into power, he is reconciled to them by the fact of their standing in so close a relation with the State which is sacred to him, and being in some measure identified with it.

I expect to conclude the revision of the second volume within the next few days; the printing will begin in about three weeks. This volume will be necessarily very dry; the third quite the opposite. I wonder if it will have a good sale. A very large number of works are stopped because they do not sell. Rehberg's publisher will not continue the printing of his works. I have been requested to write a review of them, but can not do so without expressing my disapprobation of his rancorous speeches about Goethe; and also of his having thought it sufficient reparation to insert in his preface an apology for his former attacks upon Prussia, while he allows writings to be reprinted "containing what" he "would not write now." If he will consent to this, I shall joyfully recognize their many excellencies. But it is very lamentable that authors of whom we ought to be proud should be thus neglected.

* Berüf unseres Zeitalters zur Gesetzgebung.

In these last few days, I have been reminded very forcibly how much beautiful poetry came out thirty years ago or more (particularly the poems of Voss and Stolberg), of which we hear no more now—which is, indeed, quite forgotten......

CCCLIX.

BONN, *12th February*, 1829.

......The passages in my History, referring to the Irish Catholics have made me to some extent a political authority in England, and I am quoted with favor or bitterness, but for the most part with favor. On this account I have been requested, by a member of parliament, to write my opinions on the subject. Formerly, I should have responded to the request with eagerness, but my old love for England is very much cooled. Personally, I have no reason to feel estranged from the nation; from none do I receive so many proofs of esteem—sometimes of a very odd kind.

The contract for the purchase of the house was signed the day before yesterday. It is a great disadvantage for us that the severity of the winter will hinder its completion; still the main building will be quite habitable by the middle of May......

CCCLX.

BONN, *26th April*, 1829.

In the house which we are about to leave, I have spent more happy days than have been awarded to me for many years; just at present I feel rather depressed.* If I could make up my mind to leave Gretchen and the children for some months, and to spend so much money upon myself, a journey to London or Paris would afford me the refreshment I need.

[Our new house] is really such a pleasant and comfortable dwelling that it leaves nothing to wish for......

Under other circumstances I should set about the change in excellent spirits. I hope that it will deceive the Fate which seems to have decreed that I shall never live more than seven years in one place. I have often remembered with a heavy heart, that in August I shall have passed six years here already. A summons to Berlin has been long out of the question......

Read by all means Goethe's Correspondence with Schiller. In the third part, you will again find some of the most pleasing passages that have ever proceeded from Goethe's pen, and which show his personal character in as fair a light as one could wish. More of this hereafter. The contrast between him and Herder is very remarkable, as well as his indignation at the latter for never taking hearty pleasure in any thing, but always trying to limit and modify his praises, that they might not be joyful. Nothing is easier than to do this, and to show that even the production in question is not faultless; he who rejoices in it knows this too; Goethe knew it too, where Herder's superciliousness stepped forth with such a wise air. But he also knew, that without the joyful satisfaction which lets well alone, we should have a miserable existence in this world. Such passages alone would make this letter a jewel to me.

* The first part of the letter gives an account of Madame Niebuhr's dangerous illness.

CCCLXI.

BONN, 14*th June*, 1829.

You have probably seen in the newspapers that my English translators have been defending me against an attack in the "Quarterly Review." I have received some copies of their article, and will send you one when I have an opportunity. A certain Dr. Granville had mentioned in his Travels to St. Petersburg by way of Berlin, that I had remodeled my book into an entirely new work, adding, that a decisive influence on the rebellious disposition of the students was attributed to my earlier work. It is extremely likely that this was suggested to him by H. C. The "Quarterly Review" has taken this up, and accompanied it with a note, in which it pronounces it a crime, that clergymen of the Church of England should have translated a book containing the most disgusting scoffs at religion that have been written since Voltaire's time; they ought at least to have appended remarks in refutation. But, perhaps, they thought it unnecessary, because it must be allowed that my scoffs were "*as dull as pert.*" Upon this, they have been obliged to answer for themselves, since their prospects of patronage and promotion in the Church were endangered, as I foresaw would be the case; for it makes the Anglican hypocrites furious, that the historical character of the Jewish history should be contemplated in its true light. The defense is written in a most affectionate spirit as regards myself, and for the sake of this affection, you will pardon the prolixity which other readers will set down to my account, as well as to that of the English writers. Further, with many readers, their extreme veneration will inevitably produce a reaction.

I enjoy uninterrupted health, but am not in an energetic state of mind, and it is with great toil that I have dragged myself through the second volume so far that I can now see land, and look forward to the printing.

Let me recommend a book to you, dear Dora, if you have not yet read it, which I pronounce excellent; Ranke's History of the Servian Revolution. There is no other historical work in our language, in which the materials obtained from oral accounts are so satisfactorily and luminously treated: the events take place—it is not the author who relates, and we give him our unconditional credence. Ranke has given himself such elaborate mental cultivation, that he is certain to remain an excellent writer. Count Platen's "Romantischer Œdipus," I should rank far below the "Verhängnissvolle Gabel," even if the passages, written in a spirit of animosity to Berlin, did not extend themselves to the whole of Prussia, and if they had been expiated by apology, as they have been with regard to Berlin itself. Still there are some clever things in it. If you happen to meet with Travels in the United States, by Duden (printed at Elberfeldt), do not forget to read it; it is the best and most instructive book of the kind. What he says of the Germans there, and of the evil consequences of their persisting in a barbarous separation from English culture, may remind you of what I have said, when I was with you, on this subject. I think you did not perceive that I was right, but were not angry with me for my opinion, as has often been the case in other instances.

You must read Bourrienne's Memoirs when you can get them. I look at things of this kind more particularly on account of my lectures;* they

* The lectures on the French Revolution.

excite undiminished interest, and my lecture-room is crowded to suffocation. I dwelt long in exhibiting the development of the various events of the eighteenth century, and the condition of Europe before the Revolution. The first five lectures were attended by a French eccleciastic, a tutor of the Duke of Bordeaux, who is perfectly acquainted with German, and to all appearance, is traveling as an emissary of the priestly party. There may be some more birds of this feather; but no one shall be able to lay any thing to my charge, unless he puts forth downright lies and fabrications. The aspect of the political world is very threatening: the appearance of the emperor at Berlin, reminds one alarmingly of 1805. Else, on the whole, things look much better now in Germany than they did some years ago. An immense change has taken place in the feeling toward Prussia; not, indeed, in Hanover, but in the whole Southern and Central Germany; in Saxony likewise, to an incredible extent. The Zollverein with Darmstadt has begun; the treaties with South Germany will complete it.

CCCLXII.

BONN, 20*th June*, 1829.

Torrents of foreigners are pouring along our river-highway, but happily very few come near me; a reputation for inaccessibility protects me. Professor Wunder from Grimma has arrived to-day, and will spend the evening with us. We had lately an agreeable visitor in a certain Chevalier Andraym, Spanish embassador at Brussels, a frank and intelligent man, whose conversation afforded, what is to me about the greatest attraction with strangers, information about public events, bearing the unmistakable stamp of accuracy. It had an extraordinary effect, to hear a Spaniard relating with indignation anecdotes of the bigotry in Brabant. With us, this spirit only displays itself in insignificant instances as yet, but it certainly ought to be watched. As we hear, it manifests itself in Saxony in a really insane manner. Many Saxons are almost in despair about it, and people who have been hitherto my bitter enemies, ever since the Congress of Vienna, are now rather disposed to obtrude their complaints upon me. It is very remarkable how the perception is spreading, that the small States are an evil now; great advantage might be taken of this to the promotion of the true welfare of Germany, but it will not be done. In these Rhenish provinces, the beneficial results which Darmstadt has experienced from its union with us have produced a crisis. Far as we are from perfection, our condition is in every respect undeniably superior to that of the neighboring German countries: all classes are full of activity and enterprise, and both town and country are flourishing. Foreigners, who are best able to learn the real sentiments of the inhabitants, assure me, that they now find in general great contentment even here, where formerly the feeling of estrangement toward the new rulers was so strong. One must not, indeed, look too far forward into the future, for there is reason to fear that the immense manufacturing population on the Lower Rhine will also experience their share of bad times, and when these have come, no lasting remedy can be found.

......I send you the "Vindication,"* dear Dora, and at last a copy of the "Kleine Schriften"† also, for yourself, as well as for Twesten and

* "Vindication of Niebuhr," by Hare and Thirlwall.

† His own "Minor Writings."

Dahlman. Have I told you that this collection is prohibited in Austria? On the other hand, I am assured that a larger number of copies have been ordered in France than of any learned German work before. However, a hostile review of my History has appeared there also. It will stand firmly enough nevertheless; but the way in which people make use of it in Germany to fabricate apparently original works, is almost ridiculous.

I should lead a very pleasant life, if my head were brighter, and Gretchen's state more encouraging.

CCCLXIII.

BONN, *6th September.*

......I confidently hope that your apprehensions about your fate in Holstein are groundless. Hanover is a pledge that England will scarcely involve herself in a war—and a war, however successful, could bring no positive gain to her, although the nation in its universal uneasiness desires it. This is the general opinion in all the great money markets, and my own, which keeps me easy. So I hope we may be able to hobble on for some time longer. England can not wish to involve Prussia in a war with France, because an attempt on the part of the latter to press forward to the Rhine, would break up the Netherlands, whose existence is universally considered by the English indispensable to their interests. That the French, and *now*, more especially, the so-called royalist party, harbor the idea of reconquering the Rhine frontier, is by no means doubtful to us *in these parts*, nor yet a secret. Even in this university, there are persons well known to be in communication with the priests in France, who are seeking to excite rebellion against the heretical government; attempts which would be simply laughable, if it were not for the unsatisfactory aspect of things in Belgium. It is not without an object that the Duke of Bordeaux is learning German. We have no reason to complain of the liberals; that is, of the native ones; and altogether I am without fear, as the people see more clearly every day that they are very well off under the German government, and contrast their prosperity and light burdens not only with the Netherlands, but also with France, where at present both agriculture and manufactures are in a very bad state as compared with ours.

In about a week, I shall make an excursion to Mayence, to visit an old friend, General Von Carlowitz. This change is really necessary for me, and while I should have been obliged to consent to the journey in order not to hurt an old friend, I take it for my own pleasure also, as well as from the feeling that I could not do without it; traveling always does me good. The world is going to sleep; not that there is any lack of exciting occurrences, but they leave men passive; the indifference and lethargy which have diffused themselves since I returned from Italy are shocking: I must make some effort not to be overcome by this universal somnolency......

CCCLXIV.

BONN, *27th September*, 1829.

......Besides my good old friend General Von Carlowitz, there is also in Mayence one of my hearers, who is very much attached to me, and is now staying there in the house of his parents. There is always a class among the students who can not do too much for their tutors, and they reward one for one's pains. To the Rhinelanders and Catholics, what they hear from me is quite new; if they lay it to heart, one essential element of their real reunion with Germany, and reconciliation to Protestantism will be gained. For every thing good must proceed from individuals in whom the right spirit has been awakened. The opposite party are working might and main to widen the breach. The Catholic faction in France are just as much bent upon the conquest of Belgium and the Rhenish provinces, as the Imperial party. Toward the end of my lectures, induced by the complaints made by young Protestants of the attempts to stir up sedition among them, I publicly attacked this treasonable spirit, and pronounced a woe upon those who, instead of promoting the union of the German races, are actively endeavoring to make their differences a source of hatred and division; I have exclaimed to them, "Get thee behind me, Satan!" and thus put an end to hypocritical complaisance, and openly proclaimed hostilities; but it would have been cowardice to have avoided it. Fearlessness makes a very good impression on the higher class of minds among the young Catholics

In spite of the miserable weather, there was never perhaps so much traveling on the Rhine as there has been this summer. At the end of the season, I had a visit from a Parisian *littérateur*, a M. St. Hilaire, belonging to the romantic school, who take it for granted that we Germans are particularly delighted with their productions, and ought to be thankful to them for having thrown off the old French classic style; which is, however, impossible, since their performances turn out so extremely trivial, and they give up precisely that which constitutes the peculiar excellence of the French literature (wit and subtlety), to hunt after that for which neither they nor their language have any aptitude. Wisdom and modesty would lead us to rejoice in what another can do, without forthwith coveting to do the same thing ourselves; it is moreover because a contrary course, or else a depreciation of foreign performances, is the most usual one, that an acquaintance with foreign literature does so much injnry, and cripples talent. I say to the French, "Once for all, you will never have a Goethe, but delight yourselves in him; we shall never have a Voltaire nor a Béranger, but I take pleasure in them;" (do you know his for the most part seditious and sometimes wanton, but still genial "Chansons?") I hear that a faithful translation of Othello (in Alexandrines indeed) is just going to be performed at the Théâtre Français. Now this is a good thing;—but my literary friend means to bring a tragedy on the stage in which an angel appears to King Alphonso, and consoles him for the murder of a Jewish mistress, and that will be ridiculous.

The older, really liberal, literati regard this school with very unfriendly feelings, for in politics it professes the liberal creed, but by its Romanticism with respect to faith, places itself pretty much at the mercy of the Church. For the rest, it seems certain, that the priests do themselves infinite injury by their extravagant pretensions, and that the number of their opponents increases. According to St. Hilaire's account, the appointment of the present unfortunate ministry is explained by the report, that the clergy refused the eucharist to the King except on this condition.

The peace will not be very fruitful in good results; infinite misery for the poor countries that were the seat of war, unredeemed by any prospects of a brighter future. Still I am glad of it, because our provinces will be spared the sufferings of war for the present, which would not have led, in the long run, to any thing better. When one is getting old, it is perhaps wisest to wish that outward things may remain, on the whole, as they are.

One of the leaders of the English radicals has sent me a clever pamphlet written for the common people (price 3*d.*), in the *fourth stereotype edition*, the inflammatory tendency of which is shown still more by the vignette than the contents: a repulsively ugly woman, whose head-dress is composed of the crown and mitre combined, is feeding with a spoon a bloated child, already deformed by over-feeding, while five starving and ragged children are standing below crying piteously for food, or sitting in sullen despair on the ground. This is in truth a picture of society in England: God grant that it may not come to this with us also!

I recommend Bourrienne's Memoirs warmly to you, dear Dora, if I have not done so already. There you see Napoleon as he was. The book is a Waterloo for his memory; the liberal journals too are as still as mice about it. On the other hand, my lectures have led me again to speak still more directly of the immortal Mirabeau; I should like to raise a monument to him.......

CCCLXV.

Bonn, 20*th December*, 1829.

The revision of the second volume is at last rapidly approaching its conclusion. I have been terribly slow over this volume; the work was far more difficult than in the first, which related to general institutions, with the consideration of which I had often been able to occupy myself during my stay in Rome, where I was surrounded by objects calculated to throw light on them. The present volume treats of detached facts, with respect to which we have generally but very few external sources of correction; and arbitrary institutions, the traces of which are very scanty and indistinct. My time has not been spent in vain. I have freed the history from the year 260 (490 B.C.) onward, from all falsifications, and in its restored state it will no longer be liable to suspicion or accusation; there is not a single chasm left in the successive steps by which the constitution was developed; in fact I think that no single question which might be suggested by intelligent reflection remains unanswered. But this I have only been able to attain very gradually; the most important points are the result of sudden flashes of light and divinations, with regard to which it often seriously crossed my mind, whether I had not been inspired by the spirits of the ancients, as a reward for my faithful efforts on behalf of their memory. But this I would on no account say to *any one* but yourself; besides, I do not say it in earnest *now*.

I have separated the principal legends from the annals which had become suspicious through their intermixture with these, have restored them to their proper shape, and recovered the pure outline of the annals themselves. It is incredible how rich and uncorrupted they are.......

CCCLXVI.

TO SAVIGNY.

Bonn, 19*th February*, 1830.

My Dear Friend—You will not require an account of the calamity which has befallen us. The history of the conflagration you have learnt through our friends. The whole lies already like a frightful dream beyond my historical remembrance.

You will know that the copy of the second volume, in which I had introduced a multitude of additions, was lost and has been recovered. This was a great consolation! The actual manuscript part, so far as the book had been entirely remodeled, or received extensive additions, has indeed been saved, as well as the sketch of the third volume. One sheet has been found too of the manuscript that was ready for press, and should have been sent on the next day. It is the introduction and first chapter. I shall begin with all energy to restore the missing portions as soon as I have finished cataloguing the books that are saved, for the insurance offices to make their estimates.

At first, my wife stood the shock of the misfortune—of the fright and the severe cold to which she was exposed, half-clothed, better than I had hoped. But afterward the mournful task of looking over the articles we had saved, and which were in great part rendered useless, so affected her nerves and exhausted her strength, that the joyful feeling is now over, with which I had buoyed myself up for some months past, that her health was much better than usual at this time of year.

We have not lost heart, my old friend. Our thoughts are fixed upon the rebuilding of what has been destroyed, with enlargements and improvements, for the sake of which we look forward to the milder season with impatience. We hope to be able to add a third story, which would afford me winter rooms with the sun, and a view over the town toward the Kreuzberg, and sideways toward the Siebengebirge.

The Holwegs have treated us in the most affectionate manner. God reward them for it. We have experienced many proofs of affection from all kinds of people; from such as we know to be friends, and from many who were almost strangers to us; from the towns-people too. The students have done every thing in their power, and richly rewarded my affection for them; by dint of inconceivable exertions, they have saved almost the whole of my library, though they were not able to prevent its suffering great injury. All the books in which I had written collations and emendations of importance are safe.

It is now my most ardent wish that we may be able to remove into our new house in the autumn, and remain in it many years. I could not conceive a better lot for the whole of our life, and would not ask for a happier life than that which I have led here since my return from Berlin in 1825; particularly during the glorious southern climate we had here in the years 1825 and 1826.

I have already told you that the printing of the second part should have begun immediately. It had been delayed just at last, and this printing of the volume, which would have been thicker than the first, would not have been finished before the autumn. I intended afterward to take flight and visit Berlin, in order to see you, my dear friend, and the Crown Prince, and to convince the latter that it is not the long journey, nor yet caprice, that prevents my coming, but that I will not again be separated from my wife and children as I was that winter. Now, of course, the journey is out of the question. But I regret being compelled to give it up all the more, because any thing that thus excites and diverts the mind is such an extraordinary benefit and help, and my route would lie through

Thuringia and Saxony. Hermann has behaved so frankly and nobly, and one of his favorite pupils, Professor Wunder, has attached himself so warmly to me, that I thought with pleasure of a day at Leipsic; and Goethe too is still so fresh, that it would not have been too late to make his acquaintance. Are you not as thoroughly delighted as we are with his Correspondence with Schiller, and the new volume of the Travels in Italy? Goethe's greatness—in all its versatility and depth—shines forth beyond my expectations from the whole of this collection, and in his letters he is as great as Cicero. Schiller too I understand and like much better since reading these letters. You will remember, perhaps, that I did not share the idolatry of him, which was universally prevalent at one time; but that man had a thoroughly noble nature who was never rendered arrogant by such adoration, which exalted him far above Goethe, but willingly and cheerfully recognized the superiority of his friend, and paid him affectionate homage.

How barren and dumb is our literature now! How apathetic are all hearts! We, however, who know how to enjoy, are made much richer by these publications than we were thirty years ago, or our fathers fifty years ago. Thus it was with the Greeks after Alexander's time, at the beginning of the Peloponnesian war.

CCCLXVII.

TO MADAME HENSLER.

Bonn, *4th August*, 1830.

I sit down to write to you to-day, as in the war times, when we sought intercourse in writing to our dearest friends, because the events happening around us made it impossible for us to pursue our ordinary occupations, though at the same time they made us lose sight of the personal affairs which form the usual subject of our communications. This will sound like an enigma to you, dearest Dora, as you will scarcely, if newspapers and letters reach you together, look into the former first, nor have heard already, through any other channel, what has come to our ears early this morning; viz., that an insurrection had broken out at Paris on the 27th and 28th of July, the issue of which was still quite undecided. If the newspapers have already been brought to you, you will very likely learn at the same time that you receive this, what we shall not know till to-morrow. I scarcely think you will learn the decision as yet, but perhaps what may to some extent enable you to divine it. It is possible that the insurrection may be quelled by a massacre, if the troops of the line stand firm to the King, which seemed, however, doubtful on the 28th at noon; it is possible that they may join the people, and overpower the guards; it is possible the Court may take flight as after the 14th July, 1789, and even that the King may abdicate. In this case, the whole spell of royal power is dissolved, and the King will be as impotent as Louis XVI., and the best thing that could happen then would, undoubtedly, be the elevation of the Duke of Orleans to the throne. A new dynasty can begin its career with incomparably more authority than the old vanquished one. If the rebels get the upper hand, and the Court does not give way, we may expect that the Deputies now sitting at Paris will constitute themselves, form a government, and restore the National Guard. A happy result is in no case conceivable; no one will be carried away by a delirium of passionate sympathy and hope, as in 1789. Foreign powers will not be so mad as to interfere, but in the general ferment, any slight occasion may impel the French to begin a war.

The Protestant feeling of our King is the surest guarantee that he will not suffer himself to be implicated; for without fail Protestants will be murdered in the south. Austria has probably encouraged the government to venture on their bold attempts, but will scarcely have promised assistance. I will not deny that I should sooner have expected the sky to fall, than an insurrection to take place, and I was led to this opinion by the expressions of liberal Frenchmen. People of this party, who were certainly in a very good position for judging, confessed last autumn, that if the Polignac ministry had attempted a *coup d'état* immediately on its accession to power, at the same time not sparing money, any thing might have been possible. The sentence "*le peuple a donné sa démission*" had become a proverb, and as there are now so many families who have property to lose, and nobody builds castles in the air as in 1789, I decidedly believed that they would be able to muzzle the nation. I lamented the "*ordonnances*," because they introduced a detestable misrule, but that they would succeed *for the present* I did not doubt. I certainly thought it would only be for the present, that in the long run they could not be maintained, and even that the dynasty might probably fall in a few years; that is, if the priests went too far. The government have made a mistake in waiting for a year without checking the freedom of the press, and now all at once heaping every thing together that was calculated to embitter and exasperate the people.

I remembered too, how easily the Parisians suffered themselves to be dispersed in October, 1795, and how insignificant were the occurrences in June, 1820: and hence, I did not give them credit for allowing themselves to be so far excited by political feelings as to risk their lives. They have proved themselves more manly than I thought. The insult to the citizens of depriving them of the right to vote, hitherto obtained by taking out a license to trade—the fear of retaining only a phantom of representation, which might be used to procure a sanction to the most odious decrees, and abhorrence of the priests, have all combined to drive the people to madness. This does not prove that they will hold out; if the troops of the line make a decisive advance, Paris will surrender. One of your first thoughts, dear Dora, on hearing of these events will be, that the greater part of our property is invested in France. If the liberals win the day, it is safe: to pay the State creditors is the interest and the system of this party: it could only be in danger if a civil war broke out.

We may hear the decision of the fate of Paris so early as to-morrow, and can hardly be without it longer than the day after. We have a daily post from Paris here, and learned on the twelfth, that Algiers had surrendered on the fifth.

In the midst of such engrossing excitement, I get on but badly with composition; and I am already at least a quarter of this volume behindhand with the materials I have to work out. For more than the last three weeks I had already found it very hard work, on account of the excessive and continuous heat. And now in September comes the annual review of the troops and afterward our removal. I long to finish this volume, not, as with the first, in order to see it before me a finished creation, but to have got rid of the arduous labor. When I look through the proof sheets now, I rejoice indeed in the richness of their contents, and the discoveries, through which the history of Rome, during a period when it seemed lost in impenetrable obscurity, has been fully restored and established on a solid foundation; but I can not believe that it will be an attractive work. Those who wish to find fault, and they are generally the majority, will find room for complaint that so many minutiæ and such an expenditure of research should be found in the history of a trivial age.

Have I told you lately that a very impertinent review of my history has appeared in the *Débats*, on occasion of the translation? No doubt by that empty sciolist Villemain, whose weak head has been turned by the plaudits of the public. One must try to become hardened against things of this kind. This man, like other fools who will make themselves heard, always goes back to the earliest times, and he in particular tells me it is nothing new to refuse to regard these as historical. These people are actually unable to understand, that the value of my exposition consists in my having shown why and how each circumstance has been invented.......

CCCLXVIII.

BONN, 16*th August*, 1830.

However strongly the present events excite the desire to interchange my thoughts with you, it is yet difficult to find the necessary leisure and quietness of mind, as I am obliged to prepare manuscript and correct proof sheets. I feel almost stupefied with all I have to attend to, and a letter which I was obliged to write a short time ago turned out so badly in consequence, that I wish it had never been written. With you, dear Dora, I need not fear this; I do not shrink from your seeing me half asleep.

I was not quite unprepared for the way in which danger and calamity of all kinds are now every where breaking in. I have enjoyed the happiness of the years gone by, with the presentiment that it could not last. The revolution I did not expect; indeed, I thought it impossible. I expected individual calamities, such as the comparatively mild one which has befallen us, and the dreadful one which has befallen the Brandis family.*......

If peace last, I think there is no fear but that our dividends will be paid us. The government will make extraordinary reductions in the budget, and although the bankers will assuredly not retain forever such overweening influence as they now possess, in a representative state public opinion and self-interest will secure the payment of the dividends. A reduction to four per cent. will no doubt take place, and that is fair, and is occurring every where. If the cabinets were mad enough to engage in a war, then indeed both capital and interest would be endangered; and as, in all probability, the war would take the same course as that of the revolution, our property and our whole existence here would be abandoned to destruction. I do not know how far one can reckon upon the fact of the danger being so apparent; the impossibility of a result ought to strike all. The sovereigns may perhaps be led astray by the example of 1815; the rest of us, you at a distance, we on the frontiers, are not liable to this delusion.

* In Kiel, where the brother-in-law of Professor Brandis lost his life, together with his son, in the burning of his house.

Simple people leave this unanswered, and are forever harping upon one string—the danger that threatens all Europe. Yes, in truth, danger does threaten; the revolution which had been defunct for years, has started into new and most vigorous life; in many respects, indeed, it is widely different from that of 1789, but still in essence it is the same, and armed with the same strength. But who can believe in these days that it will be conquered because it is so fearful? Neither does it avail any thing to curse those who have made it inevitable—who have exorcised, and conjured till the spectre which they thought to lay, has risen out of the earth and annihilated them. I have delivered my sentiments on this subject publicly; on the impiousness of the jesuitico-aristocratic factions, which took their rise in 1821, and how they ought to be execrated; but it has been without effect. Still, every honest man, whose voice has any weight whatever, is bound to cry aloud against the sympathy and commiseration expressed for fallen majesty.

I will not deny that I think the Parisians heroic, the moderation of the victors not simply theatrical, and the discretion of the deputies, even of the extreme Left, worthy of high respect. Every thing has gone on better than in 1789, and by this it is evident that the nation has really improved. I only wish old La Fayette and echoes of him were out of the way!

That the scholars and literati among the French have changed, is shown by the way in which they receive the translation of my History. A second edition of it is in the press, although the first consisted of 1600 copies. Paris is the only place in which a regular course of lectures has been delivered on the work. They manage it rather awkwardly, but still show much good-will.

I will leave off here to go out; the air does me good. If the revolution had not happened, in all human probability, in the course of this year, *i.e.* before August, 1831, I should have gone to Berlin, and very likely to see you.

CCCLXIX.

BONN, *7th October*, 1830.

I have not been so long without writing to you since I can remember, dearest Dora; but neither have I experienced such a paralysis of the soul since 1806 and 1807, as during the last five or six weeks. Even in 1806 and 1807, when calamities we now only foresee had actually occurred, I did not feel so vulnerable to the strokes of fate as I do now. We were childless, I was young and full of life; now I am old, shall probably in a few years leave a widow and children unprovided for behind me.......

Since the loss of Belgium, the seat of war is brought within a few marches of us, and though every thing is still perfectly quiet in our province, and all who have property recognize that their salvation depends on the maintenance of the existing order of things, we are, notwithstanding, threatened with an outbreak on the part of the populace, if an opportunity offer. Added to this, there are fears for the safety of our property since the outbreak of the revolt in Belgium. I have decided to sell more than two-thirds of our French stock, and to invest the price in various places, so that at all events we may not lose all with one blow; the rest I shall leave in France for the same reason. No man can advise himself or others with certainty in such cases. My uneasiness about these affairs is certainly no mean love of money, but a most justifiable anxiety on the part of the father of a family, in such times; as also the other question—how to invest the money. I have resolved to dispose of a part of it in Russian bonds and certificates. I have decided to take these upon conviction, because we can not conceal from ourselves, that while all these movements may add to the overthrow of Germany, they will extend the dominion of Russia, and because this power, invulnerable from without, finds support within from the size of its population, grows yearly, and will always be able to bear a much heavier national debt than her present one. This is not a question of sentiment but of facts, and upon these I act. The Norwegian funds are likewise now no contemptible property, as there is, perhaps, no State less threatened with war, and, after the example of Holland, Sweden will, no doubt, perceive that it is her policy to give way, if Norway should wish to loosen still more the bond between them.

The fate of our town, in case of war, situated as it is between two fortresses, I need not picture to you. For we can not deceive ourselves as to the fact, that the war would be disastrous to us, that we should be driven back, since a great part of Germany, far from supporting us, would receive the French with open arms. Our resting-place will therefore not remain here in that case; and I have made up my mind to our leaving, as soon as the war breaks out. It would then certainly be a great pity that we have the house. Meanwhile, whenever I go into it and see how beautiful it looks in its new condition, it has such a charm upon me, that I should bring myself to give it up with great difficulty.

I have breathed more freely for the last two days, because I have finished the preface to the second volume. I can not describe what a torture it was to me to be obliged to compose every week manuscript sufficient for two printers' sheets, not to speak of correcting the press, in this state of anxiety and depression, and with my thoughts so differently occupied. The printing might have been delayed, but Reimer was urgent that the book should be finished in October, and I too was anxious to bring it to an end. I am conscious that the part which has been written since the 1st of August, betrays the state of mind in which it has been produced, while the first two-thirds may, perhaps, be considered as a successful effort, notwithstanding the dryness of the subject-matter. I have said this in the preface, as also that my hopes of following it up with a third volume after a short interval of rest, had been frustrated by the unhappy state of public affairs.*

* "At another season the delay [in the printing of this volume] would have had no influence on the execution of my work: but only two-thirds of it were completed when the madness of the French court burst the talisman which kept the demon of the revolution in bonds. The remainder has been written under a feeling that it was a duty not to leave what I had begun unfinished, amid constant efforts to repel the harassing anxiety ever pressing upon me from the prospect of the ruin which menaced my property, my dearest possessions, and my happiest ties. The first volume was written when every thing was smiling around me, and I was thankfully and heartily enjoying it in the most perfect unconcern about the future. Now, unless God sends us some miraculous help, we have to look forward to a period of destruction similar to that which the Roman world experienced about the middle of the third century of our era—to the annihilation of prosperity, of freedom, of civility, of knowledge. Still even though barbarism should for a long season scare the muses and learning entirely away, a time will come when Roman history will again be an ob-

My expressions about the impending future, its retrogression toward barbarism, the flight of the sciences and muses, will be recognized by posterity as the view of an unprejudiced contemporary; at present they will raise the clamors of the dazzled multitude. Very few know whither they desire to go; the greater number start up and run headlong away, like people taking a walk who only want to give themselves exercise; they are completely under the influence of declamation and visionary ideas; yet among them are honorable men, and even authors of talent.

While I was lamenting over these infatuated revolutionists, I received a bullying letter from *, because having occasion to write to him, I had freely declared that this resuscitation of the revolution was entirely to be ascribed to the priestly party and a perverse aristocracy. He flies at me as if he would tear me to pieces for "seeing such phantoms and defending the liberals." There is a priestly aristocratic party here, small in numbers, but which has a nest in Coblentz, by which he suffers himself to be befooled. However dear the friendship of any man may be to me, I can not purchase its continuance at the sacrifice of truth.

Gretchen has a good thought about our emigration, if it *must* be; to turn our steps to Halle, where we have a friend in Bluhme, and have also other acquaintances.

After the perfect apathy which reigned as long as the great tendencies which were the precursors of present events might have been calmly set forth, is there now with you, who have nothing to fear for yourselves, the same universal exulting garrulity on the course of public events, which prevailed forty years ago? Here, even the liberals, with few exceptions, are full of anxiety, and many judge very sagaciously. Political follies have had little influence so far. A state of prosperity is hardly possible in France, even if peace lasts: if war comes, there can be no security for any thing in the general breaking up. It is all over with the Imperial party, but it can not be absolutely affirmed that republican anarchy may not lead back to the Duke of Bordeaux. No one can deny that the people of Brunswick and Hesse Cassel have right on their side, in the main also, the people of Dresden; but with them the imitation of the French is already grievous and disgraceful; the risings of the peasantry are horrible.

The absence of every kind of joy, hope, and illusion is a peculiar feature in these revolutions, particularly that in France, as compared with 1789. Every thing bears the impress of age and decrepitude; the aged La Fayette, who still dreams that he is in the olden times, stands like a spectre in the midst. There is much more self-consciousness than there was then; the lowest rabble have their eyes bent on their own immediate advantage. Forms are a matter of indifference, except to a few young visionaries. It is very possible that such a dissolution of society as that in South America may take place even in France. The mercantile class, heartily as it detests the priesthood, would be only too glad if the revolution had never happened. I held it to be impossible, because I knew that the upper classes thought of nothing but their own advantage, and cherished no dreams. It was to be foreseen that they could never expose themselves to the bullets, and so it has turned out; they have let loose

ject of attention and interest, though not in the same manner as in the fifteenth century."—Preface to the second volume of the History of Rome. (Hare and Thirlwall's Translation.)

the mob, and in Paris it has behaved not only with heroic courage, but for a mob most admirably. The misery and the scarcity of food are now indescribable, and things can not improve.

We have passed several days in immediate anxiety. Now we have our garrison again. The day on which the news of the insurrection at Aix-la-Chapelle reached Bonn was horrible; just like the air before an approaching storm, or in the south, before an earthquake, when all animals are full of terror. On the previous evening, similar tidings had come from Liège, at nine in the morning they came from Aix-la-Chapelle; an hour after, a fellow stood up here in one of the squares and exhorted the mob to insurrection; the populace eyed us of the higher ranks with looks of defiance and scorn; in the afternoon, we learnt that a disturbance had broken out at Cologne. Our house is opposite to a large manufactory, whose master is universally hated, from which we are only separated by a broad open street, and moreover we had neither a garrison nor a national guard, nor any one who knew how to form one. For the present we are quite safe. We shall remove into our new house in a fortnight at furthest, unless great changes take place between now and then. The repairs are very nearly completed......

CCCLXX.

TO SAVIGNY.

BONN, 16*th November*, 1830.

......The preface expresses my views about the future, with that strict correspondence with my thoughts, which I always endeavor to observe. It is my firm conviction that we, particularly in Germany, are rapidly hastening toward barbarism, and it is not much better in France.

That we are threatened with devastation, such as that two hundred years ago, is, I am sorry to say, just as clear to me, and the end of the tale will be, despotism enthroned amid universal ruin. In fifty years, and probably much less, there will be no trace left of free institutions or the freedom of the press throughout all Europe, at least on the Continent. Very few of the things which have happened since the revolution in Paris, have surprised me. Before the revolution, a Frenchman had started the question in a newspaper, what I should say to Cæsar's death?

I am just sending this reply to him; "As I do about the ordonnances; submission was impossible, and yet both now and then, it was a calamity that the attempt succeeded." You will not find this paradoxical......

[The following extracts from some of Niebuhr's letters written about this time, are given in the Lebensnachrichten, without a date:]

"In my opinion, what constitutes a royalist, is to believe that the State is no arbitrary association;—that the whole is before the parts;—that government is of God;—that government is the first necessity, and that government and liberty must be combined;—that they may be so under the most diverse forms;—that forms which set bounds to the pretensions of the mass of mediocrity are salutary; those which do not, intrinsically bad;—that attempts to alter the constitution by insurrection, are not merely irrational, but criminal. And on all these grounds I can acquiesce in the mistaken measures of the aristocracy, although I am often keenly alive to their errors. But if I am required to acknowledge any tyranny as sacred, and to pronounce every endeavor to break the yoke, rebellion, even where commanded by the most urgent distress, I can not yield my assent; and when I see folly and ignorance at the helm of affairs it rouses my indignation, and I do not conceal my sentiments.". . . . . .

"Our disease is far too deeply seated to be removed by mere changes in the constitution: for, from no change made in these times, and by the men of this generation, can we venture to hope for that legislation, which might bring us into a healthful and progressive condition, by transforming our habits and our entire social circumstances. What we want, is as certain and clear to me as my own existence, and to a great extent I could express it, but it were to talk to the winds, and I do not choose to be dragged through the mire to no purpose. 'They have Moses and the Prophets, and hear them not.' Were I in power, I would act, and with vigor, in God's name, even if it brought danger to myself.". . . . . .

"Many royalists are not so in the same sense as I and my fellow-thinkers; they regard that as admirable and praiseworthy, which we only defend as necessary in principle, without denying that in the actual state of things it often works very ill, and, therefore, while we maintain that if it fall, every thing must go to ruin, yet, we prophesy that no human power can uphold it, unless a reform take place, and a new life be infused into it. For example, we say there must be an aristocracy, indeed, an aristocracy of many grades; but we add, at this moment there is no tolerable aristocracy existing, and that which calls itself such, is a phantom from which all vital energy has fled. The other party are satisfied with this aristocracy as it is, and fancy it is only necessary to compel obedience. We say, make proper regulations, and obedience will not be wanting if a good example is set to the people. They think to accomplish all by repression, and we demand free scope for movement, in conformity with the law. We say, when the governments understand their vocation of ruling, the subjects will soon return to theirs of obeying. And so on without end.

"In this, our two parties (if I may so call them) agree, that revolution is rebellion, and that of the most ruinous kind that can befall nations; and likewise, that we despise the liberals beyond all expression for their shallowness and wickedness. But I do not thereby abrogate my conviction that it is only the despotism now inseparable from it, owing to the monstrosity of the ruling ideas of the present day, which renders revolution so utterly execrable, that it can bring forth nothing but evil, and that a sensible man ought to risk every thing even for a bad government, sooner than submit to it. My conviction is, that ere the despotism of liberalism became all-powerful, there were perfectly justifiable revolutions, in which one power was victorious in the struggle with the usurpations of another power, as in England and the Netherlands. Lastly, that tyranny, under all circumstances and in all ages, remains tyranny; and that where this exists, nature takes her course, though under our present conditions, that course can lead to nothing but slavery. Many good men call such principles dangerous, and although they may be far from mistaking the motives of one who maintains them (like myself, who, in order not to acquire an unmerited reputation, have fully developed them in my report to the government) yet they can not help feeling a little terror at his openness and temerity. This may make it clear in what sense I am an unconditional, true, and faithful royalist, and that I have not swerved in the least from the principles of which I am an avowed adherent."

"Had I lived in ancient Rome, and had it been possible for a Tribune to propose such a regeneration of the State as the short-sighted people of our day desire, I would have helped to strike him dead in God's name; and if I lived in a State where one constitutional element of the whole was injuriously repressed, whether it were the democratic, or a truly aristocratic element, I would strain every nerve to give it fair play, and put it in possession of its rights.

With us Germans, aristocracy can never become so sickening as a superficial liberalism. The hot fever has burnt itself out, like a plague that at last vanishes spontaneously; still we shall have repose, and be able to return to the quiet life of our grandfathers, who were not, indeed, like ourselves, threatened with a barbarian yoke.

Constitutional forms are of no use among an enervated or foolish nation. What avails the choice of representatives, when there are no men fit to represent the people? Is it answered, "Let them learn by practice;" that is, indeed, to sport with the gravest matters. I say; give them free communal institutions, and let them, in the first instance, learn by practice within a sphere with which they are acquainted. Believe me (but that *you* know already), I know how to prize a free constitution, and am certainly better acquainted than most with its meaning and worth; but, of all things, the first and most essential is, that a nation should be manly, unselfish, and honorable. If it is that, free laws will grow up of themselves by degrees."

CCCLXXI.

TO MOLTKE.

End of November, 1830.

...... Instead of the She-wolf, there now stands in the room which I have taken for myself a bust which must be familiar to your remembrance of Paris in 1790, which you have probably possessed yourself, the mention of which will call up that whole period to your mind—Mirabeau, by Houdon. I do not know if it has reached your ears, that I gave a course of lectures last year, on the History of the Revolution. On that occasion I read the "Opinions et Travaux," and my heart beat so strongly for the demon, the mightiest of all the men whose lifetime has coincided with my own, that I commissioned a person in Paris to purchase his bust for me. It was not to be found; no one inquires for it now, just as no one now *reads* this Demosthenes. A full half year passed before my commissioner was able to hunt up a replastered, varnished copy; but even this is valuable to me. Now the fact that Mirabeau had vanished from the eyes and the thoughts of the people, was a proof to me that the revolution was done with; and I inferred this still more decisively, from the manifest certainty that no one cherished any longer those hopes of better, if not golden times, by the dreams of which our youth was buoyed up; and who could have thought it possible that in an utterly unpoetical age—one like that which Petronius paints, when men, if they sacrificed at all, offered gold in ingots to the gods, to spare the cost of moulding it—people would risk wealth and comfort in order to wreak their anger? It is so, nevertheless, and I have been a false prophet; but it must be allowed that it was insane conduct which drove the people mad with intolerable oppression; and even as it is, the result has been very different from that which took place in those years of youthful enthusiasm. Tremendous catastrophes have come to pass, and there is no resistance, not a semblance of great men, no joy or enthusiasm, no hopes for the future—except that the time will one day come, when, by means of mutual instruction, every peasant boy shall be able to read. The truth of the thing is the unvailed destitution of the populace, who are resolved to bear it no longer; and this again paves the way for a revision of property; which is not, indeed, something new under the sun, but has been unheard of for centuries past, and even now seems quite inconceivable to our politicians, who have set property, in the place of God, in the Holiest of Holies. We have fallen into the state of Rome after the times of the Gracchi, with all its horrors, and he who can not see this is blind; he who thinks the question has any thing to do with freedom is a fool; forms will no longer hold things together; we shall bless despotism if it protects our lives, as the Romans blessed that of Augustus. That it was possible for reasonable men to do this, I had comprehended long ago; now, it is perfectly, vividly clear to me; and now I also understand Catiline.

This would be mournful enough if it only affected our contemporaries in foreign lands, and we were able to retain those good things of life which Livy, Horace, and Virgil enjoyed after the battle of Actium, and through whose possession they were able to keep their mind serene and fit for creative efforts; namely, security, leisure, the power and splendor of the State. But in our poor Germany, hopeless confusion is breaking forth in all directions, and delivering us unarmed and defenseless into the hands of our hereditary enemy, who is already revenging himself by insolence and scorn, for the short time during which he has lain bound, and broods over no less a design than the restoration of his tyranny, and the sacking of all neighboring countries. I could have resigned myself to the dissolution of the present order of things, though it would bring a miserably inefficient set of men into the place of those who now hold the reigns of government, and set before them a far more difficult task, but that it would inevitably lead to the wreck of our independence amid the fearful storms of war.

And let no one delude themself with the idea that, at all events, free constitutions would spring from the convulsion: it will lead very quickly to an absolute military despotism, which will scarcely trouble itself with outside decencies even so much as that of Napoleon. In Holstein also the people are already beginning to agitate. These men are perhaps still greater strangers to you than to me. Respecting the enterprise and its consequences there can be no difference of opinion between us, except of a little more or less indulgence. God help us to endure what we can not avert! Gretchen asked me lately in earnest, whether I still, as in the time of Napoleon, thought of going to North America. "If it were not for the children," whom I would rather see Germans, even under a Russian rule than Anglo-Americans! Farewell, dear friend. Shall we not see each other again somewhere? You have never answered my invitation to the Rhine, and now that is out of the question. Remember me to your sons; I have received Magnus's circular; wish him success in my name. My wife sends her kindest regards to you, she braces herself up to bear what is inevitable.

Your old NIEBUHR.

CCCLXXII.

TO PERTHES.

BONN, 17*th December*, 1830.

......3. The sudden demand for my old translation of the Philippic is as inexplicable to me as to you. I can not have the slightest objection to your republishing it; instead of the dedication, which is now inapplicable, I should like you to insert after the title page what is written on the inclosed sheet.*

With this my answer to your inquiries is ended, and now comes my turn.

1. I thank you very much for sending me the further parts that have appeared of your great series of historical works. Stenzel's book treats indeed of a field which I have explored less than any other, but so far as I may presume to express a judgment notwithstanding, I think it very excellent, and hope it will be received as it deserves.

2. You know Lardner's Cabinet Cyclopædia, to which Sir J. Macintosh's, Sir Walter Scott's, &c., historical works belong. In the same collection will appear the History of Greece up to Alexander, by my translator Thirlwall. It will be no erudite work, but the work of a truly erudite and intellectual man. Before the outbreak of the revolution, I begged the author to send me proof sheets, which Classen should translate under my eye; I intended to add a preface and a continuation up to the Roman period. We had agreed to offer you the work, my dear friend: I wished that something of consequence from my hand should be published by Perthes, and your fellow-citizen Classen had the same feeling. Thirlwall very modestly declined sending the sheets to me, saying that they were not worth the trouble. Under other circumstances, I should boldly advise a publisher to get the book as soon as it appears (which is so easy in Hamburgh), and to announce that a translation of it by Classen would appear with a preface and a continuation. But now, I can not promise you a continuation; if we are fugitives, where shall we find a secure resting-place where I could work? And now will you venture the announcement with the addition "in case I should not be prevented" from giving the continuation? And send for the book? And how much could you afford to pay Classen for it? Under other circumstances it would be an uncommonly good article, for there is at present no book of the kind at all.

3. My burdened heart would fain relieve itself by some admonitions to the Germans, at which your last letter hints: prudence counsels silence—says it would make little impression. If I write, and am satisfied with my performance, I shall send it to you. Never has Germany been so treacherous to herself as now; and since the revolution in Poland, not only has salvation through our own efforts become impossible, but even for a miracle there is no place left, which is always indispensable before a miracle can interfere in the course of earthly affairs.......

CCCLXXIII.

TO MADAME HENSLER.

BONN, 19*th December*, 1830.

......I do not mean to question that the administration of justice is

* Published in his "Nachgelassene Schriften." The last words he ever wrote for publication.

in a bad condition, but the multiplicity of the systems is the least part of the evil; the most lamentable circumstance is the character of the judges themselves, who seem to have laid aside the old characteristics of their order. This is the case wherever you inquire; the old severe gravity has vanished from the tribunals, whose members for the most part simply endeavor, like other officials, to expedite the work allotted to them with as little trouble as possible, and have no conscientious feeling that they ought to administer *the Right*, an idea which is quite foreign to the professors of jurisprudence. I by no means wish to do away with Codes of law altogether. I should rejoice to see a complete revision of the existing system of laws in Holstein, but the reformers would not be satisfied with this. They want one single new Code, just as, when they talk of Chambers, they want an entirely new representation, and such a Code can not possibly succeed. There is no human being who could frame it. And, above all, from a Code of criminal law, may God preserve every country! even if the jury were not to be immediately introduced in criminal cases, which is however an immediate consequence of the principles of these people. You have no doubt received the copies of my History, and read at the least the preface in your own copy. This has created a sensation of which I had not the least idea, when I was writing down the statements of my convictions, or, perhaps, I might have omitted it. It has roused a clamor, not only among those who rejoice in disturbances and destruction, and already regard as rebellion any lamentations over the state of things which they promote, at least with their wishes, but also among those who do not like to think the evil quite so great as it is, and many who do me the honor to think themselves wiser than I. What is said of me behind my back rarely comes to my ears, but I have accidentally heard something of it which makes me very indignant. It is said that I can not bear that any one should differ from me in opinion. This is not true; on the contrary, no one can in practice more completely concede to others the liberty to have what opinion they choose: I condemn none, and defend—how often—the sentiments of my greatest opponents. But I require that no one should take the liberty of blaming me for having my own, especially on subjects into which I have more insight, and on which I can form a better judgment than those who set themselves up for wiser, and who allow me no voice whatever in things belonging to their sphere. Meanwhile, I have a rich compensation in the unlimited approbation of Hermann, who is equally convinced with me that the present tendency of the world is toward barbarism.

My sadness, quite apart from the misfortune which is impending over us personally, is caused by the degeneracy of our nation, no less than by the prospect of its servitude and devastation. It is impossible not to perceive that the noble qualities which were the glory of our nation are disappearing—depth, sincerity, originality, heart, and affection—that shallowness and impudence are becoming universal. This can not be charged upon the circumstances of the times; things are pursuing an ordinary course, such as other nations have witnessed before; and if there were nothing else, I should calmly work on for other ages, from which a book written now can not be quite kept back, even if Germany should be desolated by Hunnish ravages. But when we contemplate the present, when we look at the tiger in the West waiting with glaring eyes to pounce upon his prey: and the tone of feeling pervading all Germany (with the exception, for the most part, of our old provinces), which furthers the design of the enemy, dissolves all bonds, makes resistance impossible, opens outstretched arms to the French! "Give us freedom," say they, "and we are ready to withstand the foreigner:" but this freedom is chaos, and the sway of madmen or fools; and since their demands neither can nor will be granted, and there is no great man living to win the people to himself and carry them away with him, to all human foresight, the loss of the left shore of the Rhine to France, the inundation of the rest of Germany by French hordes, the destruction of the existing States, and the formation of servile republics under the guidance of traitors, has become quite inevitable after the insurrection of the Poles. I will not blame these latter; the blame is due in the first place to the absurdity of forming them into a State, organizing their armies, and then sending them a ruler, who would have driven the mildest nation to despair. But while we lay no blame on them, and under other circumstances might even rejoice to see their revolt, he must be a wrong-headed man, who would not now think of the salvation of Germany in the first place.

The French are always talking of defense, and their whole line of conduct points to attack; and in Germany no voice is raised to exclaim that *no one has threatened them;* the most that has been shown is a determination not to suffer them to seize on Belgium. The German press is only an echo *against* Germany! How willingly would they seek a pretext against Prussia, who does not, however, afford them the least, yet the "Correspondent" repeats the lying statement of an English journal, that the execution of the "bloody work" of subjugating Belgium was assigned to Prussia! It would lighten my heart to write; the effort to smother my feelings quite deadens my faculties; but if no great result could be expected, it would be a piece of knight-errantry to come forward singly. I have written a few words which may at least find an echo in the hearts of well-disposed but undecided persons, by way of preface to a reprint of the oration of Demosthenes, which Perthes wishes for: a demand has suddenly arisen for it in South Germany, and all the copies in stock have been sold.

The Russian bonds have received a great shock, which may lead to very bad consequences. Neither has the French credit been strengthened by the extension of French power, for further revolutions are, I think, inevitable What a change within five months! What a conclusion for this year! how will the next end? God protect you, my beloved Dora, and us! You will find a refuge, I trust. Give our love to all our friends and relations. Most likely I shall not write to you again in the old year. You will, I hope, pass a tolerably merry Christmas in spite of every thing; I wish you may skim over a little of my book during the holidays. I embrace you tenderly once more in the old year.

Your old NIEBUHR.

ON THE CHARACTER OF NIEBUHR.

BY PROFESSOR BRANDIS, OF BONN,

AUTHOR OF THE "HISTORY OF THE ARISTOTELIAN PHILOSOPHY," ETC.

NIEBUHR was considered passionate, and his feelings, his predilections, and his dislikes were, no doubt, expressed with a warmth, or rather a vehemence, which, untempered by deliberation, could not fail either to carry all before it, or to hurt the feelings of others. Not alone the narrow-minded or ill-disposed, who might feel themselves justly rebuked, but men of nobler nature were often wounded by his passing ebullitions of temper, or the sharpness of his expressions. Even his most valued friends did not escape these passionate outbursts, which for the moment were deeply felt. Still it can be affirmed, that he never inflicted a deadly wound on friendship; the shaft that pierced knew in like measure how to heal, not by explanations, too often fruitless, but by proofs of love, which, in general, followed speedily and unsought, and were therefore indescribably touching. His anger was easily borne, even when unjust, or partly unfounded, because it was but the transient flash of an inward fire, which otherwise could not have shone forth so brightly in good-will and friendship.

It was the same with the love and hatred which were evident in his judgment on the past, and on the present, from which he was personally remote. To a man of his deep and strong feelings, it was impossible to observe and judge the occurrences of social life with the same coolness and impartiality as the necessary sequence of natural events. Great and noble sentiments, or eminent powers of mind, filled him with love and admiration; narrow and interested motives or aims, arrogant little-mindedness or vanity, he despised and disliked, whether they met his eye in the present or the past. His indignation against a Xenophon was as ardent as though he had even now left a noble father-land to its fate, in times of heavy need, and had nevertheless attained a false fame; for whether it was the present or the past against which Niebuhr's anger was directed, it never arose from selfish considerations, wounded vanity, or an envious wish to detract. No one could more thoroughly and cheerfully appreciate excellence of every kind; no one could value those excellences more highly in which, often through a touching self-depreciation, he thought himself deficient. But the injustice of contemporaries or posterity hurt, nay exasperated him, as being at once the ungrateful disparagement of well-founded claims, the sign of a despicable want of independent judgment, and the hindrance to all lasting influence. To confound good and evil, to place great and small things on the same level, was absolutely repulsive to his nature, whether it were the result of a deficiency in warmth of feeling, or in the acuteness of the moral sense; for he was firmly convinced that only where the bad, the impure, and the base, are alike hated and despised, can the great and noble be truly reverenced and loved, and thus exert a purifying and elevating influence on the character. Hence he placed his standard, with regard to the formation of opinion, far higher than most men; earnestness of mind, he considered, ought to be shown, above all things, in pronouncing a judgment, that the faculty of judging might be thereby developed. Inconsiderate or hasty expressions with regard to remarkable men or events, he did not easily allow to pass uncensured.

It was impossible for Niebuhr, so thoroughly pervaded by moral earnestness, to contemplate history otherwise than from the centre of his own nature, and he looked upon the actual relations of life from the same point of view. To be misunderstood or depreciated affected him deeply; and however ready he might be to admit contradiction, those truths which he had once grasped with living conviction, became portions of himself, and were as sacred in his eyes as moral and religious principles, with which, indeed, they were always more or less bound up in his mind; certainly they always had their origin in the pure love of truth. How frequently he tested them, and how readily he relinquished those which would not bear re-examination, is most fully proved by the second, and by parts even of the third edition of his History of Rome. What classical work has ever undergone so searching a revision? But contradiction which, without a thorough examination of the subject, opposed mere assertion to convictions which he had founded on deep research—a setting up of bare possibilities, without real insight into the conditions, through which alone they could have come to pass—wounded him bitterly, especially when accompanied by arrogance. It wounded him because it implied a refusal to recognize the conscientious earnestness of his investigations, and because it deprived those truths which he believed himself to have established, of the reception which he desired for them, on behalf of science.

It is not surprising that he now and then adhered with some obstinacy to opinions not so important nor so well-grounded, but this never arose from dislike to acknowledge error, nor from petty vanity. On the contrary, as he never adopted or expressed an opinion without the most careful examination and thorough mastery of all the facts relating to it, he could not give it up until it had received the most complete refutation. It was kept firm in his mind by the same profound love of truth from which it had originally proceeded, until a higher truth had dawned upon his sight. Men of more flexible intellect find it easier to sacrifice their earlier sentiments; but are not their views, for this very reason, deficient in completeness and power? Besides, it must be remembered that Niebuhr's opinions were most intimately connected with, and organically dependent upon each other, so that if one were given up, its successor must equally be brought into due relation to what remained behind; while his more important principles were of a kind that could scarcely be renounced, but, at most, only undergo modification. Such a habit of mind could exist only in one whose convictions were ever present to him as a whole; it was at least the chief cause why Niebuhr almost invariably attained a higher insight by his own efforts, rarely by the aid of others, though a well-timed suggestion would quickly rouse him to fresh researches. Another cause lay in his early habit of resorting immediately to the fountain-heads, without availing himself of the labors of his predecessors. Nothing less than that incredible mastery over his materials, which he derived from an almost unexampled grasp and certainty of memory, combined with the most brilliant reflective powers, could justify him in despising aids, which are indispensable to a less comprehensive and original mind. It was not indeed so much that he despised them, as that he seldom had occasion to make use of them. Up to his seventeenth year, the classical authors had formed almost his sole reading, and he was already as much at home in their world, as most learned men in their mature years. He next turned with like eagerness to modern science and literature, to which he was led by an intimate acquaintance with Dante. He followed modern history through all its details; for him it reflected a light over the records of the past, and drew forth electric sparks from every pebble on the shore of antiquity; nay more, it gave an early maturity to his judgment, and he was not carried away by the intoxication of the French Revolution, because he clearly comprehended the nature and conditions of freedom in ancient times, and the necessity of introducing it step by step, and not by sudden leaps. From his residence in England and Scotland, and his active participation in public business, sometimes of an important nature, he gained a practical view of affairs in which the merely learned historian so often fails. He was so fully engaged in official life, from his twenty-second or twenty-third year, to the year 1810, that he could scarcely devote more than his hours of relaxation to study. No leisure remained for researches with an extensive apparatus of learning, but he attained the same end, without fixed purpose, simply by applying his practical knowledge of circumstances and affairs to history, and never resting until he was able to form as distinct and vivid a picture of those portions of history, which had most attracted his interest, as men in general retain only from the experience of the present.

Had he kept to the ordinary track, had he combined the study of the original sources with an examination of the principal attempts to inspire them with fresh life, he might still indeed have found single facts confirming or modifying his representations, but he would scarcely have opened a new career to historical investigation. Other great scholars before him have treated of the history of Rome; other adepts in political science have made it their study, and how warmly, how gratefully were the labors of Machiavelli, Gronovius, Perizonius, Montesquieu, and Gibbon acknowledged by Niebuhr! His claim to be the pioneer of a new path in science, rests upon the fact, that he threw broad flashes of light across the darkness that vailed the early history of Italy;—that he espied a thread of truth in the tissue of fictions and embellishments, detected history in legends, and marked out the respective domains of the legendary and the historical;—that from the scanty and unconnected details belonging to history, he was able to draw clear and correct outlines, by displaying their relation to each other; finally, that by a close comparison of the results thus obtained with analogous conditions of society in periods better known, he gradually filled up these outlines till they presented a picture that spoke to the heart and mind of his readers. And we may fairly say that the opening of this new path has been, and will be, productive of still greater results than even the important discoveries to which it conducted Niebuhr, and by which he proved its correctness. It is a path which can not be closed again to science, however many may be the stumbling-blocks it presents to those who attempt to pursue it with ill-trained powers, who set apparent, in the place of real possibilities guaranteed by striking analogies—external resemblances in the place of internal relations, and mistake fortuitous conceptions for views founded on a consideration of facts.

We leave it to those better fitted for the task, to define the nature and value of Niebuhr's method of treating history, and its influence on the present state of historical research and opinion. As we confine ourselves within the limits of a biographical sketch, it is enough for us simply to bring into view whatever may tend to exhibit the peculiar features of his mind.

A more comprehensive and trustworthy memory, or greater control over it, can scarcely have been possessed by Joseph Scaliger, and other heroes of mnemonics; it certainly was never combined in any instance with clearer powers of reflection. Niebuhr was a close observer, and found some connecting link between all the manifold external and internal perceptions which came before him; hence he mastered languages and sciences, signs and the thing signified, with equal ease, and with such certainty, that with his mind's eye he saw each in its own individuality, separate from its fellows, and yet intimately and variously related to them. No sufficient explanation of his memory is furnished either by the pretended laws of the association of ideas, or of the reproduction of representations, or by any logical dependence among the ideas themselves. It was equally retentive of perceptions and thoughts, of views and feelings, of sights and sounds; whatever came within the sphere of his recognition took up its due relative position in his mind with equal certainty and precision.

A great part of the Greek and Roman poetry had imprinted itself so indelibly on his memory, that he could frequently recite hundreds of verses without stumbling, and could answer on the spot every allusion or quotation from the Latin poets in the notes and letters of the younger Valckenaer, who was most deeply read in those authors; even in his later years he retained every poem which appealed strongly to his heart, whether it were a modern Greek or Servian ode, or a song of Goethe, Count Platen, or others. In his later years, at least, we scarcely think that he ever learnt any thing by heart; whenever a poetic thought which had vividly seized upon his mind was clothed in the form perfectly adapted to it, both the form and its inner spirit implanted themselves firmly within him, without the necessity of any mechanical assistance.

When a youth, Niebuhr had made himself master of French, and, perhaps, still more completely, of English, and wrote and spoke both languages with great fluency and correctness. In his riper manhood, while the cares and occupations of the fatal years of war were undermining his health, he learned several of the principal dialects of the Sclavonic languages; in his fortieth year, he began to write and speak Italian, in which, up to this time, he had read nothing but historical works and poetry; and, with a rapidity that put his younger companion to shame, he acquired no slight command of this language, at the very time when he was accustoming himself to a new sphere of action, and devoting his leisure to antiquarian and historical researches. During his residence in Edinburgh he had occupied himself with the natural sciences, particularly chemistry, but had never afterward found time or opportunity to pursue these studies; yet in subsequent years he was able to form the most distinct conception of out-of-the-way or complicated details, to the astonishment of men versed in the subject. Hence he was strongly interested in the natural sciences of antiquity. The meteorology, natural history, &c., of Aristotle, the botany of Theophrastus, and the ancient writers on agriculture, were perfectly familiar to him. His memory was no less certain and comprehensive with regard to impressions of sight and numbers. As referee of the consular business, at the Danish Board of Trade, he once gave a very detailed report, full of calculations, without the slightest hesitation, though, as his neighbor remarked, he had brought with him by mistake, instead of his notes, a paper which had nothing to do with the matter in hand. But even numbers did not imprint themselves on his memory mechanically, but because the facts expressed by them were never destitute of some point of connection with other facts, within the wide compass of his historical and practical sphere of vision. Thus, too, the statistics of the finances, at least of the more important States, were so present to his mind, that he not unfrequently predicted great alterations in the paper currency with an accuracy most surarising to financiers and the thinking men engaged in trade.

ON THE CHARACTER OF NIEBUHR AS AN HISTORIAN.

FROM A LETTER BY PROFESSOR LOEBELL, OF BONN,

AUTHOR OF A "UNIVERSAL ANCIENT HISTORY," ETC.

. . . . . . YOU request me to furnish you with Niebuhr's characteristics, as an historian, within the compass of a few pages. This compels me to content myself with indicating some of the most important points, for the development and establishment of which, a small book would be necessary.

When great men step forth as the authors of a revolution in their peculiar department of science, and as the discoverers of new paths, on which others follow them, it generally is because they have been the first to recognize, in its true depth and significance, some want, vague indications of which have already betrayed themselves in the great tendencies of the age, and to supply which, they bring the eye and the gifts of genius.

At the period when Niebuhr took up the idea of re-investigating and remodeling the history of Rome, certain movements and aspirations had developed themselves in two provinces of intellectual activity, which could not fail to exert great influence on historiography. These provinces were classical philology and politics; that is, the internal civil life of a people. In classical philology, within the last ten years of the preceding century, there had grown up in Germany a new method of criticism, which for boldness, acuteness, and delicacy, was superior to all that had gone before it. This found its earliest manifestation, and one that excited the greatest attention, in the famous disquisitions of Wolf, concerning the origin and authors of the Homeric songs. In its wider and more general application, this method of criticism led to the conviction, that even the authority of ancient testimony is not sufficient to determine the author and the date of a work, unless it coincides with internal signs and evidence. Whenever these principles were applied to history, it was inevitable that the criticism which lies at its foundation should take a new form. It was seen that the use of any sources of history must be preceded by researches into their genuineness, and not merely into the genuineness of those which we possess, but also into the genuineness of those which are lost to us, but from which authors still extant have drawn their statements.

The other influence which helped to give a new form to historiography, proceeded from the great historical events of the age —the American and French revolutions. These revolutions first brought men to feel that, in the history of a State, the chief stress ought not to be laid on those things which had hitherto been almost its sole topics—wars, treaties, internal disturbances and struggles, and the personal relations of princes—but on the growth of its form of government and constitution—on every thing which serves to throw light on the relation of the whole people to the life of the State. How completely had this been neglected up to that time! Even in your England, where the idea of free citizenship had long ago awakened to active and conscious life, a thinker like Hume could assign such topics their place in appendices which he entitled "Miscellaneous Transactions." How long was it ere a Hallam conceived the idea of a "Constitutional History!" And a profound and spirited description of the condition of a people, in relation to its political principles and endeavors, such as is presented by the third chapter of Macaulay's admirable work, is the product of the present age alone.

Permit me to draw your attention, however, to the fact, that in this field too, the Germans were the first to break the soil. Soon after the outbreak of the first French Revolution, Spittler, of Göttingen, wrote a very clever and profound Hand-book of the History of the European States, in which their history is treated altogether with reference to their constitutional development, but which is, after all, a mere sketch, a skeleton, which the lectures of the author were to clothe with flesh and blood.

Some other writers on history had also begun to assign to this most important subject, a more prominent place than it formerly occupied. Thus, to some extent, Niebuhr had predecessors in this direction, when he placed the Roman constitution, and the struggles to which it gave rise, in the very foreground of his picture. But he had none in the application to history, of the method of criticism which had made such great advances in philology. And what is still more, he was the first to combine both tendencies, a combination for which he possessed endowments rarely found in any age.

In his History of Rome, Niebuhr commenced the erection of an edifice, in the construction of which he would not employ the very smallest stone until he had carefully examined its fitness. Furnished with a comprehensive and profound acquaintance with the languages and literature of antiquity, he was fully qualified to apply the principles of the new tendency in philological criticism on a far wider scale, by the most acute examination and analysis of the original sources of history. What had hitherto (with a few exceptions which attracted no attention) been termed historical criticism, consisted partly in a reckless skepticism, which rejected entirely the remains of whole periods—as Hume says, "The first page of Thucydides is, in my opinion, the commencement of real history"—partly in testing contradictory statements in the accounts of the narrators of isolated events, by their greater or less probability. Another step had been taken shortly before Niebuhr's time. Instead of credulously receiving, or absolutely rejecting the whole, an effort was made to pick out the kernel of historical truth, from the midst of the mythical elements with which it was mixed up in tradition. But Niebuhr did not stop here. He comprehended in the fullest extent the changes which the objective, positive, and actual historical truth must undergo, in its subjective transmission, and the influence of which perpetuated itself to after-ages. Hence arose the following questions, which the true method of criticism must answer, before deciding on the trustworthiness of the original sources: What would such a century, according to its modes of thought, be able and desirous to hand down to posterity? How has that which has been thus transmitted, been by later historians received, added to, or altered? 1. According to some general conception of the earlier period which had become current in their day. 2. According to their greater or less ability to test what they have received. 3. Or according to their political party-spirit, which often throws its own coloring over men's views of the past? These critical principles lead to the most fertile results. It follows from them, among other things, that narrations of events must be estimated, not merely by their own intrinsic degree of credibility, but also by the whole position of the narrator; a principle which had formerly been applied, only where the veracity, or want of veracity, in an author was already generally acknowledged. Further, that some fragments of an account, accidentally preserved, and overlooked or rejected by later writers, may contain the truth in far greater purity, than a detailed narration which has come down to us in its integrity. To seize the true meaning, and supply the deficiencies of such a fragment—from which Niebuhr sometimes extracted the most astonishing results—certainly demanded his delicate appreciation of style, and his power of divination. In the way in which he sometimes brought some important relation to light from a few mutilated lines, he resembled such a naturalist as Cuvier, who from the fragments of a bone, determined the conformation of an extinct species of animals.

But Niebuhr was no less pre-eminently qualified for the political part of his task. He had early entered the invaluable school of public life, where he had acquired an unusually keen and penetrating eye for all political relations, and where many things came within the circle of his personal experience that can never be learned from books. He made himself acquainted with the most various spheres of action; scarcely any thing which could be rendered instructive from any point of view, was without interest to his ever eager thirst for knowledge. Hence he was able to take a practical and technical view of subjects, which most learned men know only by name, or from superficial descriptions.

Thus he made far higher demands than most on archæology, or a knowledge of the conditions and circumstances of the nations of antiquity. That bare acquaintance with particular usages or forms, unaccompanied by insight into their meaning, with which the merely book-learned content themselves, went for very little with him; on the contrary, he strove to attain such a conception of ancient institutions, that their mutual dependence, their application, their practical working seemed to be preserved, in all their living activity, to his eyes. In accounts where his predecessors, who had made no such demands, had found no difficulties, nothing problematic, he encountered chasms, difficulties, impossibilities. In the attempt to remove these, and to form to himself a consistent picture of the whole, he was often compelled to forsake established opinions, and to throw out new hypotheses, which he was enabled by the rich variety of his learning, the acuteness of his criticism, and his genius for combination, to suggest and maintain. Criticism here showed itself as not merely negative, but as the stimulant and assistant to creative energy, while a vivid imagination helped the author to perfect his production. For imagination, if understood, not in the sense of an absolutely unfettered invention, but as the gift of restoring distinct outlines and coloring to dim and faded forms, is as essential to the historical inquirer as to the poet, who does not decorate the materials furnished by history at his own free-will, but colors the given outlines, according to conditions involved in their very nature.

The great and excellent qualities of Niebuhr's historiography grew from the same roots, which by a certain inward necessity produced the defects which may be laid to its charge; they are the inevitable shadow which accompanies, and exists only in virtue of, the dazzling light. If Niebuhr sometimes brought forward too daring hypotheses with the greatest confidence, it was because he was carried away by the extraordinary vividness of his conceptions; if, at a later period, he nevertheless exchanged these opinions for others, it was but in consequence of his never-wearied enthusiasm and love of research; if his narrative is often interrupted and disturbed by long disquisitions, the cause must be sought in the power and importance of the analytical and critical element, which according to Niebuhr's method, necessarily formed the chief basis of his History. And the same cause necessarily occasioned the inequality of his style and language.

The writers who were incited through the influence of Niebuhr to new researches into the Roman history, occupy very different positions in relation to him. With some, reverence, admiration, and agreement preponderate. Among these is your fellow-countryman, Dr. Arnold, who, had a longer life been granted him, would no doubt have been the most worthy to carry forward the immortal work. Others concede to Niebuhr only a certain portion of his results, and set up other views in opposition to the remainder; others again controvert almost all his opinions. But all, with very rare exceptions, are standing on his ground; they have appropriated to themselves his critical method, and are fighting a great author with weapons which they have borrowed from himself. I share the conviction of many very clear-sighted men, that the most important of Niebuhr's results with regard to the earlier portion of the history of Rome, will remain as an enduring possession to science. But supposing, even, that all the positive results of these researches proved untenable, it would still be a great and glorious victory that his very antagonists had been forced to adopt his method: this method alone would secure a high position in all ages for Niebuhr's efforts in the development of science.

Inquiries into other periods have also yielded fair fruits to men who have prosecuted them after his example, and following in his footsteps; though many are unaware of the influence of this model on others, and even on themselves. For it is the highest victory of a new method, when it carries away with it a man of intellect without his becoming conscious whence the tendency which he is obeying is derived. No doubt, many would shake their heads over some of these assertions, and would say that the principles of criticism, which I have ascribed to Niebuhr, had long been acknowledged and applied. But this is a mistake; they confound the presentiments and vague intimations of the right method, and an occasional application of it, with its full admission into science. It would be easy for me to prove this by a series of examples, did space permit.

LOEBELL.

BONN, 3*d of October*, 1851.

NIEBUHR AS A DIPLOMATIST IN ROME.*

BY THE CHEVALIER BUNSEN.

To sketch a picture of Niebuhr's life in Italy, is a task as attractive as it is difficult to the friend in whose inmost soul this picture reposes like a jewel among the treasures of a happy and eventful past. Whether it can ever be attempted to present something not quite unworthy of this picture and this past, must, like so many other things, be left to futurity and fate. That it can not be done now, is as certain as, that if it could be done, this is not the place for it. In the Introduction prefixed to this section of the letters, by the friendly hand that accompanied this great mind with faithfulness and affection through this changeful outward and inward life, a delineation has been given equally dignified and simple, which will suffice for a general understanding of his history during the embassy in Rome. Enough lies before us, in this collection of letters, which is perhaps the most valuable presented to the world, in this country or in any period: lastly, any one who has lived in the present age, which forms the setting to this remarkable and venerable picture, may know enough of it to enable him, with the assistance here afforded, to trace the outlines without further aid, and from them to derive a fresh insight into, and a deeper knowledge of himself and his times. But it is beyond the province of any one section of his biography to fill up these outlines into a complete picture, to give an account of every single feature, of every accidental circumstance, of every apparent contradiction—to exhibit the facts in connection with each other, and with the present age. Niebuhr's intellect and inmost life were moulded at one cast, and the profoundest explanations of each portion lie in the whole. But such a one is at present, in my opinion, quite impossible. Niebuhr's inmost life is more intimately connected with the deepest movements, combinations, and struggles of suffering humanity in his own day, than that of

* This Essay was written for the Lebensnachrichten, where it will be found, vol. iii. p. 303.

any other great writer of his nation, or, I venture to say, of his age. He felt as a man, and sympathized with, observed, and thought for his fellow-men. While in so many memoirs, with which the present age is inundated and the future is intended to be deceived, the individual endeavors to represent himself to us as the centre of the events with which he was connected, a true biography of Niebuhr, on the contrary, would exhibit him as profoundly occupied with the universal weal and woe, finding solace and light upon the clear mountain-summits of antiquity, and erecting his rostra amid the noblest scenes of departed ages. It is a task imperative upon his future biographer to trace this influence in his writings as in his life. But just in so far as such a delineation would bring into prominence the great and significant features of his mind and life, it must be evident that, at the present time, it is impossible to proclaim that verdict upon human relations which they echo to the age just fled, and to the present, which will soon be numbered with it. Niebuhr took a position at once decided and modest, with regard to these times. While the antiquity which he described stood before his mind's eye like the present; so the present, in which he lived, was to him history, and, in all essential matters, he never surrendered himself to it in any other sense than the historian does to the past ages, on which he sits in judgment: loving it, but with the repressed sorrow of aspiration; sympathizing with it, but not enjoying it; combating folly and wickedness, but, for the most part, without any expectation of benefiting those whom he judges; with scarcely a hope of victory for himself and the friends and fellow-thinkers to whom he utters his prophetic cry: yet, with all this, always susceptible to every breath of life that blows upon him in the sultry atmosphere of reality—thankful for every glance of hope that casts a passing radiance on his dark and weary path. From such visitations he gathers fresh life; the former feeling constantly depresses and paralyzes him. The destiny of humanity, the welfare of his father-land, and the fate of its friends, these great points, without externally influencing his personal condition, affect him not less than the life of his own friends and the welfare of the dear ones to whom he has given his full heart of love; and if he expresses himself less frequently and fully about the former than about the latter, or for long together suppresses all mention of them, his inward feeling for them is but the stronger and more oppressive. This is the key-note which vibrates through every part of Niebuhr's mature life, and that began while he was a mere youth.

To catch this tone from his own mouth, documents would have to be printed which it is to be hoped that our children will see; nay, if we were but to follow its echo through the extracts from his correspondence now lying before us, it would be necessary to consider relations belonging to the present as well as the past, and to place under the focus of history those confused and fluctuating, erroneous and false representations of his contemporaries, which distressed Niebuhr, and against which he combated. Let him do this who can. Here we shall not even attempt to give a picture of any part of that dark and mournful section of his life, comprising seven years and a half, which was so highly unfavorable to his fertility as an historian, and yet, in many respects, so important to himself, to science, and the world. In this essay we shall only endeavor briefly to characterize Niebuhr as a diplomatist in Rome—his conduct in diplomatic life, and his views of the relations themselves which he was called upon to discuss and regulate, so far as it appears necessary to an understanding and justification of his letters.

Niebuhr's views of the diplomacy and diplomatic life of our times, were by no means ideal. The prevalence of hollow phrases, instead of a diplomatic survey of each circumstance as it presents itself—the growing rarity of a knowledge of civil and international law, and their application in the intercourse of nations, with the spread of general, abstract modes of speech, open to the misconstructions of caprice and the passions of the day—these fancied miraculous expedients of a great part of modern diplomacy, were not less repugnant to his inmost nature than were the inanity and tedium to which the social intercourse of the higher circle in most parts of Europe is condemned, sometimes by fancied notions of propriety, sometimes by irresistible attraction of mutual affinity. He used often to say, in jest, "The name diplomatist is a striking proof that the once favorite derivation of words from their contraries (as *lucus a non lucendo*) is not quite to be rejected; for it is evident that the greater part of the diplomatists in our day are only called so because they do not know how to read a diploma (*a non legendo diplomata*)."

The customary diplomatic mode of life he used to term *fuga vacui*, and to say of it what he had said in his youth of the great parties at the otherwise so agreeable house of his amiable friend Count Schimmelman, and which any one who chooses may hear from his own lips. Idle talk upon matters of lofty import, and a dwelling with pleasure upon trifling topics, were equally abhorrent to him. I shall never forget how Niebuhr spoke at a princely table in Rome, during the bloody scenes in Greece, of Suli and the Suliots, and the future of the Christian Hellenes, in much the same terms as he has spoken to posterity in a passage of his Roman history, which breathes a noble indignation and a sense that the brand of infamy still cleaves to us. The prince, a high-minded, amiable, and intelligent man, listened, as did his guests, with attention and sympathy; a serious mood seemed to come over the whole party. A pause occurred. One of the guests, a diplomatist of Mephistophelian aspect and species, took advantage of it to turn the conversation. One of the eternally repeated trifles of the day, a so-called piece of news that must be repeated to the prince, was skillfully used as a stepping-stone, and in ten minutes the whole table was alive with a dispute between the spokesman and another person who had contradicted him upon a most important point:—what "Aurora" signified in the slang of the Roman coffee-houses, whether a mixture of chocolate with coffee or not. Niebuhr was silent. At last, with quiet earnestness and dignified mien, he spoke these words:—"What heavy chastisements must be still in store for us, when, in such times, and with such events occurring around us, we can be entertained with such miserable trifles!" All were mute, and Niebuhr also; a long pause ensued, and the mysteries of the Café Nuovo and the dwarf Bajocco were not mentioned again that day.

"Those were, after all, different times," he would say, "when Hugo Grotius lived in the great world; indeed we might be well pleased if intellectual conversations, like those described and handed down to us from the times of Louis XIV. and his successors up to the French Revolution, were not banished from our diplomatic dinners as *de mauvais ton*. Who was ashamed then to speak of an important intellectual production as of an event?—to express his enjoyment of literature, his interest in intellectual life? The taste of that age was not indeed worth much, but it was at least a sign of life. There are, however, good and sufficient reasons for the phenomenon: much is owing to the alternation of political excitement and exhaustion, much to the endless divisions and diversions of society and to the prominence of the politics of the day, and yet on this topic very few can go beyond the hollow phrases of our time, and no one will talk except in a *tête-à-tête*." The ostentation, the extravagance, and the ruinous habit of contracting debts necessarily involved in such a mode of life, were naturally not less intolerable to him. "Where will all this end," he often exclaimed, "but with the universal bankruptcy toward which Europe is tending in the first general crisis?" "No diplomatist should lay by a penny of the salary which he receives in order to do honor to his country in his station, and to show hospitality to his countrymen," was another of sayings: "with most there is little danger of this; but no one has a right to demand of him that he should spend his own property in addition, least of all for such objects."

The sacrifices he entailed upon himself by such views—and views were with him inflexible principles and maxims of life, a confession—the annoyances that awaited him, the misconstructions, nay slanders, to which he exposed himself, were by no means unknown to him when he decided upon accepting the embassy to Rome. But he had probably not fully realized what an oppressive influence they would actually exercise upon him, a pressure like that of a sultry and unhealthy atmosphere. It must, however, be remembered that he had never reckoned upon remaining more than three or four years absent from Germany. A wide sphere of activity was not only in itself as much a necessity to his mind, as leisure for the investigation and representation of antiquity in a circle of beloved sympathizing friends or fellow-workers; he had been used to it from his youth up, and even his most learned investigations were based upon the contemplation of those public and social relations which are more or less perfectly expressed and mirrored in the circles of diplomatic life. I believe I may venture to say that no eminent practical statesman in Europe, whose name will be mentioned with honor after his death, ever left Niebuhr after a conversation upon either past or present political relations, without the highest respect for his intellect and heart; in fact I have never heard the most distinguished of them speak of him but with admiration of his intellect and knowledge, and reverence for his exalted sentiments, however much they might differ from him in social habits or national views. This frank appreciation of Niebuhr by distinguished statesmen gave great pleasure, although it sometimes pained him to find himself better understood, and his views regarded with greater sympathy in England and France, than in Germany and among Germans.

His motto, "*Tecum habita*," his own ill health, and still more that of his wife, together with his limited means, kept him from living in an expensive manner, and led him to take no larger a share in the diplomatic parties and festivities than was rendered necessary by his position, or might be or appear conducive to the service of the King and the objects of his mission. And in this respect Niebuhr recognized the peculiar advantages afforded by Rome for his habits and views of life. What in other capitals and courts is a necessity (although not to the extent it is said to be), the joining in the social whirl that involves still more loss of time than money, and deadens the intellect still more than it wastes the time, is in Rome of no political importance whatever. "What a blessing it is," he used to say in his merry moods, "that there are no court ladies here; it is so difficult for me to discover one from another." He generally declined the invitations of foreigners of distinction, because he could not return them; this hindered him from forming family connections, but not from intercourse with the distinguished men who sought his society. He never frequented entertainments among the Italians; he was to a certain extent glad that that nation who bore so little resemblance to their great forefathers, had not the remotest suspicion that the historian of Rome and the greatest scholar of the age was living in the midst of them. He was much obliged to them for leaving him in peace as a quiet "filosofo," and contenting themselves with occasionally imparting instruction to him. In reference to the instruction thus imparted in long calls and similar molestations, he used to say, "We do the Romans injustice when we say that not a true word comes out of their mouth; they say at least one true thing in every call, namely their farewell formula, '*adesso le livrò l'incommodo*.'"

During the first part of his stay he was ready to associate with the scholars of Rome, properly so called, in their own peculiar sphere, and it was enough for him to learn that Nibby (a young man alluded to in one of the foregoing letters, from Rome) was studying Greek for the sake of carrying on antiquarian researches, an unheard-of circumstance at that time among the professed antiquarians, to induce him to invite him frequently in the evenings, and encourage him in his labors. But even this connection with the learned men of influence was not of long continuance. How much sympathy and enthusiasm real Italian genius inspired in Niebuhr, and what a deep feeling he had for its peculiar greatness and elegance, was displayed most touchingly when he met with Count Giacomo Leopardi. I still remember the day when he entered with unwonted vivacity the office in which I was writing, and exclaimed, "I must drive out directly to seek out the greatest philological genius of Italy that I have as yet heard of, and make his acquaintance. Just look at the man's critical remarks upon the Chronicles of Eusebius. What acuteness! what real erudition! I have never seen any thing like it before in this country. I must see the man." In two hours he came back. "I found him at last, with a great deal of trouble, in a garret of the Palazzi Mattei; instead of a man of mature age, I found a youth of two or three and twenty, deformed, weakly, and who has never had a good teacher, but has fed his intellect upon the books of his grandfather in his father's house, at Ricanati; has read the classics and the heathens; is at the same time, as I hear, one of the first poets and writers of his nation, and is withal poor, neglected, and evidently depressed. One sees in him what genius this richly endowed nation possesses." Capei has given a pleasing and true description of the astonishment experienced by both the great men at their first meeting; of the tender affection with which Niebuhr regarded him, and all that he did for him. This and the subsequent fate of this great and noble-minded man, who ended his joyless life in 1837, do not belong here; but the trait we have mentioned is characteristic of Niebuhr's social life in Rome, and important for the prevention of misunderstandings which might be occasioned by isolated passages in his letters. Especially characteristic, however, was his affection and concern for the Prussian and German disciples of art and science who were in Rome with him. He considered it as his duty, and an agreeable part of his vocation to render them assistance, to encourage and further them in their studies, and to devote to them the time of which he was so sparing toward men of mere show and fashion. To Niebuhr belongs the glory of having been the first to recognize the men who have founded the German historical school of painting; which after philosophy, poetry, and philology, is of all the manifestations of the German mind of this epoch, the most important to the history of humanity; of having loved them; of having encouraged them with a devoted friendship as modest as it was generous, and rendered them pecuniary assistance when necessary. They are now appreciated and admired both in their own country and abroad; at that time they were the martyrs of an exalted and noble aspiration that had to fight its way through the wickedness not less than the shallowness of the times, and against which, the low and false taste of the leading connoisseurs and patrons of art of that day, had joined in a conspiracy with the licentiousness and incapacity of most of the artists. Niebuhr recognized in these associations of men like Cornelius, Overbeck, Philip Veit, and William Schadow, aspirations which had hitherto given but few outward signs of their existence, a fresh impulse closely connected in essence with the other great movements of the nation—of that re-awakened and life-begetting genius of Germany, which had formed Lessing, Kant, and Goethe—had prepared a new spiritual epoch of humanity by means of a profounder philosophy and a living historical science; and finally, had animated the noblest minds, and through them the whole nation, with a self-sacrificing public spirit, and had led them, amidst national songs and hymns, with joy and faith, to battle and to death, for the cause of their king and their father-land. The remembrance of 1813 was still warm in every heart when Niebuhr came to Rome, as it was in him to his last hour. The modern German art, the only one which deserves this name, came into being at the same time, after similar mental struggles; and though it arose in a foreign land, yet it was impressed with the spirit of the nation, and labored in its service. That this school alone had struck out the right path, and was pursuing the proper aim, could not but be recognized by him who had already so early perceived and admired in the great historical artists from Giotto to Raphael, the compeers of the ancient Hellenic schools of art—brethren in spirit of Dante and Goethe. In spite of the individual defects and incompleteness of the early works of this modern school, Niebuhr perceived in its founders and their productions, the vital principle which animated them in their opposition to the spirit of the age, and had confidence in that creative power which had united itself with clear insight and a determined will. To this faith he adhered with unshaken firmness, and on it he acted at a time when the germ from which he expected and announced a great and historically important development was wholly unknown or unappreciated in Germany, while in Rome it was despised, derided, and vituperated, as it would be even now in many parts of his own country, if men dared to give vent to their secret aversion. This recognition of a spiritual phenomenon in its first beginnings, is one of the numerous and most remarkable prophetic traits in Niebuhr's mind, and all the more striking, because of all spiritual phenomena, none lay further from him, judging from his peculiar cast of mind and the history of his life, than the arts of painting and sculpture. It is not only meritorious but worthy of fame in after ages, when the powerful ones of the earth protect and encourage the great and noble productions of science and art; but it is a much rarer and more blessed thing —only given to the open eye of genius, and to the quiet and humbly-listening ear of a noble-minded man, to recognize greatness in its bitter root, in its harsh and repulsive husk, and to tend the future all-conquering genius with love and reverence, when his young pinions lie as yet folded in inactivity. When, further, such a faculty is found at an advanced period of life—in a state of mental depression, when the magic of youth has vanished, the bloom of life faded, the eye, to use a touching expression of Niebuhr's, is filled with sand; then such an enthusiasm as Niebuhr experienced and expressed, and unalterably retained for those efforts, becomes worthy of all reverence. Certainly, and very naturally, this enthusiasm took a personal character; Niebuhr knew no other, because he believed in no spiritual power apart from personality, and looked upon all else as only its embryo, or husk, or scoria; but Niebuhr did not love the art because he had a blind personal love for those who confessed and sought to establish it; he loved its disciples, because he recognized that which they adored, to be true art, living and putting forth proofs of its power in them. A personal prepossession might, perhaps, have been able to blind him for a time, but the delusion would soon have found its own punishment, and the undeserved favor have been changed into decided aversion. This distinction is absolutely necessary in order not to misunderstand Niebuhr: he hated what he considered as evil with conscientious vehemence, but he loved what he deemed worthy of love with passion, and what is rarely united with it, constancy.

Such were Niebuhr's views of diplomatic life, and such was his own life as a diplomatist. Who could wish that he should have applied differently the leisure that remained to him for social intercourse? How many still bless him to whom he devoted this leisure in order to elevate their minds, to purify their hearts, to warn them against the perils of the age, to be a brother and a father to them in counsel and deed? And who of the rest would now thank him for having invited them to balls and dinners? Niebuhr, however, was extremely ready to show honor and hospitality to all his countrymen, according to his ability, when he was not repelled in the first instance by vulgar arrogance; this was the case sometimes, and to this refer expressions such as those of the 7th of April, 1821 (p. 407); but he never experienced any thing of the kind from foreigners. Once during the time he was in office he had occasion to give a great entertainment; it was on the visit of the Chancellor of State, Prince Hardenberg, in 1821. Its object was, to make the Prince acquainted with the Roman nobility, and the rest of the high society in Rome, and at the same time to present his countrymen to him. Niebuhr could not bring himself to give a ball. It was, therefore, necessary to contrive a musical entertainment. Niebuhr abhorred the modern Italian operatic music. It seemed to him appropriate to have the music which is peculiar to Rome, and is unlike any thing else in the world, performed before the Chancellor; this was all the more natural, as it is considered a part of *bon ton* throughout Europe, that every foreigner should have heard the celebrated singing in the Sistine Chapel during Passion week, although most of these hearers do not care the least about the matter in their hearts, but hate it as much as the modern composers despise it; like Voltaire, who smiles superciliously at the Iliad. A few weeks before, he had had the same music performed for his former *chef* and warm friend, the noble Baron Stein (see p. 404), which had made a deep impression upon the two friends—who were both in general comparatively insensible to the influence of music—as well as upon the assembled company. The idea was, therefore, carried out on the present occasion, with augmented appliances. Prince Christian of Denmark, and his consort, honored the festival with their presence. The conversation which preceded the music was very animated; the arrangement and entertainment received applause. But when afterward, the gay assemblage repaired to the brilliantly lighted saloon of the palace, where the choir awaited them in a gallery in the back-ground, and suddenly sixteen singers from the Chapel filled the apartment with the sublime strains of another world, the assembly was evidently seized with a peculiar feeling. Many grew quite uneasy when speech suddenly died on the lips; jests and playfulness found no response; some were positively driven out of the saloon and the house by the serious turn which the affair had taken, and all found in a different mood from that in which they had entered the room, or which they had anticipated. The satisfaction of the Prince and Princess, and the joyful thanks of several fellow-countrymen and a few foreigners, rewarded Niebuhr for the ungrateful task of providing a more worthy entertainment for his guests than they were used to, and for the mortification of being reminded by the ill-humor of others of a certain scriptural lesson respecting pearls. Had Niebuhr wanted any further consolation, he would have been amply satisfied by the circumstance, that in the following year his King expressly requested that this music might be performed before him at the entertainment given him by Cardinal Gonsalvi, on which occasion the company was never weary of praising the music and the taste of the selector.

In the foregoing letters Niebuhr briefly mentions having received the grand cross of the Leopold Order from the Emperor of Austria. The cause of this mark of distinction deserves to be more particularly mentioned. When the van of the imperial army had reached Rome by forced marches, and an instant attack on the passes of Antrodoro appeared to be the surest means of putting an immediate and bloodless end to the Neapolitan revolution, the military chests were found to be exhausted. Some hundred thousands of florins were absolutely necessary if operations were to be carried on. The house of Torlonia, to whom application was made, declared themselves ready to advance the sum if Niebuhr would give bills for the amount on the Seehandlung in Berlin. The imperial embassador laid the state of the case before him. Niebuhr recognized its urgency, and undertook the responsibility without hesitation; nay, in order to obtain the full amount desired, he took up a considerable sum, on his own personal credit, from the Prussian consul-general Valentini. By this means the business was settled in a few days, and the progress of the undertaking secured. The government at Berlin sanctioned the proceeding of their envoy, and the Emperor expressed his gratitude by the above-mentioned mark of distinction.

But we must hasten to conclude our sketch of Niebuhr's diplomatic life, if we are not to exceed our intended limits. Before we proceed to the second part of these notices, we wish to say a few words about Niebuhr as a diplomatic man of business. Few men of so much genius have ever conducted business with such order. Niebuhr's conscientiousness affected in a higher sphere what in others is done by habit and outward rules. His business style was peculiar without being *doctrinnaire;* his reports and notes will always appear, to us at least, a model of clear and business-like writing, unless we are to take the clumsiness of the usual German business style, and the hollow poverty of the ordinary diplomatic notes as our ideal. Those who only know Niebuhr's style from his writings, would be inclined to expect too great brevity, and a somewhat obscure conciseness, but quite erroneously. The statement is throughout flowing and easy, purely business-like and addressed to the practical statesman; although as some one has naïvely remarked of his conversation, one must take care not to let one's attention be distracted. His political memorials are unequaled models of statesman-like writing, even apart from their varied and weighty contents. Their straightforwardness and frankness give a faithful representation of the manner in which Niebuhr constantly applied his rich treasures of knowledge, experience, and reflection to the requirements of the present, kept the universal war in view, and brought all that occurred to him in the progress of his own development to bear upon the welfare of his father-land. A time will come when the circumstances treated of in those reports and memorials will become a matter of history, and most of the contemporary diplomatic papers will be left to moulder in oblivion. Not till then will it be really known what Niebuhr was. His written narratives and expositions were also a faithful picture of the manner in which he conducted verbal negotiations and deliberations. The greatest honesty appeared to him the highest wisdom, assuming that the negotiator is perfectly acquainted with his own wishes and claims, and as much so as possible with the aims and powers of the other party. With this principle Niebuhr commenced his career in Rome, and never forsook it; and, if we may judge from the results, never had cause to repent of his fidelity to it.

This naturally leads us to the second point on which a few hints and explanations seem indispensably necessary; namely, Niebuhr's views respecting the negotiations with Rome, and the relations of Protestant governments in general to the papal chair. Even during his lifetime Niebuhr was censured and misunderstood by some of his early friends, on account of his views on this subject; and it may be foreseen that now, when that point has become one of the vital questions of the day, nothing will be left untried, particularly by the opposite party, on the one hand, to bring him into opposition with himself, or with the government which he served with all the powers of his mind and soul; and on the other to weaken, by calumnies, the testimony of the first historian of Europe respecting that of which he was a witness. Some might, for instance, attempt to infer from the expressions in the letter to Perthès of September, 1815, (p. 296), that he had submitted to become the organ and defender of a system of government, with reference to the Romish Church, that in his conscience he disapproved. To obviate this and similar misconceptions, and to give a correct idea of Niebuhr's position in Rome, is the sole object of the following remarks, and will form a sufficient justification of him to every unprejudiced person.

That letter to Perthès is certainly a most remarkable one. It is written in the period succeeding Amelia's death, in which Niebuhr was living, as it were, in the presence of the loved departed one; his heart was full of sorrowful affection, free from bitterness or violence, but also without hope or care for the concerns of this life. This state of mind often allows his prophetic gift with regard to his own future to appear with peculiar prominence, and those lines exhibit a very striking instance of it. But to understand rightly what he there says of the conflict with his convictions in which his official duties in Rome would place him, we should first look at the extremely important letter to Mrs. Hensler, of the 15th of October, 1815 (p. 299), which develops his ideas more clearly. Then, too, it must be remembered, that Niebuhr had not at that time received his instructions, which were not sent to him till the summer of 1820, after he had been learning the position of affairs in Rome, from personal observation, for nearly four years, and fully expressed his views in all respects to his government, and come to an understanding with them; so that the dispatches which reached him at last may be said to have been the result of this understanding. Much light is thrown upon these circumstances by the confidential expression of his wishes and counsels, with regard to some leading principles, contained in the important and beautiful letter to Nicolovius of the 22d of January, 1817 (p. 336). His expressions on the termination of the negotiations are not less conclusive against such a supposition, as may be seen by comparing the passage (March 28, 1821), with the terms in which he speaks of what had been accomplished. See pp. 351 and 352, written in June and July of the same year.

In order, however, to understand all such expressions as those here referred to, as fully as every reader would wish to do, especially at the present moment, it is necessary to give a general outline of Niebuhr's position with regard to the views most prevalent in Germany, which each can fill up afterward for himself. Niebuhr has stated his sentiments on this subject so often, and to so many by word of mouth, as well as in writing, that it is scarcely necessary expressly to remark, that what is here said flows from no source which might be considered as belonging to official secrets, though its amplification would have to be sought in Niebuhr's dispatches and memorials.

Niebuhr found two views prevailing at that time among writers as well as public men respecting the relation of the state to the Roman Catholic Church, neither of which satisfied him, but on the contrary were offensive to him as a philosopher, an historian, and a statesman, inasmuch as they appeared to him to have proceeded from the decomposition of the vital elements of the Church and State, and to be a consequence of the decline of sound views and doctrines, respecting them. I will here only briefly mention, merely for the sake of those who do not know or do not understand his great historical work—and such it must be confessed form the majority, especially in Germany—that Niebuhr possessed a well-digested view of the State, which had become a living picture in his mind, and by which his scattered expressions respecting history and public affairs, as well as his whole political life, are to be interpreted. It was this idea of the State, which was a philosophical, no less than an historical and practical one, although he had not wrought it out into a well-founded and complete system, which he as a youth opposed with healthy aversion to the negative and destructive doctrines and opinions which prevailed at that time, consciously or unconsciously, in society and the literary world, and to the widespread jacobinism which he utterly abhorred. It was essentially the same view which he as a statesman and philosopher, in the full feeling of his superiority, opposed, now with a smile of pity, now with indignant rebuke, to the shallow, one-sided, stubborn attempts to restore political science by means of the crude negations of jacobinism, or a few elementary, abstract, pliant propositions. Now, among the views respecting the relative position of the civil and ecclesiastical powers, with which he came in contact, that one was especially repugnant to him which teaches that the highest wisdom of a government consists in exercising a sort of minute and centralized police surveillance, and administrative control over the Roman Catholic Church. Niebuhr was firmly convinced of the contrary, and often expressed this in very strong terms, unconcerned, as it became such a man, respecting the laughable misconceptions, and even the malicious constructions, to which it exposed him. The limitation of this oversight of the Roman Catholic Church to the preservation of the independence of the State, and the evidently indispensable protection of the government against an unlimited ecclesiastical power, external to the national life and the commonwealth, this, which appeared to him the leading fundamental idea of the existing laws, and the object to be aimed at in practice, seemed to others a treason against the principles of the Prussian Code, and an abandonment of the ideal of monarchy. But Niebuhr was neither to be disconcerted by the appeal to the so-called "good principles," which the passions of men have in every age made their watch-word, nor yet by the bugbear of the Prussian code. He knew that many general phrases and expressions, which had crept into the code from the one-sided, often quite untenable doctrinary views of the day, had through the force of circumstances, and the justice and mildness of the government, become a dead letter, which a practical statesman was bound to leave, like so much else, unrevived, inasmuch as a dead letter is always infinitely better than one "that killeth." But Niebuhr did not conceal from himself that the practical influence of these hostile views might greatly paralyze and interfere with his discharge of the duties of his office, and to this the words in the letter to Perthès are to be referred: "The embassador is merely the instrument of carrying out the orders which he receives, and how little these orders are likely to be in accordance with my convictions, I can already foresee." The letters referred to above show, that while his convictions underwent no alteration, his apprehensions were not justified by the event. Among others the well-known fact may be referred to, that upon his proposal made from Rome, the government immediately consented to the direct transmission of the Roman Catholic requests for dispensations of marriage from the bishops to the embassy charged with their presentation and advocacy, and to the immediate transmission of the papal rescripts to the bishops—a measure which produced a most desirable simplification of nine-tenths of the current business between Prussia and Rome.

But there was yet another view at this time, from which Niebuhr very distinctly dissented throughout the whole course of his mission. It was this, that the government ought to favor the wishes expressed for an internal remodeling of the Roman Catholic Church in Germany, abstain from all negotiation in Rome, or even declare itself the organ of those views to the Papal court, and carry them into execution. Niebuhr did all to the individuals of this party who were really in earnest about the main point—the religious and moral elevation of their church—and did not simply desire to carry out the impracticable theory of a German Hand-book of Canonical Law, in opposition to the Pope, or to set up for popes themselves. But as a philosopher and historian he held their aims impossible of attainment, and as a statesman, the highest wisdom, as well as justice seemed to him to demand that a Protestant government should, of all others, be the last to enter on such a course. On this point also Niebuhr had every reason to be fully satisfied with the part he had taken.

Niebuhr's own view was based entirely on the three leading traits of his character—conscientious piety, incorruptible integrity, and burning patriotism. His reverence for the views of Christianity which friends and pious men such as Stolberg and Fénélon held sacred, made him regard a tender and reverent handling of every thing connected with these views as an imperative duty in the case of individuals as well as that of nations. I remember his once saying to me, in reference to this, "How much easier to myself, I could make my position in Rome, and how much more satisfaction could I give in various quarters, nay, even reap applause, if I were but an atheist!" A deep text suggesting many reflections. The respect for the rights of others, which was with Niebuhr a second nature, never allowed him to forget the duties which a Christian government had taken upon itself with reference to the Roman Catholic population by the very rights which she claimed with regard to their church. Finally, his love for his German father-land, both in the narrower and wider sense of the term, strengthened these sentiments. Niebuhr saw in the "truce of God," between the members of the two confessions—whom a calamitous war on the plains and mountains of their primitive home had left as rival bodies, and yet spiritually and by affinity one nation—the only guarantee for the unity of the Germans, and consequently for the preservation of their freedom and independence. On this ground he wished to avert every thing that might disturb that peace, and call up the lurking demons. What he said in his famous address to his beloved hearers in 1830, on this point, flowed from a loving heart, oppressed, nay sometimes uncontrollably agitated by the vehemence of its emotions, which never belied itself in this or any other portion of his life. No statesman of any age or nation who has a heart in his bosom, and feels the sorrows of humanity and the heavy burdens of the past and present, can see without emotion how strong a sympathy and interest Niebuhr felt as a fellow-countryman and Christian, in all that he recognized as the real wants and essential rights of his fellow-citizens of the Roman Catholic Church, from the poverty of the parish priest on the Rhine, to the elective rights of the German cathedral chapters, nor fail to remark the contrast this spirit presented to Napoleon's niggardly spirit, and the right which he claimed to the arbitrary nomination of the bishops, as it exists in nearly all Roman Catholic countries.

In Niebuhr's opinion, the government was bound to provide for the institutions necessary to the existence and efficiency of that Church in the land. With respect to public instruction he considered it indispensable that it should bear a character of nationality, combined with a due consideration of the religious and ecclesiastical wants; and regarded every admixture of a foreign exclusive and separate influence on the great educational institutions of modern times, as pernicious; while on the other hand, he deemed the ecclesiastical character of the episcopal seminaries for the conclusion of the clerical education, judicious and wholesome.

But with respect also to strictly spiritual relations, he held that the government, guided by the principles we have indicated, ought, in the first instance, to take counsel with their own consciences and their Roman Catholic clergy and statesmen, and then to establish whatever their paternal solicitude might point out to them as their duty.

Further, Niebuhr believed that negotiations with the Roman court were the surest and most natural means of attaining these noble and desirable ends, and of laying the foundation of more flourishing conditions of the Church. The conclusion of a concordat he had considered from the first as an altogether inadmissible idea, because he knew that in the present position of a fully organized European state to the Romish ecclesiastical power, no concordat whatever can be concluded with honesty, even apart from the peculiar case of Protestant governments. With his principles, and his character as a Roman historian and a German statesman, had he not brought this conviction with him to Rome, it would have been forced upon him by the negotiations and proceedings of which he was a witness and judge during his residence there. The statements of his views on these subjects will one day prove a mine of gold to the reflecting statesman, and the historian conversant with public life.

In Niebuhr's opinion, the negotiations with Rome ought to have no other object than to give solemnity to the establishment of the resolutions that should be adopted after mature deliberation, as the result of an open and sincere understanding respecting the individual practical points, the canonical forms, and the modern development of the Roman Catholic Church in Germany. Both parties he considered must seek a basis for their friendly relations, not afforded by their conflicting principles, in the common interest felt in the object of their cares, and the practical importance of the points concerned in their deliberations; further, in the still greater importance of the fact of an honest understanding between them being possible. He believed that such an understanding would be a benefit to both Church and State, and a security to universal peace, beneath whose fostering wings the life of European nations might attain its full development. In all these, to him, fundamentally important views, Niebuhr had the satisfaction of finding the fullest concurence on the part of the Prussian government during his negotiations. If he was deceived—if it was an error to suppose that a Protestant government, conscientiously acting with a view to the highest welfare of its subjects, might carry its enlightened views with regard to the Roman Catholics, into effect by means of an understanding with Rome—if in spite of these pure intentions, malignant agitation and priestly pretensions now threaten with fresh storms, the repose of Germany and of the world, which it was hoped would be secured by these relations—Niebuhr's ashes may still be suffered to rest in peace. He shared this error, if such it was, with the noblest minds of his nation, and he and they will, perhaps, be all the dearer to posterity for the sake of this very error. Trust and patience are never thrown away, especially in the case of a powerful government; and extended historical experience can never be bought too dearly by those who remain true to themselves.

Further, it must be said, that in the views we have portrayed, Niebuhr thought as a practical statesman, who takes reality as he finds it.

He said once to a very distinguished English statesman, still living, who had consulted him while in Rome with reference to similar relations with the court of Rome, "Do every thing in your power for the benefit of your Catholics; give their clergy salaries, and have them well educated at home, but never keep an embassador in Rome."

That he did not conceal from himself the perils of the future; that he well knew how much of the then peaceable intentions of Rome was owing to the personal character of the pious Pope, and his excellent cabinet, and the instructive discipline of a period of tribulation, is sufficiently proved by his expressions in his letter to Madame Hensler, of the 4th May, 1822.

I can not conclude these lines, written in England, without expressing the pleasure I have derived from the appreciation and high esteem with which my ever revered master and fatherly friend is here regarded by statesmen and scholars—and especially from the pure enthusiasm with which he has inspired the most earnest and noble portion of the youth of this country. His influence, which is apparent to every observer, is not adequately represented even by the fact that a much larger number of copies of the English translation of his Roman History have been sold than of the German original, though many of the latter have also found their way to England. Niebuhr's incomparable superiority to all the critics of modern times—the deep truth of his historical views and political maxims—the pregnant solidity of his earnest earnest and dignified, if not easy style—the elevation of his moral views of the world—all this had long been acknowledged, in the homage paid to the Roman historian by the most distinguished men of every party in Church and State. But the pure human greatness of his noble heart—his unspotted life—his unwavering courage amid ill-health and disappointed or overclouded hopes—the devoted love of such a mind—the elevating and childlike faith in the divinity of virtue and truth—the union of qualities and capacities of heart and intellect so rarely seen in combination—in a word, the image presented in the letters before us, has raised that esteem to personal attachment, and the seeds of knowledge and virtue so richly scattered through them have fallen on a good and fruitful soil.

Well may we Germans term this joy a sorrowful one, when we turn our eyes to the disgraceful efforts of little-minded men, who, humbled beneath the grave and piercing glance of genius, have fallen a prey to their mean passions, and conspired with the disciples of impiety and the apostles of every thing un-German, to spy out the weak points of a great man with malicious joy, and use them with Mephistophelian address for their own ends; but it is so ordained that meanness and wickedness must hate nobleness and greatness, and Niebuhr's chief failing—that of yielding in such cases to immoderate vexation, shall not be imitated by his friends.

LONDON, 28*th February*, 1839.

THE END.

Layard's Discoveries at Nineveh.

Popular Account of the Discoveries at Nineveh. By AUSTEN HENRY LAYARD, Esq. Abridged by him from his larger Work. With numerous Wood Engravings. 12mo, 75 cents.

Lectures on the History of France.

By Sir JAMES STEPHEN, K.C.B., LL.D. 8vo, Muslin, $1 75.

Wesley, and Methodism.

By ISAAC TAYLOR. With a new Portrait. 12mo, Muslin, 75 cents.

A Lady's Voyage round the World.

By Madame IDA PFEIFFER. Translated from the German, by Mrs. PERCY SINNETT. 12mo, Paper, 60 cents; Muslin, 75 cents.

Sixteen Months at the Gold Diggings.

By DANIEL B. WOODS. 12mo, Paper, 50 cents; Muslin, 62½ cents.

London Labor and the London Poor,

In the Nineteenth Century. A Cyclopedia of the Social Condition and Earnings of the Poorer Classes of the British Metropolis, in Connection with the Country. By HENRY MAYHEW. With numerous Engravings, copied from Daguerreotypes, taken, by Beard, expressly for this Work. Publishing in Numbers, 8vo, Paper, 12½ cents each. Vol. I. ready, Muslin, $1 75.

Chalmers's Life and Writings.

Edited by his Son-in-Law, Rev. WILLIAM HANNA, LL.D. 4 vols. 12mo, Paper, 75 cents per Volume; Muslin, $1 00 per Vol.

Pictorial Field-Book of the Revolution;

Or, Illustrations, by Pen and Pencil, of the History, Scenery, Biography, Relics, and Traditions of the War for Independence. By BENSON J. LOSSING, Esq. With over 600 Engravings on Wood, by Lossing and Barritt, chiefly from Original Sketches by the Author. Publishing in Numbers, 8vo, Paper, 25 cents each. The work will be completed in two vols. Vol. I., handsomely bound in Muslin, is now ready, price, $3 50.

Moby-Dick;

Or, the Whale. By HERMAN MELVILLE. 12mo, Muslin, $1 50.

A Latin-English Lexicon,

Founded on the larger Latin-German Lexicon of Dr. WILLIAM FREUND. With Additions and Corrections from the Lexicons of Gesner, Facciolati, Scheller, Georges, &c. By E. A. ANDREWS, LL.D. Royal 8vo, Sheep extra, $5 00.

Lamartine's History of the Restoration

Of Monarchy in France. Being a Sequel to the "History of the Girondists." By ALPHONSE DE LAMARTINE. Vol. I., 12mo, Muslin, 75 cents.

Robinson's New Testament Lexicon.

A Greek and English Lexicon of the New Testament. A new Edition, Revised, and in great part Rewritten. By EDWARD ROBINSON, D.D., LL.D. Royal 8vo, Muslin, $4 50; Sheep, $4 75; half Calf, $5 00.

Buttmann's Greek Grammar,

For the Use of High Schools and Universities. By PHILIP BUTTMANN. Revised and Enlarged by his Son, ALEX. BUTTMANN. Translated from the 18th German Edition, by EDWARD ROBINSON, D.D., LL.D. 8vo, Sheep, $2 00.

The Nile-Boat;

Or, Glimpses of the Land of Egypt. By W. H. BARTLETT. With Engravings on Steel and Illustrations on Wood. 8vo, Muslin, $2 00.

Comte's Philosophy of Mathematics,

Translated from the Cours de Philosophie Positive of AUGUSTE COMTE, by W. M. GILLESPIE, A.M. 8vo, Muslin, $1 25.

History of the United States.

By RICHARD HILDRETH.——*First Series.*—From the First Settlement of the Country to the Adoption of the Federal Constitution. 3 vols. 8vo, Muslin, $6 00; Sheep, $6 75; half Calf, $7 50.——*Second Series.*—From the Adoption of the Federal Constitution to the End of the Sixteenth Congress. 3 vols. 8vo, Muslin, $6 00; Sheep, $6 75; half Calf, $7 50.

Louisiana:

Its Colonial History and Romance By CHARLES GAYARRE. 8vo, Muslin, $2 00.

The Lily and the Bee:

An Apologue of the Crystal Palace. By SAMUEL WARREN, M.D., F.R.S. 16mo, Paper, 30 cents; Muslin, 37½ cents.

The Queens of Scotland,

And English Princesses connected with the Regal Succession of Great Britain. By AGNES STRICKLAND. 6 vols. 12mo, Muslin, $1 00 per Volume. Vols. I. and II. ready.

A New Classical Dictionary

Of Greek and Roman Biography, Mythology, and Geography. For Colleges and Schools. By WM. SMITH, LL.D. Edited, with large Additions, by CHARLES ANTHON, LL.D. Royal 8vo, Sheep extra, $2 50.

The English Language

In its Elements and Forms. With a History of its Origin and Development, and a full Grammar. By WILLIAM C. FOWLER. Designed for Use in Colleges and Schools. 8vo, Muslin, $1 50; Sheep, $1 75.

Harper's N. Y. & Erie R. R. Guide:

Containing a Description of the Scenery, Rivers, Towns, Villages, and most important Works on the Road. Embellished with 136 Engravings on Wood, by Lossing & Barritt, from Original Sketches made expressly for this Work, by WM. M'LEOD. 12mo, Paper, 50 cents; Muslin, 62½ cents.

The English in America.

Rule and Misrule of the English in America. By the Author of "Sam Slick the Clockmaker," "The Letter Bag," "Attaché," "Old Judge," &c. 12mo, Muslin, 75 cents.

The Literature and Literary Men

Of Great Britain and Ireland. By ABRAHAM MILLS, A.M. 2 vols. 8vo, Muslin, $3 50; half Calf, $4 00.

A Greek-English Lexicon,

Based on the German Work of Passow. By HENRY G. LIDDELL, M.A., and RICHARD SCOTT, M.A. With Corrections and Additions, and the Insertion in Alphabetical Order of the Proper Names occurring in the principal Greek Authors, by HENRY DRISLER, M.A. Royal 8vo, Sheep, $5 00.

The Recent Progress of Astronomy,

Especially in the United States. By ELIAS LOOMIS, M.A. New Edition. 12mo, Muslin, $1 00.

Cosmos:

A Sketch of a Physical Description of the Universe. By ALEXANDER VON HUMBOLDT. Translated from the German, by E. C. OTTE. Complete in 3 Vols. 12mo, Muslin, $2 55.

Bickersteth's Memoirs.

A Memoir of the late Rev. EDWARD BICKERSTETH, Rector of Watton. By Rev. T. R. BIRKS, M.A. With a Preface, &c., by Rev. STEPHEN H. TYNG, D.D., of New York. 2 vols. 12mo, Muslin, $1 75.

Foster's Christian Purity.

The Nature and Blessedness of Christian Purity. By Rev. R. S. FOSTER. With an Introduction by Bishop JANES. 12mo, Muslin, 75 cents.

Elements of Natural Philosophy.

Designed as a Text-book for Academies, High-Schools, and Colleges. By ALONZO GRAY, A.M. Illustrated by 360 Woodcuts. 12mo, Muslin, 70 cents; Sheep, 75 cents.

Lord Holland's Foreign Reminiscences.

Edited by his Son, HENRY EDWARD LORD HOLLAND. 12mo, Paper, 60 cents; Muslin, 75 cents.

Curran and his Contemporaries.

By CHARLES PHILLIPS, A.B. 12mo, Paper, 75 cents; Muslin, 87½ cents.

The Irish Confederates,

And the Rebellion of 1798. By HENRY M. FIELD. Portraits and a Map. 12mo, Paper, 75 cents; Muslin, 90 cents.

The Harmony of Prophecy;

Or, Scriptural Illustrations of the Apocalypse. By Rev. ALEXANDER KEITH, D.D. 12mo, Muslin, $1 00.

The Bards of the Bible.

By GEORGE GILFILLAN. 12mo, Muslin, 35 cents.

Abbott's Illustrated Histories:

The following Works of the Series are now ready: Josephine, Cleopatra, Madame Roland, Xerxes the Great, Cyrus the Great, Darius the Great, Charles I., Charles II., Hannibal, Julius Cæsar, Alfred the Great, Maria Antoinette, Queen Elizabeth, Alexander the Great, William the Conqueror, Mary Queen of Scots. 16mo, Muslin, with Illuminated Title-pages and numerous Engravings, 60 cents per Volume.

Abbott's Franconia Stories:

Comprising Malleville, Beechnut, Mary Bell, Wallace, Mary Erskine. 16mo, beautifully bound in Muslin, Engraved Title-pages and numerous Illustrations, 50 cents per Volume.

Kings and Queens;

Or, Life in the Palace: consisting of Historical Sketches of Josephine and Maria Louisa, Louis Philippe, Ferdinand of Austria, Nicholas, Isabella II., Leopold, and Victoria. By J. S. C. ABBOTT. With numerous Illustrations. 12mo, Muslin, $1 00; Muslin, gilt edges, $1 25.

A Summer in Scotland.

By JACOB ABBOTT. With Engravings. 12mo, Muslin, $1 00

Five Years of a Hunter's Life

In the Far Interior of South Africa. With Notices of the Native Tribes, and Anecdotes of the Chase of the Lion, Elephant, Hippopotamus, Giraffe, Rhinoceros, &c. By R. GORDON CUMMING. With Engravings. 2 vols. 12mo, Muslin, $1 75.

Sydney Smith's Moral Philosophy.

An Elementary Treatise on Moral Philosophy, delivered at the Royal Institution in the Years 1804, 1805, and 1806. By the late Rev. SYDNEY SMITH. 12mo, Muslin, $1 00.

Travels in the United States, etc.

During 1849 and 1850. By Lady EMMELINE STUART WORTLEY. 12mo, Paper, 60 cents; Muslin, 75 cents.

Dealings with the Inquisition;

Or, Papal Rome, her Priests, and her Jesuits. With Important Disclosures. By the Rev. GIACINTO ACHILLI, D.D., late Prior and Visitor of the Dominican Order, &c. 12mo, Muslin, 75 cts.

Leigh Hunt's Autobiography,

With Reminiscences of his Friends and Contemporaries. In 2 vols. 12mo, Muslin, $1 50.

Campbell's Life and Letters.

Life and Letters of Thomas Campbell. Edited by WILLIAM BEATTIE, M.D. With an Introductory Letter, by WASHINGTON IRVING. 2 vols. 12mo, Muslin, $2 00.

Doctor Johnson:

His Religious Life and Death. 12mo, Muslin, $1 00.

Southey's Life and Correspondence.

Edited by his Son, Rev. C. C. SOUTHEY, M.A. Portrait. 8vo, Muslin, $1 75.

Southey's Common-place Book.

Edited by his Son-in-Law, JOHN WOOD WARTER, B.D. 3 vols. 8vo, Paper, $1 00 per Vol.; Muslin, $1 25 per Vol.

History of Greece,

From the Earliest Times to the Destruction of Corinth, B.C. 146; mainly based upon that of Bishop THIRLWALL. By Dr. L. SCHMITZ, F.R.S.E. 12mo, Muslin, $1 00.

History of Rome,

From the Earliest Times to the Death of Commodus, A.D. 192. By Dr. L. SCHMITZ, F.R.S.E. With Questions, by J. ROBSON, B.A. 18mo, Muslin, 75 cents.

A Treatise on Popular Education:

For the Use of Parents and Teachers, and for Young People of both Sexes. Printed and Published in accordance with a Resolution of the Senate and House of Representatives of the State of Michigan. By IRA MAYHEW, late Superintendent of Public Instruction. 12mo, Muslin, $1 00.

The Conquest of Canada.

By the Author of "Hochelaga." 2 vols. 12mo, Muslin, $1 70.

Health, Disease, and Remedy,

Familiarly and practically considered in a few of their Relations to the Blood. By G. MOORE, M.D. 18mo, Muslin, 60 cents.

Hume's History of England,

From the Invasion of Julius Cæsar to the Abdication of James II., 1688. By DAVID HUME. A new Edition, with the Author's last Corrections and Improvements. To which is prefixed a Short Account of his Life, written by Himself. With a Portrait of the Author. 6 vols. 12mo, Cloth, $2 40; Sheep, $3 00.

Macaulay's History of England

From the Accession of James II. By THOMAS B. MACAULAY. With an Original Portrait of the Author. Vols. I. and II. Library Edition, 8vo, Muslin, 75 cents per Vol.; Sheep extra, 87½ cents per Vol.; Calf backs and corners, $1 00 per Vol.—Cheap Editions, 8vo, Paper, 25 cents per Vol: 12mo (uniform with Hume), Cloth, 40 cents per Vol.; Sheep, 50 cents per Vol.

Gibbon's History of Rome.

History of the Decline and Fall of the Roman Empire. By EDWARD GIBBON. With Notes, by Rev. H. H. MILMAN and M. GUIZOT. Maps and Engravings. 4 vols. 8vo, Sheep extra, $5 00.—A new Cheap Edition, with Notes, by Rev. H. H. MILMAN. To which is added a complete Index of the whole Work, and a Portrait of the Author. 6 vols. 12mo (uniform with Hume), Cloth, $2 40; Sheep, $3 00.

History of Spanish Literature.

With Criticisms on the particular Works and Biographical Notices of prominent Writers. By GEORGE TICKNOR. 3 vols. 8vo, Muslin, $6 00; Sheep, $6 75; half Calf, $7 50.

Pictorial History of England.

Being a History of the People as well as a History of the Kingdom, down to the Reign of George III. Profusely Illustrated with many Hundred Engravings on Wood of Monumental Records; Coins; Civil and Military Costume; Domestic Buildings, Furniture, and Ornaments; Cathedrals and other great Works of Architecture; Sports, and other Illustrations of Manners; Mechanical Inventions; Portraits of Eminent Persons; and remarkable Historical Scenes. 4 vols. imperial 8vo, Sheep, $12 00; half Calf, $13 50.

The War with Mexico.

By R. S. RIPLEY, U.S.A. With Maps, Plans of Battles, &c. 2 vols. 8vo, Muslin, $4 00; Sheep, $4 50.

Ancient and Mediæval Geography.

For the Use of Schools and Colleges. By CHARLES ANTHON, LL.D. 8vo, Muslin, $1 50; Sheep extra, $1 75.

Findlay's Classical Atlas

To Illustrate Ancient Geography. Comprised in 25 Maps, showing the various Divisions of the World as known to the Ancients. By ALEX. FINDLAY, F.R.S. With an Index of the Ancient and Modern Names. 8vo, half Bound, $3 25.

A First Book in Latin.

Containing Grammar, Exercises, and Vocabularies, on the Method of constant Imitation and Repetition. By Prof. M'CLINTOCK, of Dickinson College. 12mo, Sheep, 75 cents.

A First Book in Greek.

Containing full Vocabularies, Lessons on the Forms of Words, and Exercises for Imitation and Repetition, with a Summary of Etymology and Syntax. By Professor M'CLINTOCK. 12mo, Sheep, 75 cents.

A Second Book in Greek.

Containing Syntax, with Reading Lessons in Prose; Prosody, and the Dialects, with Reading Lessons in Verse; forming a sufficient Greek Grammar. By Prof. M'CLINTOCK. 12mo, Sheep, 75 cents.

The Pillars of Hercules;

Or, a Narrative of Travels in Spain and Morocco in 1848. By DAVID URQUHART, M.P. 2 vols. 12mo, Paper, $1 40; Muslin, $1 70.

The Valley of the Mississippi.

History of the Discovery and Settlement of the Valley of the Mississippi, by the three great European Powers, Spain, France, and Great Britain; and the Subsequent Occupation, Settlement, and Extension of Civil Government by the United States, until the Year 1846. By JOHN W. MONETTE. Maps. 2 vols. 8vo, Muslin $5 00; Sheep, $5 50.

Moral and Political Philosophy.

With Questions for the Examination of Students. By WILLIAM PALEY, D.D. 12mo, Muslin, 60 cents.

History of the Confessional.

By JOHN HENRY HOPKINS, D.D., Bishop of Vermont. 12mo, Muslin, $1 00.

History of the American Bible Society,

From its Organization in 1816 to the Present Time. By Rev. W. P. STRICKLAND. With an Introduction by Rev. N. L. RICE, and a Portrait of Hon. E. BOUDINOT, LL.D., first President of the Society. 8vo, Cloth, $1 50; Sheep, $1 75.

Gieseler's Ecclesiastical History.

From the Fourth Edition, Revised and Amended. Translated from the German, by SAMUEL DAVIDSON, LL.D. Vols. I. and II., 8vo, Muslin, $3 00; Sheep, $3 50.

History of the Girondists;

Or, Personal Memoirs of the Patriots of the French Revolution. By A. DE LAMARTINE. From Unpublished Sources. 3 vols. 12mo, Muslin, $2 10.

History of the French Revolution.

By THOMAS CARLYLE. Newly Revised by the Author, with Index, &c. 2 vols. 12mo, Muslin, $2 00.

Letters and Speeches of Oliver Cromwell.

With Elucidations and connecting Narrative. By THOMAS CARLYLE. 2 vols 12mo, Muslin, $2 00.

Past and Present, Chartism,

And Sartor Resartus. By THOMAS CARLYLE. A new Edition, complete in One Volume. 12mo, Muslin, $1 00.

Latter-Day Pamphlets.

Comprising, 1. The Present Time; 2. Model Prisons; 3. Downing Street; 4. The New Downing Street; 5. Stump Orator; 6. Parliaments; 7. Hudson's Statue; 8. Jesuitism. By THOMAS CARLYLE. 12mo, Muslin, 50 cents.

Not so Bad as we Seem;

Or, Many Sides to a Character. A Comedy in Five Acts. By Sir E. BULWER LYTTON. As first performed at Devonshire House, in the Presence of her Majesty and Prince Albert. 16mo, Paper, 30 cents; Muslin, 37½ cents.

Sketches of Minnesota,

The New England of the West. With Incidents of Travel in that Territory during the Summer of 1848. By E. S. SEYMOUR. 12mo, Paper, 50 cents; Muslin, 75 cents.

History of the Conquest of Peru;

With a Preliminary View of the Civilization of the Incas. By WILLIAM H. PRESCOTT. 2 vols. 8vo, Muslin, $4 00; Sheep, $4 50; half Calf, $5 00.

History of the Conquest of Mexico,

With the Life of the Conqueror, Hernando Cortes, and a View of the Ancient Mexican Civilization. By WILLIAM H. PRESCOTT. With Portraits and Maps. 3 vols. 8vo, Muslin, $6 00; Sheep, $6 75; half Calf, $7 50.

History of Ferdinand and Isabella,

The Catholic. By WILLIAM H. PRESCOTT. With Portraits, Maps, &c. 3 vols. 8vo, Muslin, $6 00; Sheep, $6 75; half Calf $7 50.

Harper's Illustrated Shakespeare.

The complete Dramatic Works of William Shakespeare, arranged according to recent approved Collations of the Text; with Notes and other Illustrations, by Hon. GULIAN C. VERPLANCK. Superbly Embellished by over 1400 exquisite Engravings by Hewet, after Designs by Meadows, Weir, and other eminent Artists. 3 vols. royal 8vo, Muslin, $18 00; half Calf extra, $20 00; Morocco, gilt edges, $25 00.

Herman Melville's Works.

TYPEE; 12mo, Paper, 75 cents, Muslin, 87½ cents.——OMOO; 12mo, Paper, $1 00, Muslin, $1 25.——MARDI; 2 vols. 12mo, Paper, $1 50, Muslin, $1 75.——REDBURN; 12mo, Paper, 75 cents, Muslin, $1 00.——WHITE-JACKET; 12mo, Paper, $1 00, Muslin, $1 25.——MOBY-DICK; 12mo, Muslin, $1 50.

The Country Year-Book;

Or, the Field, the Forest, and the Fireside. By WILLIAM HOWITT. 12mo, Muslin, 87½ cents.

Dark Scenes of History.

By G. P. R. JAMES. 12mo, Paper, 75 cents; Muslin, $1 00.

www.ingramcontent.com/pod-product-compliance
Lightning Source LLC
LaVergne TN
LVHW021232110826
845150LV00002B/309
9781425562687